THE
CHARLEY-MAN

◆

THE CHARLEY-MAN

◆

A History of
Wooden Shipbuilding
at Quebec
1763–1893

◆

Eileen Reid Marcil

◆

Quarry Press

Copyright © Eileen Reid Marcil, 1995.

All rights reserved.

The publisher gratefully acknowledges the support of an anonymous friend, The Canadian Council, the Ontario Arts Council, Canadian Heritage, and The Ontario Publishing Centre.

Canadian Cataloguing in Publication Data
Marcil, Eileen
    The Charley-Man : a history of wooden shipbuilding at Quebec, 1763-1893

Includes bibliographical references.
ISBN 1-55082-092-3 (bound)
ISBN 1-55082-093-1 (pbk.)

1. Shipbuilding — Quebec (Province) — Québec — History. 2. Ships, Wooden — Quebec (Province) — Québec — History. I. Title.

VM27.Q8M37   1993   338.4'76238207   C93-090519-9

Cover art by Caroline Soucy, a watercolor based on an engraving of a drawing by Coke Smythe, for *Sketches in the Canadas*, published by Thomas McLean, London, England, c. 1840.

Printed and bound in Canada
by Best Book Manufacturers

Published by Quarry Press, Inc.
P.O. Box 1061, Kingston, Ontario, Canada K7L 4Y5.

Acknowledgements

Three men whose paths I had the good fortune to cross many years ago strongly influenced the writing of this history: Jack Richardson, who initiated me in the field of research and from whose sustained interest I have benefitted ever since; Terry Ruddell who introduced me to the subject of shipbuilding and made my early work in the area possible; and Professor Jean Hamelin of Laval University, who suggested that I undertake a major study of 19th century shipbuilding at Quebec and gave me valued guidance and encouragement. To all three I offer my most sincere thanks.

I am grateful, also, to Jean-Claude Dupont for his support while Director of the CELAT at Laval University, and to Bernard Bouchard for his kindness in lending his comprehensive card file on shipbuilding to a complete stranger. I acknowledge with thanks the work done by François Morel in the course of a student summer work project organized by the National Museum of Man (now the Museum of Civilization), Ottawa.

In the course of my research I had occasion to consult many archivists, librarians, historians and others who responded generously, and I thank in particular those who are listed below. If I have forgotten someone, I apologize for the omission.

Charles Armour, Robert Aspinall, Jocelyn Beaulieu, Jean Belisle, Mary Blackwood, André Bonneau, Wayne Chimenti, Peter Clibbon, John Cook, Lesley Couper White, Caroline Craig, Robin Craig, Edward Dahl, Peter Davies, Cynthia Dooley, Alec Douglas, Marie Elwood, Hélène Espesset, David Flemming, Antoinine Gagnon, Claire Gagnon, Basil Greenhill, Jean-Claude Hébert, Patricia Kennedy, John Keyes, Marc Lafrance, André Laflamme, Marthe Laliberté, Pierre-Louis Lapointe, Norma Lee, Reynald Lessard, Nathan Lipfert, Peter McClelland, Kenneth McKenzie, Gertrude and Colin McMichael, Monique Mailloux, Eva Major Marotte, Michael Moss, Mary Murphy, Alan Pearsall, Richard Rice, Ladrière Samson, Anthony Slaven, Maurice Smith, Mike Stammers, Georgina Stinson, Stanley Triggs, Yves Tessier, Marc Vallières, Fred Walker, Garth Wilson and Annette Wolff.

Most of my research was carried out in the manuscript department of the Archives nationales du Québec, whose staff showed great patience at all times. Marthe Chercuitte, Ginette Renaud, Denis Giguere, Yves Robert, and Jean-Paul de Beaumont bore the brunt of my heavy demands, and I thank the librarians Marjolaine Thibault and Mlle Barry, also.

Without the information and photographs from private sources and descendants of shipbuilders this book would lose much of its interest, and I am particularly grateful to Archibald and James B. Beatson, Peggy Bolenbaugh, Jean-René Breton, Stewart Brodie, Gustave Charland, Roger Coulombe, Gordon Davie, Henri Dion, Jean-Claude Ernst, James Fairrie, John Fry, Anne-Marie Garneau, Pierre Gingras, Ainslie Goudie, Paul Gourdeau, Paul Hudson, Serge Joyal, Colin McMichael, Gertrude Simons McMichael, Clayton, Edith and Edward Nesbitt, James O'Hearn, Florence Oliver, the Omell Gallery of London, G. Kenneth and Harriet Parke, Russell Payson, Alice Rawstron, Reginald and William M. Ray, Robert Reid, Ruth and Elspeth Robinson, Jacques Rosa, Harry Ross, Marc Rouleau, Mildred Russell, May Scott, Duncan Stacey, Mike Stammers, Lucy Webster and Fleur Whitworth.

The photographs that are credited to the National Museum of Man are the work of Harry Foster and Cedric Pearson, and I thank them for their care. I am grateful to Caroline Soucy, for her watercolour on the cover and her pen and ink drawings, and to Simon Carmichael who kindly turned my figures into graphs. My special thanks to R.D. Wilson, for permission to reproduce his fine drawing of the Port of Montreal.

Nor do I forget those who provided a bed and other creature comforts during my research trips away from home, especially the Tamas family, Diana and John Cooper, the Cooks, the Ruddells, and the Marine Museum of the Great Lakes at Kingston, where a warm welcome and a bunk aboard the *Alexander Henry* was enjoyed on several occasions.

I thank my family for their constant interest despite my neglecting them at times, in particular my husband George, who helped in many capacities and has been supportive throughout, Tony, who frequently offered sound advice and found a great many ways to contribute, Susie, who gave a big hand with the plans, Paul and Ian, and also my niece Jennifer Blake who together with George rendered yeoman service with paste and scissors in the preparation of the original manuscript.

I am grateful to Roger Morris, who vetted the technical details in the manuscript, and to Margaret Gulliver for her careful work. And finally, my special thanks to Skip Fischer, who was not only among those who urged that I get the history published, but by adding the reading of the manuscript to his already busy schedule, took the initial step.

But writing a book is one thing and securing a publisher is another, and the roadblocks were finally pushed out of the way by a generous sponsor who has asked to remain anonymous and a publisher who was willing to take a chance on what was considered by others to be insufficiently academic to be an academic book and too academic to be a trade book. If parts or the whole of it are read and enjoyed, then my goal has been reached.

Charlesbourg, Quebec

Toponomy

At the end of the eighteenth and during the nineteenth century, a great number of British businessmen arrived in Quebec, many of whom settled there permanently, and through their efforts and with the financial backing of the British houses they represented, Quebec became an important shipping and commercial centre. Combined with the appointment of many English-speaking official, this led to a considerable degree of Anglicization of the town.

Many places were given English names by their English-speaking owners or occupiers, and English equivalents were frequently used for places that already had French names. Although most of the English names are no longer in use, it would not be logical to write this history with such terms as "rue Saint-Pierre" or "rue Prince Edouard," when the vast majority of maps and documents on which it is based refer to Saint Peter or Prince Edward street. Moreover, to use the French names would counter the effort that has been made to reflect the reality of nineteenth century business Quebec, while to use one or the other would obviously be confusing. English names that were commonly used in the nineteenth century are therefore used throughout.

Table of Contents

ACKNOWLEDGEMENTS 5
TOPONOMY 6
TABLE OF CONTENTS 7
LIST OF ILLUSTRATIONS 10
LIST OF TABLES 12
LIST OF GRAPHS 12
LIST OF MAPS 12
LIST OF SHIPYARD PLANS 13
LIST OF ABBREVIATIONS 13

INTRODUCTION 15 Previous Studies • The Project • Sources • The Plan

CHAPTER 1 37 *The Timber Trade*

The British Market • Conditions at Québec

CHAPTER 2 51 *Quebec Background*

CHAPTER 3 73 *The Shipbuilders*

Origins • Shipbuilders and "Shipbuilders"
The Shipbuilder in the Community

CHAPTER 4 97 *The Shipyards—Location*

During the French Regime
From 1763 on – The Quebec Waterfront
The New Yards in the Palace Area 1815–1819
The Quebec Waterfront
Près de Ville

The North Shore of the Saint Lawrence River
Saint Roch and Saint Sauveur
The North Bank of the Saint Lawrence River
The South Shore of the Saint Lawrence River
The Isle of Orleans • Summary

CHAPTER 5   161   *The Shipyards—Facilities*

The Building Slip • Grid Irons
Floating Docks and Marine Railways • Saw mills
The Mould or Moulding-Loft • The Forge
Steam-Houses and Steam-Boxes
Tradesmen's Lofts and Shops • The Boiler Shop
Sheds or Stores • The Counting House
Shipyard Equipment
The Shipbuilder's Home • Fences and Booms
Maintenance and Cost

CHAPTER 6   187   *Shipbuilding Business*

Ship Brokerage • Classification
Shipbuilding Contracts
The Shipyard Workforce
Division and Cost of Labour
Prices • Profit and Loss

CHAPTER 7   219   *Materials and Equipment*

Timber • Canadian Timber • Spar Wood
Equipment and Finishing Wood
Wood Supply
Iron and Other Metal
Increasing Use of Metal in Wooden Ships

Standard Requirements
Supply • Sails • Cordage
Ship's Boats • General Quality

CHAPTER 8   251   *The Trades*

Sawyer • Ship Carpenter • Planker
The Caulker • Ship Joiner
Ship Carver • Shipsmith
Glazier and Painter
Blockmaker • Mastmaker
Pump Maker • Ropemaker
Sailmaker • Rigger

CHAPTER 9   315   *The Ships*

Description — rig, tonnage, proportions,
decks, plans, deckhouses, stern,
sails, name, figurehead
Distribution
Milestones

CONCLUSION   359

APPENDIX A	363	Table of the Shipbuilders
	364	Notes for Appendix B & C
APPENDIX B	367	Sailing Ships Built at Quebec
APPENDIX C	385	Outport Construction of Square-Rigged Vessels and large Schooners and Sloops
APPENDIX D	392	Table of the Shipyards
APPENDIX E	395	Contracts and Other Documents
BIBLIOGRAPHY	417	
INDEXES	425	Index of Ships' Names
	431	General Index

Illustrations

Fig. Pg. Image

1. 23 Quebec 1759
2. 24 Geographical limits of study
3. 27 Apprenticeship Indenture
4. 29 Ship *Maldon* of 1855
5. 30 Ship *Caribou* of 1864
6. 33 Ship *Benguela* of 1876
7. 40 Wolfe's Cove, near Quebec
8. 41 Cape Diamond and Timber Depot
9. 42 Loading Timber
10. 43 View at Wolfe's Cove
11. 45 Timber Coves in 1890
12. 46 Timber Handling Tools
13. 47 Horses Drawing Timber
14. 51 Jean Talon
15. 52 René Noël Levasseur
16. 52 Schooner building on the Isle of Orleans
17. 54 John Molson
18. 55 James Goudie
19. 55 P.S. *Royal William* of 1831
20. 57 Steamboat Tariff
21. 57 Towboat Tariff
22. 58 John Goudie 1775-1824.
23. 59 *View of Amherstburg, 1813*
24. 60 Plan of HMS *Princess Charlotte* of 1813
25. 62 Model of *Confiance* of 1814
26. 63 HMS *St. Lawrence*, built at Kingston
27. 63 Engagement of Shipyard Workers
28. 64 Black and Campbell Shipyard
29. 64 Ship Laborers' friendly society
30. 64 Bateliers' friendly society
31. 65 Diamond Harbour
32. 68 Montreal Harbour
33. 73 Thomas Hamilton Oliver
34. 74 Thomas Oliver's ship Enterprise.
35. 75 Captain James Fairrie
36. 76 Captain Patrick Beatson
37. 77 Captain William Beatson
38. 77 Captain John Beatson
39. 78 John James Nesbitt
40. 79 Saint Roch shipyards
41. 82 Louis Shickluna
42. 84 Pierre Vincent Valin
43. 85 Pierre Toussaint Valin
44. 86 Captain Lauchlan McKay
45. 87 Captain Henry Warner
46. 89 Narcisse Rosa
47. 89 Page from Narcisse Rosa's book
48. 90 Barquentine *Niagara*
49. 91 Guillaume Charland
50. 91 Jean-Elie Gingras
51. 98 Site of John Black's Shipyard
52. 102 Launching of the *Cordelia*
53. 106 The Hermitage
54. 108 *Neptune Inn, Quebec*
55. 108 *Lower Market Place*
56. 109 *Lower Town, Quebec*
57. 111 Captain Beatson's gravestone
58. 111 The Beatson and Munn homes
59. 115 Cape Cove Shipyard from the River
60. 115 Cape Cove Shipyard later
61. 116 Henry Dinning
62. 116 Barque *Anna*, ex *Elizabeth Yeo*
63. 117 George Black jr.'s Account
64. 118 Cape Cove Shipyard
65. 119 Wolfe's Cove, 1808
66. 122 Allan Gilmour
67. 122 Gilmour Shipyard and Timber booms
68. 123 Suburb of Saint Roch 1793
69. 127 Goudie's Mill beside his Shipyard
70. 128 Walter Gilley Ray
71. 128 Ray's Business Card as a Shipwright
72. 128 Ray's Business Card as a Surveyor
73. 129 Valin's Shipyard above Dorchester Bridge 1866
74. 129 After the Fire of 1870
75. 134 Ship *Bucephalus* of 1854
76. 134 Upper Saint Charles River
77. 135 The McKay and Warner Shipyard
78. 135 William Bell's House
79. 141 Allison Davie
80. 141 Elizabeth Taylor Davie
81. 141 George Taylor Davie
82. 143 Allison Davie's Home and shipyard 1847
83. 144 Etienne Samson
84. 144 Ship *Emblem*
85. 144 Barque *Cambria* of 1885
86. 145 Alexander Russell
87. 145 Alexander Russell's Home
88. 145 Vestiges of the Russell Shipyard
89. 148 Ship *Montagnais*
90. 149 Sharples' and Dobell's Coves
91. 150 Ship *Helen*, 861 tons
92. 151 Raft-Ship *Columbus* of 1824
93. 152 Plan of *Columbus*
94. 162 The ship *Shannon* prior to launching in 1878
95. 163 Rotherhithe Floating Dry Dock
96. 165 Russell's Floating Dock
97. 165 Davie's Floating Dock and Marine Railway
98. 166 Remains of Davie's Floating Dock
99. 168 Morton's Patent Slip
100. 169 *East India Floating Dock*
101. 172 Crows' Nest Model of the PS *Royal William*
102. 172 Half-model for ships built by Walter G. Ray
103. 174 Advertisement - Black & Shaw
104. 176 Grounds and Residence of Geo. D. Davie's home
105. 178 St. Roch fire 1870
106. 178 The ship *Lady Lisgar* of 1870
107. 178 The Gilmour Shipyard
108. 179 John Munn's Residence
109. 179 Description of John Munn's Property
110. 179 George H. Parke's Residence
111. 182 Timber Boom
112. 188 Service of Plate Presented to Edward Oliver
113. 195 Henry Fry
114. 195 Fry's Ships *Mary Fry* of 1861,
115. 195 *Rock City* of 1868
116. 195 *Cosmo* of 1877
117. 196 James Gibb Ross 1819-1888
118. 198 Ross Bros & Co. Chandlery
119. 199 Certificate of Testing of Anchor Chain
120. 199 Attestation of Amount of Salt used
121. 208 Sale from James E. Oliver to Getty Bros
122. 209 The Notary Archibald Campbell
123. 209 The Duties of a Notary
124. 210 Money Box from the Russell Shipyard

#	Page	Description
125.	210	Advertisement for Sparmakers
126.	219	Trees Suitable for Shipbuilding Timber
127.	220	Timber Advertisement
128.	221	Midship Section Plan showing species of Timber
129.	233	Kedge Anchor Account for barque *Culdee*
130.	234	Russell Shipyard Account
131.	234	Order for Ship's Knees
132.	238	Sails for ship *Shannon*, 1878
133.	244	Ships' Boats
134.	253	Pit saws
135.	254	Sawyers at Work
136.	254	The Mould Loft
137.	255	Laying the keel
138.	255	Deadwood, etc. in forebody
139.	255	Deadwood, etc., in afterbody
140.	256	Futtocks
141.	257	Deck openings
142.	257	Hull in frame
143.	258	Midship Section of wooden-kneed vessel
144.	258	Midship section of iron-kneed vessel
145.	258	Single Twist Augers
146.	259	Spiral and Shell Augers
147.	260	Ship Carpenters' Tools
148.	261	Steam-box
149.	263	Ship Planking
150.	264	Caulking Mallet and Irons
151.	265	Horsing Irons and Beetle
152.	265	Coppering Hammer
153.	267	Chequering Mill
154.	268	Prisoners Picking Oakum
155.	269	Caulking the Planking
156.	271	The Captain's Cabin
157.	272	Dragon Knee-head
158.	272	Figurehead Design for the *Royal Edward*
159.	275	Figurehead of the brigantine *Salmon*
160.	275	Figurehead, Barque *Highlander*
161.	276	Figurehead, Barque *Edmonton*
162.	276	House of the Sculptor Louis Jobin
163.	276	Chisels belonging to Louis Jobin
164.	278	Mast Hoop
165.	278	Midship Section of the ship *Oliver Cromwell*
166.	279	Building a ship at the Gilmour Shipyard
167.	280	Ship construction at the McKay and Warner Shipyard
168.	282	Parts of the Block
169.	282	Tackles
170.	284	Upper and Lower Deadeye
171.	284	Machine-made Blocks
172.	285	Fitted Block
173.	285	Blockmaker's Inventory
174.	286	Turning lathe
175.	286	Clave
176.	288	Shaping a Mast
177.	288	Masts of the Barque *Saint Lawrence*
178.	290	Mastmaker's Compass
179.	290	Mastmaker's Tools
180.	291	Dressing a Mast
181.	292	Pump Boring Equipment
182.	295	A Spinner
183.	295	Ropemaking
184.	296	Rope Walk in the Outskirts
185.	296	Saint Sauveur Rope Walk
186.	297	Sailmaker Richard Hudson and Family
187.	298	Square Sails
188.	300	Sailmaker's Palms
189.	300	Sailmaker's Fids
190.	301	Sailmaker James O'Hearn
191.	301	Sailmaker's Needle Boxes and Needles
192.	301	Home of the Sailmaker Peter Simons
193.	302	Sailmakers' Tools
194.	303	Advertisement of the Sailmaker James Hunt
195.	304	Sail Plan for the Schooner *Thistle*
196.	304	Getting in a Lower Mast
197.	305	Lower Mast and Shrouds
198.	305	Shrouds and Chainplates
199.	306	Mast with Rigging
200.	306	Topsail Yard Rigged
201.	307	Hull and Standing Rigging of a Ship
202.	308	Hull and Running Rigging of a Ship
203.	309	Treenail Makers or "Mooters"
204.	309	A Borer
205.	310	Oak trunnels
206.	310	Typical Moot
207.	311	Butting Timber
208.	316	Square Rig and Fore-and-Aft Rig
209.	317	Square-Rigged Vessels
210.	317	Fore-and-Aft Rigged Vessels
211.	321	Revenue schooner *La Canadienne* of 1855
212.	321	Crew of *La Canadienne*
213.	325	Ship *Lord Elgin* of 1847
214.	327	Comparison of Hull Proportions
215.	328	Ship *Ocean Monarch* of 1854
216.	332	Ship *Peter Joynson* of 1863
217.	334	Plan of the Surrey Commercial Docks
218.	334	Surrey Commercial Docks, London
219.	336	Captain Joseph Elzéar Bernier
220.	336	Barque *Felicitas* of 1874
221.	337	Ship *Calcutta* of 1874
222.	338	Barque *Royal Visitor* of 1860
223.	339	Ship *Germanic* of 1878
224.	340	Barque *Secret* of 1867
225.	340	Midship Section plan of the barque *Secret*
226.	341	Figurehead of the ship *Indian Chief*
227.	342	Canada Docks, Liverpool
228.	343	Arrangement for setting up bunks for emigrants
229.	343	Ship *Thornhill* of 1855
230.	344	Barque *Hope* at Porthmadog Harbour in 1890
231.	345	After the launching
232.	345	Quebec 1874
233.	346	George Taylor and Commemorative Cup
234.	347	Launching of the P.S. *Royal William* in 1831
235.	348	Rue Champlain
236.	348	Chemin du Foulon
237.	349	Shipping at Hall's Booms
238.	350	Ship *Stafford* of 1877
239.	352	Bark *Edinburgh* of 1883
240.	353	Barquentine *White Wings* of 1893
241.	369	Quebec Customs House

Tables

Fig. Pg. Image

1. 189 Liverpool prices of Quebec-built vessels
2. 192 Prices obtained for Vessels Built in Quebec in 1864 whose Masters Carried Instructions Authorizing Them to Sell Them at Not Less Than a Fixed Amount in Britain or Elsewhere
3. 204 Numbers of Workers in Saint Lawrence, Saint Charles \ and Pointe-aux-Trembles Shipyards 1840-1866
4. 206 Number and Tonnage of Vessels under Construction and Number of Workers in Quebec Shipyards, February 1840
5. 211 Comparative Salaries at Quebec Shipyards that Operated for Seven, Eight or Twelve Months in 1880
6. 228 Relative Stiffness and Strength of Different Timbers
7. 229 Lloyd's Classification of Quebec-Built Ships
8. 240 Sail Outfits of Vessels Surveyed from 1852 to 1880
9. 289 Spars of the 275 ton barque *Saint Lawrence* of 1819.
10. 318 Annual Production, 1787-1893
11. 319 Percentage of Total Production, Number and Average Tonnage, by Rig, 1765-1893
12. 319 Production of Liverpool, Bath and West Bath, Me., Saint John, N.B. and Quebec Shipyards 1815-35
13. 319 Tonnage of Largest Vessels Built 1787-1893 and Name of Builder
14. 320 Production of Quebec, Saint John and Bath, Maine, Shipyards 1839-1885
15. 322 Average Length, Breadth, and Ratio of Length to Breadth, by Rig, 1765-1893

Graphs

Fig. Pg. Image

1. 69 Quebec Production of Wooden Vessels 1850-1885
2. 70 British Production of Wood and Iron Vessels 1850-1885
3. 80 Operating Years and Origin of Leading Quebec Shipbuilders
4. 81 Production of leading Quebec Shipbuilders
5. 153 Maximum Number of Yards by Decade 1790-1899
6. 212 Annual Tonnage Built at the Port of Quebec 1800-1893
7. 322 Average Tonnage of Vessels of Different Rig 1765-1893
8. 324 Production by Decade and Rig 1780-1890

Maps

Fig. Pg. Image

1. 96 Quebec and its Environs
2. 99 The City of Quebec 1759
3. 103 The City of Quebec 1822
4. 110 The North Shore of the Saint Lawrence River 1822
5. 124 The South Bank of the Saint Charles River circa 1776
6. 125 Shipyards in the Seigniory of Saint Roch in 1840
7. 131 The Lower Saint Charles 1854
8. 133 The North Bank of the Saint Charles River 1865-6
9. 137 The South Shore of the Saint Lawrence
10. 139 Glenburnie Cove and Lauzon Shipyards 1864-5
11. 147 The Isle of Orleans 1822
12. 387 Shipyard Sites

Ship Yard Plans

Fig. Pg. Image
1. 100 Saint Nicholas Dockyard 1739
2. 104 The King's Wharf Shipyard in 1800
3. 105 John Bell's Shipyard in 1823
4. 110 Diamond Harbour 1804
5. 113 Diamond Harbour 1821
6. 114 Cape Cove 1831
7. 121 Wolfe's Cove 1866
8. 126 John Munn's Extended Shipyard in the 1850s
9. 130 Thomas H. Lee's Shipyard, 1847
10. 140 The Russell Shipyard 1882

Abbreviations

ACQ	Archives civiles de Québec
ADM	Admiralty records
AHDQ	Archives de l'Hôtel-Dieu de Québec
AHGQ	Archives de l'Hôpital Général de Québec
ANQ	Archives nationales du Québec à Québec
ANQM	Archives nationales du Québec à Montréal
APQ	Archives du Port de Québec
ASQ	Archives du Séminaire de Québec
AVQ	Archives de la Ville de Québec
BRH	*Bulletin des recherches historiques*
DCB	*Dictionary of Canadian Biography*
GR	Greffe of the notary – (at ANQ, unless otherwise indicated)
L.S.	Lloyd's Survey Report
MG	Manuscript Group
MMA	Maritime Museum of the Atlantic
NA	National Archives of Canada
NMC	National Museums of Canada
PRO	Public Record Office, Kew, England
RAPQ	*Rapport de l'archiviste de la Province de Québec*
RG	Record Group
RHAF	*Revue d'histoire de l'Amérique française*
RPQ	Register of the Port of Quebec (originals at PRO at Kew, and NC)
SRO	Scottish Record Office, Edinburgh
U.L.	Université Laval

Dedicated to

The Shipbuilders

Introduction

The launching of the little barquentine *White Wings* from a Lauzon shipyard in 1893 brought an end to the construction of square-rigged sailing ships at Quebec,[1] an industry which at times had provided work for several thousand of her artisans and labourers. With its passing, it was soon forgotten, and of some sixteen hundred stately ships that were built there, not one was conserved as a reminder of sailing ship days. No maritime museum was created at Quebec to keep its history alive and serve as custodian of things that are now lost or scattered. Today, few Quebeckers can name even one of the vessels built by their ancestors. Yet, there were times when as many as twenty-eight shipyards were in operation. There were shipyards where four or five vessels waited side by side for their launching at the first spring tides. And there were years when as many as fifty or sixty vessels sailed from Quebec on their maiden voyage laden with timber and masts from Canada's heartland.

My interest in this part of Quebec's maritime history began in 1976 when the History Division of the National Museum of Man in Ottawa required a ten thousand word essay entitled *Shipbuilding in Quebec, 1760–1850*, for publication in a "popular" series. It was to include a brief historical introduction to shipbuilding in New France, give the reasons for its growth in nineteenth century Quebec, describe its major characteristics, discuss its significance in the Quebec economy and include a description of the tools and techniques employed. Moreover, because budgetary considerations did not allow for research in primary sources, for the most part secondary sources would have to be used. But the few and limited secondary sources that existed did not answer enough questions and raised many others. The subject was fascinating and deserved more attention. The archives beckoned, and soon I was deeply involved.

Previous Studies

Shipbuilding in the Port of Quebec began in 1665, the year that the newly appointed Intendant Jean Talon arrived in the colony.[2] Unfortunately, the first Royal Dockyard was short-lived and little is known about it, but a second Royal Dockyard founded in 1739 was more successful, giving rise to an important period of government shipbuilding. This dockyard was the subject of an article by Pierre-Georges Roy entitled "La construction royale de Quebec" (1946),[3] and was further examined by Jacques Mathieu in his Master's thesis, published as *La construction navale royale à Québec 1739–1759* (1971). Both these studies are based mainly on correspondence between the governors, intendants and master shipbuilder at Quebec,[4] on the one hand, and the Minister of the Navy on the other.[5] Because French authorities kept such tight control over the Quebec yard, the details in the dispatches cover a wide range of matters, which together with what can be learned from the ordinances of the intendants and other official documents has allowed a portrait of the industry to emerge. The choice of shipyard sites, accounts of progress in establishing the yard and in the construction of vessels, problems in obtaining skilled labour and building materials, particularly timber, are among the many administrative and technical subjects covered, while the regulations in the ordinances which deal with smoking, the men's movements in and out of the yard (mainly to control the surreptitious removal of timber or chips), frequent visits to nearby taverns and similar matters add insight into disciplinary issues.[6] In spite of the serious nature of many of the problems the Master Shipbuilder faced, several large ships measuring from five to seven hundred tons were built at the yard before construction was brought to a standstill in 1759.[7]

Roy saw the closing of the shipyards as the result of the Intendant Bigot's corrupt rule:

No sooner had the wretched Bigot taken up his appointment as intendant of New France that all kinds of favouritism, thievery and dishonest dealings infiltrated every branch of the administration, including the Royal Dockyard. Mr. Levasseur, an honest man, could do nothing to prevent it. He was under the orders of the intendant, and had no control of the shipyard's expenses. The intendant administered the supply of workers and materials and fixed their cost. When the English invaded the colony, work at the yard halted, but the Conseil de Marine had decided two years previously to discontinue the construction of naval vessels in New France.[8] (my translation)

Mathieu attributes the closing to the fact that the industry was not planned in the interest of the colony. Naval construction at Quebec was by its nature—its financing and purpose, its methods and structure—a metropolitan industry. Top level decisions were made in France, and were conceived for and in the interests of the metropolis, not the colony. Maurepas insisted that ships be built of a size that bore no relation to the forest resources of New France. Imported methods were not successfully adapted to Canadian conditions; nor were French artisans able to draw Canadians out of their self-imposed seclusion. Whether it was due to their attitude of superiority, to the influence of the Indian or to the lifestyle that had been adopted in the colony, Canadians preferred the easy life on the farm to the long hours of the shipyard, cockcrow to the shipyard bell. They soon lost their initial enthusiasm and made no further efforts to increase their competence.

The entirely artificial character of the industry was largely responsible for the difficulties it faced. (translation)[9]

Mathieu attaches a great deal of importance to the problem of the timber supply—particularly the difficulty of obtaining single sound pieces of timber that were large enough to build a vessel of the size ordered, and indeed a full third of his study is devoted to the fundamental timber question.[10] Had the colony remained in French hands, whether the yard would have closed within two years, as Roy suggests, or carried on, importing materials such as cordage, sailcloth, tar, and iron from France, as is Mathieu's contention, is open to conjecture. Having survived for twenty years and produced an acceptable product despite all the difficulties, it might well have survived. However, had Bigot's intendancy continued and had he persisted in raiding the supply of specially seasoned timber, in depriving the yard of labour and in other tactics of which Levasseur complained, or, had the production of the domestic Royal Dockyards been able to fill Naval requirements,[11] the operation might well have been closed down.

The detrimental effect of the royal dockyards on the private shipbuilding industry, to which Mathieu draws attention,[12] has been underscored in Réal Brisson's more recent thesis in which he reviews the development of shipbuilding in New France, with the records of Quebec notaries as his main source.[13] Between them, Mathieu and Brisson provide an overall picture of both government and private shipbuilding at Quebec during the French regime.

The royal shipyards did not continue as naval yards after the change of regime in 1759, and private yards gradually took on importance. Private enterprise could not afford to be hamstrung by excessive trans-Atlantic consultation, so no body of documentation comparable to the official despatches of the French period is available to students of nineteenth century shipbuilding history. Instead, the history of the industry has had to be pieced together from a variety of sources, and much has been lost, for contemporary historians seem to have shunned the subject. The story of the two huge timber droghers, the *Columbus* and the *Baron of Renfrew*, which were built at the Isle of Orleans from 1823 to 1825, survived as history rather than as a legend due to its extensive coverage by both the Canadian and the British press.[14] The exploit of the *Royal William*, launched at Cape Cove in 1831, the first vessel to cross the North Atlantic entirely under steam, might well have become difficult to uphold had not Captain F.C. Wurtele, the Honorary Librarian of the Literary and Historical Society of Quebec, collected together sworn testimonials and other documents supporting the claim, which were tabled as a reliable record in Appendix G of the *Report of the Secretary of State for Canada for the Year ended 31st December 1894*. The *Royal William*'s exploit was thus ensured a place in international maritime history.[15]

Then in 1897 the retired Quebec shipbuilder Narcisse Rosa (1823–1907), realizing how quickly Quebec's shipbuilding years were slipping into oblivion, published a few pages of reminiscences in a little book entitled *La construction des navires à Québec et ses environs*, the major part of which was devoted to a list of the ships measuring over one hundred tons that were built in the Quebec City area between 1797 and 1896. His recollections, though brief, are precious, for he is the only shipbuilder of the town to have left some impressions of the lives of the shipyard workers and descriptions of a few aspects of the trade. Through his eyes we are able to glimpse the human side of the shipyard and to learn that despite the days of strikes and angry rhetoric, of unemployment, of low wages, there were also happy times when "the worker raised the frames of a ship as briskly and lightheartedly as if he had been building his own home."[16] (translation)

Unfortunately, Rosa's list of vessels supposedly

built at Quebec includes a large number that were built in places as far apart as Whitby in North East England and Bermuda and were merely registered de novo (re-registered) at Quebec, while at least forty-two vessels, that were built at Quebec between 1827 and 1829, have been omitted. It was, nevertheless, the only published list until recent years,[17] and in spite of obvious differences with annual Board of Trade totals, has been widely used and cited.[18] A revised list is included as the main appendix to this study.

Following Rosa, over a quarter of a century elapsed before the publication in 1924 of a volume entitled *Wooden Ships and Iron Men*. Its mariner-author, Frederick William Wallace (1826–1958) wrote in the forward:

The compilation of this record was undertaken as a labour of love and to save from oblivion the facts regarding an era of maritime effort and industry which is one of the most inspiring pages in Canadian history, but which, even today, has not been adequately appreciated. The gathering of the information presented in the following pages has been carried out under many handicaps. To be really comprehensive, it should have been written fifty years ago . . .

Wallace, who had been collecting the material since 1912, tells us that he made use of every scrap of information on shipbuilding and shipping in Quebec and the Maritime Provinces that had come his way. This resulted in a book of which one third, or about one hundred pages, is devoted to shipbuilding at Quebec and comprises biographical notes on shipbuilders and details from the careers of the ships they built, in both cases from about 1840 on. A very brief run-down of the period 1800 to 1840 is included and there are half a dozen portraits of Quebec-built ships. Wallace hoped that his work would serve as a basis for future research workers in the field. Though he did not immediately succeed in inspiring others to take on the mantle, he received so many documents, photographs and personal recollections as a result of the publication of his best-selling *Wooden Ships and Iron Men* (1924), that he himself was able to write a second volume, *In the Wake of the Windships*, published in 1927. The important Quebec shipping agent, Henry Fry, for instance, had written a little volume for his son entitled "Reminiscences of a Quebec Shipowner," which the younger Fry allowed Wallace to draw from for his second book.[19] Fry's reminiscences are now in the hands of his grandson, and will be preserved, but some of the other material Wallace received might have disappeared on the death of its owners, the heirs having no use for it. By saving so much from oblivion, Frederick William Wallace made a priceless contribution to the maritime history of Quebec and of the maritime provinces.

Fortunately, Wallace lived long enough to see his work taken up in the Maritimes. Louis Manny's *Ships of Kent County* (1949) and *Ships of Bathurst* (1951) were the modest beginning in New Brunswick. At Wallace's suggestion and with his help and encouragement,[20] Captain John Parker compiled the record and story of the large cargo schooners of Atlantic Canada in *Sails of the Maritimes* (1960), following this up with *Cape Breton Ships and Men* (1967). An overview of the era of square-rigged vessels in the maritime provinces Stanley T. Spicer's *Masters of Sail* (1968) appeared next, and then Charles A. Armour and Thomas Lackey's *Sailing Ships of the Maritimes* (1975) and Esther Clark Wright's *Saint John Ships and Their Builders* (1976). All had the same motive as Wallace and Rosa before him, namely to record whatever was still possible to record about an industry and the men who worked in it whom they admired. A great many sources were used, shipping registers, newspapers, diaries, family and official records. Basil Greenhill and Ann Giffard's *Westcountrymen in Prince Edward's Isle* (1967) had already dealt with shipbuilding in that Province within a rather wider context, which embraced the island's bond with Devon, whence many of the islanders came and with which they kept a strong trading connection.

Meanwhile, Captain Joseph Elzéar Bernier' shipmaster and Arctic explorer, had written his memoirs recounting his life afloat and ashore, which through a series of misfortunes were not published until 1939, after his death. In *Master Mariner and Arctic Explorer: A Narrative of Sixty Years at Sea from the Logs and Yarns of Captain J.E. Bernier,* he corroborates Rosa's description of cheerful shipyard workers:

The men came trooping in between six and seven, each man checking off his name in a book kept for the purpose, for in those days there were no time clocks. Nor was there reluctance to begin a few minutes before seven o'clock, especially on the part of the jobbers, who were paid on a piece-work basis. By seven, there would be four hundred or more men busily engaged and the sounds of mallet and hammer, adze, axe and saw, echoed up and down the St. Charles Valley, to the accompaniment of similar sounds from half-a-score other shipyards.

Practically all shipyard work was done in the open, even on the coldest winter days. Workmen were hardier then, and less exacting. And they were more cheerful at their work. Throughout the day there was much singing and humming of old Canadian folk-songs. Some lusty voice would break into a familiar *chanson* and the gang would join in on the choruses. If there was a heavy piece of timber to carry or to haul along the ground, the regulation song was the "Charley-Man". The gang-leader would sing out: "Charley was a good man, " and the gang would add in unison, "Charle,–man," drawing out the first syllable to keep time with the length of the pull required. Sometimes, in the case of a very heavy piece of timber, or of a large section like the stern frame, one hundred men would be pressed into service to pull on the ropes. The Charley-man" was then most impressive and could be heard for miles around.

Bernier's narrative, published more than forty years after the last wooden sailing ship was built, was the last eye-witness account of shipbuilding at Quebec, following which the subject was left to historians.

In 1956, in a paper presented at the Annual Meeting of the Canadian Political Science Association,[21] "The Decline of Shipbuilding at Quebec during the Nineteenth Century," Albert Faucher undertook a historical revision of the interpretation of the decline which, he believed, rested on half-truths:

The attempts to interpret the decline solely in terms of iron, steam and steel, or labour and sales methods in the British market sound quite admissible, but they rest on the assumption that shipbuilding at Quebec was structurally affected in the late sixties only instead of ten years earlier.

. . . . with due respect to chronology, it would be difficult for the historian to ascribe the decline of shipbuilding at Quebec to technological changes as a factor of primary or sole importance. Clapham, with Lubbock and with Kennedy as authorities, mentions the Aberdeen White Star Line as building its first iron clipper in 1869, the Orient Line in 1873. On the Clyde, a fifteen-ton iron sailing ship was launched in 1875.[22]

While agreeing with Faucher that the decline of shipbuilding had many contributory factors, I do not share his difficulty in accepting that technological changes were of primary importance. Sir Westcott Abel wrote, "The era of iron shipbuilding may be said to have been fairly established when the 'Great Britain', 322' in length, was built in 1843 to the designs of Mr. Brunel."[23] The first iron and steam Cunarder the 390-foot *Persia* was built in 1855 and the 680-foot *Great Eastern* in 1859.[24] By 1862, as much metal tonnage was being built in Britain as wooden tonnage[25] and by 1866 over a million tons of iron vessels had British registry.[26] Moreover, Lloyd's classified their first iron ship, the *Sirius*, in 1837; by 1855 their Registers carried rules governing the scantlings and construction of iron ships as a matter of course; and in 1866 fourteen hundred and thirty-seven iron vessels were listed. It would appear that iron shipbuilding was far more advanced than Faucher realized.

Even established metal shipbuilding areas, such as the River Thames, had succumbed to the tremendous surge in the iron industry of the Clyde and Northeast England, which, with large deposits of coal handy, with numerous metalworks built up over the years, a nucleus of dedicated far-sighted metallurgists in charge and far less militant unions, could build a cheaper product. These areas lead in the innovations that were constantly required in the development of the new technology,[27] leaving every other European country, the United States and British North America far behind. (History would be repeated in the next century, when Japan found ways to build more efficiently and collared the market, leaving shipyards in Britain to suffer the same fate.) As in all other businesses, profitability was the bottom line in the ship owning business. Advances in technology were responsible for the low cost at which British shipyards could produce the more economical metal ship, and were, I believe, not only an important factor, but the *most* important factor in the decline of shipbuilding at Quebec.

In 1971, the formation of the "Maritime History Group," whose mandate was to "acquire documents relating to the fisheries and shipping on a world wide basis, to undertake research into this field and to assist others in their research,"[28] gave a great boost to the study of Canadian maritime history. Located at Memorial University, St. John's, Newfoundland, its archives contain the original crew lists and agreements and the official Log Books of all merchant ships registered under the British flag from 1863 to 1939, with a few exceptions.[29] Much of the information in these and in their other collections is now in a computer data bank. Members of the Group have produced a large number of articles and papers covering many different aspects of Eastern Canada's maritime history, for example, David Alexander, "Output and Productivity in the Yarmouth Ocean Fleet, 1863–1901;"[30] Rosemary Ommer, "Anticipating the Trend: The Pictou Ship Register, 1840–1889."[31] Lewis Fischer, "A Good Poor Man's Country: Trade, Shipping and the Prince Edward Island Economy, 1802–1873."[32] Studies have been made or are under way on such topics as the "disposal and sale of Canadian built vessels in British and

European Markets," "patterns of desertion" and "the commercial activities of major investors in shipping."[33] From 1977 until 1982 conferences were held annually which attracted maritime scholars from many parts of North America, from Britain and continental Europe. The published proceedings of these conferences and many other studies of the members of the Group have made and continue to make a most valuable scholarly contribution to Canadian maritime history.

Back in Quebec, Luc Guinard's "Evolution dans la localisation des chantiers navals sur la rivière Saint-Charles 1840–1870," (1972),[34] examined the industry in that area using the local newspapers[35] and listings in city directories as the main sources. His account covers seventy-two shipbuilders or shipbuilding partnerships operating shipyards on the Saint Charles River during those thirty years. Guided by surveyors' plans, he prepared his own, which showed the location of most of the shipyards in 1840, 1854, 1859, 1864 and 1870. They are of considerable interest, particularly his plan of 1854 on which the position of the building ways can be seen.

For his doctoral thesis, "Shipbuilding in British America, 1787–1890: An Introductory Study" (1977), Richard Rice examined Quebec shipbuilding in its British North American and British context with regards to production, and as a colonial export which depended on British markets, capital and technology. He also gave some attention to the trade itself, contending that the shipyard was a manufactory rather than an industry and challenging the validity of applying the staples theory to shipbuilding. His figures for Canadian tonnage are based on his own transcriptions of the registers of the Port of Quebec from 1787 to 1855 and of the Port of Saint John from 1812 to 1813 and 1817 to 1855, together with the reports of customs officials. He concludes:

The linkages of shipbuilding to the timber trade, and in general to British navigation and trade policies were determined to be key conditioning factors in its growth, while the alterations in the timber duties and subsequent stagnation of that trade, plus the opening of the British ship market to foreign vessels combined to bring that growth to an end. Concurrently the depleting of ship-timber stocks, and changing ship technology – in the latter of which British America had little part – sharpened the changing structure of British American shipbuilding. In the end, the collapse of the British market in wooden sailing vessels brought British American shipbuilding down. The failure of the new state of Canada to pursue an active programme of encouragement of shipbuilding remains as a subject inviting inquiry.[36]

However, the first published study of shipbuilding at Quebec since Rosa based on the port registers was "La construction navale à Québec 1760–1825: sources inexplorées et nouvelles perspectives," (1981).[37] In this, Pierre Dufour, divides the shipyards of the Saint Lawrence valley and the Gaspé peninsula into three areas, which he describes as the estuary, mezzo-fluvial and fluvial areas, and, having determined the important shipbuilding localities in each, provides shipbuilding figures for them. He also compiles statistics for the disposal of Quebec-built ships on the British market over the sixty-five years. His breakdown of sales to various regions underscores the principal problem in the industry, the instability of the market.[38]

The register transcriptions and Dufour's analysis

of the register-books became the spring-board for a chapter on shipbuilding in Jean Benoit's doctoral thesis on credit in the nineteenth century economy of Quebec. Using the credit reports of the Mercantile Agency, and the reference books of R.G. Dunn & Co. and John Bradstreet and Son, he examined the financial relationship between the shipbuilding industry and wood trade. He concludes that the wood trade satellized the shipbuilding industry in its own interests and was responsible for its misfortunes, rather than being its "engine of growth" and "key element in its economic structure," as maintained by Rice, who considers that shipbuilding was "subject to the wider influences of trade and shipping."[39]

Since then, in 1984, in his spirited account, *Québec à l'âge de la voile,* Paul Therrien considerably broadened the day to day local and overseas background against which both the timber and the shipbuilding trades had previously been described.[40] While Marc Rouleau's recently published *La construction navale à Québec et à Neuville au XIXe siècle* allows a great deal of valuable insight into the operations of the shipbuilder and shipowner Hypolite Dubond and in particular those of his shipyard at Pointe-aux-Trembles (Neuville).[41] Finally, biographies of several Quebec shipbuilders and others closely related to the industry, such as René-Nicolas Levasseur, Patrick Beatson, John Black, John Goudie, James Hunt (the sailmaker), Charles Wood, George Black, John Munn, Allan Gilmour, Henry Dinning, James Gibb Ross, William H. Baldwin, Henry Fry and Pierre Valin appear in the first twelve volumes of the *Dictionary of Canadian Biography,* each offering a fresh perspective to the history of shipbuilding at Quebec.

The Project

It was not entirely virgin ground that I was stepping on, then, when I undertook to chronicle the Quebec wooden sailing ship industry, not from the point of view of its place in the economy of Quebec, nor as a colonial enterprise with all its political implications, nor in terms of the technological development of Quebec-built ships or the destiny of those ships, all of which would, however, come into it, but as the sum total of the effort of the individuals who built them. There was no intention to prove or disprove any theories, although this might occur along the way. The years between 1760 and 1840 had received the least attention from historians, but I felt in no way bound to restrict my work to those, as 1840 did not appear to be a natural cut-off point. The fact that it marked the union of the two Canadas had no direct influence on the shipbuilding industry. That it was a peak year for construction was no doubt due to the harvest failure of 1839 and the need to transport grain, and it was followed by the inevitable slump. Moreover, many important shipbuilders such as George Black, John Munn, John James Nesbitt and Thomas Oliver were half-way through their careers. I was attracted to study the far longer but neat package 1760-1893 that covered the era of square-rigger construction for the British merchant fleet, and which I saw as a whole. It is therefore those years that mark the temporal limits of this study.

Figure 1: *Quebec 1759. The unfinished frigate* Le Québec *on the stocks at the foot of the cliff. Detail from* "A View of the City of Quebec, the Capital of Canada...," *Capt Hervey Smythe, engraved by P. Benazech. Photo: Québec XVIIe Série B9, GH 470–136, courtesy Archives nationales du Québec.*

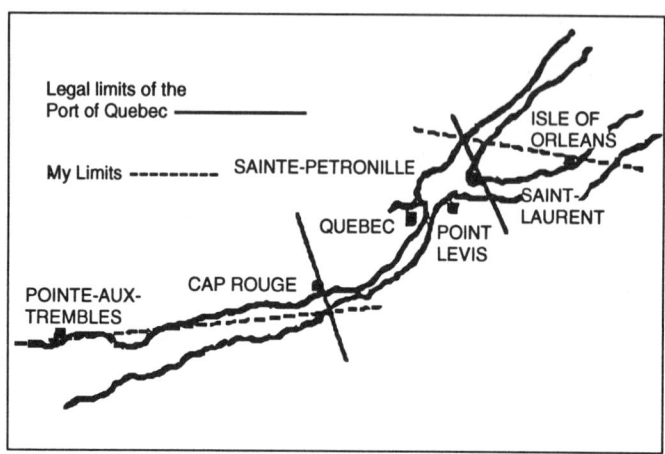

Figure 2: *Geographic limits.*

The "Port of Quebec" encompasses the Saint Lawrence River and its banks between a line drawn in a S.E. 15° E. direction from the western abutment of the bridge which crosses the Cap Rouge River to its intersection with the high water mark on the south bank of the river, and a straight line drawn from the east bank of the mouth of the Montmorency River passing through the Church of Saint-Petronille on the Isle of Orleans to its intersection with the high water mark on the south bank of the river, and includes those parts of its tributaries which the tide reaches between those two lines. With two exceptions, the major shipyards of the Quebec City area were contained within these limits. Both of the exceptions were within twenty miles of Quebec, and at both, ships were built for Quebec interests. It seemed logical therefore to extend the area covered by this study a distance of twenty miles to the west of the limits of the port on the north bank and twenty miles to the east on the south bank, so as to include Saint Laurent on the Isle of Orleans and Pointe-aux-Trembles (Neuville) upriver from Quebec.[41]

And finally, because I felt that this little known part of Quebec's history should be more readily available to all Canadians, and in particular to descendants of Quebec's shipbuilders and shipyard workers now scattered throughout the country, I decided to present it in a straight-forward manner acceptable to the general public.

Sources

The first general registration act which made it obligatory for all decked British ships of fifteen tons and upward to be enrolled in the statutory register-book at the Customs House of her home port, was passed in 1786.[42] The register-books of the Port of Quebec that came into being as a result of this and subsequent laws[43] are preserved at the Public Archives of Canada and are available on microfilm.[44] They contain copies of the initial registries of ships built at Quebec and elsewhere on the River and on the Gaspé coast, and exceptionally from other places, as well as of the "governor's passes" issued in some cases in lieu of a certificate of registry.[45] Also in the register-books are copies of registrations, or registries "de novo," of vessels that had changed hands and changed their home port or had had extensive repairs, and of vessels captured and condemned as lawful prizes.

The Registers were the principal source for my research and are the basis of my own register and data bank (now a computer bank) of all ships built and registered in the port. Moreover, they served to identify the vast majority of Quebec shipbuilders. The data taken from them includes the controlling details – the port number and date of registry, the name of the vessel and after 1855, the official number; descriptive details – the rig, tonnage, measurements, number of decks, number of masts, type of stern and particulars of galleries and figurehead; and details of build.[46] In noting them, it was disappointing to find that though the year and place were always given in the registry, and in some cases even the exact location, the builder's name was not. Not only are there periods during the 1810s and 1820s and again in the 1850s when the name is missing, but at times the name of the financer of the construction is given instead of that of the builder. It was necessary therefore to use other sources to fill as many of these gaps as possible.

Being very conscious from the outset of the length of the period I had chosen to cover, I had made determined efforts to restrict my study to shipbuilding and to avoid confronting the subject of shipping, which would extend it even further, but I found out that the two cannot easily be separated; I could not ignore what happened to a vessel after her launching. So details of ownership were also transcribed and endorsements on the certificates giving the date and port of a registry "de novo" or of a loss or wreck.

The statutory shipping registers, particularly when the series is as complete as that of the Port of Quebec, are an excellent source of accurate information, ideal for quantitative analysis. Each certificate is the proof of a fait accompli, that the vessel as described has been built and launched and, in the case of an endorsement to the effect, has sailed to and received new registry at a different port. Furthermore, with a few exceptions mostly in the early days, only those vessels so registered have been built at the port in question. My own registers became a basic tool which I referred to frequently. From their pages, I was able to see at a glance the evolution in vessel types, the progression in measurements, the variation in tonnage figures, the changes in figurehead preference, the transition of the square to the elliptical stern, the pattern or demand as shown by the registries de novo, and where each ship fitted in to them.

Following the registrations, the next most important source used is the collection of notarial "greffes" at the Archives nationales du Québec. Unlike the certificate of registry, the notarial contract, unless it has a corollary stating that both sides have carried out their responsibilities or proof has been found elsewhere to that effect, guarantees neither that the terms of the contract were in fact executed, nor that there were no changes made by mutual consent or otherwise, nor that a resiliation or amending contract was not made before a notary whose records one has not searched. It is only a document of original intent.

A contract to build a ship might have been privately cancelled, or contracted to a different builder by the commissioner, or even sub-contracted to that builder by the original contractor, so that finding a contract to build a vessel is not necessarily proof that it was indeed a part of the contractor's production. Again, changes in materials or even in measurements might have been agreed to privately; changes in requirements might have affected the price. The date of delivery could have been altered or the construction postponed for a year. The name of a vessel was rarely given in a building contract, and even in cases where it was, it was often changed before registry took place making identification difficult or impossible. Moreover, there is by no means a complete set of notarial shipbuilding contracts for any given period: many were built on speculation, others resulted from contracts drawn up privately, others from a few figures on a scrap of paper and still others from a handshake. But all this does not mean that the notarial records are not an invaluable source of information on the types, quality, outfits, prices, etc of vessels, only that they provide fragmentary information. They cannot always be matched to a particular vessel in the official register and, in particular, if they do contain divergences with details in the registries, the latter should be considered correct.

By contrast, not only can one rely on the accuracy of the description of shipyard sites in deeds of sale, but often the deeds include details of several previous sales and in principle the ownership of the sites can be traced throughout the period under study. Such difficulties as may present themselves can generally be overcome, and certainly from the 1850s when the cadastres were introduced, to do so is simple. However, tracing the landlord does not necessarily lead to the shipbuilder, who may be only a tenant and whose lease may or may not turn up in the search. When it does not, census returns, evaluation roles and city directories can help. The names of owners are important in following the development of river front areas and finding out why some became shipbuilding sites at one time and others at another.

Unless a plan accompanies the deed, the layout of the yard is generally not clear, nor are all buildings necessarily identified according to their usage: moulding lofts and smithies, for instance, can be camouflaged under the generality of "dependencies." However, sufficient information can be gleaned from among a substantial body of maps and plans in various archives, and failing that, from leases, inventories or mortgages, to recreate many of the layouts. Inventories made on the death of a builder or his wife, or, in the case of a business reversal, to present to his creditors, offer excellent descriptions of the contents of building yards.

Other business deeds which the shipbuilder may have concluded before a notary include reports of surveys, partnership agreements, arrangements for personal or business loans and discharges, or loans to enable him to build a particular vessel, which sometimes took the form of mortgages, contracts for repairs to vessels and for work other than shipbuilding, contracts to buy timber or spars, protests over materials or work improperly done or behind schedule and, on an even unhappier note, agreements with his creditors. Contracts for the sale of vessels disposed of in Canada are neatly tied in with the statutory registers, as the law required the certificate of registry to be "truly and accurately recited in words at length" in any bill or instrument transferring the property or any part of it.

Unfortunately, shipyard work was rarely the subject of a notarial contract. A certain number of apprenticeship indentures, engagements and work contracts occur up until 1825, showing the manner in which labour was hired or contracted for at the time. After that, with few exceptions, only apprenticeships and contracts for out-of-town work are covered. Could the sudden change be due to the shipbuilder insisting on an agreement signed before the notary when there was a shortage of skilled labour, in order to protect himself against late delivery penalties? That after 1825, obtaining labour was no longer a problem? Or were later contracts written into a yard journal? The almost total absence of contracts to supply sails, blocks, sculpture, etc. is also surprising. A suit of sails, for instance, was worth several thousand dollars. Notarial contracts were made for much smaller amounts.

This lack of labour contracts is particularly disappointing because no complete private shipyard records appear to have survived to provide the answers to the many questions that present themselves. Typical of these are the variation in the number of workers

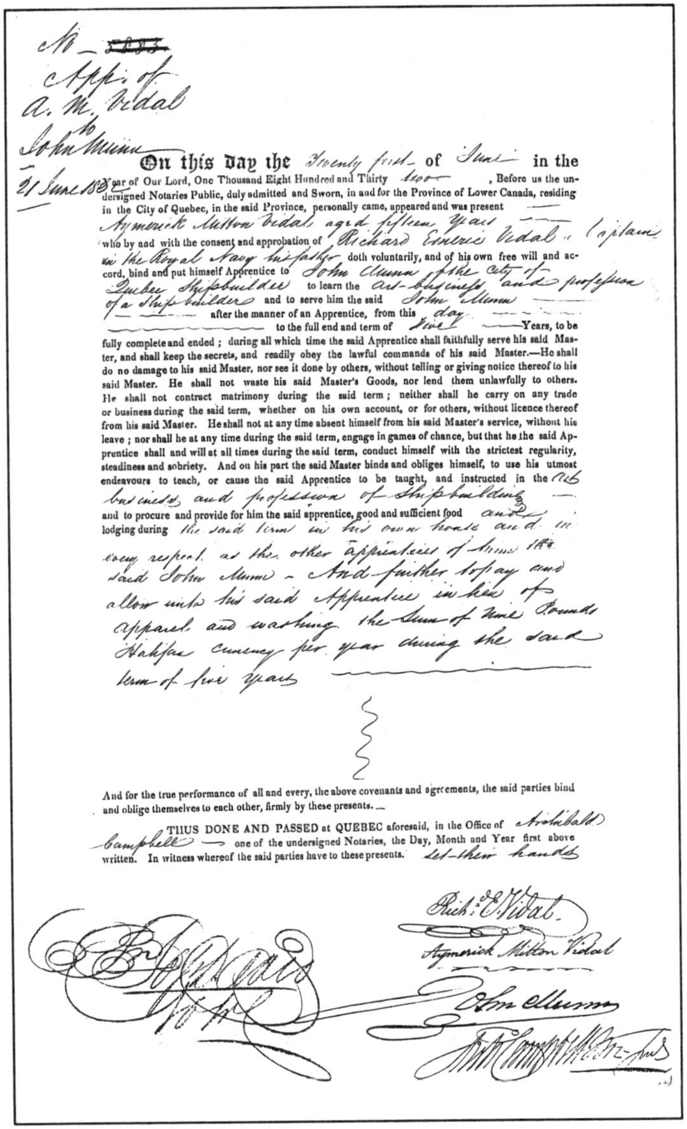
No —
App. of
A. M. Vidal
to
John Munn
21 June 1832

On this Day the Twenty first of June in the Year of Our Lord, One Thousand Eight Hundred and Thirty two, Before us the undersigned Notaries Public, duly admitted and Sworn, in and for the Province of Lower Canada, residing in the City of Quebec, in the said Province, personally came, appeared and was present Aymerick Mitton Vidal aged fifteen years who by and with the consent and approbation of Richard Emeric Vidal Captain in the Royal Navy his father doth voluntarily, and of his own free will and accord, bind and put himself Apprentice to John Munn of the city of Quebec Shipbuilder to learn the art business and profession of a Shipbuilder and to serve him the said John Munn after the manner of an Apprentice, from this day to the full end and term of Five Years, to be fully complete and ended; during all which time the said Apprentice shall faithfully serve his said Master, and shall keep the secrets, and readily obey the lawful commands of his said Master.—He shall do no damage to his said Master, nor see it done by others, without telling or giving notice thereof to his said Master. He shall not waste his said Master's Goods, nor lend them unlawfully to others. He shall not contract matrimony during the said term; neither shall he carry on any trade or business during the said term, whether on his own account, or for others, without licence thereof from his said Master. He shall not at any time absent himself from his said Master's service, without his leave; nor shall he at any time during the said term, engage in games of chance, but that he the said Apprentice shall and will at all times during the said term, conduct himself with the strictest regularity, steadiness and sobriety. And on his part the said Master binds and obliges himself, to use his utmost endeavours to teach, or cause the said Apprentice to be taught, and instructed in the Art business and profession of Shipbuilding and to procure and provide for him the said apprentice, good and sufficient food and lodging during the said term in his own house and in every respect as the other apprentices of him the said John Munn — And further to pay and allow unto his said Apprentice in lieu of apparel and washing the Sum of Nine Pounds Halifax currency per year during the said term of five years

And for the true performance of all and every, the above covenants and agreements, the said parties bind and oblige themselves to each other, firmly by these presents.—

THUS DONE AND PASSED at QUEBEC aforesaid, in the Office of Archibald Campbell one of the undersigned Notaries, the Day, Month and Year first above written. In witness whereof the said parties have to these presents set their hands

Richd. E. Vidal
Aymerick Mitton Vidal
John Munn
Archd. Campbell N.P.

Figure 3: *Apprenticeship Indenture. Fifteen year old Aymerick Vidal, son of Captain Richard Emeric Vidal, Captain in the Royal Navy, is bound to John Munn as an apprentice builder for a term of five years. Gr. Archibald Campbell, 21 June 1832, courtesy Archives nationales du Québec.*

through the seasons, the percentage of regular to casual labour, the breakdown of numbers working in the various trades or as labourers, the man-hours required to build vessels of different tonnages and how this might have been affected by the season, what changes there were in the organization of labour after 1825. Despite a great deal of time spent in an effort to trace descendants of shipbuilders in the hope that somewhere a shipyard journal might have survived, I have not yet been successful.

My account of the shipyard workers is therefore based on a variety of sources, census returns, newspaper reports, government papers, etc., and also on information found in notarial contracts of different kinds such as protests, inventories, leases and settlements of shipyard accounts. The absence of labour contracts during the period of most intensive construction is all the more tantalizing because of the existence of the early ones and our inability to follow through the changes as they occurred.

Lastly, what can we learn from the notarial records about the shipbuilder himself? Very much, and yet very little. Very much from the surprising amount of detail in some of the documents; but very little because inevitably a great deal is not covered at all. In some cases, we will find an apprenticeship contract showing the builder's beginnings in the trade and probably his origin and parentage. A marriage contract is likely to, but does not always reveal his and his future wife's origin and parentage; it will give his occupation at the time, name members of his family and friends who were present at the signing, and may give some idea of his financial status, as reflected in his settlement on his bride. An occasional power of attorney may reveal not much more than the name of the person who has his confidence at the time. On the other hand, if there are many, they may point to the fact that he absented himself frequently, perhaps to arrange the sale of his vessels, or to pick up orders, or both, and other sources may provide the answer. Depending on the season, it might also show that there was someone left behind to whom he could entrust the operation of the shipyard. A will may state nothing more than that the wife is to receive the entire estate, but sometimes it will list some, even a great deal of the estate, and if it is frequently changed, expose some of the builder's anxieties. Deeds of settlement as a result of a law suit will of course give the reference to the case so that one can follow it up, should one want to. Generally speaking, however, there is no document to compare with the inventory, particularly the inventory taken after the death of the builder or his wife. The list of children, with the names of their spouses, may provide the necessary leads to help trace descendants. If the property is owned by the estate, then the land, the home and other buildings are described, and the sizes of the buildings, the material of which they are constructed and perhaps other architectural details may be given. The contents of each room of each building are minutely described and evaluated, each piece of furniture, each bit of bed clothing, often personal clothes, each ornament, each plate. Even the titles of the books in the library may be given— notaries were paid by the word. How can one fail to learn something about the man whose home one has just walked through? His conveyances too are tell-tale, his horses and other livestock. Listed among the deeds, one may find transactions of which one was unaware. Debts outstanding, both owed and owing, will reveal the way he handled his finances, in some instances the names of employees and their duties, in others those of

Introduction

Figure 4: *Ship* Maldon, *1187 tons, built by Edmund Dubord and Jean Desnoyers at Pointe-aux-Trembles in 1855. She served in the Australian and Indian trades, ending her days as a timber carrier between Quebec and Liverpool. Fonds initial, J. Scott, 616 573–59, courtesy Archives nationales du Québec.*

Figure 5: *Ship* Caribou, *1160 tons, built by I. and J. Samson in 1864. Bought by Patrick Henderson of Glasgow, she carried emigrants to New Zealand. Fonds initial, 516 1070–135, courtesy Archives nationales du Québec.*

business associates, etc., all of which together with the description of his stock in trade and shipyard will help evaluate his career. If a sale follows the taking of the inventory, as it often does, then the real value of his estate is seen.

Some two hundred notaries practised at Quebec between 1760 and 1893, some for a very short period and others extensively. Archibald Campbell, for instance, whose services were greatly sought after by shipbuilders, left fourteen thousand deeds covering half a century of practice, 1812 to 1861. Like Campbell, most of the notaries with whom the builders dealt had their offices close to the waterfront, and I used this criteria for choosing those whose files were likely to be fruitful. My data bank compiled from the notarial records contains several thousand cards, which were initially filed under the names of over one hundred and fifty shipbuilders. This arrangement, in many cases, reflected the main lines of their careers and sometimes allowed glimpses of their characters, both of which were important to my understanding of the trade. Subsequent re-arrangement of the cards grouped the material for the chapters that follow, each one of which draws heavily on this information from primary sources. Its variety and quantity compensate for the unavoidable gaps.

The last key primary source is the collection of Lloyd's survey reports of the vessels surveyed in the Quebec area. They are of paramount importance in regard to the actual construction and the materials that were used, and though hitherto largely ignored, will no doubt become more widely consulted, as interest in maritime history grows. They have allowed me to fill in many shipbuilders' names that are not in the registries for the years after 1852; they have served as a reference to the types of timber used, to the outfits of boats, sails and other equipment; and they have provided a number of plans and other documents several of which are included among the illustrations.

But like the records of the notaries and unlike ship registration certificates, the surveys do not provide a complete series of data for the entire period under study that could be used for comparative purposes. Prices paid for ships, for instance, are for vessels that differ in quality, in the amount of finish they were given, in the amount of equipment supplied, in the materials of which they were built and in some cases, in the method of calculating their tonnage. Labour contracts available for study, that is to say those made before notaries, only account for a fraction of the labour hired. It is hoped, therefore, that in the place of a series of incompatible statistics, the many actual details and facts that have been selected to support the text will serve to give a more historically accurate impression of the trade.

The Plan

Unlike most authors of shipbuilding histories, for example F.W. Wallace in his books on the ships of Quebec and the Maritime Provinces, Esther Clark Wright, *Shipbuilding at Saint John*, or travelling further afield, Grahame Farr, *Shipbuilding in the Port of Bristol* or *Shipbuilding in North Devon*, all of whom devote considerable space to records and other details from the careers of the ships, I have not done the same in the case of the Quebec-built ships. Not only has it been my intention since the outset to devote the whole of the study to shipbuilding and not shipping, but so many and such a variety of vessels were built at Quebec, that they deserve their own monograph. However, some mention of what became of them will be found in Chapter 9 where Quebec's contribution to the shipping industry is summarized.

This book is accordingly divided into nine chapters. The first considers Britain's timber trade, and why it created a demand for Quebec-built ships and how it affected it. The second examines the circumstances and background at Quebec, defines the conditions which permitted Quebec-built ships to compete successfully on the British market and outlines the developments that led to the eventual disappearance of the market. The shipbuilders are introduced in Chapter 3 grouped according to their country of origin, with some reference to its influence on the trade at Quebec. In Chapter 4, the sites on which there were shipyards are chronicled, district by district, with the names of the shipbuilders and the dates when they built there (A table & maps of the shipyard will be found in Appendix D). Chapter 5 takes us inside the yards and describes their facilities.

The burden of office business–financing, insurance, registration, sales, etc. is examined in Chapter 6. Chapter 7, on shipbuilding supplies, deals with timber and other shipbuilding materials and equipment, as well as the standard ship's "outfit" that the builder was often required to provide. The character of the supplies and its attendant problems, their origin, availability and cost, the development in the use of alternative materials, are among the points also discussed.

In Chapter 8 the work of each of fourteen shipbuilding trades or sub-trades is outlined. Accounts of techniques have been kept as simple as possible, the purpose not being to write a shipbuilding manual, but simply to point to the variety and degree of specialization in the trades, and their place in the shipbuilding process.

Chapter 9 is in three parts. The first analyses the production of Quebec shipyards, as listed in Appendices B and C. The second looks at the destination and ownership of the vessels, and discusses their quality. The third reviews some of the milestones in the history of the industry at Quebec.

Together the nine chapters add up to the hopes and achievements of a skilled and hard-working fraternity.

Figure 6: *Barque* Benguela, *669 tons, built by William C. Charland Jr. in 1876. Seen here alongside the Surrey Commercial Docks, London, July 1914 when under the Norwegian flag. Two years later she was sunk by a U-boat. Original photo by P.A. Grimshead. Courtesy Maritime Museum of the Atlantic, Wallace Collection. MP.2.16.2.*

Introduction

Notes

1. The replica of *La Grande Hermine*, which was built at the Davie Brothers Ltd. shipyard in Lévis in 1966, excepted.
2. André Vachon, "Jean Talon," *Dictionary of Canadian Biography* (hereafter *DCB*), I, (Toronto and Quebec, 1966), 614-632.
3. *Cahier des Dix*, XI, 1946, 141-90.
4. Appointed to Quebec with the title "sous-contracteur," René Nicolas Levasseur was named "constructeur" in 1743. Jacques Mathieu, *La construction navale royale à Québec 1739-1759* (Quebec, 1971), 16.
5. The correspondence forms part of the "Correspondance générale des Intendants et des Gouverneurs de la Nouvelle France" and of the "Correspondance départ ou ordres du roi," *ibid*, xi.
6. *Ibid.*, 61-2.
7. *Ibid.*, 101-3.
8. "On a là la raison de la fermeture du chantier du Roi quelques années plus tard. Aussitôt le triste Bigot installé comme intendant de la Nouvelle-France, le favoritisme, les vols, les malpropretés de tout genre se glissèrent dans chacune des branches de l'administration, au chantier du Roi comme ailleurs. M. Levasseur, qui était un honnête homme, ne pouvait rien pour empêcher ces abus. Sous les ordres immédiats de l'intendant, il n'avait aucun contrôle sur les dépenses. Quand il avait besoin d'un ouvrier, d'une fourniture quelconque, il les demandait à l'intendant et c'est celui-ci qui achetait et fixait les prix. Aussi, quand vint l'invasion de la colonie par les Anglais, les travaux du chantier du Roi furent arrêtés, mais il y avait déjà un an ou deux que le président du Conseil de Marine avait décidé d'arrêter la construction des vaisseaux de guerre dans la Nouvelle-France." Pierre-Georges Roy, "La construction Royale à Québec," *Les Cahiers des Dix*, XI, 1946, 158-9.
9. "... la construction navale royale à Québec fut une industrie métropolitaine par ses capitaux et sa finalité, dans ses méthodes, par l'encadrement de la main-d'oeuvre, en somme dans sa nature même. A l'échelon le plus important, les décisions se prenaient en France; elles étaient conçues et valables pour la métropole, non pour la colonie. Ainsi Maurepas imposa à l'intendant un type de construction qui ne convenait pas aux ressources forestières de la Nouvelle France. On ne réussit pas plus à adopter les méthodes françaises aux conditions canadiennes. Les ouvriers spécialisés venus de France n'incitèrent pas le Canadien à sortir de sa réclusion volontaire. Est-ce dû à l'établissement de rapports d'inférieur à supérieur, à l'influence de l'Indien ou à un mode de vie propre à la colonie? De toutes façons, le Canadien préféra la vie facile sur la terre aux longues heures de travail sur les chantiers, le chant du coq au son de cloche. Il perdit rapidement son enthousiasme initial et se préoccupa assez peu d'acquérir une plus grande compétence."

    "Au caractère artificiel de cette structure se rattachent presque tous les problèmes survenus dans cette industrie." Mathieu, *Construction navale*, 83.
10. Although I agree with Mathieu that the trees that were harvested for the shipyard were not large enough to supply the timbers for the large warships that were built, I do not agree that the size of merchant vessels built at the beginning of the British regime is proof of this.
11. Quebec began building for the French navy at a time when the King was concerned with the possibility of repercussions arising out of the problems of the Austrian succession, and the extreme weakness of the Navy frightened him into handing out large sums for Naval construction. Mathieu, *Construction navale*, 12. Once the Navy was up to strength, there was no guarantee that further amounts would be forthcoming to continue the operation of the Quebec dockyard.

12. *Ibid.*, 76-81.
13. Réal Brisson, "Les 100 premières années de la charpenterie navale à Québec: 1663-1763," Master's thesis, Université Laval, 1983. This was published as *La charpenterie navale à Québec sous le Règime français*. Quebec: Institut québécois de recherche sur la culture, 1983.
14. The *Times* of London published reports on the *Columbus* or *Baron of Renfrew* at least sixteen times between September 1824 and October 1825.
15. It was necessary to counteract the American claims to a first Atlantic crossing under steam which arose from the voyage of the *Savannah* to Liverpool in 1819 with the occasional use of paddle-wheels, which were lowered over the sides each time they were used. The crossing took twenty-seven days, during which the wheels were used on seven occasions, for a total of eighty-five hours. H. Philip Spratt, *Transatlantic Paddle Steamers* (Glasgow, 1951), 17.
16. "l'ouvrier tout ruisselant de sueurs travaillait à monter un navire avec le même entrain et la même gaieté de coeur qu'il en aurait mis à bâtir son propre foyer." Narcisse Rosa, *La construction des navires à Québec et ses environs*, (Quebec, 1897), 7.
17. The list was repeated by Ivan Brookes in *The Lower St. Lawrence*, (Cleveland, Ohio, 1974), 293-318.
18. See Pierre Dufour, "La construction navale à Québec, 1760-1825: sources inexplorées et nouvelles perspectives de recherches," *Revue d'histoire de l'Amérique française*, 35:2, September 1981, 235, n.17.
19. Letter, Wallace to Fry, 16 February 1825, "I wish I had known of your relationship to Mr. Henry Fry of Quebec before my book went to press as I would have liked to feature him more than I did," and 8 March 1825, "It was very kind of you to allow me to see this personal record and from it I have derived much interesting data regarding the old Quebec ship-building days." (Copies of both kindly sent to me by John S. Fry, Henry Fry's great grandson.)
20. Which consisted in providing Parker with "a wealth of material from his marine library." Parker, *Sails of the Maritimes* (North Sydney, 1960), 8.
21. And published in the *Canadian Journal of Economics and Political Science*, XXIII, 2 May 1957.
22. *Ibid.*, 198.
23. "One Hundred Years of Shipbuilding," *The Journal of Commerce and Telegraph Centenary*, 1925, 63.
24. *Ibid.*, 63.
25. B.R. Mitchell, *Abstract of British Historical Statistics* (Cambridge, 1962), 223.
26. S. Pollard, "The Decline of Shipbuilding on the Thames," *The Economic History Review*, 1950-51, 2nd series, 3: 79.
27. *Ibid.*, 79-81.
28. As defined in the introduction to the *Preliminary Inventory of Records Held at the Maritime History Group* (St. John's, 1978), compiled by Roberta Thomas under the direction of Dr. Keith Matthews.
29. Viz., a random ten percent sample retained by the Public Records Office, London, records for 1861, 1862, 1865, 1875, 1885, 1895, 1905, 1915, 1925 and 1935, which were kept by the National Maritime Museum, Greenwich, a special collection pertaining to "famous ships" housed at the Public Records Office and a selection extracted by the English Record Office. *Ibid.*, 1.
30. *Volumes not Values: Canadian Sailing Ships and World Trades*, (proceedings of the Third Annual Conference), (St. John's, 1979), eds. David Alexander and Rosemary Ommer.
31. *Acadiensis*, X, 2, Spring 1981, 67-89.
32. Paper presented to the *Conference on Land, Sea and Livelihood in Atlantic Canada*, Mount Allison University, October 1979.

33. Maritime History Group, *Atlantic Canada Shipping Project Newsletter,* December 1980, 6.
34. Mémoire de Licence, Institut de Géographie, Université Laval.
35. For which Bernard Bouchard's research was used.
36. Rice, "Shipbuilding in British America 1789-1890: An Introductory Study," (Ph.D. thesis, University of Liverpool, 1977), 198.
37. *Revue de l'histoire de l'Amérique française,* 35: 2, 1981, 231-51.
38. *Ibid.,* 248-50.
39. Jean Benoit, "Le dévélopement d'un mécanisme de crédit et la croissance économique d'une communauté d'affaires. Les marchands et les industriels de la Ville de Quebec au dix-neuvième siècle," Ph.D. thesis, Université Laval; Richard Rice, 53, 69.
40. Paul Terrien, *Québec à l'âge de la voile.* (Montreal: Asticou, 1984.) I have limited this review to publications concerning the square-rigger trade. Several articles and books on steamboats and other river craft which are not included will be found in the bibliography.
41. For vessels built outside the Port of Quebec, see Appendix C.
42. 26 Geo. 3, c. 60.
43. 4 Geo. 4, c. 41, in 1824; 5 and 6 Will., c. 56, in 1836, and 18 and 19 Vict., c. 104, in 1855.
44. Microfilms C-2058-62, 2064-68.
45. In accordance with 4 Geo. 4, c. 41.
46. See Notes to Appendix B.

CHAPTER 1
The Timber Trade

At the port of Quebec between 1824 and 1893 a great shipbuilding industry flourished and died, its course frequently curbed by depressions, yet spurred by intermittent booms, its main customer timber-hungry Britain. In the end, the very timber shortage that stimulated its extraordinary growth became a factor in its downfall, encouraging the advancement of metallurgy and the adoption of metal-hulled ships. Quebec shipbuilders, unable or unwilling to embrace the new technology, saw their markets crumble and disappear.

Far from being extraordinary, the history of Quebec's shipbuilding industry is typical of many areas in the Canadian Maritimes, Britain or the United States in which shipyards sprang up to meet the heavy though erratic late eighteenth and nineteenth-century demand for tonnage. True to the law of supply and demand, when the steel-built vessel became economically as well as physically superior, the market for new wooden ships disappeared and the yards closed. Shipbuilding at Saint John, New Brunswick, for example, closely paralleled that of Quebec. In both towns large volumes of timber exports acted as the stimulus. At Saint John, where the timber trade developed twenty years earlier, shipbuilding began that much sooner. In both ports the industry peaked in 1863, when Saint John launched forty-five large sailing vessels to Quebec's fifty-five. In both, the trade died in the 1890s and, as Esther Clark Wright wrote, "there remained the chip filled yards . . . the old man pottering by a spar."[1]

The British Market

By the beginning of the sixteenth century British forests could no longer satisfy the country's increasing appetite for timber, and large quantities had to be imported from continental Europe. The huge rebuilding programme following the Fire of London of 1666 greatly aggravated the persistent shortage, while extensive naval shipbuilding programmes which began ten years later wrought havoc on shipbuilding timber reserves. The use of charcoal for iron smelting depleted the woodlands even faster causing pig iron to be imported from Russia, Sweden, and the American colonies to a lesser extent.[2] Early in the eighteenth century, the Baltic became Britain's main source for timber, a position it maintained for one hundred years. Baltic timber helped build housing for the steadily expanding population. It served in the construction of highways, canals, docks, bridges and military fortifications, and provided pit props for the rapidly proliferating mines. It also supplemented domestic timber in private shipyards and was used in huge quantities for planking, masts and spars in naval dockyards. Baltic hardwood, however, was considered less satisfactory for ships' frames and both crown and merchant shipbuilders were obliged to scour the countryside for supplies of "compass" timber.

The perennial timber shortage resulted in frequent price increases. Imports rose 150% between 1663 and 1669, and the average price of a load of domestic oak from £3 or £4 in 1660 to £13 by 1810.[3] It is not surprising that British shipyards were unable to compete successfully with their American counterparts; by the early eighteenth century an increasing number of shipwrights left each year to work in the flourishing New England yards. Cheap and plentiful North American timber more than compensated for the higher wages in the colonies, allowing American-built ships to capture an increasing share of the British market. By 1760, one-quarter of the merchant fleet was American-built; by 1774, the proportion had risen to one-third.[4]

British authorities were well aware of the danger of relying on foreign timber and other shipbuilding materials, particularly for naval construction. A successful system of bounties had led to the establishment of a tar and pitch industry in the American colonies, which by 1754 was supplying more than ninety percent of British needs, but such incentives did not result in the production of sufficient hemp or flax for export. America's sole inroad into the Baltic timber monopoly was the supply of "great masts" for the largest men-of-war and merchantmen. No longer available in Russia due to deforestation, they had been imported since 1634 from New England, which had benefitted from a bounty first offered in 1705, as well as from the removal of import duties on all shipbuilding materials produced in the colonies, in 1721.[5] Because of high transatlantic freight rates, there was no steady market for less costly North American timber, which was carried only when a cargo of more profitable merchandise such as sugar or tobacco could not be procured.

As long as Baltic timber was available, there was no reason to import it from America. Not only were transatlantic freight rates far higher than from northern Europe but American timber was widely considered inferior. Moreover, in order to encourage a colonial industry, it would have been necessary to impose protectionist duties on foreign imports. Apart from damaging relations with Russia, such duties would have been prejudicial to British timber firms with heavy investments in the Baltic, not to mention the British consumer out of whose pocket the resulting price increase would have to be paid.

At the outbreak of the American Revolution in 1775, the precariousness of Britain's supply of shipbuilding materials and the consequent importance of maintaining large stocks was evident. Naval stores were soon affected. Shipments of Georgia tar and pitch halted and the Navy was obliged to return to European producers cap in hand. Of far greater concern, however, was the interruption in the supply of New England masts, to which the grossly inefficient administrative procedures at naval headquarters in London were slow to respond. The Saint John River valley in New Brunswick had been surveyed for large pines in 1774 and a favourable report submitted,[6] yet no one had either the imagination or initiative to cut through the bureaucratic red tape and ensure that the desperately needed masts were delivered. Instead, although the Halifax Dockyard on local initiative began receiving New Brunswick masts in 1779, British mastmakers were still wasting precious hours fitting together smaller "sticks" to form "made" or "built" masts to supplement their meagre stocks, while the condition of masts on British warships steadily deteriorated.[7] It was not until 1782 that New Brunswick masts finally reached British dockyards, too late for use in the American war.

As hostilities dragged on, interruptions to European supplies, due in part to the general lack of sympathy for the British cause and to the vigilance of enemy fleets, forced her to dig ever deeper into her reserves of tar, pitch, oak planks, masts, spars and deals, and finally to resort to the use of unseasoned timber, leading to the disastrous premature decay of many warships. When one by one France, Spain and Holland joined in the war against her, Britain lost her supremacy at sea and capitulated, officially recognizing American independence in 1783.

In the period of peace between the treaties of Versailles of 1783 and the renewal of hostilities with France ten years later, Britain replenished her naval supplies by increasing her imports from the Baltic, while at the same time seeking new sources of timber within her North American colonies. Imports from the colonies, however, remained at little over one percent of the total, of which the great majority was timber from the Maritimes, with only a fraction from Quebec.[8] In 1787, for instance, Quebec exported sixteen masts compared to New Brunswick's two hundred.[9] Samples of Quebec oak ordered by the Admiralty in 1783 were deemed inferior and unsuitable for either building or repairing ships of the Royal Navy, and in 1803 the Commissioners refused to contract for further supplies. Nevertheless, the Quebec timber industry kept growing due to the export of oak staves to Britain, southern Europe, and the West Indies, where they were used to make casks for the sugar trade.

At the same time, attention was necessarily turned to the regulation of America's new status as a foreign nation. Because Britain desperately needed all kinds of naval supplies while the people both of the Maritimes and the West Indies would suffer if their commerce with America were prevented, it was not in Britain's interest to deny her ex-colonies their former trading privileges. Moreover, the West Indies and the other remaining colonies were far closer to the United States than to Britain, and trade in the western hemisphere was difficult to control. Even before the signing of the peace treaty, two of the unrealistic prohibitory laws were revoked, and shortly thereafter a bill was passed to allow timber and naval stores from the United States to enter Britain in either American or British ships on the same terms as colonial produce.

Nevertheless, Britain was still determined to protect her shipping industry from American competition, and in spite of growing agitation by free traders the Navigation Laws were strengthened. The Navigation Act of 1660 with its amendments had given British and colonial vessels a shipping monopoly within the Empire and would continue to do so for another sixty-five years. While it had helped the British merchant fleet to outstrip its rivals, it had also led to higher shipping charges, which in turn had raised the cost of shipbuilding because of its dependence on imported supplies. The new 1786 law restricting British registry to vessels built in Britain or her colonies tightened the whole registration procedure and prevented foreign-owned or built vessels from obtaining British registry through subterfuge, thus protecting both shippers and shipbuilders from American and other foreign competition.

Secure from that competition and with the certainty of obtaining a first cargo of timber with which to load their ships, shipbuilders in Nova Scotia and New Brunswick expanded their production rapidly. In Nova Scotia, the offer of a bounty of ten shillings per ton on all new vessels of forty tons or more resulted in the

Figure 7: Wolfe's Cove near Québec. *Seen here at the time that it was leased to William Sheppard and Charles Campbell. Watercolour James Pattison Cockburn. A 53 74 D. Archives nationales du Québec/Neuville Bazin.*

launching of twenty-three vessels between 1785 and 1787, while in 1788 another twenty-one were built despite the lowering of the bounty for craft over seventy-five tons to seven shillings per ton. In New Brunswick, which benefitted from the immigration of Loyalists with shipbuilding experience, no such incentives were necessary, and ninety-three square-riggers were sent down the ways between 1784 and 1793. The cheap and plentiful timber supplies enabled the two colonies to surpass New England as the home of British North America shipbuilding; by 1792 there were reported to be nearly as many square-riggers in the Maritimes as there were in all the United States.[10] As far as British shipbuilders were concerned, however, their competition had merely moved further north, and they were still heavily disadvantaged by the high timber prices.

During the long French Revolutionary and Napoleonic Wars which followed, Britain's vital timber supply from the Baltic once again suffered frequent interruption, presenting an opportunity for the British North American colonies to increase their share of the market. Because the ten shillings per load duty on Baltic timber which had been imposed in 1795 (increased to twenty-five shillings under a new tariff in 1805) did not fully compensate for the higher transatlantic freight rates on BNA wood, contracts for American timber were awarded by the Government to private firms at prices that assured profits. As a result imports from BNA grew from 235 loads in 1795 to ten thousand loads in 1805.[11] But the following year, when Napoleon succeeded in imposing an almost complete blockade of the Baltic, cargoes of European timber to Britain were reduced to a trickle. Since the British North American colonies were not yet able to satisfy British demand, within a few years the price of timber

Figure 8: Cape Diamond and Timber Depot in Wolfe's Cove, Quebec. *Watercolour by an unknown artist. Courtesy National Archives, Ottawa, neg. C 131920.*

Figure 9: *Loading ships with square timber at Wolfe's Cove in 1872. Quebec, L078158 (2). Photo: Notman. Courtesy McCord Museum.*

in Britain had risen three hundred percent,[12] and by 1809, when Russia renounced her treaty with Napoleon and ended the blockade, stocks had sunk to dangerous levels. Though Britain immediately resumed the importation of Baltic wood and tar, she was determined never again to find herself at the mercy of the Baltic countries, and took measures to stimulate the colonial trade. All tariffs on colonial wood were removed while the duty on northern European timber was raised in 1810 from twenty-five shillings to thirty-four shillings and eight pence, and again in 1813 to sixty-five shillings, in both cases with temporary wartime duties added as well.[13] The door was thus flung open to importers of colonial timber and a huge fleet of timber ships assured its transport.

Though the Maritimes supplied a vast amount of timber, Quebec now provided even more. In seemingly inexhaustible forests in the Ottawa valley, along the Saint Lawrence and its tributaries, and from both sides of the border on Lake Champlain, trees were felled and lashed into great rafts which were floated down streams and over rapids to the Saint Lawrence and on to Quebec. In 1799, Quebec had sent seven masts and 1,078 loads of oak and pine timber to Britain as against 5,121 large and middling masts and 149,049 loads of timber sent from the Baltic. In 1811, with important London timber firms such as Scott, Idles and Company and their rivals Henry and John Usborne now operating in Quebec, she shipped 19,025 masts, 24,469 loads of oak and 52,888 loads of pine.[14]

By the end of the Napoleonic Wars in 1815, military expenditures had cost Britain £1000 million. Heavy government borrowing had driven up interest rates, and taxes and prices had skyrocketed.[15] A brief period of prosperity ensued, but then the hard times returned once again, and with them high unemployment. Faced with a deep depression, many argued that the preferential tariff on Baltic timber imposed too heavy a burden on the British consumer and that the time had come for the principles of free trade to be allowed to prevail. Others, however, clung to older mercantilist ideas. Memorials and petitions from timber merchants, shipowners and others abounded. In 1821, in a conciliatory gesture, the duty on northern European timber was lowered by ten shillings a load to fifty-five shillings, while a ten shilling duty was imposed on Canadian timber, thereby giving North American timber an effective thirty shilling per load price advantage after transportation charges had been met. Both sides drew comfort from these new arrangements. While free traders interpreted the reductions as the beginning of the end of protectionism, timber merchants saw them as a continuing commitment to the North American industry. As a result, many lost their fear of investing in British North America, and soon close to six hundred ships were departing from Quebec annually, their holds and decks laden with timber.

Not surprisingly, the timber trade wrought radical changes on the slow-paced provincial town of Quebec. Each spring it erupted with increasingly raucous vigour when the break-up of the ice announced the beginning of the season and brought the Saint Lawrence River to life: a rowboat towing a mast to one of the shipyards, a fishing vessel off to the Labrador coast, the pilot schooner casting off for Bic with a contingent of pilots and apprentices while another set out to moor the Trinity House buoys, flat-bottomed boats piled high with farm produce or firewood, and others loaded more soberly with Pointe-aux-Trembles stone, single-masted coasting sloops and twin-masted schooners, and among them an assortment of ferries

Figure 10: View at Wolfe's Cove, looking upriver, with Messrs. Gilmour & Co's booms for loading timber, and a ship under construction beside the mould loft. (left image of stereogram). Quebec, c. 1860. Photo: William Notman. Courtesy National Archives, Ottawa, neg. PA 149074.

crisscrossing the river–steamers, horseboats, rowboats and canoes. But the season had not really begun until the first winter-built vessel had splashed into the river, the first steamboat had arrived from its winter quarters in Sorel, the first timber raft had come sweeping to the end of its long downriver journey, but above all until a favourable east wind brought a forerunner around Point Levy with the message that the "spring fleet" was close behind. Then in a parade of white sails the fleet itself appeared, and with it the cosmopolitan flavour that had left Quebec at the close of navigation the previous year.

Once again the townspeople found themselves sharing their sidewalks and streets with strangers, as passengers and seamen streamed ashore. Polyglot bands of sailors shambled to the nearest tavern to join in rowdy conviviality with the timber raft crews. Groups of immigrants gazed at the unfamiliar sights and wondered at the foreign voices as they headed for the steamboat wharf and the next stage of their journey. Old friends, long-time captains on the Quebec run, exchanged greetings before going to the notary's to file a protest against the weather or perhaps to sign a contract for their return cargo with a timber stower.[16] And merchants quickened their pace as they hurried between the coffee houses, their favourite rendezvous for business deals, and their counting houses on Saint Peter Street, where clerks perched at tall desks hour after hour scratching business records into letterbooks and ledgers. The customs and port officials were called upon to hasten required procedures to avoid unnecessary and costly delays in port, and, as auctioneers disposed of cargoes that were landed daily, store shelves filled with new merchandise.

In coves along the river banks, winter damage was surveyed and teams of workers with adze and axe set to work repairing wharves and booms, dressing leftover timber, and checking the moorings for the ships already arriving to load. Others opened the outer booms to receive new timber rafts and, following the culler's inspection, sorted the timber for shipment. Meanwhile, gangs of stevedores set up their blocks and tackles and began the long and laborious process of stowing it.

Here and there on the waterfront, carpenters bolted huge timbers together to form cages, which were then filled with stone and sunk to make new wharves or to enlarge old ones. Besides creating new loading berths, each helped to extend the crowded shelf around the cape on which the Lower Town was built until eventually wharves and landfill had doubled the area of the Lower Town and allowed a convenient road (Saint Paul Street) to be built to the rapidly expanding suburb of Saint Roch.

Throughout the six summer months, the creaking of hundreds of wooden ships rocking at anchor set up a continuous background chorus to the hubbub and clatter of the town, to which the occasional staccato outburst of commands and the snapping of wind in the rigging added a brisk accompaniment. During the long daylight hours, shipyards responded with the chant of caulkers' mallets, the whrrr of long pit saws, and from time to time the men's deep melodious voices singing in unison as they strained to move a great piece of timber forward step by step.[17] Quebec had become one of the world's great timber ports; she had geared herself to the timber trade, and was ready to embrace shipbuilding with equal enthusiasm.

Conditions at Quebec

It has often been stated that all that was needed to build a wooden sailing vessel was a sheltered, sloping beach close to deep water, a good supply of suitable timber, some skilled carpenters with trained shipwrights to guide them, and a few simple tools, all of which were available at Quebec. Along the Saint Lawrence, from Cap Rouge to L'Ange-Gardien on the north bank and from New Liverpool to Indian Cove on the south; along the meanders of the Saint Charles that skirted the city to the northwest; and in protected bays on the Isle of Orleans were many beaches offering ideal sites for shipbuilding. Local farmers were able to provide the necessary knees and a large local labour force existed. Each carpenter owned his axe and adze; each caulker his mallet and irons. The shipbuilder generally supplied the other tools, many of which he imported in the timber ships along with his order of sails, cordage, rigging, iron bars, anchors, paint, and special equipment such as compasses.

The Quebec City area was therefore well-suited for the construction of wooden ships. But a major, largely speculative, shipbuilding industry which could compete in Britain and was sufficiently flexible to survive the slumps and surges of that notoriously erratic market, required a considerable infrastructure of services. Because Quebec was the port of exit and entry for both Upper and Lower Canada and a major timber harbour clearing more than six hundred vessels annually, many were already in place.

There were four main requisites for the creation of a stable and prosperous shipbuilding industry. First, both the shipbuilders and their men must have the means to survive the slumps. Second, access to the

Figure 11: *Timber Coves in 1890. Fonds initial, Québec — Sillery – Sillery 516 470-68, courtesy, Archives nationales du Québec.*

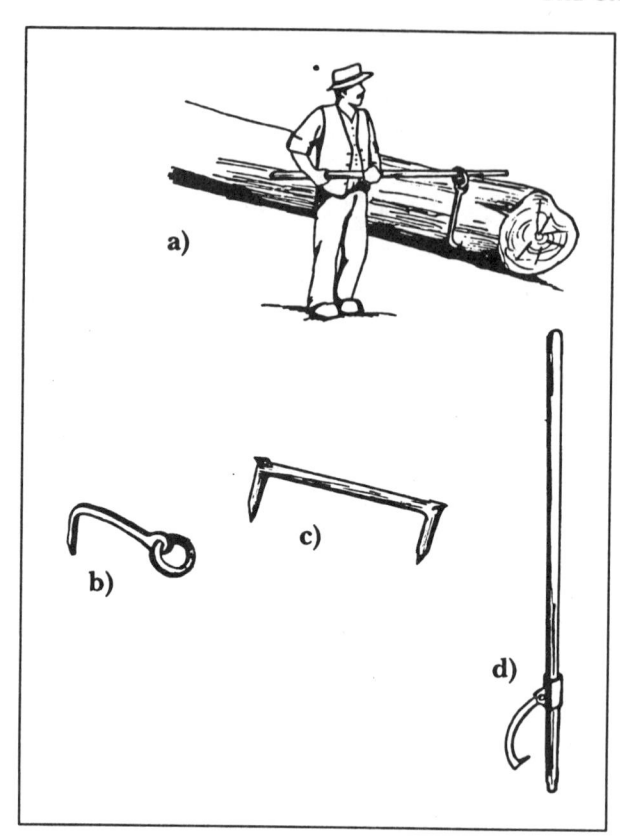

Figure 12: *Timber handling tools. a) Ring Dog with pole; b) Ring Dog; c) Dog; d) Cant Hook. Drawing by Caroline Soucy.*

required financing was essential. Third, despite the sporadic nature of the industry, it had to be efficient enough to be competitive. And finally, the services of shipbrokers to find freight or a charterer for the first voyage and to handle the sale of the ship and its cargo had to be available. The majority of Quebec ships were built during the winter when there was little competing demand for labour. This was a time when the timber coves lay dormant and the river traffic was at a standstill. The men were naturally happy to find work, even at low wages. A strong market allowed the shipbuilder to build in the summer as well and to pay higher wages, but weak demand would even cut into winter construction and cause serious hardship. When that was the case, there was sometimes construction work to be had in Montreal, Sorel (William Henry) or any of the many small villages on the Saint Lawrence or Gaspé coasts, or the builder might be able to secure a civil engineering contract to build facilities such as roads, bridges or wharves. At times builders would even shoulder the risk and lay down keels solely to provide work, regardless of the market. But at others there was no escape from the soup kitchens and many builders had their yards and even their personal possessions seized to pay the bills. The men would find work with the opening of the summer season and hope that the market would improve so that the next winter would be better. The builder would be dependent on his family and business friends to help him start again. And if such help were not forthcoming, he might never again be able to build on his own account.

In the early part of the nineteenth century, the bulk of shipyard production was built for and financed by local merchants, many associated with British firms. During the second quarter-century, Irish orders increased significantly and speculative building became prevalent, financed mainly by firms in the timber trade with British connections. It was from concerns such as Pemberton Brothers, Gillespie Jamieson, Robert Harrison, Atkinson and Company, Forsyth & Bell, G. Burns Symes, Anderson & Paradis, H. & E. Burstall[18] that shipbuilders sought their financing. By the 1860s many of the earlier lenders had departed, leaving only James G. Ross, merchant and shipbroker, who handled the vast majority of the shipbuilders' business until the end of the sailing ship era.

But wherever financing was obtained, the risk was taken by the shipbuilder, who had no way of knowing what the state of the market would be when his vessel was offered for sale, often nine or ten months after the keel had been laid. Terms of the loans were heavily weighted in favour of the lenders. This was natural, for had it been otherwise, they would have looked elsewhere for more secure or profitable investments. As far as the builders were concerned, if they had no contract there were few alternatives that would allow them to practise their trade, so they accepted the money and with it the risk.

The efficient management of the yards was largely dependent on the availability and cost of labour and materials. Though men were readily available in winter and wages were low, in times of peak activity tight organization, particularly in scheduling the work of various tradesmen at the proper time, became crucial. Delays and uncertainties were costly, and if a penalty clause was invoked, the impact could be disastrous. Quebec shipbuilders were fortunate, though, in having several thousand local shipyard workers from whom to choose, as well as new immigrants looking for work and casual workers, at times, from other parts of British North America where the industry was in the doldrums. The sheer size of the force engendered specialization and a high degree of

Figure 13: *Horses drawing timber. Drawing by Caroline Soucy.*

organization, and the few "protests" that were registered indicate that serious cases of work being delayed by a labour shortage were exceptional. The same was true for materials. Even though the builder might have to call on several timber merchants to put together his stock of various kinds of wood, at least they were close at hand.[19] The density of shipping at Quebec spawned a number of chandleries; newspapers carried advertisements for all manner of shipbuilding supplies and equipment. A host of sailmakers, block and mastmakers, shipsmiths and riggers offered the materials of their trade.

Moreover, over the years a number of institutions and services on which the shipbuilder depended had come into existence. One of the earliest, the Customs House, established in 1762, allowed on the spot vessel survey and registration when it became obligatory in 1787 for all vessels fifteen tons and over having a deck and belonging to a British subject. The location of the Customs House favoured Quebec shipbuilders and shipowners over those of Montreal and elsewhere, who had to journey to Quebec to obtain registry or even to grant the necessary bonds when the master of a vessel belonging to that port was replaced.

Also to the shipbuilders' advantage was the founding in 1805 of Trinity House at Quebec,[20] for as traffic on the river grew, the need to have a specialized body to regulate it became apparent. One of its roles was to see that there were no encroachments on shipping channels by either unlawful construction or abandoned shipwrecks. Launching problems on the narrow and winding Saint Charles River, for instance, could have been seriously aggravated had wharf construction along its banks been uncontrolled. Similarly, shipwrecks could lead to major blockages of traffic, and it was one of Trinity House's responsibilities to see that men such as Michael Stevenson, who showed no signs of moving the hull of an old ship that had been left across the north channel off the Saint Charles River, complied with the laws.[21] The increasingly important domains of navigational aids, lighthouses, buoys and all aspects of pilotage also came under its control.

The Saint Lawrence River steamboats were another valuable asset to shipbuilders. Far from regarding the early steamboats as threats to their livelihood, shipbuilders were delighted with the dependability of their regular service on the Quebec-Montreal run. Their value in towing was soon recognized, and they were used increasingly to tow materials to the yards, to restrain and tow vessels during their launch, to tow vessels up or downriver when the wind was unfavourable for sail, and eventually to tow rafts, too.

In 1809, at the suggestion of the members of the Committee of Trade of Halifax, Nova Scotia, similar bodies were founded by merchants in Quebec and Montreal. At the same time the Committee of British North American Merchants was founded in London to serve as a lobby to protect colonial interests at the seat of government.[22] Provoked by the lack of support from their own Legislative Assembly, the Quebec and Montreal committees wasted no time in sending to the Colonial Office the first of many representations listing their grievances.[23] Over the years, the Quebec Committee (which changed its name to the "Chamber of Commerce" when it was incorporated in 1840) became a strong advocate of the shipbuilders, one which they, like the timber merchants, would frequently use.

In the domain of banking, the unqualified success of Army Bills issued during the War of 1812 and their subsequent full redemption helped to overcome the long-standing opposition to the establishment of chartered banks that had its roots in the French Regime when paper money was constantly devalued. In 1822, the charters of the Bank of Montreal and the Bank of Canada in Montreal, and the Bank of Quebec at Quebec finally received royal assent; shipbuilders, along with all who engaged in economic activities, benefitted greatly from their services. The banks were empowered to receive deposits, discount notes, deal in bills of exchange and gold and silver bullion, and to issue promissory notes payable in gold or silver coin.[24] Many of the previous difficulties in handling payments of all kinds were thus overcome.

Another valuable service for shipbuilders was that of the shipbroker, a service that was generally obtained through the same merchants that arranged the financing and formed part of the same contract. At times, however, shipbuilders preferred to make their own arrangements, particularly when they had suitable connections in Britain or with visiting captains. Quite often, the builder would advertise his ship for sale or charter, or to take on freight, in the local newspaper. Dispensing with the shipbroker in this way may have proved economical in some cases, but in general, unless he had strong British connections it was more practical to bear the cost of the brokerage commissions in exchange for the necessary expertise.

Above all these considerations was the great support that shipbuilders received from the hundreds of masters whose ships called at Quebec each year. During the weeks that vessels were in port, builders were able to discuss the shipping market with their captains, and to learn the advantages and disadvantages of new developments in shipbuilding practice or ship design. Some of the vessels would be of special interest. Comparisons could be made and information on the effect of modifications obtained first-hand. The more fortunate builder might be given an order for a new vessel with which the captain had been entrusted by his employer. Another might try to convince him to use his influence to procure a contract for him on his return, for owners relied heavily on their captains' judgements when purchasing tonnage.[25] A builder could show off his yard and the quality of its work. He could also arrange for supplies and equipment for a ship he was building or was about to build to be sent out to him, and until it proved impractical, for the crew as well. And, though some of the shipbuilders made frequent trips across the Atlantic to handle their own affairs and therefore were less dependent on these services, the shipmasters brought with them current maritime information and were active links not only with Britain but also with many ports in other countries. The value of their presence to the shipbuilding community was immeasurable.

In short, the timber trade was responsible for a large part of the infrastructure of services the shipbuilder needed being in place. Trade in wood products not only provided many of the building materials but also mobilized workers, offered financing, supplied cargoes, and filled the port with shipping, thereby providing repair work and stimulating auxiliary shipbuilding trades and services. Timber merchants also added their strong voices to those of shipbuilders when their interests were threatened. Without the timber industry, ships would still have been built at Quebec – as they had been since the colony's beginning – but without its stimulus it is doubtful that the flourishing mid-nineteenth-century shipbuilding industry would have existed.

Notes

1. Esther Clark Wright, *Saint John Ships and Their Builders* (Wolfville, N.S., 1976), 29.
2. Herbert Heaton, *Economic History of Europe* (New York, 1936), 317, 499; Ralph Davis, *The Rise of the English Shipping Industry in the Seventeenth and Eighteenth Centuries* (London, 1962), 42.
3. A.J. Holland, *Ships of British Oak* ((Newton Abbot, 1971), 42.
4. Davis, *The Rise of the English Shipping Industry*, 67-68.
5. *Ibid.*, 292; see also Gerald Graham, *British Policy and Canada 1774-1791: A Study in 18th Century Trade Policy* (London, 1930), chapter 7.
6. W.O. Raymond, *The River Saint John* (Sackville, 1910), 234-235.
7. Robert Greenhalgh Albion, *Forests and Sea Power: The Timber Problem of the Royal Navy, 1652-1862* (Cambridge, Mass., 1926), 286, 293, 296.
8. J. Marshall, *A Digest of All the Accounts* (London, 1833), 71-72, 203.
9. Albion, *Forests and Sea Power*, 348.
10. Stanley Spicer, *Masters of Sail* (Toronto, 1968), 19-23.
11. Albion, *Forests and Sea Power*, 357.
12. Gerald Graham, *Sea Power and British North America, 1783-1820: A Study in British Colonial Policy* (Cambridge, Mass., 1941), 147.
13. 49 Geo. 3, c. 98; 50 Geo. 3, c. 77; 51 Geo .3, c. 93; 52 Geo. 3, c. 117; 56 Geo. 3, c. 29, cited in *ibid.*, 148.
14. Albion, *Forests and Sea Power*, 353-357, 420-422.
15. Peter Matthias, *The First Industrial Nation: An Economic History of Britain, 1700-1914* (London, 1969), 44.
16. After a stormy passage, it was common practice for a captain to sign a notarized document "protesting" the weather, thus protecting himself against charges of negligence should any of his cargo be found damaged. See, for example, J. Beatson, "Protest," 13 June 1783, greffe J. Beek, ANQM, (brought to my attention by A.J.H. Richardson); "Contract for Stowing Cargo," Decaro and Mathieu with Capt. J. Beatson, 13 October 1813, greffe A. Campbell, ANQQ [henceforth all greffes at the Archives nationales du Québec à Québec just gr with the name of the notary]; Morland with Burns, 10 August 1854, gr W.D. Campbell.
17. The sailors' shanty, "The Charley-Man," was said to be the popular shipyard song; see Narcisse Rosa, *La construction des navires à Québec* (Québec, 1897), 7.
18. Typical shipbuilding contracts include, 25 March 1828, 13 May 1826 and 23 March 1836, gr L. McPherson; 21 August 1827, 24 December 1828, 18 February 1845, 9 October 1846 and 23 January 1847, gr A. Campbell.
19. Letter from John Hart of Madawaska to Pickersgill & Tibbits, 18 May 1847, re carpenters looking for work at Quebec. Shipyard accounts often contained the names of several timber suppliers. Five were listed in Etienne Samson et frères' account for the ship *Iona*, 24 November 1857, gr S. Glackemeyer.
20. 45 Geo. 3, c. 12. It was modelled on the first Trinity House at Deptford, London, established in 1565; see Hilary Mead, *Trinity House* (London, 1934), 1.
21. 16 November 1840, gr E.B. Lindsay.
22. P.G. Roy, *La Chambre de Commerce de Lévis 1872-1947* (Lévis, 1947), 7; Fernand Ouellet, *Histoire économique et sociale du Québec 1760-1850: structures et conjoncture* (reprint, Montréal, 1971), 195.
23. D.G. Creighton, *The Empire of the St. Lawrence* (Toronto, 1956), 170.
24. Craig McIvor, *Canadian Monetary Policy, Banking and Fiscal Development* (Toronto, [1958]), 4-10, 25-29.
25. See, for example, Sholto Cooke, *The Maiden City and the Western Ocean* (Dublin, n.d.), 75. "He [Captain Bryson] is a good judge of what will suit our trade..."

CHAPTER 2
Quebec Background

Having settled on the banks of a great waterway which served as the sole highway linking their villages and homes, it was natural that boat and shipbuilding should become part of the heritage of the French Canadian people, and indeed it did. Scores of seventeenth and eighteenth century notarial contracts record the construction of all manner of vessels, from dugouts and canoes to coastal and sea-going ships. Three hundred and fifty ton ships were laid down in the private shipyards of New France, and 72-gun warships were built in the Royal Dockyards.[1]

When Jean Talon, the newly-appointed Intendant of New France arrived in Quebec in 1665, he envisaged a shipbuilding industry, the pillar of the colony's economy, supported by such ancillary trades as sailmaking, ropemaking, tar and ironmaking. The industries would serve as trade schools where boys would be apprenticed to local masters and specialists from France. But the intendant did not anticipate the extent of the problems he would encounter. The shortage of skilled labour acted as a constant barrier, and the industries he promoted during his two short terms of office remained on a fragile footing, which disintegrated when he left. The closing of the Royal Shipyard led to the decline of the tar-works and ropery. The projected ironworks remained only a project.[2]

In 1739, as part of an extensive programme to strengthen France's badly depleted Navy, a new Royal Naval Dockyard was set up on the Saint Charles River at the foot of Palace Hill, and operated there until 1748 when the main part of the yard was moved to the Cul-de-sac in the Lower Town. Under the able direction of the experienced French shipbuilder, René Noel Levasseur, nine warships were launched from the two sites over a period of seventeen years, the three largest each exceeding 700 tons. It is greatly to Levasseur's credit that under unaccustomed winter conditions, despite frequent deficiencies in the supply of labour and materials, confronted by countless problems in the domestic auxiliary industries and though surrounded by forests, often unable to obtain the "great" timbers for the larger ships he was required to construct, he succeeded through perseverance and improvisation in building vessels that drew approval from both French and British naval experts.[3] But the escalation of hostilities between the two countries led to the Siege of Quebec and work at the yard ground to a standstill, with the unfinished hull of his last ship, the frigate *Le Québec*, still on the stocks.

Though Canadian artisans and labourers formed the bulk of the Dockyard's labour force, a nucleus of skilled French tradesmen provided the expertise. It was hoped they would eventually be replaced by Canadians, but there were only a few cases where this

Figure 14: *Jean Talon (1625–1694). Intendant of New France from 1665 to 1668 and 1670 to 1672. Oil painting by the Recollet Frère Luc (Claude François), 1672-3, in the possession of l'Hôtel Dieu de Québec. Courtesy Archives nationales du Québec. Neg. E.6.7/NN.78.65.*

Figure 15: *René Noël Levasseur (1705–1784). Director of the Royal Naval Dockyards at Quebec from 1738 to 1759. Unknown artist. Courtesy Archives nationales du Québec.*
Neg. P600 – 6/N.277.55.

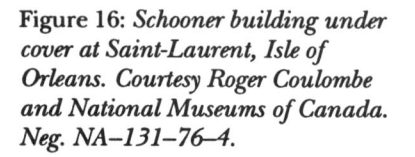

Figure 16: *Schooner building under cover at Saint-Laurent, Isle of Orleans. Courtesy Roger Coulombe and National Museums of Canada.*
Neg. NA–131–76–4.

occurred. Exceptionally, Louis Pierre Poulin, Sieur Cressé, advanced to the rank of Assistant Shipbuilder with the charge of a small shipyard on Lake Ontario, where he was required to supervise the building of two corvettes. Generally speaking, the Canadian and Metropolitan workers were jealous of the others' perceived privileges, and the disharmony between them aggravated the tendency to disinterest on the part of the Canadian workers who generally preferred life on their own farms to the discipline of the yard. When Levasseur's son was sent to build gunboats on Lake Champlain, the government was unable to muster the one thousand workers needed to operate all three yards, and work at the Quebec yard was halted.

Nevertheless, the Royal Shipyards, especially the longer lasting eighteenth-century yard, provided hundreds of labourers and tradesmen with a unique opportunity to learn or improve their skills under expert guidance in a superior, professional establishment. Though the workers had little interest in attaining the high standard of skill expected in a royal shipyard, there can be little doubt that they profited from the experience, from the most competent tradesman to the general labourer, and that skills were taken to other parts of the colony when the workers dispersed, to be passed down later from neighbour to neighbour and father to son. By the end of the French Regime, both private and government shipyards had played their parts in forming a shipbuilding tradition.

After the arrival of the British, domestic shipbuilding continued in much the same way on sheltered beaches around the Province, leading in the early nineteenth century to the development of the characteristic flat-bottomed Quebec river schooner or *goelette*.[4] Though some of the builders were professionals, much of the industry was a part-time occupation for fishermen and mariners who took part in the construction of a vessel during the winter in which they would earn their living in summer. In general, the timber was selected and felled in the autumn and left to season for a year or two. Meanwhile, the lines of the vessel, based on an earlier craft, became the subject of much discussion among those with an opinion until eventually a final version of a wooden halfmodel embodying all the accepted improvements was completed. Friends and neighbours then joined with members of the family in construction under the guidance of an experienced builder.

In this way, thousands of vessels were built and launched over the years from the beaches of the Saint Lawrence until the day when, like the larger wooden sailing ships, the familiar *goelettes* were superseded by metal craft. But the steel-hulled vessels were not their only competition. Improved transportation methods, including the airplane, long-distance truck and increasingly larger vessels did the rest. By the 1960s, domestic wooden shipbuilding had almost disappeared. It was to the end very much a grass-roots operation, coloured by tradition, its many facets forming an important part of the history of the Saint Lawrence. When it died, a direct link with the early days of the colony was lost.

Another branch of the domestic shipbuilding industry was steamboat building. After two hundred years of wooden shipbuilding with relatively few changes in shipyard techniques and only gradual developments in ship design, the impact of the widespread inventive spirit of the last half of the eighteenth century and the simultaneous proliferation of applications of steam power in mines, factories and flour mills began to have repercussions in the shipbuilding industry. By 1800, steam had reached Britain's Portsmouth Dockyard, taking the place of horses to work the saws and to pump out a new dock; shortly thereafter, it was harnessed to a ropewalk, to the iron and copper workshop and to a new blockmaking works. Experiments with steam afloat, which had been carried out for decades in Britain, France and America, crystallized in 1802 with the successful performance of William Symington's steamboat *Charlotte Dundas*, which towed two barges on the Forth and Clyde Canal against a strong breeze at three miles an hour.[5] Five years later, Robert Fulton made history when his passenger steamer, *North River Steamboat* (later renamed *Clermont*), steamed 150 miles upriver to Albany from New York at four and one-half miles an hour. Within a few years travel by steamboat became an economic reality. The engineer laid claim to his place in the shipyard and the revolution in ship design began.

Meanwhile, at Quebec traditional time-consuming methods had begun to give way to more scientific and productive ones. Peter Patterson's sawmill at the Montmorency Falls and Henry Caldwell's grist and sawmills on the Etchemin River, both in operation in the early days of the nineteenth century, were said to be among the largest and best-equipped in the world.[6] And the shipbuilder, John Goudie, who in 1811 projected a sawmill at Montmorency Falls,[7] opted for steam power instead and built at his shipyard in Saint Roch what was probably the first steam-powered sawmill in Canada, opening it for business in 1818.[8]

In marine engineering Montreal took the initiative, with the launching of the first paddle steamer on the Saint Lawrence, the *Accommodation*, by John Molson at Montreal in 1809, and retained the lead. Though the *Accommodation*'s engine was too weak for the strong river currents, it was the forerunner of many larger and more powerful craft.[9] By 1819 a regular steam service between Montreal and Quebec was provided by seven steamboats: P.S.S *Malsham* (1815), *Lady Sherbrooke* (1817) and *New Swiftsure* (1818), which were operated by John Molson, and the *Car of Commerce* (1815), *Caledonia* (1817) and *Telegraph* (1818) which belonged to his rival, Thomas Torrance. With the exception of the *Quebec*, built by Goudie, all were Montreal-built.

Unlike contemporary British steamboats, many of the early Canadian craft were remarkably large, perhaps as a result of Fulton's influence. On the river, tall-masted sailing ships towered above them, but at the waterline the steamers were both longer and broader in the beam. In 1823, for instance, the average sailing vessel calling at Quebec measured 233 tons or about 90' x 24', while with the exception of the smaller *Telegraph*, the steamboats averaged 144' x 30'. According to Merrill Denison, the original *Swiftsure* was planned as the largest steamboat in the world, but delays in building cost her the honour.[10] Nonetheless capacious, she was used frequently as a transport during the War of 1812 and is known to have carried as many as four hundred officers at one time.[11] Nor were these early steamboats lacking in comfort. According to one contemporary report,

Figure 17: *John Molson (1763–1836). Brewer, banker and operator of the Accommodation, Canada's first steamboat.*

there are no less than seven steam-boats which constantly ply on the St. Lawrence between Quebec and Montreal, five of which are nearly as large as a 40-gun frigate. They are fitted up in a very elegant manner for the accommodation of the passengers. On each side of their cabins, some of which are large enough to accommodate one hundred persons, there are two rows of berths, one above the other. The berths are supplied with excellent bedding and running curtains. Separate from the gents' cabin is one in each boat for the ladies; in which however they only sleep, for they take breakfast, dinner and tea, in the common room with the gentlemen. Every possible attention is paid to passengers on board of these boats. Servants of every description are always in waiting; and tables are daily laid out, exhibiting all the delicacies of the season, and every luxury which this fruitful country affords. In a word, their accommodations of every kind are not at all inferior to those which are to be met with in the most respectable hotels in Europe.[12]

The passage cost two pounds ten shillings downriver and three pounds for the longer return trip. Both running time and fare were steadily reduced as the boats improved in design and horsepower. The *Swiftsure*, for example, took twenty-two and a half hours for the trip to Quebec, an improvement of thirteen and a half hours on the *Accommodation*'s thirty-six. But the notorious Saint Mary's Current at Montreal, which had long been the bane of sailing vessels, defied the boats with relatively low engine power, and teams of as many as forty oxen were required to tow them past it, lengthening the already longer upriver time considerably.[13]

In 1815, Molson added two new wharves to his recently acquired property at Quebec to serve as his steamboat terminal,[14] and three years later Goudie's large deep-water wharf at the foot of Saint Antoine Street was ready to serve as the terminal both for Torrance's steamers and the new Quebec-Lauzon steam ferry service which Goudie inaugurated that Spring.[15] In keeping with the high standard of the service offered on the river steamboats, "large and commodious" accommodations with stabling for 150 horses were offered to the ferry passengers at the new hotel at the Lauzon terminus. According to an inventory taken after Goudie's death in 1824, the

Figure 18: *James Goudie (1809–1892), son of John Goudie. Designer and superintendent of the construction of the P.S.* Royal William. *Photo courtesy Ainslie Goudie.*

Figure 19: P.S. Royal William *of 1831. The first steamship to cross the North Atlantic. The Quebec shipbuilders John Bell, George Black, J.S. Campbell, Allison Davie, Hyppolite Dubord, John Munn and George Taylor were among the shareholders, as were Henry, Joseph and Samuel Cunard, giving rise to the opinion that she was the forerunner of the Cunard steam fleet. Oil painting by Samuel Skillet, 1834, Musée du Québec. Photo: Courtesy OFQ.*

hotel boasted twenty-three bedrooms, a billiard room, tap room, bar, pantry, kitchen, stable and coach house.[16]

Another pioneering step was taken in 1823 when Thomas Torrance launched the *Hercules*, the first steamboat on the Saint Lawrence built exclusively as a tug. Her one hundred horsepower engine was designed to allow her to tow even fully-rigged sailing ships past Saint Mary's Current. The construction of this vessel had a special significance. Because the engine of the *Accommodation* had been too weak, Molson had ordered the engines for his other steamboats from Boulton and Watt in Birmingham. With them had come a succession of recommended mechanics and steamboat captains. The engine of the *Hercules*, however, was built at the Eagle Foundry in Montreal, a shop set up in 1820 by the Vermonter John D. Ward. Moreover, another foundry and machine shop, Saint Mary's Foundry, had been established by John Bennett, a former Boulton and Watt and Molson employee, and his partner, John Henderson, to produce steamboat engines and equipment. For many years these two foundries and the Molson foundry supplied the machinery for the majority of steamboats on the Saint Lawrence.[17]

Between 1809 and 1899, the river industry produced more than four hundred steam vessels, varying from squat hard-working tugs to multiple-decked luxurious cruise boats. Of this number, forty-six percent were built in Montreal, thirty-seven percent in Quebec and the south shore opposite, and seventeen percent at Sorel.[18] Some disappeared quickly into oblivion while others left more enduring marks. The most illustrious, the paddle steamer *Royal William*, built under the supervision of James Goudie at the Campbell and Black shipyard at Cape Cove in 1831, was the first steamboat to cross the north Atlantic. The longest-lived, the Montreal-built *Richelieu* of 1845, was finally abandoned in 1954 after a career spanning one hundred and nine years.[19] To Quebec went the honour of producing the first screw-propelled steamer on the Saint Lawrence, the *Jenny Lind* of 1849,[20] and in 1865 the industry reached its peak output with the launching at Sorel of the 3056-ton *Quebec*, the largest of the nineteenth-century river steamboats.

Like the domestic schooner industry, this was another distinct marine industry producing for the home market and operating alongside (and in some cases in the same yards as) the larger sailing ship trade. Much of the technology of sailing ship construction was used in the fabrication of the wooden steamboat hulls, although after 1820 Charles Wood's revolutionary design of the steamboat *James Watt* led to a radically different hull design. The high quality finish of their joinery, cabinetry and furnishings, like the building and fitting of their machinery, was probably mostly carried out in Montreal, at least in the early days.

Despite the many accidents as the new technology was mastered both by builders and operators, the steamboats retained a special place in the hearts of Quebeckers, especially those who remembered the uncomfortable overland or lengthy sail-boat trips between Montreal and Quebec. Their arrival in the Port of Quebec each year from their winter quarters in Sorel was eagerly awaited and enthusiastically reported in the newspapers. Thus, the *Quebec Mercury* reported on 4 May 1821:

Quebec Background

Figure 20: *The Steamboat Tariff for passengers between Quebec and Montreal in 1831.*

Figure 21: *The rates of the Molson and Torrance Steam Tow-Boat cartel in 1842.*

RATES OF PASSAGE

PER STEAMBOATS

BETWEEN

MONTREAL AND QUEBEC,

AND INTERMEDIATE STOPPING PLACES.

CABIN PASSAGE.

From Montreal to Quebec or Batiscan	20s.
Do. to Wm. Henry or Berthier	5s.
Do. to Three Rivers	10s.
Wm. Henry or Berthier to Three Rivers	5s.
Do. to Quebec or Batiscan	15s.
Three Rivers to do. or do.	10s.

CABIN PASSAGE.

From Quebec to Montreal	25s. 0d.
Do. to Three Rivers or Batiscan	12s. 6d.
Do. to Wm. Henry or Berthier	18s. 9d.
Three Rivers to do. or do.	6s. 3d.
Do. to Montreal	12s. 6d.
Wm. Henry or Berthier to Montreal	7s. 6d.

Wing or Fore Cabin Passengers one half Cabin rate, (meals not included.)

STEERAGE PASSAGE.

From Montreal to Quebec or Batiscan	7s. 6d.
Do. to Wm. Henry or Berthier	2s. 6d.
Do. to Three Rivers	5s. 0d.
Wm. Henry or Berthier to Three Rivers	2s. 6d.
Do. to Quebec or Batiscan	7s. 6d.
Three Rivers to do. or do.	5s. 0d.

STEERAGE PASSAGE.

From Quebec to Montreal	7s. 6d.
Do. to Batiscan or Three Rivers	5s. 0d.
Do. to Wm. Henry or Berthier	7s. 6d.
Three Rivers to do. or do.	2s. 6d.
Do. to Montreal	5s. 0d.
Wm. Henry or Berthier to Montreal	2s. 6d.

Children from three to twelve years of age half the above rates.
Children under three years of age one quarter, in the Cabin only.
Gentlemen's Servants in Fore Cabin or Wing Births, (provided with Bed and Board,) two thirds Cabin fare.

Montreal, 1831

MONTREAL GAZETTE OFFICE.

ST. LAWRENCE AND MONTREAL STEAM TOW-BOAT COMPANIES.

Rates of Towing Vessels

BETWEEN

QUEBEC AND MONTREAL,

FOR THE SEASON OF 1842.

BREADTH OF BEAM. OLD MEASUREMENT.	Nine Feet Draught.	For each additional foot.	Ten Feet.	Eleven Feet.	Twelve Feet.	Thirteen Feet.	Fourteen Feet.	Fifteen Feet.
	£ s. d.	£ s. d.	£ s. d.	£ s. d.	£ s. d.	£ s. d.	£ s. d.	£ s. d.
20 Feet.	33 6 8	3 6 8	36 13 4	40 0 0	43 6 8	46 13 4	50 0 0	53 6 8
21 do.	35 0 0	3 15 0	38 15 0	42 10 0	46 5 0	50 0 0	53 15 0	57 10 0
22 do.	36 13 4	4 3 4	40 16 8	45 0 0	49 3 4	53 6 8	57 10 0	61 13 4
23 do.	38 6 8	4 11 8	42 18 4	47 10 0	52 1 8	56 13 4	61 5 0	65 16 8
24 do.	38 8 6	0 4 16 0	43 4 0	48 0 0	52 16 0	57 12 0	62 8 0	67 4 0
25 do.	40 0 0	5 4 0	45 4 0	50 8 0	55 12 0	60 16 0	66 0 0	71 4 0
26 do.	41 12 0	5 12 0	47 4 0	52 16 0	58 8 0	64 0 0	69 12 0	75 4 0
27 do.	43 4 0	6 0 0	49 4 0	55 4 0	61 4 0	67 4 0	73 4 0	79 4 0
28 do.	44 16 0	6 8 0	51 4 0	57 12 0	64 0 0	70 8 0	76 16 0	83 4 0

Any vessel taking the Boat at any intermediate distance between Quebec and the Church at Batiscan, will pay the full Towage, as if towed from Quebec. If taken in tow between Batiscan Church and the wharf at Three-Rivers, to pay three-fourths of the full towage. If taken in tow between the wharf at Three-Rivers and Sorel, to pay two-thirds of the full towage. If taken in tow between Sorel and the Church at Pointe aux Trembles, to pay one-half the full towage ; and from the Church at Pointe aux Trembles, or any intermediate place above the said Pointe, to Montreal, to pay one-third the full towage. It being understood that when towage is engaged for vessels at Quebec, as they have a preference over others, the full towage to be paid for, whether the whole, or part, or none of the towing is performed. The deduction made referring only to vessels for which towage has not been previously engaged at Quebec.

DOWNWARD TOWAGE, ONE HALF OF UPWARD RATES.

Passengers on board vessels taken in tow, to pay one-half the Steam-boat steerage rates.
Masters of vessels to furnish Tow-lines and Hawsers.
Not less than nine feet to be charged as draft water.
The greatest draft of water to be taken as measurement.
Should the masters of Boats, from any just reason, deem it necessary to cast off a vessel, no deduction to be made on the towage, provided they are re-taken by the first opportunity.
Vessels towed from Montreal, or any place above Sorel, to Three-Rivers, to be charged three-fourths of the towage to Quebec, and from Three-Rivers or above Port Neuf, to be charged two-thirds towage.
All Pilotage to be paid by the Masters or Consignees.
In the event of any vessel grounding when in tow, in consequence of being too deeply laden, or from the fault of the ship's pilot, the detention to be paid for, also the tariff rate, for freight taken out.
N. B.—The Proprietors notify to masters of vessels and others, that they will not hold themselves liable for any damage that may be done to vessels, or their warps, either in taking in tow, towing or casting them off.

TOWAGE PAYABLE ON DEMAND.

JOHN TORRANCE, & Co. Agent M. S. Tow-Boat Company, Montreal.
JOHN MOLSON, Agent St. L. S. Boat Company, do.
H. E. SCOTT, Agent, Quebec.

MONTREAL, 1842

J. C. BECKET, PRINTER.

On Saturday last our harbour presented a gay and animated spectacle, in the arrival of none less a number than eight Steam Boats with flags flying and guns firing, from their winter quarters in William Henry [Sorel] – the *Swiftsure, Montreal, Lady Sherbrooke, Caledonia, Malsham, Quebec, Telegraph* and *Car of Commerce*.

Quite distinct from these domestic shipbuilding industries was the export-oriented sailing ship industry. Largely dependent on British and foreign capital, it originated in the 1760s when the first vessels built for British ownership were laid down and ended when the last square-rigged sailing ship was launched in 1893. Sometimes prospering and sometimes depressed, the trade was twice brought to a halt by an American invasion, forcing shipbuilders and shipwrights to leave home for a while and build vessels of war at Government Dockyards on the Lakes.

On the first occasion, the new shipbuilding industry had barely begun to put down its roots when the port was blockaded by the Americans, who sought to persuade the Canadians to join them in their fight against Britain. When the siege was lifted, it became a supply port for the British army, to whose needs all its activities were subordinated.[21] French Canadian carpenters were put to building *bateaux* alongside dockyard workers sent from Halifax,[22] and shipyard workers were sent to Saint Johns, on the Richelieu River, where they worked beside men from the Portsmouth and Chatham Dockyards, seamen from both naval and merchant vessels at Quebec, and conscripts from the surrounding areas. Together they built or re-constructed thirty fighting vessels within a period of six weeks, among them one had been taken apart at a private yard at Quebec where it was under construction and

Figure 22: *John Goudie (1775–1824). Quebec shipbuilder, and Naval Contractor during the War of 1812. Garrit Schipper. Miniature. Photo courtesy Peggy Bolenbaugh.*

Figure 23: *This detail from Margaret Reynold's "View of Amherstburg, 1813"* shows HMS Detroit, *builder William Bell, just before she began her short-lived career in the British Lake Erie fleet. Courtesy Environment Canada: Parks Service, Fort Malden National Historic Site.*

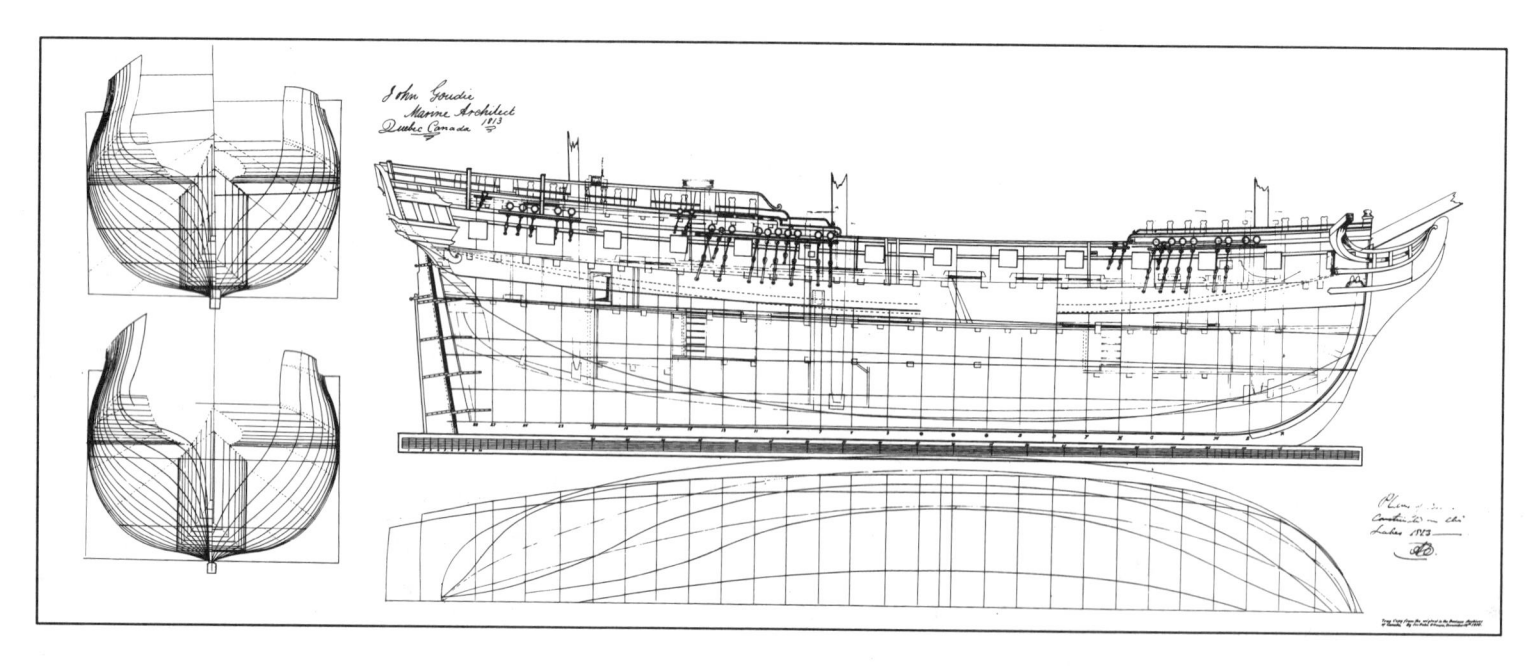

Figure 24: *Plan of HMS* Princess Charlotte *launched at Kingston by John Goudie 14th April 1814.* GOUDIE/81203–41/item 1, National Museums of Canada 78463, National Map Collection. Courtesy Ainslie Goudie and National Archives, Ottawa.

sent to Saint Johns for re-assembly, and another, the eighteen-gun brig *HMS Inflexible*, the largest vessel on Lake Champlain, built in twenty-eight days with frames sent from England.[23]

On the second occasion, during the War of 1812, not only was the extent of the shipbuilding far greater but it took place at dockyards on Lakes Erie and Ontario as well as on the Richelieu River. Immediately upon the outbreak of war, the master shipbuilder George Taylor led a first group of 128 shipwrights and other workers from the shipyards of various Quebec timber merchants to bolster the dockyard labour forces at Kingston, Amherstburg and York (Toronto).[24] The dockyards were run at that time by the army, the naval force on the Lakes being then little more than an army transport service known as the "Provincial Marine" which was unprepared for the task ahead of it.[25] According to an official return dated September 1811, the Marine's strength comprised the 20-gun ship *Royal George* on the Saint Lawrence, the 10-gun brig *Earl of Moira* and the 10-gun schooner *Duke of Gloucester* on Lake Ontario, the 16-gun ship *Queen Charlotte* and 10-gun schooner *General Hunter* on Lake Erie and the 8-gun schooner *Saint Lawrence* and six gunboats, "lately repaired but not armed." Furthermore, the same report noted that the carronades for the *Queen Charlotte* and *Royal George* were on their way up from Quebec except for six 24-pounders that were brought back to arm the gunboats, and that the *Royal George* had at that time twenty short 12-pound carronades and the *Queen Charlotte* fourteen 12-pounders. Three months later, Lieutenant Colonel A.H. Pye described the condition of the vessels as "very sorry."[26]

Duly alarmed, Sir George Prevost, governor-in-chief, immediately obtained permission to proceed with an emergency shipbuilding programme and gave orders for a frigate to be laid down at each of the three dockyards in Amherstburg, Kingston and York. Meanwhile, arrangements were made for the building and operation of the fleet to be taken over by the British Navy in May 1813. But Canada was caught unprepared and when York fell to the Americans in April, the new frigate *Sir Isaac Brock* was burned on the stocks to prevent her from enhancing their fleet. This was followed two months later by the loss of the second of the new frigates, the *Detroit*, built by William Bell at Amherstburg, which surrendered with the rest of the British establishment on Lake Erie when Amherstburg capitulated. Of the dockyards on the Great Lakes, only Kingston then remained in British hands.

At this critical time, Prevost appealed to the Quebec shipbuilder John Goudie to go to Kingston and "devote his considerable shipbuilding and entrepreneurial skills" to building up the fleet.[27] Responding immediately, Goudie left for Kingston in June with a first contingent of five foremen shipbuilders, one foreman joiner and one hundred ship carpenters, joiners, blacksmiths, sawyers and axemen recruited in Quebec.[28] The 23-gun frigate *Wolfe* had been launched at the dockyard in April under the direction of the master shipbuilder George Plucknett, and the smaller 14-gun brig *Lord Melville* was under construction.[29] Goudie immediately set his men to fitting out all available merchantmen for service, and then laid down the 56-gun frigate *Prince Regent*, which was draughted by Patrick Fleming.[30] The master shipbuilder George Record had contracted to build the smaller 36-gun frigate *Princess Charlotte*, but following his resignation in October that work was taken over by Goudie. Both vessels were launched on 14 April 1814.[31] Goudie then commenced work on another vessel, which was draughted by William Bell and was to be by far the largest that

Figure 25: *The 37-gun frigate HMS* Confiance *of 1814, named after the French Privateer that was captured by Captain Sir James Yeo, Commander-in-Chief on the Lakes, at Muros Bay and became his first command. The* Confiance *was built by William Simons at Ile-aux-Noix and launched on the 25 August 1814. Taking part in the Battle of Plattsburgh Bay, she was forced to strike her colours on the 11 September 1814. Model at the Glasgow Museum of Transport. Photo courtesy Gertrude McMichael.*

had been or would be built on the Lakes. *HMS Saint Lawrence* mounted 112 guns on three decks and was comparable in size to Nelson's *Victory*. Her 157 foot keel was four feet longer than *Victory*, her 52-foot beam a foot wider; her depth of hold only three feet less. She was launched on the 10 September 1814 to a royal salute from the batteries. She measured 2,300 tons compared to *Victory*'s 2,162.[32]

Meanwhile, William Simons, the founder of an important Greenock shipbuilding firm who had built four large merchantmen at Montreal between 1810 and 1813 for the merchant James Dunlop, visited the Isle aux Noix, on the Richelieu River, in July of 1813 to help in the valuation of captured American vessels. At that time he offered to build a sixteen-gun brig in six weeks; his offer led to contracts to build the 1200-ton frigate *Confiance*, the sixteen-gun sloop *Niagara*, later re-named *Linnet*, and two gunboats. Among those he employed at the Isle aux Noix were many shipyard workers from Quebec.[33] Under pressure from General Prevost, the *Confiance* was hurriedly launched on 25 August 1814. Hauled into the stream on the 7 September, shipwrights still worked as she sailed, her powder towed alongside in a *bateau* while her magazine was completed. Badly disabled at the Battle of Plattsburg only four days later she was forced to strike her colours.[34]

In February 1815, Goudie was awarded new contracts for a seventy-four-gun ship to be built at Kingston, as well as two frigates, a provision vessel, two brigs and eleven gunboats to be constructed at Isle aux Noix. Yet barely a month later the contracts were dissolved and he was asked to complete only the gunboats as the war had ended and the Admiralty had decided to stop construction of the rest. Goudie and James McDouall, the

Quebec Background

Figure 26: HMS St. Lawrence, *120 guns.* Built by John Goudie during the War of 1812, but served only as a transport, the war having ended soon after she was completed. To the left is shown the lugger-rigged gunboat *Buffalo,* and the tender-schooner *General Vincent* is at right. Drawing by Owen Staples, courtesy Baldwin Room, Metropolitan Toronto Library. Neg. T 15243.

Figure 27: *Engagement of Ship carpenters and others to Government.* A page from one of the many group contracts signed from 1813 to 1815. See, in particular the greffe of F.W. Scott at the Archives nationales du Québec. Photo Courtesy National Museums of Canada 76–4689.

Figure 28: *Descending to Campbell's Yard under the Plains of Abraham 1828, where the P.S. Royal William was built. Shipyard workers, left, on their way home with their customary perks, a bundle of firewood, turn to pose for the artist. James Cockburn, Watercolour (detail), (I–115). Photo courtesy National Archives, Ottawa, C 12629.*

Figure 29: *Rules and By-Laws dated 1862 issued to members of the Ship Laborers' Benevolent Society of Quebec. Courtesy John O'Connor.*

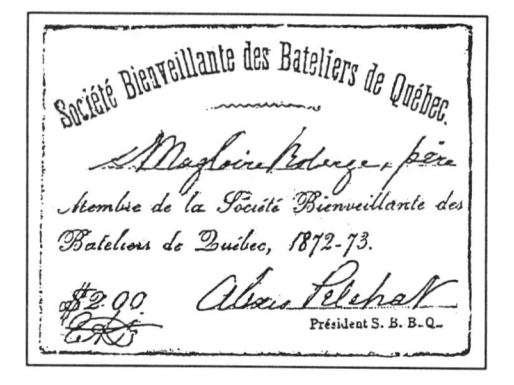

Figure 30: *Membership card of Magloire Roberge, père, in the Société Bienveillante des Bateliers de Québec, for the year 1872–3. Courtesy Hazel Taschereau.*

partner he had taken, received £13,000, one-third of the contract price.[35]

After the Rush-Bagot Agreement, the great *HMS Saint Lawrence* was laid-up for many years and finally sold at auction in 1832. She was bought for £25 by a Kingston contractor and merchant, who took off two of her three flush decks to recuperate the iron and sank the hull to make a wharf on which to pile cordwood for passing steamers, a testament to the folly of war. On the positive side, the Naval Dockyards on the Lakes, like their counterparts during the French Regime, enabled both builders and workers to gain valuable experience while earning good money. Their efforts were not entirely in vain, because it was on their shoulders that the weight of Quebec's developing shipbuilding industry in the second quarter of the century would fall.

Thus, of the three distinct types of vessels built by Saint Lawrence shipbuilders before 1815, almost all the small boats, sloops and schooners were laid down on sheltered beaches away from the large centres; steamboats were primarily built and equipped at Montreal (though the Port of Quebec came a close second); and square-riggers were constructed mainly at Quebec, which was advantaged in its shipbuilding capability in many different ways, and sent its builders to the Lakes to build there when the need arose.

The end of the Napoleonic Wars brought a brief period of general prosperity that gave way to a deep depression which lasted into the 1820s. In the post-depression boom that followed, ship production at Quebec rose from 840 tons in 1821 to 1,820 tons in 1823 and 18,357 tons in 1825. Then, having made up their fleets, shipowners cut back on orders and demand once again declined. By this time, however, the port had changed. The people were more sure of themselves, more aware that science and engineering were offering new tools that could be made to serve. The town had discovered that it had a unique role to play. The construction of the Citadel by the Royal Engineers was a landmark event in itself, which shared the limelight, however, with Charles Wood's two ship-rigged rafts *Columbus* (3690 tons) and even larger (5294 ton) *Baron of Renfrew*, launched from the southeast tip of the Isle of Orleans in 1824 and 1825. The Canada Floating Dock, laid down in Montreal in 1826, was another marked achievement.[36] Towed to Quebec the following spring, it was the first of the special facilities that allowed the port to operate an efficient ship repair and salvage trade. Before long headlines were made with the launching of the P.S. *Royal William* in 1831 and its successful passage to Britain in 1833.

Labour and waterfront services also became more "organized." Ship masters, whose business it was to turn their vessel around quickly, were frustrated with the excessive demands of the stevedores and timber stowers, and even more so with their inability to retain a full crew, without which they were not allowed to sail. In addition to the requirements for sailors of visiting ships, mainly to replace those that had deserted, crews had to be found for locally-built vessels. Native Quebeckers were disinclined to become deep-sea sailors, and to make up the numbers the "crimps," who supplied sailors by questionable means, operated in a fertile field. Sailors hired at Quebec earned £4 per month, or the equivalent "by the [one-way] run," whereas the rate in Britain, where the supply of sailors seems to have been virtually unlimited, was only one-third or one-quarter of this amount, so seamen were set upon by crimps, in connivance with boarding housekeepers, tavern owners and others who induced

Figure 31: *Diamond Harbour after the shipyards fell silent. courtesy Archives nationales du Québec-Q. Fonds Philippe Gingras, Rue Champlain, P 585, Neg 80–1–239. Courtesy Archives nationales du Québec.*

them to desert the ship on which they had arrived, wheedled whatever they owned of value from them, got them to pledge a good part of what they would earn in the future, and then offered them for hire on another ship at the Quebec rate. In the 1830s and 1840s, crimping was done "legally" by charging the captain with failing to uphold his side of the employment contract, often on a technicality, and having the sailor's contract legally dissolved. John Wilson, a lawyer, who ran his own hiring agency, boasted that he had shipped upwards of 1,700 sailors in 1846. He supplied every Quebec shipbuilder, he wrote, except the Gilmours and John Munn, but supplied their old ships as well as many others. When the Act for regulating the Shipping of Seamen was passed in 1847 in an attempt to redress the matter, John Wilson lobbied for post of official (and sole) shipping master. He claimed he was the best qualified to carry out its provisions, and if appointed, would make honest men of some of the crimps. The Bill, he said, would not work to cure the evil complained of unless by proper management at the outset. When he was refused the appointment, supposedly because he was the owner of a tavern, and could no longer ship sailors legally, he continued to work outside the law. He was one of many, though perhaps the most important. The series of laws that were passed from 1847 on in an attempt to solve the problems of crimping resulted in an increasing number of desertions in place of "legal" contract breaking as Wilson had foretold, and led to extreme violence. The whole waterfront was under the iron fist of the crimps. Sailors who opposed their wishes were beaten and shanghaied; those who sought to redress the situation were attacked and intimidated. The situation culminated in the fatal shooting of a reluctant deserter by the crimps and the axing of a crimp by a shipmaster in 1872,[37] and ended only with the decline of port activities.

The hiring of ship labourers was another serious sore in the port. Although on occasion the labourers earned as much as four dollars a day, they complained of difficulties in getting the pay that was owed them, sometimes from the ship masters and other times from the stevedores.[38] In 1862, Irish labourers formed a Benevolent Society,[39] which proposed in its union-like articles to raise ship stowage charges by forty percent and to give its members a monopoly of port labour. French Canadian labourers, who preferred low pay to none at all were prepared to undercut them, and eventually formed a rival society in 1865.[40] Violence between the two groups broke out frequently and on several occasions reached serious proportions. Like crimping, it was only toward the end of the century when the port declined in importance that the dispute lessened in intensity, and the men of both unions agreed to the same scale of wages, ranging between $1.50 and $2.50 per day.[41]

This was the age of combinations and as the years passed more were formed. Tow-boat companies, which had engaged at times in cut-throat competition, chose the more remunerative paths of joining forces in partnership or dividing up the territory and respecting each others' rights.[42] In 1855, shipsmiths banded together to establish minimum charges for the loan of landing gear,[43] and small boat owners, or *bateliers*, agreed together to restrict both the load sizes and tariffs.[44] In 1867 the ship riggers formed a union which adopted very tough closed-shop rules.[45] From 1840, the voices of ship carpenters, caulkers and other shipyard labourers were frequently heard demanding better wages or shorter working hours; on several occasions they backed up their demands with strikes.[46]

But all these were minor irritants compared to the cyclic nature of the shipping market, an unfortunate fact of life for shipbuilders. Sudden heavy demands for tonnage to move people or freight obliged owners to increase their fleets, which were left with surplus capacity when the demands subsided. The extra vessels replaced those lost through normal attrition until the size of the fleet stabilized, and until then new ships were not required. The tragedy of shipbuilding booms was that they always led to years of rock bottom prices and reduced demand. There was little for shipbuilders to do but adapt to the cycles as best they could, making the best of the booms as they occurred. In 1839, for instance, five thousand ship voyages were required to carry five million quarters of grain to Britain, where the harvest had failed, and the excessive tonnage which resulted depressed shipping values by as much as fifty percent.[47] Gold rushes to California in 1849 and to Australia two years later once again stimulated the market by diverting a large number of vessels to the longer Pacific runs. In 1854, the heavy demand for transports for the Crimean War was responsible for filling shipyard ways in Britain and America. Then the government decided to charter steamers instead of sailing ships, and the Liverpool shipbroker, Edward Oliver, was caught in a saturated market with ninety-eight sailing ships on his hands.[48]

Each time the market suffered a reverse and prices fell below costs, the shipbuilder was in trouble. As Peter McClelland wrote of a similar situation in New Brunswick, the shipbrokers provided many services for the builders, but one they did not provide was taking the price risk. That was left for the builder and every now and again another fell by the wayside.[49] Still, as long as the market for wooden ships lasted, there were shipbuilders who were willing to carry on their trade at Quebec, and conditions remained relatively good for them to do so. Captain Lauchlan McKay, brother of the celebrated American clipper builder, Donald McKay, and himself also a shipbuilder in the United States, operated a shipyard at Quebec from 1863 to 1873. He then returned to the United States, but was once more building on the Saint Charles River in 1877. By then, however, no matter how good building conditions might be at Quebec, the wooden sailing ship market was fast shrinking, as improved steel ships proved their worth.

In 1817, when John Goudie plugged up the flues of the boilers for his new mill and floated them around to his shipyard, many of the onlookers were amazed to see that iron could float. They were no doubt unaware that an iron canal boat had been built in Britain thirty years earlier, that others had followed over the years and that experiments were then taking place that would lead to the first iron sea-going vessel, the steamer *Aaron Manby*, crossing from London to France in 1822. Yet one might say that the decline in shipbuilding in Quebec began at that time, even before the rise. For, although Quebec's greatest shipbuilding years lay in the half century ahead, when events around the globe would create unprecedented demands for shipping, nothing could stop those who were committed to the development of iron and steel. Drawn together by this common interest, they worked ceaselessly to improve their techniques. They were so successful that they lifted the British iron industry ahead of that of any other country, and its product became the cheapest in Europe. Output rose from 156

Figure 32: *View of Montreal Harbour commemorating the 100th anniversary of CP Ships. With thanks to the artist, R.D. Wilson, and Canadian Pacific.*

tons in 1800 to almost four million by 1860, while between 1856 and 1870 developments in technology pushed the production of steel up six-fold and its price down by almost half.[50] In 1862, for the first time the tonnage of iron ships built in Britain equalled that of wooden ships. Seven years later, it represented more than three-quarters of all new construction.[51]

In shipbuilding, the substitution of iron for wood was only a first step, for iron lacked the necessary strength after a certain size. Nor was steel the answer until a mild steel with the necessary properties was produced by Siemens in an open hearth furnace and at a reasonable cost in 1875 in response to an Admiralty request.[52] In 1877, Lloyd's published its first rules for steel construction; by 1889, over a million tons of steel ships were laid down.

In the 1860s, when metal became the prime shipbuilding material, the dominance of northeastern England and Clyde shipyards began. London yards, which had for so long basked in their acknowledged superiority and had been at the forefront of early experimentation in both marine engineering and metal shipbuilding, experienced an outburst of frenzied activity during the American Civil War before falling into lasting decline. By 1892, not only were three-quarters of the world's tonnage built in Britain, but fifty-six percent of British production was on the northeast coast and thirty-one percent on the Clyde.[53]

The devastating effect of the new technology on the wooden ship market, though tempered in the early 1860s by heavy demands for tonnage during the American Civil War, exacted its toll on shipyards in which wooden vessels were built on both sides of the Atlantic. While those more heavily engaged in ship repairing were better able to stave off their closing, all knew that the industry was dying.

Quebec shipyards shared in the heady days of 1862 and 1863, producing record tonnage figures before the final decline began. For a few years, sales to French customers helped delay the inevitable. Then, in the last twenty years of diminishing construction, one man's efforts kept the industry alive. The Quebec merchant James Gibb Ross not only arranged the financing of most new vessels but through his connections in Liverpool, Glasgow and London, and his considerable shipping acumen ensured that they were no longer sacrificed on a depressed market but operated as traders until an opportunity for a more profitable sale occurred. Thus the shipbuilders were able to carry on for a few more years, while thousands of man-hours of labour were provided in the shipyards and sail-lofts.

In 1885, the last of Quebec's large sailing ships, Etienne Samson's 1252-ton barque *Cambria* and the 1307-ton *Cheshire*, built by Guillaume Charland, Sr., left their respective shipyards in Levis. For the next eight years, no square-rigged vessel was built in the port. Then Charland sent a little postscript down the ways in the form of the 395-ton barquentine *White Wings*, after which Quebec's great days of sailing ship construction were over.

Not only did wooden ship construction come to an end, but so too did Quebec's position as Canada's Atlantic terminal. With the completion of the Saint Lawrence Channel in 1853, ocean shipping could safely reach Montreal. As the hub of a wheel whose spokes reached down the Saint Lawrence to the sea, along canals to New York and into the heart of the American continent, with railway connections to Brockville, Toronto, Portland, Rivière-du-Loup and

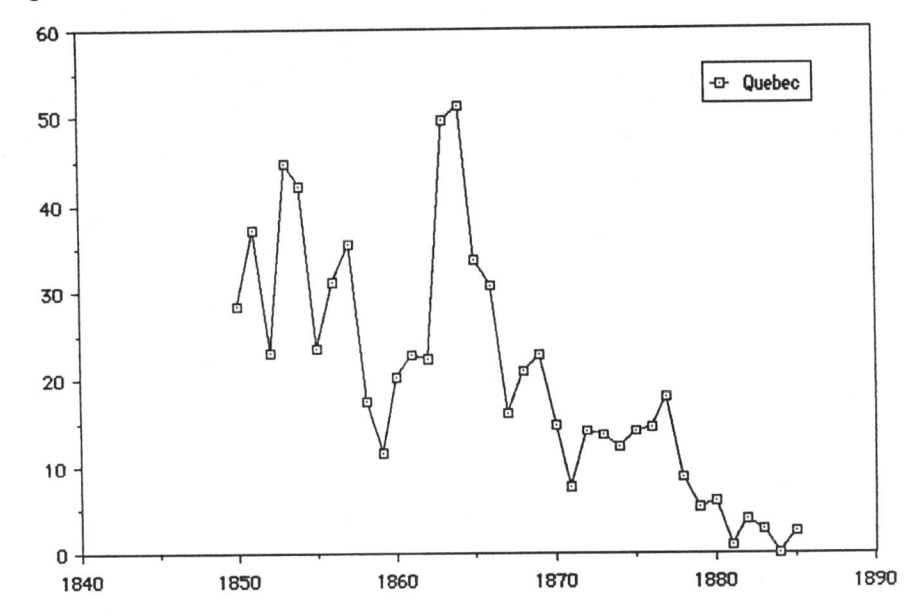

Graph 1: *Production of Wooden Vessels at the Port of Quebec, 1850-1885.*

Source: *Quebec Shipping Registers, 183-98, 202-3, 267-71, 375-78, RG12, NA.*

Note: *Graph 1 should be read bearing in mind the effect of the change in the method of measurement in 1855.*

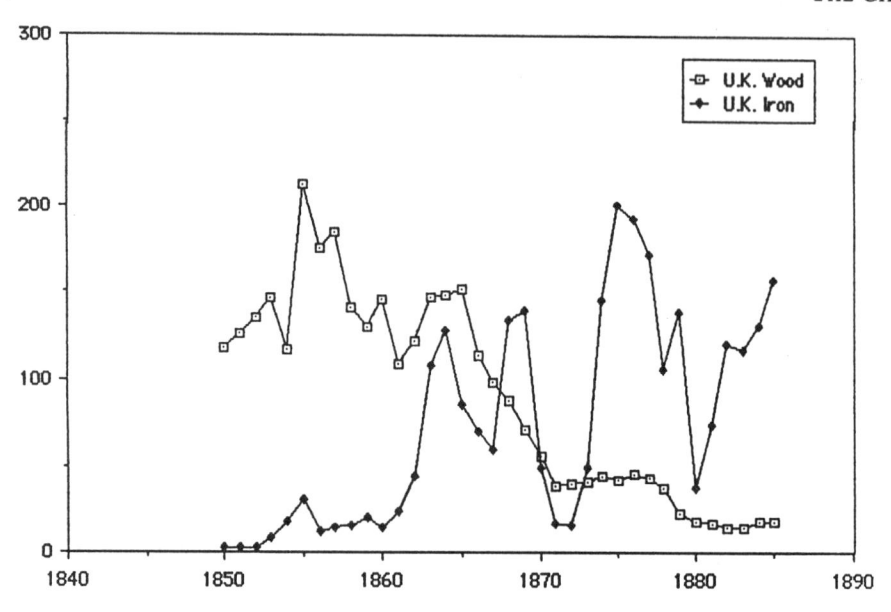

Graph 2: *British production of wood and iron vessels, 1850-85.*

Source: *B.R. Mitchell* Abstract of British Historical Statistics *(Cambridge, 1962), 223.*

elsewhere, Montreal's growth was assured. Industrial firms and commercial houses opened in quick succession and the population exploded from 35,000 in 1839 to 90,323 in 1861 and 219,616 in 1891.

Quebec, on the other hand, was no longer the hectic port with a hinterland stretching west to the Great Lakes and south to Lake Champlain, no longer the huge timber depot, the garrison town, the seat of the colonial government. Railways were slow to reach Quebec and river traffic still came to a halt during the winter. Many of the shipyard workers had emigrated to Ontario or the United States. The population, which had doubled between 1839 and 1860, rose by only three thousand in the next thirty years. The leather trades replaced the wood trade, and between 1880 and 1890 employed three thousand workers in shoe factories alone, although traffic on the river allowed two or three ship repair yards to survive, and steamboats were still built.[54]

Though different, the town was far from dead. An impressive Provincial Parliament building took shape between 1879 and 1885, and two years later construction of the new Law Courts began. Before long, a fine new City Hall would be built. The Lorne Dry Dock at Lauzon, across the river, which allowed Davie's shipyard eventually to enter the metal shipbuilding business, was completed in 1889, and old dreams were realized when the Princess Louise Wet Dock at the mouth of the Saint Charles, the beginning of efficient docking facilities at Quebec, received its first vessel a year later. Like the age of the fur trade, the age of the timber trade was almost over, and in keeping with her new role, Quebec had a new face.

Notes

1. Réal Brisson, *La charpenterie navale à Québec sous le Régime français* (Québec, 1983); Jacques Mathieu, *La construction navale royale à Québec 1739–1759* (Québec, 1971).
2. Jean Hamelin, *Economie et société en Nouvelle France* (Québec, 1970), 23, 26; André Vachon, "Jean Talon," *Dictionary of Canadian Biography* (Toronto, 1966), I:614-632.
3. Mathieu, *La construction navale*, 67; Robert Gardiner, "Frigate Design in the XVIII Century," *Warship*, I:3.
4. Michel Desgagnés, *Les goelettes de Charlevoix* (Ottawa, 1977), 30–35, 44–46.
5. *Annals of Lloyd's Register* (London, 1934), 30.
6. J.M. Duncan, *Travels Through Parts of the United States and Canada in 1818 and 1819* (New York, 1823), II, 198-205; Benjamin Silliman, *Remarks made on a Short Tour between Hartford and Quebec in the Autumn of 1819* (2nd ed., New Haven, 1824), 250; Louisa Anne, Lady Aylmer, "Recollections of Canada, 1831," *Rapport de l'archiviste de la Province de Québec* [hereafter *RAPQ*] (1934–35), 306–307. All of these are cited by A.J.H. Richardson, "Indications for Research in the History of Wood-Processing Technology," *Bulletin of the Association for Preservation Technology* [hereafter *APT*], VI:3 (1974), 74–75.
7. See "Contract to Build Mill," Winchell with Goudie and Black, 25 February 1811, gr J. Belanger.
8. *Quebec Gazette*, 5 March 1818.
9. Merrill Denison, *The Barley and the Stream. The Molson Story: A Footnote to Canadian History* (Toronto, 1955), 64–99, *passim*.
10. *Ibid.*, 81.
11. *Quebec Gazette*, 11 and 13 August 1814; Transports, Provincial Marine, C-Series, 1816, 374:208-9. See also 1826, 376: 144-5, NA.
12. Allen Talbot (ed.), *Five Years Residence in the Canadas* (reprint, New York, 1968), I, 79.
13. "Agreement," Government with Molson, Transports, 374: 208-9; Denison, *The Barley*, 66, 69, 83, 91–92; *Quebec Gazette*, 17 August 1826.
14. Construction contracts, 25 October 1815, 26 July 1816 and 27 September 1817, gr J. Voyer.
15. *Quebec Mercury*, 12 May 1818.
16. 10 January 1825, gr T. Lee. See also Aylmer, "Recollections of Canada," 313.
17. Denison, *The Barley*, 82–83; Shipping Returns for the Port of Quebec, II, 1 July 1849, RG 4 B32, NA.
18. These figures are derived from John M. Mills, *Canadian Coastal and Inland Steam Vessels, 1809–1930* (Providence, R.I., 1979). His list, however, does not include ships used exclusively in trans-ocean services or highly-specialized craft such as dredgers, icebreakers, lightships, etc.
19. The hull of the *Richelieu*, which was built of "fine British iron," was lengthened from 125 to 167 feet in 1902. Her name was changed to *Belmont* in 1886, back to *Richelieu* in 1893, and she ended up with the name of *Beauharnois*, which she acquired in 1906. *Ibid.*, x, 101.
20. Built as a barge, she was fitted as a steamer in 1852 and became a barge again in 1863; *ibid.*, 61.
21. The army made constant demands on the local population. For example, in November 1782 a naval force was unable to sail because there were neither bread nor water casks with which to outfit the transports; every baker and cooper in town was put to work to remedy the situation. 30 November 1782, ADM 49/21.
22. James Thompson's Journal, 2 July 1776, 19, microfilm 2312, NA, courtesy A.J.H. Richardson.
23. Robert Beatson, *Naval and Military Memoirs of Great Britain from 1727 to 1783* (London, 1804), IV, 143–146; RG4 A1 (S series), 7515, NA; ADM 42/2151, PRO.
24. George W. Haws, *The Haws Family and their Shipbuilding Kin* (Dunfermline, 1932), 158–160.
25. W.A.B. Douglas, *Gunfire on the Lakes* (Ottawa, 1977), 4.
26. Report of H.M. Provincial Marine on the Rivers and Lakes in Upper and Lower Canada, Quebec, 16 September, Transports, 373: 28 and 31: 5, British Military Records, microfilm C-29321, NA.

27. *Quebec Morning Chronicle*, 24 January 1883; see also, Prevost to Jas. Yeo, 12 October 1812, RG8, Military C-series, 1281: 182, NA.
28. Patrick Fleming, William and James Grant, Peter Leitch and John Hendry were the foreman builders; Jacques Laurencelle the foreman joiner. Group engagement contract, 22 June 1813, gr J. Belanger.
29. Military C-series, 729: 169; 14 October 1814, Vol. 1997, ADM 106, Canadian Yards, Admiralty Documents, PRO.
30. Report on the fleet on Lake Ontario, 14 October 1814, B-1001, ADM 106, Vol. 1997, PRO.
31. Estimates of the Naval Department at Kingston, 10 April 1814, Military C-series, Vol. 732, 171-2.
32. Plan of *HMS Saint Lawrence*, #75, Kingston Naval Yard plans, Admiralty.
33. Port of Quebec Shipping Registers, 1810–13; William Wood (ed.), *Selected Documents, War of 1812*, II, 230; Ile-aux-Noix pay lists, 1814, ADM 42/2167; Upper Clyde Shipbuilders (Simons-Lobnitz), U.C.S.4, Glasgow University Archives, with thanks to Michael Moss, archivist; information received from William Lind, Business Archives of Scotland.
34. Wood (ed.), *Selected Documents*, 122.
35. Robert Hall to Commissioners of the Navy, 12 March 1815, ADM 106/1997. Agreement, McDouall with Goudie, 4 February 1815, gr H. Griffin, ANQM.
36. Sale and transfer, Farrington to Forsyth, 19 January 1827, gr H. Griffin, ANQM.
37. Judith Fingard, "Those Crimps of Hell and Goblins Damned: The Image and Reality of Quebec's Sailortown Bosses," in Rosemary Ommer and Gerald Panting (eds.), *Working Men Who Got Wet* (St. John's, 1980). See also Fingard, *Jack in Port: Sailortowns of Eastern Canada* (Toronto, 1983) correspondence.
38. *Morning Chronicle*, 9 July 1866.
39. Quebec Ship Labourers' Benevolent Society, 25 Vict. c. 98.
40. Jean Hamelin and Yves Roby, *Histoire économique du Québec 1851–1896* (Sainte-Hyacinthe, 1971), 309–310.
41. *L'Evénement*, 22 August 1879.
42. E.g., Agreement, Jas. McKenzie and St. Lawrence Steamboat Co. with Steam Towboat Co. of Montreal, 18 April 1840, gr L. McPherson; Agreement and co-partnership, Gilmour with McKenzie, 2 June 1847, gr A. Campbell.
43. Agreement between twelve Quebec shipsmiths, 19 June 1855, gr J. Hossack. However, Robert Webb's advertisement in the *Quebec Gazette* 1 November 1856 casts some doubts on the success of the agreement.
44. Agreement, 16 May 1857, gr J. Hossack.
45. Association of the Quebec Riggers' Company, signed by thirty-five members, half French-speaking and half English-speaking, 18 July 1867, gr J. Childs.
46. See reports of strikes, *Quebec Mercury*, 5 December 1840; *Morning Chronicle*, 3 October 1867; *Courrier du Canada*, 27 September 1890.
47. R.S. Craig, "British Shipping and British North American Shipbuilding in the Early Nineteenth Century, With Special Reference to Prince Edward Island," in H.E.S. Fisher (ed.), *The South West and the Sea* (Exeter, 1968).
48. *Liverpool Telegraph and Shipping Gazette*, 2 January 1855.
49. Peter McClelland, "The New Brunswick Economy in the Nineteenth Century" (Unpublished Ph.D. thesis, Harvard University, 1966), 188.
50. Heaton, *Economic History of Europe* (New York, 1936), 500.
51. B.R. Mitchell (comp.), *Abstract of British Historical Studies* (Cambridge, 1962), 221.
52. Leslie Jones, *Shipbuilding in Britain: Mainly between the Two World Wars* (Cardiff, 1957), 22–23.
53. David Dougan, *The History of North East Shipbuilding* (London, 1968), 221.
54. M.A. Bluteau, *et al.*, *Les cordonniers, artisans du cuir* (Montréal, 1980), 100.

CHAPTER 3
Shipbuilders

Thomas Hamilton Oliver was eleven years old when he arrived at Quebec in 1821 from Glandormatt in County Derry. His father was a land surveyor with excellent prospects, but he died the following year, leaving his widow with eight young children. When their oldest son, Thomas, reached his fifteenth birthday, he was formally apprenticed to the master shipbuilder George Black for four years.[1] Not only was he in good hands but he seems to have had a great affinity for the trade, for only five years after completing his term, he laid down a vessel in his own yard. His brother, Edward, served as his foreman until 1837[2] when he too set up for himself. In 1840, however, Edward left for Liverpool where he established himself as a shipbroker, leaving his shipyard in the hands of a third brother, James Erskine. James ran the yard until 1857, at which time he also gave up shipbuilding for shipbrokerage and Thomas took it over. Thomas remained a shipbuilder to the end, enjoying a long and prolific career in the course of which he outbuilt every other Quebec shipbuilder both in the number of vessels he laid down and in their total tonnage. The 699-ton barque *Mary Graham* of 1877 was his 123rd and last. All told, he constructed almost eighty-eight thousand tons.

Origins

The Olivers were three of more than one hundred and fifty men and women who built large sailing ships at Quebec between 1763 and 1893. Many were born there of French, Scottish, English, Irish or, in one case, German ancestry. Others were immigrants from Britain or Ireland, a part of the continual stream of shipwrights that poured across the Atlantic to work in North American shipyards from the mid-seventeenth century on. A few were American-born.

The first relatively large vessel, the snow *Cordelia* launched in 1765, and the two others that followed in 1768 and in 1773,[3] were built under the supervision of Zacharaiah Thompson, Captain of the Port and a former ship's carpenter in the Royal Navy.[4] The local ship carpenter Louis Parent may have been their builder, as he was of the 250-ton *British Queen* and of two smaller vessels, all launched in 1774.[5] When the American invasion closed the Quebec yards in 1775, he left for Ile aux Noix with Thompson and others to help build up a British fleet on Lake Champlain. He was still active following the war, building the 257-ton ship *Betsey* at Sorel in 1797 and the 127-ton brig *General Prescott* at Baie Saint Paul in 1799,[6] but the rest of his production is unidentified. It is likely that Parent, who

Figure 33: *Thomas Hamilton Oliver (1810–1880). Courtesy the late M. Oliver, photo G. Marcil.*

Figure 34: *Thomas Oliver's ship* Enterprise, *1515 tons, of 1875. A fast ship, she sailed from Bic, Gulf of St. Lawrence to Greenock in 17 days in 1888. Her last years were spent under the Norwegian flag. Courtesy Maritime Museum of the Atlantic, Wallace Collection, MP1.73.1.*

came from a Beauport shipbuilding family, gained his experience in the French Naval Dockyards at Quebec.

When America became an independent country, British shipowners, who were prevented by the Navigation Laws from buying foreign ships, looked northward instead to Nova Scotia, New Brunswick and Canada to build up their fleets. This resulted in the influx of a number of Scottish ship carpenters, who might formerly have chosen to go to the United States.

One of them was a shipbuilder, referred to simply as "Mr. Fraser," who was shot dead on New Year's eve 1775 during the American siege of Quebec. Whether he had already engaged in his trade at Quebec, we do not know. Captain James Duncanson, a native of Irvine in Ayrshire and a shipmaster familiar with the port, left more evidence behind him.[7] When he came in 1785, it was to set up a yard at Diamond Harbour on the southern outskirts of the town. With a contract from Captain James Fairrie, a fellow townsman, and another from Captain Robert Crosbie of Liverpool, he laid the keels of two vessels. His workforce was composed of Scottish ship carpenters sent over for the purpose.[8] Although he then went back to sea, two of the lads who had worked in his yard, John Black and William King, remained in Canada, moving to the Baie des Chaleurs, Gaspé, where they built for the merchant Henry Rumphoff before returning to Quebec and going into business together. But their association was short-lived and left King insolvent. Black, however, managed to establish his own shipbuilding and repairing business on the other side of town, where he is said to have employed as many as sixty workers between 1788 and 1798.[9] Black may have been a good shipbuilder, but he ran into many difficulties on account of his controversial political views with regard to French Canadian dominance of the House of Assembly, which he sought to end. He had a high opinion of himself and was constantly seeking favours from men in high places, who repeatedly turned him down. In 1808, for instance, he went to England to request that the lease for the Forges Saint Maurice be given him, that he be appointed to the position of superintendent of the King's ship and batteaux yards, inspector of all the timber expended in the military departments and by the civil governments, and agent of the Seigniory of Sorel. As an alternative, he requested that he be provided for in the Canada establishment. Castlereagh, however, considered him a man of neither capital nor credit and did not recommend him for any office. Black was not a man who gave up easily and was still searching for favours in 1810[10] He was not typical of Quebec shipbuilders, who generally carried on their businesses without seeking political advantage.

Meanwhile the ships of the Montreal-based North West Company left each year for Britain laden with furs and returned each spring with military stores and goods for the Indian trade. Among the officers they employed were Captains William, Patrick and John Beatson, sons of Captain John Beatson of North Leith. For many years William was in command of the famed *Eweretta* which spent the summer season in Montreal, serving there on occasion for receptions, and left at the end of the season with her cargo of furs and other goods. He was described as a "capable commander and genial host" by Robert Hunter, Jr. Patrick, who went to sea at the age of fourteen, had served seven years in the Baltic and the North American trades as seaman and mate, and another seven in command, before spending a year and a half in East India Company ships on the India run, after which he returned to the Quebec run. John, the youngest, served on his brother William's ship before getting his own command, and was so highly considered that he was entrusted with the passage of Lady Dorchester, wife of the Governor and four of their children at the age of twenty. He would later become an important shipbreaker in Rotherhythe. In 1793, the three brothers set up a shipyard at Quebec and Patrick left the sea to run it. He employed a nucleus of Scottish tradesmen, and in 1798 stated that he had ten or twelve shipwrights and blacksmiths sent out from Scotland each year.[11]

It was not long before Beatson was joined by other Scottish shipbuilders who like Duncanson, Black and perhaps King were natives of Irvine. Alexander, John and David Munn were sons of the master shipbuilder John McMunn, or Munn, of the Half-Way, Irvine.[12] John McMunn was a contemporary and fellow-townsman of Robert Burns, and the poet's words on his tombstone, "An honest man the noblest gift of God," are an indication of the moral principles which he instilled in his sons. Alexander and John Munn arrived in the 1790s, each establishing his own shipyard, and were joined later by John Jr., John's son. David, who was considerably younger than his brothers, followed after a few years and built briefly at Quebec before settling in Montreal around 1806. A fourth brother, James, who practised his trade in Scotland for a number of years while acting as agent for his brothers, emigrated to New Zealand in 1824. Like Duncanson and Beatson, the Munns also brought many shipyard workers over from Scotland, and all three brothers enjoyed successful though short careers, for they all died in their forties.[13] The younger John, however, who began as his father's partner and lived to the age of seventy, became a pillar of the community and eventually owned one of the finest shipyards in Quebec.[14]

Other Clyde shipbuilders who came to Quebec include John Goudie of Kilmarnock. Goudie was

Figure 35: *Captain James Fairrie of Irvine, Ayrshire, subscribing owner of the 205 ton ship* Alfred, *built for Fairrie and some Greenock merchants by James Duncanson at the Diamond Harbour shipyard in 1787. Unsigned, undated ivory miniature. Photo courtesy James Fairrie, his direct descendant.*

Figure 36: *Captain Patrick Beatson (1758–1800). Oil painting, photo courtesy Archibald Beatson.*

foreman of the works at the naval dockyard on the River Thames in Upper Canada before setting up his own shipyard at Quebec[15] and as a naval contractor at Kingston during the War of 1812 was largely responsible for Canada being able to hold its own against the Americans. Like so many other shipbuilders, however, he did not reach his fiftieth birthday. Lastly, Allan Gilmour and Company from Mearns, Glasgow, who were important timber merchants in Quebec and New Brunswick, were also first class shipbuilders, and many of the finest Quebec-built vessels were laid down in their yard under the direction of Allan Gilmour, Jr., and later John Gilmour.

Scottish shipbuilders from the east of Scotland included George Black, who arrived in Quebec in 1813 from Aberdeen and worked for John Munn before entering into partnership with John Saxton Campbell and running the important Campbell and Black shipyard at Cape Cove. The brothers William and John Bell came from Aberdour in Fifeshire. William, the older brother, spent almost his entire career in government service. William was sent to the Amherstburg Dockyard on Lake Erie in 1799 as a shipwright and rose to the position of Master Shipwright on the Upper Lakes. When the Americans forced the British to retreat from York in 1813, he joined the dockyard staff at Kingston and in 1815 was appointed Assistant to the Master Shipwright in Canada, a post from which he was retired on pension the following year.[16] John, who was also stationed at Amherstburg in 1800 and built a vessel for the North West Company at Kingston in 1806, began building at Quebec in 1810 and continued to build there with one or two interruptions until 1836. He worked in partnership with the French Canadian shipbuilder François Romain in 1810 and 1811 and made an effort to work in partnership with his brother William in the 1820s,[17] but the latter soon after turned his back on shipbuilding and bought a farm.[18] John was obsessed with the idea of leaving his shipyard to his closest namesake, but although he married three times, he had no son to whom he could give his name nor was his wish otherwise fulfilled.[19]

Another Scot, William Henry Baldwin, was one of Quebec's finest shipbuilders. His grandfather, Henry Baldwin, also from the east coast of Scotland, was foreman of the Beatson yard and later built on his own account.[20] Henry's two sons, a cabinetmaker and a blockmaker, died young, but their sons William Henry and Peter both became shipbuilders.[21] William Henry, who was the senior by twelve years, had an impressive record as a shipbuilder. Peter worked with him for many years before starting out on his own when Quebec's shipbuilding days were almost over, launching his last vessel, the *Keewatin*, in 1881. He put his experience to good use, however, for in 1887 he began an important new career as superintendent for the Quebec Steamship Company in New York, which lasted until his retirement in 1911.[22]

William G. Russell, who was also of Scottish origin, was co-founder with John Nicholson of an important shipyard at Levis. Other Scots included Walter Gilley Ray, who descended from shipbuilders on both sides and capped his career as a builder by becoming Surveyor for Bureau Veritas in 1864;[23] and William Simons, naval architect, son of the Quebec sailmaker, Peter Simons, and grandson of the Greenock shipbuilder William Simons. He followed Walter Ray as Surveyor for Bureau Veritas and then became Port Warden of Quebec in the 1880s.[24]

This list of Scots who played important roles in Quebec shipbuilding would not be complete without the names of two other men, Charles Wood and

Thomas Menzies. Wood was a native of Port Glasgow and a celebrated naval architect who built the two huge timber droghers *Columbus* and *Baron of Renfrew* during the two years he spent at Quebec between 1823 to 1825.[25] Menzies did not build at Quebec, but he greatly influenced shipbuilding practice in the port through his office as Lloyd's Surveyor. Menzies was from Leith and his family shipyard, founded in the seventeenth century, was the oldest in that port.[26]

Quebec's shipbuilding trade remained almost exclusively in the hands of Scots until shortly before the War of 1812, when a first group of Englishmen arrived among the shipwrights brought over by timber merchants. They included Sam Finch, William Gilley and George Taylor, all of whom left for dockyards on the Lakes when war broke out and returned to Quebec after the peace to set up their own yards. In 1825, Taylor, who had been superintendent of the Patterson, Dyke and Company shipyard at the Isle of Orleans and had established his own yard about 1817, was joined by his new son-in-law, Captain Allison Davie, reputedly the condition under which Taylor gave him the hand of his daughter, Elizabeth.[27] Other Englishmen, such as John Nicholson, the Jeffery family, and many of the sailmakers, including James and William Hunt, were from Devon.[28]

Although most Irish shipbuilders began building at Quebec at a comparatively late date, their overall contribution to the industry was also significant. Until the 1820s there had been strong business ties between the shipbuilders at Quebec and shipowners in Scotland and London, to whom most of the vessels built in the port were consigned, but from the 1820s vessels were built for Irish shipowners through their local agents. The first Irish shipbuilder in the port was John James Nesbitt, who came to Canada in 1817 at the age of fifteen and was apprenticed to John Goudie.[29] He launched his first ship in 1836 and began building at his own yard the following year. He built up to four ships a year until 1856 when he was obliged to give up his shipyard because of financial reverses. He then turned to ship repairing and surveying. Later he showed his versatility, taking on a variety of building contracts for the Public Works Department. Many of his early ships were built for George H. Parke from Stewartstown, County Tyrone, who served as agent in Quebec for both his brother-in-law, the prominent Belfast shipowner David Grainger, and other Irish merchants or shipowners. Besides handling their exports and imports, Parke built or contracted for the construction of a large number of vessels for their fleets.[30] In 1832 another family, whose infant son was destined to become a leading Quebec shipbuilder, landed at Quebec from Stewartstown. In partnership with William H. Baldwin from 1850 to 1856, with his father James from 1858 to 1865, and then on on his own account,[31] Henry Dinning's ouput ran the gamut from building fine-quality traditional wooden sailing ships to assembling metal steamboats manufactured in Britain.[32] In addition, he did a large volume of salvage and repair work. A compassionate man, he was concerned with helping shipyard workers faced with the prospect of a winter with no work and fellow shipbuilders who encountered lean times. In this respect his friendship with the shipowner and shipping agent Henry Fry stood him in good stead.

Horatio Nelson Jones, who operated a shipyard between 1849 and 1859, was another important member of the Irish community. He came from Waterford and had been engaged in the lumber trade at the mouth of the Saint Charles before expanding his business to include shipbuilding. His yard was run by

Figure 37: *Captain William Beatson (1753–1816). Oil painting, photo courtesy Archibald Beatson.*

Figure 38: *Captain John Beatson (1765–1849). Oil painting, photo courtesy James B. Beatson.*

Figure 39: *John James Nesbitt (1803–1882). Oil painting, photo courtesy Edith Nesbitt.*

William Simons, who was already mentioned among the Scots. Finally, we have Thomas Dunn, who came to Quebec from Kilkenny around 1839, and worked in the Nicholson and Russell shipyard for many years before building eighteen vessels during the 1860s and 1870s in partnership with Etienne Samson.[33]

The lone shipbuilder of German descent was Antoine Ernst, son of Johann Ahrens, a Brunswicker who fought for Britain during the American War of Independence and was one of many who decided when it ended to remain in Canada. Antoine was born at Quebec and worked at Government Dockyards on the Lakes during the War of 1812. In the 1820s, he was working in partnership with Paul Benjamin Viger, and later was employed by J.S. Campbell.

Like many other Quebeckers, a number of shipbuilders and shipwrights who worked in Quebec moved to the United States and settled there. The renowned American shipbuilder Henry Eckford, for instance, served his apprenticeship at Quebec in the shipyard of his uncle, the master shipbuilder John Black, before making his name south of the border. In later life James Goudie, superintendent for the construction of the P.S. *Royal William*, carried on his trade in Chicago. But the road was not a one-way street and some made the journey north instead. Among the United Empire Loyalists who settled in Quebec were several whose sons or grandsons became successful shipbuilders. One was John Saxton Campbell, inspector of cullers as well as a shipbuilder, shipowner and merchant.[34] He spent considerable sums of money setting up the fine shipyard at Cape Cove that was run by his partner, George Black, to whom he later sold it, and financed many other shipbuilders. He also built a shipyard at Saint André, in the lower Saint Lawrence, where he owned a sizeable property. In 1840, however, he retired to Cornwall, England, as his Cornish wife did not enjoy the Canadian lifestyle.[35] His brother, Charles Campbell, was also a shipbuilder at one time, while another brother, Archibald Campbell, was one of the shipbuilders' principal notaries. Thomas Conrad Lee, who made a name for himself with the fine clipper ships built at his Saint Charles River shipyard, was also of American origin. He retained close connections and a strong love of his former country. On his clipper ship *Shooting Star*, the trail boards on one side represented a lion crouched on a Union Jack, and those on the other an American eagle and shield.[36] And Edmund W. Sewell, grandson of the Chief Justice, Jonathan Sewell, was among the few builders who also claimed the title of "ship architect." He designed and built steamboats and sailing ships, including the winter ferry *Northern Light*, a screw steamer contracted for by the Dominion government for winter navigation of the Northumberland Strait and the Gulf of the Saint Lawrence and put into service in 1876.[37] Other Americans who came to Quebec in the mid-nineteenth century included William Power, brought from the US by Thomas Lee to design and build clippers, and the clipper captains and shipbuilding partners, Henry Warner and Lauchlan McKay. The latter, like his brother, the leading New York clipper designer and builder, Donald McKay, was Nova Scotian-born. William Lampson, Jr. of Boston,[38] at one time the lessee of the King's Posts, was another American. He built sailing ships between 1838 and 1844 and ran an extensive ship repairing business.

Meanwhile, an increasing number of French Canadians shipwrights became shipbuilders. At the beginning of the nineteenth century there had only been one or two, such as François Robitaille and his brother Romain. Later Louis Labbé set up his own yard. The expansion of the industry in the 1820s and 1830s provided opportunities for advancement from the ranks, and several French Canadians who had acquired experience as yard foremen launched out on their own. In the 1860s, French Canadian builders, including , Jean-Elie Gingras, William Charland, Pierre Vincent Valin, Pierrre Valin, Narcisse Rosa, the brothers Etienne, Isidore and Julien Samson, F.X. Marquis, Pierre Brunelle, Toussaint Valin and Edouard Trahan outnumbered the English speaking builders, and in the end not only accounted for one-third of the thirty-five most prolific Quebec builders of large sailing ships, but their names appear frequently as the builders of the largest vessel of the year. Many of these men were fine shipbuilders, and in later years, due in great measure to the efficient services of the shipbroker James G. Ross, several were able to make good livings as shipowners as well. Among the most prolific were Guillaume Charland at Lauzon, Jean Elie Gingras on the Saint Charles, and Hyppolite Dubord. Hyppolite Dubord, however, was unique among the French Canadians in that he was an important shipbroker who kept shipbuilders busy building for him under contract over a period of fifty years. He is credited with handling the construction of fifty-six vessels by such shipbuilders as J.O. Brunet, J. Lemelin, William Power, Olivier Chartier, and Antoine St Jean, James Goudie, Edouard Desnoyers, Charles Jobin, the partnership of Louis Laroche, Edmond Dubord and Joseph Angers , and Angers alone. Besides being active as a shipbuilder, he ran a flour mill at Pointe-aux-Trembles (Neuville), where many of his vessels were built, and carried on an export and import business.

Figure 40: *Across the Saint Charles river piles of lumber lie on the beach waiting to be loaded, while at the adjoining shipyard we see the hulls of two sailing ships nearing completion on the stocks. Detail of an engraving by Hubert Clerget in the collection of the Archives of the Hôtel de Ville, Quebec. Québec depuis Beauport, 1864. Archives de la Ville de Québec – collection iconographique; Hub. Clerget: No 10649 (Detail).*

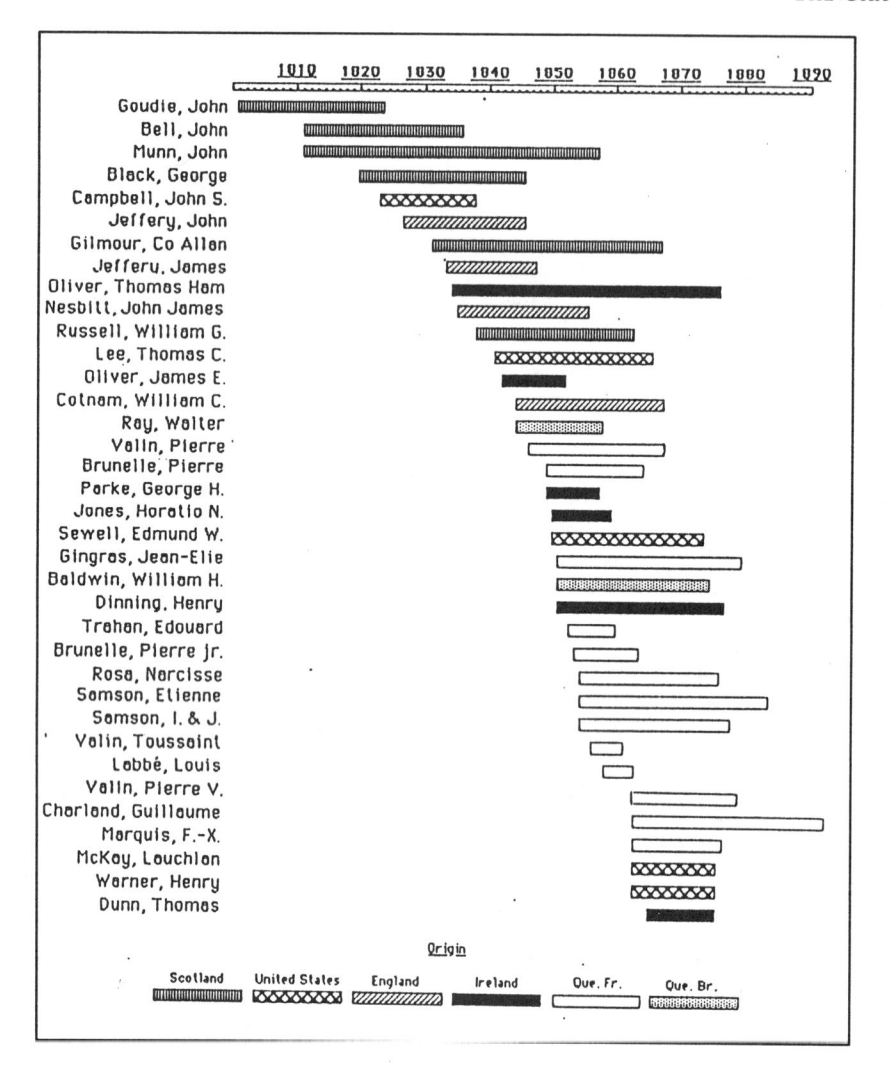

Graph 3: *Operating years of leading Quebec shipbuilders and origin.*

Source: Quebec Shipping Registers, *183-98, 202-3, 267-71, 375-78, RG12, PAC.*

Although he did not build very long on his own account, Pierre Brunelle, whose son Pierre went into business with him, received the greatest recognition for high quality design and construction of sailing ships and steamboats. Apart from the steamboats *Rowland Hill* and *John Munn*, which he built for John Munn, he built the fully-rigged ships *Dalriada, Tara, Coriolanus, Epaminondas, Asia, Africa, America, Persia* and *Arabia* for G.H. Parke before setting up his own yard. Work carried out in his shipyard was compared by the Lloyd's Surveyor to work done in the Royal Dockyards and his ship *Brunelle* was rated by her captain as one of the fastest vessels afloat. It is perhaps on account of the cost of the extra quality that he put into his ships, that his business failed. We cannot leave the French Candian shipbuilders without mentioning Captain J.-Elzéar Bernier, who acted as superintendent of Peter Baldwin's shipyard during the 1870s and was not officially a shipbuilder, but could no doubt hold his own with most of them. He wrote:

Superintending a shipyard was an interesting but arduous occupation. To a shipmaster there could be nothing more interesting than to see the members and planking of a staunch ship rise under his eyes, almost under his own hands, and for a man who loved ships and knew them the watchful attention to the small details of the finishing, the rigging, and the outfitting, became almost a labour of love.[39]

Bernier not only superintended the construction of the ships, rising at five in the morning to prepare his lunch pail and trudge two miles to the yard like the men, but also looked after the "clothing" and outfitting, and then doffing his master's cap, sailed the new ships across to Britain and sold them there for Baldwin.

It is evident that the nineteenth century sailing ship industry was an imported industry, set up by shipwrights from overseas on British lines, who used British capital to build ships of British design for the British market. It was neither the continuation of the naval shipbuilding nor of the merchant shipbuilding during the French Regime, though there was carry over in the trades. Without the strong infusion of skilled shipwrights from overseas, it is unlikely that Quebec shipbuilding would have developed into the important industry it became, but neither would it have had the strong potential to grow without the large number of native workers whose skill with the adze and axe was a firm basis for shipyard work. It was from their considerable ranks that the majority of shipbuilders of the last half of the nineteenth century emerged.

Shipbuilders and "Shipbuilders"

A man could qualify as a "shipbuilder" in various ways, and being able to build a ship was not always a requirement. However, most shipbuilders could do so, and many had learned the trade as an apprentice in a shipyard. Some had served their time in private or naval dockyards in Britain, but others received their training at Quebec. The adaptation of the traditional apprenticeship system for shipwrights, which was already losing uniformity in Britain, to the different local conditions led to considerable latitude in the terms under which apprentices were hired. A six-year apprenticeship was as common as a seven-year one, and a number of apprentices, such as Antoine Saint-Jean, Thomas Oliver and Edouard Trahan, served only three or four-year terms, during which they were given a ten shilling weekly

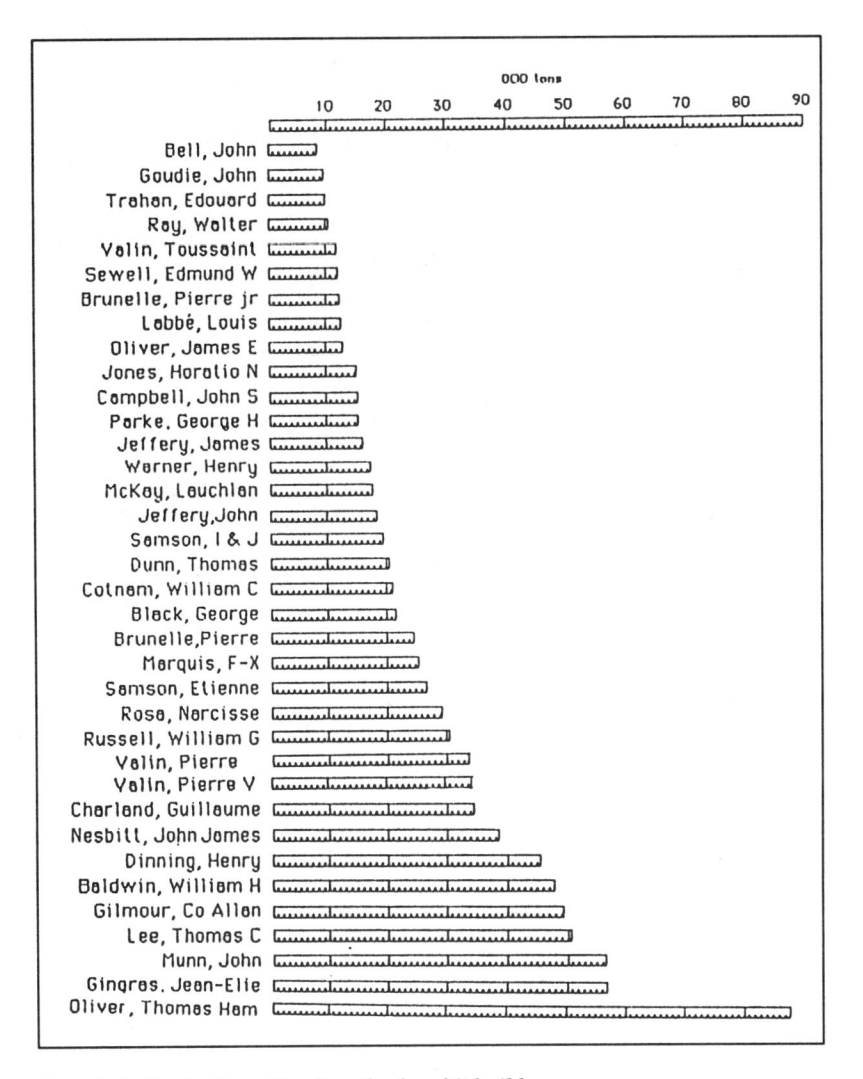

Graph 4: *Production of leading Quebec shipbuilders.*

Source: Quebec Shipping Registers, *183–98, 202–3, 267–71, 375–78, RG12, PAC.*

Figure 41: *Louis Shickluna (1808–1884). Born in Malta, Shickluna was engaged as a shipwright for the construction of the PS Royal William before establishing his own highly successful shipyard on the Welland Canal. Courtesy Donald Holmes.*

boarding allowance instead of living with their masters.[40] All three were either eighteen or nineteen years old when they were taken on, and probably had had previous shipbuilding experience, although not necessarily as formal apprentices.[41]

Clauses in the indentures also varied with regard to clothing and tools. An early indenture drawn up in 1787 between Dugald Gray, son of the wharfinger Gilbert Gray of Carolina, and the ship carpenter Silas Pearson required Pearson to provide

> sufficient Meat, Drink, and Cloathing Lodging and Washing, fitting for an Apprentice, during the said Term of Six Years and at the end . . . a full and Compleat Suit of Cloaths and also that He shall during the time of his Apprenticeship give him sufficient Education & instruct him as a Draftsman as far as the Apprentice has Capacity to learn and also at the end of his Apprenticeship a compleat Set of Tools as an Apprentice out of his time is Customary.[42]

But not all the apprentices received clothing. In some cases it was replaced by an allowance that varied from £3 to £10, or more if it covered both laundry and clothing. Exceptionally one apprentice was assured that if he could not make do with £10 for "cloathing and washing," they would be provided to him instead.[43] Working clothes consisted of a linen canvas jacket and trousers in summer and woollen garments in winter.[44] The apprentice might receive a complete Sunday suit at the end of his term, but details of what individual pieces this may have comprised have not been found in any of the contracts.

In the same way, the apprentice was sometimes given the basic tools of an axe, an adze and maul and a tool allowance of as much as £3 per annum for the rest of his tools, or if he were less fortunate, he might be expected to buy all his own tools with an allowance in some cases as low as £1 3s 4d per annum.[45] Yet in many of the contracts no mention was made of either clothing or tools and presumably the apprentice received whatever was customary at the time. The clothing and tool allowances were the only cash payments that the apprentice who lived in could expect to get, but neither was he required to pay his master the fee that was often exacted in the old world.

There were two holidays during the year apart from Sundays. Other time off was generally expected to be made up on the basis of two days for each one lost, although this did not necessarily apply to days lost through sickness.[46] Only occasionally was it written into a contract that the apprentice was to be sent to school in winter,[47] but it is evident that they were, for illiterate shipbuilders were rare. Nor is reference usually made to instruction in drafting, although most must have had this.[48] On completing his term, which generally ended when he was twenty-one, he was expected to be able to build a vessel from the laying down to the delivery, and the several Quebec shipbuilders who were building on their own account at a very young age are testimony to the good training they received.

Unfortunately, no official record of the apprenticeships served in Quebec shipyards was kept, so that with few exceptions our knowledge is limited to those for whom contracts were drawn up by notaries, and only a few of the indentures of future Quebec shipbuilders are among them. However, we do know that William Simons, son of the master sailmaker Peter Simons, who became foreman shipwright of H.N. Jones' shipyard, was apprenticed to John Munn; also that George Taylor Davie, after being apprenticed to Munn, rose to be his shipyard manager and was thus trained to take over the yard of his late father, Allison Davie. Davie's training stood him in good stead, for his is the only early nineteenth-century yard that still survives. The shipbuilders, Antoine Saint-Jean and Aymerick Vidal, also served their time in Munn's yard.[49] John J. Nesbitt was one of John Goudie's apprentices. It was agreed in his indentures that because he was "too young and too weak to work in the shipyard," he would be employed as a servant in Goudie's house during his first two years.[50] However, Nesbitt more than overcame whatever handicap he may have had on account of his size, for he is said to have been exceptionally strong, a giant of a man weighing over three hundred pounds! Edouard Trahan learned the trade in John Bell's yard;[51] Thomas H. Oliver and Walter Ray were apprenticed to the highly-reputed shipbuilder George Black.[52]

In some cases shipbuilders sent their sons back to Britain for special training. Those who did so include John Goudie, whose son James served his time at William Simon's shipyard in Greenock and learned to build steamboats as well as sailing ships. William Russell's son, Alexander, who is known to have gone to school in Scotland, may also have been apprenticed there.

Some Quebec shipbuilders, however, had a very different type of training. These were men, such as Patrick Beatson and Allison Davie, who left careers at sea to establish shipyards. Lauchlan McKay, brother of the celebrated American clipper builder, Donald McKay, and himself a clipper captain before becoming a shipbuilder at Quebec, wrote a treatise on the trade in which he described some reasons why shipmasters were well qualified to become shipbuilders. Many a shipmaster, he wrote, was well acquainted with the

Figure 42: *Pierre Vincent Valin (1827–1897). Shipbuilder and Shipowner. From the collection of Jean-René Breton, with thanks.*

science of shipbuilding and understood the operation and action of the wind and water upon different hulls and sails even better than did some shipbuilders. He procured information in foreign countries, acquired technical books and used his leisure hours at sea to study. He thus came to understand the structure of a ship and to know its strengths and was able to take advantage of circumstances not only to sail her in the best possible manner but also to be sure she was always properly laden. Moreover, wrote McKay, he was able to supervise repairs and have them done in a correct, thorough and economical manner.[53]

He might have added that such a shipbuilder would also have practical knowledge of the use of shipyard tools, for in order to become a shipmaster he began by serving on the lower deck and had been bound by his articles of agreement to carry out ship repairs, such as replacing broken timbers, trimming a spare spar to replace one that had been broken, caulking, and mending rigging or sails. Moreover, as a captain he would have acquired experience in handling men, purchasing supplies and in general business organization, all of which would stand him in good stead in running a shipyard. Several other shipbuilders besides Beatson and Davie were referred to as captains, including David Vaughan and John Henley. We do not know whether they also had shipyard training.

Other shipbuilders learned the trade neither through apprenticeship nor experience at sea. These were the builders who began working as a timber framer, general carpenter, or at some other trade, and made the change to ship carpentry, successfully working their way up. Others started by helping in the construction of schooners or other small vessels, learning eventually to build them and then moving on to build larger vessels.

Finally a so-called "shipbuilder" might not even know how to swing an axe, for the title was also given to a man who alone or jointly assumed the financial responsibility for building a vessel or vessels; who contracted out for their construction; or, in those cases where he was described as a shipbuilder on a registration certificate, who had a loan outstanding on the vessel in question. Such "shipbuilders" include George and William Hamilton and Horatio N. Jones, who were merchants and timber cove owners and became "shipbuilders" by hiring shipwrights to build for them,[54] and certain women–Elizabeth Taylor Davie and Catherine Russell, for instance, who as wives or widows of shipbuilders took charge of their husbands' affairs because of their absence, death or insolvency. There are also certain shipbuilders, particularly Hyppolite Dubord and George H. Parke, who have vessels credited to them that were in fact contracted out to other shipbuilders, their part in the operation being that of an agent or broker rather than a builder. Wherever they are known, the names of the actual builders have been added behind those of the official builders in the appendices. And finally, among those who were named "shipbuilder" on one or more registration certificates, we find men such as James Gibb Ross and Charles Wilson, who financed ship construction.

While the title "shipbuilder" was conferred on many non-builders, ironically it was not given so readily to shipwrights who ran yards for others and had full responsibility for building and launching the ships. They often had to content themselves with being referred to as the foreman, superintendent or master shipwright of the yard, while their employer was described as the shipbuilder. Typical among these was H.N. Jones' superintendent, William Simons. Captain

Figure 43: *Pierre Toussaint Valin, father of Pierre Vincent Valin. From the collection of Jean-René Breton, with thanks.*

Figure 44: *Captain Lauchlan McKay (1811–1895), the Nova Scotia born clipper captain who later built ships on the St. Charles river. He was a brother of the famous American clipper designer, Donald McKay. Photo from F.W. Wallace.* In the Wake of the Windships.

Joseph-Elzéar Bernier, who superintended Peter Baldwin's shipyard on the St. Charles River in the 1870s described the work as an interesting but arduous occupation."

There were also anomalies in the use of the term "ship carpenter" which, like the title "shipbuilder," had different connotations. The Scottish shipbuilders, who did not favour the term "shipwright," were generally referred to as "ship carpenter" or "master ship carpenter" until they had opened their own yards, and sometimes even after that. Proud of their trade, they had no pretentions on this score, even though the same title could be earned in Quebec through a three-year apprenticeship in a shipyard or even be assumed by a house carpenter who took his place beside the other ship carpenters in the yard.

Having finished his training, in the course of which he assisted in the construction of a number of vessels, it was normal for the young shipwright to aspire to the day when he would lay down his first ship. In most cases he had to wait many years before achieving this goal. Yet there were exceptions, and both Aymerick Vidal and Walter Ray launched their first vessel within three years of completing their apprenticeship at the respective ages of twenty-three and twenty-four. In Vidal's case he paid his master, John Munn, the compliment of naming the vessel after him.[55] William H. Baldwin was another early beginner. Entering into partnership with Henry Dinning at the age of twenty-three, he immediately took responsibility for running the shipyard. Whatever training he had, included serving as apprentice to his uncle Henry, a blockmaker, for four years of an original seven-year term between the ages of fourteen and eighteen.[56] But these were the exceptions; most shipbuilders had served long stewardships as yard foremen before a chance to launch on their own presented itself.

A sudden improvement in the shipping market led not only to more vessels being laid down by established builders but also to opportunities for those waiting in the wings. Often at such times a group of shipwrights would contract jointly to build. This occurred notably in the 1810s and the 1850s, with the difference that in the earlier years the groups joined informally in single ventures, while in the latter the partnerships were generally for a number of years and were recorded by notarial deed. The firm Michel Laprise and Company, for instance, which launched its first vessel in 1855, was made up of the ship carpenters François Drouin, Michel Laprise, Pierre Letarte and Edouard Gobeil; and F.X. Fortier joined with François Laurencelle and Arsène Vezina to form F.X. Fortier and Company in 1854.[57]

Partnerships were often formed between members of a family, and far more often between brothers or brothers-in-law than between fathers and sons. Father and son teams include the John Munns, Pierre Brunelles and Edouard Trahans. J.E. Gingras had two sons with whom he was associated at different times. Among the teams of brothers, we have Isaie, Joseph and Louis Julien, who with their brother-in-law Pierre Labbé made up the firm of Isaie Julien & Company, and Isidore and Julien Samson, who worked with a third brother Etienne for a while. Robert and William Carman were brothers, as were Andrew and William Parke. Among brothers-in-law who were partners, there were George Bell and John Neilson, Guillaume Charland and F.X. Marquis, John Nicholson and William Russell, Lauchlan McKay and Henry Warner, and Sheppard and Campbell. On occasion the firm comprised mixed family groups of two generations, notably the Jobins and the Jefferys. On the other hand,

Figure 45: *Captain Henry Warner (1821–1893). Like his shipbuilding partner, Lauchlan McKay, he was a former clipper captain. Photo from F.W. Wallace,* In the Wake of the Windships.

shipbuilders in the same family did not always work together in partnership. The three Munn brothers, for instance, each had a yard of his own, while Toussaint and his son, Pierre Vincent Valin, William Charland Sr. and Jr., and at one time both Sam Finch Sr. and Jr. and John Jeffery Sr. and Jr. also worked independently.

Many aspects of the shipbuilding trade are described in the following chapters, which will provide some idea of the scope of the shipbuilder's work, the problems he faced and what he achieved. In the paragraphs that follow we will look at other sides of his life. What of the shipbuilder, for instance, who did not work at his trade, either because he was not in a position to lay down a ship or because he decided to do something else. To what might he turn?

Certainly he would have no trouble carrying out other kinds of carpentry. Indeed, there is considerable evidence of men having done so, both at their own shipyards and as contractors. John Goudie, for instance, contracted with the Inspector of Roads to build wood-lined "canals" along Saint John Street and other roads in town in 1821. John Nesbitt and the joiner François Julien erected a 106-foot wharf in front of James McKenzie's Hotel in Levis in 1829. John Bell built a wharf at Saint Paul Street for the Department of Roads in 1824, and John Neilson another for the trustees of the new market in 1833. The shipbuilder Charles Jobin built a 120-foot boom for the stevedore Thomas Burns in 1856. William Russell built a pontoon for passenger traffic at the Grand Trunk Railway wharf at Point Levy in 1859. William Cotnam was given the contract for a pontoon for the jury landing at the Findlay Market in 1874. Valin and Company carried out the repairs to the wharf at the Quarantine Station at Grosse Ile in 1875.[58]

Competent shipbuilders were also always in demand for ship survey work, and no one was better qualified for the job. In his letter of introduction the Lloyd's Surveyor, Thomas Menzies, was described as "a highly respectable Ship-builder who has carried on business for many years at Leith."[59] Later the Quebec shipbuilders Walter Ray and William Simons would both be Surveyors for Bureau Veritas.[60] There was a great deal of work for independent surveyors, too, especially before the arrival of surveyors from the classification societies when surveys of vessels under construction and of general shipping on the river were required. Some shipbuilders even tried their hand at formal teaching. Patrick Fleming, for instance, inserted an advertisement in the *Quebec Gazette* on 18 December 1828 offering "lessons in the Art of Shipbuilding—and the manner of preparing Canadian Timber for Ship-building," with the addendum, "N.B. Ships' Drafts made on the best models."

A few of the official positions at the Port of Quebec were best filled by a competent shipbuilder. For example, Zacharaiah Thompson, a ship's carpenter, was the first Captain of the Port appointed by the British, and over a century later, the shipbuilder Pierre Brunelle was given charge of the government dry dock at Lauzon. In the 1880s, William Simons became the deputy Port Warden, and in 1890 the Port Warden at Quebec.

Another type of work to which the shipbuilder might gravitate was ship brokerage. Both Edward Oliver and John Jeffery Jr. became brokers in Liverpool, and William H. Jeffery teamed up with his brother-in-law H.J. Noad under the name H.J. Noad and Company to carry on the same profession at Quebec.[61] As commission merchants they handled a considerable amount of shipbuilding business.

Sometimes, however, new work meant moving away. In 1887, for instance, when the days of sailing ship construction were over at Quebec, Peter Baldwin went to New York to take up a position as agent for the Quebec Steamship Company, with which he enjoyed a very successful second career. Besides superintending the arrival and departure of steamers, he was responsible for surveys and inspections and the direction of repairs. He was also responsible for purchasing new additions to the fleet and superintended their construction. At the time of his death, the *Nautical Gazette* wrote that no man in New York enjoyed a higher reputation for integrity combined with a thorough knowledge of his work.[62]

But doing something else did not always mean giving up shipbuilding. A number of builders managed to keep building by taking on sufficient ship repair and salvage work. Apart from the well-known instances of men such as Dinning, Russell and Davie, whose yards were equipped with special repair facilities including floating docks, there were others such as the Julien brothers who did a considerable amount of salvage work on the side over the years.[63] Many became timber forwarders, sometimes having their cargoes financed as part and parcel of the loan for the construction of the vessel that would carry them, and thus were able to survive the bad years and build again when the market improved.

There is little doubt that what the real shipbuilder sought above everything else was to be able to lay down a keel, and in spite of the difficulties due to severe market fluctuations, thirty-five shipbuilders succeeded in laying down a minimum of twenty-five vessels or 10,000 tons of shipping apiece.

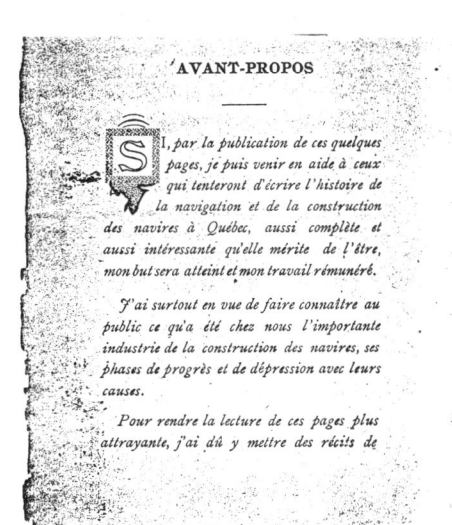

Figure 46: *Narcisse Rosa (1823–1907). Photo courtesy Jacques Rosa.*

Figure 47: *The opening passage from Narcisse Rosa's Book* – La construction des navires à Québec et ses environs.

Figure 48: *Barquentine* Niagara, 672 tons, built by Narcisse Rosa in 1866, and seen here at Dover, England. Courtesy Maritime Museum of the Atlantic, Wallace Collection, MP3.16.1.

The Shipbuilder in the Community

Generally speaking the shipbuilder was a democratic person, anywhere from twenty to seventy years old, who lived in close proximity to his yard and his workers. He enjoyed good relations with the men and at least in the early days strikes or other labour disputes were rare. In 1897 the shipbuilder Narcisse Rosa nostalgically recalled his days as a ship carpenter, probably in the 1840s, and the happy atmosphere that reigned in the yards at the time. This knew no bounds, he wrote, when a heavy piece of timber had to be moved and every man in the yard put his shoulder under it to advance it slowly step by step while singing the heaving shanty "Charley-Man."

Later days were less carefree. Larger vessels were built, the labour force was larger, and more money was at stake when the market faltered. The potential for an accident was greater, and the occasional newspaper report of a large stick of timber that had slipped, causing the death of one or two men, or of a worker who tripped and fell on his axe, reminds us that shipbuilding was arduous and the shipyard a dangerous place. To counter this, sloppy practices that might lead to serious or even fatal accidents had to be minimized. It was important that the shipbuilder should be in firm control and have the confidence of his men.

This he appears to have had, as well as to have succeeded in handling a mixed workforce from English and French-speaking backgrounds without the bitter conflicts that characterized relations between the two elements of "ship labourers," or dockers. It would seem that disputes that arose from time to time between builders or their workers were not reflections of divisions along linguistic or religious lines. The fierce rivalry that existed in the last half of the nineteenth and perhaps the early twentieth centuries between the Davie and Russell shipyard workers and led to raiding parties being organized, for instance, sprang from the competition for contracts between the two yards and the difference it made to the wage packets. Nor do there appear to have been religious or linguistic divisions in the relationships among the builders, their common trade and concerns being strong binding factors. Many of their marriage partners were, in fact, of a different religion. Undoubtedly there were hard feelings at times, such as when James Jeffery lured John Munn's shipyard workers away from him by topping any amount Munn was willing to pay with higher offers, or when George Black bucked the current and raised the wages at his yard,[64] but it is far easier to find examples of shipbuilders standing together, helping each other out of difficult times, or standing surety for each other.[65]

Whatever his background, the shipbuilder earned his place in the social strata of businessmen, not through memberships of a craft guild, but through his ability to run his very challenging business. As a relatively large employer, he had a high profile in the community–one to which the considerable responsibility he bore with regard to the soundness of his vessels and in particular to the lives of those who took passage on them, not to mention the several thousand dollars that rested on the single moment of the launch, could only add. Each vessel that left a Quebec shipyard was an ambassador, not only for him and his yard but for the Quebec shipbuilding industry as a whole. It was natural that he should be held in high esteem, and when we read of the funeral cortege of Henry Dinning and later of George T. Davie, which were said to be among the largest the City had seen, it is evident that they were.[66]

Many of the builders took an active part in public affairs and represented their community on a municipal, provincial or even federal level. John Goudie, John Munn and George Black were among those who were Justices of the Peace. John Munn, Henry Dinning and George Taylor Davie were town councillors, while John Black, John Munn, Jean-Elie Gingras and Pierre V. Valin were members of the Legislative Assembly, and Valin was also a member of the Canadian Parliament.

Apart from political office, the shipbuilders held various public or semi-public offices. Some became wardens of Trinity House, others bank directors, and yet others officers in the militia. They served as trustees of the markets, on Council committees and committees of the temperance union, of school societies, etc. They were particularly active in the Chamber of Commerce, which served as their loud collective voice. They helped form or belonged to professional associations, such as the Mechanics Union. For instance, members present at a meeting of that society in 1834 included John Munn, John Bell and George Black, who was reported by the *Montreal Gazette*, to have given an excellent address.[67] George Taylor Davie was listed among the members of the Chambre des Arts et Manufacturiers in 1878.[68]

The shipbuilders also found time for activities of a more recreational nature, enjoying such exhilarating sports as tandem racing and yachting, as well as such genteel diversions as family picnics and musical evenings. Perhaps they were able to relax the most immediately following a safe launching, at which time they celebrated the event either in their homes or at the yard. They were generally well-travelled persons,

Figure 49 : *Guillaume Charland (1824–1901). Photo courtesy Gustave Charland.*

Figure 50: *Jean-Elie Gingras (1804–1891). Courtesy Archives nationales du Québec, GH–670–123.*

aware of what was going on elsewhere in the world. Men such as Narcisse Rosa and Pierre V. Valin crossed the Atlantic repeatedly, often, it should be said, aboard steamships. P.G. Labbé, for instance, left for England in September 1864 aboard the steamship *Jura* "with the intention of visiting the principal ship-yards on the Mersey, Clyde, etc., also those of note in France."[69]

Yet in spite of their lifestyle, they lived on the lip of a volcano. Their business depended on a market that was rarely steady and in which troughs and crests were extreme. When beset with their own financial difficulties, they were constantly aware that the livelihood of a large segment of the population depended on their laying down a keel. Certainly in the last half of the century, few shipbuilders could have wished the uncertainties of the industry on their sons.

Notes

1. Apprenticeship indenture, 22 April 1825, gr A. Campbell.
2. Protest, George V. Oliver, 11 August 1835, gr A. Campbell, in which it was stated that Edward was acting as his brother's foreman.
3. *Quebec Gazette*, 4 August 1768, 24 May 1773.
4. *Ibid.*, 25 July 1765; letter from Colville, Northumberland, Halifax Harbour, to John Cleveland, Esq., Secy's Dept, In-Letters, B 1355, 139, Admiralty, PRO. A serious shortage of ship carpenters in the port was not helped when thirty R.N. ship's carpenters were lost on 18 December 1759, when they boarded a French ship that ran ashore off Quebec, which blew up. General Murray's Letter Book, 24 December 1759, microfilm C-2225, NA.
5. Contract, Parent with David Strachan and Co., London, 4 July 1772, gr L. Panet. *Quebec Gazette*, 12 May, 30 June and 28 July 1774.
6. Register of the Port of Quebec [henceforth RPQ], 1797 and 1799, NA.
7. Register of ship arrivals and departures, brig *Jenny*, 12 July 1779, and ship *Elizabeth*, 24 August and 15 September 1780, Port de Québec, APG 208/17, ANQ.
8. Notice of public auction of land occupied by Duncanson, *Quebec Gazette*, 15 June 1786; agreement with ship carpenters, 23 February 1787, gr Chas. Stewart; contract to build vessel, Duncanson with Crosbie, 6 July 1786, *ibid.*; contract to build vessel, Duncanson with Farrie, 23 February 1787, *ibid.*; report of launching of *Alfred*, *Quebec Gazette*, 24 May 1787; Robert Craig and Rupert Jarvis, *Liverpool Registry of Merchant Ships* (Manchester, 1967), Registry of ship *Roman Eagle*, 12/1787, 55.
9. Announcement of dissolution of partnership, *Quebec Gazette*, 4 August 1791; Assignment of King's liabilities and assets, *ibid.*, 28 November 1792; J. Young's correspondence with H.W. Ryland, 9 June 1798, CU 42, 3, 468-75, c-series, NA, brought to my attention by A.J.H Richardson.
10. Q113, 21 July 1808, 12 September 1809, Vol. 70, no. 21; 8 January 1810, no. 99, NA.
11. 26 July 1798, RG1 L3L 39: 19505-8, NA.
12. They were probably related to the shipbuilder, John Black, who was also from Irvine and whose mother was a McMunn. Black's marriage contract, 14 May 1801, gr F. Têtu.
13. Advertisement re. Alex Munn's estate, 18 June 1812; inventory of the late John Munn, 15 September 1814, gr A. Campbell; Register of the Parish of St. Gabriel, Montreal, 13 March 1829.
14. Description of the yard of the late J. Munn, *Morning Chronicle*, 4 March 1859.
15. Petition of John Goudie, shipwright. RG1, L3, 203: 19, "G" bundle, microfilm C-2027, NA.
16. Copy of Memorial and Petition from W. Bell, 10 June 1818, MG24 F3, Vol. 1, NA.
17. Contract, Bell and Romain with Derome and Desnoyers, 1 August 1810 and Apprenticeship Indenture, Bourgette with Bell and Romain, 6 May 1811, gr J. Belanger.
18. William Bell Correspondence, MG24, F3, Vol. 3, *passim*, NA.
19. Will, John Bell, 22 November 1825, gr L. McPherson.
20. Letter, H. Baldwin to Wm Bell, 21 December 1800, Wm Bell Correspondence, 1800-1836, MG24 F3, Vol. 11, NA.
21. Parish Register, St. Andrew's Church, Quebec, baptism of Patrick and Henry, 21 April 1799, 12 January 1817, of William, 3 November 1827. Chalmer's, Quebec, baptism of Peter, 7 April 1839.
22. *New York Nautical Gazette*, 8 November 1911.
23. *Morning Chronicle*, 29 August 1864.
24. Gertrude Simons McMichael, "The Simons Family in Canada," unpublished manuscript. Correspondance du Bureau Veritas, Port de Québec, AP-P-17, ff. 1-751, ANQ; Port Warden's Letter Book, 1890-99, F0002-6, ANQ.
25. E. Marcil, "Charles Wood," *DCB*, VII, (1988); "Ship-Rigged Rafts and the Export of Quebec Timber," *The American Neptune*, VIII-2 1988, 67-76.
26. James Scott Marshall, *The Life and Times of Leith* (Edinburgh, 1986), 21.
27. George W. Haws, *The Haws Family and Their Shipbuilding Kin* (Dunfermline, 1932), 159; other family sources.

28. Marriage Bond, 5 September 1827, Nicholson with Russell, 34: 794, NA.
29. Indenture, Nesbitt to Goudie, 16 July 1817, gr J. Belanger.
30. Mrs. Daniel McPherson writes "in the course of twenty-five years he had built for himself seventy-six large ships by different ship builders, which cost and was paid for out of his office over three millions of dollars, apart from his other business." *Old Memories: Amusing and Historical* (Montreal, n.d.), 112-113. Brought to my attention by A.J.H. Richardson.
31. Co-partnership, Baldwin with Dinning, 27 March 1851, James with Henry Dinning, 1 June 1858, and Wm Dinning with W.H. Baldwin, 28 December 1859, gr J. Clapham,; Notice of dissolution of partnership, H. and Jas. Dinning, *Morning Chronicle*, 30 November 1865.
32. K. Mackenzie, "Dinning, Henry," *DCB*, XI (1982): 290-291.
33. Pierre-Georges Roy, *Profils lévisiens* (2ième série, Levis, 1948), 86-87.
34. Appointment of J.S. Campbell as Master Culler and Measurer of Staves, *Quebec Gazette*, 19 May 1808; appointment to Board of Examiners of persons applying to be Measurers and Cullers at Quebec, *ibid*, 19 May 1823.
35. Georges Desjardins, "Un chantier naval à la Pointe-Sèche de Kamouraska," *Mémoires de la Société généalogique Canadienne-Française*, XXI (1970), 212. Brought to my attention by A.J.H. Richardson.
36. Description of the *Shooting Star*, *Morning Chronicle*, 30 July 1853.
37. Contract, Sewell with Minister of Marine and Fisheries, 15 May 1876, gr W.D. Campbell.
38. Marriage Bond, 5 October 1825, 32: 468, NA.
39. Frederick William Wallace, *Wooden Ships and Iron Men* (London, 1924), 92. J.-E. Bernier, *Master Mariner*, 169.
40. St. Jean with Munn, 12 July 1824, gr J. Belanger, Oliver with Black, 22 April 1825, gr A. Campbell, Trahan with Bell, 2 March 1829, gr E.B. Lindsay.
41. For instance, when John Black took on two apprentice shipbuilders it was stated in their indentures that they had already served three years as apprentice carpenters, but their earlier indentures have not been found. Manning with Black, 25 September 1792, gr P.L. Descheneaux, Girard with Black, *idem.*
42. 24 October, gr Chas Stewart.
43. Apprenticeship indenture, Marcot with McIntosh, 5 May 1825, gr A. Campbell.
44. See, for e.g., Indenture, Iffland to Anderson, 17 May 1810 and Robertson to Anderson, 26 July 1810, gr J. Voyer.
45. E.g., see indenture, Myers with Munn, 25 February 1815, gr A. Campbell, Simard with Taylor, 23 March 1825, *ibid.*
46. See, for instance, indentures, L. Gaulin with Goudie, 29 November 1809 and A. St Jean with Munn, 12 July 1824, gr J. Belanger.
47. Those that did, include J. O'Neil with Goudie, 15 June 1810 and Nesbitt with Goudie, 16 July 1817, gr J. Belanger.
48. Covering clauses are found, however, in some such as G. Aird with Goudie, 16 May 1809, gr J. Belanger, and M. O'Brien with Ernst, 7 June 1838, gr A. Campbell.
49. Indentures, Munn with St. Jean and Vidal, 12 July 1824, gr J. Belanger and 21 June 1832, gr A. Campbell.
50. Indentures, Nesbitt with Goudie, 16 July 1817, gr J. Belanger.
51. Indentures, Trahan with Bell, 2 March 1829, gr E.B. Lindsay.
52. Indentures, Oliver with Black, 22 April 1825, gr A. Campbell, and Ray with Black, 12 April 1836, gr E. Glackemeyer.
53. L. McKay, *The Practical Shipbuilder* (New York, 1839), 4.
54. Contract, Wm Grant with G. and W. Hamilton, 6 August 1810, gr T. Lee, Contract John Ray et al. with Patterson, Dyke and Co., 27 November 1811, gr J. Belanger.
55. Apprenticeship contract, Vidal to Munn, 21 June 1832, gr A. Campbell, Ray to Black, 12 April 1826, gr Ed Glackemeyer.
56. Indentures, Baldwin to Baldwin, 7 December 1841, which

was annulled 4 November 1845, gr E. Glackemeyer.
57. Société, Laprise, Drouin, Letarte and Gobeil, 4 June 1854, gr Germain Guay, Société, Fortier, Laurencelle, Vezina, 27 March 1854, gr F. Huot.
58. Contract, Goudie with Larue, 23 August, 1821, gr R. Lelièvre; Contract, Nesbitt and Julien with McKenzie, 10 August 1829, gr E.B. Lindsay; Agreement Bell with Larue, 5 August 1824, gr Ls Panet; Agreement, Neilson with Trustees for new market, 15 January 1833, gr A. Campbell; Contract, Jobin with Burns, 28 May 1856, gr J. Hossack; Russell with G.T.R., 12 February 1859, gr J. Hossack; Contract, Cotnam with the Corporation of Quebec, 8 July 1874, gr A.-B. Sirois-Duplessis, in which two other shipbuilders, P.V. Valin and Gonzague Vallerand, acted as joint security for him; Transfer of contract, Valin and Co. from J. Richard, 25 September 1875, gr W.D. Campbell.
59. Letter, Chas Graham to A. Gillespie, 22 August 1851, appended to agreement, Quebec Board of Trade and Lloyd's, 5 March 1852, gr L. McPherson.
60. Announcement of Ray's appointment, *Morning Chronicle*, 24 August 1864; Correspondance du Bureau Veritas, Port de Québec, AP-P-17-21, ANQ.
61. Co-partnership, Noad with Jeffery, 30 March 1844, gr J. Hunt, see also, Agreement, Lee with Noad, 31 December 1860, gr A. Campbell.
62. *Nautical Gazette*, 8 November 1911, brought to my attention by Ken Mackenzie.
63. See, for instance, purchases of wrecked vessels, Julien from Walsh, 10 October 1849, gr Saxton Campbell, ACQ; Julien from Kent, 30 May 1861, gr A. Campbell and Julien from Lamond, 24 June 1868, gr W.D.Campbell.
64. Narcisse Rosa, *La construction des navires à Québec et sea environs* (Québec, 1897), 10-14.
65. For example, Dinning's efforts on Trahan's behalf. Henry Fry, "Reminiscences," (Unpublished mss., 1891), 29.
66. Though men such as John Beatson were members of the Worshipful Company of Shipwrights of London. *Morning Chronicle*, 5 May 1876; *Quebec Chronicle*, 5 September 1907.
67. Reported in the *Kingston Whig*, 19 December 1834.
68. *L'Evénement*, 4 September 1878.
69. *Morning Chronicle*, 12 September 1864.

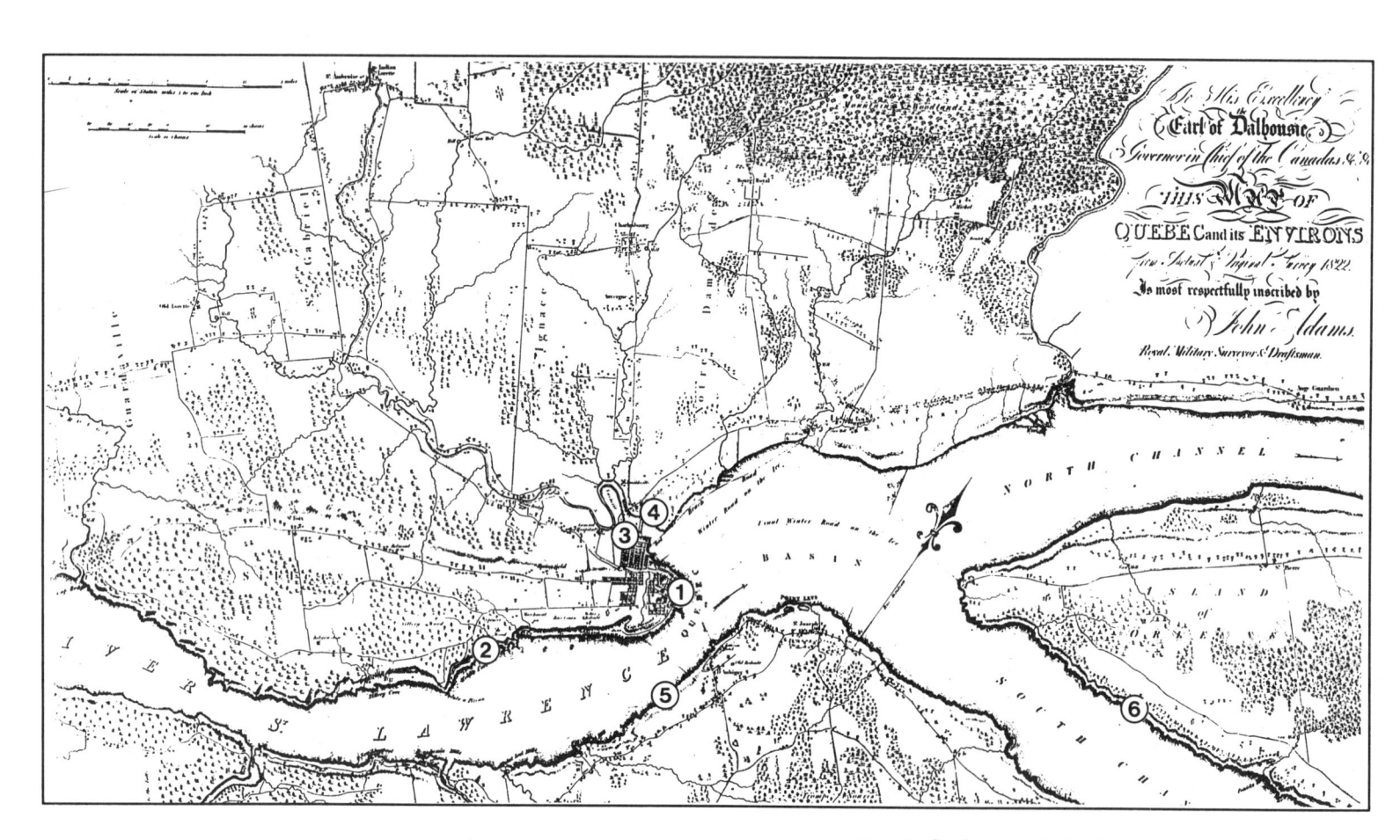

Map 1: *Quebec and its Environs*
1. The Town itself
2. The North Shore of the St. Lawrence River
3. The South Bank of the St. Charles River
4. The North Bank of the St. Charles River
5. The South Shore of the St. Lawrence River
6. The Western end of the Isle of Orleans

CHAPTER 4

The Shipyards—Location

Like the shores of most important rivers, those of the St. Lawrence have hosted countless shipyards over the years. Some were temporary installations that were reclaimed by nature after the launching of a single vessel. Others served occasionally, mostly for the construction of schooners and sloops. But some, particularly in the larger centres, were well-established permanent yards. Of these the large majority were at Quebec, where the four shipyards that were operating in 1799 had increased to twenty-seven by 1854.

Although Quebec was the centre of the large wooden sailing ship industry on the St. Lawrence and vessels of less than one hundred tons were rarely laid down in her yards, it was by no means the only place on the river where large ships were built. The Shipping Registers of Quebec and Montreal list five hundred and twenty-nine large ships laid down at one or other of seventy-nine other localities, including one hundred and twelve at Montreal, sixty-one at Pointe-aux-Trembles, twenty-five at Grondines, twenty-four at Sorel, nineteen at Les Eboulements and the rest in smaller numbers elsewhere, see Appendix C. But for every one of these vessels three were launched at Quebec, and for every ton, seven and a half times the tonnage.[1]

In this chapter, we will examine where the Quebec shipyards were located, and when and by whom they were operated. We will note their changing distribution, due sometimes to the sites becoming too valuable for shipyard use, at others to the need to expand into larger premises, and at yet others to a conscious effort to promote the trade by opening some new riverfront to shipbuilding. For the purpose of this survey, we have considered the shipyards of the French Regime first, and then from 1763 on we have divided the port into six sections, comprising: the water front of the town itself, the north shore of the St. Lawrence River (to the south of the town), the south bank of the St. Charles river (the suburbs of St. Roch and St. Sauveur), the north bank of the St. Charles, the south shore of the St. Lawrence and finally, the western end of the Isle of Orleans. Taking each section in turn, the location of the yards where large sailing vessels were built has been pinpointed and the chain of shipbuilders that operated them established. No one source could provide this information, but by putting together disparate data from leases, deeds of sale, shipbuilding contracts, letters patent, maps and plans, newspaper reports and ship registries, a fairly comprehensive picture has emerged. Profiles for the important shipyards and their tenants or owners were relatively easy to assemble, but some of the information needed to do the same for the smaller yards was more elusive, especially when there had been a frequent turnover of shipbuilders or when the yards were in operation for a short period only. Nevertheless it has been possible to determine the builders and building

Figure 51: *The site of John Black's shipyard in the 1790s. Detail from George Heriot's watercolour, c.1790. Courtesy National Archives, Ottawa, C 12744.*

places of the great majority of the vessels.

At Quebec's shipyards, particularly those on the St. Lawrence River, a considerable amount of ship maintenance, ship repair and salvage work was undertaken, and in some instances steamboats and barges were built. Either of these subjects warrants a monograph of its own and neither of them has been included in this study. Only shipbuilders of new square-rigged sailing ships or schooners of over one hundred tons and the shipyards they occupied have been taken into account. Moreover, in this chapter and elsewhere, an unqualified "sailing ship" refers solely to vessels in the over one hundred ton class and "shipyard" only to yards where such vessels were built. So, bearing in mind these limitations, we begin our review by looking at the sites where there were shipyards during the French Regime.

During the French Regime

Throughout the French regime the waterfronts of the St. Lawrence and the St. Charles rivers were quite distinct. The front doorstep of the town was on the St. Lawrence, at the landing place in the Basse Ville or Lower Town. Around it, stretching northward to Pointe-à-Carcy, were the port and business districts, the homes and offices, warehouses and workshops of the merchants, artisans and others who drew their livelihood from the river. Beyond the Point, a narrow strip of beach known as the Canoterie continued North-westward. It was used for drawing up small boats and canoes and there, in contrast to the crowded lower town, only a few houses stood against the cliff. At its far end the beach widened into the comparatively spacious Palace area or suburb of St. Nicolas, where the Intendant's Palace, various government buildings and homes of other officials enjoyed a degree of seclusion. Beyond them was the Recollet property on which stood the "Petit Hermitage," or "Chapelle Saint-Roch," and further on lay the farmlands of the Seigniory of Saint Roch. Southwestward from the landing place, a trail at the foot of the cliff led to the anse-des-Mères or Diamond Harbour, the first of the coves outside the town. Bordered by a few houses, the district it passed through was known as "Près-de-Ville."

Until the waterfront was built up, vessels were frequently careened on its beaches for repairs, and there was room for the occasional sloop or schooner to be laid down between the wharves. The construction of larger vessels took place on the more open beaches at either end of the town. The details of much of this period of shipbuilding are unknown, but we do know

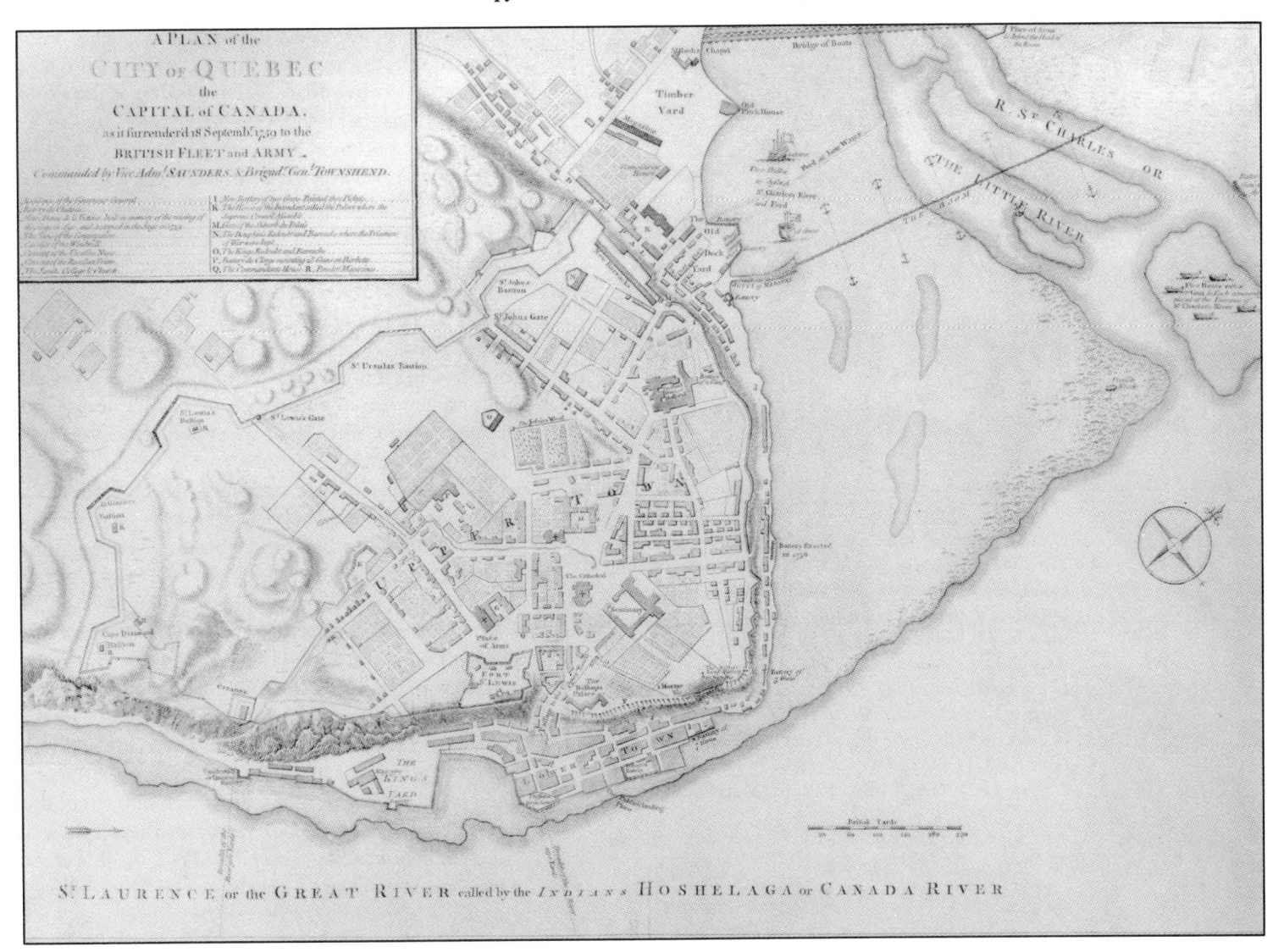

Map 2: *A Plan of the City of Quebec —
the Capital of Canada . . . , 1759*
*As it was at the end of the French Regime. Unidentified
are the Landing Place, to the right of The King's Yard,
bottom left of centre, Pointe-à-Carçy, at the extreme
eastern point of the City, and the Canoterie continuing
northwestward to the old French Royal Naval Dockyard.
Jetty of stones, and St. Roch's Chapel, top centre.
P600-4 Collection initiale, B-342-Québec-17590,
ANQQ.*

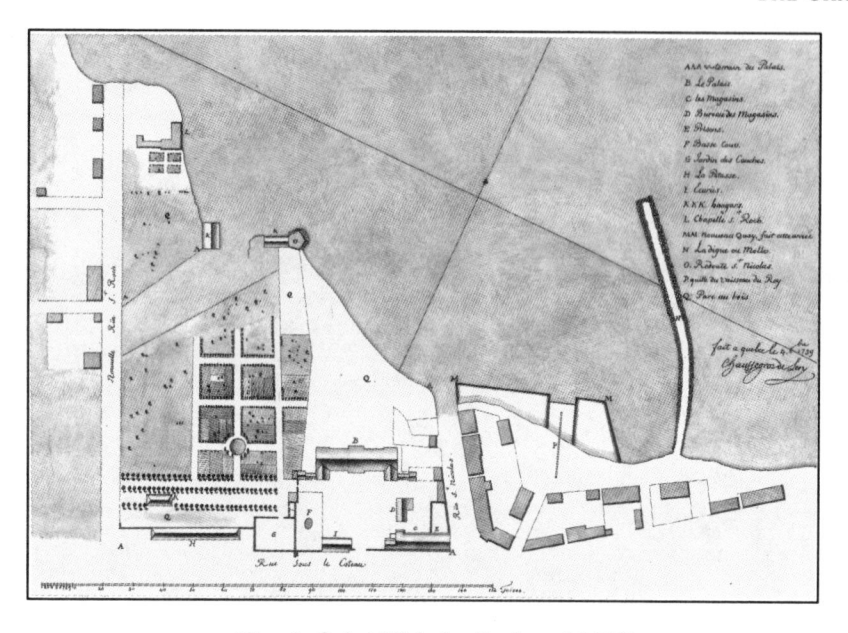

Plan 1: *Saint Nicholas Dockyard 1739*
The French Royal Naval Dockyard immediately to the east of the Intendant's palace established in 1739. It served as the main yard until 1748 and then as an auxiliary to the new yard at the Cul-de-sac. Showing the dyke (N), the new wharf (MM) and the building ship (P). The Chapel of the Recollets, or Friars of Saint Francis, is on the extreme left (L). Drawn by Chaussegros de Léry, 4 October 1739 Archives Nationale Paris, colonies, C11A-126-Pièce, 8 copied by C A Beaudouin, August 1931. Neg # 1603, National Map Collection, NA.

that the first large vessels to be built at Quebec were three merchant ships laid down between 1666 and 1672 under the Intendant Talon's orders at the Royal Dockyard "near the Palace." They were built at or near where merchant ships were still being built in 1731, four or five arpents from the Palace, on the St. Charles River, beyond the Hermitage of St. Roch – apparently to the east of St. Roch street and probably between St. Francis and St. Joseph street.[2] Launching into the swift St. Charles River, however, was difficult, and as part of a policy to encourage shipbuilding in 1733, a curved dyke was built to the east of the Palace, thus creating a protected harbour into which vessels built on the beach could safely be launched. Such problems were not encountered at the Anse-des-Mères, or Diamond Harbour, just beyond the town, where a 350-ton frigate was launched in 1712 and a 180-ton ship in 1739.[3]

In 1738, following the decision to have warships built at Quebec for the French Navy, the site that was being used for private shipbuilding had to give way to a Royal Naval Dockyard and the Palace area underwent considerable upheaval. A large quay was erected on each side of the building slip, old structures were torn down, and workshops and stores were set up in new and restored buildings. The river bed was dredged in front of the building slip, the channel to deep water cleared of rocks, the beach in front of the Palace became the timber yard and the whole was closed in behind a high fence.[4] By 1742, the first of six naval vessels that were built there, the 500-ton forty-gun flute *Canada*, was ready for launching. And though she finally reached the water safely, her launch had to be postponed day after day for two weeks because the wind was in the wrong direction. As a result, and because the French government insisted that even larger vessels be built, modifications were made to the yard, including the lengthening of the wharves a further 150 feet into the river. But even this could not provide an acceptable depth of water for launching naval ships of five hundred tons and over, and it was finally decided to move the main part of the yard to the Cul-de-Sac on the other side of the town. The Palace shipyard, known as the St. Nicholas shipyard, became an auxiliary yard, where rigging, spars and other equipment were prepared, while the building slip was used for repairs and maintenance.[5]

A dozen properties were expropriated at the new location, and the beach, on which a small community of ship carpenters had earned its livelihood since at least 1674, together with an adjoining part of the Cul-de-Sac, disappeared under the extensive wharfing of the new yard. Once again, existing buildings were made over as workshops and offices, and a number of buildings were torn down. Later, a large forge was added to the yard. But as the shipyard workers and other horrified spectators discovered when the first vessel was sent down the ways, there had been a miscalculation, for the 60-gun frigate *L'Orignal* broke her back and sank on reaching the river. The improvements that were then undertaken allowed two ships to be safely launched at the new dockyard before the Seven Years War brought all shipbuilding at Quebec to a halt.[6]

The Hermitage beach, l'anse-des-Mères and the two Royal Dockyards are the only places at or near the town where naval or large merchant ships are known to have been built during the French Regime.[7] Because an important consideration in choosing a site for a shipyard is its suitability for safe launching, it could be expected that shipbuilding would continue there after the change of government, and for a while it did.

From 1763 on –
The Quebec Waterfront

After Quebec was taken by the British and her fate decided by the Treaty of Paris in 1763, the townspeople began rebuilding their lives under the new regime, and the first merchant ships that would sail under the British flag were laid down. During the twelve years leading up to the American Revolution, fifteen one to two hundred ton vessels and some that were smaller were launched.[8] There is information on six of the fifteen in the *Quebec Gazette*.

Thus we know that the launching in 1765 "at St. Rochs...[of] the Snow *Cordelia*, begun and carried on by the Direction of Mr. Thomson, Captain of the Port," was "the first at that place since in the Hands of the English," and presume that the "place" referred to is the Hermitage site. Whether any construction had occurred elsewhere in the town since the change of government, as the text seems to imply, is not known. By 1774, the local shipwright Joseph Parent was definitely building at the Hermitage, while Thompson had moved to the old Naval Dockyard near the Palace,[9] but the work of both would come to a sudden stop the following year when Canada was invaded by American forces.

To meet the emergency, facilities were commandeered and every available shipwright and many of the sailors from ships in port were sent to Lake Champlain where under the command of Lieutenant John Schanck, R.N., they helped build up the Canadian fleet. With them they took the frame of a 300 ton ship that was on the stocks which was taken apart and rebuilt there. The extent of ship and boatbuilding at Quebec over the next eight years is unclear, though we know that a large number of *bateaux* needed for the

Figure 52: *Report of the launching of the snow Cordelia, Quebec Gazette, 25 July 1765.*

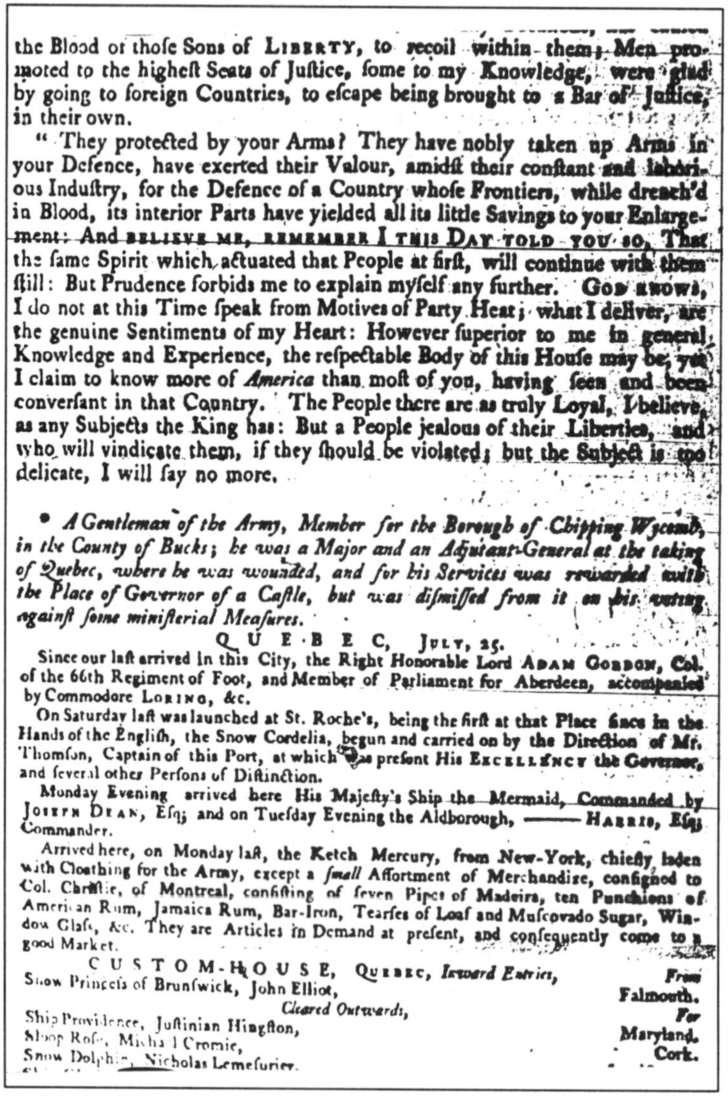

the Blood of those Sons of LIBERTY, to recoil within them; Men promoted to the highest Seats of Justice, some to my Knowledge, were glad by going to foreign Countries, to escape being brought to a Bar of Justice in their own.

"They protected by your Arms? They have nobly taken up Arms in your Defence, have exerted their Valour, amidst their constant and laborious Industry, for the Defence of a Country whose Frontiers, while drench'd in Blood, its interior Parts have yielded all its little Savings to your Enlargement: And BELIEVE ME, REMEMBER I THIS DAY TOLD YOU SO. That the same Spirit which actuated that People at first, will continue with them still: But Prudence forbids me to explain myself any further. GOD KNOWS, I do not at this Time speak from Motives of Party Heat; what I deliver, are the genuine Sentiments of my Heart: However superior to me in general Knowledge and Experience, the respectable Body of this House may be, yet I claim to know more of *America* than most of you, having seen and been conversant in that Country. The People there are as truly Loyal, I believe, as any Subjects the King has: But a People jealous of their Liberties, and who will vindicate them, if they should be violated; but the Subject is too delicate, I will say no more.

* *A Gentleman of the Army, Member for the Borough of Chipping Wycomb, in the County of Bucks; he was a Major and an Adjutant-General at the taking of Quebec, where he was wounded, and for his Services was rewarded with the Place of Governor of a Castle, but was dismissed from it on his voting against some ministerial Measures.*

QUEBEC, JULY, 25.

Since our last arrived in this City, the Right Honorable Lord ADAM GORDON, Col. of the 66th Regiment of Foot, and Member of Parliament for Aberdeen, accompanied by Commodore LORING, &c.

On Saturday last was launched at St. Roche's, being the first at that Place since in the Hands of the English, the Snow Cordelia, begun and carried on by the Direction of Mr. Thomson, Captain of this Port, at which was present His EXCELLENCY the Governor, and several other Persons of Distinction.

Monday Evening arrived here His Majesty's Ship the Mermaid, Commanded by JOSEPH DEAN, Esq; and on Tuesday Evening the Aldborough, —— HARRIS, Esq; Commander.

Arrived here, on Monday last, the Ketch Mercury, from New-York, chiefly laden with Cloathing for the Army, except a *small* Assortment of Merchandize, consigned to Col. Christie, of Montreal, consisting of seven Pipes of Madeira, ten Puncheons of American Rum, Jamaica Rum, Bar-Iron, Tearses of Loaf and Muscovado Sugar, Window Glass, &c. They are Articles in Demand at present, and consequently come to a good Market.

CUSTOM-HOUSE, QUEBEC, *Inward Entries,*   From
Snow Princess of Brunswick, John Elliot,   Falmouth.
            Cleared Outwards,   For
Ship Providence, Justinian Hingston,   Maryland.
Sloop Rose, Michael Cromie,
Snow Dolphin, Nicholas Lemesurier.   Cork.

The Shipyards – Location

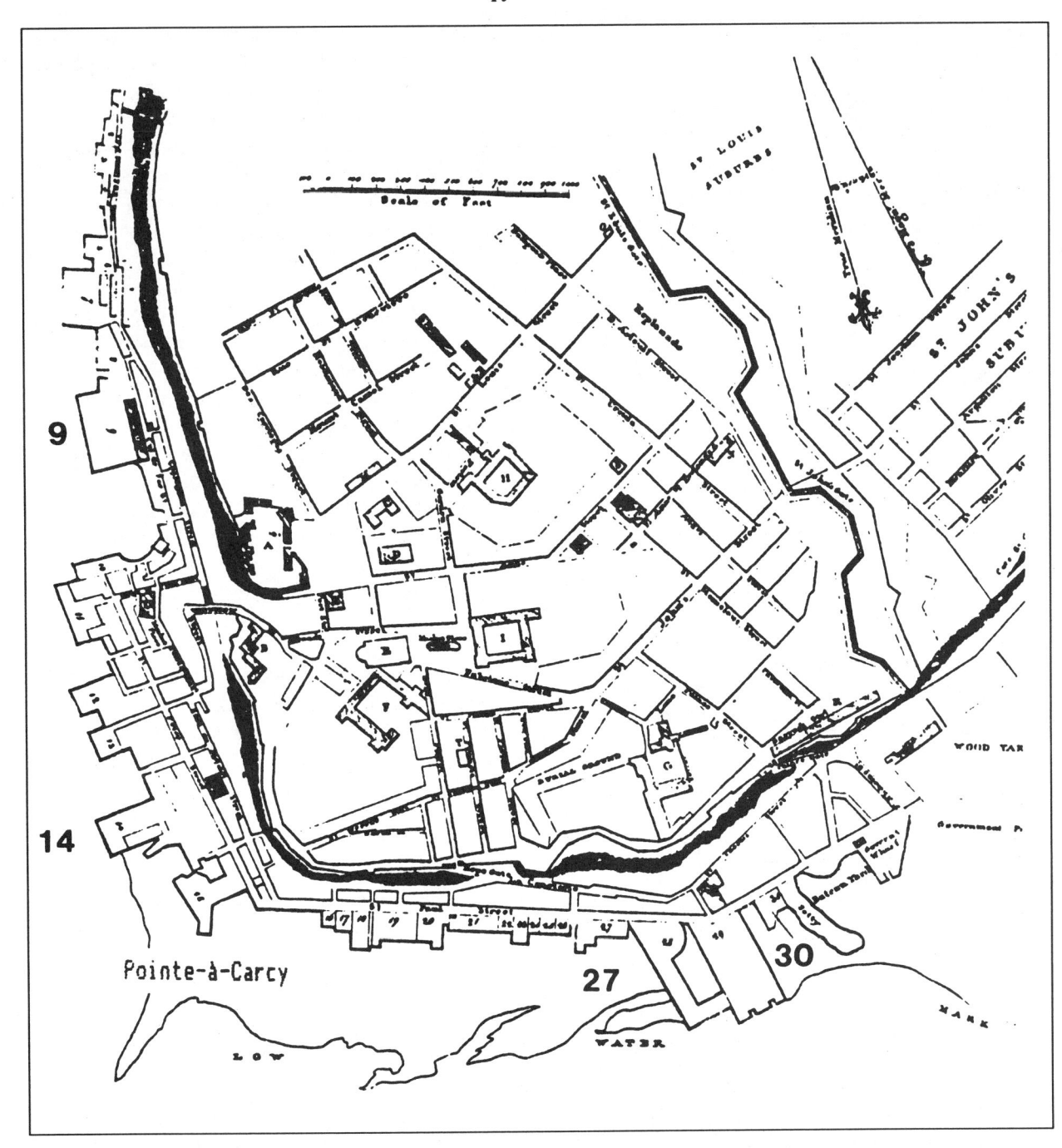

Map 3: *The City of Quebec 1822. Showing the Government Wharf, (bottom right) site of the French Naval Dockyard, (30) Bell's and (27) Taylor's shipyards, (14) Goudie's Wharf, the first built out into deep water, and (9) the King's Wharf, site to which the main part of the French Naval Dockyard was moved and of Alexander Munn's Shipyard. (Top left), just off the map, the Carman shipyard. City of Quebec, engraved by E. Bennet, in The Quebec Directory for 1822...., T. H. Gleason, Quebec, Neilson & Cowan, 1822.*

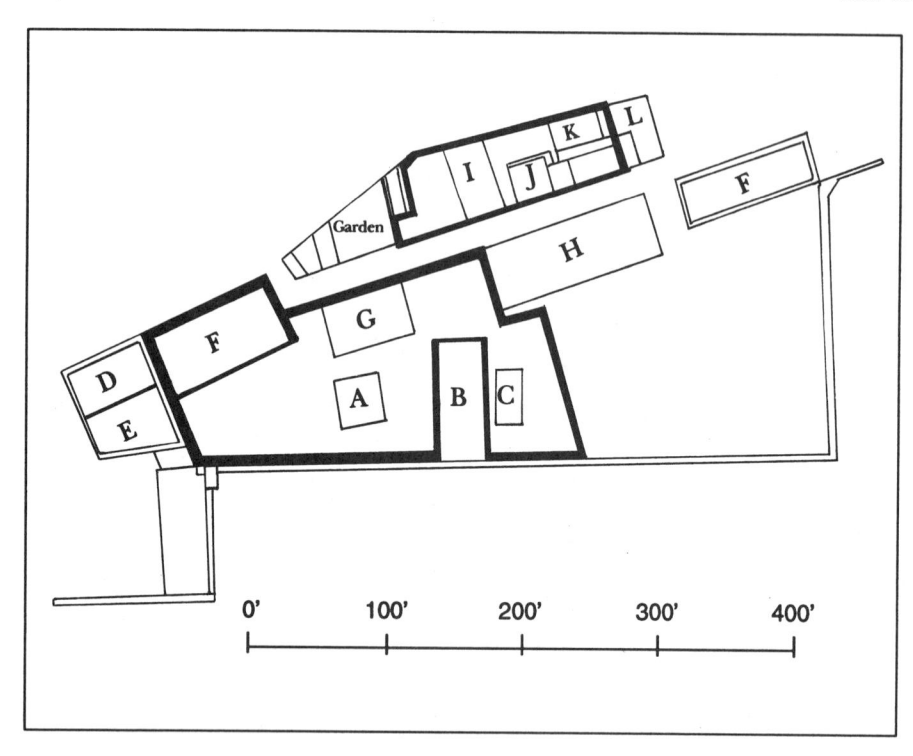

Plan 2: *The King's Wharf Shipyard in 1800*
The parts of the King's Wharf leased by the government to the shipbuilder Alexander Munn in 1800. A) wood pile B) building slip C) old wooden shed D) Messrs Johnston & Purss' house E) garden in front F) stone-built store G) wooden store H) wood store built on stone foundation I) boathouse or workshop J) wooden shed K) stone house L) reserved for a guardhouse. "Plan of the King's Wharf." Redrawn from the original by Samuel Holland that accompanied letter of 19 July 1800. Seignieuries, 5B07-1800B, #45, ANQ.

transshipment of men and supplies were built at the King's Shipyard beside the Palace by local carpenters and artificers brought from the Halifax dockyard.[10]

In 1788, the war was over and private shipbuilders were back in business. John Black, who was building at Diamond Harbour, extended his operations to the beach in front of the Hermitage, setting up a ship repair yard there. He built one new vessel, however, the 316-ton ship *Prince Edward* of 1792, the first to be laid down in the town since the war. In 1798 it was reported that he had "four ships under his charge repairing, sixty carpenters and sawyers, with a number of labourers."[11] But when he petitioned for a grant of the land on which he was building, his request was refused on the grounds that it belonged to the Recollet Order which was allowed to hold property, and the last surviving member, Father Berry, was still alive.

In 1798 Black left on a visit to England and found on his return that Father Berry had died, after conceding the property to a wood merchant. This did not prevent Black from renewing his petition for the land, but without success.[12] His days of shipbuilding at the Hermitage beach were over. Though Black's had been essentially a repair yard, it was there, nevertheless, that John Goudie, the Canadian naval contractor during the War of 1812, and Henry Eckford, the great American shipbuilder, learned their trade. It is ironic that the two friends were destined to pit their skills against each other in the war.[13]

Black's petition for the Hermitage property was one of his several attempts to set up a shipyard in the Palace area. He had his eye on a piece of ground on the other side of the King's Woodyard, but the request he and his partner William King made in 1790 for permission to fence in and lay down a keel there was refused. He also tried his luck in 1792, petitioning to build a dry dock at the same place because "the want of such a dock is daily experienced by merchants and others." The government replied that the land was needed for drawing up rafts of firewood for the garrison, and suggested that he apply for land elsewhere, but he chose not to pursue the matter any further.[14]

Although the government was determined not to give up any ground in the Palace area, it did not plan to set up a naval dockyard at Quebec and had designated the Cul-de-Sac yard a public wharf, which was renamed the King's Wharf. In 1770 it had called for tenders for a thirty-year lease from a "person or Persons of good Substance, Credit and Ability" who were willing to put it into "good and substantial repair" and operate it in accordance with its regulations. The merchants Johnston and Purss were the successful bidders. According to the terms of their lease, the wharf was to be kept open from sunrise to sunset with free access to the public from the 1st of May to the 15th of December, except Sundays and Holy days, and a charge for wharfage was allowed according to a fixed reasonable tariff. It was stipulated, moreover, that the slip was to be made good and kept in proper condition for building and launching.[15]

In 1794 the merchant shipbuilder Alexander Munn sub-leased a small forty by thirty-foot portion of the wharf, with "permission to erect a shade for his convenience," renting a further fifty by 135 feet the following year, with several wooden or stone buildings. He was given permission to erect a crane, and the "liberty in common of said slip or launching place for building vessels or hauling timber." Here he ran a shipping business, carried out ship surveys and repairs, and built the 242-ton ship *London* in 1796, followed by one or two new vessels of two to three hundred-ton each year thereafter. When the government's lease with Johnston and Purss expired in 1800, it rented the space directly to him.[16]

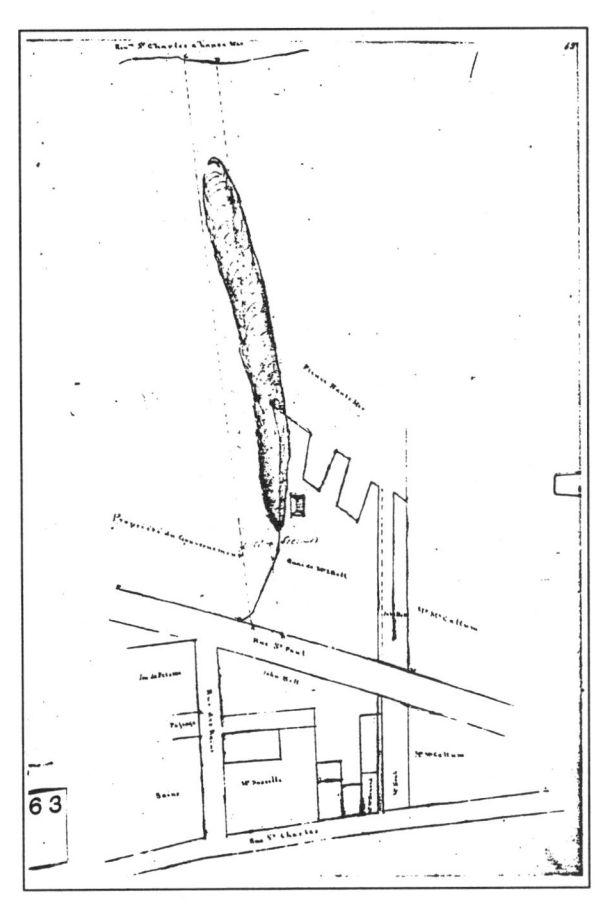

Plan 3: *John Bell's Shipyard in 1823*
Its wharfing encroaching slightly on the old mole, which had disappeared entirely under extensive new wharfing three years later. Here we see the shipping berths and beach beside the long wharf, and one unidentified small building. J.B. Larue, 1:62-3, Le Palais, AVQ.

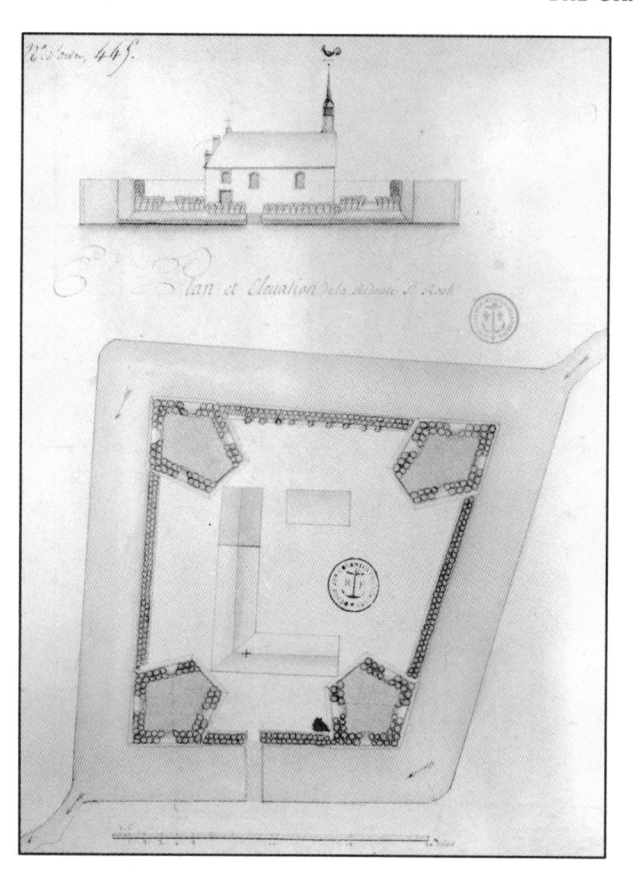

Figure 53: *The Hermitage. Courtesy National Archives, C 15898, with thanks to Juliette Cloutier.*

In 1798 his brother John joined him at Quebec and settled on the other side of town, putting together a shipyard from a collection of rented spaces to the east of the stone jetty on the St. Charles: two sheds, the ground floor of another, half an attic, part of a cellar, four rooms in a house, some beach front, and the wharf to the east of Young's brewery. Of his various leases, only one had a three-year term; for the remainder he had to accept one-year or even shorter terms.[17] His first vessel, the 250-ton ship *Caledonia*, was registered in July 1799, and he continued to build at these makeshift premises until 1803 or 1804, when he moved his shipyard to the land he had purchased in the suburb of St. Roch.

Alexander made his move away from rented premises in 1806, buying the Diamond Harbour shipyard from the Beatsons' bankrupt estate.[18] Not only was he thus freed from the tyranny of a lease, but as Jacques Mathieu makes clear, the Cul-de-Sac had two distinct disadvantages. Launchings could only take place when the tides were at their highest, and the current was stronger there than anywhere else at Quebec.[19] After Munn's departure the King's Wharf shipyard was rented occasionally for ship repairs and dressing masts, and blockmakers had their shops there, but it does not appear to have been used for building ships again.

The timber trade was now gathering momentum, and extra ships were urgently needed to transport the huge quantities of wood from the coves at Quebec to British ports across the Atlantic. Since local shipyards, which were already working to capacity, could not meet the increased demand, several timber merchants solved the problem by setting aside a section of their timber coves or forwarding wharves for shipbuilding, and arranging for skilled tradesmen to be sent over from Britain to supplement the local supply. With the added help, between 1806 and 1812 a total of sixty-one vessels were built in the port, of which two were launched from timber coves for every three launched from regular shipyards. But this situation was short-lived, for following the invasion of Canada in 1812, the vast majority of shipwrights left to work at government dockyards on the Great Lakes and Lake Champlain.

The New Yards in the Palace Area, 1815–1819

By 1815, when the war ended, the shipyard community at Quebec had lost two of its senior members – both Alexander and John Munn had died. John's son, John Jr., inherited half his father's yard and, buying the other half from his stepmother, leased the whole to Sam Finch, while he himself took charge of his late Uncle Alexander's yard at Diamond Harbour.[20] John Goudie, who had distinguished himself as a naval contractor during the war, emerged as the strong leader. Having recognized the importance of steam, a large part of his efforts at this time were directed to furthering the application of steam power both ashore and afloat. Several of the other shipbuilders in town who had served in the dockyards during the war were eager to settle down and start building on their own, and in spite of the weakness of the shipping market, Samuel Finch, John Bell and George Taylor succeeded in doing so in the 1810s.

Samuel Finch became a shipowner and exporter, and built three small vessels during his six-year lease on Munn's yard, increasing his production after 1821 when he moved to the adjoining premises that belonged to John Campbell's estate.

Before the war, John Bell had built under contract both on his own account and in partnership with Romain Robitaille at various rented premises, and in 1809 had managed to buy a small lot with a sixty-foot frontage to the west of the jetty. On his return, he leased the land between his lot and McCallum's brewery from Joseph Drapeau, and was able to buy it from his widow in 1819.[21] During his shipbuilding days, his yard evolved considerably. When the city decided to locate a market beside it to the west, he donated a fifteen-foot strip bordering their property, on part of which he in turn was given a contract to build a thirty-foot wide wharf that jutted 440 feet into deep water over the old stone jetty. In addition to the work that this gave to his men, the additional moorage and protection from the elements that the wharf provided was undoubtedly an advantage for his yard. Plans show only one small store or hangard on the wharf. The rest of the buildings were on the other side of St. Paul Street. When Bell gave up shipbuilding in 1836, he gave the shipwrights John Nicholson and William Russell a nine year lease on the yard, but Bell died in 1841 and two years later the lease was broken.[22]

And finally there was George Taylor, whose rented premises were to the east of John Bell's yard and immediately to the west of St. Thomas Street on the Canoterie. John Black had bought the property and set up a shipyard there in 1801 after all his attempts to get a grant in the Palace area had failed, but had been in business there only five years when he went bankrupt.[23] The merchant brewer Pierre Brehaut, who acquired it at auction, gave short-term leases to several shipbuilders in succession, and after his death Taylor leased it from the estate and established his shipyard there. The property was described at the time as having 130 feet of frontage, a stone house with a blacksmith's shop at one end and a stable adjoining, and a stone hangard seventy feet long by thirty-two feet wide.[24] In 1825, following Taylor's daughter's marriage to Allison Davie, Davie became

Figure 54: Neptune Inn, Quebec. *Watercolour, James Pattison Cockburn, I–205. Courtesy National Archives, Ottawa.*

Figure 55: *Quebec with the arrival of* HMS Hastings, *conveying the Earl of Durham Governor General of Canada, May 1838. Drawn by Captain Digby Morton, Lithographed by ?Day and Haghe, London, 1838. With thanks to Colin McMichael.*

his partner, and the last two ships launched on that site were built under the direction of Davie, who had taken over the yard when Taylor fell ill in 1828. In 1830 the lease was relinquished and Davie moved to the south shore.

The Quebec Waterfront

As the years passed, the shipyards were gradually squeezed out from the waterfront at Quebec. After the others had gone, Joseph, Isaie and Louis Julien and Pierre Labbé, working under the name Isaie Julien and Company, operated a successful shipyard on the land between the former Bell and Taylor yards, which they leased from the malt brewer Paul Lepper.[25] Here, immediately below the Hôtel Dieu they built by far the largest vessels that were laid down on the Canoterie, crowning their efforts with the launching of the 1344 ton *Amoor* in 1855, a vessel that must certainly have looked impressive standing on the stocks at the foot of the Côte de la Canoterie, and whose unusual crocodile figurehead must also have elicited some comments. Their last vessel, which was considerably smaller, was launched in 1857.

And so almost two hundred years of sailing ship construction in the town itself came to an end, but we have only to look at the ship that is featured on the crest of the City of Quebec to be reminded of the important part that the industry played in its affairs.

Près-de-Ville

Passing the King's Wharf in a southerly direction, we come to Près-de-Ville, the building block complex of wharves and warehouses that extended the waterfront of the Lower Town. Like the Lower Town, it's contours were constantly changing as merchants, shipowners and tradesmen increased their precious feet of river front by building on new wharfing. At the turn of the eighteenth to nineteenth century, a small property near its western end had belonged successively to the shipbuilders William King, Patrick Beatson and Alexander Munn, serving as an annex to their shipyards.[26] In 1815, it was one of several adjoining properties bought by the Montreal brewer and steamboat operator, John Molson, to make a Quebec terminus for his river steamboats. He was able to build the wharves and workshops he needed at Quebec at a time when he was refused a permit to build wharves in Montreal. In 1822, when the owners of steamboats on the Quebec-Montreal run amalgamated their operations, forming the St. Lawrence Steamboat Company, and Molson's terminus became redundant, he rented it. James Cockburn's watercolour, Figure 56, shows the property when William and Robert Carman, the former a merchant and the latter a shipwright, were his tenants. Their lease ran from 1824, but when Robert died in 1825, the shipbuilding side of their concern foundered and their stock-in-trade was divided among their creditors.[27] The yard was then sub-divided into twenty foot building lots. It would seem that this stretch of waterfront was not suitable for shipbuilding. During the 1840s, part of it was rented to Thomas Oliver, who like John Munn, the owner of seven hundred feet of frontage at Près-de-Ville, were important shipbuilders on the St. Charles and required berths for outfitting and loading the many vessels they built or managed.[28] Munn's wharves later became a part of the extensive premises acquired by the Montreal Ocean Steamship Company for its Allan Line of steamers.

Figure 56: Lower Town Quebec. *Près-de-ville*. On top of the large building, centre left, is the sign of the Robert and William Carman shipyard on Molson's wharf. It is evident that these are cramped quarters for shipbuilding. *Watercolour, James P. Cockburn, s.d., 951.82.3. Courtesy Royal Ontario Museum. From* The Drawings of James Cockburn: A visit through Quebec's Past, #22, page 41.

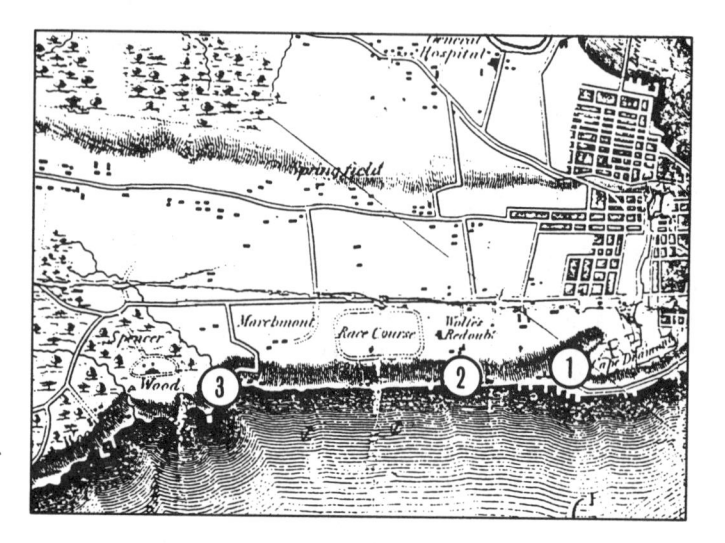

Map 4: *North Shore of the Saint Lawrence*
The three coves that were actively engaged in shipbuilding, within a mile and a half of each other, close to the town, (1) Diamond Harbour, (2) Cape Cove and (3) Wolfe's Cove. Detail from The Map of Quebec and its Environs, Adams (Map 31).

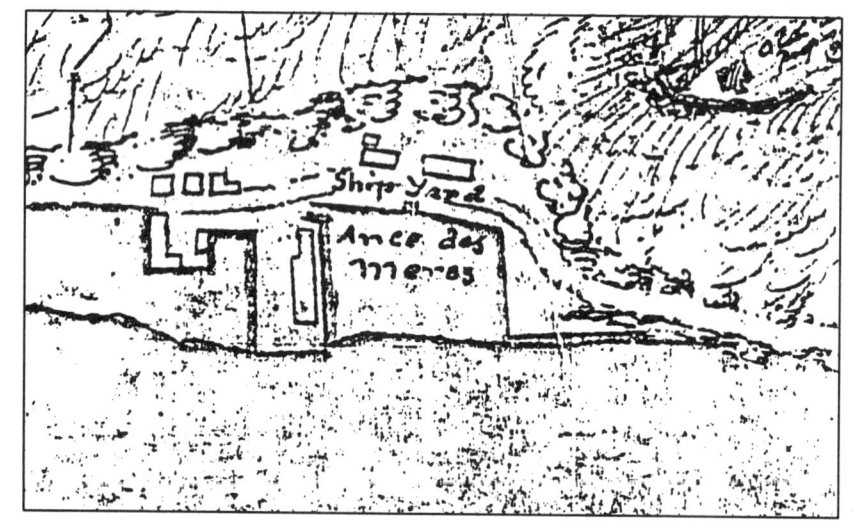

Plan 4: *Diamond Harbour 1821*
It was being used as a shipyard by John Black and William King in 1791, and two years later would be occupied by Patrick Beatson. Bought by Alexander Munn in 1806, in 1821 it was rented by his widow to his nephew John Munn. "Plan of the City and Fortifications of Quebec." drawn by E.W. Durnford, 1821 (portion) BO, IGF, NA. seen 615.966

The North Shore of the Saint Lawrence River

At the beginning of the nineteenth century timber exporters began vying for the coves to the southwest of Près-de-Ville[29] and by the 1830s the entire shoreline had become one vast woodyard. From Diamond Harbour to Sillery, and at Crescent, Dalhousie, Cap Rouge and Alexandria Coves, huge stocks of timber covered the beaches extending into the river, where they were restrained by floating fences or "booms" anchored across and between the coves. On the periphery, timber ships loaded their cargoes alongside large rectangular piers marking the deep-water lots, while others rode at anchor awaiting their turn. From time to time, a part of a timber cove would give way for a year or two to shipbuilding. Among the timber coves, lying within a mile and a half of each other and close to the town, were three important shipbuilding sites: Diamond Harbour or l'anse-des-Mères; Cape Cove, also originally known as l'anse-des-Mères; and Wolfe's Cove or l'anse-au-Foulon, at all of which shipbuilding would take place continuously for many years.[30]

It was at Diamond Harbour that the first ships were laid down after the American Revolution. Contracts issued by the Commissary General at Quebec, which handled a large part of the wartime provisioning, were largely responsible for its development as a small industrial centre and outport, where corn was dried, flour was milled, bread and biscuit were baked, fish was packed – and ships were repaired and built. It grew to comprise two substantial wharves, ten buildings, including a storage shed two stories high and 150 feet long, a smithy, cooperage, and three large dwelling houses and stables.[31]

Figure 57: *Patrick Beatson's tombstone at the "English Burying Ground" beside St Matthew's Church, Quebec. Photo by Cedric Pearson, courtesy National Museum of Man M17/15A.*

Figure 58: *Below Cape Diamond, the substantial masonry house in the foreground was built by Alexander Munn. Beyond is the long low timber house where Patrick Beatson lived. Watercolour, 1829, James P. Cockburn, I–187. Courtesy National Archives, Ottawa, C 40011.*

Between 1785 and 1791 five vessels varying from 104 to 204 tons were built there, the first two by Captain James Duncanson and the three others by two of the ship carpenters he brought from Scotland, John Black and William King.[32]

In 1793 Captain Patrick Beatson, a native of Leith and frequent visitor to the port, retired to Diamond Harbour after twenty-one years at sea, becoming a shipbuilder and shipowner in partnership with his brothers, Captains William and John Beatson. Under Patrick Beatson's direction their shipyard became the first important private yard at Quebec. The thirteen square-rigged vessels launched in the space of seven years included the 497-ton ship *Queen* of 1795, one of only three three-decked merchant sailing ships ever to be built at Quebec, and the even larger 646-ton ship *Monarch* of 1800. But in December 1800 Patrick died, and, as neither of his brothers was prepared to settle at Quebec and run the yard, John saw to the completion of the two large vessels that were on the stocks, and then built two smaller ones and used up the lighter timber for repairs, before leaving in 1803.[33]

An emphyteutic lease granted by the Ursuline sisters on adjoining land to the west had increased the frontage of the yard from 832 to 1,192 feet during the Beatson tenure, but the inventory taken after Patrick's death does not allow us to pinpoint any major improvements to the shipyard, nor is there evidence of any in contemporary plans. Ironically, Patrick's brothers had honoured his private commitment and bought the property from Louis Dunière in 1802, the year before they gave up the yard.[34]

When Alexander Munn bought the Beatson shipyard in 1806, he moved his family into the old wooden house that had been Patrick Beatson's home. Business prospered, and in 1811 he ordered the construction of a two-story stone house, the new family home that he was destined not to enjoy, for the following spring, Alexander Munn, like his predecessor, died prematurely. His family remained at the new home and his widow managed the property over the next twenty-seven years, renting it first to her brother-in-law David and nephew John, and then parcelling it out to a succession of tenants and sub-tenants. Part was leased as a timber cove, and part as one or two shipyards. Her shipbuilder tenants included Louis Labbé and Jean Desnoyers, and the shipmasters Ed Henley and James Clint, who supervised the construction of their own vessels there in 1824 and 1825, respectively. Other short-term tenants included James Young, and Paul Benjamin Viger and Antoine Ernst in 1827, while the brothers James and John Jeffery rented from 1831 to 1836 before moving to St. Roch to pursue separate careers. Even with two shipyards, there was room for the shops of riggers, blacksmiths and boatbuilders and the homes of all the workers, while the wharves were used among other purposes for dressing and shipping both staves and masts, and for a while a building in the west end of the cove housed a tobacco factory, which burned down in 1826.[35]

In 1839, ownership of the entire property and the emphyteutic lease passed out of the hands of the Munn family and into those of William Lampson, a native of Boston, a shipbuilder, fur trader, land developer and entrepreneur. He was also the agent for the new Floating Dock Company that leased part of the yard. Lampson's financial position was strained at the time, and it was the merchants Forsyth and Bell who bought the harbour property in trust for him and also obtained the letters-patent for the four deep-water lots in front, before they ceded it to him the following year. Lampson kept the central part of what had been the Beatson shipyard for his own shipyard and floating dock installation, erecting a large new moulding loft with a store below on the north side of Champlain Street and a new smithy at the head of the central wharf, which he enlarged.[36] In 1840, he extended his holdings by buying the property immediately to the west, known as Cap Blanc, which increased his frontage by five arpents and eight perches. This he leased out to timber merchants.[37] Meanwhile, having transferred his shipbuilding activities from St. Roch to Diamond Harbour in 1839, he launched three vessels each year for the next three years and finally a schooner in 1844. In later years he built a number of barges and steamboats. His main contribution to the trade however was in the construction of floating docks which he either operated or rented, and in which a large number of vessels were repaired and many wrecks rebuilt. He had a number of shipbuilder tenants, among them Pierre Valin, David Vaughan, John J. Nesbitt and Jacques Blais,[38] and changes in the division of the property were frequent.[39] Although shipbuilding had a very mixed history at Diamond Harbour and not nearly as many vessels were launched there as were launched at many other shipbuilding sites, at no other site were ships built over such a long period of time.

By contrast with Diamond Harbour, Cape Cove, which adjoined Cap Blanc to the west, had a relatively stable history. It belonged to the Augustine Sisters of the Hôtel Dieu and lay undeveloped until 1815, when a thirty-nine year emphyteutic lease was granted to the Montreal timber merchant, Benjamin Viger, and a local ship carpenter, Olivier Trahan. The terms of the lease required Viger and Trahan to build a thirty to

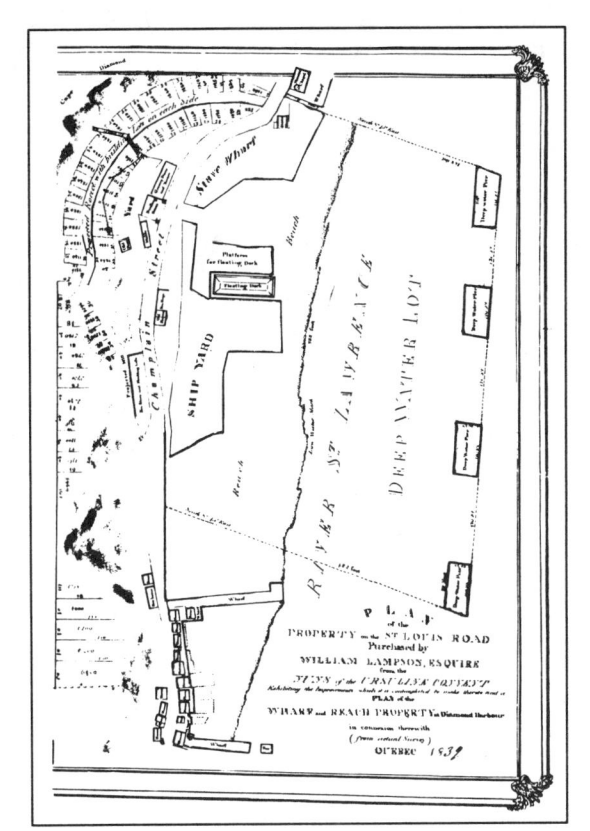

Plan 5: *Diamond Harbour 1839*
Showing the improvements proposed by Lampson, including a floating dock and platform, a large new mould loft on the north side of Champlain Street and a new forge. The four new deep water piers are also shown. "Plan of the Property . . . Purchased by William Lampson Esquire from the Nuns of the Ursuline Convent . . . the Wharf and Beach Property at Diamond Harbour in connexion therewith (from actual Survey) Quebec 1839." Anon. BO. H2/340/Quebec/ 1839, NMC, NA.

Plan 6: *Cape Cove 1831*
The shipyard is in the centre with mould loft beside the quay. Right, the steam sawmill wharf with timber yard behind. The office, workshops and shipbuilders and workers' homes are below the cliff on the other side of the road. Plan attached to the deed of sale from Campbell to Erle Henry Hall, 25 January 1831, gr F.X Garneau. "Plan of a Beach Property in the Occupation of J.S. Campbell Esqr. shewing the Wharves Roads Buildings & which have by him been constructed, as the same now exist." Signed John Adams Surveyor & Archt. Quebec 18th Octr. 1831, ANQ.

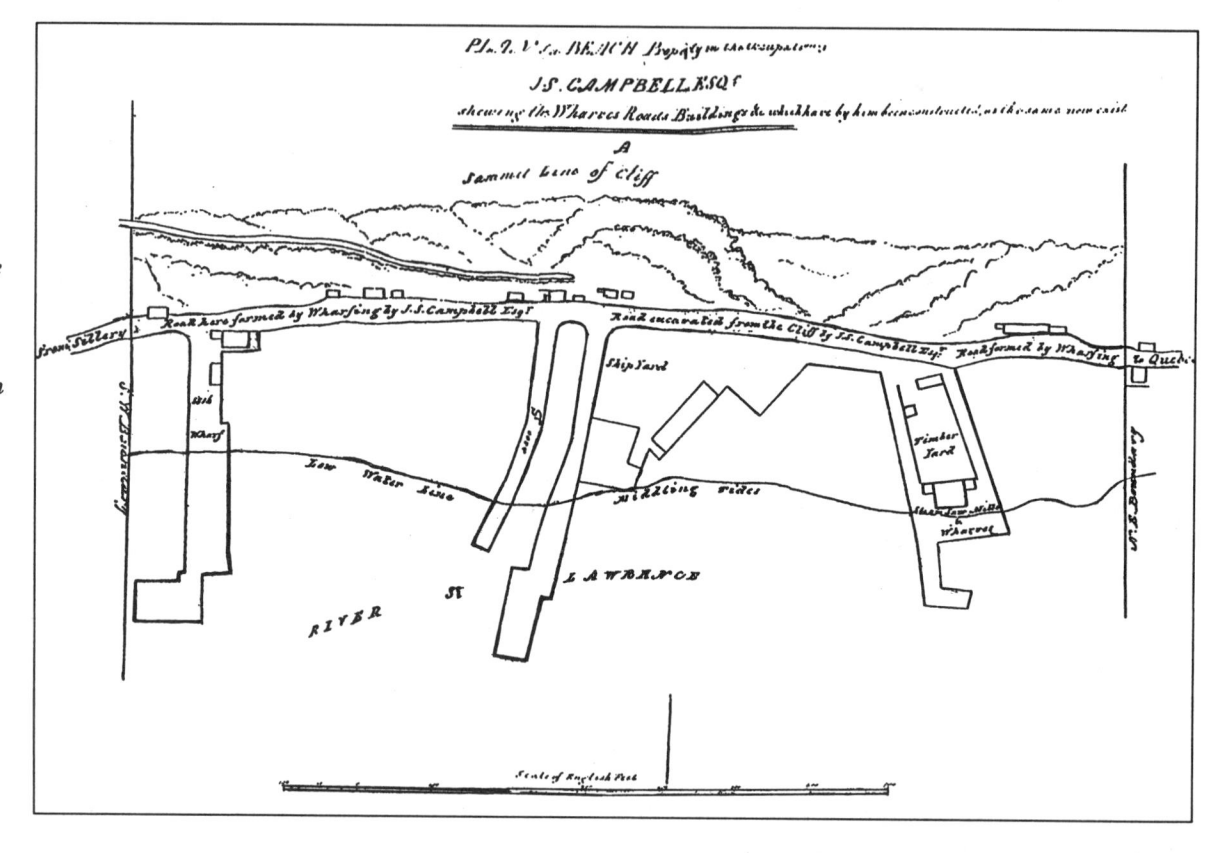

forty foot wide wharf reaching the low water mark, another with 137 feet of frontage within three years, and a third with sixty feet of frontage within fifteen. In fact, Viger and Trahan occupied the property for four years, during which time they erected a house, shed, smithy and steamhouse, and built a 212-ton vessel in 1818, after which Trahan took on a new partner, the ship carpenter Jean Martin dit Beaulieu.[40] In 1825, the remainder of their lease was taken over by John Saxton Campbell, son of the United Empire Loyalist Archibald Campbell and brother of the notary of the same name. J.S. Campbell had entered the wood trade with his father and had qualified as an inspector of cullers. A dynamic man, by 1825 he was operating on his own and showing a particular interest in shipping and shipbuilding. Going far beyond the requirements of the lease, he wasted no time in laying down a good road across the property, for which it was necessary to cut

The Shipyards – Location

Figure 59: *Cape Cove Shipyard from the River. Courtesy National Archives, Ottawa. Neg. C 12472.*

Figure 60: Cape *Cove Shipyard from the River. Shipbuilders' new home below the cliff, left, to which they moved from their quarters above the office in the centre building. Floating dock, foreground left. Courtesy late Reginald G. Ray.*

Figure 61: *Henry Dinning (1830–1884), shipbuilder at Cape Cove. From F.W. Wallace,* In the Wake of the Windships.

Figure 62: *Barque* Anna, *ex fully-rigged ship* Elizabeth Yeo, *895 tons built at the Baldwin and Dinning Shipyard at Cape Cove in 1856 for William Yeo of Appledore, Devon. The builders accepted the wreck of the* Princess Royal, *another Yeo ship in part payment. Watercolour, unsigned, London, 1877. Courtesy Duncan Stacey, great grandson of the sailmaker G.T. Crump, who made a suit of sails for her in his loft at Ratcliff, London, in 1877.*

back the cliff on the one side in places and build up the beach in others. He then put up two good wharves, with a steam sawmill on the easterly one, and leased the lower part of the cove with the sawmill to a certain John Fernie. On the central part he set up a shipyard, taking the Aberdonian shipbuilder George Black as his partner to run it while he looked after the business end. It was their highly-respected shipyard that was awarded the contract for the construction of the renowned paddle steamer *Royal William* in 1830, the year that the first term of their partnership expired. The yard had acquired a floating dock in 1827 (see next chapter) which had proved highly successful and added significantly to their business. Black's handsome share of the profits for the first five years amounted to £4,000, and the agreement was extended for another ten. In 1832 Campbell acquired the Cove including the deep-water lots in front as a concession from the Hotel Dieu. By then he had added to the wharfing and had successfully petitioned for the right to extend three of his wharves into deep water, having argued that

"the building of Wharves at the extremity or at the North East and South West points of the respective coves from l'Ance des Mères to Cap Rouge would be of general benefit and advantage to the Trade of the Country, as it would prevent the North East and South West winds from breaking up the Rafts of Timber, which are hauled up in the said coves for the purpose of being shipped on board of the Vessels lying in the Stream."

In 1837, when the Campbell and Black partnership was dissolved, Campbell sold the Cape Cove property to Black, and it was a flourishing business that Black handed over to his son George in 1846.

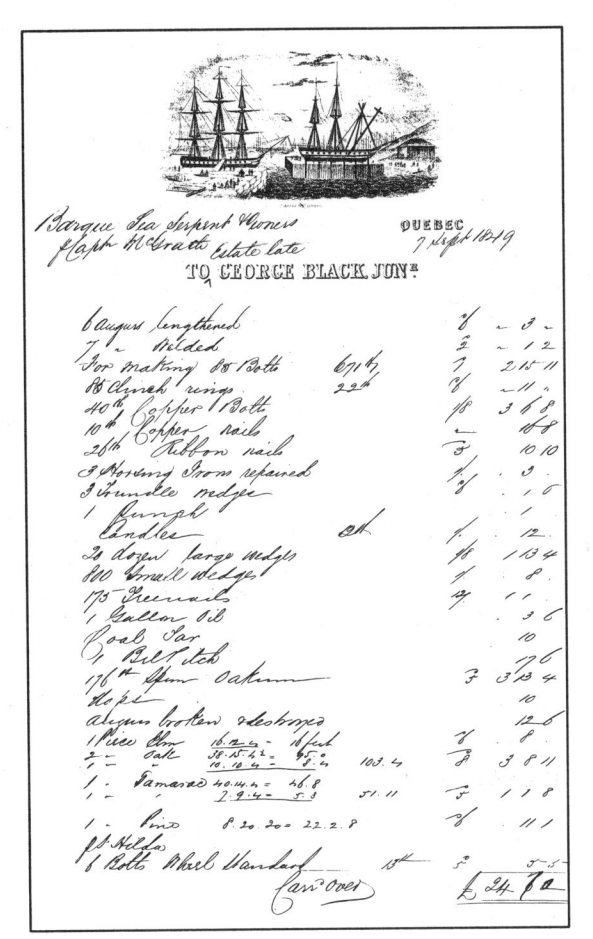

Figure 63: *Account owed to the estate of the late George Black for materials used in the repair of the barque* Sea Serpent, *dated 7 September 1849.*

Figure 64: *Cape Cove Shipyard. In the centre, the steepled mould loft, with small floating dock on its bed on near side, and ships under construction on far side. The large brig in the foreground is apparently in a floating dock. Cap Blanc and the Diamond Harbour Shipyard beyond. Alongside the deep water piers ships wait patiently for their loads of timber. Courtesy National Archives, Ottawa. (with thanks to Henri Dion). Neg. PA 103102.*

George Black, Jr. did not have the chance to make his mark, for he died three years later. Black's other sons were not qualified to take over the business, and the yard, complete with two floating docks, houses, wharves, slips, gridirons, booms, beaches and deep-water lots, was let to his nephew William Henry Baldwin, a blockmaker, and his partner Henry Dinning.[41] During the two four-year terms of their association they built ten vessels averaging 1,100 tons, maintaining the high quality for which the yard was known. Then Baldwin left to open a yard on the St. Charles River. George Black had hoped that one of his sons would eventually run his shipyard, and in 1858 his third son Edmund took a lease on it in partnership with James Gibb Shaw, but their association was short lived and they gave up the lease the next year. In the spring of 1859 Dinning once again rented the yard, this time in partnership with his father James, and they worked there together until 1865, when James retired and Henry, who had bought the yard in the meantime at auction in 1862, continued on his own.[42] Henry Dinning built a total of thirty sailing vessels at the Cape Cove shipyard, of which the last two, the 1220-ton ship *Cosmo* and the 1244-ton *Lorenzo*, were launched in 1877. Barges and steamboats were also built, and a vigorous salvage and repair business was carried on until his death in 1884. The Cape Cove shipyard is known to many as the yard where the P.S. *Royal William* was built, but first and foremost it was the birthplace of scores of classically-elegant square-rigged sailing ships, such as the *Ocean Monarch*, which was featured in the *London Illustrated News* in 1854.

Two timber coves, Ottawa North and Ottawa South, lay between Cape Cove and Wolfe's Cove, the choice large bay fronting the property sold by the Seminaire to General Murray in 1762. Beyond it to the

Figure 65: "View of Waterfall at Wolfe's Cove, Quebec, ca. 1808" *from* "Drawings — Heriot." *The wood trade had barely begun to intrude on the beaches to the southwest of the town when George Heriot painted this watercolour. To the extreme left, sawyers are at work splitting a huge log into planks. Watercolour by an unknown artist. Courtesy National Archives, Ottawa, neg. C 12723*

west was Spencer Cove, which at the turn of the eighteenth century was often considered to be part of Wolfe's Cove or l'anse-au-foulon. It is for this reason that we cannot be sure whether it was at Wolfe's Cove or Spencer Cove that Michel Chartier de Lotbinière was required to land the rafts of curved white oak timber and planks for shipbuilding ordered by Acklom Bondfield in 1770, nor from which of the two coves the 103-ton brigantine *Sisters* was launched by G. Bradford Lane in 1795.[43] Around that time, the cove, like others between Sillery and Quebec, was frequently used for the delivery of rafts of timber ordered not only by its legitimate owners or tenants, but by all and sundry, and it was to put an end to this free-for-all that the *Act for the Better Regulation of the Lumber Trade* was passed in 1808. This law laid down penalties for those landing rafts at a cove and leaving them there for more than six days without the owner or tenant's permission.[44]

For some time in the hands of Henry Caldwell, Wolfe's Cove was acquired by Paterson, Grant and Greenshields in 1810 and was being exploited by John S. Campbell in partnership with Robert Ritchie in 1812. In the winter of 1814–1815, vessels were repaired and built there for James Dunlop of Montreal, under the supervision of a shipwright named William Simons, who would later become the foremost shipbuilder in his native Greenock. From 1819 to 1830, Campbell's brother Charles, in partnership with their brother-in-law William Sheppard, operated a lumber and shipbuilding business from the cove, and for the last five years of this period vessels were also being built there by others for John S. Campbell himself. In 1826, however, Sheppard and Campbell were requested to "vuider les lieux et faire place nette" (give up the property) by the first of May following.[45]

It was then that Allan Gilmour and Company took over the cove, first as tenants and from 1834 as the new owners. This new branch of the well-established timber firm Pollok, Gilmour and Company of Glasgow was entrusted to Allan Gilmour, Jr., who brought with him the accumulated experience of the firm's operations and his own experience in the Baltic and in New Brunswick. Besides becoming the largest timber exporter in Quebec, Gilmour established a first-class shipyard where as many as four vessels were sometimes on the stocks, almost all of which were destined for the Pollok, Gilmour & Company fleet. In all, fifty-seven superior vessels were launched from the Gilmour-Wolfe's Cove Shipyard before it was sold to John Roche in 1868.[46]

There were no long-term shipyards to the west of Wolfe's Cove, although some ships were built here and there sporadically; the most active yard was at Sillery Cove belonging to the Jesuit Estates. It was there that the first ship built in Sillery, the 284-ton *Mercator*, was launched by Walter Gilley for Anthony Atkinson and Company in 1811. After other owners and tenants, the timber firm of Henry Sharples Company occupied the eastern part of the cove and had a number of vessels laid down during the 1830s and 1840s, most under the supervision of their "Mr. Milling."[47]

Further west in Cap Rouge, the 403-ton ship *Crescent* had been built at Crescent Cove in 1810 for Francis and William Hunter by the shipbuilder, James Morrison, who had come to Quebec with a contract to build ships for John Behan and Francis Kenny of Dublin, but was left high and dry when he was discharged from their service before his first ship was launched. Then, between 1825 and 1830, when Anthony Anderson had a timber yard there, François

The Shipyards – Location

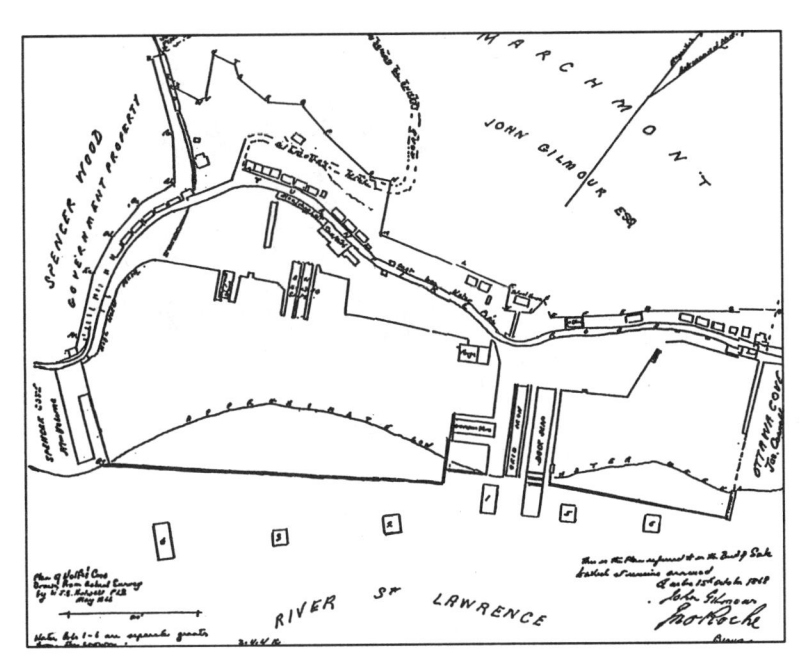

Plan 7: Wolfe's Cove 1866
The well appointed shipyard developed by the Gilmours. Plan forming part of the conveyance of Wolfe's Cove from John Gilmour to John Roche, 15 October 1868, gr Wm Bignell. "Plan of Wolfe's Cove." Redrawn from the original by W.J.S. Holwell, P.L.S., Quebec, May 1866, ACQ.

Figure 66: *Allan Gilmour (1805–1884) Some of Quebec's finest ships were built in the Gilmour shipyard at Wolfe's Cove by his Mr. McCord and subsequently, Mr. Dick.*

Figure 67: The Timber and Shipbuilding Yards of Allan Gilmour and Company at Wolfe's Cove, Quebec, Viewed from the West. 1840 *Robert C. Todd, oil on canvas. Courtesy National Gallery of Canada, neg. 29695. (detail)*

Robitaille superintended the construction of four ships for him, the last by Sam Finch, Jr.[48]

With the launching of Dinning's *Lorenzo* in 1877, the construction of square-riggers on the north shore of the St. Lawrence came to an end. The shipyards lingered, building an occasional steamboat or barge and carrying out repair work. But gradually those contracts too petered out and the proud shipyards fell into disrepair and were abandoned. Landfill and asphalt have since done their work, and today they lie in common anonymity under Champlain Boulevard, with only an occasional name, such as Gilmour Hill, linking them with their history.

Saint Roch and Saint Sauveur

Many fine ships were built on the St. Lawrence, but it was the riverfront of the Seigniory (later the Suburb) of St. Roch that became the heart of the wooden sailing ship industry.[49] At its height, each shipyard rubbed shoulders with the next, the building ways and moulding lofts giving the appearance of one vast shipyard. Upstream where the river was narrower the yards were often hidden from view, and here and there a set of two or three masts thrust upward one behind the other seemed to be growing out of the town itself.

At the turn of the century, more than half St. Roch's inhabitants, or about five hundred souls, lived on St. Vallier street, the road along the foot of the cliff on its southern boundary. The rest of the seigniory was given over to farming and milling. When the mill lots on its northeast and northwest borders became shipyards, the fields were sub-divided into small concessions to house the workers. By 1805, the population had risen to 1,500; between 1805 and 1818, it tripled to 4,600.[50] By 1822, the entire suburb had been laid out

Figure 68 : *Saint Vallier street, Suburb of St. Roch, 1793. Watercolour, George Heriot. Courtesy National Archives, Ottawa. C 12743.*

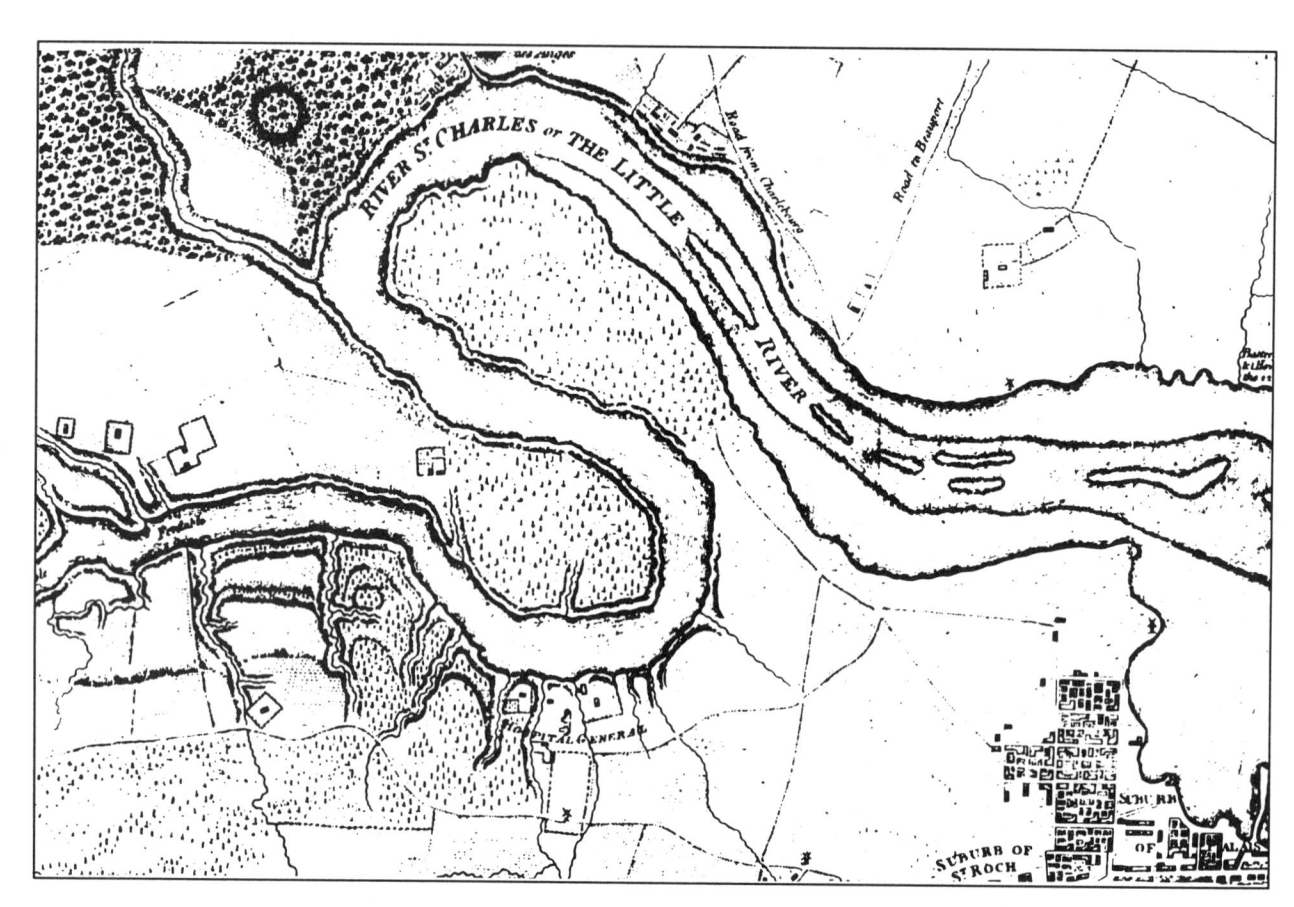

Map 5: *The Saint Charles River c. 1776.*
Showing the suburbs of Saint Roch and Le Palais, bottom right. At this time, the people of Saint Roch lived in the small built-up area near the Palace or along the foot of the cliff that led toward the General Hospital. The shipyards gradually spread along the south bank of the St. Charles and in 1847 began their encroachment on the north bank. Plan of the City and Environs of Quebec, engraved by William Faden, 615.966 1776. Cartothèque, UL.

The Shipyards – Location

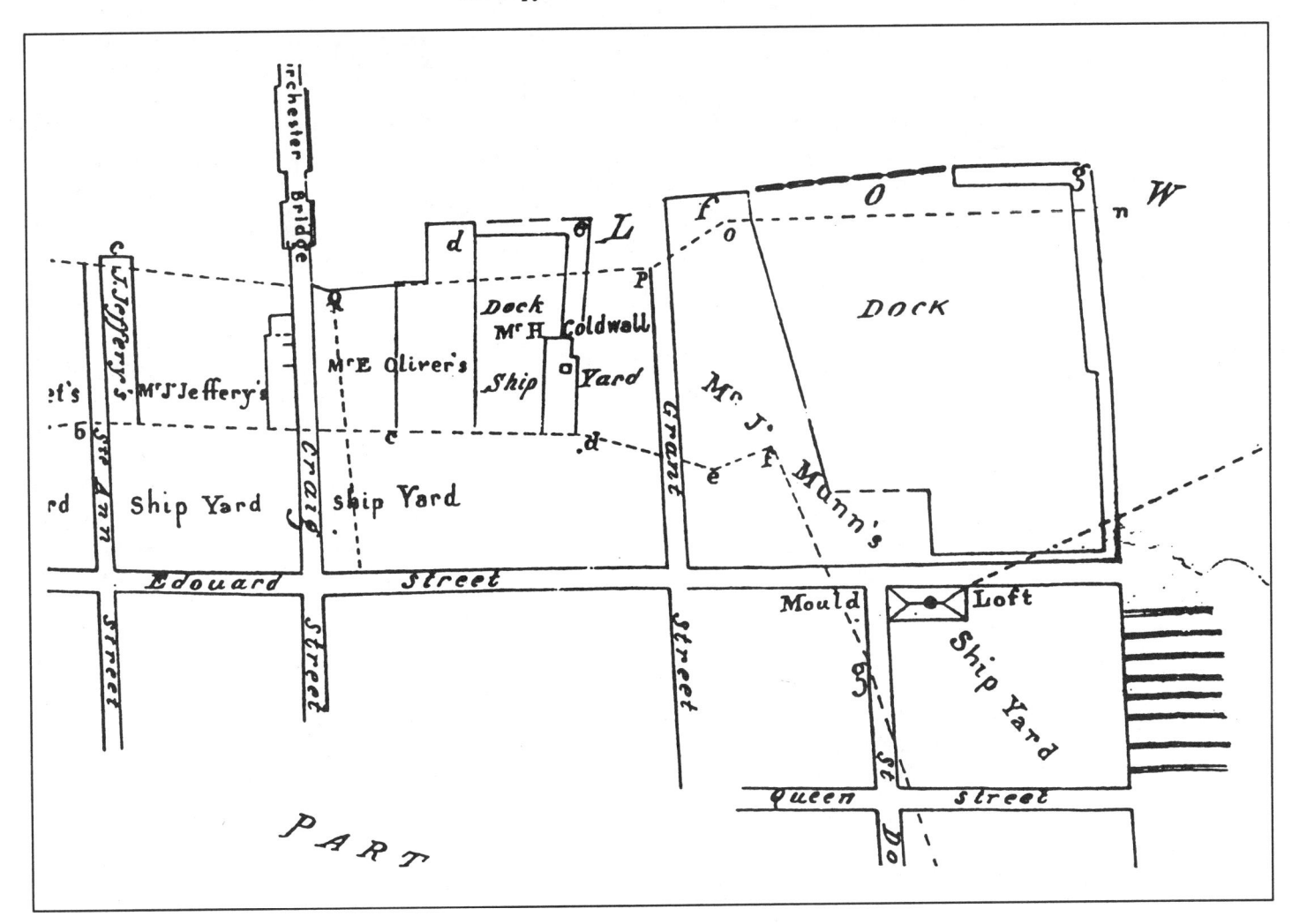

Map 6: *Shipyards in the Seigniory of Saint Roch in 1840 The wharving of the continuation of Saint Roch Street has created a large timber pond. Munn's shipyard between Grant and Saint Roch Street from King Street to the River is identified, and his mould loft is shown. Plan of the beach on the south side of the channel of the River Saint Charles surveyed June and July 1840 by Joseph Bouchette Junior, Deputy Survr. Genl., 10 August 1840. 615.966 1840, Cartothèque, UL. "True copy of the original Public Works Office Montreal 26th October 1846 (signed) G.F. Baillairgé Asst. Draft," only a portion is shown here).*

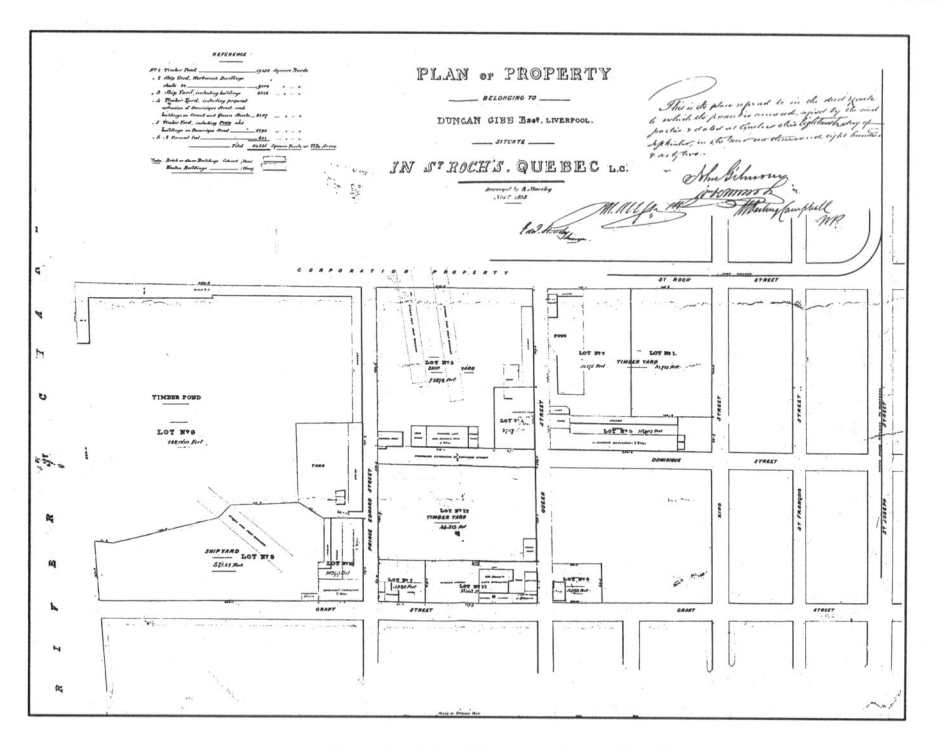

Plan 8: *John Munn's Extended Shipyard*
Drawn by Edward Staveley in 1858 after Munn's losses had obliged him to surrender his property, which then included two self-contained shipyards. Copies of this plan, are attached to many different agreements, in this case to the lease of the shipyard to the shipbuilders Patterson & Shaw, 18 September 1862, gr W.D. Campbell. "Plan of Property belonging to Duncan Gibb, Bart., Liverpool situate in St Roch's, Quebec L.C." CN1-51/7, ANQ.

with streets, and a new Dorchester bridge spanned the river at Craig (Dupont) Street half a mile below its former emplacement.

John Munn's and John Goudie's shipyards were in the north end of St. Roch, with the mill dam property of the timber merchant John Campbell between them. John Goudie's was to the west of it, and John Munn's to the south.[51] During the early part of the century, both builders were able to benefit from the timber yard beside them, from the strong shipping market, and from their activities as shipowners. In addition, Goudie ran a profitable ship salvage and repair business. While Goudie was able to enjoy the profits from his shipbuilding contracts with the government during the War of 1812, Munn died soon after his brother Alexander in the winter of 1813-1814. The John Munn that is referred to henceforth is his son, who became his partner shortly before he died. Goudie first, and then Munn, would greatly increase their holdings in St. Roch over the years.

Goudie needed beaches on which to draw up his rafts of shipbuilding timber, of sawlogs for the steam sawmill that he set up in 1818, and of timber for export purposes, and was constantly on the alert for additional river frontage above his shipyard. When he died in 1824, he owned the whole of the northern riverfront of St. Roch from Grant Street to the Vacherie. But Goudie had too many irons in the fire and apparently there was no one else capable of handling them. His oldest son was a law student, the second apprenticed to a notary, the third had just begun to serve his time in a shipyard in Scotland and the youngest was eight. His estate was grossly mismanaged, and his properties were sold at auction for far less than their worth.[52]

For his part, John Munn patiently assembled the lots to the east of Grant street, his major acquisitions being the lots to the south of his original property, that he obtained at auction from Goudie's estate in 1829, and the corner lot, acquired from John Campbell's heirs in 1835. He took full advantage of both when he rebuilt and expanded his facilities following the fire of St. Roch in 1845. At that time both he and Thomas Oliver gave strips of land to the town so that the streets could be widened to form more of a fire break.[53] The description of the facilities at his double shipyard when it was offered for sale in 1859 gives a clear indication of the stature of its highly respected owner and the scale of his yard. During his career, Munn launched ninety-four sailing ships, and in this regard was surpassed only by Thomas Hamilton Oliver, his neighbour to the west for twenty-five years.

Following Goudie's death, his shipyard, together with his three other lots on Prince Edward street (two on either side of Dorchester Bridge), were bought on speculation by the merchant David Burnet, who kept them rented to shipbuilders until the opportunity for a profitable sale arose.[54] The first occurred a little over a year later, when he disposed of the steam sawmill lot to Henry Caldwell, but within a couple of years Caldwell had given up milling and rented the property in 1834, complete with the mill, to the young shipbuilder Thomas Hamilton Oliver. Oliver converted the mill into a mould loft and spent the first part of his very prolific career there. In 1859, he moved to the adjoining yard to the west which his brothers Edward and James Erskine had bought from Burnet and had occupied for twenty years, and pursued his trade there until 1877.[55] Between them, the three Oliver brothers made a substantial contribution

Figure 69 : *John Goudie's sawmill beside his shipyard, and to the left, John Munn's mould-loft with a steeple. It is probable that a bell hanging in the steeple marked the shipyard hours. Detail from a watercolour by James P. Cockburn, s.d., I–241. Courtesy National Archives, Ottawa, neg. C 40342.*

Figure 70: *Walter Gilley Ray (1820–1893), who after his shipbuilding days at Quebec was named Agent for the Bureau Veritas at Quebec and later at Halifax. Photo courtesy late Reginald Ray.*

Figure 71: *His business card during his shipbuilding days.*

Figure 72: *His business card as a Surveyor for the Bureau Veritas.*

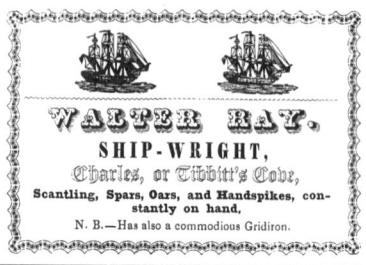

to the overall shipbuilding production of the St. Charles over a period of forty years.

The yard immediately above Dorchester Bridge was bought by John Jeffery in 1836 after a seven-year lease that he and his brother James had negotiated for Sillery Cove fell through. Both a culler and a shipbuilder, John had worked at Diamond Harbour for the timber merchant James Hamilton on a commission basis and had then entered a shipbuilding partnership with his brother that had lasted from 1833 to 1836. When the lease fell through, the partnership was dissolved, and John struck out on his own. Like so many shipbuilders, he ran into serious financial problems, and in 1843 the sailmaker James Hunt lent him the money to buy back his own bankrupt estate. Following this, his son John Jr., who worked for him, became his partner and represented their shipbuilding and shipowning association in Liverpool until 1846, when the death of his father brought him back to Quebec.[56] He gave up the shipyard two years later, and it was rented to a succession of shipbuilders including Pierre V. Valin, Walter G. Ray and William Cotnam.

In 1837, a year after Jeffery acquired his yard, John J. Nesbitt rented the water front lot next to it, buying it outright in 1842. Until 1846, he built almost exclusively for Irish shipowners through their Quebec agent George Holmes Parke and did not lack for work, after which his good name attracted a wider base of different customers. During his eighteen-year career there, he built an average of three ships a year, and like the other shipbuilders ran into his share of financial problems. Although he managed to buy back his yard from the assignees when he was declared bankrupt in 1848, he was unable to weather a second business reversal in 1856 and gave up the shipyard, though

The Shipyards – Location

Figure 73: *Pierre Vincent Valin's shipyard above Dorchester bridge 1866. Photo: Québec - Vues – "La ville du pont de la Saint-Charles, d'après un cliché de Leggo, 1866." Ancienne collection Paul Gouin. courtesy Archives nationales du Québec, BB–7. (detail)*

Figure 74: *Saint Roch and Saint Sauveur following the fire of 1870. Bottom, ship under construction at Baldwin's shipyard; above, the Vacherie timber cove and shipyard site; upper right, the Marine Hospital. Photo by Augustin Leggo, courtesy Archives nationales du Québec, P600–6/GH 273–41.*

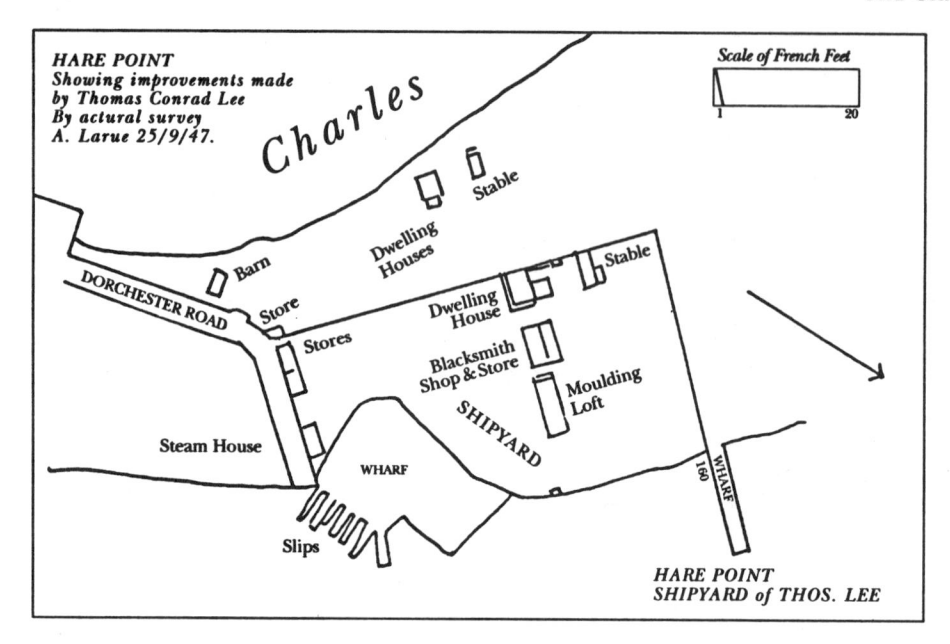

Plan 9: *Thomas H. Lee's Shipyard*
Where James Jeffery and his brothers built throughout the 1840s and made substantial improvements, and Thomas H. Lee had his shipyard after that time. A) shipyard B) wharf C) moulding loft D) blacksmiths' shop and store E) steamhouse F) dwelling house G) stable H) stores. "Showing improvements made by Thomas Conrad Lee." Redrawn from the original by A. Larue 25 September 1847, CA1-27-4, ANQ.

not the property, which he rented to William H. Baldwin.[57] There for the next ten years Baldwin built the quality ships that he had previously built at Cape Cove, but in 1866 when fire once again swept St. Roch and the shipyard was burned to the ground, he moved upriver to the yard that had belonged to his late father-in-law, Thomas Lee, one of several yards on the meanders of the St. Charles.

Beyond Nesbitt's shipyard was the former Jesuit land of the Vacherie,[58] consisting of the Vacherie farm and the peninsula known as Pointe-aux-lièvres, or Hare Point. In 1834, the beach, which served as a timber cove, was divided into two sections. The easterly one was leased by the timber merchant Thomas Conrad Lee from 1837 until 1861, during which time he sub-let it to at least one shipbuilder, William Power.[59] The westerly section became the emplacement of the new Marine Hospital, and a part of it, which was earmarked for the expansion of the hospital and adjoining cemetery, was rented to Andrew Neilson in 1838 to serve as a shipyard. Neilson died two years later, however, and his lease was assumed by T.C. Lee, who began a second career, as a shipbuilder, laying down fourteen ships there during the nine years he occupied it. In 1849, he moved to his own yard that he had let to the Jefferys (see below), subsequently sub-letting the Marine Hospital shipyard to others, including Pierre Valin, William Power and P. G. Labbé.[60]

The yard to which Lee moved, which would become known as "Lee's Shipyard," was immediately to the west of the southern end of the original Dorchester Bridge on Hare Point. Lee, who held the land under lease as a timber cove, had sub-let it in 1839 for ten years to James Jeffery, his brother Richard and son, William Henry, who were partners.[61] Their

The Shipyards – Location

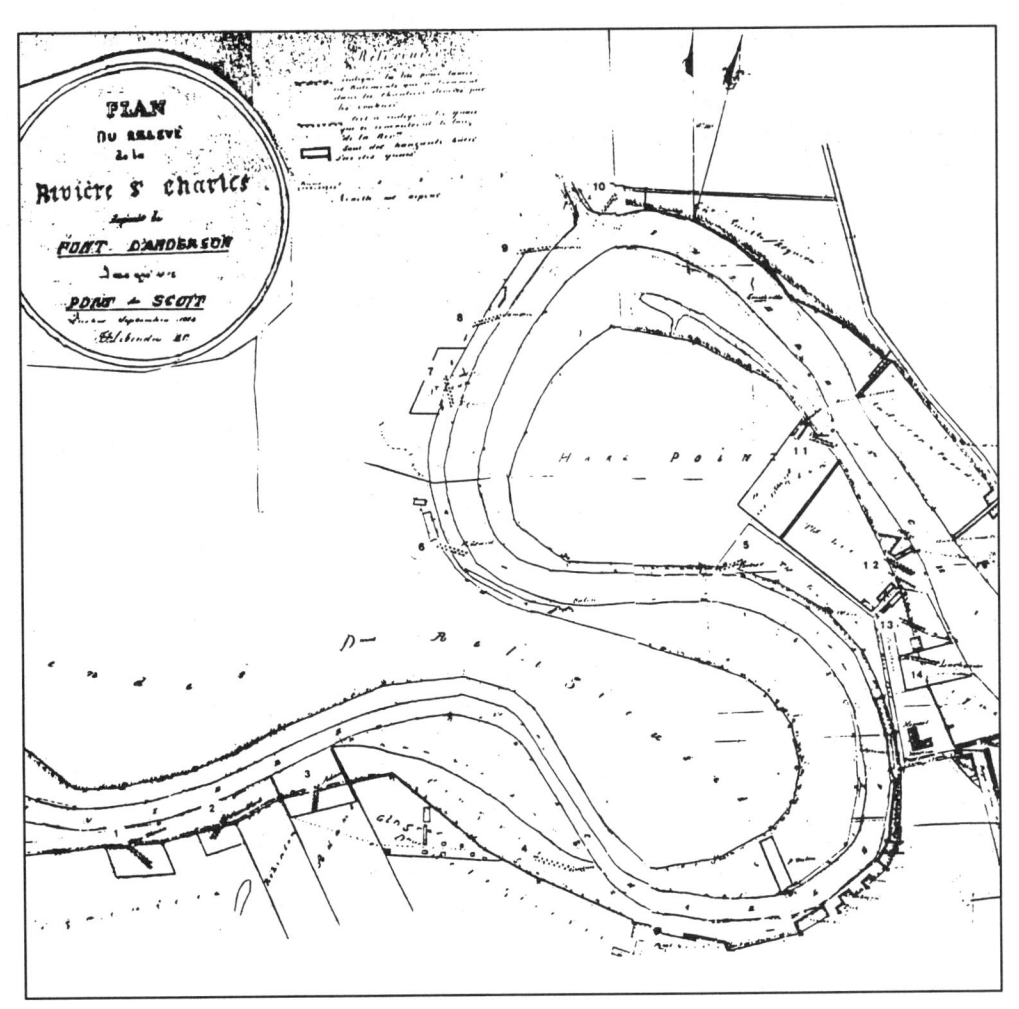

Map 7: *The lower Saint Charles showing the shipbuilding ramps.*
Plan du relevé de la R. St. Chas., depuis le quai Anderson jusqu'au pont de Scott, *Legendre, 1854, PR-123-1854-01, APQ.*

1. Blouin	6. Rosard [Rosa]	11. Valin
2. Standford	7. St. Jean	12. Lee
3. Adam	8. Samson	13. Drolet
4. Gingras	9. Laprise	14. Drolet
5. Fortier	10. Parke	15. Lachance

tenancy of the yard was marred by family quarrels and financial difficulties. A settlement did not reconcile the partners and within two years the association was dissolved.[62] James and Richard continued independently in the trade, but William Henry went into business with his brother-in-law H.J. Noad as merchants and shipping agents. Between them, in various associations, the Jefferys built twenty ships during their ten years at Hare Point. When the Jeffery's lease came to an end in 1849, Thomas Lee moved into the shipyard and laid down another forty-six ships there, including some fine clipper ships built under the supervision of William Power, whom he had hired in the United States. Later Power built nearby on his own account before moving to Kingston.[63]

Beginning in 1850, there were several other yards further upriver, some on land leased from the Augustine Sisters of the General Hospital and some on adjoining properties. A few years later as part of government policy to encourage shipbuilding, the rest of Hare Point, the peninsula of the Vacherie, was sub-divided into eight lots each approximately 350 by 450 feet, which were auctioned off in 1854, though the sales were converted later to leases.

For their part, in leasing land to French Canadian shipbuilders at a low rent, the Augustine Sisters' sought to help them compete in an industry that had until then been largely dominated by anglophones. The man who benefitted most from this was Jean-Elie Gingras, who in 1850 obtained the lot immediately above the Hospital with six arpents of frontage and built over 55,000 tons of shipping there in the course of his thirty-year career, some on his own, some in partnership with one or the other of his sons, and some with F.X. Martineau.[64] Fortunately, launching into the narrow and winding St. Charles does not appear to have been a serious problem for him or the other builders there; in fact, a few ships were built on land even further upstream during the 1850s and 1860s.

Although Hare Point was only sub-divided for shipyard use in 1854, we know that the Jefferys had been building there from 1839, and it appears that Pierre Valin had been on lot number one immediately beyond them since at least 1848. The improvements on the lot were such that he paid £4,000 for it at the auction in 1854. Valin was the first important French Canadian shipbuilder, and this was one of several shipyards at which he built either on his own account or in partnership. He put Léandre Dugal in charge of this yard in 1860, taking him as his partner in its operation. There were no other shipyards on the north side of the point, but there was a sawmill immediately to the west of the Valin and Dugal yard.[65]

Several shipbuilders had yards on the south side of the point, including Narcisse Rosa, who having succeeded in obtaining orders and financing from France, moved his shipyard from across the river in 1862 and set up five building slips on lot number six. Beside him on lot number seven, George Lemelin built six ships between 1861 and 1864, and was followed by Edmund Sewell who laid down four more in 1865 and 1866. The last lot, number eight, was rented by Joseph Trahan, who worked in the early sixties with his father, Edouard. A former apprentice of John Bell, Edouard Trahan was considered "one of the cleverest shipbuilders in the province for many years, and a conscientious and unassuming man," by the shipowner Henry Fry, who financed his construction. But the Trahans did not build there for long, for Edouard died soon after.[66]

This completes the list of shipyards on the south bank of the St. Charles. What a sight they must have been at the height of the shipbuilding industry, and what a pity that it did not occur to artists and photographers to leave a detailed record of them. With few exceptions, the shipyards were only considered an interesting subject when they were lying smoldering following a fire. Nor have civic officials recognized their historical importance. Lee had a street named after him during his lifetime, and on the north bank there is a rue Julien, but the other shipbuilders responsible for the livelihood of so many of the inhabitants have been forgotten. At one time known as St. Charles Street and at another as Wolfe Street, the street on which many of the shipyards stood was eventually named Prince Edward Street. It was called the "rue des chantiers Goudie" by the Curé Signay in his census of the town in 1818, a name that would have served its history far better had it survived.

The North Bank of the Saint Charles River

At the beginning of the nineteenth century, the riverfront of the two seigniories of Notre Dame des Anges and St. Joseph on the north bank of the St. Charles was lined with large farms on which cattle and horses were bred.[67] The villages of the seigniories lay several miles inland. By 1815, some of the beaches were used for timber storage, but the river acted as a natural barrier to industrial development, and except in the area immediately around Robert Dalkin's ropewalk at Beauport, the population was slow to increase. Half a century elapsed from the time Goudie laid down his first ship in St. Roch until shipyards of the north bank began contributing to the port's production.

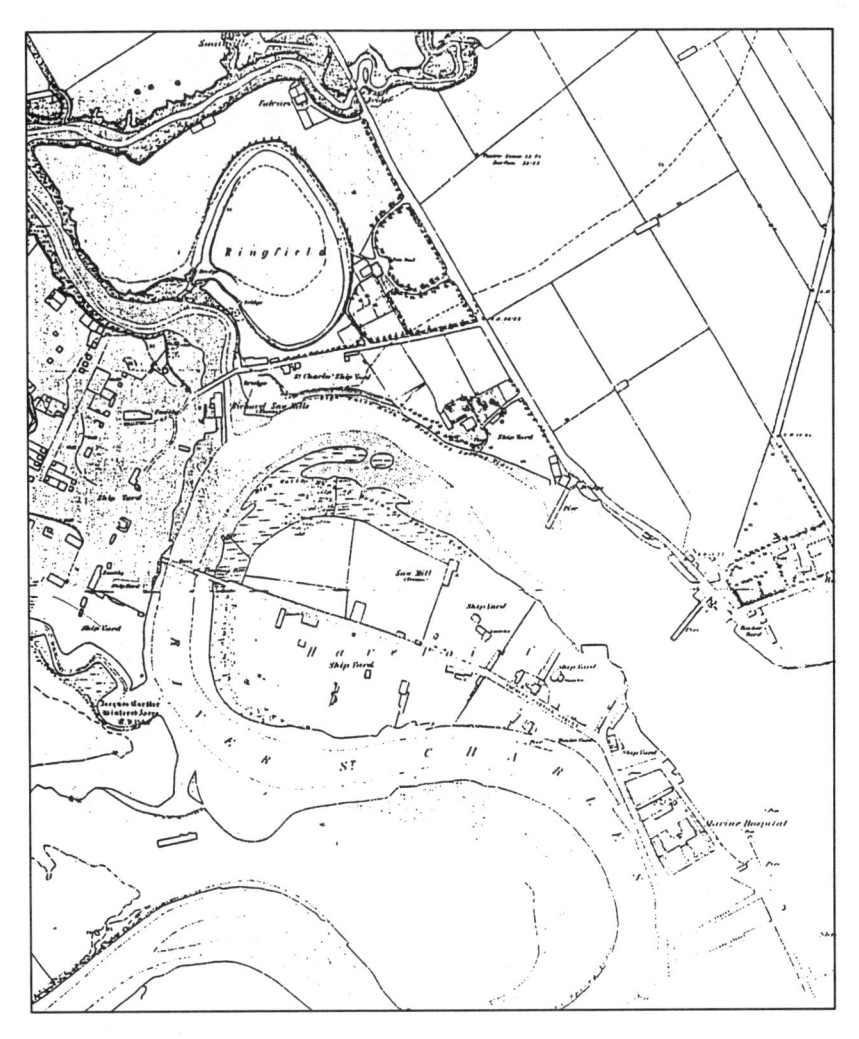

Map 8 : *North Bank of the Saint Charles River*
The shipyards of the north bank of the St. Charles River from (right centre) New Waterford Cove at the river mouth, to a point (bottom centre) on the Pointe-aux-Vaches immediately opposite the laundry of the General Hospital. Part of Fortification Surveys, Fortification Surveys/Quebec/sheet iv(1,2 and 5)/1865-6, NA.

Figure 75: *Ship* Bucephalus, *1197 tons, launched by Jean Lemelin jr from his shipyard on Hare Point, on 16 August, 1854. W. Clealor. Oil. Courtesy Serge Joyal.*

Figure 76: *The upper Saint Charles River with several sailing vessels already masted waiting for their launching. "Village Saint-Sauveur vers 1875"(detail). Photo: L.-Prudent Vallée. Inventaire des oeuvres d'art, Québec vues, S-12, fiche 14813.*

The Irishman Horatio Nelson Jones had established a timber cove and sawmill at the mouth of the St. Charles in 1843 to which he gave the name New Waterford, and like many other timber merchants he reacted in 1849 to the favourable shipping market by establishing a well-equipped shipyard. From this cove, his foreman, William Simons, nephew and namesake of the Greenock shipbuilder, launched thirteen vessels averaging over a thousand tons during the 1850s, but the yard did not survive into the 1860s.[68] His was not the only short-lived shipyard near the mouth of the river, however; others had even shorter lives.

The more successful yards were further upriver, where the local shipbuilding establishment welcomed into its midst at "Smithville" the American clipper captains Lauchlan McKay and Henry Warner. They built there over a period of nine years, from 1863 to 1872, and again in 1876 and 1877. McKay had a considerable reputation as a shipbuilder. He had served in the best yards in the United States, and in 1839 had written the first American book on ship design, *The Practical Shipbuilder*. He and Warner lived in the large old house at the yard with their wives, the Coombe sisters, who owned the property. Together they laid down a total of twenty-nine large and small vessels, many of the smaller ones on contract, but the larger ones to operate themselves. Of three others, launched in 1877, two were on account of a new partnership between McKay and Charles Dix, and the third for Warner alone.

Immediately beside Smithfield was the property known as Ringfield, of which it had once formed part. It belonged to George H. Parke, the agent from 1832 for a number of Irish shipowners, including David Grainger, his brother-in-law and a leading Belfast shipowner. At first Parke contracted for replacements for their fleets with local shipbuilders, but after 1847, when he established the St. Charles shipyard on his

The Shipyards – Location

Figure 78: *The shipbuilder, William Bell's, house on the upper St. Charles or, as it was known locally, the Little River. "The old Bell house near the bridge at St. Sauveur, City of Quebec." National Museums of Canada Photographic Collection, C. Marius Barbeau Collection, neg. 76454.*

Figure 77: *The McKay and Warner shipyard, 1869. Their home is on the left, and close by there are two vessels on the stocks. The sawmill is behind the square-sterned barque, centre, which is being rebuilt. From F.W. Wallace.* In the Wake of the Windships.

property he had ships built there, too. The first year he took the young builder Pierre Valin as his partner, but due to financial difficulties their first vessel was also their last. Valin's successors in the 1850s were Pierre Brunelle, James Nelson, and Alexander and William Parke, while those of the 1860s included Robert Maxwell and Edmund Sewell.[69]

Further upstream a new area became available for shipbuilding in 1850 in the seigneurial farm of Notre-Dame-des-Anges facing the end of Hare Point when thirty arpents of the farm's river frontage were fenced off to be leased to the trade. The three or four yards located there were beside one of the most historically significant places in Canada, where Jacques Cartier anchored and spent the winter of 1534. Although George H. Parke, who rented the northernmost section from 1850 to 1853, was the first to take advantage of the new sub-division, they are mostly associated with William Cotnam, the Samson brothers and Julien and Labbé, all of whom built there for many years. Antoine Saint-Jean, who was granted a ten-year lease, did not build there himself, sub-letting instead to a group consisting of the master ship carpenters M. Laprise and E. Gobeil and the master joiners P. Letarte and F.X. Drouin, who carried on their business under the name Michel Laprise and Company.[70] In 1862, the division of the yards was changed and William Cotnam moved northward from the lot he had rented since 1850 and continued his career until 1868. His yard has a special significance as the site from which Peter Baldwin launched the last square-rigged sailing ship built on the St. Charles, the 792-ton barque *Keewatin* in 1881. The southwesterly yard alongside the St. Michel stream was leased to Theophile St. Jean in 1850, but in 1853 he sub-let the rest of his ten-year term to the Samson brothers. After a new division of the property was made in 1862, there was room for P.G. Labbé to run a shipyard between the Samsons and Cotnam. Many of the ships built in this area were probably planked with wood prepared at E.O. Richard's sawmill on the lot between Cotnam's yard and the Lairet river.

Immediately to the west of these yards was the land belonging to the General Hospital known as the Pointe-des-Vaches, where Pierre Valin built in partnership with Gonzague Vallerand from 1854 to 1856 on the right bank of St. Michael's stream, and then sublet it first to Narcisse Rosa and then to P.V. Valin's father, Toussaint Valin. It was described as having a five hundred foot frontage and being 350 feet deep, with stores, blacksmiths' forge, steamhouse, small house and dependencies, and is shown on Legendre's 1854 map (Map 7).[71]

Finally, we come to a four hundred by two hundred foot lot on the opposite side of the peninsula facing the hospital laundry, which Narcisse Rosa rented from 1857 to 1864 for his first shipyard.[72] This is where he proved himself before moving across the river to Hare Point. A prolific builder, he launched over thirty thousand tons in the twenty-two years he operated on his own account, and must be remembered for his efforts to keep the French market open to Canadian shipbuilders.

Two settlements provided housing for the north bank shipyard workers. In the first half of the nineteenth century, some of Anderson's land on the Canardière was sub-divided to form the village of Hedleyville, or St. Charles Village. Originally intended for those who worked in the timber coves or at the ropewalk, it later sheltered many shipyard workers' families, too. During the last half of the 1860s, the area behind the Stadacona shipyards was sub-divided by Hammond

Gowen and Thomas Bickell to form a community of about 140 families that was probably more completely dependent upon the shipbuilding industry than any other in Quebec. The heads of family listed in the Quebec Directory of 1871 include four shipbuilders, thirty-nine ship carpenters, ten sawyers, sixteen labourers, three blacksmiths, one painter, six joiners, six boatmen, three caulkers, one carter, one watchman and one accountant, as well as various other members of the families and their lodgers, all of whom probably earned their living in the shipyards. Moreover, it was on their custom that the butcher, baker, seven grocers and one sausagemaker, four shoemakers, two dressmakers, two gardeners and the tavern keeper depended. One cannot help wondering how they fared after the last ship was launched on the St. Charles ten years later.

The South Shore of the Saint Lawrence River

The south shore of the St. Lawrence, from the mouth of the Chaudière in St. Romuald to Indian Cove, Lauzon, comes under the jurisdiction of the "Port of Quebec." The whole of this area was given the name Pointe Lévy by Champlain, and later became the lower part of the Seigniory of Lauzon. Today it consists of the newly amalgamated municipality of Lévis-Lauzon, officially "Lévis" to the east of the Etchemin River, and the town of St. Romuald between the Etchemin and the Chaudière.[73]

The central section of this coastline, a solid ledge of rock, falls abruptly into thirty to fifty feet of water and was, as it still is, ideal for launching large ships. At either end are wide sandy beaches, well-suited for use as timber coves. Unlike the north shore, where large tracts belonged to religious institutions, most of the

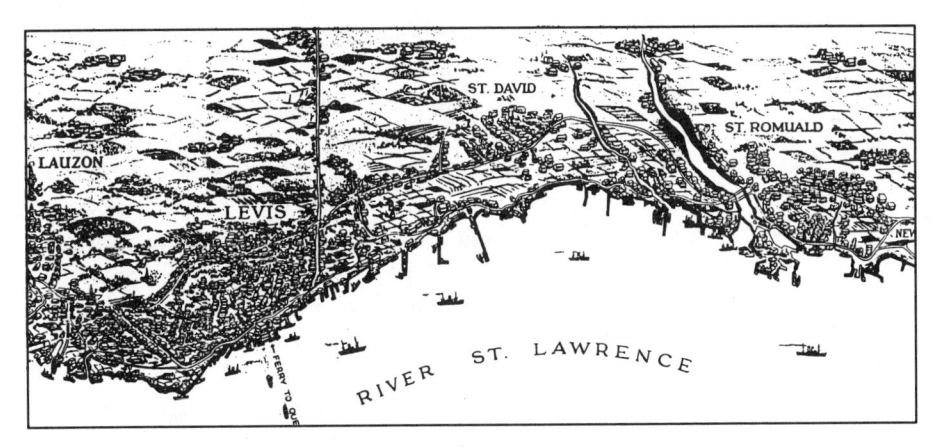

Map 9: *South Shore of the Saint Lawrence Bird's eye view of the south bank of the St. Lawrence in the early twentieth century from the beaches of New Liverpool to the dry docks at Lauzon, showing the centres of population and the extent of the development of this part of the Port of Quebec, attributable in part to the shipbuilding and repairing industry. Topographical Plan of the District of Levis [1927], published by the Chamber of Commerce of the District of Levis in* Industrial District of Levis.

south shore was granted in small concessions. Those who lived along the waterfront looked to the river to earn or supplement their living. Some were fishermen; some mariners; others offered a ferry service by canoe or boat. It was from these individuals that the timber merchants and shipbuilders who built on the south shore had either to lease or buy the beaches on which they carried out their business.

Although several vessels had been built on the south shore for the Hamiltons and other wood merchants before the War of 1812, shipbuilders were slow to set up shipyards. Even in 1825, at the height of the shipping boom, when "the wharf and extensive beach at Point Levy, at the foot of Labadie's Hill, well adapted to the purpose of shipbuilding" were offered for rent,[74] the owner was unable to tempt a shipbuilder across the river. It was not until 1829 that Allison Davie bought some beach lots a short distance to the north of the ferry landing and set up his shipyard, settling his family into their brand new home in 1832.[75] And if no new keels were laid until the 1840s, certainly there was a steady flow of ships that received attention of one kind or another on the patent slip that Davie put into operation in 1832.[76] He died in 1836 without having built any ships at his new shipyard, but his son George, who also devoted his main efforts to ship repairing, laid down five square-rigged sailing ships for the British market and a salvage schooner for his own use between 1853 and 1883. Though not many, they are enough for us to be able to say that tall ships *were* built in the yard, and thus it has its place among the handful of surviving shipyards in North America where tall ships were built, and is indeed the oldest.

Within a few years other shipyards were in operation on the South Shore. In 1839, for instance, the merchants Pickersgill and Tibbits, who were in the shipping business, fitted out a shipyard with a floating dock at Charles' (Tibbit's) Cove to the west of the ferry landing.[77] And in 1843, John Nicholson and William Russell towed their floating dock from the Canoterie and set up beside them. Unfortunately, only four ships had been built by Pickersgill and Tibbit's master shipbuilder Walter G. Ray when their business failed and the yard was closed, but the Nicholson and Russell shipyard survived.

The shipyard property which Nicholson and Russell had patiently acquired a few perches at a time from its various owners had 440 feet of frontage extending to low water.[78] On it they built two 150 foot wharves, a main shipyard building of over 140 feet and an office building; they were ready to expand further when Nicholson passed away in 1845,[79] leaving Russell to complete the yard. Having done so, he enjoyed a twenty-year career during which he built one or two sailing ships each year and his floating dock was kept constantly busy. When he died in 1864, his son Alexander was only thirteen and it was his wife Catherine who had the two vessels left on the stocks completed, after which two more were built. Catherine then leased the yard to two of her husband's former foremen, Thomas Dunn and Etienne Samson, in return for one-third of their profits, while Andrew furthered his education. From 1865 to 1877 Dunn and Samson continued to build the quality vessels for which the Russell yard was known. In 1877 their partnership was dissolved and Catherine entered into a partnership with Etienne Samson alone, which lasted for two years. By then Alexander was ready to take over, and he ran a busy and successful repair yard into the twentieth century.[80]

When wooden sailing ships were no longer built in the port, the rivalry between the Russell and Davie

The Shipyards – Location

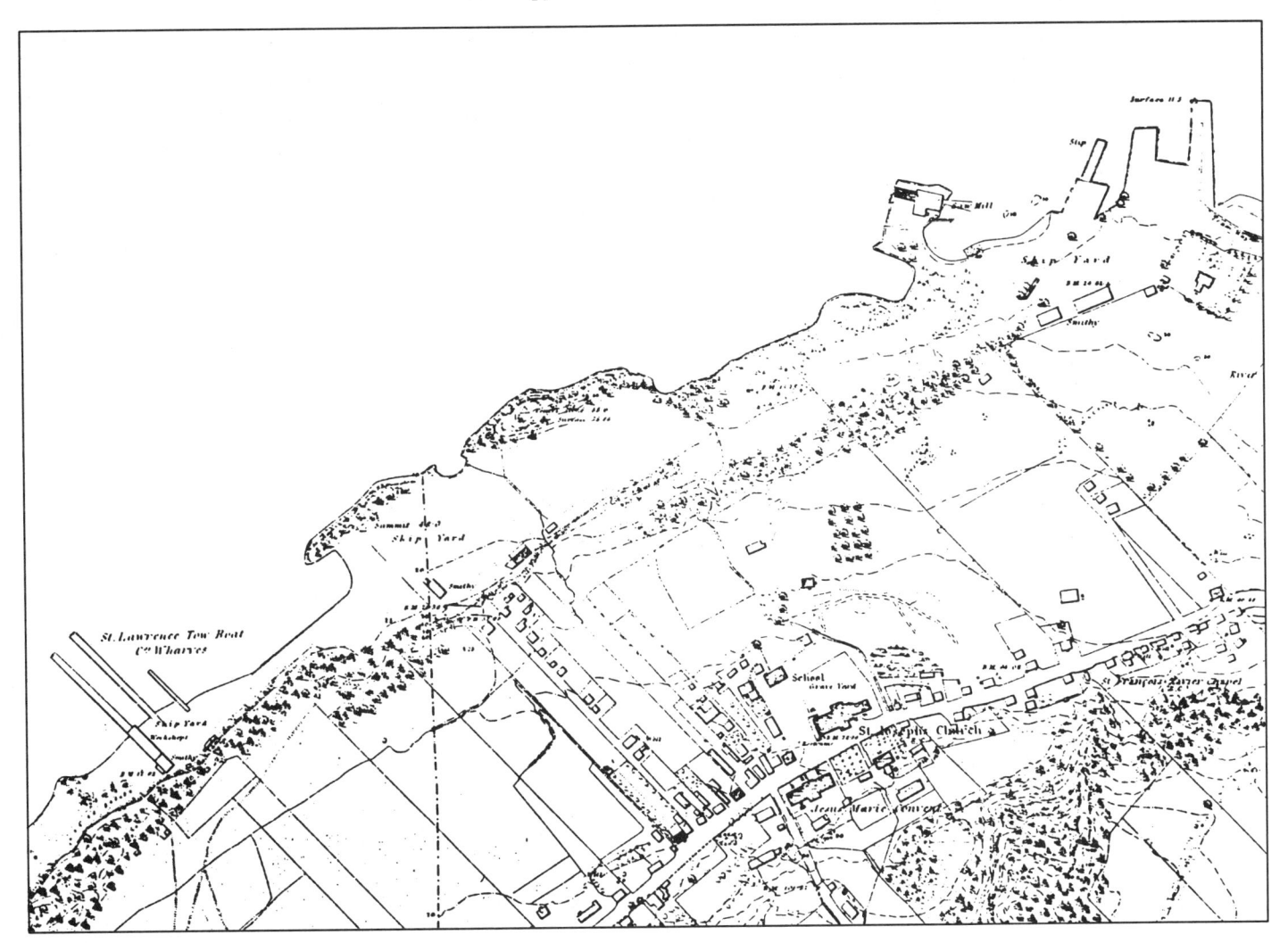

Map 10: *Glenburnie Cove and Lauzon Shipyards*
The northeast section of the south shore with the St. Lawrence Towboat Shipyard, formerly Brunelle's, the adjacent shipyard of Charland & Marquis, and further north in Lauzon, Duncan Patton's shipyard, then under the superintendence of Pierre Brunelle. Part of Fortification Surveys ..., Fortification Surveys/Levis/sheet(iv)3/1864-5, NMC 19705, NA.

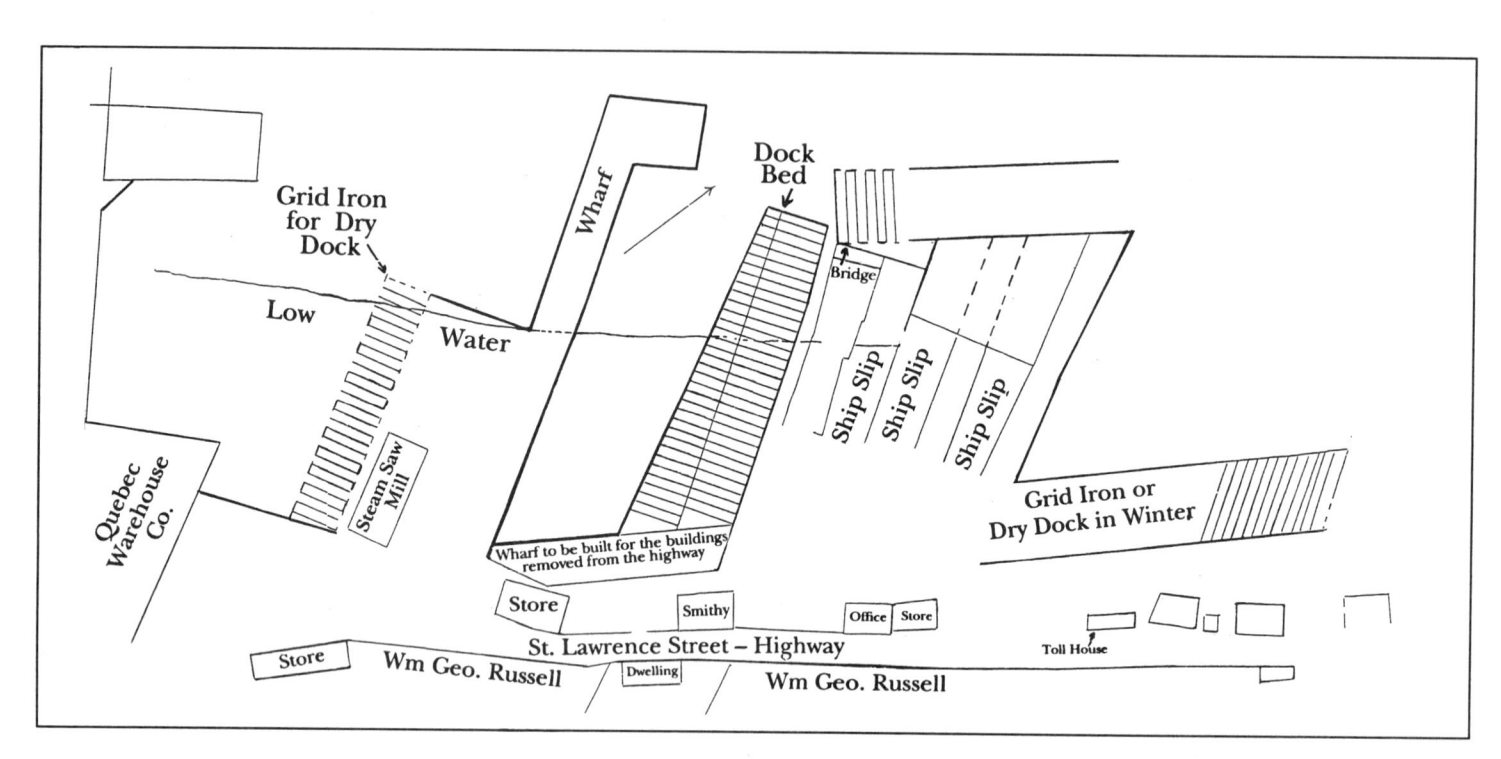

Plan 10: *The Russell Shipyard 1882*
There are now four building slips and two dock beds for the floating docks and two other grid irons. Although a steam sawmill is shown beside the most westerly grid iron, there is no sign of the mould loft, which was probably the building removed from the highway that was to be re-erected on the new wharf to be built (centre). "Wm Geo Russell Esq St Lawrence Ward Levis." Redrawn from the original by Alexander Sewell, Quebec, October 1882, ANQ

yards intensified over both repair work and the few available contracts for steamboats. When the railway was put through his property, Russell, like Davie, was able to use the expropriation award to make improvements, but left his shipyard to become Port Warden and continued working until his death in 1926. The yard is shown as it was in 1882 at the time of the expropriation, with its extensive grid system, two floating dock beds, steam sawmill, new wharves and shipyard buildings, but unknown to Alexander Russell he had built his first and last ship.

To the north of the Davie shipyard the long cove known as Glenburnie stretched all the way to Indian Cove. It was there in 1853 that Pierre Brunelle, who had been John Munn's supervisor of steamboat construction at St. Roch, founded a shipbuilding business with his son Pierre, proudly advertising four years later that they had "just completed a substantial and capacious SLIP... 350 feet in length and 65 feet wide; and ...[could] therefore receive any vessels belonging or trading to this port." It was, they claimed, "the only thing of the sort in Quebec, where Vessels of any length...[could] lie in safety, it being constructed for its whole length on the solid rock." Although according to the Lloyd's Surveyor Brunelle's work was comparable to that done in naval dockyards, their business was unable to weather the tough shipping conditions, and after launching nine fully-rigged ships, their's was one more shipyard that failed. The yard and stock in trade were auctioned in 1862.[81]

The cove was sold to the merchants J.W. Withall and Ross and Company, and the shipyard itself was resold with one arpent of frontage to the St. Lawrence Towboat Company as an upkeep and repair depot. The rest, which had eight arpents of frontage, was

Figure 79 (left): *Allison Davie (1796–1936). Founder of the Davie shipyard at Levis. Photo Moderne.*

Figure 80 (bottom left): *Elizabeth Taylor Davie (1803–1860) Allison Davie's wife, and herself a shipbuilder. Photo Moderne.*

Figure 81 (below): *George Taylor Davie (1828–1907). Founder of the existing Davie shipyard at Lauzon. Photo: courtesy Marie Anne Garneau.*

THE CHARLEY-MAN

The Shipyards – Location

Figure 82: *The Davie shipyard at the time that Elizabeth Davie was in charge. The oldest shipyard in North America, the Davie yard has been acquired by the City of Levis and will become a museum.* A Panoramic View of Quebec from Pointe Lévis. *1847–1849. George Seton. Watercolour over pencil. Courtesy National Archives, Ottawa, neg. C–96432-96434.*

Figure 83: (below left) *Etienne Samson (1815–1893)*. He built in partnership with his brothers on the St. Charles and later with Thomas Dunn and on his own account on the South Shore. Photo from F.W. Wallace, In the Wake of the Windships.

Figure 84: (right) Ship *Emblem, 1151 tons, built by Etienne Samson in 1880.* Courtesy Maritime Museum of the Atlantic, Wallace Collection. MP1.83.1.

Figure 85: (below right) Barque *Cambria, 1252 tons, built by Etienne Samson in 1885, and launched the same day as William Charland's* Cheshire. *Captained by Joseph Elzéar Bernier on her maiden voyage, the* Cambria *left Quebec two days after the* Cheshire *and arrived at Liverpool one tide ahead of her. Both she and the* Emblem *ended their days under the Norwegian flag.* Fonds initial, courtesy Archives nationales du Québec, fonds initial, 070–132.

The Shipyards – Location

Figure 86: (below right) *Alexander Russell (1851–1926), son of the Lévis shipbuilder William G. Russell. Photo Courtesy late Mildred Russell.*

Figure 87: (left) *Alexander Russell's home in Lévis. Archives nationales du Québec, P600–6/PN–287/1.*

Figure 88: (below left) *Vestiges of the Russell shipyard, the heavy timbers still embedded in the beach. Photo Marcil.*

leased and sold a year later to the shipbuilders Guillaume Charland and F.X. Marquis. After working together until 1869, Charland and Marquis divided the land and continued independently, Charland keeping the southern half.[82] In 1875 his son, Guillaume Charland Jr., began building on his own account at the western end of Lauzon, but the sailing ship market did not encourage him to continue for long. F.X. Marquis also soon gave up, sending his last ship down the ways in 1878, but Charland Sr. kept building until 1893. Over a period of thirty years, fifty vessels were built at the Charland and Marquis shipyards and another eight by Guillaume Charland Jr. on his own.

George T. Davie and his brothers had set up a second shipyard in 1866 on a beach lot with three arpents of frontage located immediately to the south of the St. Lawrence Towboat property.[83] This lot, which they bought at a time when many shipyards were without work, appears to have been acquired to serve as a yard for steamboat repairs, but for some reason from at least 1873 it was rented to other shipbuilders. Here Edmund W. Sewell built the 1097-ton ship *Forest Belle* in 1874, followed by the winter steamer *Northern Light*. The latter, which was intended to carry mail, passengers and freight in the winter navigation of the Northumberland Straits and Gulf of St. Lawrence, was also fitted out as a towboat to be able to render assistance to stranded or ice-bound vessels.[84] Her construction was something of a landmark. Her builder, a strong promoter of winter navigation, regarded the undertaking "as the initiatory step towards the greater scheme of winter steam communication between Quebec and Europe."[85] After that, George T. Davie's brother, Allison, ran a repair yard there.

Finally we come to Duncan Patton's timber cove at the western end of Indian Cove, where Brunelle built three ships and a barque for Patton in the period 1863 to 1865 following his own business failure.[86] Today it is contained within the only shipyard still in operation at Quebec, the MIL Davie shipyard at Lauzon, offspring of the original Davie shipyard at Levis and Canada's largest shipyard.

It is no accident that it was on the south shore that shipbuilding survived the change to steel, for metal work and marine engineering flourished there in the nineteenth century, side by side with wooden shipbuilding. Overall, the South Shore shipyards accounted for approximately ten percent of the production of wooden ships in the port, with the Russell and the Charland & Marquis shipyards each building about one-third of the South Shore ships.

Isle of Orleans

Familiarity with the river resulted in many of the inhabitants of the Isle of Orleans becoming mariners and pilots. For those who preferred to work ashore boatbuilding was a popular trade, particularly in the nineteenth century when the construction of so many large sailing ships close-by created a strong demand; even ships built as far away as Kingston are known to have been outfitted with boats from the Isle of Orleans. The boatbuilding shops, in which so many islanders earned their living, were generally set up in small wood-shingled premises not far from the river, but were sometimes under the family roof itself in a section of the house set aside for the purpose.[87]

The Shipyards – Location

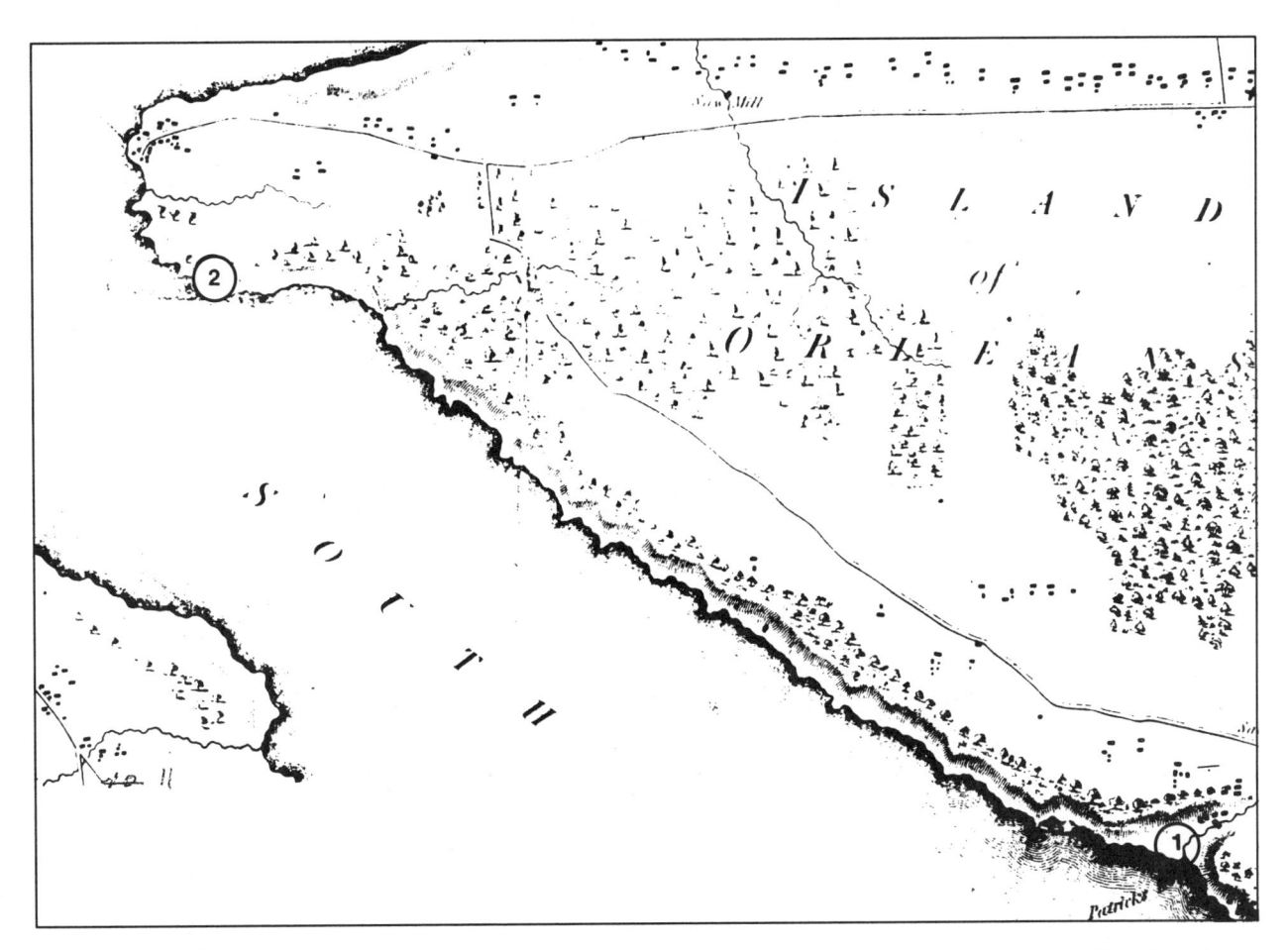

Map 11: *Isle of Orleans*
The southeast part of the island. On the extreme right (1), the deep sheltered cove known as St. Patrick's Hole, which offered safe anchorage to a large number of vessels and where sailing ships were built in the years immediately before the War of 1812 and again in the mid-1820s. Lower cove, top left (2), St. Pierre, now Ste Petronille, where the timber droghers were built, 1823-5. Part of The Map of Quebec and its Environs, John Adams, 1822, published 1826, D-36, 1822, AVQ, neg. 79943, NMC, NA.

Figure 89: Ship Montagnais, *1297 tons, of 1879. She was built by Etienne Samson and Alex Russell in Levis. Courtesy Maritime Museum of the Atlantic, Wallace Collection, MP.1.86.1.*

Once in a while, these men used their boatbuilding skills in the construction of larger craft. There are two sites on the island where vessels are known to have been built during the nineteenth century, though strictly speaking one of them, St. Patrick's Hole, is a little outside the port of Quebec. It seems appropriate, nevertheless to mention it here. It was at St. Patrick's Hole that the timber merchants Benson, Newberry and Copper operated a shipyard between 1810 and 1814. A building described as 100 feet long and forty feet wide, with three pairs of doors and four windows on each side, two pairs of doors at either end, and ten garret windows to throw light on the mould loft floor above, was erected for storage and shops. And five large timber ships of 370 to 570-tons were built under contract there by several teams of shipwrights under the supervision of the master shipbuilder George Taylor before the War of 1812 put an end to their activities. The remaining stocks of shipbuilding materials were auctioned off in 1815. Ten years later, the cove came to life again with the sound of ship carpenters' axes and two, perhaps three, large ships were built by Joseph Barallier before it fell silent again. When the property was offered for sale in 1855 as a "superb shipyard," it was bought by the Lloyd's Surveyor Thomas Menzies and the merchants James Gillespie and James Dean. Menzies used it as a country retreat; Gillespie and Dean's purpose in buying it we do not know, but it seems that it was not a practical location for a shipyard.

The second and more historic site was the anse du Fort at the southwest tip of the island, the large cove where the engineer Chaussegros de Léry had suggested in the 1740s that a dry dock be built. The cove, which was "three arpents eight perches in width at the extremity of its depth, but of greater width along the

Figure 90: *Sharples' and Dobell's Coves, Sillery, Quebec. Booth's raft of Pine Timber with last of Sailing Ships. Photo: John Thomson, 1891. Copy W.B. Edwards.*

Figure 91: *The 861 ton ship* Helen *of 1840, Captain Thomas Hunter, owned by the merchants Sharples and Jones of Liverpool. She was built at the Sharples timber cove at Sillery. Unsigned, undated, believed to be the work of Samuel Walters. Courtesy the Trustees of the National Museums and Galleries on Merseyside.*

Figure 92: The Columbus, *Captn Wm. McKellar. The 3690 ton* Columbus *built in 1824 by Charles Wood on the Isle of Orleans, registered and described at the time as a four-masted ship, but later sometimes referred to as a four-masted barque. She was more than a third longer than the* Prince Albert, *then the largest ship in the British Navy. Drawn on stone by Joseph Harweed, lithograph S. Vowles. Courtesy William S. Scott, with thanks to Mary R. Scott.*

Figure 93: *Plans of the* Columbus. *Presented to the Governor General of Canada, Lord Dalhousie, by Charles Wood. Inscribed in pencil, "Mr Woods and Mr. McKellar told me that she would contain - timber in the ship frame 3000 tons, do. of cargo 7000 tons," signed D. "An Elevation of a Timber Ship built on the Island of Orleans, 1824." Dalhousie Collection, 85.119.22, neg. N–15, 194. Courtesy Nova Scotia Museum, Halifax, with thanks to Marie Elwood.*

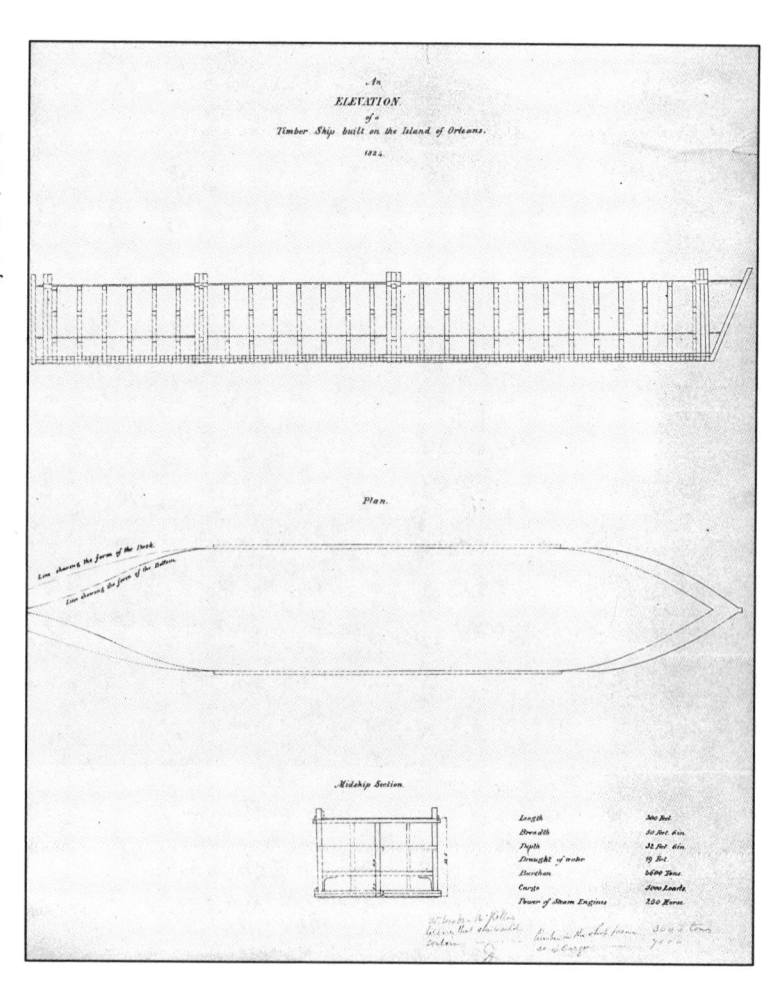

The Shipyards – Location

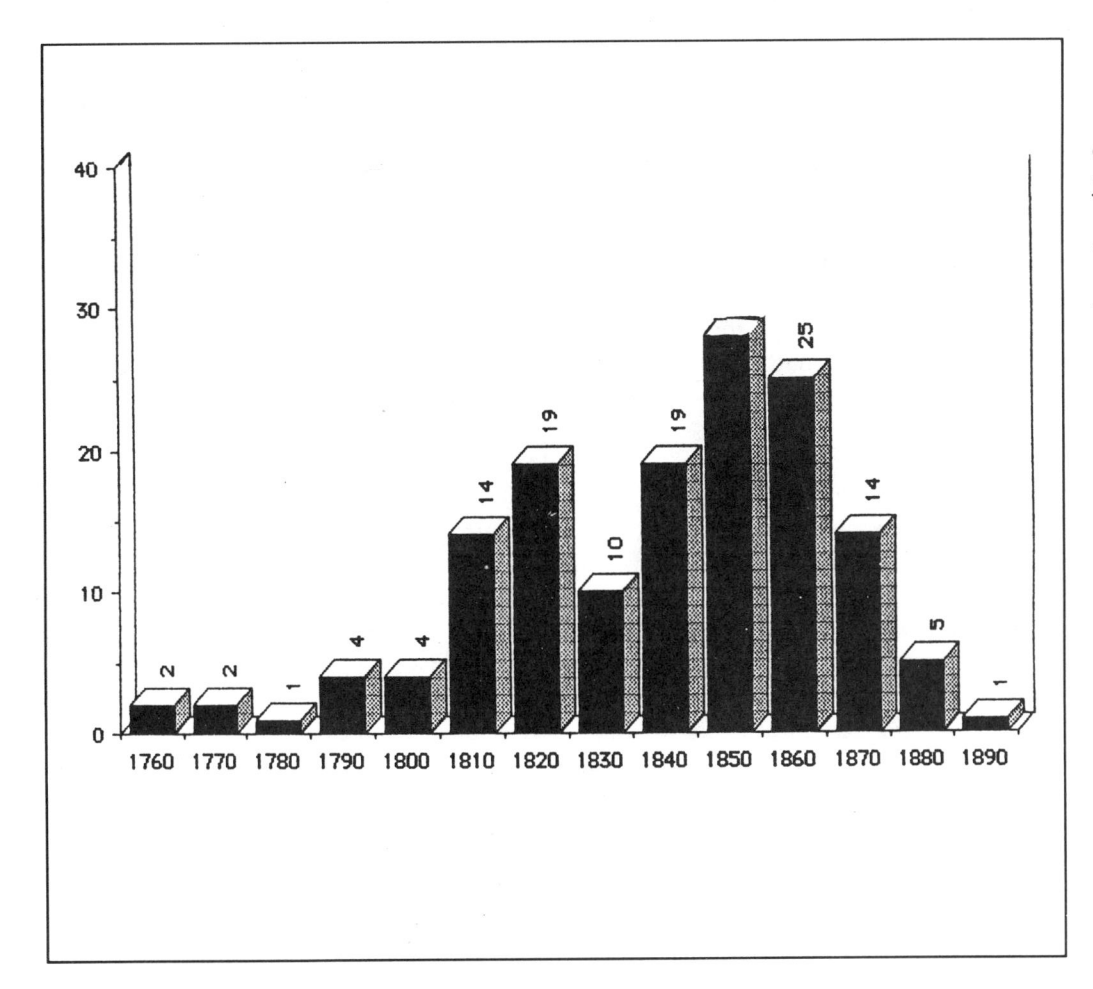

Graph 5: *Maximum number of yards by Decade 1790–1899*

Source: Quebec Shipping Registers, *183-98, 202-3, 267-71, 375-78,* RG12, NA

River St. Lawrence" was leased by Charles Wood for the construction of the two huge timber droghers, the 3690-ton *Columbus* and the 5294-ton *Baron of Renfrew* of 1824 and 1825. Although he was given the right to cut trees and to erect such buildings, pits and works as he might see fit, and in spite of the numerous shipbuilding facilities with which he lined the cove, the construction of no other large ship has been traced to this site.

Summary

We have seen that as the nineteenth century advanced, the centre of activity moved away from the town, first westward to the north shore of the St. Lawrence, then to the St. Charles River, ending up on the south shore of the St. Lawrence.

When the upswing in the economy in the mid-1820s brought work for the shipyards, the main expansion in the base of operations was west of the town on the north shore of the St. Lawrence, the prime promoter being John Saxton Campbell. The number of homes along the "Foulon" increased rapidly from the thirty-six enumerated from Diamond Harbour westward in 1818 to 136 by 1833.

During the 1830s, the focus of the industry swung to the St. Charles River, remaining there until the 1870s, the yards on the south bank of the St. Charles helping in the development of the suburbs of St. Roch, St. Vallier and St. Sauveur. This was the decade in which Allan Gilmour and Company took over Wolfe's Cove, and for the next thirty-four years maintained a first-class shipyard there, while the other yards on the north shore also improved their facilities. Across the river, the south shore began developing its own shipbuilding potential with the laying down of the marine railway at Davie's Yard in Levis.

Although several new yards on the St. Lawrence north shore built sailing ships during the 1840s, it was above all the acceleration of production at the St. Roch shipyards and in particular at Thomas Oliver's yard that sent the figures for Quebec-built tonnage soaring to three times those of the 1830s.

At the beginning of the 1850s, shipbuilding finally moved to the north bank of the St. Charles and helped feed the families of Limoilou and Stadacona from 1850. In 1854, with new yards further upstream on both banks of the St. Charles as well as in Lévis, Lauzon, and even on the Canoterie, the shipyards reached their maximum number of twenty-seven, following which came the decline. In the 1870s, there were only fourteen yards spread thinly through the area. The volume of construction had dropped dramatically on the St. Charles, where in the 1880s only two vessels were built, by P.V. Valin and Peter Baldwin, respectively. Thirteen others were subsequently laid down on the south shore of the St. Lawrence, where the yards remained actively engaged in salvage, repair work, and steamboat construction, and it was there that the wooden sailing ship industry finally came to an end in 1893.[88]

Notes

1. Registers of the Port of Quebec, 1764-1900.
2. Ignotus, "La construction des vaisseaux sous le régime français," *Bulletin des recherches historiques* [hereafter BRH], X, No. 6 (1904), 179-187.
3. Réal Brisson, *La charpenterie navale à Québec sous le Régime français* (Québec, 1983), Annexe B, 217-243.
4. André Charbonneau, Yvon Desloges and Marc Lafrance, *Québec, The Fortified City: From the 17th to the 19th Century* (Ottawa, 1972), 369.
5. The engineer Chaussegros de Léry had proposed that the shipyard be set up opposite the Palace, where the water was 13 feet deep, 3 feet deeper than at the chosen site. Archives nationales, France, Colonies, C^{11}, 78: 335-6, cited by Charbonneau, Desloges and Lafrance, *Québec, The Fortified City...*, 139, n. 166; Jacques Mathieu, *La construction navale royale à Québec 1739-1759* (Québec, 1971), 17-21.
6. Mathieu, *La construction royale*, 102.
7. *Ibid.*, 17-23, 101-3; Brisson, *La charpenterie navale*, 225, 236.
8. Registers of the Port of Quebec, *Lloyd's Register...*, 1767 to 1775.
9. 25 July.
10. An account of claims against Government... William Wilson for James Wilson and Son of Kilmarnock in Scotland for a Ship on the Stocks at Quebec taken to pieces by Government and carried to Lake Champlain and reconstructed there. RG 4, A1 (S Series), p. 7515, (microfilm C-2999), NA.
11. Correspondence, Young to Ryland, 7 June 1798, 3: 468-7, Military C-series, NA, brought to my attention by A.J.H. Richardson.
12. Black's petition, 8 August 1800, ff. 21706-9, Vol. 43, Lower Canada Land Papers [LCLP], RG1 L3L, NA.
13. Howard Chapelle, *The History of the American Sailing Navy* (New York, 1949), 248.
14. Black bought 3,796 sq. ft. from Ralph Gray, 1 February 1792, gr C. Voyer. Although the second of the petitions refers to the "Canoterie," it is clear from the description that the land was on Saint Nicholas Street. Petitions, ff. 21701, 21703, Vol. 43, LCLP, RG1 L3L, NA.
15. Lease, Carleton to Johnston and Purss, 30 July 1770, Reg. Gen. Records, Liber C, Imperial Commission, RG68, Reel C-3921-2, NA.
16. Leases, Johnston and Purss to Munn, 15 February 1794 and 23 April 1795, gr C. Stewart; Milnes to Munn, Reg. Gen. Commissions and Letters Patent, 1: 494, microfilm C-392; At the same time, the blockmaker Thomas Allen petitioned the government for a small piece of the northerly part of the wharf, as Munn required the part of the wharf that Allen had previously held under a sub-lease. LCLP, 30: 16018, RG1, L3L, NA.
17. Leases, Laflèche to Munn, 30 September 1798, gr C. Stewart, 15 September 1801, gr J. Voyer and 23 November 1802 and 7 October 1803, gr Bart Faribault.
18. Indenture of sale of 15 September 1806, Sheriff to Munn, 24 November 1808, filed 22 December 1825, gr A. Campbell.
19. Mathieu, *La construction*, 23.
20. Lease Agnes Munn to David Munn, 1 July 1814, gr A. Campbell; Lease, Agnes Munn to John Munn, 3 March 1815, *ibid*, 11 March, 1815 sale Farrie to Munn gr. Belanger.
21. Sale, Laflèche to Bell, 3 October 1810, gr Faribeault; Lease Drapeau to Bell, 4 November 1817, gr Belanger; Sales Robichaud to Bell, 1 September 1818 and Drapeau to Bell, 28 September 1819.
22. Lease Bell to Nicholson and Russell, 18 May 1837, gr J. Hunt.
23. Sale Descheneaux to Black, 29 July 1801, gr F. Têtu.
24. Sheriff to Brehaut, 14 May 1806, gr Berthelot; Rawson to Brehaut, 4 October 1806, gr F. Têtu; Lease, Brehaut to Taylor, 14 March 1817 and 1818, gr L. McPherson.
25. Lepper to Julien, 18 March 1854, gr N. Bowen.
26. Sales, Vigneau to King and Lacroix to King, 16 September 1789, gr P. Descheneaux; King to Beatson, 24 March 1794, idem. Lease, Munn to Smith, 28 December 1810, gr J. Voyer.

27. Sale Munn to Molson, 25 October 1815, gr J. Voyer. Lease, Molson to Carman, 25 November 1824, gr L. McPherson. Agreement, Carman with creditors, 4 September 1826, gr L. McPherson.
28. According to the lease with Molson's heirs, Oliver was to build out the wharf so that there would be 18 foot of water at low tide, 17 December 1840, gr E. Glackemeyer. In 1845, Oliver sublet the wharf, retaining the right to put three ships at the upper pier in the Spring and two in the Fall, 27 February, gr J. Hossack.
29. The first seems to have been the sale of Spencer Cove, heirs of P. Beatson to H. Usborne, 15 October 1801, gr F. Têtu.
30. The first named after the Ursulines and the second after the Hospitalières who were previous owners, though Cape Cove is described as Anse des Maures in Provost, *Recensement de la Ville de Québec en 1818 par le Curé Joseph Signay*, 90, 157. Both Ottawa Cove North and South were also described as Anse des Mères, see Sale, Fraser to Bonner, 16 November 1835 gr A.A. Parent and Fraser to Petry, 16 November 1835, *ibid.*, also Lease, Petry to Dalkin, 25 January 1852, gr S. Glackemeyer. From 1710 to 1734, the Seminaire ran a fulling mill at the foot of the rivulet that empties into Wolfe's Cove, hence the word "foulon."
31. Lease, Ursulines to Dunière, 15 November 1796, gr J. Planté; Inventory, 15 December 1800, gr C. Voyer; Sale, Dunière to Beatson, 15 March, 1802, gr F. Têtu.
32. Agreements, Duncanson with Crosbie, 6 July 1786, Duncanson with Fairrie, 10 July 1786, and Fairrie with John Black et al, 23 February 1787, gr C. Stewart; launching announcement of, *Alfred*, *Quebec Gazette*, 24 May 1787.
33. Sale, Fraser to Dunière, 21 October 1791, gr C. Voyer.
34. 15 March, 1802, gr F. Têtu; E. Marcil, "Patrick Beatson capitaine et constructeur de navires – Patrick Beatson shipmaster and shipbuilder 1758-1800," *De la voile à la vapeur – From Sail to Steam* (Montréal, 1982), and "Beatson, Patrick," *DCB*, IV, 48-49.

35. Leases Agnes to David Munn, 1 July 1814 and to John Munn, 3 March 1815, Munn to McDonald, 17 March 1824; McDonald and Hows to Labbé, 30 July 1825; Engagement Denoyé, 9 May 1825; Lease, McDonald and Hows to Henley, 7 June 1824; Contract, McDonald and Hows with Clint, 5 July 1825; Young with Dalkin, 13 March 1827, all gr A. Campbell; Viger and Ernst with Thompson, 19 June 1827, gr L. McPherson; Lease, Hamilton to Jeffery, 26 April 1831, gr A. Campbell; Lease Munn to Farlin, 5 April 1836, *ibid.*; Discharge, Agnes Munn to Quebec Fire Assurance Co., 28 November 1827, gr A. Campbell.
36. Lease, Floating Dock Company to Colford, 14 March 1838, gr J. Childs; Sale, Munn to Forsyth, 21 January 1839; Letters Patent, 5 June 1839; Cession, Forsyth to Lampson, 2 December 1840, gr E.B. Lindsay.
37. Sale, Fraser to Lampson, 4 November 1840 gr AA Parent; Lease, Lampson to Atkinson, Usborne and Company, 1 May 1841, gr A. Campbell.
38. Lease, Lampson to Vaughan, 25 August 1847, gr A. Lemoine; Announcement, Nesbitt, *Morning Chronicle*, 12 May 1857; Lease, Turner to Blais, 20 February 1856, gr P. Shaw.
39. See also, Contract, Valin with Henry, 7 December 1844; Lease, Lampson to Vaughan, 25 August 1847; Announcement, Nesbitt, *Morning Chronicle*, 12 May 1857; Lease, Turner to Blais, 20 February 1856, gr P. Shaw.
40. 17 August 1815, gr J. Belanger; Lease, Hôtel Dieu with Trahan and Martin, 24 December 1819, gr Boudreault. Because the builders of a number of vessels of this period have not been identified, it is not known whether Trahan built other vessels with either Viger or Martin.
41. Lease, Hôtel Dieu with Campbell, 7 March 1825, gr J. Belanger; Lease, Campbell, Campbell with Fernie, 11 March 1825, gr C. Huot; Private agreement between Campbell and Black of 22 April 1825, forming part of the agreement of 8 April 1831, gr F.X. Garneau; Agreement, Black with Campbell, 8 April 1831, *ibid.*; Concession, 20

August 1832, gr A.A. Parent, confirmed by Letters Patent, 11 February 1833; Petition to Government, 25 March 1829, RG1 L3L, 55: 27913-16, NA; Campbell and Vivian, his wife, to Black, 24 January 1837, gr F.X. Garneau; Lease, Black to Baldwin, 6 November 1846, gr A. Campbell; Lease, Baldwin to Jobin, 26 October 1849, gr J. Hossack; Lease Jobin to Jeffery, 6 April 1850, gr Saxton Campbell; Co-partnership, Baldwin with Dinning, 27 March 1851 (effective 1 April 1850), gr J. Clapham.

42. Lease, Heirs Black to Black and Shaw, 14 August 1858, gr W.D. Campbell; Partnership, Jas and H. Dinning, 1 June 1858, gr J. Clapham; Lease, Heirs Black to J. and H. Dinning, 29 April 1859, gr A. Campbell; Announcement of expiration of partnership of H. and Jas. Dinning, *Morning Chronicle*, 30 November 1865.

43. Contract, Lotbinière Bondfield, 14 September 1770. When P. Beatson bought Powell Place, the deed of sale referred to "the Chatellenie de Coulonge, commonly called Le Foulon or otherwise Wolfe's Cove and now known as Powell Place." Powell to Beatson, 31 October 1796, gr C. Stewart. Yet, there was obviously some confusion, because when Beatson's inventory was taken 4 years later, it was said that there were "at l'Ance des Mères, Wolfe's Cove, Powell Place and Pointe au Piseau more oak timber, pine logs, oars, spars & handspikes lying in the snow," 15 December 1800, gr C. Voyer. Beatson's heirs sold Spencer Cove to H. Usborne, Deed of Sale, 15 October 1801, gr F. Têtu.

44. *Statutes of Canada*, 48 Geo. 3, c. 27, 17.

45. Sale, 12 November 1810, gr J. Planté; Lease and covenant of co-partnership, 21 October 1812, gr J. Belanger; Notification, Grant and Greenshields to Sheppard and Campbell, 29 October 1829, gr L. McPherson.

46. Sale, Grant, per Paterson and Greenshields to Gilmour, 24 October 1834, gr L. McPherson; David S. MacMillan, "Gilmour, Allan," *DCB*, 11: 305; Sale, Gilmour to Roche, 15 October 1868, gr W. Bignell; Notice of Sale, *Morning Chronicle*, 21 April 1868.

47. Lease, Patterson to McAlpine and Richardson, 14 November 1823, gr A Campbell; Lease Patterson to Wright, 10 December 1825, gr A. Campbell; Contract, Picard and Lapointe with Wright, 22 November 1825, gr J. Belanger; Assignment to creditors, Wright, 12 October 1826, gr A. Campbell; e.g., see report of launching by Milling, *Quebec Mercury*, 27 June, 1835.

48. Desistment, Behan and Kenny vs. Morrison, 22 September 1810; Shipbuilding contract, Chamberlain et al with Atkinson, 16 November 1824, gr A. Campbell; Report of the launching of a vessel of upwards of 300 tons from Mr Atkinson's shipyard at Cap Rouge, *Quebec Gazette*, 8 June 1826; *ibid.*, 24 June 1830.

49. The Seigneur, William Grant, bought the eighty-six arpents that comprised the seigniory from Magdeleine Josephte Hiché, Dame Ignace Perthuis, daughter and sole heir of Henri Hiché, by private contract registered 24 June 1766, English Register A, p.277. Letters Patent were granted to the trustees of his estate to allow the beach to be reclaimed along the continuation of Saint Roch Street on 5 March 1811, compare maps 5 and 6.

50. "Les dénombrements de Québec faits en 1792, 1795, 1798 et 1805 par le curé Joseph-Octave Plessis," *RAPQ, 1948-49*, 156, 212; H. Provost, *Recensement de la Ville de Québec en 1818 par le curé Joseph Signay*, 278.

51. Goudie's lot measured 240 feet on the southwest side and 156 feet on the northeast, in all 60,232 sq. ft. in area. According to the contract of sale, Goudie had been in possession since the summer of 1802 following Grant's verbal promise to sell, and had built a house, hangard, forge and other buildings, Grant to Goudie, 4 March 1807, gr J. Belanger. Munn's land was originally conceded in five 50' lots to three different parties, from whom they were bought by John Black, who in turn sold them to Munn. Grant to Hall, 26 October 1801, Grant to Campbell(2), 22 December 1801, Grant to Anderson(2), 24 December 1801; Campbell to Black, 18 October 1802, Hall to Black, and Campbell to Black, 30 April 1803; Black to Munn, 12 May 1803, gr F. Têtu.

52. Goudie's inventory, 10 January 1825, gr T. Lee; Records of the Superior Court, Quebec Bank v. Jane Black, S.C. 909 in 1828, ANQ.
53. Letter, Munn to Inspecteur des chemins, 21 October 1845, referring to his proposal of 8 August 1845, Lettres reçues, Reg. 1, 1840-46, Travaux Publiques, Les Archives de la Ville de Québec [hereafter HVQ].
54. Except for those he owned to the south of Munn's shipyard, which Munn bought. Sheriff to Burnett, 27 June 1829 (Quebec Bank v. Jane Goudie, sale took place 3 November 1828); Sale, Burnett to Caldwell, 18 February 1830, gr L. McPherson; Lease, 5 August 1834, gr L. McPherson; unsigned deed of sale Burnett to Lampson, 2 December 1840, gr E.B. Lindsay; Lease, Lampson to Oliver, 15 March 1839; Sale, Burnett to Oliver, 6 May 1841, gr L. Provost. Auction purchase of land 180' wide by David Burnett, 27 June 1829; Lease Burnett to H. Caldwell, 18 February 1830, gr L. McPherson; Lease, Lampson to Oliver 15 March 1839, gr E.B. Lindsay; Sale, Burnett to Oliver, 6 May 1841, gr L. Provost.
55. Sale, Burnett to Oliver, 6 May 1841, gr L. Provost; Sheriff to Oliver, 15 December 1853 and Oliver to Oliver, 31 December 1853, gr J. Clapham and 12 December 1864, gr W.D. Campbell
56. Engagement Jeffery to Hamilton, 9 December 1829, gr L. McPherson; Sale, Burnett to Jeffery, 22 August 1836, gr L. McPherson; *Quebec Mercury*, 25 July 1842, announcement of auction; Sale, Assignees of Jeffery bankrupt estate to John Jeffery jr, 9 August 1842, gr A. Campbell; Agreement, Hunt and Jeffery, 16 May 1843, gr L. McPherson; Release Hunt to Jeffery, 27 May 1844, *ibid*; Partnership Agreement, John Jeffery and Son, 9 October 1845, *ibid*; *Quebec Mercury*, 14 June 1849, announcement of bankruptcy.
57. The shipyard was held by Nesbitt under verbal loan from David Burnett until 1842, as stated in Sale, Burnett to Nesbitt, 24 February 1842, gr Ed. Glackemeyer; Sale, Nesbitt to Baldwin, 26 April 1856, gr J. Clapham.
58. Administered by the Commissioner of the Jesuit Estates.
59. Eleven-year lease from 1 October 1848, Jesuit Estates to Lee, 24 May 1849 and deep water lot opposite, 7 March 1851, gr Ls. Panet.
60. Leases, Dubord from Parish of St. Roch, 200 x 88 feet, 3 September 1836, gr A.B. Sirois; Lease, Dubord from Marine Hospital, 21, 136 feet of land, obliged him to build a wharf there, 14 October 1837, *ibid*; Transfer of leases, Dubord to Neilson, 12 September 1838, *ibid*.
61. Lease, Lee to Jeffery, 9 July 1839, gr A. Campbell; Co-partnership, Jas, Richard and Wm Henry Jeffery, 23 September 1839, gr J. Hunt; Agreement with creditors, 1 May 1842, gr A. Campbell; Assignment and agreement, Jas. and Wm. Henry and Richard Jeffery, 26 January 1844, gr L. McPherson.
62. The difficulties were resolved in 1842 when their creditors agreed to accept 6/8d in the pound within three months or 10/- in instalments. 1 May 1842, gr A. Campbell; Protest, Shaw, Jeffery and Co. v. Jas Jeffery, 19 July 1848, gr E. Glackemeyer; Protest, Jas. Jeffery vs. Richard Jeffery and John Shaw, 18 May 1849, gr A. Campbell.
63. Advertisement, Wm. Power, marine architect, *Quebec Gazette*, 1 November 1856; Hypothecation of a vessel (under construction on land between Dorchester Street and the Marine Hospital), Powers to Stafford, 7 January 1857, gr E. Lindsay; James Lemoine, *Quebec Past and Present*, 439; H.I. Chapelle, *National Watercraft Collection*, (Washington, D.C., 1960), 60.
64. *A Cyclopaedia of Canadian Biography*, Jean-Elie Gingras, 660; 8 July 1840, gr J. Clapham; Act of Union of Creditors, 28 September 1858; Ls Labbé is described as the maternal uncle of Gingras' children in an account filed 23 November 1859, gr E. Glackemeyer; Partnership, Gingras with Gingras, 22 December 1856, gr A. Campbell; Partnership, Gingras with Gingras, 5 December 1878, gr S. Glackemeyer and Gingras with Martineau, 30 September 1879, *ibid*; decision to lease six arps to Gingras for £30 per annum, 3 December 1850, p. 71,

Délibérations du Chapitre, 1821-1858, 13.3.2, 1.8.3, HGQ, and subsequent documents.
65. Contract, Valin with Atkinson, 23 June 1849, gr A. Campbell; Partnership, Valin with Dugal, 11 May 1860, gr W.D. Campbell.
66. Leases from Jesuit Estates, P. Valin, 23 February 1865, gr L. Panet; Narcisse Rosa, 8 May 1862 and 8 April 1865, *ibid.*; George Lemelin 30 May 1865, *ibid.*; Sewell from Lemelin, 6 September 1865 and 21 July 1866, gr W.D. Campbell; Joseph Trahan, 6 April 1865; Apprenticeship, 2 March 1829, gr E.B. Lindsay; Henry Fry, "Reminiscences," 29, 31.
67. When a nine year joint lease was granted on the Farm of Notre Dame des Anges to Anderson and Smith by the Com. for the Jesuit estates, 27 April 1811, gr R. Lelièvre, Smith already was in possession of the land to the northeast of it. Afterwards, the farm continued to be rented by Chas. Smith, Lease, 4 May 1820, gr A. Campbell, who also leased Hare Point, and then by Thornton R. Smith until 1856, when the lease was obtained by John Campbell. Ten years later, the property had been acquired by Thos. Bickell and Hammond Gowen.
68. Power of Attorney, Jones to Simons, 22 February 1858, gr J. Clapham; Deed of Composition, Jones to creditors, 23 September 1852, *ibid.*; Declaration, H.N. Jones, 21 March 1859, *ibid.*
69. The land belonged to George Holmes Parke's wife, Annie Smith, according to her marriage contract. See Assignment, Parke to Grainger, 14 December 1848, gr W. Bignell; Obligation and Mortgage, Valin to City Bank, 12 February 1848, gr L. McPherson; Contract, Maxwell with Stevenson, 7 September 1863, and Sewell with Stevenson, 27 April 1864, gr S. Glackemeyer.
70. Lease Smith to St. Jean, 19 May 1854, gr A.B. Sirois; Lease, St. Jean to Letarte et al, 22 May 1854, gr G. Guay. The shipyard equipment sold by St. Jean at this time, i.e., 1 cabestan, 2 grosses poulies, 8 douzaine de bouches, 6 palans blancs, 4 pièces à lit de vaisseaux, etc., may have been brought to the yard from Pointe aux Trembles, where St. Jean had been building.
71. Délibérations du Chapître, 1821-1858, 17 November 1852, HGQ; Hospital to Valin and Vallerand, 3 April 1854, gr Chas Parent, (Délibérations du Chapître, 28 March 1854, p. 91, HGQ); Lease, Valin to Rosa, 14 January 1857, gr A. Campbell; Dissolution de Société, Valin and Vallerand, 12 March 1860; lease, HG to Valin and Vallerand, 8 September 1863, gr Falardeau; Sub-lease Vallerand to Valin, 8 October 1863, gr S. Glackemeyer.
72. Délibérations du Chapître, 17 July 1857, p. 125 and lease, Hôpital Général to Rosa, 16 September 1863, gr Falardeau. The yard measured 400 by 200 feet according to the first, and a little larger according to the second.
73. "Pointe Lévy" was also used to designate the point of land where the Lorne Dry Dock was built. "Point Levy Cove" was the name given to the cove immediately to the west of Labadie Hill.
74. *Quebec Gazette*, 8 November 1825.
75. Sale, Carrier to Davie, 2 December 1829, gr L. McPherson; Sale, Thomson to Davie, 28 December 1830, gr L. Panet; Confirmation of titles, King's Bench, 17 April 1830 and 20 June 1831.
76. Inventory of Allison Davie's property, 19 July 1836, gr L. McPherson, in which it is stated that the land at Lévis was bought to carry out the business of shipbuilding and repairing, and particularly for setting up a Patent Slip.
77. Bourassa to Charles, 26 January and Samson to Charles, 3 February 1810, gr F. Têtu; Samson to Charles, 27 March 1810, gr J. Voyer (the Cove appears to have been known as New Wicklow Cove at that time); Assignment, Tibbits to Pickersgill, 11 December 1847, gr L. McPherson; Lease, Samson and Son to Tibbits, 21 November 1839, gr L. McPherson.
78. Sales, twenty-two perches and 16 ft. in all, Guenard(1) and Rodrigue(1) to Nicholson and Russell, 13 February 1843, gr J. Hunt; Nadeau to Nicholson and Russell, 14 February and 22 November 1843, 9 March(2) 1844, and

Nadeau and Ruel to Nicholson and Russell, 15 April 1844, idem.
79. This includes three vessels launched under his widow's name in 1864 and 65, the last named after him, the 1264 ton ship *W.G. Russell.*
80. Lease, Morrison to Dunn and Samson, 26 November 1868; Dissolution of partnership, Samson and Dunn, 5 November 1877; Co-partnership and Dissolution of Partnership, Morrison and Samson, 8 January 1878 and 20 November 1879, gr Austin; RPQ 5/1879.
81. *Morning Chronicle,* 11 September, 1862.
82. Sales, Lecours to Brunelle, 29 October 1853, gr S. Glackemeyer, and Montmigny to Brunelle, 13 August 1855, gr F.H. Guay. Sale, Brunelle to Withall, 23 May 1863, gr S. Glackemeyer; Lease, Withall to Charland and Marquis, 18 August 1863, *ibid.*; Sale, Withall to Charland and Marquis, 28 September 1866, *ibid.*; Division of property, Charland and Marquis, 16 November 1869, gr S. Glackemeyer.
83. Sale, Benson to Davie brothers, 17 September 1863, gr W.D. Campbell.
84. Sale, Sewell to de Wolf and Powell, 17 September 1873, gr S. Glackemeyer; Contract, Minister of Marine and Fisheries with Sewell, 15 May 1876, gr W.D. Campbell.
85. *Canadian Illustrated News,* 2 December 1876.
86. *Morning Chronicle,* 29 May 1865.
87. David Gosselin, *Figures d'hier et d'aujourd'hui, à travers St. Laurent, I.O.* (Québec, 1919).
88. The lesser yards that have been left out will be found in the complete list of shipyards, Appendix D, in which all yards with known locations are included.

CHAPTER 5
The Shipyards—Facilities

When the shipwright Matthew Reed stated in 1811 that he had counted sixteen shipyards as he sailed up the Saint Lawrence, he felt confident that he had spotted them all.[1] They were easy to pick out with their tell-tale slips leading down to the water, large curved timbers strewn around the construction and pairs of tall sawyers' trestles. If he had made the journey forty or fifty years later, many of the out-of-town sites would have looked much the same, but he would certainly have noticed a difference in Quebec, where the yards had grown both in numbers and size in keeping with the growth of the industry. Because the ship repairing business was flourishing, the special facilities that had been added to many of them were strongly in evidence. Nevertheless, the basic shipbuilding yard was largely unchanged.

The Building Slip

The fundamental requirement for a shipyard was a gently sloping beach where a slip could be built that was long enough for a vessel to gain enough momentum on launching so as not to get stuck on the ways. Ideally the length of the slip above the high-water-mark was one and a half times the vessel's keel, with room for a staging around the construction and space alongside for handling and hoisting materials. Increases in the size of vessels and consequently in the length of their keels brought a corresponding one hundred percent increase in the length of the slip; where a 150-foot slip was ample for the sailing ships built at Quebec in the 1790s, those of the 1850s with two hundred-foot keels required a slip three hundred-feet long. If a beach did not allow the launching of vessels in the traditional manner stern first, it was possible to lay the keel blocks along it and launch the vessel broadside, provided that the river frontage was sufficient and suitably oriented. The launching ways, placed at right angles to the keel, were then considerably shorter and steeper. On account of the river's narrow winding channel, many shipbuilders on the Saint Charles River laid their building ways obliquely to the river to take advantage of the deepest parts, launching their vessels at the highest tides.

The slip required a firm and even foundation for the keel blocks, which were sometimes dogged to "grounds" or bed logs in rows parallel to the river which were in turn dogged to piles driven into the beach. Although it was possible to alter the angle of the slip in laying the blocks, it was preferable to begin with a suitable slope. It was also necessary for the river bed at the foot of the slip to be cleared of rocks and debris and for the water to be deep enough over a sufficient distance for the vessel not to run aground before it was

Figure 94: *The ship* Shannon, *1155 tons, just before launching at the F.-X. Marquis shipyard at Lauzon, with most of the shores removed. She was named after the British frigate that captured the US frigate* Chesapeake *off Boston in 1813. Photo from F.W. Wallace,* In the Wake of the Windships, *GH 1070–90, courtesy Archives nationales du Québec.*

restrained. Special care taken in preparing the site was amply repaid at the time of launching.

A row of upright poles or bare tree trunks planted in the ground were used both to attach the shores supporting the vessel and to erect the staging used by the gangs of plankers, borers, caulkers, painters and others as they completed their work. In addition, wide sloping gangways were set up as needed to provide the required access.

Grid Irons

Once a ship had been launched, special facilities were needed for any work that had to be done to the hull below the water level. Traditionally, ships were heeled over on one or other side on the beach and the work was carried out between tides. This was far from satisfactory for several reasons: the vessel had to be unloaded to lessen the strain on the hull; only one side of the hull could be worked on at a time; the hull had to be made watertight each time the tide came in or suffer a soaking twice daily and unfinished work had to wait for the tide to recede again to be resumed. An improvement to this method was the use of a grid iron or tidal grid, a series of bed logs lying parallel to the river crossed with other heavy timbers onto which a vessel could be floated at high tide to be shored up and worked on. While grid irons did not allow repairs to be carried on around the clock, both sides were exposed at the same time and they were practical for minor repairs and inspections. It was, and in many places remains, a widely used expedient, particularly for smaller vessels such as schooners, about which Basil Greenhill wrote in 1968 "most minor repairs on vessels are made on grids to this day."[2] Figure 88, page

145 shows a part of the two hundred foot long Russell grid at Levis, where the huge timbers are still imbedded in the beach.

Nineteenth-century shipyards at Quebec that were equipped with grids include Diamond Harbour, Cape Cove, Wolfe's Cove (322 feet long) and the Charland and Marquis yard at Lauzon, whose slip was built in 1857 by the shipbuilder Pierre Brunelle. "The slip," he advertised,

is 350 feet in length and 65 feet wide; and can therefore receive any vessels belonging to or trading in this port. As it is the only thing of the sort in Quebec, where Vessels of any length can lie in safety, it being constructed for its whole length on the solid rock; Vessels can undergo repairs without the slightest risk of straining or deranging their sheer.[3]

Drydocking Facilities

In many of the Quebec shipyards salvage and repair work was undertaken as well as new construction, and for many years it was carried out without the benefit of special facilities. The damaged vessel was careened or shored up on the beach in the old inefficient manner. Ships that were surveyed at Quebec in 1817, for example, were variously described as "lying on the ground alongside Messrs Patterson & Mure's wharf," "lying on blocks (or 'lying on a platform of planks') at the Cul de Sac," or "lying on her larboard bilge on the ground at Diamond Harbour."[4] It was not that the use of dry docks was unknown. The first dry dock was built in Portsmouth by Henry VII in 1495, and was followed in the seventeenth century by others in British and Continental European ports.

Figure 95: *This old hulk, possibly at the Beatson shipyard on the River Thames, serves a new purpose after its days at sea were over, as the Rotherhithe Floating Dock. Docks such as these were the forerunners of Quebec's wooden floating docks. Drawn by L. Francia. Engraved by J.C. Allen, published 1829 by W.B. Cooke. 071 515 1162. Courtesy Museum in Dockland Project, London, with thanks to Robert Aspinall.*

But dry docks were expensive to build, and with no earth-moving machinery to help dig out the huge basin, often involved brutally hard work. Though the important powers considered them essential for the maintenance of their navies, even the United States was without one as late as in 1827. A committee of experts there deplored the fact that their country presented "the only instance existing of a great commercial people, destitute of dry docks for building, coppering, examining, cleaning and repairing their national and commercial marine." American merchants, it stated, were "sometimes compelled to send their vessels to the dry docks of Europe... employing the shipbuilders of foreign, and sometimes hostile nations..."[5] It is not surprising that there was no dry dock at Quebec though the question of building a dock was considered during the French regime, and the idea was revived in 1792 by the young Scottish shipbuilders John Black and William King.[6]

Once the advantages of using dry docks had been established, many attempted to invent less costly methods of dry docking. In some parts of Europe, for instance, a graving dock was made from a hulk by beaching it, weighing it down with a large amount of ballast, and then cutting off the stern and fitting doors in its place. Obviously, its U-shape did not make a stable foundation. In the State of Maine, . . . a rectangular trunk, was substituted for the hulk, but it was discovered that the least inequality on the surface of the soil on which it rested endangered its stability by causing it to warp and jeopardize the safety of the vessel inside it. Moreover, the need for pumps, unless the tide rose and fell many feet, was considered a serious drawback.[7]

Meanwhile, hulks were being used on the Thames not as graving docks, but as *floating* dry docks,[8] a practice that may have originated at Kronstadt, during the reign of Peter the Great, where an English shipmaster is said to have made a floating dry dock by gutting an old hulk, cutting off its stern and fitting a watertight gate in its place[9]. From the early 1820s, floating dry docks were no longer tolerated on the Thames because they encroached on the river, but the idea did not die. Not only are ships still being converted into floating docks today,[10] but the converted hulks became the direct ancestors of a simple type of purpose-built floating dry dock, such as was built in the nineteenth century at Quebec. The 1280 ton *Canada Floating Dock* was the first.

Built by Joseph Farrington at his shipyard at Montreal, it measured 120.5 feet in length and fifty-two feet in width, with an inside depth of fifteen feet. According to the specifications the floor timbers were of oak, the foothooks of tamarac, and the top timbers of white pine. It had two keels amidships and two others on either side, and was planked throughout with red pine - four and six inches thick on the bottom, and four and three inches on the sides. The ceiling reached to the lower of three gangways. It was finished with the required joinery, caulked and painted.[11] After its launching, it was towed by the towboat *Hercules* to the Campbell and Black shipyard at Cape Cove, and can clearly be seen in James Cockburn's watercolour of the launching of the *Royal William*, figure 234 page 347.

Like its ancestors, it had no watertight compartments to lift and submerge it, but relied on the floatability of wood and the tide. The principle was simple. A dock with an end-gate open floated naturally in the River a little below the water level, allowing a ship afloat to enter. If the draught of the vessel was too great for it to do so, the dock was ballasted – a ballast scow being part of the dock's equipment. With the vessel properly shored, the dock was then floated onto its bed at high tide and securely moored there. After the tide had receded and most of the water had drained out, it was pumped dry and the gate was closed and caulked, and work could proceed.

That the floating docks were well suited to local conditions is evident from the way they proliferated in later years. There was plenty of timber lying in the timber coves to build them, and no shortage of experienced men to handle them. The fifteen foot tide greatly cut down the work of the pumps. They were generally found in the important St. Lawrence river shipyards, where there was plenty room for manoeuvering them, rather than in the closely hemmed in yards on the St. Charles river. At least nine docks were in operation in the port during the nineteenth century, some of which were still in use in the twentieth century, long after Quebec's first graving dock had been built.

Their strongest advocate was William Lampson, who as agent of the Floating Dock Company, put a first one into operation at Diamond Harbour in 1837 and a second, capable of taking in a ship with a 165-foot keel, in 1843. It took forty thousand feet of timber to build it, "mostly oak of large dimension and all of the best description and quality."[12] Lampson's connection with the Floating Dock Company is not clear; it was his financial status and not that of the company that obliged him to sell the two docks a few years later when one was moved to the Pickersgill and Tibbits' shipyard on the south shore. Nevertheless, his interest in floating docks remained strong and he launched an even larger 230-foot dock in 1856. Though most of the others were owner-operated, the *Diamond Harbour* (or *Anse-des-Mères*) *Floating Dock* was sometimes leased as part of a small shipyard there. In 1848, when it was

Figure 96: *Russell's pontoon-type floating dock. Collection Livernois, N976–73, courtesy Archives nationales du Québec.*

Figure 97: *Davie's submerged box-type floating dock and marine railway. Photo: courtesy Paul Gourdeau.*

Figure 98: *Remains of an old floating dock at the Davie shipyard at Lévis. Photo: Marcil.*

rented for four years to David Vaughan, he was required to caulk, tar and paint it regularly, for the wooden floating docks required the same upkeep as wooden hulls. An "Inventory of Sundries" belonging to the dock lists among other equipment: 11 lanterns, 50 augers, ropes, chains and blocks and caulking gear, a boat and a ballast scow. A new dock, built in 1856, was leased to John James Nesbitt, who advertised that it was "prepared to make repairs of every description to ships and steamboats," and was "capable of receiving vessels of 226 feet keel."[13]

Meanwhile, the shipbuilders John Nicholson and William G. Russell had completed a 161-foot dock at their Saint Paul Street shipyard in 1843, which they towed to their new shipyard across the river at Levis later that year. It measured 180 by fifty-three feet, and accommodated vessels 190 feet long drawing twelve to fifteen feet. Thomas Oliver, the only St. Charles River builder to operate one, exploited his dock, the *East India Floating Dock* at the East India Wharf, at Pointe-Carcy, only moving it to his building yard on Prince Edward street in the late 60s when the shipbuilding industry there was winding down. After almost thirty years of service, it was bought by George T. Davie in 1872, who placed it beside the dock that he had acquired from James Tibbits twenty years earlier.[14] During the winter of 1848, the Gilmours followed the trend and built their own 212-foot floating dock. It was taken over by John Roche when he bought the Wolfe's Cove shipyard from them in 1868. The last of these huge wooden structures, a dock 225 feet long and fifty-two feet wide, was built in the Russell yard in 1878. Those who made by far the greatest use of them, however, were Henry Dinning, who in 1864 owned the large dock at Diamond Harbour and two smaller ones at Cape Cove (which he used as collateral for his settlement on his bride),[15] and George T. Davie and his sons, who continued to use them until the 1930s. The remains of the last one can still be seen at his shipyard at Levis, Figure 98.

Another type of repair facility, a "Patent Slip" (or marine railway), was installed by Allison Davie at his South Shore shipyard in 1832. It was built under licence to its Scottish inventor, Thomas Morton, according to his patent of 1819,[16] and was the third to have been set up in America, the first, at Salem, dated from 1824, and the other, at New York, from 1827.[17]

The public was kept informed of Davie's enterprise by the local paper, which wrote:

Captain Davy's Marine Railway constructed at Pointe Lévi, opposite the lower town landing place, was tried for the first time on Saturday, when one of the Steam Companies' barge was hauled up. We believe this is the first establishment of the kind formed in British America. It will be very useful. The principle is that of a common railway, the carriage on which the vessel is taken at high water, moving on iron rollers & being drawn up by an iron chain, the largest vessels may be drawn up in this manner.[18]

The following spring, when the brig *Rosalind* was taken on, the Patent Slip justified the highest expectations. Before long, ships were waiting their turn in the stream.[19]

The experienced wharf builders, Francis and James Wiseman, built the inclined wharf under the railway of tough hemlock timbers filled between with stone, according to the plans and model supplied by Davie.[20] It was five hundred feet long and twenty, increasing to forty, feet wide, with a slope of three-quarters of an inch per foot. The local founders, Thomas Tweddell and Weston & Galbraith, made the castings.[21] A sign over the office door at the shipyard announced that it was the "Patent Slip Office," and in fact Davie's shipyard was generally referred to as "The Patent Slip."

Unlike the United States marine railways, which were horse-driven, Davie's slip was originally actuated by Algonquian Indians, who were in the habit of camping at Point Levy each year. Members of the band of all ages joined in the sport of manning the capstan in return for refreshments and other considerations. Within a short time, however, both Davie's and many of the United States railways were driven by steam.[22] An important extension to the slip was soon added in the form of a horizontal plane across which vessels were side slipped from the launchway on transfer trucks, sometimes merely to make room for others to be hauled out, but also for wintering them. Davie's marine railway can still be seen at his shipyard in Levis, the only early nineteenth-century shipyard in Canada that has survived.

The early success of the Patent Slip prompted George Black, the operator of the *Canada Floating Dock*, to "set out for Philadelphia to procure the best model of a railway for hauling up vessels and repairing them,"[23] but he came back empty-handed having no doubt learned of the loss of the ship *Panther* due to a docking accident. Unlike the U.S.A., where many marine railways continued to be built during the second quarter of the nineteenth century, Davie's railway remained the only one in the port until F.-X Marquis built his in the 1880s. In addition to the floating docks and railways, a three hundred by sixty-four

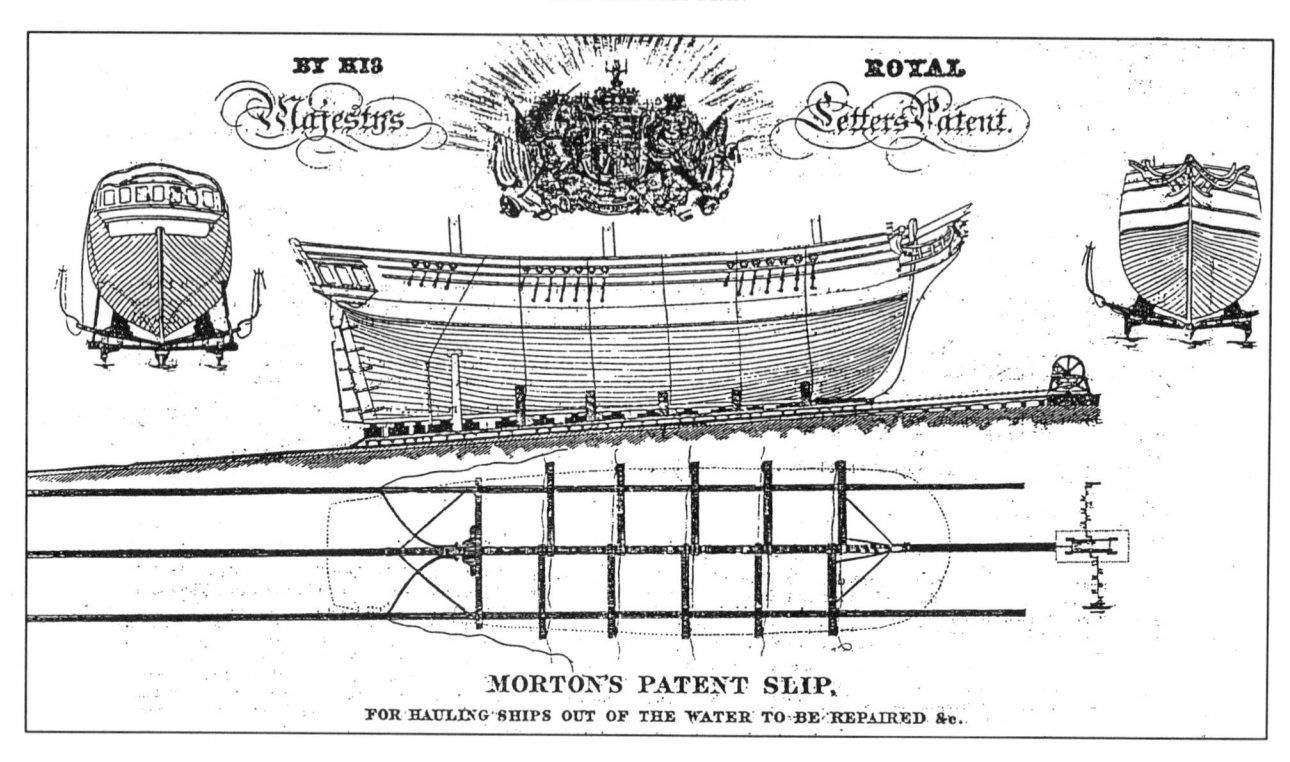

Figure 99: Morton's Patent Slip. *Courtesy Royal Society of Civil Engineers.*

MORTON'S PATENT SLIP,
FOR HAULING SHIPS OUT OF THE WATER TO BE REPAIRED &c.

foot graving dock at the Wolfe's Cove shipyard is listed among them in the 1890s, but I have found no further details of it.

Very much a part of the Quebec harbour scene, the dry docking facilities ensured a considerable amount of labour-intensive work each summer. This "old work" was profitable both for the shipbuilder, who could calculate his costs without having to consider the possibility of market fluctuations, as well as for the workers, who not only were paid on a higher scale than when they were doing "new work" but, because the shipmaster was generally in a hurry to get his ship operational again, did a large part of it at overtime rates. The floating docks and Patent Slip were therefore an important part of the shipyard facilities. Though they had little to do with the production of large sailing ships, as they only held the occasional new ship that was coppered at Quebec or was taken in for a special survey, they allowed the shipbuilder to make up for the losses he frequently incurred on construction, by undertaking ship salvage and repair.

Saw Mills

When George Gale wrote that every shipyard had a sawmill as an adjunct,[24] he overstated the case, for though shipyard sawmills existed, they were far from universal. The attitude of sawyers towards them may have been partly responsible, but another explanation is that running a sawmill was a different business from shipbuilding and sawn lumber was available from a large number of local mills.

By the end of the eighteenth century, sawmills were not only accepted but had become fairly common in North America. In Britain, on the other hand, they continued to meet with strong opposition from sawyers, and as late as 1769 a newly-erected mill at Limehouse, London, was torn down.[25] But the resistance of British sawyers could only delay but not prevent their construction and by 1799 the Navy had set up and was operating a steam-powered sawmill at its Portsmouth Dockyard.

At Quebec, mill-sawn planks were used in shipbuilding during the French Regime, and there is no reason to suppose that the practice came to an abrupt end with the arrival of the British. When George Allsop wrote to his son in 1795 suggesting that they acquire the land at Montmorency to put up a sawmill as "I have for many years thought of providing ship plank, oak and fir, for shipping and exportation,"[26] there is no hint of expected opposition. We do not know where the shipbuilder Patrick Beatson intended to set up the "woodwork for a sawmill" listed among his stock-in-trade in 1800. Nor is there reason to surmise that the "large steam engine adapted for sawing timber," offered for sale by Patterson & Dyke in 1814 at their combined wood and shipyard at Saint Patrick's Hole on the Isle of Orleans had not been used to cut

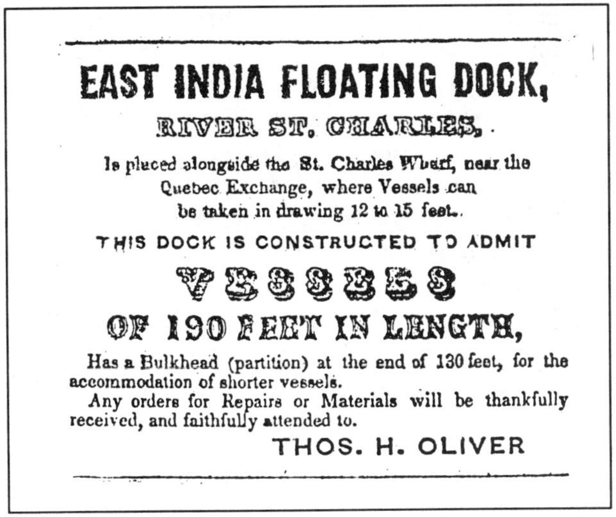
EAST INDIA FLOATING DOCK,
RIVER ST. CHARLES.
Is placed alongside the St. Charles Wharf, near the Quebec Exchange, where Vessels can be taken in drawing 12 to 15 feet.
THIS DOCK IS CONSTRUCTED TO ADMIT
VESSELS
OF 190 FEET IN LENGTH,
Has a Bulkhead (partition) at the end of 130 feet, for the accommodation of shorter vessels.
Any orders for Repairs or Materials will be thankfully received, and faithfully attended to.
THOS. H. OLIVER

Figure 100: East India Floating Dock *Announcement in Quebec Directory, 1844.*

planking for the vessels that they had had built there.[27] Similarly, it would seem logical to conclude that Henry Caldwell's sawmill at Etchemin cut plank for his shipyard nearby and that Peter Patterson's at Montmorency provided the plank for the vessels he ordered. It does not seem possible that with the shipyards working to capacity and timber merchants vying with each other for their services they would not have used at least some milled plank. Yet, that immigrant sawyers would have left all their prejudices with regard to mills behind in Britain is too much to expect.

Because the saw frames in the saw mills were wooden the danger of fire was very real. On a visit to the Montmorency Mills, J.M. Duncan noted that the frames were smoking profusely, in spite of all the care taken to keep them well greased and the fact that they were made of the softest pine to cut down on friction.[28] It is not surprising that so many mills caught fire. When John Goudie in 1818 erected perhaps the first large steam-powered flour and sawmill in Canada at his shipyard at Saint Roch, the sawyers reacted to this threat in the militant manner of their British counterparts: after several abortive attempts, they succeeded in burning it to the ground. The *Quebec Mercury* of 11 May 1819 denounced the "cause that checks the progress of that spirit of enterprize by which Mr. Goudie is so eminently distinguished," but Goudie was not intimidated and built an even larger mill.[29]

It was run by a fifty horsepower engine with the capacity to cut two hundred sawlogs a day. It had a large walking beam, a flywheel twenty-seven feet in diameter and a chimney over one hundred feet high. Engineers and tradesmen came from Scotland to set up the machinery, and its three large boilers were brought over from Glasgow on the deck of a trader.

The sawmill had four gates, each with a gang of twenty-two saws and eight circular saws to make shingles and laths. A nail-making department with two nail-cutting machines was added in 1821.[30] We do not know what percentage of the milled plank was used by the shipyards. A carefully worded advertisement offered "plank, boards, scantling, flooring and laths, etc. so true and clear that in applying them to house or any other use, they will at least save 25% of the labour."[31] But it took Goudie's indomitable spirit to keep the mill in production. Not only were there the sawyers to contend with, but replacement parts had to be sent from Scotland with resulting delays that ran at times into several months. After his death, it was operated by Henry Caldwell until at least 1832, at which time it was reported that the numerous sets of saws worked with prodigious velocity, driven by a steam engine of considerable power. But within a year or two it had ceased its milling activities. By 1825 John Saxton Campbell had followed Goudie's lead and set up his own steam sawmill at the north end of Cape Cove. Although it was adjacent to his shipyard, it was not a part of the operation and was leased to the merchant John Fernie for nine years.[32] No record has been found of its operation, although its chimney is shown smoking in the water colour of the launching of the *Royal William* by James Cockburn.

Like so many other tradesmen, the sawyers eventually had to accept the reality of steam power. By the mid-nineteenth century, the battle had been lost. Steam had penetrated many Quebec industries – breweries, foundries, a printing works, soda water works and a soap and candle factory – and steam sawmills had begun to proliferate. In 1853, one was erected by the wood merchant William Price at Hadlow Cove on the south shore and another by the merchant Gabriel Valin on the Saint Charles River.[33] By 1857, a sawmill driven by a twenty-five horsepower engine in H.N. Jones' shipyard at New Waterford Cove was driving "gates or upright saws capable of sawing the largest and longest timber which this or any province can produce for export, for making oil vats and for local shipyards."[34] In fact, as early as in 1855, Lloyd's surveyor reported that the timber for the H.N. Jones' 1239-ton ship *Tricolour* was all sided at the saw mill on the premises. By 1866, a steam sawmill was in operation at the Gilmour shipyard, while in 1871, another at the McKay and Warner shipyard at Stadacona was standing, but out of order.[35] A plan dated 1882 shows a steam mill at the Russell shipyard. Yet, many of the shipbuilders stuck to shipbuilding and bought their planks from a mill nearby. Like the sawmill in H.N. Jones' shipyard, the one at the Drum furniture factory in Saint Roch was producing large quantities of wood for shipbuilding in 1873.[36]

But there was still work for the sawyers and a considerable number continued to earn their living in the shipyards. As Gale wrote "it was nothing unusual to see as many as two score of men sawing away at immense pieces of square timber."[37] In the few surviving photographs of Quebec shipyards, their tall trestles, sheerlegs and saw sharpening horses can generally be seen. The equipment did not belong to the shipbuilder, but to the pair of sawyers who worked together and generally owned it in partnership. In fact the sawyer Alexis Fluet's inventory shows that he had not one, but two partners with each of whom he owned a pit saw in partnership. When he died, some of his equipment was in one shipyard, and the rest in another.[38]

The Mould or Moulding-Loft

The nerve centre of the whole shipbuilding operation was the "mould" or "moulding" loft, which offered the large uninterrupted floor space required to lay down the plans for the full-size patterns or "moulds" used to shape the ship timbers. Ideally, it was half the length of the largest ship to be planned and a little wider than half its maximum breadth, though with some improvisation a smaller loft could be made to serve. Both Thomas Oliver's and William Lampson's lofts were 120 feet long. Some mould lofts on the Saint Charles, such as those on the north bank between the Lairet and Saint-Michel Rivers, were shared by two or more shipyards. Ten years after John Goudie's death, his steam sawmill was given new life as a mould loft by Thomas Oliver.[39]

Mould lofts were required to be free of encumbrances and to have a clean floor, which was restored by sanding or painting between each laying off of plans. Inventories show that they had little furniture – one or two tables and an occasional chair. Equipment included drawing instruments, sweeps and sets of ribbands, and a good supply of tacks. Plans were kept in chests, while the ubiquitous iron stove countered the chill. Half-models from which vessels had been built hung on the walls. Long after the vessels themselves had sailed, the models served both for reference and as a physical reminder of the past achievements of the yard.

At the time that Captain F.C. Wurtele was gathering evidence on the trans-Atlantic voyage of the paddle steamer *Royal William*, the respected shipbuilder William H. Baldwin vouched for the authenticity of the

Figure 101: *Crow's nest model of the paddle steamer* Royal William. *From the* Report of the Secretary of State of Canada for the Year ended 31st December 1894, *Appendix G. Photo: OFQ.*

Figure 102: *Half-model that served for ships built by Walter G. Ray. Courtesy John Ray, photo National Museums of Canada.*

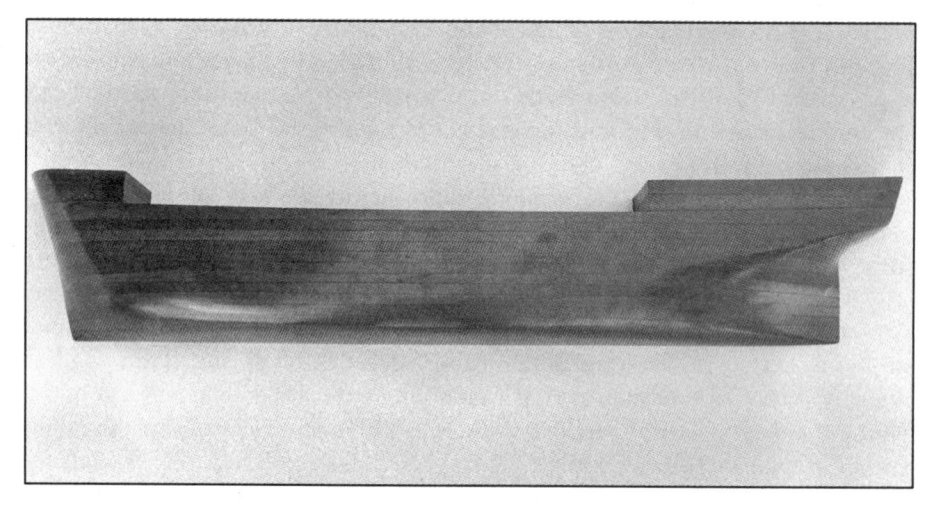

model. He had visited the Cape Cove shipyard in 1846, he said, and "in the moulding loft there were numbers of models, and amongst the rest that of the steamer 'Royal William.' The name was on her model, and Mr. George Black, who was then alive, proudly showed it to [me] . . . as being the model of the first steamship that crossed the ocean propelled by the motive power of steam."[40]

Models were not necessarily regarded as private trophies of the builder. Often they were considered a part of the shipyard and remained in the mould loft when the yard changed hands. An inventory taken when the Gilmour yard was sold in 1868 listed seventy ship models left to the new owner in the mould loft. In the shorter-lived Brunelle shipyard at Lauzon, there were six.[41]

The Forge

Second in importance to the mould loft was the shipyard forge, for far from being dependent on wooden fastenings, as wooden sailing ships became larger, they were increasingly strengthened with iron bolts, knees and other fittings, many of which were custom made. The shipbuilders provided their blacksmiths with a fully equipped forge and a supply of coal. In 1800, the Beatson shipyard forge occupied a twenty-four foot square house on the wharf beside the building slip. Inside its thick stone walls was a twenty foot square workshop area containing[42]

    3 anvils
    6 sledge hammers
    7 small hammers
    4 sett hammers
    3 vices
    1 beck iron

4 plate screws
1 pr. callipers
5 punches
1 iron square
3 files
5 cold chisels
6 hot chisels
11 nail tools
16 pr. tongs
1 pr. shears
1 pr. nippers
1 brace
5 iron gauges
1 iron bevil
1 draw knife
4 drag irons
1 two handed hot iron rubber
1 tool for rounding iron
3 rounding hooks
4 pr. smiths' bellows
1 large crane hook
1 iron beam and scales
2 fire engines with hose and pipes

The inventory of the Gilmour yard in 1868 lists a clock, desk, stool, a small scale and weights, a large beam, scales and weights, a vertical boring iron, etc., an iron platform for bending iron knees, a trip hammer, two vices and benches, three bellows, seven anvils, two swedge blocks and horns, two mandrels, a wheelbarrow and an unstated number of hand tools.[43] The blacksmith's work was still laborious, but the steam-driven trip hammer greatly eased his work. The platform for bending knees had become essential in the 1850s, from which time the large iron knee riders were installed in the vessels at Quebec rather than in Britain.

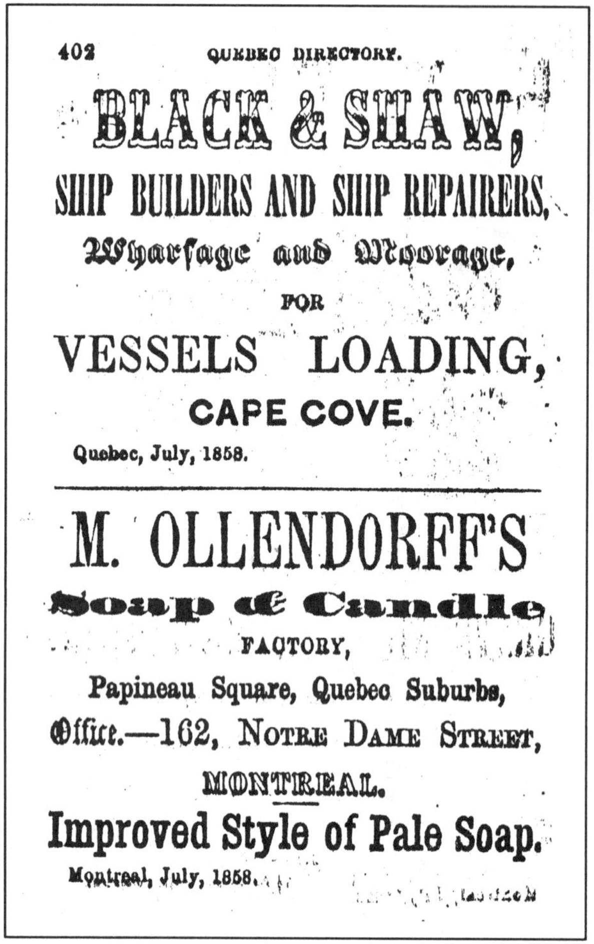

402 QUEBEC DIRECTORY.

BLACK & SHAW,

SHIP BUILDERS AND SHIP REPAIRERS,

Wharfage and Moorage,

FOR

VESSELS LOADING,

CAPE COVE.

Quebec, July, 1858.

M. OLLENDORFF'S

Soap & Candle

FACTORY,

Papineau Square, Quebec Suburbs,

Office.—162, NOTRE DAME STREET,

MONTREAL.

Improved Style of Pale Soap.

Montreal, July, 1858.

Figure 103: *Announcement of Edmund Black and James Gibb Shaw's short-lived partnership at Cape Cove, in the Quebec Directory of 1858.*

Perhaps the best equipped forge was in H.N. Jones' shipyard at New Waterford Cove, which contained "five fires, rapping out morning and evening, patent trusses, iron tillers, wrought iron caps, hoops for masts, and everything in the iron way, indeed, except anchors," both for its own use and for that of other shipyards.[44]

Steam-House and Steam-Box

A steam-house and steam-box in which planks were softened before being fastened to the ship's frame were other essential features of the shipyards, although like the mould-loft, the steam-house was sometimes shared. Large iron kettles or boilers hung over well-tended fires in the steam-house to produce the steam, which was led off to a steam-box outside. The boxes were made of heavy planks securely fastened and caulked at their ends. Wood being plentiful, they could be readily made up by the workers. They are easily recognizable in shipyard photographs, and one in the Nesbitt yard is very similar to the steam-box used in the construction of a schooner at Saint-Joseph-de-la-rive in the 1950s. This was another facility that could be shared by adjoining shipyards, as it was by the Lemelin and Valin shipyards on Hare Point in 1854.[45]

Tradesmen's Lofts and Shops

There is good reason for the workplaces of sailmakers and riggers to be known as lofts, or perhaps I should say for their working in lofts. Not only did they need the best light possible, as well as warmth to keep their fingers from becoming numb, but because of the danger of spontaneous combustion to which damp canvas or hemp rope are susceptible, dry quarters were also essential from the point of view of the stores. The sailmakers' lofts, or sail lofts, were not to be found in the shipyards, however, though occasionally directories and censuses list a sailmaker or two who lived close to a shipyard and may have worked there. Generally speaking, they were in the Saint Peter Street district of the Lower Town where they were handy to their wider clientele from visiting ships that needed replacements and others built outside Quebec. Riggers, on the other hand, were far more likely to have a designated area at the yard in which to carry out their work. Since riggers required a long narrow space in which to lay out their work, they might in some cases have occupied the length of a building, leaving the adjoining space for the joiners or other shipyard tradesmen.

The designation of a certain area as a "joiners' shop" can be found on shipyard plans from around the middle of the nineteenth century, though undoubtedly they existed before that. The joiners' shop at the Jeffery shipyard had five joiners' benches, a vise and a lathe. The latter served for the pump and blockmakers' work, as well as for turning balusters, the spokes of ships' wheels and belaying pins. In later years more sophisticated powered tools were added to the shops. At Gilmour's yard, for instance, there were moulding, tenoning and mortising machines, as well as a circular and a jig saw.

The Boiler Shop

It is perhaps surprising to find a boiler shop listed among the facilities in shipyards where wooden ships were built, and certainly they were not common. However, both the Munn and the Dinning shipyards had them. Both built steamboats with wooden hulls for which boilers were needed, and it is likely that all kinds of other metal work including foundry work were also carried out there.

Sheds or Stores

Other buildings found on plans of shipyards are usually labelled either "sheds" or "stores," but we know that in some, the loft and/or ground floor did duty for one or more tradesmen's shops, the remainder of the building being used for storage. In some, the lower level was open on at least one side. Many were of extremely large dimensions, for a great deal of space was required for the huge quantities of shipbuilding materials, and perhaps outfitting supplies, that had to be kept on hand, but with one exception which ended disastrously when a fire ravaged the neighbourhood, they were not used as covered slips. The builders were well aware of the advantages of building under cover and keeping the construction dry, for from the beginning of the nineteenth century all vessels built in the dockyards in Sweden and many built at Brest and Venice were built under cover.[46] Presumably the practical disadvantages outweighed the advantages at Quebec. Plans of the later years show fewer anonymous sheds; they are labelled "treenail house," "spar house," "paint store," "salt shed" or "oakum room," instead.

The Counting House

In most yards a small building was set aside as a counting house or office, where a clerk kept painstaking accounts of labour, building supplies and business transactions of all sorts. A stove, tall desk and stool

176　THE CHARLEY-MAN

Figure 104 : *Plan of George D. Davie's Grounds and Residence beside the shipyard at St. Joseph de Lévis, or Lauzon, which testifies to his obviously comfortable life style. Surveyed and drawn by G.K. Addey, 12 May 1915, Collection des Cartes et Plans, Archives nationales du Québec, Québec, CA1–62,318B.*

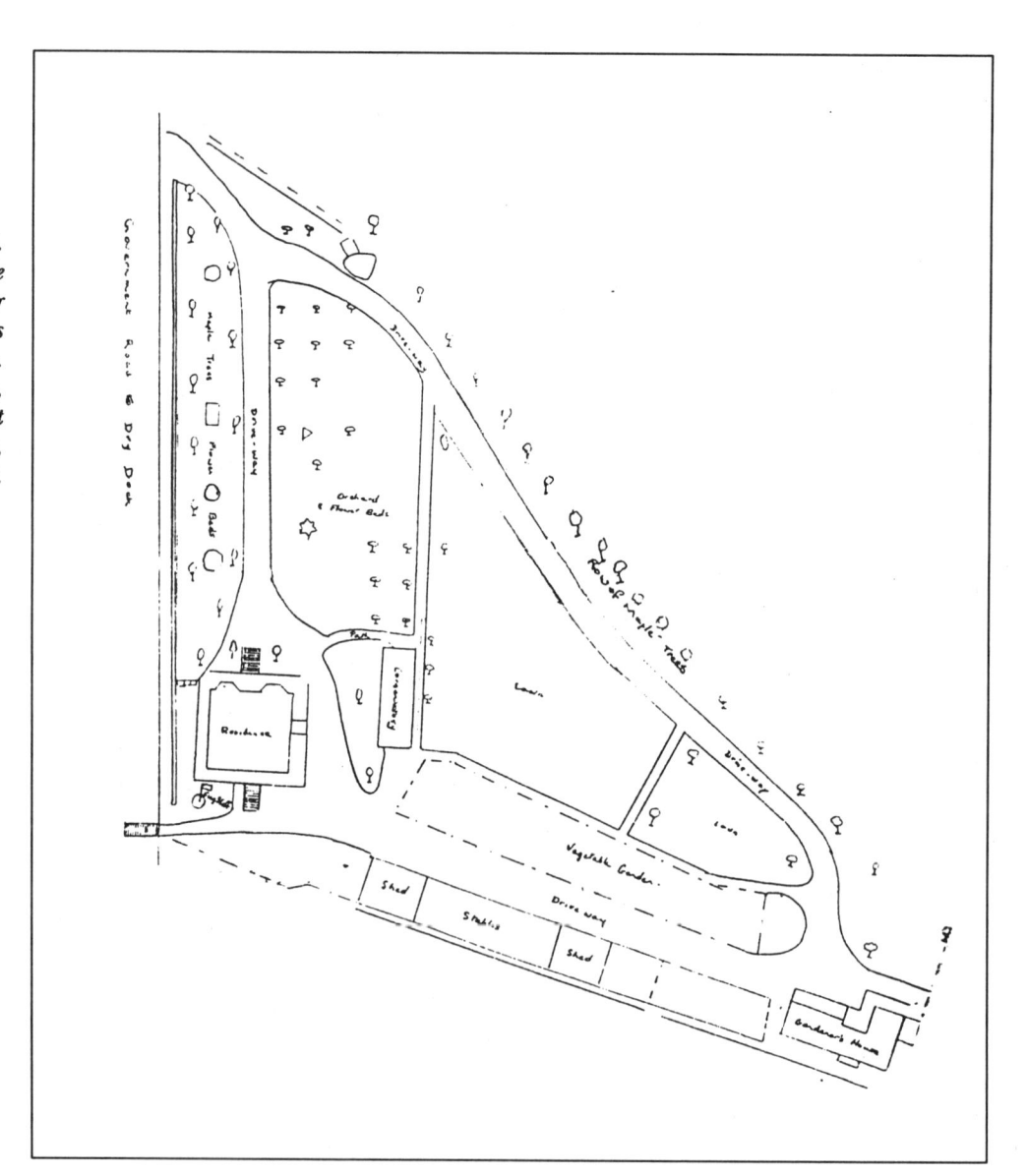

were the standard furnishings, sometimes accompanied by a small bed or cot and a clock.

Shipyard Equipment

Shipyard equipment was unsophisticated – some wheelbarrows and shovels, some ladders, cable and rope, a good selection of blocks, gins and a few tackles and cant hooks for moving timber, and dogs and cramps to keep it in place. The carpenters provided their own axes and adzes, but the shipbuilder usually supplied the cross-cut saws and augers, hawsing irons and beetles, and a treenail mill or mills. He also had on hand a grindstone or two and pitch kettles and ladles. Usually there was a crab or winch to help with the heavy work and sometimes an elementary crane or swinging boom on the wharf. Alexander Munn, for instance, was given permission to install a temporary crane for hauling wood when he leased the shipyard on the King's Wharf,[47] and others can be seen in early photographs. A speaking trumpet quickly got the attention of any worker on the job. But with vessels on the stocks worth thousands of dollars in labour and materials and extensive stocks of timber and other inflammable supplies on hand, the risks posed by the open fires used to heat tar or boil water made the fire engine one of the most important pieces of shipyard equipment. Together with a relay of leather fire buckets, it was no doubt a requirement of the fire insurance companies, although obviously a common sense requirement as well. At the Beatson yard in 1800, twenty-five leather buckets, of which twelve were "painted with the Phoenix Arms," and seventy-eight wooden buckets were stacked on the gallery and in the entry of the house, while the fire equipment at the Gilmour yard was stored in a special "engine house," and included besides the engine, six hundred feet of canvas hose, sixty-eight buckets, two copper jet pipes, two hose reels on two pairs of wheels, with alternative sleighs for winter use, six long ladders and a large pole and hook, and twenty-six feet of leather suction pipe.[48] It is a tribute to the order and discipline of the shipyards that although a few buildings were lost to fires over the years, no serious shipyard fires began in the yards themselves. Major destruction was always due to general conflagrations that spread from elsewhere in town.

The Shipbuilder's Home

Unlike the timber merchants, who almost without exception resided in fancy villas set in large estates above their timber coves, the shipbuilders lived in or beside their yards, close to their work and to their workers' homes. Homes of young shipbuilders who were struggling to establish themselves at the beginning of the nineteenth century were often of modest construction, their garrets and cellars greatly encroached upon for extra storage space for shipyard supplies, but as the years went by the successful builders tended to have more substantial stone or brick residences built, allowing greater comfort while at the same time sending out the signal that theirs was a well-established and not a temporary or mediocre yard. Their houses were large enough to accommodate a pair of apprentices, who were brought up as part of the family, and some incorporated a private office where important customers could be received.

The inventory taken after Patrick Beatson's death in 1800 reveals the lifestyle of a certain type of shipbuilder, one who turned to shipbuilding after a successful career at sea. His long, low, galleried house overlooked the Saint Lawrence at anse-des-Mères, his

Figure 105: *The St. Roch fire of May 24th 1870. Valin's ship, right, is spared, but Baldwin lost the two ships he was building under cover.* Canadian Illustrated News, *June 4 1870. Courtesy National Archives, Ottawa, neg. C 48832.*

Figure 106: *William Baldwin's answer to the fire of 1870, in which he lost two ships, the ship* Lady Lisgar, *1241 tons, of 1871, named after the wife of the Governor General. Photo from F.W. Wallace,* In the Wake of the Windships.

Figure 107: *The Gilmour shipyard at Wolfe's Cove. Note the very long mould-loft with the lower floor open on one side, probably used for dressing masts as well as for other purposes, compare with plan 7 Neg. Courtesy National Archives, Ottawa, neg. 103089.*

The Shipyards — Facilities

Property of the late John Munn
For Sale, most valuable freehold property in St. Rochs.

This well known Town Property, formerly owned by the late JOHN MUNN, Esquire, containing in one block 11 1/4 acres, dimensions by accurate survey as follows:—

No. 1. The convenient Timber Booms on the River St. Charles, in good order, superficial contents 19,125 square yards.

No. 2. A Ship-Yard, Workmen's Dwellings, etc., consisting of one Brick Terrace, two stories high, with good Garrets, fronting 80 feet on Grant Street and 140 feet on Prince Edward Street, covered with slate, has good back yards and hangars complete, capable of accommodat"ing thirty-two tenants and families, and the Houses on Prince Edward Street are supplied with Company's water, and fittings for this purpose. There is also from the end of this building a good wooden shed 300 feet long, and three or four Ships may be built together here, the superficial contents being 9,204 square yards. The timber booms are connected with this lot.

No. 3. Another Ship-Yard on which is a fine brick workshop 200 feet long by about 38 feet wide, two stories high and high attics, and covered with slate - principally now used as a boiler maker's workshop, with two wooden buildings at the east end, one 60 feet long the other 135 feet long; also a large stone building two stories high, with high attics and covered with slate, adapted for rigging and moulding lofts, blacksmith's shop, etc, length 75 feet and width 35 feet, to which is attached a steam©house at one end, at the other end an iron store, and at a small distance a treenail shop about 40 feet by 27 feet. Several Ships may be built together on this property, the superficial contents being 8326 square yards.

No. 4. Is a fine Timber and Lumber Yard between St. Dominique Street (the part newly extended) and Grant Street, and Queen Street and Prince Edward Street, all well fenced in and containing 8407 square yards.

No. 5. Is another splendid lot, which includes a Stone Terrace, two stories high, covered with tin and slate, will accommodate twenty families, on St. Dominique Street, bounded at one end by Queen Street, and extending towards King Street 345 feet. The Company's water is in part of these premises. In the rear of these buildings is a fine Timber and Lumber Yard, with the convenience of a tide dock to float timber to the premises. Superficial contents 8793 square yards.

No. 6. Is a fine corner lot of land, fronting on Grant Street 96 feet and on Queen Street 45 feet, suitable for a yard, or house building purpose.

No. 7. Is a splendid Brick Mansion, covered with tin, fronting on Grant Street 50 feet by 40 feet back — a small garden in front planted with trees, and a kitchen and flower garden north end, fronting on Grant Street 182 feet by 65 feet back, partly planted with fruit trees, and at the south end of the house bounding on Grant and Queen Streets, is a brick Coach house and Stables, and brick Offices, all covered with tin and slate and all fenced in.

The House has breakfast, dining and two entertaining rooms on the first floor, and on the second flat a splendid drawing room, and, with the folding doors, may be extended the whole depth of the house, or about 36 feet by about 19 feet, with an abundance of bed rooms. Their [sic] are large cellars and kitchen the whole size of the foundation, and two Russian stoves for heating through the house, put up at great cost, and the Company's water is efficiently carried in. The whole of this fine property runs along Grant Street from the River St. Charles in an unbroken line 975 feet, and is but 500 feet, on the City side, from the Toll Bridge on the St. Charles, and on the south side of the property from King Street to the Saint Charles is 1115 feet, and protected by wharves to this river. This, or east side of the property, is bounded entire by Corporation property, and the south corner is but 300 feet from the new bridge of the North Shore Railway. The whole property is well fenced round, and fenced also in divisions.

For further particulars, please apply to DUNCAN GIBB, Esq, the owner; to Messrs. Allan Gilmour & Co., Quebec, or on the premises to Hugh Mackay.

Morning Chronicle
March 4th, 1859.

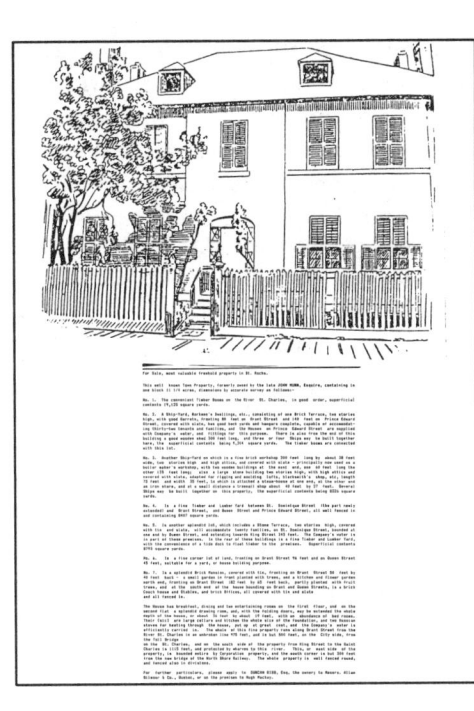

Figure 108: *The home of the shipbuilder John Munn on Grant Street after his death, when it was being used as a synagogue (with thanks to A.J.H. Richardson) From Jos. Trudelle,* Les jubilés et les églises et chapelles de la Ville et de la banlieu de Québec 1608–1901, *2:278.*

Figure 109: *Description of John Munn's property that appeared in the* Morning Chronicle *on the 4 March 1859, shortly after his death.*

Figure 110: *"Ringfield," home of George H. Parke. Photo courtesy Kenneth Parke.*

garden was neatly delineated by thirteen posts with link chain between and dotted with carronade and guns. His home was filled with possessions reflecting his former career, his love of the sea, the style of a successful shipmaster, and his familiarity with the east. The large rooms were amply furnished, the windows neatly curtained, the walls of the drawing-room and sitting-room crammed with upwards of sixty paintings, among which pictures of shipping predominated. The portraits included naval heroes, such as Lord Nelson, whose career was still young when his ship *HMS Albermarle* escorted an Atlantic convoy to Quebec in 1782. In the dining-room, the place of honour was reserved for a large painting of the pier at Leith, a reminder of Beatson's boyhood days. A smaller picture of the pier hung in his study, the sole exception to the engravings, prints and drawings, all ship portraits, that hung around the walls. It was this room that held the large deal drawing table, on which he drafted the plans for the ships he built. This is where the paraphernalia for that purpose, including ninety-six pearwood sweeps and squares, paints and brushes, and even printing type, was kept.[49] His library showed a preference for history, particularly naval or Scottish history, but politics, geography and literature, even poetry, were also well-represented, as well, of course, as books pertaining to his trade. It is unlikely that John Munn, who was of a far more austere nature, owned the quantity of paintings, prints and knick-knacks of all sorts that adorned Beatson's house. His home, however, reflected the standing he had attained in his profession. John Jeffery's home, which unfortunately was gutted by the fire that swept Saint Roch in 1866, was also sober and substantial, as were, undoubtedly, those of many of the other builders.

The stable was always close at hand and served as quarters for one or two cows as well as for the horses that drew the family conveyances and helped with the pulling and carrying in the yard. In the outlying areas, oxen were sometimes used instead. Sleighs or carioles and sometimes a berline served for winter travel, while two-wheeled carriages were the general choice for summer. Beatson, who had a fondness for fine things, succumbed to his whim of having two carriages decorated by the local Paris-trained painter and sculptor, François Baillairgé, who also sculpted the figureheads and other carved work for the ships he built. The Jeffery brothers owned a four-wheeled carriage, which was unusual not only among shipbuilders but also among the general population. For shipyard work, the horses were most frequently harnessed to a "pair of wheels," though carts, "trucks," and drags were also used in the yards. The "timber carriage," noted in Goudie's inventory, probably had some kind of lifting apparatus incorporated. No mention is made in shipbuilders' inventories of dogs or other family pets they may have owned; yet there are two peacocks listed in Allison Davie's inventory,[50] which must have struck an exotic note strutting around the yard.

In a partnership business, it was not unusual for the partners to share the dwelling house. William Baldwin and Henry Dinning, for instance, lived together at the old Black home at the foot of the cliffs at Cape Cove in the 1850s, and Lauchlan McKay and Henry Warner, who had married sisters, occupied the house known as "Smithville," on the north bank of the Saint Charles during the 1860s.

The shipbuilder's home was an integral part of the shipyard. If he came upon hard times and was forced to give up the yard, he had also to give up his home;

Gr. Hossack, 28 May, 1856.

Specification of Boom to be built by Mr. Jobin.

To be 120 feet long. to be built of good Cull White pine Timber – to be four pieces wide – and the timber to be 17 & 18 Ins in girth. the foregoing forms the body of the booms – which is to be fastened with 16 bolts of 1 1/2 inch round iron penetrating through and clinched in plate of 3/8 x 3 in. flat iron at each end.

Bordages to be put in each side of the boom   the whole length to be of Oak Timber 12 in in depth by 6 In in width to be fastened into the body of boom with 18 bolts of round Iron 1 Inch with plate of flat iron 2 1/2 x 1/4 In. on each bolt – In order to prevent the head of bolts from working through bordage   Two p. Oak to go across the boom 16 Inches wide by 6 Inch in depth – at each end. And 2 p. of Oak for   as per plan. Two holes to be bored at each end of boom about 15 and 10 feet respectively – each hole to be fitted with a metal flange suitable for 1 5/8 inch chain –

Figure 111: *Plan and specifications for a timber retaining boom to be built by the shipbuilder Charles Jobin for Thomas Burns. Gr. Hossack, 28 March 1855, Archives nationales du Québec.*

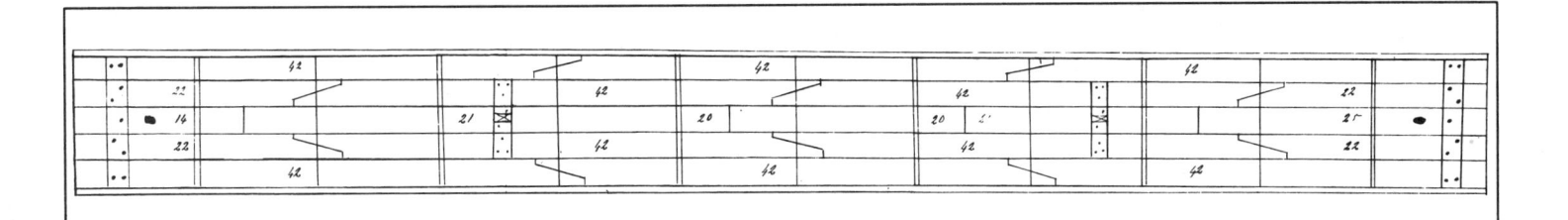

when he died, his family had to move to make way for the next owner. There were, of course, exceptions. Alexander Munn's widow was among the fortunate, for she was able to retain her brand new home and rent the shipyard with her former dwelling house, which still stood.

Fences and Booms

The shipyard complex was enclosed with a solid wooden fence enabling passage from within and from without to be controlled and preventing encroachment or trespass from neighbouring properties. This was understandable and standard practice, though not always popular with the average citizen, who saw his acquired rights to use the beach as a road at low tide suddenly denied and his access to the river at times severely restricted. The authorities, however, realized the necessity of this measure, as is evident from a petition of 1790 in which John Black and William King requested permission "to fence in and use government land in St. Roc to lay down a keel." If an unfenced piece of ground were leased as a shipyard, the responsibility of the shipbuilder to erect one was written into the lease. In fact, when leasing a part of their property, the Sisters of the General Hospital required Pierre Valin and Gonzague Vallerand to put up a fence at least ten to twelve feet high.[51]

On the river side, most shipyards had a wharf or two where vessels could tie up and land cargo, if only at high tide, while to complete the enclosure of the property, a stretch of booms held in a stock of floating timber. The booms were built of pine because of its buoyancy, but were planked on either side with oak, which stood up much better to the wear and tear. The whole was securely bolted and chains were attached with which they were anchored in place.

The boom was opened to receive deliveries of timber made at high tide by raft or moulinets, which were hauled on to the beach to be dismantled. John Munn's shipyard was particularly well appointed in this respect, with extensive wharves, a tide dock to float timber to his premises and 19,000 square yards of protected timber booms.

Maintenance and Cost

The wharves, booms, floating docks and other facilities in their exposed positions on the river banks, even those on the more sheltered Saint Charles, fell prey at times to the violence of the elements. A wharf put up by Allison Davie at his new shipyard at Levis in 1829, for instance, was carried away by ice the same year, while the sawmill of the McKay and Warner shipyard on the north bank of the Saint Charles was destroyed in a storm in 1878. Even when the damage was not as radical, a considerable amount of maintenance was required. Fortunately, with few exceptions the shipyard carpenters and labourers could do the work and there was no shortage of timber with which to do it, so that expense was minimal. In a settlement in 1853 with his partner, for £245 Baldwin not only built new timber booms (£114 4 8d), but added a new slip to the yard (£34 12 1d), rebuilt the burned joiners' shop (£33 13 4d), put new bilges in the old floating dock (£35), and shingled the blacksmiths' forge (£16), the treenail house (£4 19s) and the old dwelling house (£6 10s). It cost him a little more to put up the new dwelling house

(£307 19 1d).[52] The wharves, however, were very costly items, for as Davie found out, unless they were very strongly built and securely anchored they were liable to be torn away by the ice. This is clearly illustrated by the evaluation made of the buildings and other facilities in the shipyard following the cancellation of the five-year partnership between James, Richard and William Henry Jeffery in 1844[53].

Shipyards were so often sold by auction when shipbuilders became insolvent that it is difficult to estimate their true market value. Moreover, the shipyard was only valuable when there was a market for the ships that might be built there and a shipbuilder in a position to build them, and unfortunately the shipping market was very erratic.

Leases give us a better idea of shipyard costs. In the 1780s, a simple shipyard on the outskirts of Quebec could be rented for as little as £15 per annum, but as the demand for shipbuilding sites increased, prices were driven up. During the nineteenth century the cost was generally from £100 to £150. For example, John Munn leased his shipyard to Sam Finch for £108 10s in 1815, George Taylor paid £150 for the Brehaut yard in 1818, and McDonald and Hows sub-let the Cape Diamond shipyard to Louis Labbé for seven or eight months for £100 in 1825. In 1834, Thomas Oliver paid £120 per annum for Goudie's shipyard, while as late as 1854 it cost Pierre Valin £100 for the lease of a shipyard at Hare Point, with shared steam-house facilities. In the same year Isaie Julien and Company leased Lepper's yard on Saint Paul Street at £200, rather higher than the average, probably reflecting the advantage of berthing facilities and the fact that it was in town. When a shipyard was also equipped for ship repairing, however, its value rose steeply. When George Black retired in 1846 and his son took over the yard with its two floating docks, the rent was fixed at £800. In 1849, William Russell's settlement with his late partner's widow was based on an annual rent of their yard of £376, although the yard was on the South Shore and he had already bought out his half-share of the floating-dock for £750, and David Vaughan signed a four-year lease for the Diamond Harbour Floating Dock at £300 per annum. In 1853 the Davie yard, which had both a marine railway and a floating dock, was rented at £500.[54] Floating dock installations greatly enhanced the value of a shipyard. In fact, the dock alone, which cost from £800 to £1,500, was frequently used as collateral for a loan.

James Jeffery & Company (1839-1844)
Shipyard at Hare Point

	Cost When Built	Value Now
Dwelling house	£200	£500
Stables	25	75
Smiths' shop	100	250
Large store	150	350
Steam house	75	200
New store near gate	200	75
Shipbuilding wharves	100	1,100
Fence around yard	25	100
3 sets of launching ways and blocks	40	150
	£750	£2,800

The value of the superior yards, however, was not necessarily related to such special repair facilities. On the contrary, there were many fine owner-operated yards on the Saint Charles, including the Oliver and Nesbitt yards, where it was the prime location that made the land valuable.[55] John Munn's admittedly exceptional shipyard, of which a full description is in Figure 109, page 179, was accepted as security for a £21,000 debt.

Generally speaking, however, unless the shipyard had special repair facilities, its cost was negligible compared with the amount paid for labour and materials. Jean-Elie Gingras, for instance, built sixty-three vessels, among them some very fine ships, on a sheltered beach with a smithy and one or two sheds, and roughly half of all the large sailing ships launched at Quebec were built in rented yards that were not very different from his.

Notes

1. Matthew Reed to William Bell, 5 July 1811, William Bell Correspondence, I, MG 24 F3, NA.4.
2. Basil Greenhill, *The Merchant Schooners* (New York, 1968), 116.2.
3. Advertisement, *Quebec Morning Chronicle*, 11 July 1857.
4. Reports of Survey, gr. L. McPherson, 11, 16, 17 and 28 July.
5. "Report of the Select Committee of the Franklin Instiute on a Dry Dock projected by Comodore James Barron, and also, one by Captain Thomas Caldwell," *The Franklin Journal and American Mechanics Magazine*, 3:1, January 1827; "H. Rept. 100. Dry Docks, January 25, 1828," 20 Cong. 1st sess.
6. Petition, 26 May 1792, Lower Canada Land Papers, f. 21703, XLIII, RG1 L3L, NA.
7. "Report of a Select Committee of the Franklin Institute, on a Dry Dock," projected by Commodore James Barron, and also one by Thomas Caldwell in *The Franklin Journal and American Mechanics Magazine*, (New York, 1827) III, No. 1 (January 1827), 6.
9. *Shipping Wonders of the World*, II: 1046-1051
10. The 2575 ton pulpwood carrier *Menier Consol*, for example, built at the Davie shipyard at Lauzon in 1962, can be seen today in Toronto Harbour, where she serves her new owner The Toronto Dry Dock Corp. as a dry dock for vessels of up to 180 by 40 ft. Brought to my attention by Roland Webb.
11. Sale and transfer, Farrington to Forsyth, 19 January 1827, greffe H. Griffin, Archives nationales de Québec à Montréal [hereafter ANQM].
12. Announcements, *Quebec Mercury*, 1 July 1837 and 29 April 1843.
13. Protest, Vaughan V. Bradshaw, 31 January 1852, gr W. Bignell; *Quebec Morning Chronicle*, 12 May 1857.
14. Sale, Lampson to Pickersgill and Tibbits, 5 April 1845, gr A. Campbell; Obligation, Lampson to Nesbitt, 3 June 1856, gr A. Lemoine; Sale, S. Russell to W.G. Russell, 27 March 1849, gr J. Hunt; *L'Evénement*, 6 May 1878; Loan, Oliver from Noad, 20 November 1852, gr S. Glackemeyer; advertisement, *Quebec Directory 1844-45*, 202; Sale, Henry to Davie, 6 November 1872, gr W.D. Campbell. Resiliation of sale of dock, 16 August 1853, gr W.D. Campbell.
16. *Specifications Relating to Ship Building*, 23 March 1819, no. 4352, 65.
17. John B. Hutchins, *The American Maritime Industries and Public Policy 1789-1914* (Cambridge, Mass., 1941), 13; Robert Greenhalgh Albion, *The Rise of New York Port* (Boston, 1939), 299.
18. *Quebec Gazette*, 29 October 1832.
19. *Ibid*, 3 May 1833.
20. Building contract, F. and J. Wiseman with A. Davie, 28 March 1832, gr L. McPherson.
21. Account listed in inventory of A. Davie, 19 July 1836, gr L. McPherson.
22. G.W. Haws, *The Haws Family and their Seafaring Kin* (Dunfermline, 1932), 107; Hutchins, American Maritime Industries, 108; Albion, *Rise of New York Port*, 299; William Avery Baker, *A Maritime History of Bath, Maine, and the Kennebec Region* (2 vols., Portland, 1973), 616; *Trading and Shipping on the Great Lakes* (reprint, Toronto, 1980), 42-43.
23. *Quebec Gazette*, 26 July 1833.
24. George Gale, *Twixt Old and New* (Québec, 1915), 67.
25. John E. Horsley, *Tools of the Maritime Trades* (Newton Abbot, 1978), 75.
26. A.J.H. Richardson, "Indications for Research in the History of Wood-Processing Technology," *APT*, IV, No. 3 (1974), 69, citing George Allsopp Letter-Book, I, 75-8, MG23, III, NA.

27. Advertised for sale, *Quebec Gazette*, 29 September 1814.
28. John M. Duncan, *Travels Through Part of the United States and Canada in 1818 and 1819* (New York, 1823).
29. *Quebec Gazette*, 23 October 1820.
30. James Goudie to the editor, *Quebec Morning Chronicle*, 24 January 1883; Agreement, Goudie with Sam Culter, nail cutter and white smith, 29 March 1821, gr T. Lee.
31. *Quebec Mercury*, 23 October 1820.
32. Lease, 11 March 1825, gr C. Huot, which was cancelled 12 May 1831, with effect from 1829, "because of business losses." Fernie had previously had some connection with Goudie's mill, perhaps running it. It was he who advertised certain items for sale "at the Steam Saw Mill, St. Roch," *Quebec Mercury*, 25 July 1820.
33. Contract, Calvert, Tweddell and McMaugh with Price, 6 September 1853, gr D. McPherson; contract Richard with Valin, 7 May 1852, gr J.B. Pruneau.
34. Willis Russell, *Quebec: As it was, and As it Is* (Québec, 1857), 159.
35. Census of 1871.
36. Ovide Frechette, cited by P.L. Martin, *La Bercante Québécoise* (Montréal, 1973), 140.
37. Gale, *Twixt Old and New*, 67.
38. Inventory, Fluet, 14 October 1806, gr J. Belanger.
39. See, for example, sub-lease, T. Saint-Jean to E. Samson, 22 June 1853, gr Frs. Huot; Lease, Caldwell to Oliver, 5 August 1834 and 11 September 1835, gr L. McPherson.
40. *Report of the Secretary of State of Canada for the Year Ended 31st December 1894*, Appendix G, 76.
41. Inventory, 15 October, gr W. Bignell; Obligation, Brunelle to Gillespie, 30 November 1857, gr S. Glackemeyer.
42. Inventory, Beatson, 15 December, gr C. Voyer.
43. Inventory, Gilmour, 15 October 1868, gr J. Bignell.
44. Russell, *Quebec: As it Was*, 153.
45. Lease, Lemelin with Valin, 11 February 1854, gr Huot.
46. "Pering and Money on Shipbuilding," *Analectic Magazine*, I (1813), Philadelphia.
47. Sublease, Purss and Johnston to Munn, 23 April 1795, gr C. Stewart.
48. Inventory accompanying Deed of Sale, Gilmour to Roche, 15 October 1868, gr J. Bignell; lease, Beatson to Dunière, 13 October 1802, gr R. Lelièvre.
49. E. Marcil, "Patrick Beatson capitaine et constructeur de navires – Patrick Beatson shipmaster and shipbuilder 1758-1800," *De la voile à la vapeur – From Sail to Steam* (Montreal, 1982).
50. See inventory of Pointe-aux-Trembles shipyard in the Sale, Dubord to Angers, 18 December 1867, gr S. Glackemeyer; 20 May 1796, Baillairgé's Journal, ANQ; Goudie's inventory, 10 January 1825, gr T. Lee; Davie's inventory, 19 July 1836, gr L. McPherson.
51. Petition, folio 21700, XLIII, RG1 L3L, Lower Canada Land Papers, microfilm C-2509, NA; Lease, 3 April 1854, gr C. Parent.
52. Account for improvements to the Cove, Baldwin, 20 September 1853, gr S. Glackemeyer.
53. Agreement, 26 January 1844, gr L. McPherson.
54. See cession, Murdoch Stuart, 22 July 1785, gr J.A. Panet; Lease, S. Finch from J. Munn, at £108 10s per annum, 13 April 1815, gr J. Belanger; Lease, Brehaut with Taylor, 14 March 1818, gr L. McPherson; Sub-lease, McDonald and Hows to Labbé, at £100 for the time required to build two ships, about eight months, 26 June, gr E.B. Lindsay; Leases, Caldwell to Oliver, 5 August 1854, gr L. McPherson, and Lemelin to Valin, 11 February 1854, greffe Frs. Huot; Lease, 6 November 1846, gr A. Campbell; Sale, Nicholson to Russell, 27 March 1849, gr J. Hunt. Four-year lease, Bradshaw to Vaughan, 3 May 1849, gr J. Hunt; Lease, Bradshaw to Vaughan, 3 May 1849, gr J. Hunt; Lease, Davie and Taylor to Davie, 28 December 1854, gr D. McPherson.
55. Though Oliver had his floating dock installed at his yard in St. Roch towards the end of his shipbuilding days.

CHAPTER 6
Shipbuilding Business

The extent to which a shipbuilder was personally involved in the business side of his trade depended on a number of factors, in particular on his inclination and ability to handle commercial matters, the capital and credit at his disposal, and the terms under which he could obtain financing. At one end of the scale he might be hired to take charge of the construction of a hull, selecting his requirements of timber from a supply made available to him by his employers, along with the other building supplies, and when the vessel had been launched, he would be paid and other contracts awarded for its completion.[1] At the other, he might assume the entire responsibility for the construction and outfitting of the vessel ready for sea, finding and purchasing materials, building the hull, arranging for the masting and rigging, either by his own men or by a sub-contractor, and delivering the vessel complete with everything that comprised her equipment and outfit: sails, steering gear, compass, cabin furnishings, kitchen and table utensils, water-casks, lamps, tools of all kinds, flags, pennants, etc. Often he would also engage the captain and crew, provide supplies for the trip and make arrangements for a cargo or charter.

If a shipbuilder decided to put all his effort into the actual construction of vessels and to leave the problems of financing and disposal to others, he could either take a job as a yard foreman or supervisor or enter into partnership with someone who would handle the business side. Some highly competent shipbuilders such as William Simons, James Dodds and John Dick were content to take the first course—Simons was in charge of H.N. Jones' shipyard, the others of the Gilmour yard. Many more, including Pierre Brunelle and Walter G. Ray, were forced by business failures to do the same.[2] When the yard that Pierre Brunelle had so proudly advertised in 1853 was sold nine years later, he was hired by George Patton to superintend his shipyard, while Walter Ray found work with Henry Dinning after his business failed. George Black and John Saxton Campbell were among those who entered into partnerships and split up the shipyard and office responsibility. Their agreement, which lasted from 1825 until 1837, required Black to manage the building yard at Cape Cove and to devote his entire attention to building and repairing vessels. William H. Baldwin and Henry Dinning operated together under a similar arrangement in 1851. Baldwin was in charge of the "outdoor department" while Henry Dinning was "more particularly in charge of the office and books."[3]

Figure 112: *The "Service of Plate Presented to Edward Oliver Esqr. by Bankers, Merchants and Dealers of Great Britain and Ireland, the British Provinces of North America and of the United States as a Testimonial of their appreciation of the energy and ability which directing his spirited enterprises have rendered distinguished serviced to the Great Shipping Interest. Liverpool August 12th, 1855." Liverpool Public Libraries, 152 K/42.*

Ship Brokerage

Fortunately, professional help was available, and the person to whom most shipbuilders turned to handle at least a part of their business was the shipbroker, otherwise known as a commission, ship or shipping agent. Besides negotiating the sale of the vessels they built, a shipbroker provided working capital for the shipbuilders, found charterers for shipowners, and conversely found suitable shipping for would be charterers. He also engaged tonnage space for shippers or found consignments to make up a cargo for shipowners, made arrangements for loading or discharging, handled customs and insurance matters, sold and purchased goods, and in doing so made the necessary advances and collections, on all of which he received a commission. He belonged to a network of shipbrokers and commission merchants around the world who acted as agents for each other and whose services became increasingly efficient following the introduction of the electric telegraph in the 1850s. In short, the shipbroker knew the shipping market and was well placed to advise and assist the shipbuilder in any of the above mentioned ways.

His expertise was invaluable when the shipbuilder was considering the basic question, whether or not to lay down a ship, and he was in a good position to suggest the size and rig likely to be in demand. A competent shipbroker with his finger on the shipping pulse analysed the commodity market with an eye to future shipping requirements; knew the rate of attrition of merchant fleets; noted any new trends or tendencies of the owners in making replacements; was aware of the possible effects on shipping of pending legislation and other regulations; watched for signs of emergencies, such as crop failure or war, which might result in an abnormal demand for tonnage;

and made his recommendations accordingly. The chances of his being close to the mark were generally good, though he was not infallible, as both Quebec and Maritime shipbuilders, who relied heavily on the services of shipbrokers, found out to their detriment at the time of the Oliver debacle.

Edward Oliver, youngest of the three Oliver brothers who were shipbuilders at Quebec, had moved to Liverpool in the early 1840s and become a highly successful shipbroker and shipowner. His success was such that on 12 August 1854 a number of bankers, merchants and traders of Great Britain, Ireland, British North America and the United States presented him with "a service of plate valued at two thousand guineas" as a testimony of their appreciation of "his distinguished services to the Great Shipping Interest." In view of this special honour, his business collapse a short two months later badly shook the business world. His liabilities were placed at one million pounds and his assets at half a million. Banking on the heavy demand for tonnage at premium prices to move troops and supplies to the Crimea, he had built up a fleet of ninety-eight vessels without taking into account the fact that the demand for tonnage would plummet when the army had embarked, nor imagining that when it did pick up, the transport service would favour steam tonnage.[4] When notice was given of the "unprecedented sale of seventy-four ships" belonging to his estate, the market price of the large sailing ships that had been fetching £8 to £12 per ton, fell by 50s per ton, while that of the small ones fetching £7 to £8 10s. fell by 20 to 30s.[5] For some the drop in price was even greater. His failure had serious repercussions in Quebec. In December 1853 there had been twenty-nine ships on the stocks at Quebec; in December 1854 there were four. And though the shipping market had begun to rally by the end of 1854, no vessels were launched in 1855 by such established Quebec shipbuilders as J. J. Nesbitt, T.H. Oliver, P. Valin or J. Lemelin Jr., or by several of the lesser ones. Nor had prices begun to rally (see table 1).

Table 1
Liverpool Prices of Quebec-built Vessels 1853-1855

Sold	Built	Rig	Vessel	Tonnage	Class	$ per ton	
1853	New				6	9 10 - 10 0	
	New				7	10 0 - 11 5	
1854	New					14 0	
	1853	ba	Stamboul	1275		10 0	
	1835	sh	Indus	822		7 6	
	1851	sh	Crown	1284		8 6	
	1853	sh	British Lion	1370	7	15 0	(y.m.)
	1851	sh	Birmingham	1033		11 12	(y.m.)
						13 0	(resale)
	1853	sh	Boomerang	1823		2 14	
	1852	sh	Ebba Brake	1700	6	13 2	(y.m.)
1855	1854	sh	Typhoon	1410*	7	6 15	
	1854	sh	Bucephalus	1337*	7	7 0	
	1853	sh	Norwood	1169*	7	9 10	(y.m.)
	1841	ba	The Duke	682		3 12	
	1851	sh	Panola	965		5 8	
	1852	sh	Gulnare	1106		6 1	
	1854	ba	Mary Ann	475	5	4 4	
	1854	sh	Agnes Anderson	1185		5 0	

Source: *Morning Chronicle*, 3 February to 23 July 1855

Notes: Note the effect of the Oliver bankruptcy. Prices of as much as £15 in 1854 drop sharply at the end of the year, and 1854 production is selling from £5 to £7 in 1855.

Abbreviations: sh ship   y.m. sheathed with yellow metal
 ba barque * Old Measure

The alternative to taking a shipbroker's advice with regard to speculative construction was for the shipbuilder to rely on his own market sense and judgement in deciding if and what to build, as did the shipbuilder Henry Dinning, who presumably counted on making sufficient profit on some vessels to compensate for whatever losses he might incur on others. But as Frederick William Wallace pointed out, Dinning

continually suffered set-backs through overoptimism. Though shrewd and smart in business, good-tempered, a first class builder of ships, yet he would plunge into the construction of vessels without carefully surveying his chances of selling them.[6]

Dinning and his partner William Baldwin are said to have made a profit of $20,000 on the 1877-ton ship *Ocean Monarch*, which they sold on the stocks at the top of the market in 1854. But after their partnership was dissolved in 1856, Dinning faced serious financial difficulties on at least three occasions.[7] Ironically, it was Dinning who had been in charge of the business side of the partnership.

Once the decision to build had been taken, shipbuilders had to solve the problem of obtaining the necessary financing, and most shipbuilding agreements made before notaries were in fact loan agreements to provide funds either for a vessel that had been ordered or more often for one that was being built on speculation. In the latter case, the terms of the loan usually gave the lender the right to have the vessel sold in Britain by his agent, for which both he and the agent were entitled to a commission, while provision was made for alternative compensation should the vessel be sold in Quebec. The loans were generally secured through a mortgage on the vessel, which sometimes extended to its cargo, and it was not uncommon for the shipbuilder to have to put up some or all of his property as security as well.

Although mortgages on vessels were often granted during the first half of the nineteenth century, it was felt that the lenders were not sufficiently protected. This problem was addressed by the Merchant Shipping Act of 1854 which laid down regulations for the registration of mortgages on registered vessels. However, the act made no provision for increasing the security for loans made during construction, a deficiency that was resolved as far as Canadian-built vessels were concerned by the Act to Encourage Shipbuilding within the Province, passed by the Canadian Parliament in 1856. This act provided for the registration of a mortgage on a vessel as soon as her keel had been laid. The person advancing money or goods for her completion was granted a lien until the mortgage was repaid or until he was assigned the vessel, with the right to "give and grant" the builder's certificate and to obtain registry in his name. The mortgage agreement was made either before a notary or two witnesses and registered in the Registry Office of the county in which the vessel was built. The British Act Relating to Shipping and for the Registration, Inspection and Classification Thereof of 1873 reiterated the provisions of the Canadian Act.[8] The lender was deemed the owner of the vessel, insofar as was necessary for making the vessel available as security for the mortgage debt, and was given the right to sell it. However, he remained accountable to the shipbuilder for the proceeds of the sale over and above the amount of the mortgage. This is clearly-illustrated in an agreement between Henry Warner and Lauchlan McKay, in which the barques *Beulah* and *Verona* were listed among their partnership property and described as being held in trust by James G. Ross, subject to several amounts due to him. Ross was the "registered owner" of both vessels.[9]

The Canadian act also laid down a procedure for owners who appointed attorneys to sell their vessels. A standard form or "Certificate of Sale," was provided on which was entered the price or "not less than" amount at which the sale could be made and the date of expiry of the authorization. This was signed by the owner and endorsed by the registrar who noted the details in the port register; many such endorsements are found in the Port of Quebec register books.[10]

Although these measures may have made more working capital available to shipbuilders, the additional security does not appear to have brought about a reduction in commission rates. In his testimony before the "Select Committee of 1868 appointed to inquire into the condition of the shipbuilding industry in Canada," J. Bell Forsyth, a partner of the well-established Quebec firm, Bell, Forsyth & Company, who according to his own declaration had arranged loans for shipbuilders for some twenty or thirty years, said:

Shipbuilders pay, generally from 2% to 5% commission on moneys advanced, and 7% interest, and if the vessel is not sold in Quebec, generally from 4 to 5%, in addition; 2% commission freight is charged in England for collecting.[11]

The commission of 2% was a straight finder's fee, a percentage of the total advances to the builder arranged by the local broker, namely the payments during construction, the cost of any materials and outfit imported by the broker, and the cost of a cargo sent over in the new vessel, if it was financed by the broker. Although five percent was the usual fee, there were many instances in which two, three or four percent was charged. The rate was sometimes progressive, increasing if the loan was not repaid within a certain time, and if the vessel was sold in Quebec, provision was sometimes made for the commission on advances to be calculated on the sale price instead.

The general interest rate on all advances had risen from six to seven percent per annum in 1859, and in the 1870s as much as eight percent coupled with a low commission of 2% was charged by Ross & Company, with the proviso, however, that a five percent commission would apply on a sale made at Quebec. Sending the vessel to the British market gave the shipbuilder an opportunity to make money on a charter or cargo, almost always of timber. But like shipping prices, timber prices fluctuated, and there was the risk that the shipment would arrive when the market was weak. John J. Nesbitt reported a £1000 loss on the combined account of the ship *Anthony Anderson* and her cargo in 1843.[12] The broker, nevertheless, made a 2% commission on either the charter or the freight, while his counterpart in Britain charged 2% for collecting the amount of the freight and four or five percent on the sale of the vessel. A four percent "commission," however, might be accompanied by a further one percent "brokerage" fee.

The builders would have preferred to borrow from the chartered banks, but in the early days of banking the banks were not empowered to lend to them, nor did their directors, many of them merchants who made commissions on loans to shipbuilders, favour the idea. In 1868, answering a question before the "Select Committee appointed to enquire into the General Condition of the Building of Merchant Vessels," Thomas H. Oliver said:

Table 2
Vessels Built in Quebec in 1864 whose Masters Carried Instructions Authorizing Them to Sell Them at Not Less Than a Fixed Amount in Britain or Elsewhere

Vessel	Tonnage	n.l.t.	For sale at £/ton	Sold at £/ton	amount	Mortgage amount
Angelique	956	£8,000	8 7	8 7	£8,000	
Rosalind	547	4,750	8 13	8 10	4,649	
Thistle	683	6,000	8 15	7 13	5,250	
Indian Chief	1806	14,600	8 1	6 3	11,000	
Maythorn	641	5,500	8 11	7 11	4,850	
Mandarin	799	6,750	8 8	8 10	6,791	
Strathspey	525	4,650	8 17	7 16	4,100	
Huron	774		8 0	7 10	5,805	6,000
Superior	1375	10,000	7 5	7 12	10,464	10,000
Queen of the Lakes	1154	9,500	8 4	7 7	8,500	
Her Majesty	1342	10,000	7 9	8 0	10,736	10,000
L'Agouhanna	1115	9,000	7 3	7 17	8,780	
Rock Light	778	6,000	7 14	7 8	5,791	6,400
Mauldslie	637	5,250	8 4	7 17	5,016	2,500
Caribou	1160	9,450	8 2	7 10	8,700	
Defiant	1325	10,000	7 10	7 2	9,400	8,500
Bonniton	593	4,700	7 18	8 10	5,261	

Source: Registers of the Port of Quebec, Vols. 268-9, NA.

Note: The *Huron, Superior, Her Majesty* and Rock Light, sold by H. and J. Dinning fetched an average of £7 12 6d per ton. The *Defiant* was sold by W. Cotnam at £7 2s per ton; the other twelve by James G. Ross at an average of £7 16s.

If the banks were allowed the power of lending money to shipbuilders on the same footing as merchants now lend, there would be a clear gain to the builder of from 10 to 15 percent; for the builder, instead of buying at 6 months, could buy for cash at 10 percent less at least. But the banks are under the control of directors, who are the merchants now advancing to shipbuilders.

The shipbuilders Dunn and Samson were of the same opinion. "If the Banks were allowed to lend money at a reasonable rate," they said, "it would materially improve business." The shipowner Henry Fry, however, did not believe that allowing banks to advance money to shipbuilders on the security of new vessels under construction would solve the problems facing the industry at that time. Not only did he think that they would be unwilling to do so, but he attributed the difficulty in selling Canadian-built vessels to the rapid increase in popularity of iron and composite ships, which was "destroying all demand" for Canadian wooden ships. As a shipowner of both kinds of vessels, he *knew* how fast the wooden ship was becoming obsolete. In the 1870s, however, both the Union Bank and the Banque Nationale, and perhaps other banks, held mortgages on ships, but they too had to use the services of shipbrokers to sell the vessels, and the brokers naturally took "the usual commission."

Throughout the era of tall ship construction Quebec shipbuilders relied heavily on commission agents who had the essential trans-Atlantic connections and varying degrees of mercantile shipping savvy. They provided the financing, frequently handled part or all of the importation of equipment and, if they were timber merchants, often supplied some or all of the timber. In most cases, they also handled the disposal of the vessel, either taking over the hull as soon as it had been completed or else receiving the vessel completely equipped and outfitted ready for sea. Most of the lenders were primarily timber merchants and their names appear over and over again in loan agreements and ship registration certificates. They include such firms as Atkinson, Usborne & Company, Anderson and Paradis, G. Burns Symes, H. and E. Burstall, Forsyth and Bell, M. I. Wilson and many more, but among them two men stand out for their exceptional knowledge of maritime matters–Henry Fry and James Gibb Ross. Both earned a special place in the history of the trade.

"The love of ships, and everything connected with them, was one of the earliest of my boyish tastes, and seemed to be innate," wrote Henry Fry,[13] and he undoubtedly considered himself most fortunate when he entered Mark Whitwill's brokerage firm in Bristol, England, in 1838 at the age of twelve. After becoming a partner of the firm in 1851, he looked after its ship agency and commission business at Quebec for the eight months of each year that the port was open. In 1856, when he struck out on his own account, he was already part-owner of four sailing ships, for ship brokerage and shipowning often went hand in hand. Fry remained a shipowner for thirty years, during which he became part or full owner of another eighteen vessels and managed them himself. He used his profits to run a timber exporting business which he described as his "hobby," and did not actively finance the construction of vessels, though he did buy several Quebec-built ships either for re-sale or for his own fleet. He considered Edouard Trahan, who built four of them, "one of the cleverest shipbuilders in the province for many years, & a conscientious & unassuming man." Fry also admired the work of Henry Dinning, another shipbuilder with whom he did business on many occasions, though he deplored the headstrong manner in which Dinning decided to build a ship, without due consideration of the market. Dinning laid down four vessels to Fry's specifications, including the *Devonshire* in 1860 and the *Cosmo* in 1877, both of which were built for the express purpose of providing work for ship carpenters during particularly hard times as a result of Dinning's strong intervention on their behalf. Henry Fry's extensive knowledge of shipping matters frequently led to his service as assessor for the Quebec Admiralty Court. He crossed the Atlantic thirty-seven times in twenty-three years, often sailing in January when conditions were at their worst. Incensed by the unnecessary suffering and loss of life among sailors, which he attributed to the repeal of the law prohibiting deck-loads after October, he wrote a paper for the Dominion Board of Trade in 1872 demanding that deck-loads of timber and deals and grain cargoes be regulated–he himself did not allow deck loads on his own ships in winter–and lobbied successfully for bills of reform to be passed in both the Canadian and British Parliaments. In 1873, as President of the Quebec Board of Trade, he courageously organized a campaign to stamp out the vicious crimping system, demanding energetic measures from the government. His contribution to Canadian maritime history was recognized across the Atlantic and underscored by Basil Greenhill and Anne Giffard when they wrote,

Prominent in the agitation for the passing of this Act [limiting deck cargoes], as he had been in the cleaning up of the Quebec waterfront, was an outstanding figure in the maritime history of Canada, Henry Fry.[14]

While Henry Fry started in the shipping business at a very tender age, James Gibb Ross was gradually drawn into it. He arrived in Quebec as a boy of fifteen, and entered the highly successful wholesale and retail grocery business of his maternal uncles, James and Thomas Gibb. Besides learning the grocery business, from which he would later make a considerable fortune, he had there his first experiences of ship financing and brokerage. From 1858, when he and his elder brother John formed a partnership under the name "Ross and Company," ship brokerage and ownership, for which James G. Ross demonstrated an extraordinary flair, began occupying an increasingly greater part of his time. In 1858, Ross and Company financed three Quebec shipbuilders, Louis Labbé, T.C. Lee and Dubord, Laroche and Company, and as a consequence J.G. Ross registered the following spring the first of close to 250 vessels that were registered in his name over the next twenty-seven years. Ross' principal agents were Robert Edmiston and Alex Mitchell in Glasgow, his brother William H. Ross[15] and Alex Cassels in Liverpool and Albert Chrystie in Le Havre, but he also dealt with a number of other shipbrokers at other ports. Cassels was his agent from 1866 to 1867 and handled the larger part of his business, having also represented him for two years jointly with W.H. Ross.

James Gibb Ross' journals from the year 1868, when he withdrew from the partnership with his brother and continued on his own, record his management of 216 vessels and bear out J.G. Scott's statement that he was "King of the whole shipbuilding industry." He dealt with some forty shipbuilders for whom in most cases he provided working capital by means of a mortgage during construction. Many of the mortgages were not repaid within the prescribed number of days following the launch and thus the vessels were registered in his name. The shipping registers show that he made mortgages on others after their registration. Some of the vessels were held in trust by Ross until he was able to sell them at what he considered a fair price. Details of some of the different arrangements that were made in this respect appear in Ross' journals and other documents, but were not necessarily endorsed on the registration certificates. The *Madura*, built by F.X. Marquis in 1876, was divided into sixty-four shares, thirty-two of which were owned by W.H. Ross and Company of Liverpool, and sixteen each by Marquis and by Ross and Company; P.V. Valin's *Canada* of 1866, though registered in Ross' name, was three-quarters owned by him and one-quarter by Ross.[16] While waiting to be sold, the vessels were skillfully managed by Ross and earned their way carrying cargoes of timber from Quebec, coal from Newcastle, guano from Callao, cotton from Pensacola, and grain from Montreal–to name but a few. Although it is difficult to compare ship prices because we do not know how they may have differed, Table 2 shows that those sold by Ross' agents in 1864 fetched better prices than the vessels sold by H. and J. Dinning and William Cotnam. Like Henry Fry, Ross was not indifferent to the plight of shipyard workers when the shipping market was bad, and made advances on many occasions so that there would be work for them.

Shipbuilding Business

Figure 113: *Henry Fry, Bristol-born Quebec shipowner, who was known on both sides of the Atlantic both for his writings and courageous stand against crimping, the practice of carrying deck loads of timber in winter and unsafe bulk grain handling procedures. Photo: Courtesy Notman, with thanks to John Fry.*

Figure 114: *The vessels that flew Henry Fry's red Maltese cross, included the 986 ton ship* Mary Fry *of 1861, named after Henry Fry's wife and built by Dinning, who kept a share in her. She began her career by sailing twice to Montreal for wheat and flour that year. Courtesy Maritime Museum of the Atlantic, Wallace Collection. MP1.97.1.*

Figure 115: *The 825 ton* Rock City, *built by McKay and Warner for Henry Fry. According to his memoirs, she was the most fortunate and profitable ship he ever owned. Photo from F.W. Wallace,* In the Wake of the Windships, *Fonds initial 616 1020–89, courtesy Archives nationales du Québec*

Figure 116: *The vaunted* Cosmo, *1220 tons, built to Fry's specifications by Dinning. Photo John Stevenson Fry.*

Figure 117: *Senator James Gibb Ross (1819–1888), businessman, merchant, ship broker and shipowner, and foremost authority on shipping in Quebec. Courtesy Harry Ross.*

Although Ross played an important part in the shipbuilding industry through the 1860s and 1870s as a shipowner, shipbroker and commission agent, he still had enough energy and initiative left for other interests and the capital to invest in them. He was a founding shareholder of the Quebec Marine Insurance Company, which was incorporated in 1862, and made large investments in wood mills, paper mills and railways.[17] Naturally, he was also a timber and lumber exporter. In 1895, when no one could any longer doubt that the age of the wooden sailing ship had ended, Fry wrote, "If the late Senator James Gibb Ross were alive, he would certainly start a steel ship-building company in Quebec and make it a success."[18] Whether this statement was realistic is open to discussion. Certainly it is a tribute to the part played by James G. Ross in the shipbuilding industry from one who was well qualified to judge.

Classification

Classification, so often a thorn in the shipbuilder's side, was the natural outcome of marine insurance. It grew from the need for criteria to evaluate the risk being underwritten and had existed informally as long as marine insurance itself. It was the yardstick by which the selling price and the insurance premiums on a vessel and its cargoes were reckoned. Formal classification began in 1760, when a group of London underwriters began keeping records in their *Register of Shipping*. Under their system, hulls were designated "A," "E," "I," or "U," and equipment "G," "M," or "B"–good, middling or bad. Thus, a first-class ship with a good outfit would be classed "AG." Regulations for classification were altered from time to time, as were the symbols,[19] but as a rule, the alterations were minor. In 1797, however, new rules adopted by the society contained startling changes. Thereafter, vessels were to be classed solely according to their age and the place in which they were built, with no regard to how they were built, of what timber they were built or their condition.[20]

A Thames-built ship would be granted a first classification that was valid for thirteen years; a similar vessel built in Quebec was eligible for ten years; while one built in Wales or in northern Britain could receive no more than eight. Shipowners immediately protested the unfair system, but received no satisfaction. As a result, London shipowners broke away, formed their own rival society, and issued their own register. It was officially called *The New Register Book of Shipping*, but was commonly known as the "Shipowners' Register," or "The Red Book," as opposed to the "Green Book" as the underwriters' register was known. The problems, however, were far from solved, for the rules of the new shipowners' society were barely more equitable than the underwriters' rules. Although the classification of a first-class Thames-built vessel was reduced to twelve years, the maximum for a similar county-built vessel was still only ten.[21]

The two societies operated side by side despite the increasing dissatisfaction with both and many attempts to bring about an amalgamation, until finally in 1834 reason prevailed and the "Permanent Committee of Lloyd's Register of British and Foreign Shipping" (henceforth Lloyd's) was formed. It was made up of merchants, shipbuilders and underwriters and took over from the two societies, introducing a new set of rules and issuing the first edition of *Lloyd's Register of British and Foreign Shipping* in 1834.[22]

According to the new rules of 1834, vessels were classed "A," "Æ," "E" or "I"; anchors, cables and stores were classed "1" if satisfactory or "2" if unsatisfactory. Classification was awarded for a given number of years. Thus, the rating "10 A 1" denoted a first-class vessel with satisfactory equipment whose rating would hold good for ten years. At the end of ten years, the vessel had to undergo certain prescribed repairs and pass a thorough survey in order to retain an A character, failing which, she would be described as Æ. The E rating denoted a second-class vessel, one unfit to carry dry cargoes but safe to travel to all parts of the world, while I class ships were third-class and "good for short voyages only." The *Register* included a list of timbers acceptable for the various terms of classification, and tables of required scantlings and sizes of anchors, chains and bolts. (see Appendix E) As the maximum classification a vessel could obtain was established by the species of timber of which it was built, the builder was ill-advised to put more value into it than was required by the rules for a vessel built of that wood. The class would not be raised, the selling price was very unlikely to be higher, and the builder's profit was likely to disappear. On the other hand, if he did not observe all the requirements of the rules, the vessel could lose a year of class. For example, an A rating valid for seven years, i.e. A 7, might have its validity cut to six years and suffer the customary reduction in its selling price of two dollars per ton per year of class. An instance of such a reduction appears in a building contract between Jean E. Gingras and Henry Dinning in which the price was quoted as thirty-four dollars per ton provided the vessel was classed A 9, but thirty-two dollars if it were classed A 8 and thirty if classed A 7.[23]

Thirteen full-time and fifty part-time surveyors were appointed in British ports. Some were "shipwright surveyors," whose primary duty was to inspect vessels at three stages of their construction–when they were in frame, when the beams and some of the planking but not the decks were in place, and when all work had been completed; others were "nautical surveyors" who surveyed vessels afloat. The surveyors made recommendations, but the classification could only be assigned by the Classification Committee itself.[24]

Figure 118: *The Ross & Company establishment on St. Peter Street. Photo Courtesy National Archives, Ottawa.*

> **Instructions regarding the amounts to be paid out to shipbuilders, dated 17 February 1872, in James G. Ross' "General Memoranda Book."**
>
> *Angers & Bertrand* will require every fortnight $200 or $300 besides what they have had to date and will bring Mrs. Bertrand's order to get the $1,000 left in our hands as security. The total not to exceed the balance that will be coming to them from the *North Star*.
> *Gingras* not exceeding $500 p.w. except that he is buying some wood - total advances should not exceed $45,000 after taking off old balance.
> *Marquis* $500 - $650 p.w., with a little for purchases.
> *Charland* $500 - $500 p.w., except he is buying something and don't go too much with that.
> *Valin* should not exceed $400 - $500 p.w. unless he is planking, then 200 extra.
> *Dunn & Samson* get what they want.
> *Wilson* for new steamer may require $2,000 - $2,500 to complete her.
> *McKay & Warner* should require not over $2,000 to complete ship.

Canadian shipbuilders found the rules discriminatory and unjust. Not only were North American shipbuilding timbers classed so low that it was impossible for Canadian vessels to receive more than a mediocre rating, but vessels whose construction was not controlled by the inspections of a Lloyd's surveyor suffered in their rating on that score also. It is not surprising that in 1836 the Montreal and Quebec Boards of Trade echoed the request that had already been made by shipping interests in Rotterdam for the appointment of a Lloyd's Surveyor at the port. This was followed by a meeting in May 1837 between the Secretary and the Chairman of the Society on the one hand, and Mr. A. Gillespie on behalf of the Quebec Board of Trade, on the other, but Quebec shipbuilders had to mark time for fourteen years before Lloyd's finally took action.

At last, in 1851 Thomas Menzies, "a highly respectable Ship-builder who has carried on business for many years at Leith," was appointed surveyor of ships at the Port of Quebec. The Quebec Board of Trade guaranteed his annual salary of £300 by agreeing to make up any deficiency between the fees he received and that amount.[25] But the Board did not have to fulfil their commitment. Menzies' appointment was so successful that the following year a surveyor and two assistants were appointed to Saint John, New Brunswick, the assistants later being given their own surveyorships at Prince Edward Island and Miramichi, respectively. Within a few years, there were six Lloyd's surveyors in British North America. As each took office, it was required that all new vessels built in his district seeking classification by Lloyd's undergo the three surveys before launching as laid down in the rules of the society, or suffer the loss of a year of classification. However, the duties of the surveyors went much further than carrying out the three compulsory inspections. If a shipbuilder so desired, it was now possible to build a vessel "under special survey." This meant that, for the small sum of one shilling per register ton, the surveyor would follow a vessel's progress through every stage of her construction, which in some cases entailed forty or fifty inspections. Moreover, for a smaller fee the same service was available for ships under repair.[26] It is hard to conceive of any other measure that could have done as much to upgrade local shipbuilding practice.

The surveyors did not have the authority to award classifications but were limited to forwarding reports of their surveys with accompanying remarks, including their recommendation as to the classification of the vessel. As the years passed, an increasing number of supporting documents were required. From 1853, for instance, shipbuilders had to produce certificates of tests of cables; from 1862, certificates of anchor tests. From 1869, when an extra year was granted for thorough salting, an attestation as to the amount of salt had to be submitted as well.[27]

It was Thomas Menzies, who, determined that Quebec shipbuilders should reap the utmost advantage from his appointment, suggested to Lloyd's Committee that the words "built under special survey" be inscribed on the classification certificate of every vessel that had benefitted from the special service. They not only agreed to his proposal but, impressed by the outpouring of expressions of appreciation of the shipbuilders, decided to go one step further and adopt a symbol to distinguish the special survey vessels in their *Register Books*. The symbol, a Maltese Cross, is used for that purpose to this day.[28] Though appointed by Lloyd's and remaining under its sole orders, Thomas Menzies and his assistant and successor, Charles Coker, showed great loyalty and sympathy towards the Quebec shipbuilders throughout their terms of office. Their support was invaluable in the long battle to upgrade the classification

Figure 119: *Certificate of Testing of the anchor chain of the* Six Frères, *built by Charles Jobin and Company in 1863. Lloyd's Survey No. 527.*

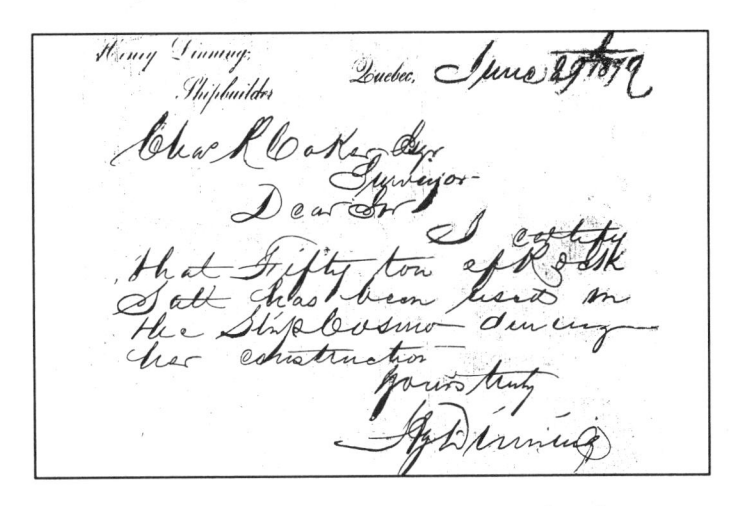

Figure 120: *Attestation of the amount of salt used in the construction of the ship* Cosmo, *signed by Henry Dinning, the builder. Lloyd's Survey No. 1047.*

of Quebec-built ships. There are many instances when a vessel might have lost one year of classification for not conforming strictly to Lloyd's rules had not the surveyor succeeded in convincing the Committee that the offending discrepancy had been more than offset in other ways.

Meanwhile, a continental classification society had been established in Brussels in 1828 under the name Bureau Veritas. Moved to Paris in 1830, it remained there for forty years before returning to Brussels. In 1864 the respected local master shipbuilder Walter Ray was appointed the first Bureau Veritas surveyor for classifications, surveys, etc. in the Port of Quebec,[29] and increasingly, vessels that were not built for the British market were classed by the French society instead of Lloyd's. As might be expected, the rules, the methods of survey and measurement, and the classification code were different. A contract signed by the shipbuilder William Cotnam with Messrs Gildermeister of Bremen, Germany in 1876 required the vessel to be classed "in the French Veritas 3.3.1.1. three, three, one, one, for 10 years."[30] It was not long before rivalry between the two societies became apparent. The Bureau Veritas system of measurement produced a lower tonnage than the Lloyd's system, according to Lloyd's surveyor Charles Coker, who indignantly described it as "a regular piece of robbery on dues." According to French law, he wrote, there were thirty-two charges on vessels, twenty-five of which were based on the tonnage, so that a vessel classed by the Bureau Veritas would pay lower dues than an identical vessel classed by Lloyd's and thus Lloyd's customers would be at a disadvantage. Moreover, because of the lower tonnage figure, the vessel in question could be built of less heavy timber than if she were registered at Lloyd's and her stores could be smaller.[31] A note in one of J.G. Ross' journals gives a different viewpoint. His agent had written that Veritas was more expensive (and therefore stricter) than Lloyd's for outfit. Forty-five fathoms of cable put aboard at Quebec had been condemned as too small by their surveyor, who also rejected two chain pipes that had to be replaced.[32]

The majority of vessels built for the British market continued to be surveyed and classed by Lloyd's until 1877 when the position was reversed. By then, the number of ships being laid down did not warrant the services of a full-time surveyor in the port, and the *Braidwood* and the *Lauderdale* of 1880 were the last large sailing ships built under Lloyd's special survey. The few vessels launched after that date were surveyed by the part-time agent for Bureau Veritas, the master shipbuilder William Simons.[33] In the Maritimes, a third classification society, the American Shipmasters' Association, was also active, but no evidence of that society having operated at Quebec has been found.

Lloyd's surveyors handled by far the greatest part of the business of the port between 1852 and 1880 and did much for the sailing ship industry. Their presence not only encouraged the British shipowner to give orders to Quebec shipbuilders, confident that they would be of the required standard, but also encouraged him to buy vessels sent to Britain from Quebec on speculation. The industry paid a heavy price for the fifteen years that elapsed from the time a surveyor was requested to the time of his actual appointment to the port.

Shipbuilding Contracts

Fortunately for the historian, Quebec ships were not always built on speculation, and the Archives contain many of the original construction contracts. They vary in length from two to as many as forty pages or more, the difference in size generally accounted for by the amount of detail in the specifications. In many cases, these were sent or brought over from Great Britain or Ireland where they had been drawn up by the purchaser or his agent, and were appended to the contract in their original form. Plans, however, were few and far between. Only a few midship section plans, one deck plan and a few drawings of details have come to light. When vessels were bought "on the stocks" the contracts were comparatively short, but among them are several with detailed lists of equipment and stores that were to be supplied.

As most vessels were sold to British customers, few contracts were signed by the prospective shipowner. They were frequently executed by a commission merchant on his behalf, and sometimes by one of his captains who might also be required to supervise the construction, particularly before the appointment of the Lloyd's surveyor in 1852. The shipbuilder signed on his own and perhaps a partner's behalf, though if he became insolvent and did not have a partner whose credit was good, it was often his wife who signed. Following Thomas Oliver's bankruptcy in 1853, for instance, the business was carried on under the name of Oliver & Company and documents were signed by his wife, Jane, and at times by Oliver himself on her behalf. When Thomas C. Lee was in the same position in 1857, his wife did the same.

The "contract to build" generally specified where the vessel would be built, "at his shipyard," "at his shipyard on the St. Charles River," or perhaps more exactly "in his shipyard ... the keel now laid on the West side of a vessel in course of construction now planking." Besides a delivery date, a launching time was generally included, "on the first Spring Tides" or "on the opening of Spring navigation" or perhaps before a given day. In most cases, delivery took place after launching alongside a designated wharf, and the time allowed for completion between the two was usually a matter of two to three weeks. The shipbuilder agreed either to supply a builder's certificate so that the purchaser could take out the registration in his name, or else to provide the registration certificate itself.

A contract signed in Liverpool in December 1849 between Edward Oliver, on behalf of his brother Thomas, and Messrs Pryde & Jones, required only a vessel built "of dimensions, model and workmanship similar to the *Maria* now in this port and not to exceed 875 tons Old Measure." She was to be copper-fastened to sixteen feet with centre bolts of iron. Thomas was to supply hull, masts, spars, studding sail booms and yards with all necessary iron work, rigging, two bower anchors, one stream and one kedge, chains, seventeen sails and three boats. She was to be fitted with a full figurehead, cookhouse, camboose, a patent purchase on the windlass, three hawsers and metal pumps. The hull, spars, etc., were to have two coats of paint, and the vessel was to be in every way up to being classed six years at Lloyd's, "with the exception of the usual iron kneeing and caulking here [in Britain]."[34]

By contrast, there were twenty-seven pages of specifications in the contract signed in 1840 by Edward Oliver while he was still shipbuilding in Quebec and Francis Jenkins, master mariner of Dublin, on behalf of Henry Daniel Brooke of Dublin and Joseph Wilson Brooke of Liverpool.[35] Despite the fact that the model was to be the "same as the *Brooke* built by Mr Oliver last year," the Brookes left nothing to chance. Oliver was told just what species of wood was to be used for each timber, what size it was to be and how it was to be fastened. Every part of the construction was equally carefully described. It is apparent, however, that no plans were provided. There is just one drawing–of the square bilge of the midship's frame.

The price of the vessel was expressed as so much per ton, very occasionally as a fixed sum, never as a cost plus amount, and after 1834 it was often conditional on her being awarded a certain classification. Because the exact tonnage could only be calculated after the vessel had been completed and measured, purchasers were apt to protect themselves against wide variations from the tonnage they had ordered by stipulating that no payment would be made for tonnage in excess of a certain amount, or that a reduced rate would be applied to extra tonnage. Payment was usually made in four or more instalments that were designed to take care of current bills for wages and materials and were scheduled either at certain stages of the construction or at regular intervals, weekly or monthly, sometimes with larger amounts payable during periods of heavy labour costs. The final instalment of about twenty percent, which represented the builder's own salary, his yard and other costs, as well as his profit, was disbursed only after safe launching and delivery. Even when it was supposedly a builders' market, he might only receive half the final payment immediately after the launching and be required to wait for two months or more before the final payment became due.

In general, vessels were built "at the risk of the contractor until safely launched and afloat." In the case of accident, the builder was either liable for the amount of the penalty for non-compliance or in some cases was required to furnish a similar vessel in the shortest time possible. Often agreements stipulated that insurance should be obtained by the builder against fire on the stocks, or that it would be obtained by the purchaser and charged to the builder. Sometimes, though rarely, the cost was shared, as when George Charles was required to bear five shillings per hundred pounds on the sum insured as his share of the premium. Vessels could not be insured against the risk of launching until the last half of the nineteenth century, when it became standard procedure. Terms of the 1855 contract between the shipbuilder William Cathro Richardson and John Jameson, which required the vessel to be insured against the risks of fire on the stocks and launching, are typical.[36] In the case of vessels built on speculation and sent to Britain with a cargo of timber, both ship and cargo were insured, the premiums varying considerably depending on the time of year. Thus, James Tibbits was charged a rate of 25/- on the twelve year old ship *Crusader* and her cargo, which he sent to Britain in April of 1847, and the same on the brand new *Thomas Fielden* and *Lord Elgin* in June. On 1 September, however, he was obliged to pay 60/- on another new ship, the *Madawaska*, and by the time he insured the *Saint Andrew* one month later it cost him 84/-. The rate had reached 210/- when he insured the *China* on 9 December, while a staggering 252/- was charged for the *Thomas Fielden* the same day, ten times the rate of her previous voyage in June.[37] One cannot help feeling that if the risk were so great, the ships should not have sailed at all.

Arrangements for arbitration in case of dispute over the quality of workmanship or materials formed part of many contracts, each party agreeing to name one arbitrator, who in the case of non-agreement could name a third. To avoid costly delays, a time limit of a few days was generally imposed. Both parties were further bound by a penalty clause for non-compliance which, though small in some cases–£100 in the contract between James Fairrie and James Duncanson in 1786[38]–was extremely high in others. For example, the penalty of £5000, specified in an agreement between John J. Nesbitt and G. H. Parke in 1839, was in excess of the sale price of the vessel.[39] In some cases the penalty was progressive. Thus a contract made in 1850 between Thomas Oliver and Messrs. Pryde & Jones called for the vessel to be completed not later than 15 June, and it was agreed that a 10s per ton would be deducted if she was not complete by then, of 20s if she was not ready by 15 July, of 30s if she was still not ready on 15 August, and of 40s if she had not been dispatched on 15 September. Moreover, if the vessel was not granted a six-year class, there would be a 10s per ton reduction in the sales price.[40]

In general, contracts to build were ironclad, though occasionally escape clauses reflected uncertain times. Contracts made in 1811 by the timber merchants Patterson, Dyke & Company with shipwrights committed to report to Naval Dockyards in the event of war were subject to cancellation should war break out, the shipwrights receiving "the amount of the work done up to that time at a fair evaluation to be made by Master Shipbuilders."[41] Though the parties must have frequently agreed to modifications in the terms of contracts or in specifications during the course of construction, it is evident that it was considered unnecessary to have such changes added to the original deeds which remained in the notaries' hands, as very few such riders have been noted.

On the whole, the terms of shipbuilding contracts were remarkably similar at any given time. It was understood that things would be done according to the custom of the port, and it was men versed in the custom, other shipbuilders and not the courts, who were generally the arbitrators in cases of dispute. Moreover, from 1852 one of the effects of Lloyd's surveys was to impose a controlled building standard and thus reduce the number of disputes regarding quality.

The Shipyard Workforce

The very nature of shipyard work imposes serious limitations on any attempt to give accurate statistics of the number of workers employed in Quebec shipyards over the years. In winter, their work was largely confined to new construction and numbers varied. In summer, yards where repair work was not undertaken often closed down.

The newspapers did not report on the labour situation in the shipyards in summer, and their winter figures have to be regarded with circumspection, particularly for the years prior to 1840. For instance, the statistics published by the *Quebec Mercury* in 1840 purporting to show the number of men who had worked in the Quebec shipyards annually over the previous twenty-two years were obviously concocted using the formula of fifty-five men for each vessel built in Quebec according to the newspaper's own production figures, which were themselves incorrect.[42] Beginning

Table 3
Numbers of Workers in Saint Lawrence, Saint Charles and Pointe-aux-Trembles Shipyards 1840-1866

	Saint Lawrence	Saint Charles	Pointe-aux-T	Total		Source
1840	810	1,565		2,375	QM	27/ 2/40
1841	730	2,130	100	2,960	QM	10/ 4/41
1842	480	950	150	1,580	QM	5/ 4/42
1843				750	QM	23/ 2/43
	373	855	30	1,420	QM	29/ 4/43
1844		395	965	1,360	QM	8/ 2/44
1845	640	1,690	100	2,430	QM	20/ 2/45
1846	823	1,090		1,913	QM	3/ 2/46
1847	630	1,501	250	2,381	QM	26/12/46
1851	669	1,515		2,184	QM	13/12/50
1861				2,000	QM	5/ 1/61
1863		2,260		2,260	MC	/10/62
				4,181	MC	24/ 3/63
1865	870	1,405		2,275	MC	27/ 1/65
1866	1,047	1,767		2,807	MC	26/ 1/66

Abbreviations: QM *Quebec Mercury*
MC *Morning Chronicle*

in 1840, an actual survey was made each winter to find out how many men were working, and from then on the figures published represent either the number working in the yards on the day the survey was made or the number that the shipbuilder or his foreman expected to hire that season, or even a combination of both. Although they were far more accurate after 1840, they should still be read with these considerations in mind.

Table 3, which gives available figures for 1840 to 1866 for the three shipbuilding districts at Quebec, shows that on average between fifteen hundred and twenty-five hundred men were employed at some time during the winter season. Exceptionally, over four thousand are said to have been working in the spring of 1863 and as many may have worked in 1864, a year of even higher production. To these figures should be added a substantial number of support workers, such as carters, and independent tradesmen–mastmakers, sailmakers, riggers and others. With a few exceptions, for which the census provides the answers, we do not know the length of time that the men worked each year. In many cases, employment lasted a few months; in some cases, for the whole year.

As vessels increased in size, the number of hands employed to build them also increased. In April 1825, it was reported that an average of thirty-five men were working on each of the six vessels building in Quebec, which averaged 389 tons, while five times the number, or one hundred and seventy-five men were working on the 5294-ton *Baron of Renfrew* on the Isle of Orleans.[43] The columns in Table 4 of the number and tonnage of vessels under construction and the number of workers employed in the various Quebec shipyards in February

1840 show that ten vessels averaging 741 tons were under construction in the Saint Lawrence River shipyards, while there were twenty-three averaging 602 tons on the Saint Charles. In both cases the number of workers hired gives us a ratio of approximately nine tons per man, while the difference in the average number of workers per vessel, eighty-one and sixty-eight, respectively, reflects the difference in the vessels' size. However, it is apparent from these figures and from data on other years that various shipyards had different policies as to the number of men they hired per ton of shipping under construction.

Moreover, the number also varied considerably through the period of construction. On a large ship, there might be as many as a hundred or more at one time and less than a dozen at another, for any of a number of reasons. It could be due to the number required to do a particular job efficiently, to the availability of labour or to the time in which it was desired or required to build it. A shipbuilder with little capital would be more apt to spread it thinly on a few workers and build one vessel slowly through the winter,[44] while one for whom capital was not a problem might employ many more men and build more than one. On occasion construction might be brought to a temporary halt. This occurred in some cases, when the vessel was in frame in order to allow the timbers to season on the stocks, thus fulfilling a requirement of the prospective buyer.[45] That this practice was beneficial is apparent from the fact that vessels built by Allan Gilmour and Company for their own fleet were frequently left on the stocks to season for more than a year. In the case of a speculative undertaking, construction might be delayed on account of a weak market, when by halting the work and delaying borrowing, the amount of future interest payments was reduced. Sometimes the delays were due to current high wages and work was resumed when the rates had dropped. In this respect, the decision was not necessarily made by the shipbuilder. In the 1860s, for instance, financing contracts of men such as James G. Ross, Jeffery, Noad and Company and W.H. Anderson gave them the right to halt construction should "unreasonable" wage increases occur.[46]

Conversely there were occasions when the shipbuilder set out to build a vessel quickly or had to hasten construction, particularly when work was behind schedule and a penalty clause might come into play. This could be the result of labour problems[47] or delays caused by an unusual number of snow storms during a winter–the winter of 1863 was particularly bad in this respect[48]–or the devastating fires of 1845 and 1866 which drove hundreds of shipyard workers from their homes. He might then hand out separate contracts for work on the port and starboard sides to the tradesmen such as the plankers and caulkers, thus doubling the number of men on the job. On at least one occasion, when additional workers were unavailable, a shipbuilder lured them from a neighbouring yard with the promise of higher pay.[49]

In general a vessel took from five to seven months to build, but there were many exceptions. Among them was the 1124-ton ship *Stag*, which had been on the stocks for twenty-three months before she was launched in 1867, and the 1200-ton ship *Pladda*, the 1435-ton ship *Westminster* and the 472-ton barque *Ravenscliffe*, all three of which had been twenty months building. Several others took over a year.[50]

Table 4
Number and Tonnage of Vessels under Construction and Number of Workers in Quebec Shipyards, February 1840

Shipbuilder	No. of vessels	No. of men	Tonnage reported	Regd. tonnage	Tons/ man	Men/ ship
St. Lawrence						
Sharples	1	100	765	861	8.61	100.0
Gilmour	3	180	2,300	2,275	12.63	60.0
Black	3	250	1,890	2,089	8.36	83.3
Lampson	3	280	2,117	2,181	7.79	93.3
	10	*810*	*7,072*	*7,406*	*9.14*	*81.0*
St. Charles						
Nicholson & Russell	2	150	940	1,071	7.14	75.0
Munn	3	200	1,540	1,639	8.19	66.0
Vidal	1	70	570	638	9.11	70.0
Oliver, Th.	3	220	1,630	1,810	8.23	71.3
Oliver, Ed.	4	290	2,158	2,363	8.15	72.5
Jeffery, John	4	205	2,200	2,276	11.10	51.2
Jeffery, Jas	3	250	2,000	2,328	9.31	83.3
Nesbitt	3	180	1,600	1,711	9.50	60.0
	23	*1,565*	*12,038*	*13,836*	*8.84*	*68.0*
Total	33	2,375	19,110	21,242	8.94	72.0

Sources: *Quebec Mercury*, 26 February 1840.

Note: These figures are consistent with those of R. Rice for February 1852, which show an average of 188 men employed in each yard, as compared to 198 here, with seventy-three working on each vessel, seventy-two here, and 8.6 to 8.2 tons of shipping per man, this despite a 50% increase in the size of the vessels over the twelve years. "Shipbuilding in British America 1787-1890: An Introductory Study."

Division and Cost of Labour

Hiring and managing the permanent staff of tradesmen, apprentices and labourers, the "gangs" who contracted to do specific jobs, and the workers, both skilled and unskilled, taken on by the day or for longer periods, was an important part of the shipbuilder's business. He normally shared this with his foreman, the man who had charge of the day-to-day management of the yard and from whom the workers as well as the apprentices were bound at times by their contracts to take orders.[51]

Shipyard foremen did not all have the same degree of competence. Sometimes the position was filled by a ship carpenter, sometimes by a shipwright. The shipwright William Grant, for instance, was employed by George and William Hamilton in 1810, the ship carpenter Jacques Labbé by Louis Labbé in 1825.[52] In many cases a shipbuilder or master shipwright was hired, instead. John Banfield, who was described as a "shipbuilder and draughtsman," became foreman of Labbé's yard in 1825, and William Simons, for many years foreman of H. N. Jones' shipyard, was described indifferently as "shipbuilder" or "master shipwright."[53] Nor was every foreman a yard foreman. He might only be responsible for the construction of a particular ship or ships. Charles Jobin was hired as foreman for the construction of two ships by the merchant Thomas Sherwood in 1863.[54] Sometimes the foreman's duties stretched beyond shipbuilding and repairing to include responsibilities in the timber yard, as evidenced by William Grant's contract with the merchants Bruce and Anderson.[55] In addition, the foreman was sometimes but not always in charge of the shipbuilder's apprentices, sometimes required to do the draughting and sometimes to teach draughting.[56] Though he might himself have to work under a supervisor—even shipbuilders did on occasion, especially before the appointment of a Lloyd's surveyor, – he might, like William Simons, be known as both foreman and superintendent of the yard.

Naturally, his pay varied also. Though a fairly common wage was the equivalent of ten shillings or two dollars a day, to which might be added either a bonus for each launching or else a percentage of the profits of the yard,[57] he did not always earn as much, and yet he sometimes earned considerably more. The wide range in amounts resulted not only from differences in experience and responsibilities but also from the effects of supply and demand. Henry Baldwin, who had been foreman of the Beatson yard and subsequently built a number of vessels on his own account, was hired by the merchants David Anderson and Company in 1806 for a four-year period at the very low rate of six shillings and eight pence per day. Yet in 1808, his successor William Grant was paid nine shillings, and when Sam Brown took Grant's place in 1809, the company agreed to give him one-quarter of the net profits of the yard, somewhat optimistically guaranteeing him a minimum salary of £500,[58] or five times Baldwin's wage. As it turned out, Brown like Baldwin did not complete his term, and after twenty-two months billed his employers for his guaranteed minimum salary, as well as £90 for the services of his two apprentices. The differences in these rates are partly explained by the rapidly increasing demand for the services of skilled shipwrights at the time,[59] yet a salary such as Brown's seems to have been exceptional. Even wartime wages paid to the foremen shipbuilders that John Goudie took to the Kingston Dockyard in 1813 – twenty shillings per day and "the usual rations"[60] – were considerably lower, though they were extremely high compared to the 7s 2d per day that the shipbuilder William Cotnam earned while building the *Mathilde Isaac* in 1850.

The foreman of the yard was seconded by a number of foremen tradesmen who, depending on the size of the yard, might include foremen carpenters, blacksmiths, joiners, riggers and perhaps others.[61] For their greater expertise and additional responsibilities they earned on average thirty-three percent more than ordinary tradesmen. Henry Mulholland, John Goudie's foreman blacksmith, was paid a daily rate of 9s in 1813. Edward Edgeley, foreman rigger of the Jeffery shipyard, received a yearly salary of £130 in 1841.

Among ordinary tradesmen, by far the most numerous were the ship carpenters, whose work began in the moulding loft and ended only after the vessel had been launched. The vast majority earned a more or less standard wage which peaked exceptionally at four dollars in the early 1850s and reached a low of forty cents in 1866, but was more often somewhere between fifty cents and $1.40. Rates of pay differed not only with the season, as was common in many trades, increasing in May when the working hours also increased, but also from yard to yard, according to whether a man was working on new construction or repairs, and even among carpenters of varying skill or experience at work on the same job in the same yard. Differences in the rates can be seen in documents such as group engagements, contracts in which it is stated that any employee whose work was deficient would have his rate of pay reduced accordingly, and shipyard accounts.[62]

In the case of the specialized trades such as joinery, carving, painting, sailmaking, rigging and mast, pump and blockmaking, a contract was generally given to the master tradesman concerned, who ran his own business. However, with the exception of sailmaking, which was generally though not always given out to the master sailmakers of the town, work of this type was also done by specialists employed by the yard, particularly in the case of the larger more permanent yards with the necessary facilities.

As to the pit sawyers, even when a considerable amount of planking was obtained from the sawmills, there was still a need for them to do the work that the mills were unable to handle. One has only to look through the 1861 census of Saint Roch to see how

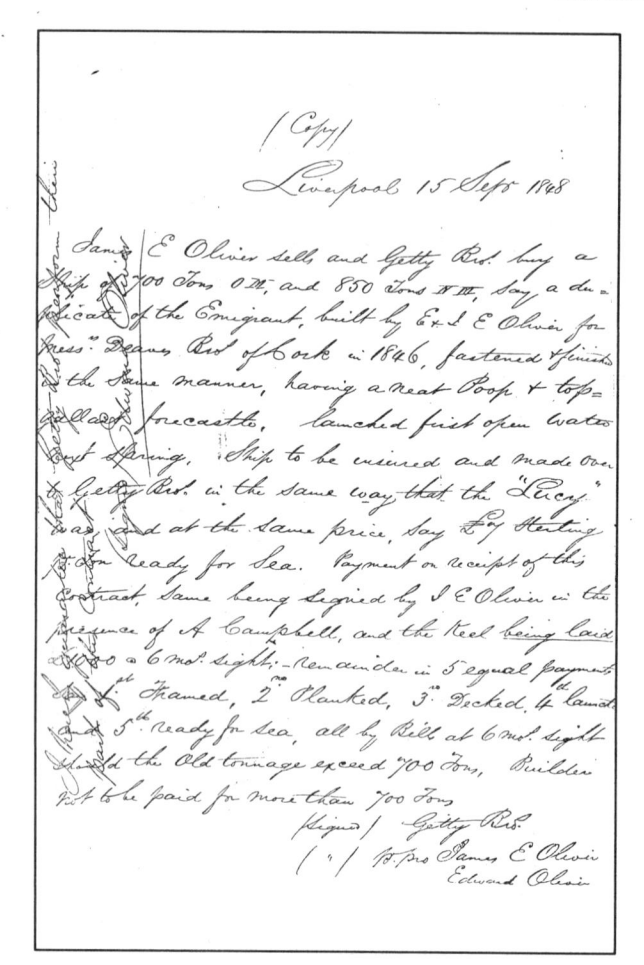

Figure 121: *Sale of a vessel to Getty Bros. signed at Liverpool on 15 September 1848 by Edward Oliver on behalf of James E. Oliver and attached to deposit and ratification by J.E. Oliver, 25 October 1848, gr A. Campbell.*

many pit sawyers there were. The sawyers worked in partnership, often owning their equipment jointly, and though in Britain the top sawyer earned more than the bottom one, at Quebec, where they had been equal partners during the French regime, the Quebec custom frequently prevailed. Some sawyers were taken on as shipyard employees, some did piece work and were paid according to the species of timber they sawed, as well as the amount, and others contracted by the job. In 1807, for instance, Goudie hired a pair of sawyers at a dollar each per day, while in 1813 David Munn paid the sawyers he engaged eight shillings per hundred feet for the oak they sawed and six shillings for pine. In 1814 his brother John paid ten shillings for oak and seven shillings for pine.[63] In the example of the contracts handed out in Pointe-aux-Trembles, p. 402, a pair of sawyers undertook to do all the sawing for the ship for a total of £178.

We come now to the apprentices, of whom there were three distinct categories: the shipbuilder's apprentices, the tradesmen's apprentices and those who are referred to here as the "shipyard" apprentices. Shipbuilders generally had two apprentices who were bound for seven-year terms. They were the elite and were considered shipbuilder "material." They lived with their master in the traditional manner of craftsmen's apprentices and though they neither received pay nor paid for their training, they were either provided with clothing or else were given a clothing allowance varying from £6 to £12 ($24 to $48) instead. The tradesmen's apprentices were also bound by the traditional terms of apprenticeship and many lived at their masters' homes even after the old apprenticeship system began to die.

The shipyard apprentices, on the other hand,

lived with their own families and with few exceptions served three-year terms during which they were trained by the foreman of the yard. They received between £20 and £40 ($80 to $160) each year, often with the rate increasing from year to year, those who had reached their majority generally getting at least £30 ($120). Many received a set of tools over and above these amounts.[64] At the end of their term they were entitled to be known as ship carpenters, though there appears to have been some qualifying period before they earned the full carpenter's wage.

These shipyard apprentices were not a feature of all yards. John Goudie, however, indentured at least thirtynine between 1802 and 1820, of which no fewer than thirty were taken on between 1802 and 1813. John Bell also engaged a considerable number, and many more were trained at the Carman and Taylor yards. This system, which is reminiscent of the way in which Jean Talon handled the shortage of skilled workers during the French regime, setting up workshops in which boys were trained to become proficient workers, had a double advantage. Not only did it increase the number of skilled workers but it also allowed the youths to become tradesmen instead of remaining common labourers earning lower pay throughout their lives. From the point of view of the local population, it was infinitely better than bringing workers from Britain to take the good jobs. Although in the long-term the shipbuilders undoubtedly benefitted from having a larger trained labour pool from which to draw, it does not seem likely that they actually profited financially in the short-term from the arrangement. They would have done so, perhaps, had the apprenticeships lasted longer than three years, but under the circumstances it would seem that the

Figure 122: *Notary Archibald Campbell (1790–1862), who practised at Quebec from 1812 to 1861, and received a great deal of the shipbuilders' business. Fonds James Thompson, O3Q P 254, N 83–7–2. Courtesy Archives nationales du Québec.*

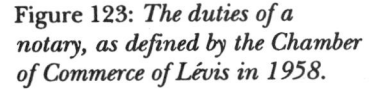

Figure 123: *The duties of a notary, as defined by the Chamber of Commerce of Lévis in 1958.*

NOTARIES

The Province of Quebec is distinct in legal matters ... Its code of Civil Law ... is in large measure based on the *Code Napoleon* of France.

[The notary] draws and keeps of record all original deeds of Sale, Mortgages, Marriage Contracts, Last Wills, Trust Deeds, Articles of Partner‾ship, Administration Accounts by Executors and Trustees, Partitions, etc; he examines titles of property, attends to registration, winds up and acts as agent for the sale of real estate.

[The notary] makes a deed "authentic," that is, in general unquestionable as to its execution, including the certainty of the date and of the signatures; he numbers and keeps the original on record in his office, delivering copies thereof which have the same legal force and authenticity as the original deed itself. This provision is particularly serviceable in connection with last Wills and Powers of Attorney.

The Editor
Industrial District of Levis
Chamber of Commerce of the District of Levis. 1928

Figure 124: *The money Box that held the gold and silver coin with which the Russell shipyard workers were paid, with W.G.R. engraved on the brass plate. Courtesy Russell Payson.*

Figure 125: *The Hamilton brothers advertise for sparmakers for their shipyard at New Liverpool during the War of 1812, a time when there is a severe shortage of skilled shipyard workers.* Quebec Gazette, *18 January 1814.*

apprentices had the best deal. In some cases, apprenticeship served an additional purpose. At least one of Goudie's apprentices was indentured to him for the express purpose of avoiding the "Press."[65]

It is interesting to note that the problem of the shortage of craftsmen was handled in the same way in New York. In his *History of New York Ship Yards*, John Morrison writes that in the mid-eighteenth century many of the shipbuilders could not afford the expense of maintaining apprentices. But prior to the War of 1812, when the industry began to show signs of improving, a shortage of skilled shipyard workers was anticipated by the shipbuilders, and they too began offering apprenticeships to a considerable number of young men. Coupled with the influx of skilled labour from Europe and Canada, their action largely overcame the shortage by 1822.[66]

Labourers, or workers who were not skilled in a craft, earned for the most part either slightly more or slightly less than half the tradesmens' wage. During the summer season from 1826 to 1828, for instance, they earned three shillings to five shillings per day, while the artisans earned five shillings to seven and sixpence. In February of 1846, when the carpenters were paid three shillings to three shillings and sixpence, the labourers got one shilling and eightpence.[67] Among the labourers there were some who did partly skilled work, such as the axemen and borers. Whether their pay always reflected the fact or whether they sometimes received the ordinary labourer's wage is not clear, but we know of many instances in which they received a higher rate. At the Anderson yard in 1810, at a time of maximum employment and high wages, axemen and borers earned from eight to eleven shillings per day, while the ordinary labourer earned six shillings or seven shillings and sixpence. As the nineteenth century progressed the gap between the wages of carpenters and labourers was sometimes far less, and the rivalry between the two classes of workers led the carpenters to object to labourers working in the yards.

Still, part or all the work of building a vessel was done not by employees, but by contractors who worked with what was known as a "gang." The contract might entail putting in the knees of one of the decks, the caulking of one or both sides, the planking, or some other job, or it might cover the entire framing. Such contracts were generally undertaken jointly by three to six workers who hired as many extra men as were needed to finish the work within the allotted time. The shipbuilder paid both the undertakers and the men they hired at the current rate of wages each week as the work progressed, and when it was finished, the undertakers shared the difference between the contract price and the amount that had already been paid out.

A fair number of these contracts both for Quebec and for out of town shipyards were made before notaries until the 1830s, and it has been possible to assemble some of the sub-contracts handed out for certain vessels, but once again, whether the rest of the work was handled by shipyard employees and if so how many there were, or if other contracts were given out that have not come to light, is unknown. Almost all the later contracts made before a notary were for out of town work; contracts for local work were probably written into the yard journals instead. George Black's journal is not only the sole Quebec shipyard journal that appears to have survived, but it contains only one example of a vessel for which he sub-contracted. I am therefore particularly grateful to Mr. Marc Rouleau, who owns a Pointe-aux-Trembles shipyard journal, and has kindly permitted me to give the details of the contracts handed out by Joseph Angers for the construction of the 900-ton ship *Bridget* through the winter of 1860-61. Both are in the Appendices.

In his description of his superintendence of Peter Baldwin's shipyard, Captain Bernier wrote:

The workmen were divided into carpenters, joiners, plankers, mast-makers, spar-makers, riggers, blacksmiths, treenail and wedge makers, caulkers, painters, carters, labourers, etc. Some of these worked by the day and some on piece-work. There were other specialists who also did job work such as the stern, the stem, the windlass, the keelson, the mast-stepping, the stringers and beams, the rudder and the deck-houses.

We can only conjecture as to the overall picture of the ratio of yard employees to sub-contractors. Whether Joseph Anger's method of building a vessel such as the *Bridget* entirely through sub-contracts was widespread, or whether the division at the Baldwin yard or some other set up was more general.

We encounter the same problem in reading Table 5, for we have no idea how the itinerant "gangs" were handled in the count. Were they included in the figures of each shipyard where they worked? Were they omitted altogether? Or, if neither was the case, how was it decided who should count them? Is the wide discrepancy in the amounts earned per month due to the itinerants, who earned part of their wages in one yard and part in another? Or is it due to a far heavier proportion of unskilled workers in the three yards where less than twelve dollars a month was earned? Or, as seems likely, are both factors involved? Unfortunately, it seems unlikely that we shall find the answer.

Table 5
Comparative Salaries at Quebec Shipyards that Operated for Seven, Eight or Twelve Months in 1880

Builder	Number of employees	Amount of salaries	Average salary	Months worked	Average per month
Julien & Labbé	150	$10,500	$70.00	7	$10.00
Samson & Co.	120	9,600	80.00	7	11.50
Baldwin	30	42,300	184.00	8	23.00
Valin	75	12,500	167.00	8	21.00
Cantin	90	8,500	94.40	8	11.80
Sawyer	36	2,500	69.40	8	8.70
Davie	25	6,500	260.00	12	21.67
Dinning	115	32,400	282.00	12	23.50
Gingras	100	24,000	240.00	12	20.00
McKay & Warner	150	37,500	250.00	12	20.83

Source: *Census of Canada*, 1880.

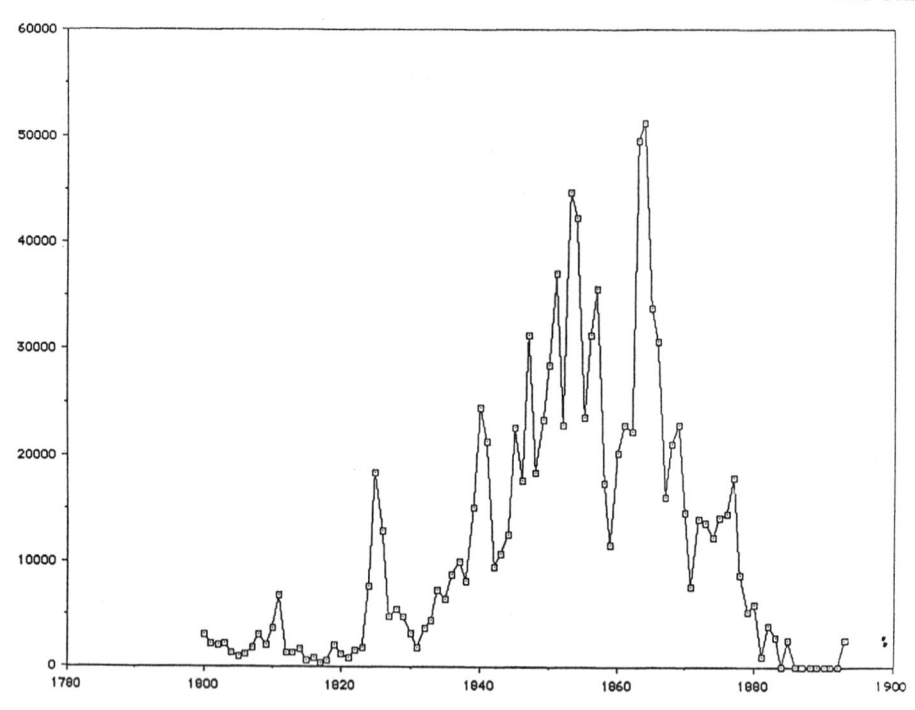

Graph 6: *Annual tonnage 1800–1893*

Source: Quebec Shipping Registers, 183–98, 292–3, 267–71, 375–78, RG12, NA

Prices

The price of a vessel was generally quoted at so much per ton. Currencies used were pounds sterling for sales in Britain, and pounds Halifax or pounds currency (worth slightly less), though sometimes sterling, for those transacted in Quebec. After the mid-1850s, the Canadian dollar was used increasingly instead.

Though the method of calculating tonnage for registration purposes changed over the years, for the purposes of construction "Builders' Measurement," later known as "Old Measurement" (O.M.) or "Builders' Old Measurement" (B.O.M.) remained very much in use at least into the mid-1860s. It was, of course, necessary to specify clearly which method of tonnage was being used and in the case of a contract in 1792 between William King and William Beatson for the construction of a vessel at Sorel, it was required to measure "two hundred and sixty seven tons and 56/96 or two hundred and seventy three tons and 26/94 should the latter be the mode of Calculation of Tunnage in the River Thames."[68]

Vessels built to order, or sold at Quebec during or after construction, generally fetched higher prices than those sent on consignment to Britain. Prices quoted covered for the most part either the cost of the hull and masts, ready for masting, or the vessel, masted, rigged and outfitted ready for loading. Due to shortages in the late eighteenth and early nineteenth century, the purchaser often agreed to provide some of the material and/or work, the value of which was either taken into account in fixing the rate per ton or else was deductible from the total price. For instance, between 1805 and 1812 the purchaser tended to supply all or some of the ironwork, and the graving, glaziers', plumbers' and block-makers' work as well as the joinery in the finish of the cabin.[69] In fact, it was customary for the latter to be carried out in Britain well into the 1850s.

Many Quebec vessels, however, were built on speculation and despatched to a broker in Britain who looked after their sale. Even though these vessels left Quebec "ready for sea," they generally had what was known as a "Quebec outfit," which was sufficient to leave the port but had to be supplemented on arrival overseas. Besides the joinery of the cabin, work done on the hull at a British port might include changing iron to copper fastenings, sheathing the bottom with metal, sometimes finishing a mast, and in later years replacing wooden masts with metal ones, adding iron knees before 1858-after that they were all fitted in

Quebec – and, on occasion, changing defective timbers. Skimpy outfits were supplemented with regulation anchors and chains, and extra boats, sails, cordage and other equipment. In 1848, a British shipowner stated before the Select Committee on the Navigation Laws that he had to spend an additional £5 10s per ton on top of the sale price of £7 when he bought a vessel built in Quebec.[70] Notwithstanding, Quebec shipbuilders complained of unjustifiably low prices.

During the years under review, the price of a vessel built in Quebec varied from a low of £4 sterling per ton for a hull without spars to what may have been a one-time high of £21 6s currency for a vessel ready for sea. At times, such as in the last half of the 1850s, there were long stretches of low prices, and there were five peak periods of exceptional output (see Graph 6) matched by high prices. The first of these was just prior to and during the War of 1812, when timber contractors to the Admiralty were avidly buying and building vessels to transport their timber, the second in 1824 and 1825 at the end of the post-war slump, the third in 1839, when the European grain harvest failed, the fourth in 1853-1854 at the outbreak of the Crimean War, and the last in 1863-1864 during the American Civil War. All were followed by a sharp decline.

During the last decades of the eighteenth century, before the Napoleonic Wars, prices paid for vessels built to order in Quebec were comparable to current Scottish prices. In 1786, for instance, James Duncanson built the hull of the 205-ton ship *Alfred* for "Four Pounds Four Shillings Sterling money [£4 13 4 currency] per Ton Carpenters measurement as customary to be built for in North Britain," and in 1792 William King contracted for the hull and masts of a 267-ton vessel at £4 17 6.[71] However, it was not long before competition for tonnage between rival timber merchants drove the prices up; by 1805, the going rate for a hull and masts excluding the graving, glaziers', plumbers', pump and blockmakers' and ironwork was £7. Within two years, it had risen by a pound and in 1809 over £11 was being paid. In 1810 and 1811, new vessels were changing hands at £12 and £14, and the peak price reached was probably £21 6s, which was paid for John Goudie's 361-ton ship *Goudies* in 1813, the year after she was built.[72] During this time labour costs also rose significantly. John Munn, who was paid £2 5s per ton to build a hull in 1798, received £4 in 1806, and François Robitaille got £6 in 1810. In 1811, John Ray was paid £4 for just the carpentry and caulking.[73] At the end of the war demand slackened and prices fell, and in 1818 John Bell built the hull with masts of the 250-ton *Saint Lawrence*, except for the pump and blockmakers' work and the finish of the cabin, for £9 6 8d per ton. The same year, Goudie's *Highland Lad*, ready for sea, sold for the equivalent of £13 6 3d currency. Like previous Quebec vessels, they were built of oak.[74]

The slump in the shipping market lasted until 1824. By then timber prices were double those of the beginning of the century, but the less conservative were able to offset this to some extent by supplementing the oak in the futtocks and planking with red pine and tamarac, which only cost half as much. Many vessels were now being fastened with copper instead of iron, at greater expense, and hulls were generally sold ready to receive the rigging and masts, all except for the finish of the cabin, although in some cases it was "finished plain." An analysis of building contracts shows that in 1825-1826 a hull sold at Quebec for £10 to £11 and a vessel ready for sea for £14. By the end of 1826, however, the market was once more falling. In

1827, shipwrights were supplying all the labour for the construction of a hull for £2 10s while the finished copper fastened hull sold for £6 10s to £8 7 6d. Through to 1838 the average vessel fetched £7 10; those supplied with rigging and sails £10 or slightly more.[75]

Prices rallied in 1839-1840 due to the poor harvest in Britain which created a demand for five thousand extra ship voyages to transport five million quarters of grain. The increment was equivalent to one-seventh of the existing merchant marine. Unrigged vessels sold at Quebec for £8 10, and once again £12 10 to £13 5 was obtained for those sold complete, ready for sea. This surge eventually produced another tonnage glut that caused a depreciation of shipping values by as much as fifty percent,[76] and it was not until the next shortage that resulted from the California Gold Rush of 1847 that the market began to recover. The first Gold Rush was followed shortly after by a second, and two others to Australia and New Zealand in 1851 and 1853. All stimulated the demand for shipping. These should have been prosperous times for the busy shipyards, and indeed some good prices were obtained, yet for the most part Quebec ships had only a five-year class and sold in Liverpool on average for £5 10s to £6 5s. The fact that Prince Edward Island ships with copper fastenings were only fetching £5 and those with iron fastenings as little as £3 10s to £3 15s was no consolation to the builders.[77]

The arrival of the Lloyd's surveyor in 1852 gave local shipbuilding a welcome shot in the arm. In March 1853 the *Morning Chronicle* reported "vessels now on the stocks are of superior material, model and finish, to any ever before built here." Although this statement may have been somewhat exaggerated, it reflected the general feeling of confidence through the knowledge that the new vessels were entitled to a seven-year rating. And happily, this coincided with a boom in the shipping market. In 1854, Baldwin and Dinning's 1832-ton *Ocean Monarch* was sold on the stocks at $53 per ton (£13 5s),[78] but by October the market had collapsed again. Although more tonnage would be built in 1863 and 1864 than ever before, the *Ocean Monarch* would remain the symbol of successful shipbuilding in the "good old days."

In the last half of the 1850s Quebec shipyards began fitting vessels with the large iron knee riders that hitherto had been fitted in Britain, as well as using iron strapping to meet the new Lloyd's regulations. Hulls were built for as little as £6 to £6 10s per ton, ready to be kneed, and vessels could be bought for £9 to £10 ready for sea, but the large majority were built on speculation to be sold on the Liverpool market, where many were knocked down at prices close to cost.

The years 1863-1864 surpassed all others both in numbers of vessels built and total tonnage, but the high prices obtained in 1863, which reached as much as £15 2s 6d per ton, were forced down by the number of United States vessels that were unloaded on the market. The official Customs report for 1865 stated that thirty-eight vessels had been exported at a value of $1,090,320, or $40 per ton.[79] Prices quoted in the 1880s were between £8 and £9 per ton.

In 1898, the shipbuilder Narcisse Rosa estimated that the cost of labour and materials in Quebec-built sailing ships over the previous century had averaged forty dollars (then the equivalent of £8 8s sterling) per ton ready for sea.[80] At our corrected tonnage figures for the port, this represents $43,779,240. Rosa had many years experience in shipbuilding and his estimate may be correct,[81] especially since Peter McClelland puts forward the same figure for the cost of New Brunswick vessels in the period 1870-1879, but from the information we have on costs and selling prices, it would seem a little high. He calculated that workers earned twelve dollars a ton, which seems reasonable and would indicate that the shipyard workers in the port earned over thirteen million dollars working on new construction. This was no negligible amount, especially since much of it was earned in winter and was in many cases a supplement to the larger summer wages.

Profit and Loss

And how did the shipbuilders fare? The four independent shipbuilders in town did very well in the years prior to the War of 1812, when ships were contracted for on an average at £10 per ton; and shipbuilders stood to make money each time that the market peaked after that. In 1854 Baldwin and Dinning sold the 1832-ton ship *Ocean Monarch* to Charles Levey and Company for a reputed $53 per ton or close to $100,000, making a profit of $20,000.[82] But this exceptional sale should not leave the impression that shipbuilding was lucrative, which was far from the case. The peaks were few, and the possibility of the market having slumped by the time a ship was completed was always present. In 1857, for example, the Samson brothers contracted to build the 889-ton ship *Iona* at £6 7s 6d or nearly $32 per ton. Their workmanship was described by the Lloyd's Surveyor as excellent, but they lost over £1,700 on the contract.[83] However, they were fortunate in that they were able to survive the loss and keep on building on their own accounts until 1879 in the case of Julien and Isidore, and 1885 for Etienne. Many shipbuilders were not as fortunate, and every now and again a meeting of the creditors of another leading shipbuilder was announced–Pierre Brunelle, Henry Dinning, J.E. Gingras, the Jefferys, Thomas C. Lee, John James Nesbitt, Thomas H. Oliver, Walter Ray, Edmund W. Sewell and many more. For some the fall was devastating. How hard it must have been for James Goudie at the age of seventy-nine, to offer to sell a model of the *Royal William* that he had "spent a good deal of time building" for twenty-five dollars, his "finances not being in very good condition."[84] Shipbuilding was a business in which the risks were great and long-term financial rewards extremely rare.

Notes

1. E.g., Agreement, Gilley with Atkinson, 5 December 1810, gr J. Voyer.
2. Evaluation of J.J. Nesbitt's stock by John Munn and Elie Gingras, 12 August 1856, gr J. Clapham; Sale of Brunelle's shipyard and equipment, *Morning Chronicle*, 11 September 1862.
3. Agreement Black with Campbell, sous seing privé 22 April 1825 and deposited 8 April 1831, gr F.X. Garneau; Agreement, Baldwin with Dinning, 27 March 1851, gr J. Clapham.
4. *Shipping and Mercantile Gazette*, London, 1 January 1855.
5. *The Liverpool Telegraph and Shipping and Commercial Gazette*, 2 January 1855.
6. F.W. Wallace, *In the Wake of the Windships* (Toronto, 1927), 114.
7. Henry Fry, "Shipbuilding in Quebec," *The Canadian Magazine*, V (May 1895), 5; Deed of composition between Dinning and his creditors, 30 April 1858, gr Jean Côté; *Quebec Official Gazette*, 18 January 1878.
8. 17 & 18 Vict., c. 104; 19 Vict., c. 50; 36 Vict., c. 128.
9. Sale and assignment, Warner to McKay, 23 December 1873, gr W.D. Campbell.
10. Form "N," 17 & 18 Vict., c. 104.
11. Canada, Sessional Papers, 31 Vict., 1868, Appendix 11, "Fourth Report of the Select Committee Appointed to Inquire into the General Condition of the Building of Merchant Vessels," 8.
12. Agreement, Nesbitt with his creditors, 28 November 1843, gr A. Campbell.
13. Henry Fry, "Reminiscences" (unpublished ms., 1891), corroborates much of the information in this paragraph.
14. Basil Greenhill and Ann Giffard, *Westcountrymen in Prince Edward's Isle* (Toronto, 1967), 192.
15. According to F. W. Wallace, this firm was one of several Liverpool shipping firms of Canadian origin. These include the Allans, De Wolfs, Roberts, Vaughans, Cruickshank and Gass, Andrew Gibson and Cunards. Wallace, *In the Wake*, 264.
16. See Ross's Journals; Inventory, Charland and Marquis, 4 September 1871, gr F. Guay, père; Sale and Assignment, Warner to McKay, 23 December 1873, gr W.D. Campbell.
17. Kenneth S. Mackenzie, *et al.*, "Ross, James Gibb," *DCB*, XI (1982).
18. Fry, "Shipbuilding in Quebec," 8.
19. Lloyd's Register of Shipping, *Annals of Lloyd's Register* (London, 1934), 6, 9-18.
20. *Ibid.*, 23.
21. *Ibid.*, 20-25.
22. *Ibid.*, 54-55.
23. 16 November 1869, gr S. Glackemeyer.
24. Lloyd's Register, *Annals*, 63-65.
25. Agreement between the Quebec Board of Trade, Lloyd's and Thomas Menzies, 5 March 1852, gr L, McPherson.
26. Lloyd's survey reports; Agreement, 5 March 1852, gr L. McPherson.
27. "Rules and Regulations Wood Ships," No. 265, 26 May 1870.
28. Lloyd's, *Annals*, 97.
29. Announcement of Ray's appointment by H. Veltman, Chief Surveyor for the Bureau Veritas of Paris, *Morning Chronicle*, 24 August 1864.
30. Contract, Cotnam with Vonrittern, on behalf of Gildermeister, 11 January 1876, gr S. Glackemeyer.
31. Private letter, Coker to Geo. Seyfang, 23 June 1865, Lloyd's Surveys.
32. Barque *Staghound*, Ship's Memoranda 2, Ross Collection.
33. Correspondence of Bureau Veritas, Port of Quebec, AP-P-17-21, ANQ.
34. Shipbuilding contract, Oliver with Pryde and Jones, 1 March 1849, gr A. Campbell.
35. 30 October, gr L. McPherson.
36. Contracts to build, Bell with Douglas, 1 August 1818, gr L. McPherson, Charland and Marquis with Wilson, 7 October 1865, gr W.D. Campbell, and Cotnam with Vonrittern, 11 January 1876, gr S. Glackemeyer; Agreement, Charles with Oviatt, 19 October 1810, gr J.

Belanger; Contract to build, Richardson with Jameson, 22 March 1855 and Rosa with Wilson, 19 May 1862, gr W.D. Campbell.
37. Pickersgill and Tibbits papers, Accounts 1847, P0202-4, ANQ.
38. 10 July 1786, gr C. Stewart.
39. 8 November, gr L. McPherson.
40. 15 February, gr A. Campbell.
41. Agreement for building a ship, William Gilley, *et al.*, with Patterson, Dyke and Co., 26 September 1811, gr J. Belanger.
42. 11 February 1840.
43. *Quebec Gazette*, 29 April 1825.
44. Pierre Thorn and Joseph L'Heureux, for instance, were only required to work with "at least fifteen ship carpenters" to build a 530-ton ship for J.J. Nesbitt over a period of ten months, 26 July 1839, gr L. McPherson.
45. E.g., contract, Goudie with Usborne, 6 October 1809, gr J. Belanger.
46. See contract, Valin with Ross, 5 September 1862, gr S. Glackemeyer; Lee with Jeffery, Noad, 14 November 1862 and Oliver with Anderson, 25 November 1863, gr W.D. Campbell.
47. See reports on strikes, *Quebec Mercury*, 10 December 1840; *Morning Chronicle*, 25 September, 25, 28, 29, 30 October, 26-30 November, 11, 13, 24 and 28 December 1867, 1 January 1868.
48. *Morning Chronicle*, 24 March 1863.
49. Narcisse Rosa, *La construction des navires à Québec et ses environs* ((Québec, 1897), 11.
50. Lloyd's Surveys [hereafter L.S.], 815, 802, 803 and 809.
51. E.g., Apprenticeship Indenture, Chas. Vermette with John Bell, 29 March 1824, gr J. Belanger.
52. Engagement contract, 6 August 1810, gr J. Belanger; *idem.*, 12 May 1825, gr A. Campbell.
53. Engagement, Banfield with Labbé, 30 May 1825, gr A. Campbell; power of attorney, Jones to Simons, 22 February 1858, gr J. Clapham.
54. 6-9 December 1863, gr S. Glackemeyer.
55. 24 February 1808, gr J. Belanger.
56. Indenture of Wm Tweddell with Allan Gilmour, 29 November 1841; engagement of Banfield with Labbé, 30 May 1825, gr A. Campbell.
57. See, for example, employment contracts, Jacques Labbé with Louis Labbé, 12 May 1825, gr A. Campbell; Adolphus St. Jean with J. Jeffery and Co., 4 October 1839, gr J. Hunt; and Chas Jobin with Thos. E. Sherwood, 9 December 1863, gr A. Glackemeyer.
58. Engagement contracts, Baldwin with Anderson, 30 December 1806, gr J. Jones and Grant with Anderson, 24 February 1809, gr J. Belanger; engagement contract, Brown with Anderson, 30 November 1809 and resiliation, 3 June 1812.
59. Carpenters in the service of John Bell in 1810 were paid "au plus haut prix qui leur sera offert ailleurs," (the highest price offered elsewhere), engagement contracts, 31 October 1809, gr J. Belanger; Anderson's carpenters earned 12/6 per day and a bounty of £5 at the end of their 5 month term, engagement contract, 13 May 1810, gr J. Voyer.
60. Contract various with government, 22 June 1813, gr J. Belanger.
61. E.g., Engagement as foreman blacksmith, Mulholland with Goudie, 25 June 1813, gr A. Campbell; Engagement as foreman rigger, Edgeley with Jeffery, 12 January 1841, gr J. Hunt.
62. An account for work done at the Gilmour shipyard bills the ship carpenters' time at eleven different rates. 17 June 1854, gr J. Clapham.
63. Contract Deschamps & Trudel with Goudie, 9 October 1807, gr J. Belanger; contracts Brown and Bradley with David Munn, 4 May 1813 and Mirian and Viancours with Munn, 29 January 1814, gr A. Campbell.
64. Compare the pay of the New York apprentice John Englis, bound to Stephen Smith in 1825, who received $2.50 weekly and $40 per annum, paid quarterly, in lieu

of meat, drink, washing, lodging, clothing and all other necessities. Robert G. Albion, *The Rise of New York Port, 1815-1860* (Boston, 1939), 301.
65. I.e., being pressed into naval service. Apprenticeship contract, Clouston with Goudie, 28 May 1809, gr J. Belanger.
66. Pp.11, 41 (New York, 1909).
67. *Quebec Mercury*, 3 February 1846.
68. 23 June 1792, gr J. Beek, ANQM. This should not be confused with Thames Measurement, or T.M., introduced by the Royal Thames Yacht Club in 1855, which also produces remainders in 94ths, Peter Kemp, *The Oxford Companion to Ships and the Sea* (Oxford, 1976), 864.
69. See contracts Goudie with Usborne, 15 November 1805, gr J. Jones and Munn with Ross, 11 October 1809, gr J. Belanger. It was unusual for the cost for finishing the cabin to be deductible from the price paid, as it was in a contract between Goudie and Mure and Joliffe, which set the amount at twenty pounds, 31 August 1807, gr J. Belanger.
70. *British Session Papers, House of Commons*, XX, part 2, 600-699.
71. Duncanson with Fairrie, 10 July 1786, gr C. Stewart; King with Beatson, 26 March 1792, gr J. Beek, ANQM.
72. E.g., shipbuilding contracts, Goudie with Pearson, 3 October 1804, gr J. Voyer; Goudie with Usborne, 16 September 1807, gr J. Jones; Goudie with Usborne, 6 October 1809, Charles with Oviatt, 10 September 1810, Goudie with Oviatt, 16 October 1810, gr J. Belanger; Munn with Whitfield Coates, 25 January 1811, gr J. Voyer; Goudie with Stewart, 1 July 1813, gr J. Belanger.
73. Contract Munn with Pearson, 13 July 1798, gr C. Stewart; Munn with McDouall, 23 August 1806, gr J. Voyer; Robitaille with Mure, 13 September 1810, Ray with Patterson and Dyke, 7 November 1811, gr J. Belanger.
74. Contract, Bell with Douglas, 1 August 1818, gr L. McPherson.
75. In 1832, George Black contracted to build a vessel complete with sails, anchors, and cables, provision it and engage the crew, pay the bill for towing her cargo of timber and the pilot's fees, for £10 10s per ton. Contract, Black with Price, 30 May 1832, gr A. Campbell; Mr. John Astle, testifying before the Select Committee on Shipwrecks in 1833, stated that the cost of a vessel ready for sea at Quebec was £10 per ton.
76. Robin Craig, "British Shipping and British North American Shipbuilding in the Early Nineteenth Century, with Special Reference to Prince Edward Island," in H.E.S. Fisher (ed.), *The South-West and the Sea*.
77. *Morning Chronicle*, 24 January 1851.
78. Frederick William Wallace, *Wooden Ships and Iron Men* (London, 1924), 73.
79. *Morning Chronicle*, 17 February 1866.
80. Rosa, *La construction*, 158.
81. Based on a variety of sources, especially New Brunswick, *Journals of the House of the Assembly*, Annual Reports on Trade and Navigation; U.S., Congress House, *Lynch Report* (1870), House Rep. 28, 41 Cong., 2 Sess., 227-8; Peter McClelland, "The New Brunswick Economy in the Nineteenth Century" (Unpublished Ph.D. thesis, Harvard University, 1966), 230, n. 112.
82. Wallace, *Wooden Ships*, 73.
83. Deed of pledge, Samson to Russell, 24 November 1857, gr S. Glackemeyer.
84. Letter to L. Hagardon, 4 October 1888, New York Historical Society.

CHAPTER 7
Materials and Outfit

Timber

The main raw material on the shipbuilder's shopping list was wood, and the bulk of it fell under the designation "timber." The term covered all pieces over eight inches thick, with the exception of spar wood. It comprised the "great" timbers, at least nine inches square, from which the keel, keelson, stern-post and beams were made; the "compass" timber, curved in its growth to the extent of more than five inches in a twelve foot length, which served for the "futtocks" or ribs of the vessel; and the specially-shaped two-armed pieces such as the breasthooks and knees, which joined the timbers lying in one plane to those lying in another. Timber sawn into planks two to eight inches thick was called "planking," and if it was over four inches thick, it was known as "thick stuff." Planking, generally thick stuff, lined both the inside and outside of the hull, forming respectively the "ceiling" and the "skin," while thinner planking served for decking.

Spar wood, or wood sold in the round for masts, bowsprits and yards, came in a variety of sizes and conformed to a specific taper, either in accordance with government regulations for timber exports[1] or else following the conditions of its sale.[2] Among the different types of spar wood, bowsprits were proportionately the thickest, increasing approximately one inch

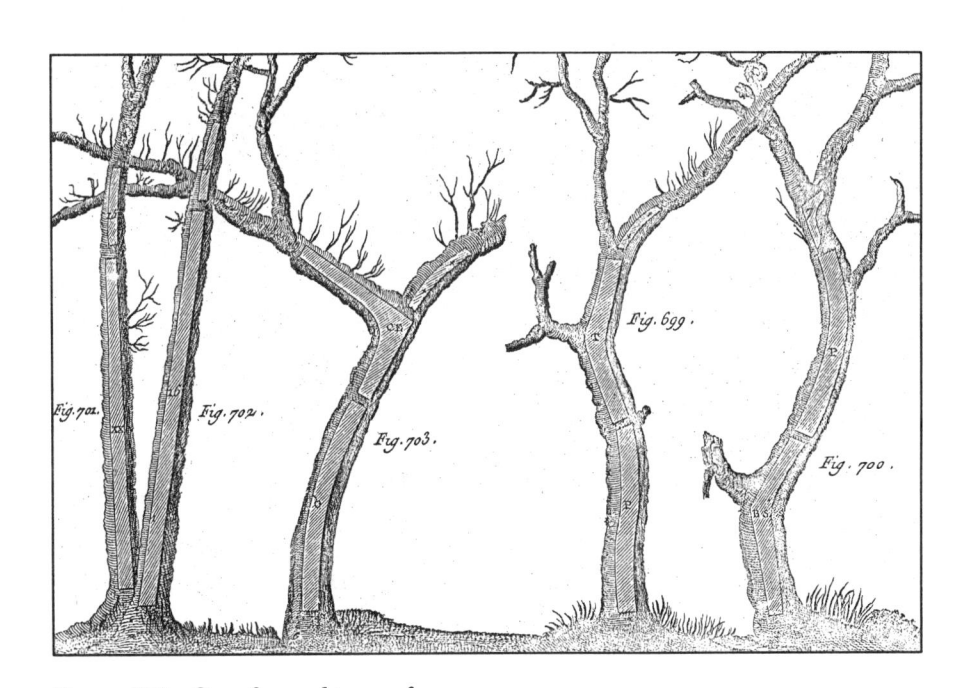

Figure 126: *One of several pages of illustrations showing the manner of obtaining ship timber from variously shaped trees in the* Encyclopédie méthodique: Marine, *4:102.*

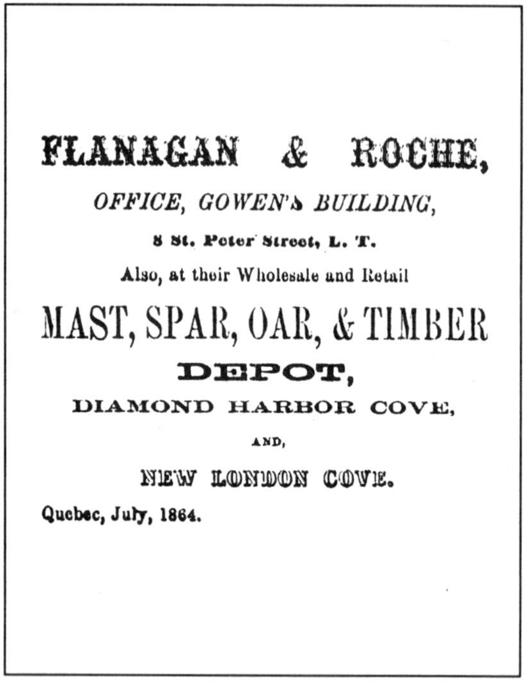

FLANAGAN & ROCHE,

OFFICE, GOWEN'S BUILDING,

8 St. Peter Street, L. T.

Also, at their Wholesale and Retail

MAST, SPAR, OAR, & TIMBER DEPOT,

DIAMOND HARBOR COVE,

AND,

NEW LONDON COVE.

Quebec, July, 1864.

Figure 127: *The wood merchants Flanagan & Roche offer masts, spars, oars and timber for sale, wholesale or retail, at their premises at Diamond Harbour.* Quebec Directory, *1864.*

in diameter for every two feet in length. Lower masts measured three feet per inch, and other spars were comparatively thinner.

Shipbuilding timber required careful selection if it was to give satisfaction over the years. The properties that the shipbuilder sought were hardness, to prevent injuries from blows or falling; stiffness, to avoid bending or warping; tenacity in holding fastenings; strength to withstand the tensile and compressive strains to which loaded ships at sea are subjected; resistance to dry rot; and lightness, for speed and carrying capacity. The relative importance of each in a particular member varied not only with its structural function, but also with its position above, below or on the waterline. The ability to stand up to wear and to the burning rays of the sun were additional requirements for deck planking. Spar wood required durability, straightness, the proper proportion of length to girth, strength as well as suppleness, elasticity and a good retention of resin to ensure a tendency to bend rather than snap under the strain of the rigging. For all these qualities to be at their best, timber had to be thoroughly seasoned, and spar wood fresh and resilient.[3] Government dockyards frequently carried out tests to check on the properties of different species of timber. Table 6 lists the results of one such test of stiffness and strength carried out on English, Baltic, "Quebec" and American wood.

The two main natural enemies of ship timber were the Teredo worm and dry rot. Encountered by European ships when they visited warm waters, Teredo worms bore their way through the bottoms of vessels and in time turned them into sieves. Many remedies were tried, but none brought a solution until the 1760s, when the hull of the British frigate *Albion* was sheathed with copper instead of the ineffective layer of planking over a mixture of tar and hair then customary. While this solved the problem of the worm, the copper sheathing caused a galvanic action which heavily corroded the iron fastenings in the hull. It was not until 1775, when it was thought that a layer of heavy waterproof paper between the bolt heads and the copper sheathing would prevent the corrosion, that sheathing was generally introduced in the fleet. But in 1783 serious defects were discovered and it was realized that the paper gave insufficient protection. Nonetheless, the value of copper sheathing had been established and with the introduction of non-ferrous copper and zinc ship fastenings, the problem was finally solved. Strangely enough, the Romans had dealt with it centuries earlier by sheathing their vessels with lead plates fixed with copper nails.

The problem of dry rot, on the other hand, was never completely overcome. The disease destroyed the tissues of the wood, either appearing as a toadstool growth on the surface or spreading undetected inside, until in either case the wood was reduced to powder. Areas of the hull immediately above the waterline were particularly susceptible. Albion lists the four principal causes of the origin and spread of dry rot as the use of unseasoned timber, the use of certain foreign woods, improper construction and lack of ventilation. His definition of "unseasoned" timber includes timber taken from the outer edge or cambium of a log, which could not be seasoned and which, if used to obtain a sufficiently large piece of timber would give trouble.[4]

The remedies tried included improved seasoning procedures, charring, "stoving" or putting the timber in wet sand and heating it, and treating it with one of a variety of substances such as sulphate of copper, sulphate of iron, salt or creosote. Of all the remedies, the use of rock salt seems to have been the most effective.

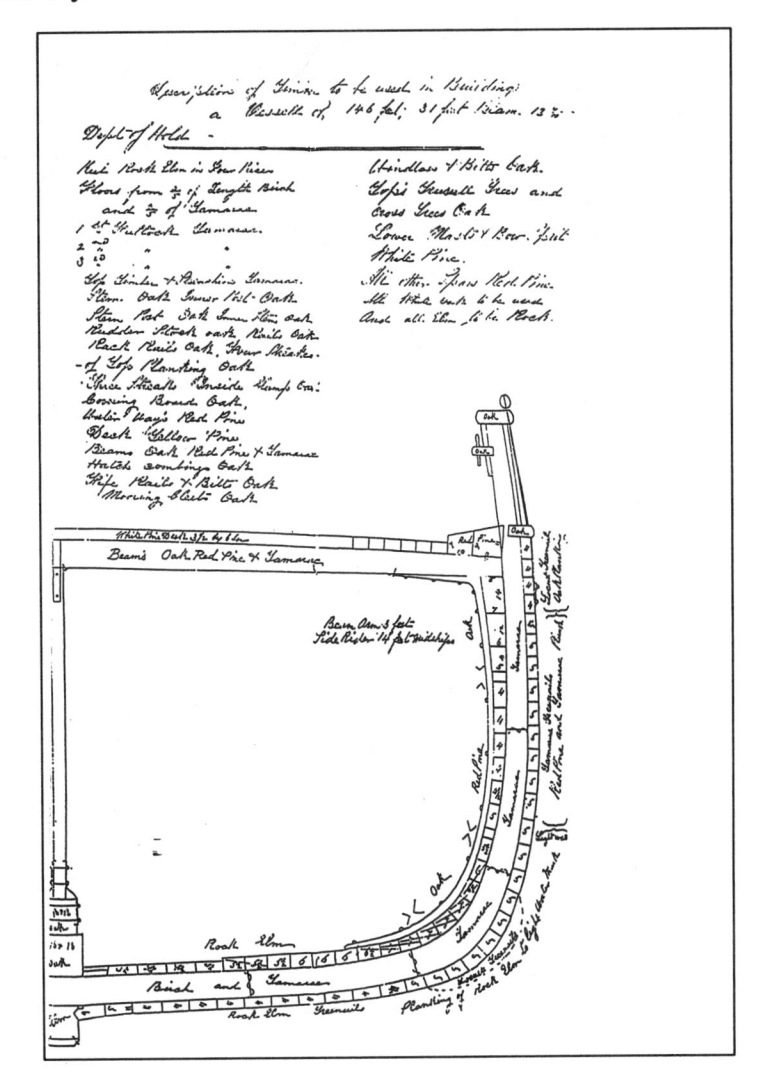

Figure 128: *Midship plan showing the timber to be used by William Cotnam in the construction of the 430 ton barque Friedrich Perthes, attached to contract between Cotnam and Von Rittern, 11 January 1876, gr S. Glackemeyer.*

Although it had long been realized that the frame timbers of salt-carrying river boats remained sound after fifty years of service, a suitable method of applying it to the timbers of large vessels was slow to be devised.[5] In 1744 fifteen hogsheads of strong brine were poured into the hold of the seventy to eighty-ton corvette *Carcajou* during its construction at the Royal Dockyard at Quebec, but the same procedure was not practical in the case of 700-ton vessels.[6] By 1831, however, "it was not unusual for builders of wooden ships to employ salt to preserve the timbers from dry-rot even to the extent of boiling them in salt water."[7]

In 1860 the ship *Reform*, built at the Gilmour shipyard at Cape Cove, was described by the Lloyd's survey as having been put in frame in the spring of 1859 and remaining "whitened with lime during the whole summer." We are not told whether this was an experiment or the standard practice of the yard. The value of filling the spaces between the timbers of the frame and transoms with salt was recognized by Lloyd's in 1869. In a circular letter dated 26 June, it was announced that an extra year or two of classification would be awarded to vessels so treated, and a year later the rule was amended to require additional salting and to lay down how it should be effected. Shipbuilders seized the opportunity to improve the rating of their ships, filling each vessel with thirty-five to as much as one hundred tons of salt.

According to Captain Bernier, "Pickling was done by the spraying of a solution of rock salt over the inner and outer surfaces of the hull . . . [which] was started as soon as the ship's hull took shape and was done every few days until launching." The Gilmour ships, which were owner insured, were not subject to Lloyd's regulations, and were treated even more thoroughly.

Large pieces of rock salt were placed in puncheons partly filled with water, and when sufficiently dissolved, it was the duty of one man to go around with a syringe about four feet in length, in the summer months, and spray the frames of the vessels, . . . with the view of hardening the wood. This work he was obliged to repeat every two weeks, Apart from that, a large piece of salt was placed on every timber head and left there to be dissolved by the rain and find its way through the pores of the wood, so that the ship would be pickled inside as well as outside. The treenails, made of locust wood, were also soaked in a solution of rock salt in a large vat.[8]

Whatever attempts were made to deal with the problem, it was never really solved, and dry-rot remained a major enemy of shipowners until they turned to metal hulls. In the meantime an increasing number of different species of timber were utilized in the shipyards, and it was found that some had greater resistance to dry-rot than others.

For centuries oak, the favourite ship timber of the great maritime nations, was used for all parts of the hull. Hard, stiff and strong, it held its fastenings well, and its high tannic content was thought to deter the destructive Teredo worm. Although on the heavy side, its strength and low splintering quality made it of special value as warship timber. Yet it was subject to dry-rot and corroded any iron with which it came in contact. By the seventeenth century, heavy demands for oak, particularly for naval shipbuilding, had caused a serious shortage. Moreover, because the weight of oak made harvesting and transportation more difficult, it was also expensive. But despite these disadvantages, oak had no peer in the opinion of shipwrights, and in

Britain native oak was considered superior to any other.[9]

By the mid-eighteenth century, the British navy, which had to compete for supplies with private shipyards, had broken with tradition and was using other timber as well as oak. By the end of the century, not only were the keels of naval vessels made of elm, but elm, beech, fir and baltic oak were all used in significant quantities for planking below the waterline. Due to the constant wars, these measures did not prevent an increased demand for oak for shipbuilding and ship repairing purposes, and as a result, a survey was made by the Commissioners of the Land Revenue during the 1790s to determine what timber might be used in its place. They came to the conclusion that larch was "the best substitute for oak that we have heard of."[10]

Larch is not a tree native to Britain, but large experimental plantations laid down by the Duke of Athol in his estates in Scotland had shown its value. It was tough, durable and strong, yet throve in poor soil, whereas oak required special soil and climatic conditions. It reached maturity in fifty or sixty years, less than half the 125 years required by oak. It was lighter than oak, and was therefore more buoyant and better suited to heavy cargoes. Moreover, it resisted attack from Teredo worms and did not corrode iron fastenings. All in all, larch was seen as the ideal timber to replace oak in many of its applications. As a practical test, a frigate was built entirely of larch. Launched in 1820, the *Athol* proved entirely satisfactory.

Yet larch did not answer all shipbuilding purposes, and the reserve of ship timber in naval woodyards continued to shrink. In 1806 the Navy Board began soliciting British government representatives abroad for samples of local wood, which were subjected to dockyard tests on their arrival. As a result, naval shipwrights were forced to admit that some of the timber was superior to British oak. The myth had finally been laid to rest and during the remaining fifty years in which wooden warships were built, they embodied an extraordinary mixture of foreign and domestic timbers,[11] a far cry from the days when only British oak was deemed good enough for the fleet.

Until 1812, however, shipping interests at Quebec and their principals overseas clung conservatively to their total allegiance to oak. "All the plank and timber to be good Sound white Oak of this Country," ran the contract for the 205-ton ship *Alfred* built by James Duncanson in 1786.[12] "Your petitioner has upon an Average, converted nearly Sixty Thousand feet of Oak timber annually to the purpose of Ship building," declared Patrick Beatson, most important of the eighteenth-century private shipbuilders, in 1798.[13] "None but the said oak timber," agreed John Goudie, would be used in the frame of the 473-ton ship *Briton*, launched by him in 1809.[14] But the supposed ideal was not always realized, and a certain amount of other timber found its way into the shipyards. The occasional shipbuilding agreement called for a pine deck, and in at least one case, pine knees were allowed if oak knees were unavailable.[15] Furthermore, though mention of tamarac knees is not to be found in any specifications, deeds of sale of red spruce knees, that is to say "tamarac," to shipbuilders indicate that they too were used.[16]

After 1815 a radical change occurred, and by 1840 the typical Quebec merchantman was raised on an elm keel, had futtocks of tamarac, planking of rock elm, red pine and tamarac, and a yellow pine deck. Yet oak was far from being entirely out of the picture, for it continued to provide many parts requiring special strength, such as the stem, sternpost and keelson. Furthermore, the old pride in an oak ship lingered on, and the occasional launching of an oak vessel was underlined by the press.

The general change in the choice of ship timber at Quebec was not brought about by a shortage of oak, as it had been in Britain, but rather by the bad name that Canadian oak had received in the dockyards there, where shipwrights had condemned it as "unfit for the Building and repairing of His Majesty's ships" and suitable only for "inferior purposes."[17] But how much this was due to inherent weaknesses of the timber, how much to improper handling and seasoning, and how much to prejudice is unclear. As Robert Albion points out, Canadian oak exported to Britain was rafted hundreds of miles to Quebec, where it was loaded dripping wet into the holds of the waiting timber ships for the warm summer crossing, conditions ideal for the development of dry rot. Moreover, it was used in the dockyards only as a last resort, when timber stocks were low and there was no time for seasoning and in the repair of old ships already decayed. And, as Albion adds, where various sorts of timber, even different kinds of oak were used together it was well recognized that dry rot was more liable to develop.[18]

The condition or quality of Canadian oak used in British dockyards cannot therefore be considered a criterion to judge the quality; instead, the service records of the ships built at Quebec of Canadian oak have to be examined. Turning to Lloyd's shipping registers we find that a number of Quebec vessels built prior to 1812 enjoyed a long life. The 98-ton brigantine *Industry* of 1774 was abandoned in 1816 after forty-two years' service, and when recovered and repaired resumed her career. The 117-ton brigantine *Iroquois* of 1793 roamed the oceans for seventy-two years before foundering in 1865, and Alexander Munn's 221-ton ship *Quebec*, launched in 1799, still plied regularly between London and Newcastle thirty-five years later.[19] Many other vessels gave their owners over fifteen years' service, sailing for the greater part of the time under war conditions and carrying the strain of their armament. Furthermore, when new regulations were adopted in Britain in 1798 by the committee of the Underwriters' Register, Quebec ships automatically received a two-year higher first-class rating than the rating given to similar vessels built in Hull, the northern ports of Britain, or Wales. This would surely indicate that at that time Quebec vessels enjoyed a good reputation.

And yet there is no doubt of the general disrepute into which Canadian oak timber had fallen by the 1820s and of the concern of Quebeckers on that score. In 1822 subscribers to the *Quebec Mercury* were encouraged to read that Canadian oak was to a certain degree held in higher estimation in England. There were at that time a number of Canadian-built vessels in the harbour, several of which were built in 1811 and 1812, which were still considered perfectly sound and staunch. They included the *Sir George Prevost*, the *Saint Patrick*, the *Harrisons*, *Christopher* and *Lord Wellington*, one or two of which, it was noted, had traded for several years to Lima and other warm climates.[20]

But far from receiving higher estimation, the regard for Canadian oak, and indeed for Quebec ships, went from bad to worse, and once again the question arises as to what extent this was justified. Certainly, British free traders and other interested parties who opposed the high duties on Baltic timber could be expected to capitalize on every possible criticism of protected Canadian timber. Yet Henry Fry, the noted Quebec shipowner of the last half of the century, definitely agreed with them. "It [Canadian oak] was very strong," he wrote "but, as a rule, it was found to be affected with 'dry rot' in about five years."[21] How can one reconcile this statement with the fact that in spite of the switch to other timbers, oak was still used for parts of the hull that required great strength? Why were they not affected with dry rot in five years? Did the complaints about Canadian oak provide the pretext to use far cheaper timber that was adequate for the job, had the advantage of being lighter, and was not as sensitive to improper handling? Was oak, if properly seasoned, stored and handled, still vulnerable to dry rot, but not nearly as vulnerable as it was made out to be? The answer would appear to be "yes." In his testimony before the Select Committee on Trade of 1821, August McGhee Brodie, a prominent London shipbroker, repairer and builder, described Quebec oak as very nearly as good as English, if properly seasoned. He reported that he used Quebec timber for repairs and did not think that using English timber would be any better. He had broken up many vessels of British oak suffering from dry rot at an early age, knew no Quebec ships that had to be broken up so early, and knew several Quebec ships already ten or twelve years old, which were not as bad. Henry Usborne, a merchant who had experience in the timber trade in both the Baltic and at Quebec, testified in the same vein. He knew of dry rot setting in when oak that was cut in the spring and immediately rafted to Quebec was shipped wet from the rafts, but any wood would do that. He considered New Brunswick timber inferior to Canadian timber and had used only Canadian timber in recent repairs to his house in England. Moreover, he claimed to have a list taken from *Lloyd's Register* of 123 Canadian ships that were over ten years old.

There is no doubt that much of the condemnation of Canadian timber in Britain originated in the Royal Navy. Dockyard officers argued that the sun could not reach the trunks of trees that grew in dense forests, as most Canadian oak did, and consequently they were more porous and prone to decay than the British oak, that grew for the most part well spaced in plantations.[22] Why was it then that carpenters and sawyers were constantly complaining that Canadian oak was so hard that it blunted their tools? Sir Robert Seppings, Surveyor of the Navy, also gave evidence in this tradition. North American timber, he said, was used at that time only for partitions and bulkheads. North American masts, yards and bowsprits were also used, but only because mast timber of proper proportions was not to be procured elsewhere. North American timber had been used by the Navy from 1807 until 1815 or 1816 and was found to be very subject to decay, particularly in generating fungi, the forerunner of dry rot. He then compared frigates built with Baltic fir around 1796, which had lasted on average for eight years, with others built of North American pine in 1812 and 1813 that had averaged only four years, stating categorically that North American timber was inferior to all Baltic timber. "I consider the English oak as superior to the American as the Baltic fir is to the fir of that country," he added. "The American oak is very bad. I think of the two, the oak is worse than the fir." Under cross-examination, however, he was forced to admit that some vessels built of English timber during the war were also affected very quickly by dry rot. Furthermore, he was unable to vouch for the manner in which the North American pine was handled and stored prior to its conversion into frigates in private shipyards.[23] His evidence, far from appearing to be an honest evaluation of the quality of the timber, smacks of ingrained prejudice. Unfortunately, he was in a position to hurt Quebec shipbuilding and it took half a century to undo the harm.

In 1870, an amendment to Lloyd's rules finally raised American white oak to the eight-year grade when used for beams hooks, transoms, knightheads, hawse timbers, aprons, deadwood, stems and sternposts. An extra year allowed for salting and another for the use of yellow metal bolts made a ten-year class possible. In Table 7 we see the gradual progression in classification leading up to 1880, when William Charland had the great satisfaction of building the only Quebec ship to be awarded an eleven-year class. Her stem, sternpost, knightheads, hawse timbers, apron, main rudder piece and windlass were of *oak*, her main keelson and deadwood, of tamarac and *oak*, her floors of birch, tamarac and *oak*.

Whatever doubt there was about Canadian white oak did not arise in the case of Canadian rock elm. Dense, tough and strong, it retained its strength even when bored through repeatedly with holes for fastenings, and the long straight sticks of this timber of remarkable resistance to water-logged conditions were ideal for keels and bottoms – as well as for ships' pumps.[24] There is no evidence of its use in the square-rigged sailing ships built at Quebec between 1763 and 1812,[25] but warships built in the Canadian Naval Dockyards during the War of 1812 were given elm keels,[26] and from the end of hostilities in 1815 elm appeared more and more in the contracts for Quebec-built merchantmen.

By 1830 it was firmly established in the local shipyards. The paddle steamer *Royal William* of 1831, for instance, the pride not only of its builders but of every other Quebec shipbuilder, was raised on a rock elm keel and all her bottom and part of her ceiling were also made of that timber.[27] Elm was used in the hulls of over three hundred anti-submarine patrol boats built at Levis in World War I, and was also used for building wooden minesweepers in Britain in World War II. Henry Fry's judgement that it was magnificent for bottoms has been upheld.[28]

Yellow or black birch, as it was often known, was the third and only other hardwood used in significant quantity in the structure of the hull. Though birch is not a very large tree, its wood is moderately heavy and tough, and being both strong and resistant to dampness, it was suitable for use below the waterline. Used frequently in the private shipyards of New France,[29] it was at first passed over by the early Quebec shipbuilders trained in Britain who had eyes for nothing but oak, but in the 1830s the disrepute of oak led them to be more receptive to other timber. Thereafter, birch was regularly employed for floors and first futtocks.

Among the softwoods, both red and white pine did double duty, serving either for spars or in the hull. Eighteenth and early nineteenth-century shipbuilding contracts rarely differentiated between the two varieties,[30] but when important timber firms began operating in Canada, a greater awareness of the differences in the qualities of North American timbers developed. Red pine, which is heavier and harder than white and therefore a better bearing timber, was inferior to tamarac as futtock timber but made good planking, ceiling and beams. Yet when it was used as decking during the 1810s and 1820s, it was found to be unsatisfactory.[31] Nevertheless, a versatile and inexpensive timber, it was a real friend to the shipbuilder and huge quantities were used in the yards. Narcisse Rosa's statement of the cost of building a 1500-ton sailing ship in 1889 underlines its importance. Red pine, the cheapest wood he listed, accounted for nearly fifty-seven percent of the timber.[32] Like Canadian oak, Canadian red pine had to overcome strong prejudice on the British market, but by 1833 the prejudice was wearing away and its importation had risen by two or three hundred percent.[33]

The softer white pine, known as Quebec yellow pine when sold as square timber, was unsuitable for framing or planking but was, even Sepping admitted, cleaner and freer of knots than Baltic timber and had the added advantage of being available in larger pieces. It carved and worked well, and was used extensively in both Canada and Britain for figureheads and other carving, as well as for joinery. In the 1830s it came into its own as the ideal decking. Its qualities were described in 1844 by Nathaniel Gould, long-time director of the Commercial Docks system in London. "Eight of the company's granaries," he wrote, "were built entirely of pine timber; and two altogether of Canadian pine, "the entire of the outside being of *yellow* pine; . . . one of these, which had been erected twenty-four years, was in as sound and efficient a state as when originally put up. No wood," he continued,

bore the alternation of weather better than American yellow pine, being most particularly free from warp and crack, and, *if allowed to be thoroughly dried before painting*, was free from rot, and remarkably durable. It had of late got into considerable consumption, for the decks of ships.[34]

Readily available because of the huge quantities being shipped from Quebec, cheap, easy to work, and excellent for the job, the choice of yellow pine as deck timber became a foregone conclusion.

The heaviest and strongest of the softwoods in eastern Canada, tamarac, or "hackmatack" as it is known in the Maritime provinces,[35] shared the qualities of larch, its European counterpart. Though translated into French as "mélèze," tamarac was generally referred to as "épinette rouge" by French-speaking Canadians, and it is under that name, or as "red spruce," that it appears in many contracts drawn up at Quebec.[36] During the 1820s Quebec builders began to use it for both futtocks and planking,[37] and in 1830 the choice of larch for the midship futtocks of the paddle steamer *Royal William* marked its official acceptance.[38] Rapidly gaining favour through the 1830s, it became the main framing timber, serving for beams as well. Unlike the Maritime shipbuilders, whose supply of tamarac ran out so that they were obliged to fall back on spruce, Quebec shipbuilders were fortunate that the timber trade brought ample supplies of tamarac from the interior as long as they built wooden ships. Henry Fry extolled the combination of strength and durability found in tamarac, claiming that "all the best modern Canadian ships were built of this fine wood." Some had been found, he said, that were "sound and tight, when twenty, thirty and even forty years old."[39] Nevertheless, tamarac ships had to fight their way gradually up the ratings from an original five-year classification laid down by the Lloyd's Register Committee in 1834. It was only in 1869 that the committee recognized the true merit of a tamarac ship, granting it a basic eight-year rating with an extra year for thorough salting and another for extra copper bolting, making ten years possible – and even this classification was exceeded in 1880 when William Charland's 1259-ton ship *Lauderdale* was granted an 11A class.

Lastly, we come to spruce which, though it served

Table 6
Relative stiffness and strengths of different timbers
according to tests carried out in the Royal Dockyards, England

	Stiffness*			Strength#	
1.	Sound Timber	261	1.	English Oak, King's Langley	482
2.	Christiana white Spruce Fir	261	2.	Long Sound yellow Fir	396
3.	Young English Oak from King's Langley, Herts	237	3.	Riga Oak	357
4.	American yellow Pine	374	4.	Christiana white Spruce Fir	343
5.	Riga Oak	233	5.	American pine from Quebec	329
6.	White Spruce from Quebec	180	6.	White Spruce from Quebec	285
7.	English Oak from Godalmin supposedly 200 yrs old	103	7.	English Oak from Godalmin	218

*   Weight required to bend timber one half inch in the middle, in lbs.
\#   Weight applied to test the strength of timber, in lbs (method of testing not explained).

Source: Minutes of Evidence of the Select Committee Appointed to Consider the Means of Improving and Maintaining the Foreign Trade of the Country, London, 1821.

only for spars and knees during the late eighteenth and nineteenth centuries, was pressed into service for both futtocks and planking during the shipbuilding booms of the 1820s and early 1830s.[40] Spruce, which dries quickly and works easily, is also fairly strong and was the natural choice when stocks had no time to season, especially as it had the advantage of being readily available. In the mid-1830s, however, it lost out to the stronger tamarac, which secured a higher rating, and it continued to play second fiddle to tamarac thereafter. When Edmund Sewell in 1874 launched the 1097-ton spruce-framed ship *Forest Belle*, he was unable to get her the eight-year classification he sought and had to content himself with seven years,[41] and the experiment was not repeated by any other Quebec shipbuilder.

As important to the ship's structure as the timbers themselves were the huge knees that served as struts and ties. Their great strength lay in their continuous unbroken grain, the result of being taken either from the intersection of a branch with the trunk of a tree or, as was generally the case, from the junction of a root with the stump. The ordinary knees belonged to one of three categories, according to the position they occupied. Placed vertically, and joining the underside of a beam to the side of the vessel, they were called "hanging" knees, though they were known as "standards" if they lay along a deck and up the ship's side; placed horizontally, they were generally referred to as "lodging" knees, though correctly speaking, if they were on the forward side of a beam, they should be distinguished as "lap" or "bosom" knees; the third classification covered those placed diagonally, which were known as "dagger" knees.

The knees varied in length from four to eight feet along the trunk of the tree and from two to four feet along the root, and could be as much as eighteen

Table 7
Lloyd's Classification of Quebec-built Ships

	4A1	5A1	6A1	7A1	8A1	9A1	10A1	11A1
Before 1834		x	x	x			x	
1834-1843	x	x						
1844-1852		x						
1853-1860			x	x				
1861-1869				x	x	x		
1870-187			x	x	x	x		
1880							x	x

Sources: Lloyd's Survey Reports for the Port of Quebec 1852-1880, NA. *Lloyd's Registers*.

Note: Incomplete for ships built before 1852.

inches thick at the bend.[42] Each vessel, however, required a certain number of knees for specific locations, including v-shaped breasthooks, which were fitted horizontally at the bow with an arm along each inside wall, crutches, which occupied corresponding positions at the stern, and the heavy stern knee, connecting the sternpost to the keel, all of which were far larger than the ordinary knee. The breasthooks of the 250-ton barque *Saint Lawrence* of 1818, for instance, were twelve feet long.[43]

Many species of tree provided the knees – oak, spruce, pine, birch, tamarac, etc. Most often spruce or tamarac were used. Spruce, which served for knees in the vessels built at the Royal Dockyard of the French Regime, remained in use and served with tamarac for lodging knees after the introduction of iron hanging knees. Some shipbuilders, however, notably John Munn and John J. Nesbitt, appear to have stuck to tamarac. By 1865, this had become universal, and no more spruce knees were used.

Wooden treenails or trunnels, fasteners driven in by the thousand, were cheaper and lighter than bolts and would not corrode, yet by general consensus metal bolts were stronger. As ships became larger and metal became cheaper trunnels were gradually relegated to fastening timbers that lay against each other. In places where extra strength was required, such as at the abutment of planks or where timbers were joined to the keel, stem, or sternpost, as well as for fixing knees, metal bolts were employed.

The trunnels varied between one and two and a half inches in diameter, according to the size of the vessel into whose timbers they were driven and, depending on the thickness of the timbers they were fastening, might be as much as three feet long. At one time they were laboriously made by hand, but over the years a wide variety of turning machines were invented for their manufacture. Some compressed the timber so that once in place the trunnel expanded making an exceptionally tight joint. Locust wood, because of its toughness and durability in conditions favourable to fungi and termites, was considered excellent for the purpose and was used extensively, particularly after trunnels of North American oak were disallowed by Lloyd's in 1834. In later years, both elm and tamarac were used for trunnels in increasing quantities, and it was common practice for the trunnels to match the species of timber into which they were driven.[44]

From 1834 the wood from which the trunnels were and were not to be made and the number to be used was regulated by the Lloyd's Committee and published in their *Register*. English or African oak, locust or other hard wood was permitted, but in no case Baltic or American oak. All planks above nine inches in width were to be treenailed double and single except where there were bolts. Narrower planks were to be treenailed single, and at least one-half of the treenails used were required to go through the ceiling.[45]

By 1866, the instructions had been extended to include the method of fabrication, and a table specified from which timbers they might be made. From then on, all planks above eleven inches wide had to be double fastened, and eight inches became the width above which the planks were to be treenailed double and single. In all cases, the treenails were to be caulked outside. A second table laid down the thicknesses to which the treenails must conform – one inch in a fifty-ton vessel up to one and a half inches in one of 1350 tons.

By contrast with the choice of ship timber, which was governed so rigidly by Lloyd's, the choice of spar wood was free of constraints other than those of the forest itself. The giant white pines provided the lower masts and bowsprits, the smaller red pine and spruce the rest of the masts and spars. The surveyor of a vessel had only to report that the spars were of good quality and sufficient in size and strength.

In his evidence before the Select Committee in 1821, Sepping maintained that Canadian masts, that is to say American or Canadian masts shipped from Quebec, were only used by the British Navy because masts of that size were not obtainable elsewhere.[46] But the fact remains that from 1609, over a period of over two hundred years, the fleet was masted with North American white pine, at first from the American seaboard to the south of New France, and later from New Brunswick and Quebec. The pines were not only large enough, their quality was obviously acceptable and, being adequate for naval vessels, they were more than satisfactory for Quebec merchantmen. In a letter to *The Times*, quoted by the *Canadian Economist* on 20 June 1846, a subscriber declared that

Yellow (white) Pine, the description of Canadian Timber which has been most abused, is the most useful timber in the world; it gives us a mast ninety-six foot long and thirty inches in diameter, cheaper by one half and as good as can be produced in any quarter... This timber for mast-yards, topmasts, and booms, is unequalled. The Baltic produces nothing like it; it is tough, clean, durable, clear of sap, obtainable in any length required, and is more free from defects than any other timber with which I am acquainted...

Good quality white pine masts from sixty-nine to 105 feet long and from twenty to thirty-two inches in diameter were sold in Quebec until the 1860s, although by then they were no longer being exported in large quantities. In the 1870s, due to deforestation, the shipbuilder was no longer assured of finding the quality he wanted. "A nice looking barque, but the masts are miserable," wrote James G. Ross of the *Tarifa* built by Dunn and Samson in 1875. The masts and spars of Guillaume Charland's *Glenalla* he found "knotty and sappy."[47] It is not surprising that iron lower masts and bowsprits were being turned out at a local boiler shop.[48]

Red pine provided strong resinous timber for top masts and bigger spars. It was generally sold in sticks forty-seven to sixty-six feet in length and twelve to eighteen inches in diameter, though larger sticks were available.[49] But in the early 1850s when vessels over two hundred feet long were built, there was a shortage of red pine large enough for their lower yards, whose size increased in ratio to the ship's length, and white pine had to be used instead.

Young spruce trees with long tough fibres, thirty to sixty feet high and only seven to ten inches in diameter, were ideally suited for the many smaller spars. Older spruce, even when big enough for large spars, were too brittle for the purpose, although for intermediate sizes, either spruce or pine would do. Thus white pine, red pine and spruce complemented each other, between them supplying all the masting timber required.

Turning to the wood used in the finish and equipment of the vessel, we come first to *lignum vitae*, a tough tropical wood essential to the blockmaker's work. Each heart, dead-eye and block sheave, and many of the block cases or "shells" through which the ropes in the rigging were passed came from a cross section slice of this unusually hard timber. Some seventy to eighty percent heavier than oak, it was strong, had high resistance to abrasion and was excellent for turning. Unlike other wood, it was sold by the pound or ton and marketed in bolts two to ten feet long and three to twelve inches in diameter.[50] By keeping a stock of logs of different diameters, the blockmaker kept waste to a minimum, as he fashioned blocks in variety as well as quantity. A 1200-ton ship, for instance, required over 450 single blocks, more than one hundred double blocks, more than a hundred dead-eyes, twenty-one hearts and close to a dozen triple blocks.[51]

The larger block shells that could not be made of *lignum vitae* were generally made of rock elm, which was also tough enough to serve for the windlass and capstan drumhead. And certainly no tree could provide long straight lengths of a more suitable timber for ships' pumps, though we also find them made of birch, tamarac and more often red pine.[52]

According to specifications in shipbuilding contracts, white oak was favoured for many of the special fixtures, including the belfry, the windlass bitts and step pieces, the windlass itself when it was not made of iron, the caps, tops and cheeks of the masts, the cat heads and belaying pins, as well as for the deck railings, though ash and rock elm also served for the railings and the windlass was sometimes made of rock elm.[53] No mention of the steering wheel appears in contracts of the late eighteenth and early nineteenth centuries. In 1840, however, the wheel of the ship *Leonidas* was to be "handsome and strong," and the *Lucinda* of 1841 was to have a "neat oak wheel." By the 1870s, at least some of the prospective owners were placing greater importance on the ornamental quality of the wheel and requiring polished mahogany wheels decorated with brass fixings.[54]

By and large, the timbers one could expect to find in a shipyard woodyard were white oak, rock elm, birch, tamarac, red and white or yellow pine, spruce and, in small quantities, locust and *lignum vitae*. There were of course exceptions. The building contract for the ship *Ultonia* in 1854 required clamps and ceiling of Savannah pitch pine,[55] a timber frequently used in British shipyards, and 2,050 feet of pitch pine are listed among the expenses for the barque *Iona* in 1857.[56] Specifications called for part rock maple floors in the barque *Elegante* of 1865,[57] but other references to the use of maple in the yards are rare. And the rather surprising statement made by the owner of the ship *Annie Jane* at the enquiry into her loss to the effect that her top timbers and part of her planking were of African teak is evidently a stenographer's error. The timber as stated in the surveyor's report was tamarac.[58]

Quebec yellow pine, which served so often for the figurehead and other carving, was also for a long time the wood most used for the panelling and finish of the cabin, whether the work was done at Quebec or, as was more frequently the case, in Liverpool.[59] But beginning in the 1850s, the joinery of an increasing number of ships was completed at Quebec and though some cabins were still soberly panelled in pine, or perhaps oak, others were enhanced with cabinet work rivalling that of the Saint Lawrence River steamboats, on which the local craftsmen had occasion to practise their skills. Handsomely finished in mahogany, rosewood, bird's eye maple, walnut, chestnut and cherrywood,[60] they were no doubt a source of great satisfaction to all Quebeckers, particularly the shipyard workers, who for so long had watched the ships on which they had laboured sail away to be completed by strangers.

Apart from the relatively small quantities carted or sledded in, shipbuilding timber arrived at the shipyard by water, some towed from the properties of habitants in the vicinity and some from further afield. Many sources were tapped for the various lots and special individual pieces needed for one vessel. For example, the tamarac in the ship *Palinurus* built by Pierre Valin in 1857 came from four different suppliers, and timber for the ship *Iona* built by Samson et frères in 1857 from six suppliers as well as from the Russell shipyard's woodyard.[61]

There were certain advantages to dealing with local timber merchants who literally brought the forests of Lake Ontario and the Ottawa, Richelieu and Saint Maurice valleys to the shipbuilders' doorsteps. The timber did not have to be ordered months ahead of time, individual pieces could be selected from large stocks on hand and it could be bought in small or large quantities. Moreover, strict laws regulating the export of timber from Quebec left merchants with stocks of rejects or "culls", that is to say timber that was either undersize or defective. It sold for considerably less than merchantable timber and much of it could be incorporated in the ships. So builders did the rounds of the coves looking for what they wanted, haggled to get the best prices possible and perhaps ended up buying from half a dozen different firms. An even better price could be obtained by buying a ready-made small raft or *moulinet(te)*, perhaps 60 by 40 feet, of assorted lengths and thicknesses of timber,[62] which was delivered to the shipyard at high tide.

Yet not all timber came from such a distance. If the forests around Quebec could not yield sticks of oak, elm, pine and other shipbuilding timber of the size that was brought down to the coves and shipyards

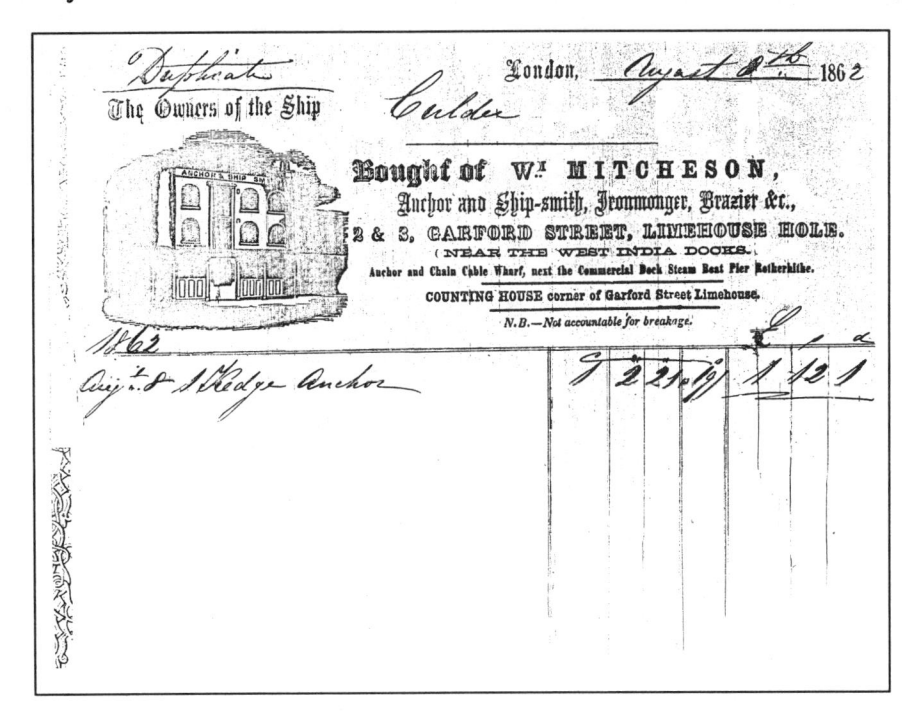

Figure 129: *Kedge anchor account for barque* Culdee, *364 tons, built by I. and J. Samson. With Lloyd's Survey No. 487, 1862.*

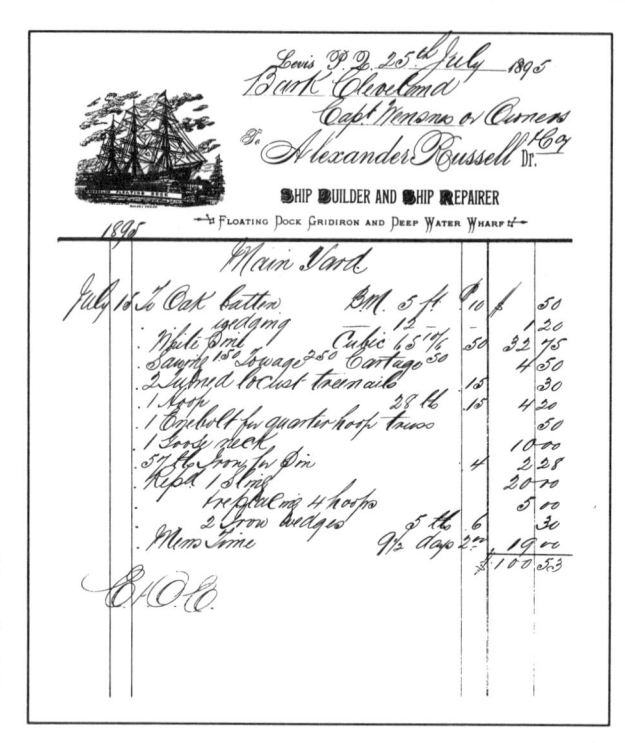

Figure 130: *Russell shipyard account for repairs to the bark* Cleveland *which includes turned locust treenails.*

Figure 131: *List of knees imported from Liverpool for the ship* Greenock *of 1873. With Lloyd's Survey No. 956.*

from Canada West or Upper Canada, they could and did supply the shipyards with smaller logs and knees and masts, futtocks of birch and tamarac, and spruce knees in quantity. George Black's list of "persons that is in the habet of breening knees and the Pleases where they live," which have come down to us in his Letter Book, clearly indicates that habitants from Ancienne Lorette, Loretteville, Saint-Henri and other areas did the rounds of the shipyards hawking their timber. Moreover, notarial files reveal many formal agreements for its sale.[63] In the case of orders for knees or futtocks, "moulds" or patterns were sometimes provided to which the pieces were to conform.[64] According to an estimate given in the *Quebec Gazette* on 17 January 1837, approximately £5000 was earned annually in this way by farmers living within a thirty mile radius of Quebec.

The supply of this type of timber was not restricted to habitants of the Quebec area. Similar orders can be found for timber from such places as the Saguenay Valley and the Montreal area, and in greater numbers from the Three Rivers area, which supplied large quantities of white spruce upper mast and spar timber and occasionally small white pine masts as well.[65] But the huge white pine lower masts and bowsprits came mainly from the Ottawa and Lake Champlain areas and, because of the special handling their size required, shipbuilders bought them as well from local merchants.

Iron and Other Metal

In the last half of the eighteenth century, iron played an important though still limited role in wooden ship construction. The shipbuilder supplemented treenails with bolts and spikes, used nails of various kinds and small iron fittings, such as shackles, hooks and eyes. The rudder was hinged with iron gudgeons and pintles, the standing rigging was fastened to iron chainplates on the hull, and masts were fitted with iron collars, caps and tops. By 1800, windlasses had iron bushings, and capstans iron spindles. There were some iron pumps, and blocks were not only iron-bushed and strapped but some were of iron throughout.[66] The huge iron bower anchors were still by far the largest metal components of the ship. As the century advanced and iron became more plentiful and less expensive, more and more instances were found where it could be used to advantage in the hull, the rigging and other parts of the equipment.

In 1791, Gabriel Snodgrass, the Chief Surveyor of the East India Company and an advisor to the Admiralty for twenty years, recommended that hulls be fitted with iron knees, standards and diagonal bracing to prevent them from working, which resulted in the publication of John Nichols' report entitled *Methods Proposed for Decreasing the Consumption of Timber in the Navy with Observations on Fastening Ships with Iron Knees* published two years later. Successful experiments in Southampton Dockyard followed, and led to their adoption not only for naval vessels but also for merchantmen, whose frames had to bear a heavy strain from the guns that the long periods of war obliged them to carry.

The first references to the use of iron knees in Quebec shipyards are in the contracts for the ships *Mary* and *Thomas Henry*, which were built for the timber merchant Peter Patterson during the winter of 1811–1812. They call for one iron knee on each upper deck beam and one iron standard knee on every lower deck beam.[67] The use of iron knees was soon followed by the use of iron breasthooks, and the iron knees supporting the hold beams gradually developed into long knee riders that reached to the ship's bottom, adding far more strength to the frame and taking up less valuable cargo space than the wooden knees. The Levis shipbuilder W.G. Russell was among the builders who went even further and installed iron lodging knees, too.

The change from hempen anchor cable to iron chain, another milestone in the development of the sailing ship, was also pioneered by the Royal Navy. Originally advocated by Sir Samuel Brown in 1808, the suggestion was put into effect in 1811 when one iron cable was issued to each ship in the fleet. While there was little difference in the initial cost, the advantages of chain were enormous. Unlike hempen cable, it could not be easily shot away, it was neither easily broken by rocks or ice nor adversely affected by being alternately wet and dry, and though it was more difficult to handle in deep water, stowing it in a locker was far easier than coiling a huge hempen cable.[68] Once again, merchant shipowners were quick to see the advantage and to follow the Navy's lead, and in 1813 Lloyd's began using the notation "iron cable" in its *Register*. The ship *Martha* of 1810 and the barque *Triton* of 1812 were among the first Quebec ships to be thus identified, though whether the chain cable was fitted at Quebec we do not know. Certainly, in the case of the *Saint Lawrence* of 1818 it was.

By the mid-1840s, many of the rope fittings on masts and yards had been replaced by iron bands, and patent iron trusses had supplanted the rope trusses of the lower yards. The use of chain had spread into parts of the running rigging: chain slings for lower yards and chain topsail and topgallant sheets and ties. In 1851 another important step was taken when William

Simons, the Clyde and former Montreal shipbuilder, introduced wire rope standing rigging, with which large merchantmen were soon being fitted as a matter of routine.[69] It was cheaper, stronger and more durable than hemp, and had less surface exposed to the wind. Although there was no question of its superiority, for once the Navy was slow to make the change. At the same time, iron lower masts and bowsprits were rapidly gaining favour and soon the masts were being crossed with iron lower yards. At least two new Quebec-built vessels were fitted with iron fore and mainmasts during the 1860s, P.V. Valin's 1188-ton ship *Saint James* of 1866 and Jean Elie Gingras' 1746-ton ship *Atlantic* of 1869. During the 1870s and 1880s there were many others. A few had iron lower yards, and both the *Saint George* and the *Edinburgh* of 1872 had an iron bowsprit too.

After the introduction of iron cordage there was a further step in its use to strengthen the frame. According to a new Lloyd's rule that came into force in 1858, certain vessels requesting classification, including those built in British North America, had to be diagonally strapped with iron plates on either the inside or outside of the hull. There was to be at least one pair of plates to every twelve feet of the vessel's length, and the plates were to be no more than eight feet apart. Extra long vessels, or those whose length exceeded six times their breadth or nine times their depth, were to be fitted with a pair of plates for every ten feet, not more than six feet apart. Quebec vessels were strapped on the outside. Until 1858, it was the custom for this to be done at Greenock or Liverpool following their maiden voyage, but following the introduction of the new rule, all vessels left Quebec complete with all their iron knees, knee riders and strengthening plates.

These requirements for stiffening the hulls of timber-framed vessels with iron are not surprising in view of the fact that composite ships, wooden vessels with iron keelson, frames, knees and deck beams, had been built for a number of years and had been proven. The first composite ship registered by Lloyd's was the *Tubal Cain*, which was registered in 1851. In 1869, William Baldwin laid the keels of two composite ships. They were the only composite ships built at Quebec, but Baldwin was robbed of his achievement, for they were destroyed in a fire that swept the neighbourhood a few weeks before they were due to be launched[70]. The 1020-ton ship *Guinevere*, built by William Cotnam for Henry Dinning in 1870 and William Baldwin's 699-ton barque *Lady Hincks* of 1871, both had iron beams, knees and stanchions, but tamarac frames, according to their surveys, and were not what is generally known as "composite" ships.

In 1807 John Munn said that five tons of iron and twelve quintals of spike nails were needed to build a 500-ton ship,[71] and he might just as well have been speaking about colonial America thirty years before. But fifty years later, the metal content of wooden ships had risen to the extent that it took forty tons to build a 900-ton barque.[72] By 1889, 126 tons of metal were needed for a vessel of 1500-tons, exclusive of the iron masts and foundry work, according to the figures in a letter from the shipbuilder Narcisse Rosa to the *Courrier du Canada*.

Most of the metal parts used in wooden ship construction were made of hand-forged iron, which was tougher and stronger than other iron, yet more elastic. It was soft enough to be pounded into shape, and bolts and spikes could be clinched. Except for anchors and knees, which were imported from Britain, the wrought iron pieces were tailor-made for individual vessels in the shipyard smithies, and most could be fashioned from round and square iron bars up to three or four inches thick and flat plates of three and a half and four inches wide.

As the use of iron spread, it became necessary to establish standards. Alongside the regulations for timber laid down by Lloyd's in 1834 were others regarding anchors, chain cable and bolts. According to these, vessels under two hundred tons were to have at least two bower anchors of "proper" weight, and vessels above that tonnage were to have three. Cables were to be of "approved" quality and their length was to conform to Lloyd's specifications, which were based on tonnage.[73]

Though their length was controlled, the "approved" quality was subject to interpretation until 1846, when Lloyd's instructed their surveyors to see that each new cable had been tested and stamped with the strain to which it had been subjected. Furthermore, from 1853 a certificate was required giving the diameter of the iron of which the links were made and the type, weight and "proof strain" of the cable. In 1858, the Committee issued a new table of their suggested standard for the number and weights of anchors and the lengths and sizes of chain cables for vessels of different tonnages. These regulations and suggestions might have ensured a proper outfit had there not been irregularities in testing. Instead, the high incidence of shipwrecks and public concern over the quality of the equipment on merchant ships brought government action. A Select Committee appointed in 1860 to enquire into the manufacture of chain cables and anchors found that the testing machines were often inaccurate and frequently under the control of the manufacturer. It was apparent that Lloyd's did not have the means to enforce its regulations, and in 1864 the responsibility for inspecting and licensing the "Proving Houses" where the cables were tested was given to the Board of Trade.[74]

Making anchors for large sailing vessels was very specialized work requiring huge forges. In the 1740s, the Intendant's efforts to have the Forges Saint Maurice provide iron knees and anchors for the French warships under construction at Quebec had to be abandoned and the pieces brought from France. There is no indication that anchors were made at the Forges in later years. Nor is there proof that any of the large anchors for sea-going vessels were made at Joseph Archer's "forge for the manufacture of anchors" described by Willis Russell in 1864.[75] Even had Archer been in a position to make them at a competitive price he would have been balked by the lack of testing facilities. These were so costly to maintain, that Lloyd's own Proving House in Poplar was closed in 1873 because of the great expense it entailed.

If anchors and chains had to be imported, bolts certainly did not and local shipsmiths made them by the thousands. The midship section plans of the 566-ton barque *Glengarry* of 1876 and the 1071-ton *Belstane* of the following year (appended to their surveys) show that two-foot bolts were far from unusual and that many were three, four or even five feet long. They measured from three-quarters of an inch to one and a half inches in diameter. A table of required sizes for bolts in vessels of 150 and five hundred tons was published in the *Register* of 1834 and expanded in the *Register* of 1861 to cover vessels from fifty to 1350 tons, but it is clear from reports of surveys that the shipbuilder did not always adhere strictly to the precise dimensions in the tables, choosing sometimes to use slightly larger bolts in one area and slightly smaller ones in another. Bolts that had to be especially tight, in the scarphs of the keel, breasthooks, knees, and shelf pieces, and every second bolt in the butts of the outside planking, were clinched over a ring made of the same metal.

Copper bolts, rings and rods listed in Patrick Beatson's inventory of 1800[76] indicate that some if not all the ships built in his yard were "copper-fastened," that is their planking below the wales was fastened with copper bolts as a pre-requisite for the copper sheathing which would be applied in Britain. However, as copper was in short supply at Quebec during the Napoleonic Wars, most vessels at that time were built with the proviso that they would be copper-fastened if the purchaser provided the copper.[77] With peace, came an end to the shortage, and in 1834 Lloyd's made copper fastening compulsory for all vessels seeking first-class classification. Yet at the same time a more durable metal, an alloy of copper and zinc invented by G.F. Muntz, of Birmingham, England, and known as yellow or Muntz metal, was being used in some shipyards instead of pure copper for both bolts and sheathing. By the 1850s Quebec founders were casting yellow metal bolts and rudder-bands for use in local yards.[78] To the end, only a very small number of sailing ships were sheathed with metal at Quebec, perhaps only those sailing directly to warm waters. For the rest, the sheathing continued to be applied in Britain.

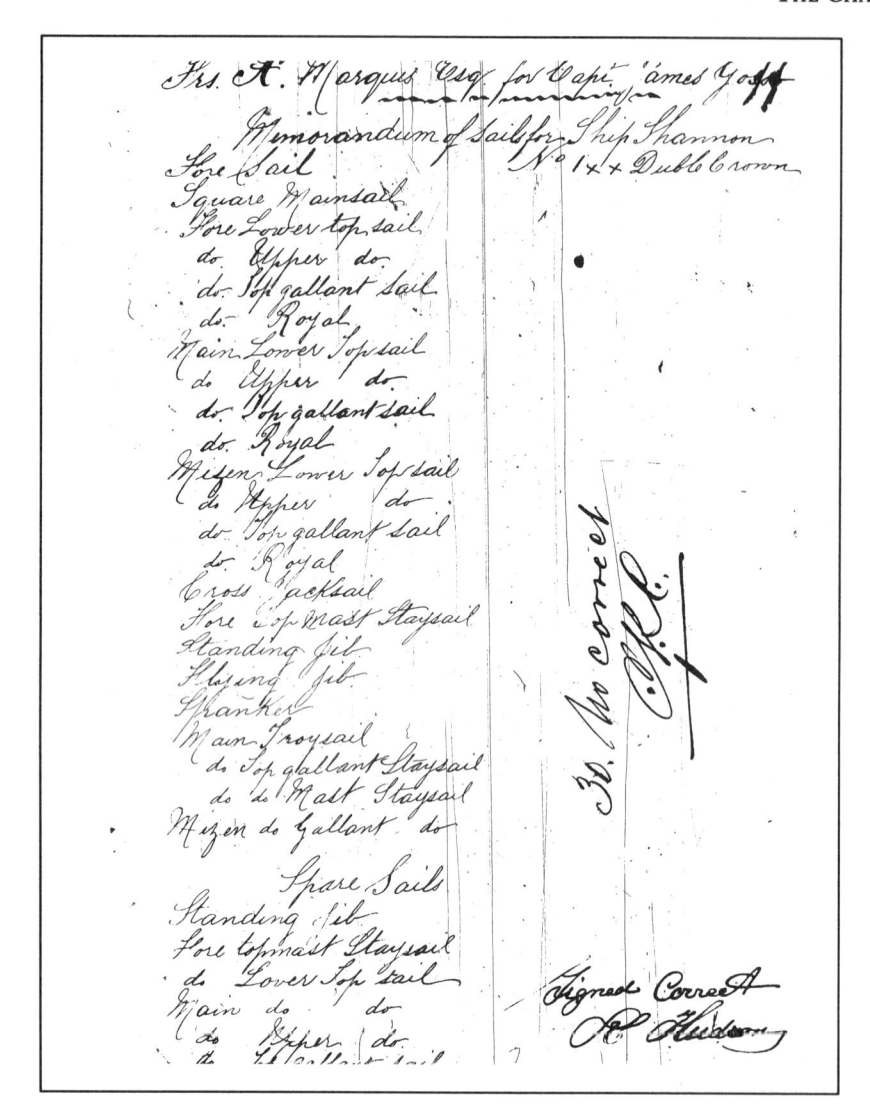

Figure 132: *Memorandum of sails for F.–X. Marquis' ship* Shannon *of 1878, signed by the sailmaker Richard Hudson. With Lloyd's Survey No. 1071.*

Sails

After timber and metal, the third largest item of shipbuilding supplies were the huge canvas sails. Originally, canvas was woven from hemp or cannabis, from which it derives its name, but later it was found that canvas made from flax was stronger and more flexible and so a delicate plant about two foot high with blue flowers and long narrow leaves became the unlikely raw material for the immense canvas sails of the windships.

The cultivation of flax, like that of hemp, was introduced to Quebec during the French Regime with limited success. And as in the case of hemp, when a good price was offered, crops were grown, sold and stockpiled. But due to the perennial shortage of both spinners and weavers, stocks remained high, prices fell and farmers lost interest in growing them because a crop of wheat fetched a better price. Unlike their efforts to promote the growth of hemp, however, the British seem to have made no effort to re-establish flax as a commercial crop. Even had they done so, it is unlikely that Quebec could have competed successfully with the industrialized British mills, whose products were readily available on the Quebec market, and were imported from Great Britain or Ireland either in the form of canvas or else already made up into sails and covers. The size of the sail outfit varied (see Table 8), but in the 1850s the standard number of sails for vessels outward bound from Quebec on their maiden voyage was considered to be twenty-one for a fully-rigged ship and sixteen for a barque, in both cases with no spares.[79] For the period for which figures are available, that is to say from 1852 to 1880, thirty-one percent of all ships and eighteen percent of barques carried fewer than the standard number, while twenty-five percent of ships and thirty-four percent of barques carried more (see Table 8). Among these were the ship *Queen of England* of 1858, which Thomas Menzies described as having "24 sails, 1 suit and 3 spares," and the barque *Far Away* of 1864 with "1 3/4 suits, 28 pieces." In the case of fully-rigged ships, the standard number of sails remained unchanged despite the introduction of double topsails in the 1860s, and this was evidently achieved by a corresponding reduction in the number of studding sails supplied. The outfit for barques, however, rose at this time from sixteen to eighteen. In many cases, we know from the surveyors' reports that additional sails were supplied to the vessels on their arrival at a British port, so that they would have two full suits, or at least a number of spares. The ship *Nugget* of 1854, for instance, left Quebec with sixteen sails and had her outfit made up to two suits in Liverpool, while the ship *Hiawatha* of 1856 was supplied with a second suit in London. Superior outfits, which included up to thirty sails or more, comprised a suit of sails, a number of spares, a bolt or two of canvas, one or two covers for each of the hatches, a cover for the steering wheel, "coats" for the masts to prevent seepage where they passed through the decks, possibly coats for the pumps and occasionally boat sails.

The sails were made from flax canvas, often Scottish or Irish; the hatch covers and mast coats from tarred hemp or "tarpaulin." Flax canvas was generally preferred by British shipowners because it was stronger than the cotton canvas favoured by the Americans, though the cotton canvas was more tightly woven and sagged less.[80] The canvas was graded according to its weight from 0000 to 12, the lower numbers being those of the strongest canvas. It was sold in bolts of forty to forty-two yards, generally twenty-four inches wide, but was also available in a thirty-inch width.[81] "Suits of sails" were of different strengths: "plain

Table 8(a)
Sail Outfits of Fully-Rigged Ships Surveyed from 1852 to 1880

No. of Sails	Suit	14	15	16	17	18	19	20	21	22	23	24	25	26	27	28	29	30+	Total
1852	4	2	2	2	1		3	1	4	1									2
1853	12	2		1	3	2	3	3	12	4									42
1854	5	2	4	2	1	2	1	3	7	6	1						1		35
1855	5		1			3	1	1	6	5		1							23
1856	14					2	1		7	1				1			(33)	(37)	28
1857						1	2	4	6	4									17
1858	11			1					1	1		2		1					17
1859	5								3		1								9
1860	1				1		1	1	11	1		2	2						20
1861						2	4		12			1	1						20
1862	4					1			4		5			2	1				17
1863			1		2	5	2		7		6	7	2		3			(31)	36
1864			1			6	2	6	12	1	6	4	2						40
1865				2		1	5	1	4	1	6	5		1	1				27
1866						1	2	1	3		3	1		1	1				13
1867							3	1	4	1								(36)	10
1868				1	1		1	1	5										9
1869						1		3	2	3									9
1870						2			2										4
1871									1										1
1872							2	3	2										7
1873							1		4	1									6
1874							1	1	3										5
1875																			
1876																			
1877								1						1					2
1878									3									(30)	4
1879)																			
1880)							1	1											2
Ships	61	6	7	9	11	29	36	32	125	30	28	23	7	7	6	0	1	5	423

Table 8(b)
Sail Outfits of Barques Surveyed at the Pot of Quebec from 1852 to 1880

No. of Sails	Suit	14	15	16	17	18	19	20	21	22	23	24	25	26	27	28	29	30+	Total
1852							1												1
1853	2				1		1		1										5
1854		1	1																2
1855	2		1																3
1856	2		1	3		1													7
1857	5		1	1															7
1858	2					1													3
1859	1											1							2
1860	1		1									1							3
1861				3	1														4
1862			2	5		1	2												10
1863		3	2	10			2	1	1						1				20
1864			1	12		2	3									1	1		20
1865				6	4	2	1					1					1		15
1866		2	1	4	1	3			1	1		1		1		2		(31)	18
1867				1	3														4
1868			3	1		3		1							1				9
1869				1	1	1	1												4
1870						5		1	1				1	1					9
1871					2	3							1	1	1				8
1872					1	2													3
1873					2	3	1						1						7
1874																			
1875																			
1876													1						
1877							1											(30)	2
1878					1	2													3
Barques	15	6	14	47	17	29	13	3	4	1	2	3	4	2	3	3	2	2	170

Source: Lloyd's Survey Reports for the Port of Quebec 1852-1880.

sails" for normal weather, "light sails" for fine weather, and "storm sails" for heavy weather. In addition, the canvas of the individual sails of a suit varied according to the strains they bore. For instance, the specifications for the 1112-ton ship *Oliver Cromwell* of 1865 called for twenty-four sails and a full set of hatch covers of "Rutherford Brothers' best long flax canvas," the fore sail, top-sails and for-top-mast-stay sail to be of canvas number 1, the main-sail, jib and spanker of number 2, the top-gallant sails and cross jack of number 3 and the royals, flying jib and others of number 4. Five thousand yards were required to fill the order. The 904 ton ship *Thomas Fielden*'s nineteen sails and tarpaulins took 3,814 yards, in addition to what was required for the three mast and 2 pump coats. Apart from canvas, the sailmakers' supplies included a considerable amount of bolt rope that was sewn around the edges of the sails, and points rope for making the reef points that secured the sails when they were reefed. For the *Thomas Fielden*, the bolt rope and spun yard amounted to 968 lbs. with 94 lbs. of tarred twine. Some leather was also needed to line parts that would otherwise be quickly worn by chafing.[82]

Shipyard stocks of cordage comprised small cordage or "small stuff," such as twine, line and yarn; medium cordage or "rope," i.e, cordage over one and under ten inches in circumference; and "cable," which is cordage ten to thirty inches in circumference, formed by twisting three or four ropes together. All cordage was measured in fathoms, one fathom being equal to six feet, and was sold in coils by the pound (lb.) or hundredweight (cwt.), with the exception of some of the small stuff which was put up in bundles, skeins or hanks. A length of 120 fathoms, the standard length of an anchor cable through the early part of the nineteenth century, was known as a "cable."

Small stuff, which was frequently referred to according to its use as "worming," "seizing," or "serving," was also known by the specific names "marline," "spun yard," "houseline," "roundline" or "hambroline" that distinguished the fibre from which it was made, whether it was tarred or not, whether it was loosely or tightly twisted and whether it had a left or a right-hand twist. Some, such as hambroline and houseline, were made from a standard number of threads, but others could vary and were then described as "4 yarn spun yarn," "9 thread ratline" and so on.

The smallest small stuffs were whipping twine, made from two threads of flax twisted together and waxed, used for whipping wormings and for winding around the ends of small ropes to prevent them fraying; and sewing twine, made of three threads of flax or alternatively of hemp or cotton, used either waxed or tarred to sew sails and other canvas goods. Most of the larger small stuff, the spun yard and the various lines, were hempen and generally tarred, as untreated hemp deteriorates quickly when left exposed to the elements. Riggers used small stuff to work, serve, lash, mouse and seize, as they transformed ropes, blocks, dead eyes and other fittings into working parts of the rigging.[83]

Until the end of the eighteenth century, the medium and heavy cordage in the outfits of Quebec ships were also almost exclusively made of hemp, which was used not only for the working ropes but also for all the cordage of both the standing and running rigging. The first half of the nineteenth century saw the introduction of manila rope which soon took the place of hemp in most of the ropes of the running rigging. For instance, the rigging of the 1037-ton ship *N. Larrabee*, built at Bath, Maine, in 1857, was made from 1,878 fathoms of hemp, 5,740 fathoms of manila cordage and 4,250 lbs. of small stuff.[84] In the 1850s, wire began replacing the hemp cordage of the standing rigging. The ship *Maldon* of 1855 was one of the earliest Quebec ships to have wire rigging. The ropemaker's outfit below, which is taken from the specifications for a barque built by William Cotnam for Messrs. Gildermeister of Bremen in 1876,[85] shows the extent to which hemp rope had been supplanted by manila, wire and chain. Anchor chains had long since taken the place of the huge hempen cables used for the bower anchors, though other working ropes, such as the stream anchor cables, the hawsers and warps were still made of hemp.

> standing rigging of wire
> running rigging of best Manilla hemp, with exception of Jibs
> fore topmast staysail downhauls of Russian hemp
> all footropes fore and aft to be Russian hemp
> chain topsail sheets, ties and runners
> chain topgallant sheets, ties and runners
> royal halyards of Russian hemp, with chain and wire runners as required
> peek ties of chain with boom lifts wire
> halyards on the end lanyards of all lower rigging to be of best Russian hemp – 3 or 4 strand
> all brace pennants, jib and stay sail pennants of wire
> bob stays and bowsprit shrouds of chain with lanyards
> rope ladder with man ropes
> hawsers according to the Rules of Veritas to be of Russian hemp
> 180 fathoms as the Rule for long course chain
> 1 log reel with log ships
> 2 log lines
> 3 lead lines 90 x 25 x 35 fathoms

The conglomeration of ropes that made up the rigging followed an internationally-accepted order so that sailors transferring from one vessel to another would "know the ropes." Moreover, manuals written by well-known authorities, such as *Steel's Art of Rigging*,[86] laid down optimum sizes for each piece of cordage. They had to be strong enough to withstand gale conditions yet no larger than required, to avoid burdening the superstructure with unnecessary weight. In Steel's 1818 edition, for example, there were twenty-seven pages of tables giving precise sizes and lengths for every piece of cordage in the rigging of merchant vessels of 330, 544, 818 and 1257 tons, respectively. Over six hundred separate measurements are given for the rigging of the 1257-ton ship, from small stuff of less than an inch all the way up to sixteen-inch four-stranded cable-laid rope. The sizes for working ropes were also given in rigging manuals and were laid down by Lloyd's, which required that its surveyors report their number, size and length. Before 1858, the outward maiden voyage from Quebec was frequently undertaken with a rope outfit below the requirements and the deficiencies were made up on arrival at a British port. Typical is James E. Oliver's 1778 ton ship *James McHenry* of 1853, which sailed with one hundred fathoms each of 1 7/8 and two-inch cable, and ninety fathoms each of six-inch tow-line, seven-inch hawser and ten-inch cable. Her chain cable was changed at Liverpool for three hundred fathoms of two-inch and 2 1/16 in. chain, and an extra ninety fathoms of six-inch cordage was added to her outfit.[87]

Local roperies in Quebec and Montreal, such as John Brown's Patent Cordage Works in Saint Roch North (Limoilou) went after the large shipyard market, not without some success. In advertisements, such

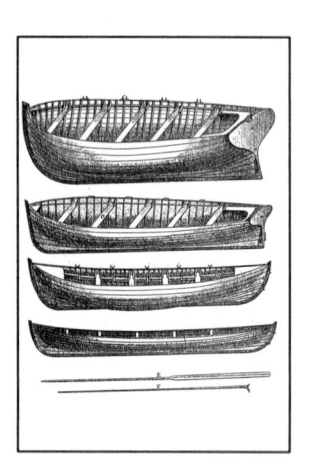

Figure 133: *Ships' boats. Top to bottom, long boat, cutter, life-boat, and gig.* **Capitaine Paasch,** From Keel to Truck: Dictionary of Naval Terms, 74.

as one in the *Quebec Morning Chronicle* of 28 November 1856, he advertised his cordage to be every bit as good as imported cordage, and though we cannot tell what proportion of the ships Canadian ropeworks supplied, the rigging or ropes of a number of vessels were described by the surveyor as being Quebec, Montreal or "Colonial" rope. But large quantities of cordage were imported from places such as Greenock, Liverpool and Belfast, some of it already made up into "gangs of rigging."[88]

Pumps, which were of such critical importance, came under special consideration by the Lloyd's Committee in 1874, which circularized its surveyors asking them to gather information respecting "the amount of pumping power deemed needful for vessels of different tonnages, also on the various descriptions of pumps in use, coupled with the opinions of practical persons as to their respective efficiency" and "the desirability of fitting a donkey engine in sailing ships of large size for working the pumps." They were directed to "seek information on the subject from Ship builders and Ship owners" and forward their suggestions. A table of minimum acceptable size of common pumps for vessels of different tonnage was provided, with an estimate of the amount of water each would discharge in an hour to serve as a yardstick against which the performance of other types of pumps could be measured.[89] Up until then there appears to have been no special control on their quality, number or size, though the surveyors reported their number (generally two), the material of which they were made (usually wood or cast metal), whether they were patent pumps, and noted at times that they were "good."[90]

With regard to ships' boats, Lloyd's from 1834 required that all vessels under 150 tons be provided with one good boat, and every vessel above that tonnage with two or more. The reports of their Quebec surveyors provide a record of the number of boats supplied to each vessel for its outward journey from 1852. The broad rule that emerges from a study of this is that one boat was supplied to vessels under two hundred tons, two to vessels of two to seven hundred tons, and three to those of over seven hundred tons. An outfit of four or five was rare. However, there were many exceptions, particularly during the 1850s, when vessels of up to 1500 tons left with only two boats.[91] Once again we find that the deficiencies were made up on the vessel's arrival at a British port. Moreover, the vessel that was not provided with one, two or even three boats over the normal Quebec outfit was the exception rather than the rule. From 1855, the number of boats on decked ships proceeding from ports in the United Kingdom was also regulated by the Merchant Shipping Act. There were several different types of boat, but typically the first boat was a long-boat and the second a pinnace. Others, in the order of frequency, are jolly-boats, gigs, cutters, skiffs and life-boats. Measurements of the boats are so rarely given that it has not been possible to establish the Quebec norm.

Nor has it been possible to find out much about the boats themselves. The item "boats" in shipbuilding specifications is generally covered by a minimal "usual number of boats" or "a long boat, jolly boat and pinnace – copper fastened."[92] Exceptionally, the type of timber is mentioned, as in a contract between Edward Oliver and Francis Jenkins, a Dublin shipmaster. It reads "two boats Iron fastened of suitable size and carvel Built of Oak frame & Tamarac plank, Oars etc complete."[93] A contract between F.X. Marquis and Francis Spaight & Sons of Limerick gives other details.

Two boats of 25 feet long and two of 20 feet long ... all fitted complete with ash oars, rudders, rowlocks and a stem band on two. With skids to stow three, one pair of davits with blocks, falls & guys complete.[94]

It must be remembered, however, that this sparse information refers to the boats of ships built to order, and there is no way of deducing whether an oak frame with tamarac plank, for example, was commonplace for such vessels, let alone for those in far greater number built on speculation. As far as the oars are concerned, we know that ash oars were exported from Quebec by the tens of thousands in the nineteenth century.

The place of manufacture of most of the boats was the Isle of Orleans where a boatbuilding industry flourished. In his *Histoire de l'Île d'Orléans*, L.P. Turcotte in 1867 put the number of boatbuilders regularly supplying ships' boats at more than forty. As might be expected, there were also boatbuilding establishments in Quebec and its suburbs, who supplied the shipbuilders, and they may also have had some boats made in their own shipyards.[95] And because the long-boat and pinnace of T.C. Lee's ship *White Rose* of 1862 are described as "English built,"[96] the possibility arises that some were imported. While the idea cannot be entirely discounted, I have uncovered no evidence of boats being imported along with the sails, cordage, iron knees and other supplies. It seems more likely that the two English-built boats of the *White Rose* were either salvaged from a wreck or else came to Quebec in some other uncustomary way.

General Quality

On the whole, Lloyd's surveyors' reports, which cover the period 1852 to 1880, leave a favourable impression about the quality of the materials with which the ships were built, although there were a few complaints. The timber itself was sometimes defective. "I had to remove several futtocks and top timbers from being shaken and sappy, and nearly all the cross chocks had to be removed or refitted. The frame is now good,"[97] wrote Menzies about a vessel framed before his arrival in Quebec. Regarding the timber of the *Agamemnon* he stated that

Several of the oak second foothooks seemed foxy and in a state of decay. They were worst on the outside near the head of the foothooks ... defective timbers I took the precaution to point out to the foreman, Mr Gingras' son that he might have them removed.

Such references, however, are greatly outnumbered by the many that refer to the timber being sound, free of sap, and of generous size, and though in early reports futtocks are sometimes described as rather heavily-chocked,[98] in many others the builder gets a pat on the back as the surveyor reports fine natural crooks of tamarac without outside chocks.[99] The lower futtocks of the 1117-ton ship *Sydney* of 1860 were "very fine tamarac well seasoned;" the 847-ton ship *Iona* of 1857 had hold beams of "oak of very large dimension well wrought to timbers."[100] Rarely did a builder risk losing years of classification by persisting in using an unsuitable species or defective timber, the main exceptions being the *Agamemnon* of 1854 built with deficient left-over timber, which received a three-year class, and the

Carioca of 1857 built with a mixture of grey and rock elm, which received only one year more (but was still afloat and on the India run nine years later).[101] And though a half dozen Quebec ships at Liverpool in 1857 were found to be wormed,[102] it is by no means certain that they left Quebec in that condition.

As to the quality of the masts and spars, complaints from the Quebec surveyor were rare. He did find that the masts of the ship *Montcalm* of 1852 appeared "to have lain Long the mizzen masts badly shaken at heel and hooped."[103] A few lower masts were found slightly decayed on arrival at Liverpool and had to be repaired or replaced. It was considered that others required fishing and that still others required re-hooping with heavier iron.[104] On the whole, however, they were considered good and at times received praise. The masts of the ship *America* of 1852 were described as "very well built indeed the oak fishing and the cheeks are dowelled to main piece finished with great care."[105]

The ironwork was generally not found wanting. Where iron was undersized, compensation had been made by placing it closer together.[106] For instance, the barquentine *Norfolk* of 1863 was built with larger iron riders and more in number than required by the rules to compensate for not putting in iron plates, and the following year McKay and Warner were obliged to obtain permission from the surveyor to put the iron strapping closer than was generally required because the ship bringing them their strapping iron had been lost and they could not obtain strapping of the right size. Nor did the rigging come in for criticism, except in one case where it was considered "too small."[107]

Unfortunately, the same cannot be said about the equipment. The whole attitude to a brand new ship pressed into service on its first run as a timber ship was that it would be outfitted in Britain, so why should good money be spent bringing out equipment that could be put aboard there? For its maiden trip, it was equipped as most other timber ships were, which meant minimally. In his report on the *Eleanor*, one of the first ships he surveyed in Quebec, Menzies stated:

The general workmanship is good. The outfit in ropes and sails, chains and anchors is bare, but such is the custom here in sending home ships for sale. It will be observed one of the chains is old also an anchor.[108]

Certainly Henry Dinning made no bones about his opinion on a timber ship's equipment, albeit one that was fifty years old, "*As this vessel is only intended for the timber trade*, I did not intend putting on board more than the customary cable."[109]

Some under-equipment was not intentional. The 1832-ton *Ocean Monarch* of 1854, for instance, left Quebec with chains and anchors that were too light, and Menzies explained in his report that no others could be got at the time and they would have to be changed in Liverpool.[110]

As far as the workmanship was concerned, there were few complaints and the surveyors frequently commented that it was excellent. In 1852, when Menzies first arrived in Quebec, he did find poor "faying" (joining one piece of timber to another) in parts of some of the ships. In T.C. Lee's ship *Montcalm*, for instance, whose overall workmanship appeared "very good," he found "the outside planking above the bilge is all

Tamarac & very fine" and "well seamed but in the Bows and Quarters above wales ... badly fayed." Even so, he had only praise for the vessels of the well-trained shipwrights, such as T.H. Oliver. He surveyed his ship *Premier*, which he found already framed when he took up his appointment, and wrote that "the frame was well put together, the timber good well squared & free from sap and well fayed and seamed. The clamps and shelves," he continued,

are well fitted and bolted & the ceiling is very good & well wrought – The treenails are well drove thou not through wedged on Timbers – The Beams are very good – The knees are full sized having the Roots upon the Beam and are well fitted & Bolted – The general workmanship of this vessel is very good.[111]

In 1854, Menzies stated that he considered H.N. Jones' clipper ship *Tudor*, built by his master shipwright William Simons, to be a very superior ship, and as a whole the best that had been built since his arrival. He also thought Brunelle's 1208-ton ship *Sardinian* and Gilmour's 1172-ton *Illustrious*, both of 1856, superior; Munn's 922-ton ship *Staffa* of 1857 a "faithful and well built ship." He undoubtedly had a high opinion of Brunelle, whose 688-ton *Anomia* of 1860 he said was "remarkably well put together and workmanship throughout is excellent."[112] There are many comments of this kind throughout the surveys, but the real proof of the quality of the vessels was the fact that many shipowners returned again and again for another Quebec-built vessel.

Notes

1. E.g., Canada, Statutes, 48 Geo. 3,c. 17; 6 Vict. c. 7.
2. E.g., (712), 18 August 1807, gr J. Belanger.
3. John G.B. Hutchins, *The American Maritime Industries and Public Policy, 1789-1914* (Cambridge, Mass., 1941), 78-9; Robert Greenhalgh Albion, *Forests and Sea Power* (Cambridge, Mass., 1941), 78-9; Samuel F. Manning, *New England Masts and the King's Broad Arrow* (Kennebunk, Me., 1979), 9.
4. Albion, *Forests*, 12-13.
5. Lloyd's, *Annals of Lloyd's Register* (London, 1934), 32.
6. Jacques Mathieu, *La construction navale royale à Québec 1739-1759* (Quebec, 1971), 41.
7. Lloyd's, *Annals*, 31.
8. J.-E. Bernier, *Master Mariner*, 171; George Gale, *Twixt Old and New*, 67.
9. Albion, *Forests*, 8, 16-17.
10. *Ibid.*, 15, 33.
11. *Ibid.*, 34.
12. Contract, Duncanson with Fairrie, 10 July 1786, gr Charles Stewart.
13. Petition for land grant, Patrick Beatson, 39: 19505-7, Lower Canada Land papers, RG1, L3L, NA.
14. Contract, Goudie with Linthorne & Joliffe, 26 October 1808, gr J. Belanger.
15. Contract to build a ship, Munn with Parker, 7 December 1812, gr W.F. Scott; Duncanson with Fairrie, 10 July 1876, gr Charles Stewart.
16. Contracts to provide knees, Frs Leblanc to J. Goudie, 7 September 1802, gr F. Tetu; J.M. Robitaille to Martin Chinic, 23 November 1799, gr J. Voyer.
17. Graham, *Sea Power*, 145. This refers to timber used at the Chatham dockyard in 1803.
18. Albion, *Forests*, 15.
19. *Lloyd's Register of Shipping*, 1818; *Lloyd's Register*, 1834.
20. 2 August 1822.
21. "Shipbuilding in Quebec," *Canadian Magazine*, V, 4 May 1895, 3.
22. Richard Pering of the Plymouth Dockyard and Wm Taylor Money, late Superintendent of the Marine, Bombay, "Perring and Money on Shipbuilding," *Analetic Magazine* (Philadelphia), 1: 1813, brought to my attention by Marsha J. Shapiro.
23. *Minutes of Evidence of the Select Committee Appointed to Consider the Means of Improving and Maintaining the Foreign Trade of the Country* (London, 1821); see also, Isaac Blackburn, *A Treatise on the Science of Ship-building with Observations on the British Navy and the Extraordinary Decay of the Men-of-War* (London, 1817), 139-149, which refers to "inferior Canadian wood."
24. This quality is also present in English elm. Drain pipes laid in London in 1613 were dug up in the 1950s in good condition.
25. Mathieu, *Construction navale*, 43. Though originally used in the French Naval shipyard at Quebec both for bottoms and for the outer shells of blocks, elm was not favoured by all and by 1745 was no longer utilized. As far as the merchantmen of this period were concerned, Brisson tells us that the bottoms were generally of birch, though he lists elm among the timbers used on occasion, *Charpenterie navale*, 186.
26. Letter from Strickland to Commissioners of HM Navy, London, 6 January 1815. ADM 106/1997, PRO refers to oak and elm being sleighed into the yard at considerable expense, viz. 2/6d per cu. ft. and white pine at 1/3d "from every settler who can bring in a few trees."
27. Contract for her construction, 3 September 1830, gr L. McPherson.
28. Fry, "Shipbuilding," 4.
29. Brisson, *La charpenterie navale*, 103-4.
30. E.g., 10 July 1786, gr C. Stewart; 24 September 1807 and 4 November 1811, gr J. Belanger.
31. See, for example, Contract, Bell with Douglas, 1 August 1818, gr L. McPherson.
32. *Courrier du Canada*, 16 July 1889.
33. Evidence of Allan Gilmour before the Select Committee on Shipwrecks, 24 July 1833, *Minutes of Evidence of the*

Select Committee Appointed to consider..., 529.
34. John Pudney, *London Docks* (London, 1975), 58-9.
35. Both are Indian names. Hackmatack in Algonquian, Tamarac in Huron.
36. In many cases one can only guess that tamarac is meant, but in a contract of 2 November 1844, gr A. Campbell, the notary has written "épinette rouge (tamarack)," leaving no doubt as to the intention. Moreover, in L.A. Belisle, *Dictionnaire général de la langue française au Canada* (Québec, 1974), "épinette rouge" is defined as "mélèze d'Amérique."
37. E.g., specifications of shipbuilding contract, Berte with Price, 3 November 1824, gr L. McPherson.
38. Construction contract, 3 September 1830.
39. Henry Fry, *The History of North Atlantic Steam Navigation* (London, 1896), 4.
40. See, for instance, Agreement, Labbé with Finlay, 19 January 1828, gr L. McPherson.
41. *L'Evénement*, 1 June 1874; L.S. 985.
42. E.g., contracts for the sale of knees, 4 September 1795, gr F.X. Dumas; 7 September 1802, gr F. Tetu.
43. Contract for its construction, 1 August 1818, gr L. McPherson.
44. Rules and regulations for fastenings *Lloyd's Register of British and Foreign Shipping, 1866*, 13, Appendix E. 18.
45. *Lloyd's Register* of 1834, 18.
46. See note 39.
47. It is clear from James G. Ross's business journals, NA.
48. Summons, Lane to Dinning and Webster, 19 January 1870, gr S. Glackemeyer.
49. Contract, Wright with Mure & Joliffe, 28 September 1807, gr J. Belanger.
50. Taylor et al, eds., *Book of Wood*, 244.
51. David Steel, *The Art of Rigging 1818* (London 1818), 137 et seq.
52. Shipbuilding contracts, 23 January 1819, gr A. Campbell; 26 April 1826, gr L. McPherson.
53. 24 March 1845, gr A Campbell; 7 October 1865, gr W.D. Campbell.
54. 8 November 1839 and 20 October 1840, gr L. McPherson; 11 January 1876, gr S. Glackemeyer.
55. 19 October 1853, gr A. Campbell.
56. 24 November 1857, gr S. Glackemeyer.
57. 7 October 1865, gr W.D. Campbell.
58. *Report made into an Investigation into the loss of the Annie Jane made by the Direction of the Board of Trade by Captain Beechey, R.N.*, (London, 1854), 1.
59. "... all joiners' work outside and inside complete, except the inside of the cabin..." is a phrase that appears over and over again in shipbuilding contracts. See, for instance 6 October 1809, gr J. Belanger. Even as late as 1853, we find "cabin to be finished in the 'rough' as usual in the Port of Quebec," 4 March 1854, gr A. Campbell.
60. E.g., see *Morning Chronicle*, 14 July 1857.
61. Atkinson with Valin, 21 January 1859, gr W.D. Campbell; Samson with Russell, 24 November 1857, gr S. Glackemeyer.
62. Contract, Clark with Munn, 1 June 1813, gr A. Campbell; *Quebec Mercury*, 1 May 1820, advertisement of H. Atkinson; J-E. Bernier, *Master Mariner*, 168-9.
63. E.g., Contract, Goulette with Goudie, 29 January 1803, gr F. Têtu, Poliquin with Gingras, 16 October 1852, gr J. Birch.
64. See Leblanc with Goudie, 1 September 1802, gr Têtu; Marchand and Lacroix with Munn, 7 December 1824, gr L. McPherson.
65. E.g., Gauvin with Campbell, 12 March 1807, gr J. Belanger; Michaud with Blais, 29 January 1856, gr J. Hossack.
66. Patrick Beatson's inventory, 15 December 1800, gr C. Voyer.
67. Shipbuilding contracts, 26 September 1811 and 7 November 1811, gr J. Belanger.
68. Naish, "Shipbuilding," 585-6.
69. Michael Moss and John Hume, *Workshop of the British Empire*, (London 1977), 147. Though Naish states that

"wire standing rigging was introduced into the Royal Navy in 1838," 593.
70. *Quebec Morning Chronicle,* 26 May 1870.
71. Contract, Munn with Mure & Joliffe, 24 September 1807, gr J. Belanger. (1 quintal = 112 lbs.)
72. "Nantissement," Samson & frères with Russell, 24 November 1857, gr S. Glackemeyer.
73. *Lloyd's Register* of 1834, 24.
74. *Lloyd's Annals,* 101-2.
75. *Quebec: as it was and as it is.* Cited by A.J.H. Richardson in "Indications for Research in the History of Wood-Processing Technology," *APT,* VI, 3, 1974, 126.
76. 15 December 1800, gr C. Voyer.
77. E.g., Shipbuilding contracts, 26 October 1808 and 11 October 1809, gr J. Belanger.
78. *Quebec Morning Chronicle,* 25 January 1859. J.W. Henry's business card.
79. Sail orders for a ship and barque, given by T.C. Lee to the sailmaker R. Blakiston in 1865, 18 August, gr S. Glackemeyer.
80. The only Quebec ships with cotton canvas sails that I know of are the barque *Constantine* of 1854, the ship *Pied Nez* and the barque *De Salaberry* of 1855. Sails provided for one of the *Shannon's* boats were also made of cotton, 16 April 1878, gr W.D. Campbell.
81. Horsley, *Maritime Trades,* 287-8.
82. Contract, 7 October 1865, gr W.D. Campbell; Pickersgill, Tibbit & Co. account with James Hunt, 8 March 1847, Pickersgill, Tibbits & Co. papers, P-202-4, ANQ.
83. Horsley, *Maritime Trades,* 289-92.
84. W.A. Baker, *A Maritime History of Bath, Maine, and the Kennebec River Region,* 1043-4.
85. 11 January 1876, gr S. Glackemeyer.
86. A treatise taken from the original *The Elements and Practice of Rigging, Seamanship, and Naval Tactics,* published in 1794, of which at least three editions were published in London, the third in 1818.
87. L.S. 61.
88. E.g., ship *Alma* of 1855, British and Belfast rigging; ship *Beaconsfield* of 1861, Scotch rigging.
89. Filed with L.S. 1050.
90. E.g., L.S. 1047.
91. The 1497 ton ship *Fanny Forsyth* of 1854 and the 1193 ton ship *White Rose* of 1862 are two such vessels.
92. E.G. Contract, Nesbitt with Parke, 8 November 1839, gr L. McPherson; Sale, Valin to Wilson, 16 January 1858, gr A. Campbell.
93. 30 October 1840, gr L. McPherson.
94. 16 February 1878, gr W.D. Campbell.
95. E.g., builders, such as Sam Finch, Louis Labbé, Sheppard & Campbell, R. & W. Carman, Wm. Bell and Geo. Taylor are listed among the customers in the accounts of the boatbuilders Usmar & McPhaden. 30 September 1831, gr L. McPherson.
96. L.S. 489.
97. L.S. 4.
98. E.g., L.S. 179, 230.
99. L.S. 72, 233, 269.
100. L.S. 400, 287.
101. L.S. 104, 294.
102. L.S. 286, 291.
103. L.S. 14.
104. L.S. 76, 198; 103, 118; 76.
105. L.S. 12.
106. L.S. 553, 848.
107. L.S. 632, 55, 118.
108. L.S. 3.
109. L.S. 1000 of Dinning's ship *Marchioness of Queensbury,* built in Hull, England, in 1824.
110. L.S. 98.
111. L.S. 16.
112. L.S. 124, 222, 252, 284, 405.

CHAPTER 8
The Shipbuilding Trades

Aware of the bustle and noise that was part of every shipyard a century ago, I was struck on visiting the Davie shipyard at Lauzon in 1978 by its deserted aspect, the lack of clutter and almost eerie quiet. But as I walked to the office, the silence was broken by a vehicle which pulled out of one of several long buildings carrying a large pre-fabricated section of a vessel. At the building slip, a crane was waiting to swing the metal section into its fore-ordained place in a ship under construction, as though placing a piece in a giant three-dimensional jigsaw puzzle. For a while welders busied about securing it, and then they were gone. Realizing that this modern shipyard or industrial plant was not where I would learn about traditional shipbuilding trades, I redirected my steps to the original little Davie shipyard at Levis, where even though old technology had been adapted to power tools, shipbuilding materials had changed and factory-made fittings and fixtures had taken the place of those formerly made by hand, it was nevertheless still possible to learn something out about the old shipbuilding tools and methods used during the days when the large wooden sailing ships were built, both from the workers and from the installation and equipment.[1]

It was necessary, however, to begin with a modicum of knowledge, and, because the craftsmen at Quebec were almost all either French immigrants to New France or later British immigrants, or their descendants, I turned to such recognized definitive works as Diderot's *Encyclopaedia* of 1762, showing French techniques up to that time, and then Steel's *Elements of Mastmaking, Sailmaking and Rigging* (1794), Captain Paasch's *Dictionary of Naval Terms* (1909) and in particular that excellent reference work, R.A. Salaman's *Dictionary of Tools of the Woodworking Trades circa 1700–1970* (1975) to cover the techniques brought from Britain. Notarial contracts, inventories and other documents, and advertisements in periodicals, helped confirm that the various tools and techniques had indeed been used in Quebec, while the Quebec tools in the collection of the National Museum of Man (Canadian Museum of Civilization) in Ottawa served as a very useful physical reference. In addition, field trips to other small shipyards and to the homes of retired shipyard workers and sailmakers provided the opportunity to further my research.

Many different tradesmen or specialists contributed to the construction of a ship, and in this chapter fourteen of them are considered: the sawyer, ship carpenter or framer, planker, caulker, joiner, ship carver, shipsmith, painter and glazier, blockmaker, mastmaker, pumpmaker, ropemaker, sailmaker and rigger. Some of the less specialized workmen are included under the heading "other shipyard workers."

Although each of the trades was a specialty in itself, two or more were often practised by the same man, particularly in the smaller yards. The carpenter might handle the planking, and even the caulking. The blockmaker was very often responsible for the masts and pumps. Here, however, each trade or specialty is examined separately – its general substance and scope, its nature in Quebec, the tools and techniques and, where possible, the workplaces and forms of training.

The Sawyer

The work of the sawyer or *scieur de long* as he is so aptly called in French, was to saw timber along its length to make planks. His motions were imitated to produce the water-driven sawmill, and the single saw blade eventually gave birth to a series of blades harnessed in parallel, known as the gang saw. In 1818 Quebec's, and perhaps Canada's, first steam-powered sawmill began production in Saint Roch,[2] and as the century advanced, more and more water or steam-driven mills, some in the shipyards themselves, took over the sawyers' work. But despite the far greater productivity of the mills, there was still room in the shipyards for a large number of sawyers, cutting planks to size as they were required and doing all the irregular jobs, such as sawing curved timbers, that the less versatile mill saws could not handle. A total of 122 sawyers were enumerated in the St. Roch suburb of Quebec in the 1861 census and ten years later there were still eighty-six.[3] Many were engaged in the shipyards, where "it was nothing unusual to see as many as two score of men sawing away at immense pieces of square timber."[4]

In Britain and other parts of northern Europe the logs were generally laid over pits to be sawn, but in France and most European countries they were sawn on high trestles. Many of the nineteenth-century Quebec sawyers were of British origin, but generally followed the local custom and used the high trestles rather than a pit.[5]

The sawyers worked in pairs. The senior sawyer was traditionally responsible for sharpening the saws and marking the log, and it was he who stood on the log holding the "tiller" or upper handle of the saw while his partner below, wearing a veil or a wide-brimmed hat to prevent sawdust from getting into his eyes, held the "box" or lower handle. How the details of the partnership were handled we do not know, as no partnership agreement between sawyers has yet been found.

Logs, which had been rough-hewn on two sides so as to lie flat, were chalk-lined on their upper side, marked down each end with the aid of a plumb line and turned over and chalked along the other side.[6] Once marked, they were lifted onto the trestles with the help of a pair of sheer-legs, and held in place by iron dogs. The sawing then began. According to George Gale, a wedge was used to split the plank off the log when the saw reached six inches from the end, and it is likely that long hanging wedges were also used behind the saw to prevent it from jamming.[7]

Until the mid-eighteenth century, the long pit saw blades were held taut in a rectangular wooden frame; after that open saw blades made from strong improved steel were imported; these required only a handle at each end, allowing the sawyers far greater freedom of action. The framed saw blades measured from four to six feet in length, while the longer open or "whip" blades were regularly manufactured in four to eight foot sizes but could reach as much as ten feet in length. In addition, narrow blades for cutting gentle curves were available from four to six foot long for both types of saw. Various round and flat files were used to keep a sharp edge on their large teeth, which were all slanted or "raked" in the same direction for cutting only on the down stroke.[8]

The sawyers, generally hired in pairs, were paid by the day, by the job, or by the amount of wood they cut, the toughness of the wood dictating the rate and the senior man sometimes but not always earning slightly more.[9] They were the first to start working on a new construction and they remained on the job as long as there were carpenters or joiners employed who might need a plank of special dimensions. If they ran out of work temporarily, they were often required to wield an axe, to caulk or do other work. Theirs was not a trade in which a formal apprenticeship was customary, nor one to which a man necessarily adhered throughout his life, but one which a habitant might take up for a short time, following which he might work as a caulker before returning to his land, or to which a sailor, carpenter or joiner might turn when he found it expedient to undergo a temporary change. The shifting occupations of a certain Simon Vaillancourt, for instance, have been traced. He appears as a mariner in the Parish "Visits" of 1795 and 1798 and as a sawyer in 1805. In 1811 he obtained a contract as a caulker, then signed up as a sawyer in 1814, and was once again working as a caulker according to the Visit of 1818.[10] Nor is his case unique. It is often said that all French Canadians were natural woodsmen. An initial survey confirms that among the sawyers there were many drawn from other occupations, who either chose or were obliged to earn their living for a while with the saw.

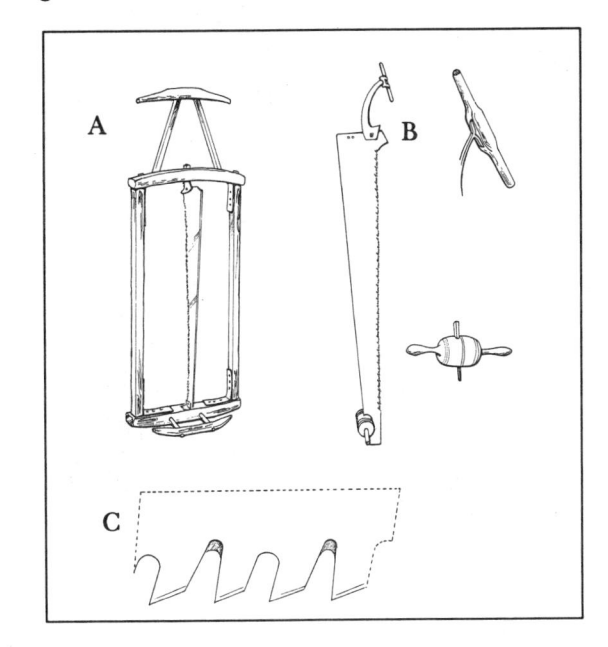

Figure 134: *Pit Saws*

a) *Framed Pit saw with narrow blade, which is tensioned by a thumbscrew at the top.*
b) *Broad bladed open pit saw with tiller and box handles.*
c) *Pit saw teeth, raked one way to cut only on the down stroke.*

Adapted from R.A. Salaman, Dictionary of Tools used in the woodworking and allied trades *c.1700–1970.*

Figure 135: *Sawyers at work in a shipyard on the Saint Charles river. Courtesy Musée de la Civilization, Quebec.*

Figure 136: *Mould Loft. Nerve centre of the shipyard, where the full-size moulds, or templates, are prepared.*

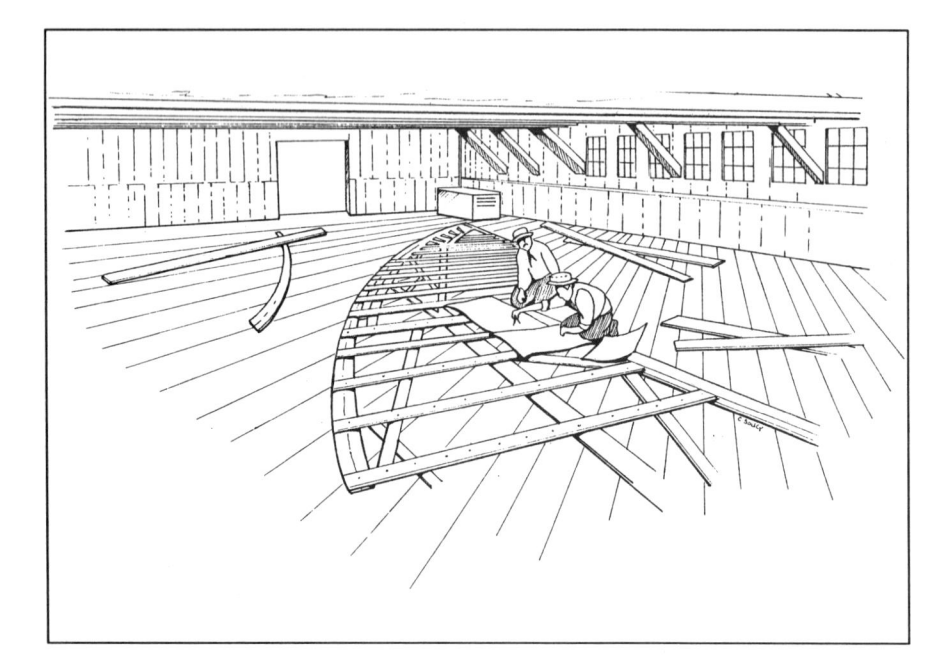

The Ship Carpenter

In every shipyard there was a "mould-loft," with an uninterrupted floor space a little longer than half the length of the largest ship to be planned there and a little wider than half its maximum breadth. The floor was painted or sanded so as to present a clean level work surface, and it was there that the work of building a ship began. A grid was drawn onto which the plans of the ship under construction were projected full-scale, following which a team of ship carpenters helped the shipbuilder or his foreman make the patterns or "moulds" for the frames of the ship. Meanwhile others prepared the building slip outside, laying the keel-blocks four feet apart, slightly inclined in the direction in which the ship would travel on launching, and taking great care to make a firm foundation on which the whole weight of the ship could safely rest.

Once the yard superintendent was satisfied with the keel-blocks, the carpenters laid the keel, which in a large ship might measure over twenty inches square. It was generally made of elm, a timber that resisted the water well and remained strong even though many bolts and fastenings were driven through it. It usually consisted of at least two or three lengths of timber "scarfed" or "scarphed" together, perhaps two or three pieces deep.[11]

When the keel was ready, a rabbet was made along its length on both sides into which the first strakes of planking would later be fitted and then each end was built up with timbers known as the "dead-wood," which were bolted into place ready to receive the stem and stern-posts. The stem-post, which was rounded on the bottom, could be built up of three pieces, but the stern-post required greater

The Shipbuilding Trades

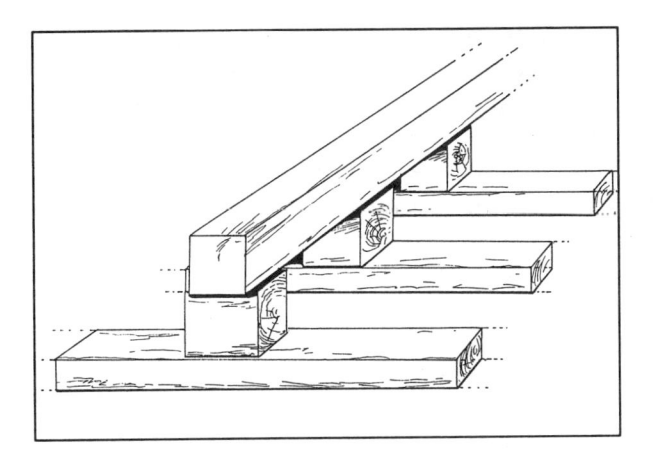

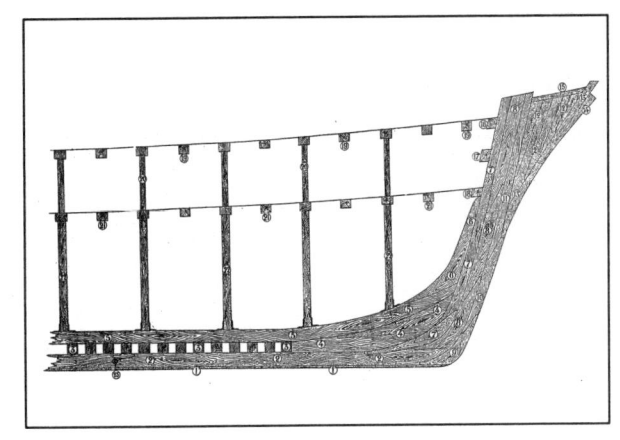

Figure 137: *The keel blocks.*

Figure 138 : *Deadwood, etc. of forward portion of keel.*

1. False-keel
2. Keel
3. Floors
4. Fore-deadwood or stem deadwood
5. Keelson
6. Stemson
7. Apron
8. Stem
9. Gripe
10. Cutwater
11. Independent-piece
12. Filling-chocks
13. Lace-piece
14. Bobstay-piece
15. Gammoning-piece

Figure 139: *Deadwood, etc. of after portion of keel.*

1. False-keel
2. Keel
3. Keel-scarph
4. Stern-post
5. Inner-post, or inner-stern-post
6. Sternson
7. After-deadwood
8. Keelson
9. Keelson scarphs
10. Floors
11. Heel-knee
12. Cant-floor
13. Cant-frame

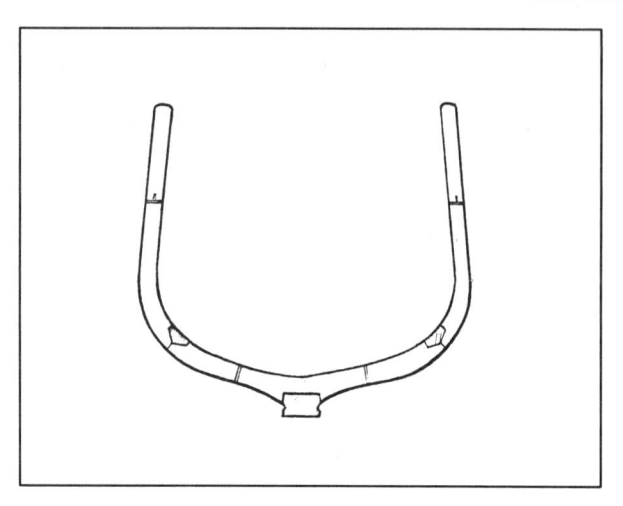

Figure 140: *Futtocks*

strength to support the rudder and was generally shaped from a single straight piece.¹²

The moulds of the frames were then matched to the curved timbers in the woodyard, and pieces were selected which would entail the least waste. Each horse-shoe shaped frame representing a cross-section of the ship comprised a piece in the centre, known as a "floor," with two or more "futtocks" followed by a "top timber" on either side.

The various sections of the frames were joined with chocks or butt-dowels. The floors were mortised to fit over the keel and all the outside edges were bevelled to present a smooth surface for the planking. The frames were then assembled on a platform and placed at equal distances along the keel, great care being taken to set the first exactly at right-angles to it and then the others parallel. The upper ends of the frames were held in place by long flexible laths or "ribbands," which ran the length of the ship, and on which the position of each frame had been marked in the moulding loft. The whole structure was supported with breast and bilge shores. A great timber, known as the "keelson," was laid the length of the ship on the floors directly over the keel and all were thoroughly bolted together. In some cases additional keelsons were then added for greater strength. When all that had been accomplished, it remained only for the timber-work of the stern to be built up for the ship to be officially "in frame."

It was then the turn of the plankers to begin their work, while the carpenters turned their attention to shaping the slightly arched beams that would support the decks and which ideally were made of a single piece of timber. At every deck-level a beam was laid across each frame, to act both as a strut to hold the sides of the hull apart and a tie to hold them together. It was supported by a stanchion at the centre and by "hanging" knees bolted to the planking under it, and was stiffened longitudinally by smaller horizontal "lodging" knees. At the stem and stern, timbers known respectively as "deck hooks" and "deck transoms" formed the bed for the ends of the deck planks.

The rest of the carpenters' work included building the steps on the keelson into which the masts would be fitted or "stepped," building the catheads and timber-work of the bow, installing the V-shaped timbers known as breasthooks that connected and strengthened the sides of the ship at the bow, and generally finishing off the carpentry of the vessel, including making the deck hatches and mast holes, stern windows and portholes.

The shipbuilder provided the heavy tools, of

The Shipbuilding Trades

Figure 141: *Deck openings*

1. Hatch
2. Hatchway or hatch
3. Hatchway coamings or hatch coamings
4. Hatchway carling or forming hatch carling
5. Headledges
6. Fore and after
7. Hatchway beams or hatch beams
8. Half-beams
9. Lodging-knees
10. Deck-stanchions
11. Mast-hole
12. Mast carlings
13. Chocks
    12. & 13. forming mast-partners
14. Mast-beams
15. Deck-planking

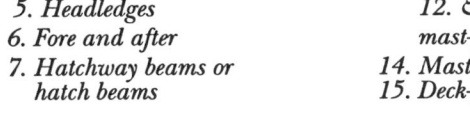

Paasch

Figure 142: *The hull in frame.*
1. Keel
2. Skeg of keel
3. Deadwood
4. Stern-post
5. Filling-chock
6. Filling-transoms
7. Wing-transoms
8. Helm-port
9. Counter-timbers
10. Margin
11. Horn-timber
12. Stern-timbers
13. Side-counter-timbers
14. Quarter-timbers
15. Fashion-timber
16. Cant-frames
17. Square-body-frames

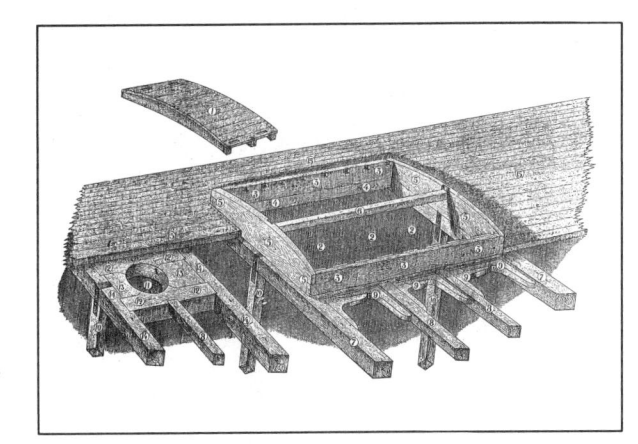

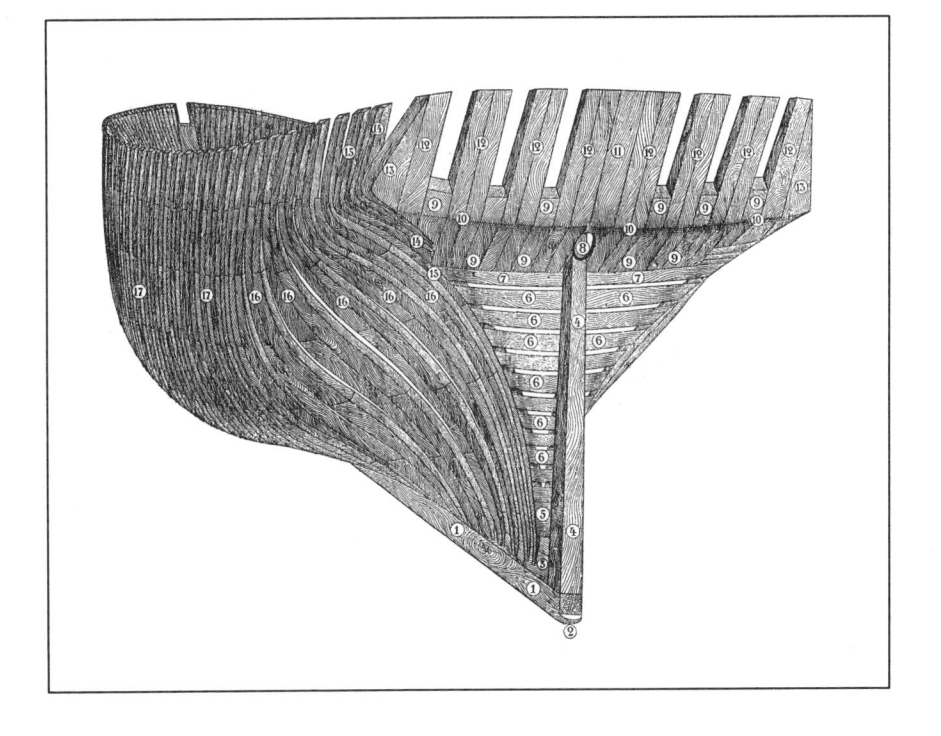

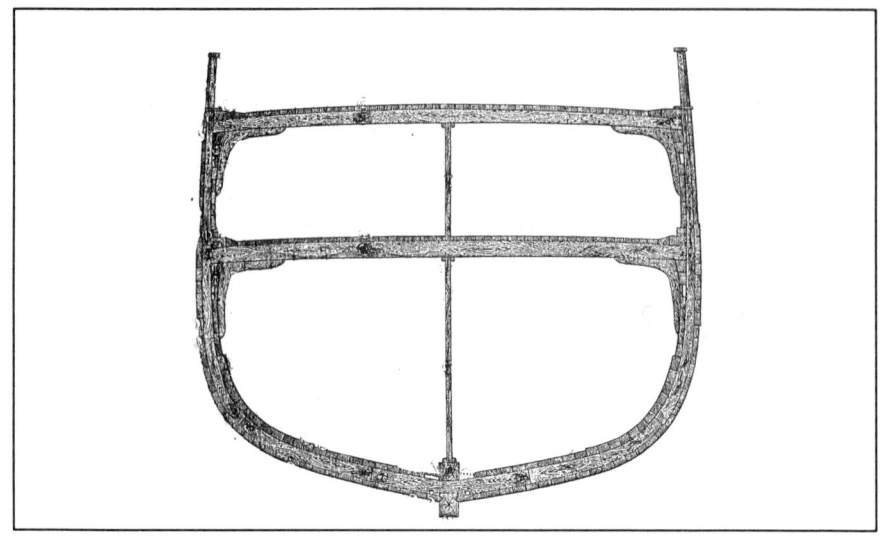

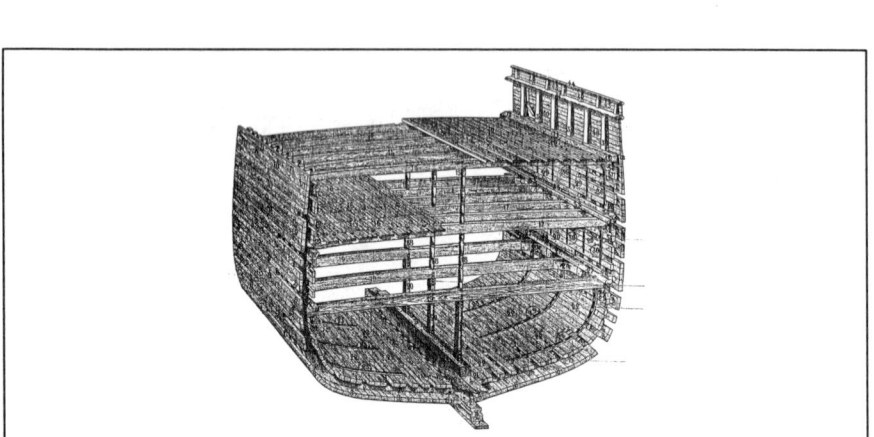

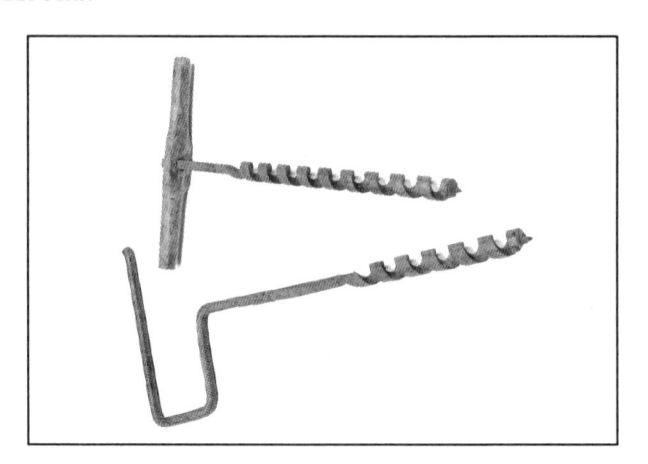

Figure 143: *Midship Section of a wooden sailing ship with two decks and wooden hanging knees.* Paasch

Figure 144: *Midship Section of a wooden sailing ship with two decks and three rows of beams, fitted with iron knees and knee riders.* Paasch

Figure 145: *Single twist augers with screw leads in the collection of the National Museums of Canada, Ottawa. Neg. NA–16–77–11*

which only augers were required in large quantities,[13] and Salaman's contention that shipwrights preferred the shell-shaped to the spiral augers because they were less liable to "wander" or follow the grain is confirmed by inventories of the contents of shipyards which only occasionally note an auger of the screw type. From twelve to twenty-seven inches long, they varied from 3/8 to over two inches in diameter. They were provided with either a bonnet or a barrel-shaped eye to receive a cross handle, a tanged shank for embedding in and clenching over a cross handle, or a plain square section shank, which could be fitted in a patent handle or else have an extension welded to it of any desired length. This sometimes took the form of a crank, enabling the worker to handle the auger like a brace.[14] They were used almost exclusively to bore holes for treenails and bolts, and were selected for use with a diameter 1/8 inch less than that of the fastener itself.

The carpenter's own tools consisted of an axe, adze, maul and handsaw which, with the auger, enabled him to carry out most of the carpentry of the hull. With his axe, he made quick work of squaring timber, while his skill with his adze enabled him to shape timber with a high degree of accuracy, to trim or "dub," and even to make some of the mortise and scarph cuts. If he came across heads of spikes or bolts when dubbing, he drove them below the surface with the peg poll of his adze. What he could not readily cut with his axe or adze, he cut with his saw. The ship maul, with a round flat face at one end of its head and a tapered pin at the other, served as an all-purpose hammer, in particular for driving fastenings, and like the adze, was turned over for use as a punch.

Some of the other tools the carpenter might

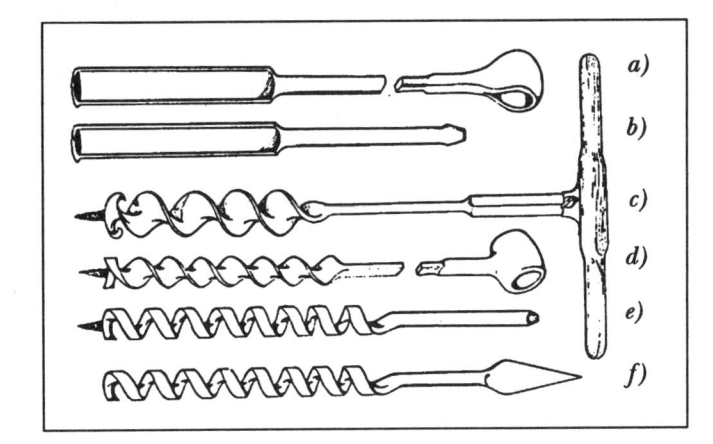

Figure 146: *Spiral and Shell Augers*

1. Single twist or "L'Hommedieu" pattern auger, *made from half-round or triangular bar iron coiled in an open spiral:-*

    a) *"Bull-nosed" (Eng.), "Shell mouth" (Scot.) or "Barefoot" (U.S.A.), i.e., with no lead. Tanged shank.*
    b) *Screw lead. Plain shank for fitting in patent handle.*

2. Double twist auger, *made from twisted flat bar:-*

    c) *"Scotch" pattern, i.e., flat cutting edge with side wings, screw lead. Barrel eye shank.*
    d) *"Gedge" pattern, i.e., cutting edge curved upward, screw lead. Patent handle.*

3. Shell auger, *with half-cylinder blade and in-bent horizontal cutter on nose, no lead.*

    e) *Plain shank for welding to extension.*
    f) *Bonnet eye shank.*

Adapted from R.A. Salaman, Dictionary of Tools used in the woodworking and allied trades c.1700–1970.

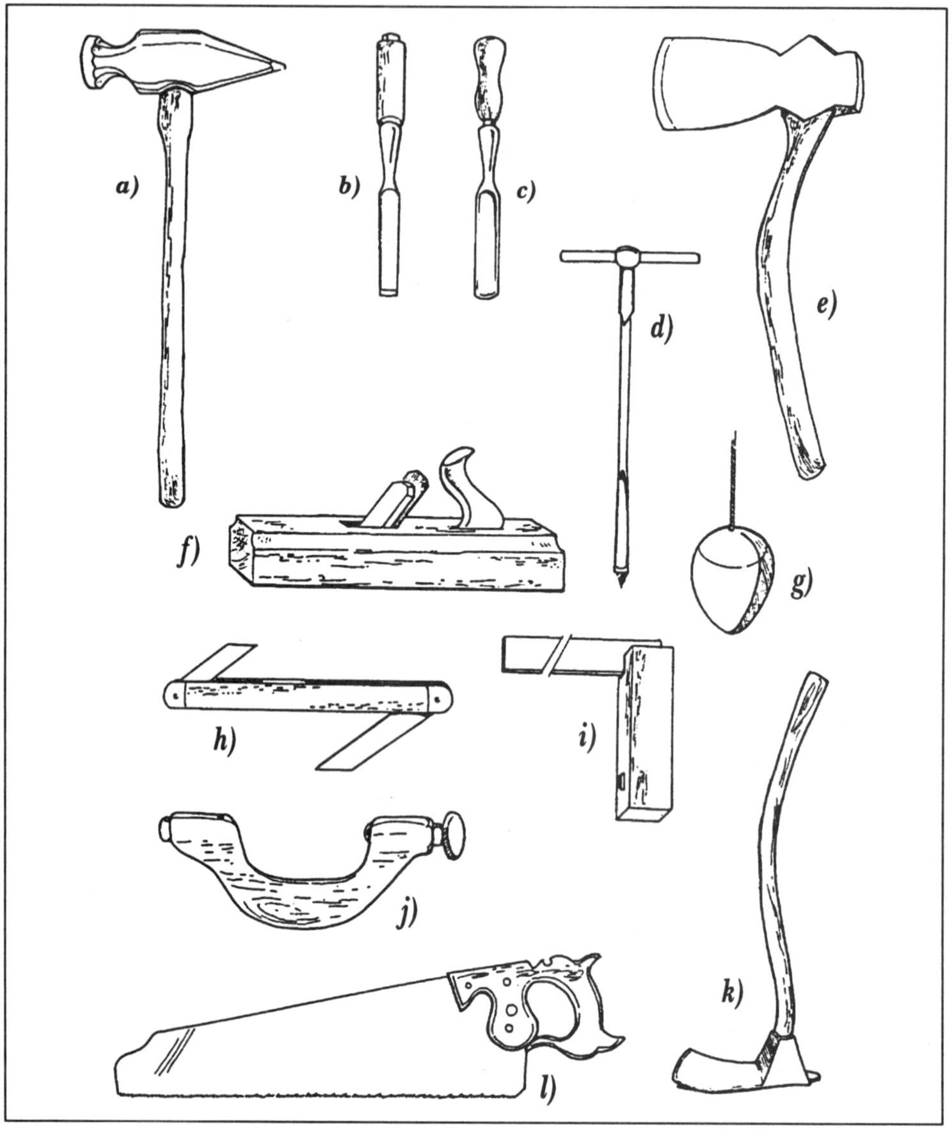

260 THE CHARLEY-MAN

Figure 147: *Ship Carpenters' Tools*
    a) *Maul (Pin Maul)*
    b) *Chisel*
    c) *Gouge*
    d) *Gimlet*
    e) *Broad axe*
    f) *Jack Plane*
    g) *Plumb Bob*
    h) *Bevel*
    i) *Try Square*
    j) *Brace*
    k) *Peg Poll Adze*
    l) *Hand Saw*

Figure Adapted from R.A. Salaman, Dictionary of Tools used in the woodworking and allied trades c.1700–1970.

carry in his bag included a chisel and gouge, not unlike the heavier socketed types used by house carpenters and measuring up to two inches in width and thirty-six inches in overall length, and perhaps a similar but wider chisel with an offset handle and a two to four inch blade, known as a "ship slice." Some shipwrights, however, preferred all-iron chisels, which resembled extra large caulking irons.[15] They were used mainly for paring down timbers where the adze could not reach and for cleaning up mortise and other joints. Many carpenters carried a Jack plane for going over some of the work of the adze, shaping beams and similar work, and perhaps a shorter roughing plane designed for removing preliminary waste. The draw knife, a favoured old-time shaving tool, would certainly be found among his tools, as would that important shipyard measuring tool, the bevel. For those responsible for trueing up timbers, a plumb bob and large try square were essential.[16]

According to a retired shipwright interviewed by Marius Barbeau in 1925, his father's apprenticeship (probably during the 1830s) lasted seven years, after which he was given a certificate qualifying him as a ship carpenter, and only then was he able to draw full pay. By the 1860s, when he himself started working in the yards, this system had died out, but he nevertheless served some kind of an apprenticeship, which began, he stated, by learning to chop an accurate cant on timbers; it was only when he was twenty years old that he was given a salary.[17] Like other ship carpenters, he would have been proud of his rank and resent any attempts to use unskilled labour for work he considered to be his. If he had sufficient skill, he might become a specialist planker.

Figure 148: *Steam box. As used to build the schooner* Mont Marie *in 1952, see Michel Desgagnés,* Les Goélettes de Charlevoix, *its design had not changed in over a century.*

The Planker

The wooden covering of the frames, both inside and out, and the covering of the beams, that is to say the decks, together made up the "planking," each ensemble of planks that ran from end to end of a vessel being known as a "strake." The strakes were fastened to the frame of the ship one on top of the other without overlapping, that is to say the vessel was "carvel" as opposed to "clinker" built. Different parts of the planking were subject to different strains and conditions and this was offset by varying the thickness of the strakes and, after it became acceptable to do so, by varying the species of wood employed.

Points of stress on the outside, particularly where the shrouds were attached and at the levels of the beams, were strengthened by extra thick strakes or "wales" which occurred sometimes as a single strake and occasionally as a solid wall of several wales. In the inner planking or "ceiling," heavier strakes were fitted immediately above and below each tier of beams and in the curved area of the bottom on which the cargo exerted a strain. On the deck, the outermost strakes were not only thicker but also especially shaped to form gutters or "waterways." The lightest planks were above the waterline, where the pressure was relatively light.

Specialist plankers were often awarded sub-contracts for planking either one or both sides of a ship, and their contracts might include other work that had to be done either after or in conjunction with the planking, such as fixing the breasthooks or helping to install the beams. The builder usually supplied the materials, scaffolding and steam, and often a man to bore the holes for the fastenings. The plankers, whose time was considered more valuable than that of most of the other shipyard workers, were not required to cut off and wedge treenails, work which was included in the caulking contracts. They were paid either by the strake or by the job. In some of the contracts it was specified that certain strakes were to be left open for a given period, either to permit inspection of the timbers or to facilitate their drying.

Before the planking was started, a flexible straight piece of wood or "ribband" was fastened to the frames along the length of the vessel, crossing the mid-ship frame at right-angles, and its position was "laid off" or marked on the edges of each frame, a line or guide thus being made along which the plank would be laid. The process was repeated at intervals of six to eight widths of strake, ensuring that the planking would be kept horizontal and even. It was customary to lay a few strakes from the top down before beginning the work from the bottom up. Every plank was tailored to fit. Its edges were bevelled to lie snugly against the adjacent plank and the outside planks were given an extra bevel to one-third of their thickness to allow room for the caulking. Once the shape of a plank was satisfactory, it was heated in a steam box and then carried still hot by a team of men to the vessel, where it was lifted into position and clamped against the frame, ready for fastening. Care was taken to stagger the butts, so that they would be several strakes apart when they occurred in the same frame. The final strake in the middle of the ship's side was carefully shaped to fit tightly and then driven into place with heavy mallets or "beetles."

In laying the ceiling, when the level of the last two strakes under each row of beams was reached, specially shaped planks known as "beam clamps" and

Figure 149: *Planking. With the top and bottom part of the planking of this vessel in a Levis shipyard already in place, the plankers are now filling in the space between.* Photo Coll. Livernois, CM 154 11531, courtesy Archives nationales du Québec.

Figure 150: *Caulking mallet and irons, with rove of oakum. In the collection of the Canadian Museum of Civilization. Photo: National Museums of Canada NA-16-77-13.*

"beam shelves" were installed which, with the knees that were bolted to them, provided strong support for the beams that were then put in place. As each tier was completed, its deck was laid (unless there was to be no deck on them), giving the men a solid floor on which to continue their work. The ceiling ended at the upper deck beam.

The planker's chief measuring tool was the "bevel," which he used to find the angle between the frame and the preceding plank and to reproduce it accurately on the plank he was preparing with his axe or adze. To clamp the planking to the frame, he appears to have used both the extra large unwieldy versions of the G-cramp and joiner's bar cramp known as the "ship cramp," and the far simpler "holdfast" made by driving wedges under each of the ends of stout wooden or iron bars held in place by ring bolts. He was equipped with a ship gimlet, which resembled a slender pod auger with a screw lead for boring holes for spikes, but used the augers provided by the shipbuilder for bolt and trunnel holes. As in the case of the framing carpenter, the maul was his driving tool.

Planking was described as "single fastened" or "double fastened" according to whether one or two treenails or bolts were driven through the plank into each frame or deck beam. It was called "double and single fastened" when alternately fastened with one and two fastenings. This type of fastening was specified in some Quebec shipbuilding contracts, and was required by Lloyd's regulations for all planks over nine inches wide. The same underwriters stipulated that all butts should be fasted with bolts and there should be one bolt through every futtock in the bilges.

The Shipbuilding Trades

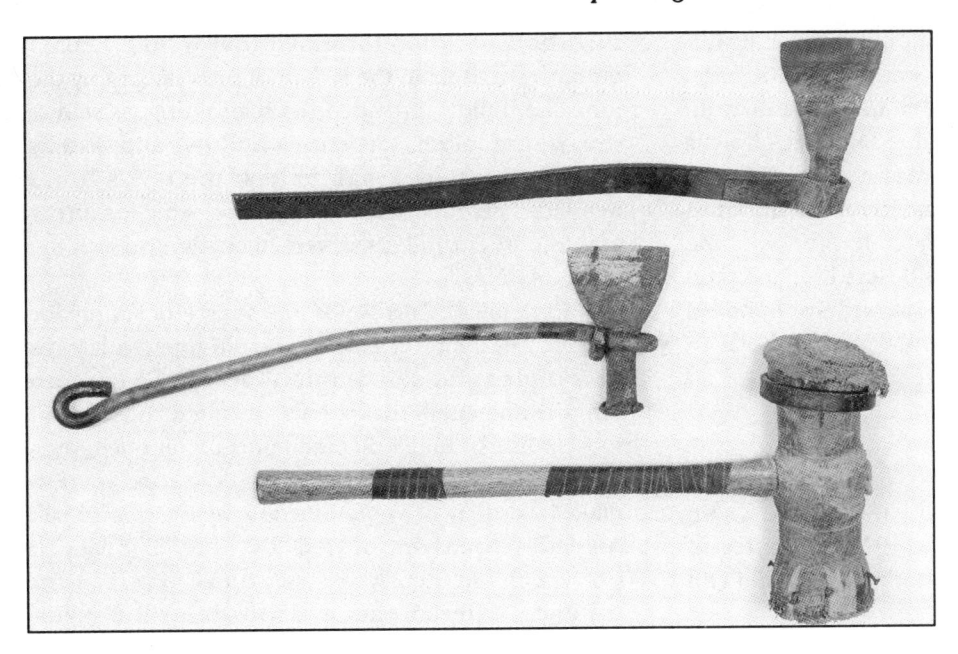

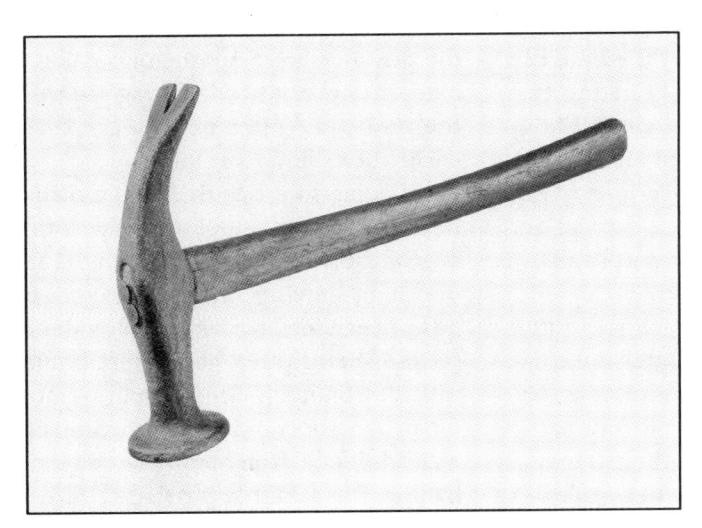

Figure 151: *Beetle and hawsing irons in the collection of the Canadian Museum of Civilization. Photo: National Museums of Canada 76–4988.*

Figure 152: *Coppering hammer from the Davie shipyard at Levis in the collection of the Canadian Museum of Civilization, Ottawa. Photo: National Museums of Canada NA–16–77–20.*

Standard bolts were made of iron but if a ship was to be copper-fastened, as was usually the case, copper bolts were used below the waterline to avoid the deterioration of iron bolts due to the electrolytic action between the two metals. As one would expect, the thickness of the bolts depended on the thickness of the planks, which in turn related to the size of the ship. Thus 5/8 and 3/4 inch bolts were used to fasten the butts of planks on ships of 150 and five hundred tons, respectively, and 5/8 and 7/8 inch bolts to secure their ceilings.

The Caulker

The all important operation which rendered a ship watertight was known as "caulking." It consisted of filling the seams between the planks with oakum and pitch, and the care with which the work was carried out could make the difference between a safe passage and one on which a vessel foundered and was lost. Besides receiving an initial caulking at the time of construction, the bottom of every ship had to be caulked once every five years to comply with Lloyd's regulations, unless it was wood-sheathed and felted, in which case it was caulked once every seven years. In addition, if a ship became leaky, she was docked or careened to have her hull examined and part or all of the caulking was replaced.

Though sometimes undertaken by shipwrights, or even sailors, at Quebec the work was often done by specialized caulkers, either shipyard employees, or men working in a team comprised of two to four partners. As in the case of the planking, the partners would contract with a shipbuilder to caulk one side or the whole of a ship for which they would be paid either by each seam the length of the vessel or by the job. The builder provided the scaffolding, as well as the oakum, pitch, turpentine and tar, and usually agreed to supply a man to heat the tar as it was needed. The undertakers were responsible for hiring as many other caulkers as were necessary to finish the work on time.[18]

Ropemaking dross was one source of supply for oakum, but the principal one was old rope, which was always plentiful and required only to be cut into lengths and then untwisted and rolled together in loose coils. In many places including Quebec, prisoners were given the job of picking old rope apart to make oakum, which could be bought at the local jail. An advertisement placed by the "House of Correction" in the *Quebec Gazette* on 20 May 1813, for instance, offered oakum at thirty shillings per hundredweight and proffered the services of the inmates for picking oakum or coarse sewing. However, the prisoners were not the only oakum pickers – old men or boys not strong enough to work generally in the yard could often be seen preparing oakum in a corner of a shipyard or loft.[19]

Caulkers were easily distinguished as they walked to work, a folding stool strapped to their back and a bag of tools hanging from a caulking mallet slung over their shoulder. The mallets were made of *lignum vitae*, beech, or live oak, often by the caulkers themselves. Their slotted heads were bound at each end with an iron hoop, which could be moved inwards as the mallet wore down, and were sometimes reinforced with additional iron hoops placed on each side of the handle. It is said that the slots on the hammer heads accounted for the cheerful chirping sound of the mallets when they struck the iron, and that if there had been no slots, the solid mallets would eventually deafen the caulker. In his bag, the caulker carried a Rave Hook to remove old pitch and oakum, a set of steel irons of varying sizes and thicknesses comprising reaming irons to open a tight seam before caulking, caulking irons to drive oakum between the planks, and making irons with flat or grooved edges to compress the oakum and make room for the tar or pitch.

To caulk the sides of a ship, the caulker first separated a few strands from a coil of oakum and with them made another coil or "rove" of loosely twisted single stranded rope. He then used his mallet and a thin caulking iron to ram this oakum into the opening between two planks formed by the slight bevel they had received, to about one-third of their thickness. If there were no opening or an insufficient one, he first used his reamer to open the seam. He worked along the opening until his coil was used up and then went back to where he had started and forced in another layer using a larger iron, continuing in this way until the seam was tightly filled and was as hard as the plank itself. The seam was then further compressed with a making iron or, in the case of very heavy planks, the work was done by two men, one holding a hawsing iron on the end of a bridle and the other hitting it with all his strength with a beetle. Following this, a mop was used to pay the seam with a heated mixture of pitch and turpentine and the excess was scraped off. Treenail heads were cut off or "dubbed" with an adze, split with an iron and wedged, before being caulked in the same way. For deck work, the caulker sat leaning forward on his stool and was grateful that the seams were not as deep as the side seams, as this position was very hard on his back. When he had finished, a ladle or a tall lipped metal jar was used to pour tar over the oakum, and again the excess was removed.

Very often the caulking was followed by "watering", or filling the space between the planking and the ceiling with water to make sure that there were no leaks. The caulkers were requested to attend, and if there were leaks, were obliged to put the matter right. Although the caulking procedure may seem simple, experience and judgement were needed; using too much oakum could force the planks apart and be as disastrous as using too little.

In an agreement made in 1841, Louis Lachance undertook to caulk four ships to the satisfaction of James Jeffery and Company, or their foreman, wedging the treenails in the manner directed, for the sum of £525. After the caulking and paying was done, the team of caulkers was to stand by for the watering and make good anywhere found necessary, and then black the bottom up to the bends. They would use their own small tools, but Jeffery would lend the reaming and horsing irons and be responsible for providing the shores and moving them as necessary.[20]

Sheathing the ship's bottom was other work done by caulkers. Although most coppering was done in Britain, a certain amount was done at Quebec both on new construction and on repairs. The new ships, however, were not sheathed on the building ways, as copper might suffer in the launching, but were drydocked for the work to be done in a floating dock or on the marine railway. Sheets of copper or yellow metal, through which nail holes had been pierced, were applied to the hull up to the waterline over a mixture of tar and horsehair or other underlay and

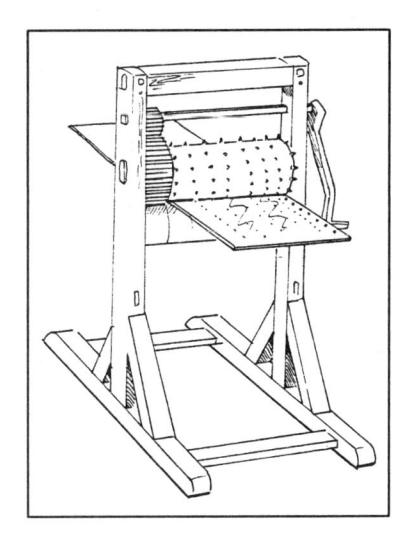

Figure 153: *Chequering mill for perforating copper sheets, in the collection of the National Maritime Museum, Antwerp. A similar mill was used at the Davie shipyard in Levis and no doubt at other Quebec yards. Drawing by Caroline Soucy.*

Figure 154: *Prisoners Picking Oakum in a Military Prison at Quebec. From a sketch by W.O.C.,* Canadian Illustrated News, *9 December 1871. Courtesy National Archives, Ottawa. C 56627.*

The Shipbuilding Trades

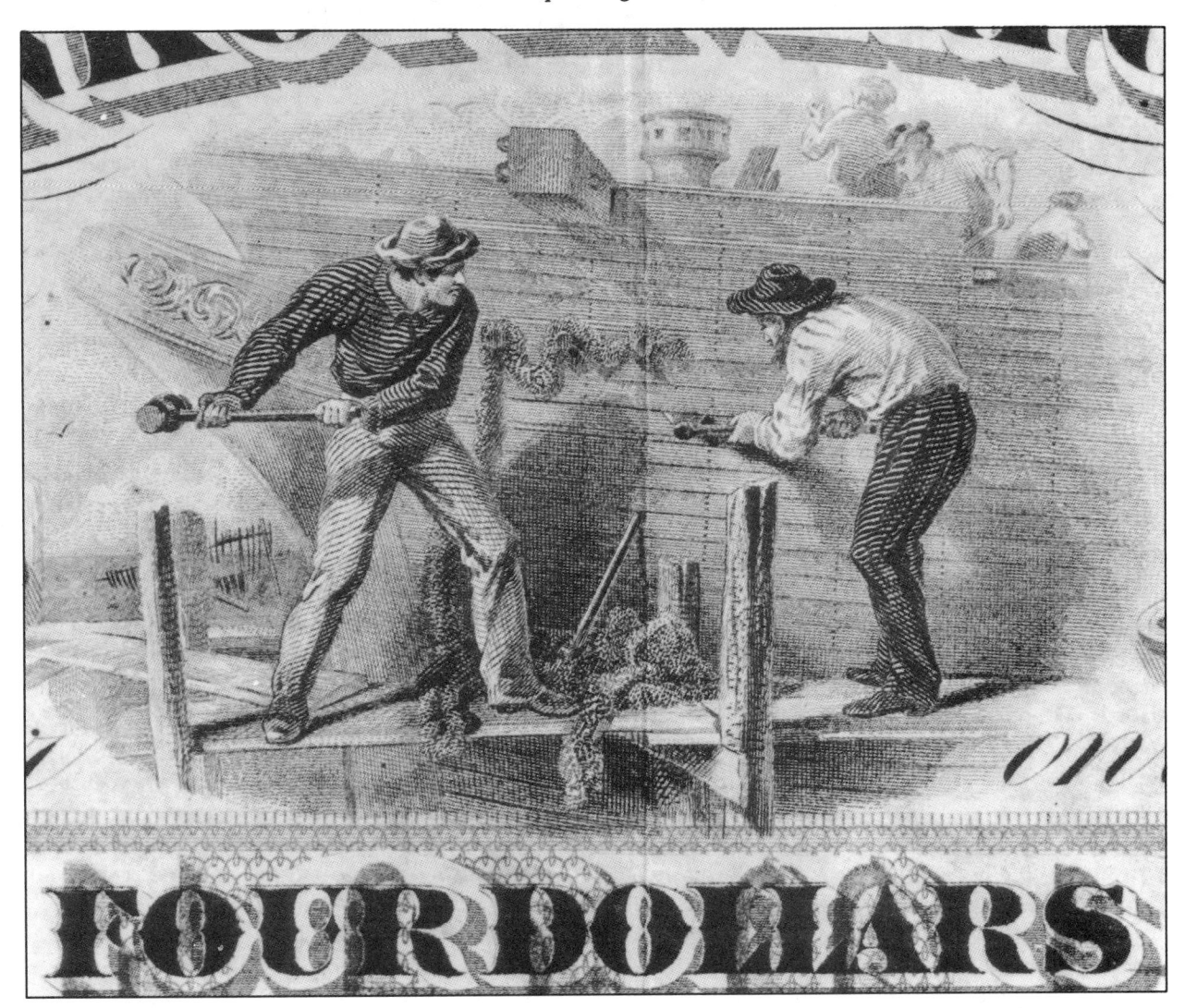

Figure 155: *A four dollar bank note of the Bank of Liverpool, Nova Scotia, 1871 showing caulkers using a horsing iron. Courtesy Maritime Museum of the Atlantic, Halifax, N.S. N 1438.*

beaten with flat-headed hammers to take its shape. This not only protected the hull from the ravages of the Teredo worm but also reduced the fouling of the ship's bottom.

The Ship Joiner

Despite the ever present risk of a vessel meeting a premature end, sailing ships were nevertheless carefully planed and bravely trimmed with mouldings and beadings to present a gracious appearance. This was the work of the joiners, who took over after the framing and planking was done, put a finish on the shipwrights' work and, with the exception of the carving, completed the woodwork of the hull.

The amount of trim varied from ship to ship according to the specifications or, if it was built on speculation, as the shipbuilder chose. The list of work to be done in a contract for the joinery of a ship built at Saint Patrick's Hole in 1812 is typical. All the exposed timbers, such as the sides and underneath of the beams, the stanchions and the cathead, were to be planed, as were the deck planking on both its upper and lower sides, the outside planking down to and including the wales, and the ceiling between decks. A bead was to be run along many of the timbers, and the channels and lower edges of the sheer strakes finished with a moulding the entire length of the ship. The stern and counter were also to be "finished," but no indication is given of the type of finish and it is likely that a design was provided. The rest of the work consisted of erecting bulkheads to separate the officers' quarters from the steerage, making staterooms for the captain and the mate, and preparing the captain's panelled day cabin complete with windows and "deadlights" or shutters. Stairs and companions were to be built and installed, and a "camboose" or galley erected on deck for the cook, but no hen coops were to be built, as were often required. That the joiner was entrusted with finishing this cabin was neither customary nor without precedent, for the cabin of John Goudie's 1806 ship *Roberts* was finished at Quebec in cherry wood, and that of his 1808 ship *Canada* "was done with Pine" and had a winding staircase.[21]

It was, nevertheless, more usual for the shipbuilding contract to stipulate that all joinery was to be done, with the exception of the cabin which, like the interior of the deck house or houses, was finished in the rough. However, when the ship *Etna* was launched by Pierre Valin in 1857, she was hailed by the *Morning Chronicle* of 14 July, as "the first vessel built at Quebec to have all the joiners' work done at Quebec." Messrs. J. O. Vallières, it noted, had fitted up work done in their shop in the cabin and stateroom in a very superior manner. The stateroom doors were panelled in a combination of mahogany, rosewood, black walnut and bird's-eye maple – very pleasing to the eye. The paper further suggested that shipbuilders and shipowners would loose nothing and might gain much by causing their cabins to be finished in Quebec. Perhaps the builders heeded this advice, for the following year the ship *Cameronian* was launched by Walter Ray with "her cabins being very elegantly got up with beautifully grained woods, stained glass windows, etc.," and we are told by F.W. Wallace that the cabins of Henry Dinning's ship *Cosmo* of 1877 were "beautifully finished in Ash and Black Walnut."[22] The time had come for the Quebec cabinetmaker to share the responsibility for the cabin with the joiner. The well-equipped furniture-making shops of Quebec

Figure 156: *The Captain's Cabin. This captain of the barque* Albania *built 1867 in Puget Sound displays his family portraits for the photographer in his traditionally panelled cabin. Photo: Wilhelm Hester. Courtesy San Irancisco Martitme Nat'l Historic Park Hister Collection. Neg. U60 12,489 no. 1.*

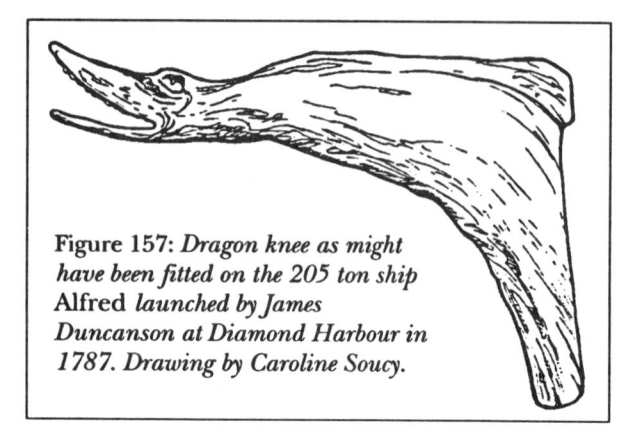

Figure 157: *Dragon knee as might have been fitted on the 205 ton ship* Alfred *launched by James Duncanson at Diamond Harbour in 1787. Drawing by Caroline Soucy.*

Figure 158 : *Figurehead of the ship* Royal Edward, *built at Saint Jean, Lake Champlain in 1793, commissioned by the government from François Baillairgé. Watercolour, F. Baillairgé, Musée de Québec. Photo: A–75–255.*

supplemented the joiners' shops at the shipyards, which for the most part contained only work benches, vices and perhaps a turning lathe, though some of the larger better-established yards had a certain number of more sophisticated machine tools.

The joiner provided his own panoply of hand tools – saws, axes, chisels and gouges, jack and smoothing planes, various moulding planes, augers and gimlets, hammers, files, bevels and try-squares and other measuring and marking tools. His tools were remarkably similar to those of the house carpenter or joiner, in fact he was very often one and the same man. Many well known joiners, such as Thomas Hunt, Jacques Laurencelle and J.O. Vallières, undertook work in either capacity.

The Ship Carver

The eyes on the bows of Asiatic, Greek and Phoenician boats, the dragons and serpents heads on the Norsemen's long ships, the men and beasts on Mediterranean craft and the gamut of figureheads of more recent years stemmed from man's common urge to attribute a living quality to his vessels, and held special importance for sailors as long as ships were driven by the wind and were very much at the mercy of the elements. Though his work often covered considerably more, it is with the figureheads that the ship carver is primarily associated.

During the sixteenth century larger ships wore a lion rampant as a figurehead, while further ornamentation was carried out by painters who picked out strips of brightly coloured designs over the entire superstructure, giving the ships a toy-like quality. As the seventeenth century progressed, sculptors became more and more involved in the decoration until at its end the whole of the stern, quarters and bows of larger naval vessels were buried under an extravaganza of carving. As a result, in the eighteenth century, both the British Admiralty and the French Minister of the Marine issued orders restricting the excessive decoration. Merchantmen were built at that time to resemble warships, and underwent the same restraint, so that there was a general decrease in the adornment of ships. However, naval shipwrights were loath to submit to the directives in their entirety and some head carvings were still elaborate compared with the sober heads of the nineteenth century or with those of merchantmen of the day.[23]

It was at this time that shipbuilding in Quebec, which had been dormant for the most part since the last years of the French Regime, was revitalized, and we are fortunate that some of the journals of the sculptor François Baillairgé (1759-1830), as well as some of his sketches for figureheads, have survived. The most interesting is his design for a group carving for the warship *Royal Edward*, built at Saint Jean, Lake Champlain, in 1793, in which Prince Edward at the prow is flanked on the trailboards by two figures representing Lower and Upper Canada, ornamented with other paraphernalia. Baillairgé tells us that he spent a total of 105 days on the design and execution of this head, perhaps the last heroic head by a Quebec carver and certainly the only one of the British Regime whose details are known to us. Among his other figureheads he lists likenesses of people and animals, as well as plain and ornamented scrolls, replaced in some instances by a decorative carved knee under the bowsprit. They include several fiddle and animal heads for Captain Beatson, two Indian figureheads for government vessels, two others for ships belonging to the merchant Louis Dunière, a replacement arm for the figurehead of the ship *Levant*, which visited Quebec in 1793, and a statue of Prince Edward, as well as catheads and other carvings for John Black's ship of that name. For the *London* of 1796, however, he carved from elm a female figure representing the City of London. She wore the dress of a Levite, gathered with a ribbon under her breast and a mural crown over her loose flowing hair, and held a Union Jack. For this seven-foot figurehead suitably painted he charged ten guineas.[24]

Unfortunately, with his entry of 11 February 1800, "Reçue ordre de Mr. Cragy, d'exécuter une figure de vaisseau representant son altesse royal le Duc de Kent en Armure avec une Renomée," our only autobiographical account of Quebec ship carving comes to an end. It is interesting to note that by this time a pattern had already been established for the nineteenth century. Decorative carving would be optional and limited to a simple figure or scroll head, trail boards with linear, floral or leaf designs, badges or sham galleries on the quarters to soften the line where the stern met the side of the vessel, a moulded or otherwise decorated panel on the counter of the stern and animal faces in low relief on the ends of the catheads. In addition, the name of the ship would be carved into the transom above the counter or into the planking at the stern and sometimes into the trail boards as well. Execution of the steering wheel and capstan would be entrusted either to the sculptor or the joiner.

Almost two-thirds of the figureheads of Quebec sailing vessels represented men or women and of these, eighty percent were full-length figures and the rest busts, among them several costumed Indians and Highlanders. Scrolls, often decorated with stylized leaf or floral designs, accounted for another third of the heads. The remaining few were mostly animals on vessels of the 1850s and 1860s, perhaps because they were then in style and there were sculptors in the town who were able to carve them successfully. Eagles and lions outnumbered the rest, which included pawed and hoofed animals, serpents, birds and fish. The ship carver James McKenzie, who supplied at least some of Thomas H. Oliver's heads and whom Abraham Joseph identifies in his unpublished diary as the sculptor of the unicorn that he had made for his sleigh during the winter of 1839-1840, carved some of them.[25] William Black (1816-1886) was another of the ship carvers. Newspaper items identify him as the author of a gilt figurehead of a wild horse made for Jean Lemelin's ship *Bucephalus*, and described his figure on the *Woodstock* of 1850 as "as classical a figurehead as ever graced a prow, which does our townsman Mr. Wm Black great credit." He was also responsible for the Indian figurehead on Edmund Sewell's *Forest Monarch* of 1851, and for a Turkish figure on Nesbitt's *Abdalla* of 1852, for which he was paid £25. Another sculptor well known in the Saint Sauveur shipyards was Jean-Baptiste Côté (1834-1907), whose father was a brother-in-law of Narcisse Rosa and foreman of his yard, and whose customers included besides Rosa, Pierre Valin and James G. Ross.[26]

The figurehead of F.X. Marquis' ship *Shannon* of 1878 is likely to have been carved by another sculptor, Louis Jobin (1845-1928), who was responsible for many of the heads of the ships built at this time on the south shore, including the figureheads of the 1298-ton barque *Edmonton*, which can be seen at the

Figure 159: *Figurehead of the 178 ton brigantine* Salmon, *built by Laprise and Letarte for Narcisse Rosa on the Saint Charles river in 1859. Drawing by P. Marcil from a photograph kindly lent by J. Burlinson.*

Figure 160: Highlander. *Perhaps from the 694 ton* Highlander *built by N. Rosa in 1864. Photo courtesy H. Dawson.*

Mariners' Museum in Newport News, and that of the *Edinburgh*, displayed in the Addison Gallery at Andover, Maine. According to the specifications, the *Shannon* was to have a two-thirds female figurehead, with scrollwork in black and gold on the stem and trailboards. A gold ornament was to adorn each cathead, and her name was to be on each bow. The stern was to be decorated with a centre shield or medallion with an arch of scrollwork in black and gold that continued around to each quarter. Finally, her name and port of registry was to be cut in on a carved scroll in the centre, and the letters gilded.[27]

Wm Black's account for his work on J. J. Nesbitt's ship Abdalla of 1852 reads as follows:

	Quebec October 1852
To a Turkish Figure	£9 10 0
To carving stern moulding Trail Boards, Poop boards, Cat heads etc.	8 10 0
To Mahogany Wheel	8 10 0
Less 3 months interest at 6% for summer	7 9
	£25 12 3

In carving these figureheads, the grain of the wood was followed as much as possible for maximum strength, and an effort was made to avoid forming pockets that would hold water; flowing clothes generally swept back. Arms, wings or other vulnerable parts

276 • THE CHARLEY-MAN

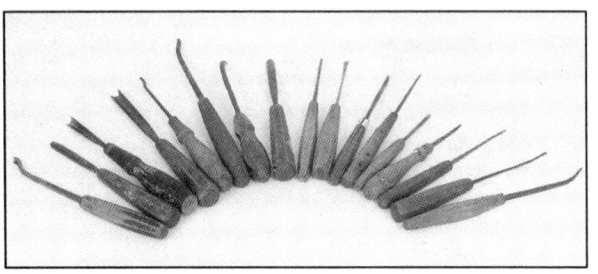

Figure 161: (top left) *Figurehead of the 1298 ton barque* Edmonton, *built by Wm. Charland in 1882, in the Mariners' Museum, Newport News. Courtesy Mariners' Museum, photo OF 29.*

Figure 162: (top right) *First workshop of the sculptor Louis Jobin at Sainte-Anne-de-Beaupré. Photo: National Museums of Canada, supplied by Musée de Québec.*

Figure 163 : (left) *Chisels belonging to Louis Jobin in the collection of the Château de Ramezay at Montreal. Photo by Patrick Altman, courtesy the Musée de Québec.*

were bolted on so that they could be unshipped at sea and replaced just before sailing into port. Yes, sailors usually took a great deal of pride in their ships. We learn from François Baillairgé's journal that models sometimes posed for his figureheads, that in some cases he submitted sketches and even clay, wood or wax models for approval, and that the first rough hewing might be done with an axe by an apprentice. In a description of American shipyards, Allan Villiers writes that "shipbuilders would draw on the [loft] floor the lines of the bow where the figure would go" and that "the carver then chalked the design on his block of pine, and set to work with hammer, chisel and gouge."[28] The figurehead was then painted in bright colours and gilt, except in the case of a clipper ship, whose full-length figure was traditionally all white.

A number of the heads and perhaps other carvings on Quebec ships were sent out from Britain or purchased in the United States. For instance, in a contract of 1809 it was noted that "if any carved work should be sent out for the said ship, the said John Goudie to fix at his expence,"[29] and on 3 February 1826 John White and Company advertised two figureheads carved in London suitable for vessels of 250 to three hundred tons. But in some cases, vessels sailed without heads or with temporary ones and had their permanent heads fitted elsewhere. The *Ringfield* and *Riverdale*, built by Pierre Valin for G.H. Parke, were both registered with "temporary heads" in 1847 before sailing for Belfast. But such ships were a minority: only one of every ten ships left Quebec with neither a figurehead nor a scroll.

The Shipsmith

There was little fundamental difference in the building materials that went into the construction of the *Santa Maria* in 1492 and those of any merchantman sailing up the Saint Lawrence three hundred years later. But the next century saw a gradual change from the wholly wooden to the all-metal ship. At each step, the serious shortage of ship timber in Britain, where most of the new techniques were developed, ensured that the next one was not far away. By the end of the century the metal worker had supplanted the ship carpenter insofar as the building of large vessels was concerned.

In the process, the Quebec shipsmith adapted to the changes. At the beginning of the century, he made quantities of bolts for fastening the frame and the side planking, square section chisel point spikes for the deck planking, joiners' nails in all sizes, and a variety of small fittings, such as shackles, hooks and eyes. He made too the gudgeons and pintles, which hinged the rudder to the sternpost, the chainplates and other fixtures used to attach the standing rigging to the hull, and he forged the mast collars, caps and tops. By 1810, many more and a greater variety of bolts were required as they were used increasingly to supplement oak or locust treenails. In 1811, the use of iron knees, which had first been experimented with in the Royal Dockyard at Southampton in the 1790s, was begun tentatively in Quebec, the building contracts for at least two of that year's ships requiring that there be "one iron knee on each upper deck beam and one iron standard knee on every other lower deck beam in

Figure 164: *Mast band in the collection of the Canadian Museum of Civilization, Ottawa. Photo courtesy National Museums of Canada NA 122–76–35.*

Figure 165: *Mid-section plan of the 1112 ton ship* Oliver Cromwell, *built by Charland and Marquis in 1866, showing the iron hanging knees in the upper deck and long iron knee-riders in the lower deck. Attached to contract and specifications, 7 October 1865, gr W.D. Campbell.*

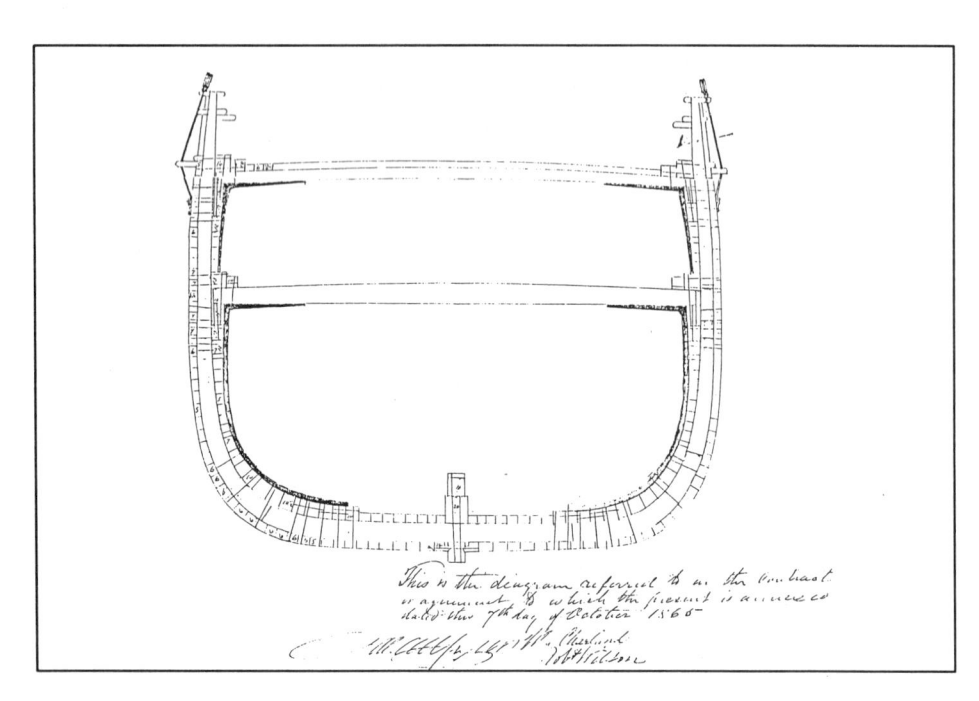

addition to the wooden knees."[30] Later, iron knees would completely replace the wooden hanging knees supporting deck beams and v-shaped iron breasthooks would serve to strengthen the bow, wrought iron spindles would be fitted to capstans, and iron necks and whelps to windlasses.[31]

Progressively through the nineteenth century new smelting techniques made better iron that was more available and less expensive, and it was used increasingly to strengthen the oversized hulls of larger wooden ships. Knees were lengthened to such an extent that they completely lined the futtocks through which they were bolted, and though the fitting of these new rider knees was done at first in Britain, by 1858 local shipsmiths were fitting them at Quebec. Although the knees themselves had to be imported, no ship left Quebec thereafter without its knee riders, nor the diagonal iron strapping that was also required. As the blacksmiths' work in the shipyard increased, so did that of the founder, the metal worker and machinist, the use of wood continuing to give ground on many fronts.

Shipsmiths, though fewer, were as much a part of every shipyard as the ship carpenters, for so much of the ironwork was made to measure that it was essential that the smithy be at the yard. Each was equipped with at least one forge with a hearth, anvil and vice, and a set of blacksmiths' tools. Anchors and chains, however, were imported. Anchors of sailing ships were much larger and heavier than those of ships using other forms of power because their sails caused a far greater surface to be exposed to the wind. Those for large sailing ships weighed as much as one and a half to two tons, and it is extremely unlikely that any of that size were forged at Joseph Archer's "forge for the manufacture of anchors," the only one in Quebec."

The Shipbuilding Trades

Figure 166: *Ship under construction at the Gilmour shipyard at Wolfe's Cove. Photo courtesy, Archives nationales du Québec, GH 372–29.*

Figure 167: *Nearing completion at the McKay and Warner shipyard on the Saint Charles river. Photo Courtesy National Archives, Ottawa. C–8042.*

A certain amount of the iron work was contracted out to local smithies, such as those described by Jean-Claude Dupont's in his comprehensive study of Quebec blacksmiths, *L'Artisan forgeron*. The shipsmiths' technology was not different from that of the regular blacksmiths he describes.

The Painter, Gilder and Glazier

Everything to do with building a large sailing vessel was of heroic proportion and the paintwork was no exception. Every inch of every surface of the hull, spars, decks and tween-decks had to be covered with two or three coats of paint, varnish or blacking of some kind. The worst part of the job, in the eyes of a young man in Maine, was painting the bottom:

Looking and holding one's arm up for hours, the green liquid from the brush running down your arm, into your neck, head and clothes. On the bottom of the brush we had to fasten a circle of leather three to four inches in diameter to catch the drippings, but sometimes when that would get full it would spill all over us ... Mornings when we had to put on these paint clothes again for the day's work, after drying off all night it would be almost impossible to get them on ... The other different painting around the vessels I liked quite well.[32]

The spars were either oiled, varnished or painted white or another light colour such as yellow. In 1824, for instance, Willima Hadden, who was given the contract for the *Saint David*, built by John Bell, was required to paint her masts, yards, booms, gaffs, tops, crosstrees, caps, blocks, bowsprit, including the whole from the truck to the deck a light Yellow. The inside including the whole in sight square from the rail Green with a few mouldings of different colour. The bottom from light water mark to the bends Copper colour with a White Ribbin of three inches at the top. The outside of the Bullwark Black. The top sides Yellow with a Black Ribbin of 4 inches and half Ports 2 Boats and Stern.[33]

Green was a favourite colour in the early days. The bottom of the paddle steamer *Royal William*, for instance, was given two coats of green paint and contrasting black wales, but as was usual at the time, this was described as the caulkers' and not the painters' work.[34]

While overall the hulls were generally black, the poops white and the bulwarks brown, there was a certain amount of variation. The paint merchants W. & J. McKay and Carey directed an advertisement to shipowners and builders in 1854 in which they announced that they were then "preparing in Small and Hermetically Sealed Canisters Drabs, Greens, Yellows and Pinks, Chromes, and all kinds of tinted colours requisite in ship painting." Rooms and passages of the vessel ordered by Von Rittern from Cotnam in 1876 were to be painted "as desired," while the cabin, as was frequently the case, was to be oak grained and varnished.[35] The paint scheme of a vessel built by Valin for the French owner Fabre in 1867, however, was strictly black and white: three coats of white for the cabin, bulkheads, ceiling and the outside of deckhouses, black paint on the nine topmost strakes of the hull, and tar on the rest "as customary in the Port of Quebec."[36]

The fancy work on the vessels varied considerably and gilding was popular. Typical specifications of a smart vessel of 1840 read:

> ... to guild scrolls to heads and that part of the trail Boards that is connected with head; to letter and guild the names on head Boards, and the Astrigals around the name; the name to be done in fancy work, and to be approved of by the said James Jeffery & Company; to do eight or more pilasters to the stern, and the Bead over the pilasters and sashes to correspond with the Beads on the pilasters; the name on the stern to be lettered and guilded, the same as the head names; and the Cats faces or Stars to Catheads to be painted and guilded.[37]

Unfortunately the original appearance of the decoration is left to our imagination, any woodwork that may have survived having been painted over many times in the intervening years according to the each owner's fancy, and perhaps no longer reflecting the character given to it by the original painter.

In closing, it should be stated that most painters were painters and glaziers. For example, it was as an apprentice house, sign and ship painter and glazier that Alexander McDonald was taken on in 1826.[38] Some painters used the title of gilder, and some were also plumbers, carrying out any work in which lead was required, such as leading window panes or fixing lead scuppers.

The Blockmaker

We come now to the work of the blockmaker, one of the few tradesmen at the shipyard who was called

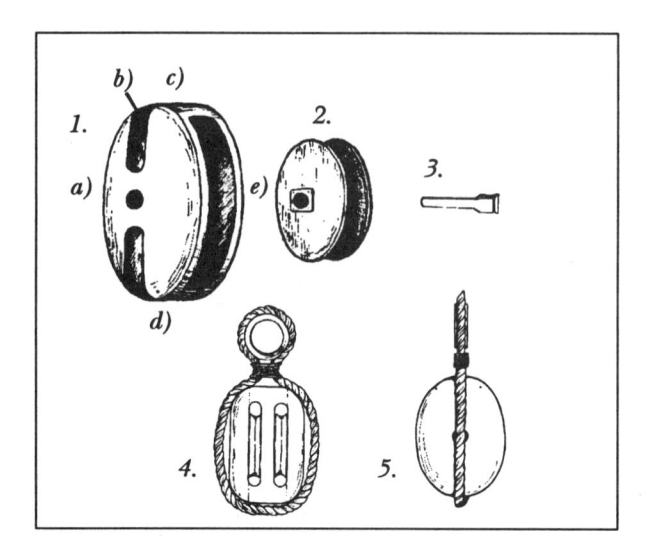

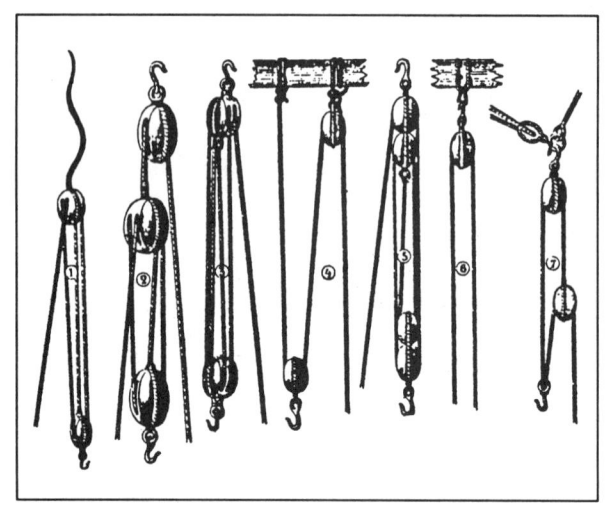

Figure 168: *Parts of the block. 1. Shell a) Cheek b) Score c) Crown d) Tail e) Swallow 2. Sheave 3. Pin 4. Strapped block 5. Double block fitted with thimble*

Figure 169: *Tackles*

upon to make a product which contained moving parts and was in fact a simple machine. During the sailing ship era, blocks, which were used extensively to supplement muscle power, were invaluable in shipbuilding in helping to lift the heavy frames onto the keel, in stepping masts, in "careening" or beaching ships on their side for repairs, and in many other ways. On board ship, they lightened the work when a sailor slackened or tightened a rope to spread a sail, brace a yard, swing a boom or hoist a weight. In fact, the whole of the running rigging passed through or "was rove" through a block, and when the standing rigging was installed, deadeyes served to achieve the correct tension on the masts.

The block itself is a very simple device, consisting of a wooden shell which houses from one to four pulley wheels or "sheaves," with either a shackle, an eye, or a fixed or swivel hook attached to the top or "crown" according to the manner in which the block is to be applied. Blocks in combination with ropes are known as "tackles" and are used not only to raise, lower or move weights but also to increase the power of an applied force. Two single blocks, for instance, will double the lifting power of a force and two treble blocks will produce a six or seven-fold increase of power.[40]

Blockmaking could be carried out in a relatively small shop equipped with a lathe, a blockmaker's low bench, or "clave," and a number of hand tools. The sheaves were made of *lignum vitae* or other hardwood, the shells of a tough wood, such as elm or ash.[39] Sawing, boring and shaping the hard woods with which the blocks were made, especially the particularly heavy *lignum vitae*, involved work that was both strenuous and precise in order to produce a smoothly operating block. One that jammed could be a serious liability if it interfered with the rapid execution of a command.

The rough shell of the block, in the form of a solid piece of wood with its corners removed, was wedged in the clave, and holes were drilled through at each end with an auger. The intervening wood was then removed with a chisel and rasp, following which the block was turned on its face to have the centre pin hole bored and the channel or "score" gouged for the rope or iron band that would eventually strap the block. Then, using the clave board to support the shell, the outer surfaces were trimmed and it was ready to receive the sheave.

A slice sawn from a log of *lignum vitae* and turned on the lathe to form a disc with a groove around its perimeter became the sheave when a hole was bored through its centre with a brace. The pintle on which the sheave would revolve was also turned on the lathe, and left with a square head at one end. The pin was then inserted through the centre of one of the cheeks of the shell, and the shape of its head was marked on it; the necessary wood was then removed with a chisel, so as to allow the head to fit into the cheek. The sheave could now be put in place and both ends of the pin were cut and smoothed flush. The more expensive blocks were metal bushed with steel pins.

The deadeye, which has no moving parts, is a variation of the block, consisting simply of a thick disc pierced by three holes, with a channel or "score" around the perimeter to accommodate a rope. Deadeyes are laced together in pairs to form fasteners, which can be slackened or tightened as required, and connect the shrouds to the chainplates attached to the hull.

Like the sheave, the deadeye was sawn from a log of *lignum vitae* chosen to match its size and thus waste as little of the valuable wood as possible. The excess was chopped off with an axe and the lathe used to turn it to the required diameter. A pattern was applied to mark the position of the three pilot holes, which were bored with a pod auger, and the deadeye was returned to the lathe where it was rounded and a groove to fit the size of rigging it would receive was turned round the circumference. The deadeye was then firmly wedged in the clave and the three holes were drilled through with a brace. It remained to chamfer or "score" the edges of these holes, so that they would not chafe the ropes and this operation, for which a long tool similar to a nose auger was used, requiring considerable skill in order to obtain the correct degree of chamfer. While all three holes of a lower deadeye were chamfered on both sides, the left hand hole on the inboard side of an upper deadeye, unlike the other two, was not scored, so that it could hold the knotted end of the rope.[41] Hearts, which were a type of deadeye used for the bowsprit rigging and for the fore and aft stays, were made in the same way as ordinary deadeyes, except that the whole centre was removed in the form of a D, and across the straight side of the D three parallel channels were gouged to hold sections of rigging.

Early in the nineteenth century, mechanized blockmaking developed by Marc Brunel was introduced in Britain's Royal Dockyards, which enabled ten men to make as many blocks as were previously made by 110,[42] and by the end of the first quarter of the century British blockmakers were reduced to making only the special sizes and types of block that the mills could not handle. The hand trade lived longer at Quebec. When Patrick Baldwin, the Canadian-born blockmaker died in 1833, there was no hint of

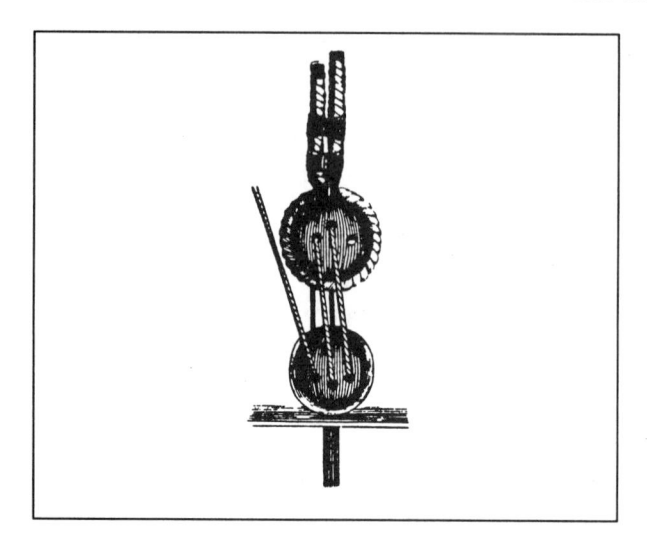

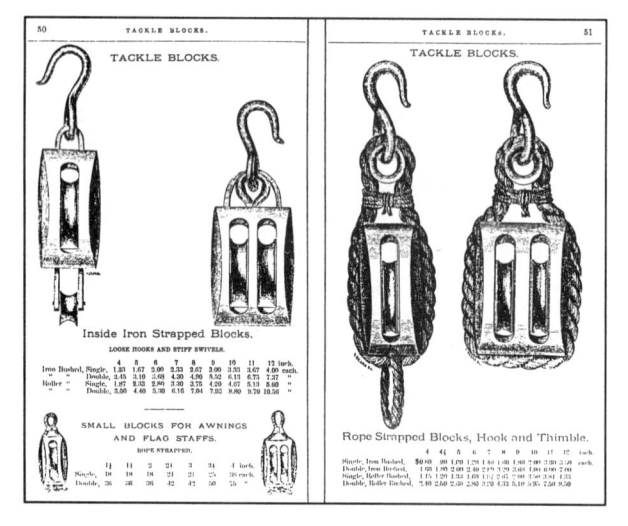

Figure 170: *Deadeyes*

Figure 171: *Imported machine-made single and double blocks.*

The Shipbuilding Trades

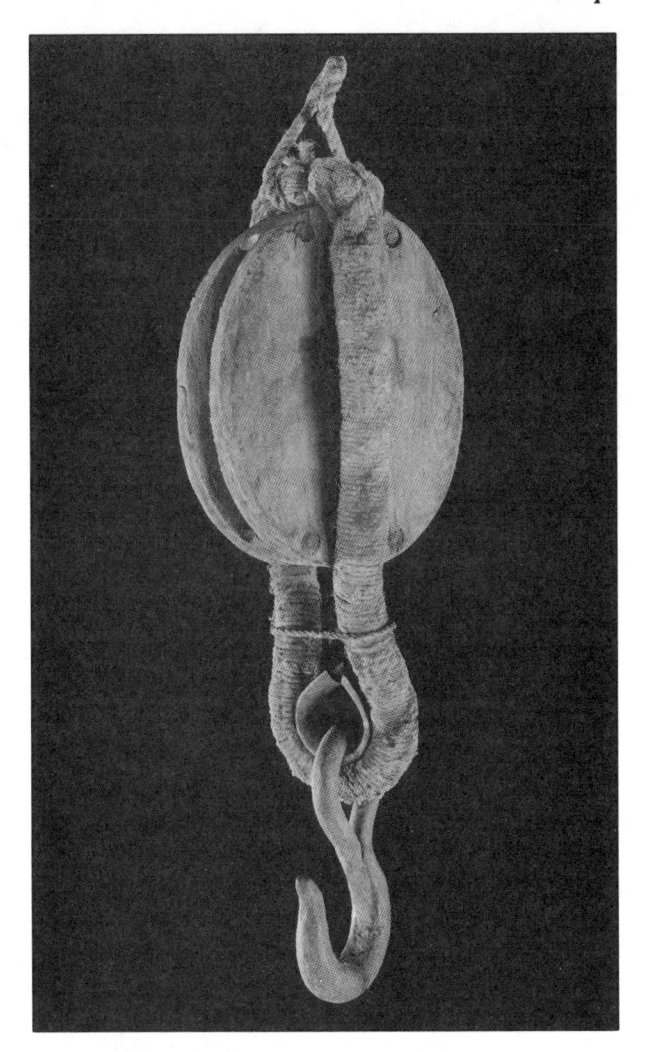

Figure 172: *Single block double stropped and fitted with a thimble and hook. Collection of the Canadian Museum of Civilization, Ottawa. Photo courtesy National Museums of Canada NA–16–77–8.*

```
STOCK IN TRADE IN THE INVENTORY OF PATRICK BALDWIN,
BLOCKMAKER, AT THE TIME OF HIS DEATH IN 1833

  Grindstone                          7s   6d
  Joiner's bench                  10   0
  Turning lathe              10    0   0
  Pump boring tools          10    0   0
  Chisels and gouges          2   10   0
  Vice - 1 dollar                  5   0
2 Cross cut saws              1    0   0
  Augers                     1   10   0
  Grindstone                       7   6
  Old rope                        10   0
  Borers and chisels          4    0   0
4 tons Lignum Vitae          24    0   0
  Steering wheel              2   10   0
  Crowbar                         12   6
  Planes                      1    0   0
  Drawing knives              1    0   0
2 Purchase blocks             5    0   0
  Sundries, old tools        40    0   0
  Blocks finished and
      unfinished             25    0   0
                          £ 130    2   6
```

Figure 173: *Blockmaker's inventory*

mechanization in his shop.[43] It was 1844 when the newcomer Andrew Butchart, who ran a blockmaking establishment on Saint Peter Street, contracted with Messrs. Freeman and Montgomery to install a 2 horsepower high pressure engine with sufficient force to drive a circular saw that would cut through a piece of *lignum vitae* measuring ten inches in diameter, and turn and drive a turning lathe and boring machine at other times as required, with a boiler proportionate in size and strength for the engine. They were also to manufacture a turning lathe and circular saw, for which a table with a double-acting slide was to be provided, as well as all the necessary pulleys and belts. The whole was to be set up in Butchart's shop within one month at a cost of £80, which included three months' servicing of the steam engine.[44]

In that very active shipbuilding period, one

might expect that the equipment would have been very much appreciated, but evidently something was unsatisfactory, for by a second contract written two months later Freeman and Montgomery agreed to remove the steam engine and all the other apparatus with the exception of the turning lathe.[45] No explanations were given. However, mechanization at Quebec was still often experimental and one may surmise that either the blockmakers were afraid the machinery would rob them of their work or else that they preferred to work at their craft in the way they knew until the machinery was more reliable, in spite of the harder work involved. In the latter case, this may have been in the year 1861 when, according to the census, Robert Greig was "in the process of erecting steam power in his two-storey blockmaking establishment on Champlain Street."

Some of the many thousands of blocks that were needed in Quebec each year both for new ship construction and for repairs, and especially the more sophisticated patent blocks with roller bearings, were imported from Britain or the United States, but many thousands of standard blocks and deadeyes were made by Quebec blockmakers at the shipyards or in their lower town shops. They shared the market with the importers of blocks and did not receive the protection of a heavy import duty, as did their counterparts in the United States. Though in most cases the blockmaker doubled as pumpmaker or mastmaker or both, all these trades relied on a somewhat erratic shipbuilding industry, which was not conducive to the establishment of a large home industry. Shops remained small, with generally two to five employees. The apprenticeship system lasted at least until the 1830s, there being often two or even three apprentices in a shop serving a three

Figure 174: *A lathe formed part of the blockmaker's equipment. A foot pedal actioned many of them, as in this nineteenth century shipyard workshop in Stavanger, Norway. Photo A. Marcil.*

Figure 175: *Clave or bench used for making deadeyes*

to seven-year turn and learning both blockmaking and mastmaking, and sometimes pumpmaking as well, as in the case of Patrick Baldwin.

The Mastmaker

A mastmaker was also, and more precisely, known as a "sparmaker," because in addition to making masts he made the bowsprit and its jib boom, all the yards, booms and gaffs that supported or extended the sails, and any cargo booms that were carried, all of which are known collectively as the "spars" of a ship. Yet, though he was sometimes given the title of "mast and sparmaker," in Quebec, as in most other places, he generally went by the name of "mastmaker," or "mast and blockmaker" when he carried out both of these trades.

Pine spars ordered by Quebec merchants were sent by boat or raft from Lower or Upper Canada, from New York and Vermont,[46] where they were dressed on the beaches for use in local shipyards or for shipment to Britain, and at that time any damage incurred on the trip down the Saint Lawrence was removed. The mast dressers worked under the supervision of a master mastmaker or qualified shipwright responsible for inspecting and sorting the spars ready for loading.[47] The spars varied in length from twenty to over one hundred feet and, because of their relatively small girth, required careful handling. As they increased in length beyond eighty feet, the price rose sharply, so that when a seventy-five foot mast cost £6 5s, one ninety-nine foot long sold for £30.[48]

A mast made from a single tree was known as a "pole mast"; when, as in the case of some of the larger masts, it was formed by several pieces of timber treenailed or bolted together and bound with iron hoops, it was called a "made" or a "built" mast. According to F.W. Wallace "most BNA vessels of the larger tonnage had 'built' lower masts," but except in relation to the days of New France, I have not found any mention of them in my research for this study on Quebec ships.

The number and the size of the spars that were required to outfit a sailing ship is impressive, each mast alone consisting of as many as four lengths known as the lower mast, the topmast, the top-gallant mast and the royal mast, erected one above the other and slightly overlapping, and equipped with its own yards and booms. If it is considered that a 275-ton barque had forty-two spars (see Table 9) and that a ship of the same tonnage had closer to sixty, the amount of work required to make her spars can well be imagined. In addition, the wooden fixtures of the masts were also the mastmaker's responsibility; these included the cheeks fixed to each side of the lower mast to support the topmasts and all the other parts required to make the masts functional, such as crosstrees, trestletrees, tops, fids and mast caps, which were delivered separately for installation by the riggers. Before delivery a tenon was cut at the foot of the lower masts to fit into mortises in the mast steps, and the upper masts were slotted or otherwise prepared for installation. A joiner could easily learn to do these various jobs. Obtaining the maximum size mast from a given tree and making it true was the specialized skill of the mastmaker.

The first step in mastmaking was to inspect the wood and make sure that there were no imperfections that would weaken the mast. Then, if the mastmaker was

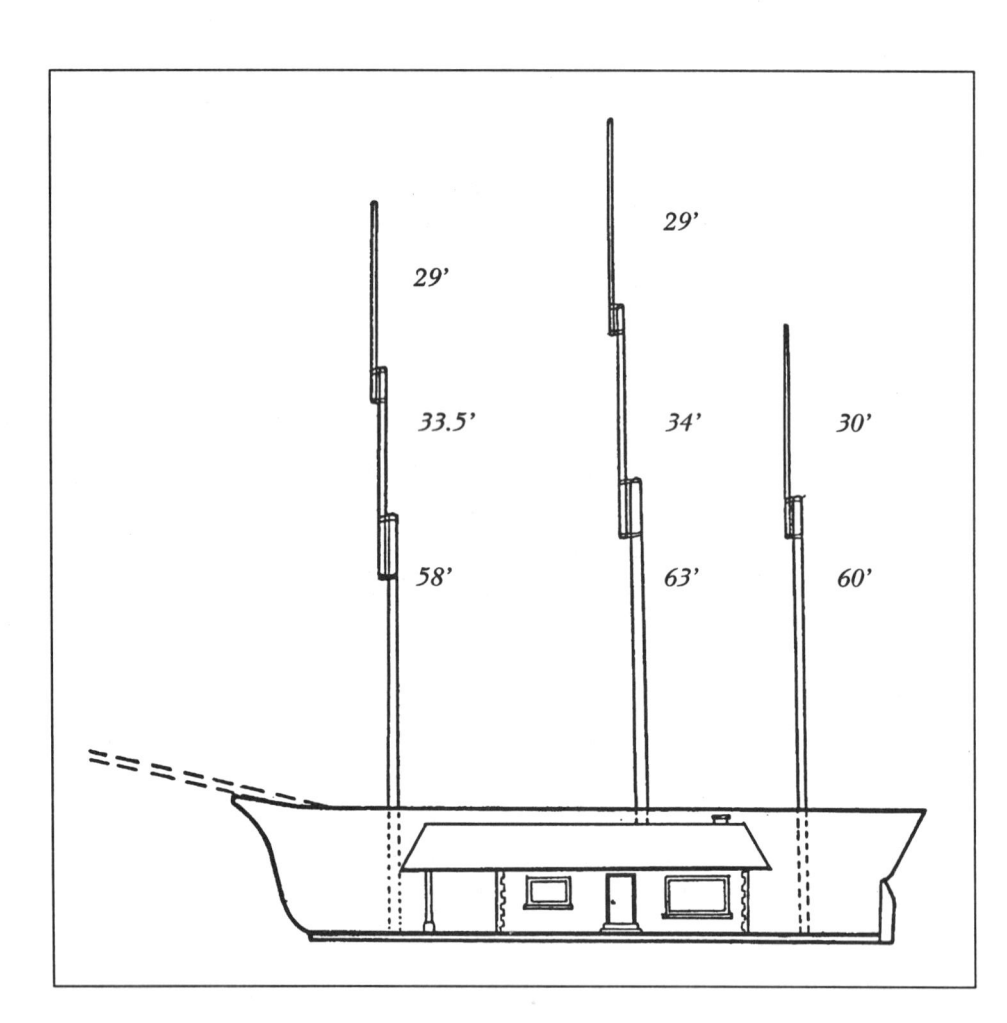

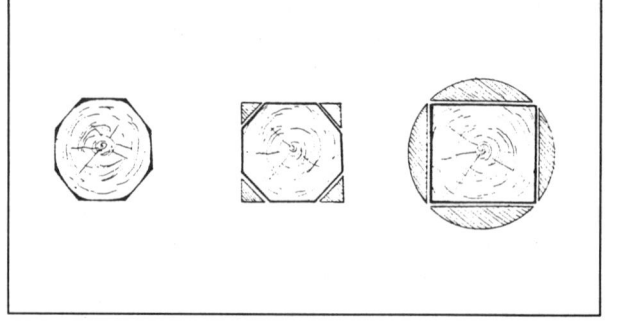

Figure 176: *The three steps in shaping a mast. After it has been squared off, the corners are removed to form an octagonal cross section, whose corners are removed to form sixteen sides. The sixteen-sides of the mast are then smoothed down to form a perfect circle.*

Figure 177: *A typical modern bungalow drawn to scale beside the masts of the 250 ton barque* Saint Lawrence, *launched in 1818 by John Bell from his shipyard on the Canoterie. This vessel had forty-two spars, of which her 63 foot lower mast weighed approximately two tons. Yet even for those days she was a small vessel, and the mastmaker, who would complete the work in about four weeks, might then find himself outfitting a far larger ship with masts 90 foot long and weighing not two, but seven tons.*

satisfied, he put it on blocks or trestles, which were known also as sparmaker's stools[49] and, marking it first with a chalk line, took off the heavy waste with a mast axe to form a long square tapering stick. The four corners of the stick were then removed on their entire length along lines whose position had been accurately marked with a mastmaker's rule, to result in an octagonal cross section, and then the eight corners were taken off to give it sixteen sides.

Great skill was required in wielding the axe, so as to come close enough to the final shape and yet not remove too much wood, for although the mast could be cut down to make a smaller mast or yard, it would still be a costly mistake, especially if a ninety-foot mast were involved. Careful shaving with a mastmaker's draw knife, or *mast shave*, which was larger and heavier than the usual carpenter's draw knife, gave the mast its final circular shape before it was smoothed, first with a jack plane and then with a hollow-soled mast plane. After the measurements had been checked with a pair of large calipers to make sure it was the exact size required, it was rubbed down with glass paper and the mast itself was finished.

A number of independent mastmakers practised in Quebec, among them Joseph Gaboury, Andrew Allen and Richard Uppington, who were active at the outset of the nineteenth century, and later members of the Baldwin family, some of whom were also shipbuilders. Their workshops were located close to the river because of the necessity of receiving the mast trees and despatching the finished masts by water. Difficult to move over land on account of their length, they could, however, easily be towed to the ship for which they were destined. Other mastmakers who were shipyard employees included John Pounder,

Table 9
Spars of the 275 ton barque *Saint Lawrence* of 1818

	Length feet	Diameter inches	Length feet	Diameter inches	Length feet	Diameter inches
Masts						
Lower	58	19.5	63	19.5	60	14
Top	33.5	11.5	34	11.5	30	7
Top-gallant	29	6	29	6	-	-
Yards						
Lower	42	12	42	12		
Topsail	32	9	32	9		
Top-gallant	24	5.5	24	5.5		
Royal	16		16			
Boom					43	10
Bowsprit	37	20.5				
Jib boom	34	9.5				
3 Gaffs	32	7				
4 Studding sail booms	25					
4 Top-gallant studding sail booms	18					
8 Studding sail yards						
2 Lower booms						
2 Trysail yards						

Figure 178: *Mastmaker's compass found on Cape Diamond. Musée Maritime Bernier.*

Figure 179: *Mastmakers' Tools.* Left to right, *Jack plane and hollow-soled mast plane, compass and mast axe, below, draw knife or mast shave*

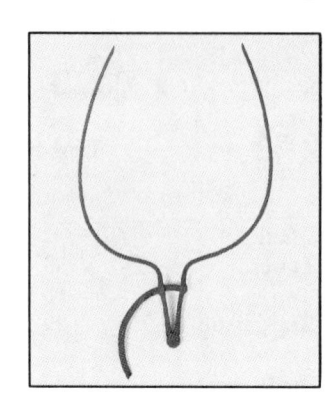

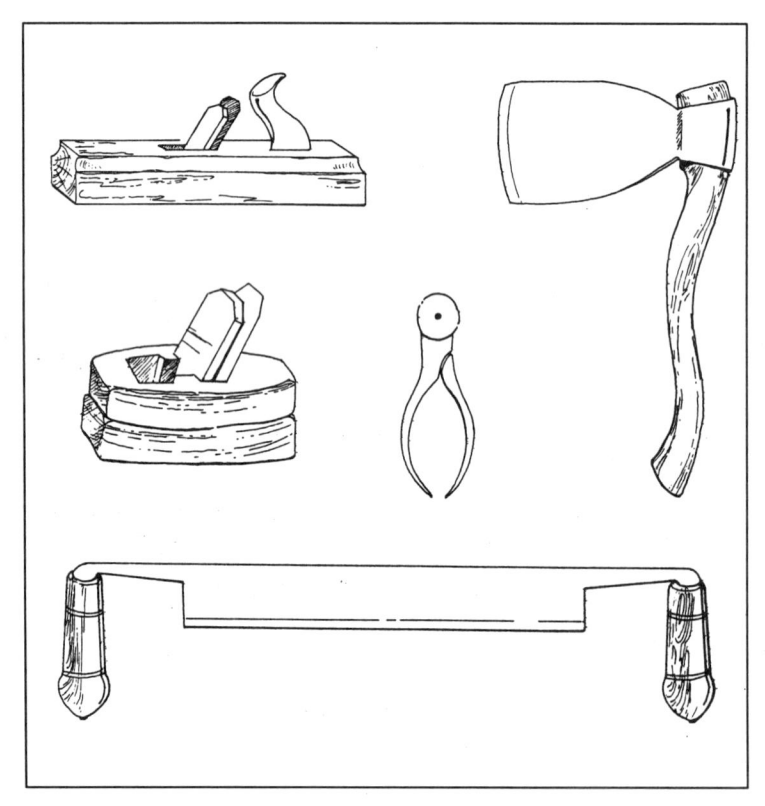

who apprenticed himself to John Munn in 1827 to learn both the mast and blockmaking trades.[50]

Masts were supposed to last twelve years before the resin dried up, depriving them of their strength; but by the 1870s good masts in the larger sizes had become difficult to obtain. Quebec ships visiting the west coast of America often had masts made of Oregon pine substituted for their relatively new masts, and other vessels had iron lower masts installed at Liverpool.[51]

The Pumpmaker

One of the main differences between a wooden and a metal sailing ship was that the former was far less likely to remain watertight. It was not necessary for her to run aground or collide; the strain of constantly riding the waves and the force of the wind tugging on her rigging took its toll. When water began to collect in the bilges, the order "Man the pumps" was given and the crew immediately obeyed, knowing that their safety might depend on it. With luck, just two rudimentary pumps would enable the ship to reach port safely.

Traditionally the pumps were made of wood. Elm was preferred because it stood up well to the constant damp to which it was subjected and was readily available in long straight lengths, but various other woods, such as birch, red pine and tamarac were also employed in Quebec ships. Not all pumps were wooden, however. At the beginning of the nineteenth century some were made of lead and later of iron and other metals. Nevertheless wooden pumps did not become obsolete; instead the simple early versions gave way to more sophisticated equipment, such as the "patent double action wooden suction ship pump," a demonstration of which was advertised in the *Quebec Morning Chronicle* in 1860.

The pumpmaker's equipment was simple. The log from which the barrel was to be made was supported on blocks or trestles, and bored with a shell auger bit on the end of a twelve foot iron shank, first from one end and then from the other. The bore was then enlarged using a series of tapered pump augers of increasing size until the hole was the required diameter; at the same time extensions were added to the handle as needed. Screw augers were not suitable for the work, because they were apt to follow the grain of the wood. As pumps were sometimes twenty to thirty feet long, it was necessary at times to make them of two pieces, which was accomplished by tapering the bottom of the upper log and recessing the lower log to receive it.

Once the barrel was ready, the pump only required a piston with a one-way flap valve made to fit the barrel and a rocker arm to operate it. The shipbuilder generally fixed the pumps, installing them side by side before the mainmast with the tops of the barrels protruding a few inches above the upper deck. When functioning, the water was sucked up on the up stroke, passed through the valve on the down stroke and as more water rose on the next stroke, flowed over the lip of the barrel onto the deck and found its way over the side. This simple and effective apparatus was still being installed in vessels well into the twentieth century.

Among those who combined the trades of mast, block and pumpmaker was Richard Uppington, who was not averse to having a few other extra items in his orders, too. For example, J.S. Campbell's order in 1819 for a three hundred-ton barque included:

Figure 180: *Mastmaker smoothing a mast with a drawknife. The mast was for the reproduction of the* Bounty *built in the Smith and Rhuland shipyard in Lunenburg, Nova Scotia, and launched in 1962. Photo courtesy Jacques Coulon.*

masts, yards, booms and gaffs complete with steering sail booms – Fore and Main top – mizzen to be like the Cross Trees – Fore and Main cross trees Bowsprit, cap and heart and cheek blocks – Two lower caps and three trucks. To make wheel, cut sheave holes in catheads, sheet blocks, gallows, stancheons and bitts, boat davitts – Set of dead eyes for iron straps for lower rigging and backstays and for the top plates the mizzen. To bore the windlass capstan and scuppers, make two red pine pumps with two sets of handles. All iron work and wood furnished by owner, sheaves, pumps and dead eyes by contractor.[52]

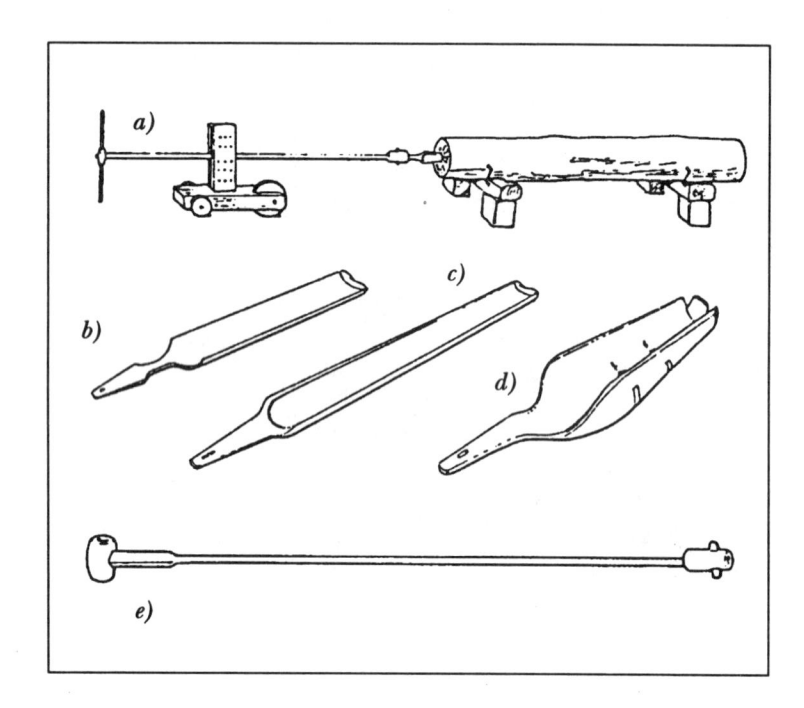

Figure 181: *Pump Boring Equipment*

a) *Shown here with a T-handle and supported by a dolly, this arrangement, on display at the National Maritime Museum, Antwerp, would seem to be ideal. Similar supports may have been used in Quebec*
b) *Shell auger bit for boring the pilot hole, about 16 inches. long and 2-2 1/2 inches. in diameter.*
c) & d) *Tapered auger bits with a cutter at the nose and one side of the body sharpened, sold in sets 2 - 8 inches. in diameter. Some were slotted so that a widening liner could be tied or bolted to them. Others were made with a hook at the nose to which a rope was attached, and the auger was then pulled through from one end of the barrel while being twisted at the other.*
e) *Turning shank 12 feet long with a socket at one end into which either a shank extension or a bit was keyed, and an eye at the other for a long cross handle, which was turned by two men. The shank of pump boring equipment owned by a retired ship carpenter on the Isle-aux-Coudres has been bent to form a crank handle instead.*

Adapted from R.A. Salaman, Dictionary of Tools used in the woodworking and allied trades c.1700–1970 *by Caroline Soucy.*

The Ropemaker

Though cordage is now made from a variety of synthetic fibres, vegetable fibres and wire, in nineteenth-century Quebec it was made mainly from hemp and manila "hemp."

Hemp grew in most temperate regions of the world, notably in Russia. It required tarring for maritime use, as its fibres would rot through exposure to salt water. Only three-quarters as strong as manila cordage, it was used almost exclusively for roping sails and also for hawsers and for running rigging, for the lanyards of the shrouds and for "small stuff." Manila "hemp," on the other hand, was obtained from the leaf stalks of the abaca, a plant of the banana family eight to twenty feet tall, which grows in the Philippines. Because its fibres were light, strong, long and flexible, and did not deteriorate in water, it did not require tarring. Considered the finest for large ropes and cables, it was too stiff, however, for small cords and twines.

From 1665, as part of Jean Talon's plan to establish a Royal shipyard complete with its supporting industries, the people of New France were encouraged from time to time to cultivate hemp. Talon not only distributed free seed, on condition that the growers turn in an equivalent amount when they harvested their crop, but also seized all the thread he could find in the colony, redistributing it to those who promised to return a stated amount of hemp. His strategy worked, and it was successfully grown and harvested in large quantities when a good price was offered.[53] But due to the lack of ropemakers the colonists did not have a steady market, and turned each time to other crops. In the last part of the eighteenth and in the nineteenth century, the farmers were repeatedly urged to sow hemp, and articles which appeared in periodicals describing methods of cultivation and harvesting seem to have been of no avail. Yet in 1866, the importation of Russian hemp was severely criticized and blamed for keeping the price of cordage so high. If the hemp were grown locally, it was said, the cost of rigging a ship would be greatly reduced and allow for some profit in the shipbuilding industry.[54] Besides the high cost of their raw material, ropemakers suffered the competition of a great deal of imported rope advertised on the Quebec market as the best available, although owners of local ropewalks maintained that their product was just as good.[55]

A picture of the Quebec ropewalks is still far from complete. One of the earliest of the post-New France period was established by John Goudie the shipbuilder in 1809 on a fifteen foot wide strip of land in the vicinity of the General Hospital. He hired two ropemakers to work from five in the morning until seven at night in spring and summer, and from eight until six in winter. This was perhaps the "old established rope manufactory" in Saint Roch suburb, with a rope walk twenty fathoms long, which was offered for sale in the *Quebec Gazette* on 2 October 1849. In 1818, Robert Dalkin erected another ropery at the Canardière, which was destroyed by fire in 1822; though re-built, it was destroyed again in 1828, this time by high tides and winds. It was re-built once again at the water's edge, but was eventually moved further inland where, according to the census, it was still operating under the name of "John Brown's Patent Cordage Works" in 1871. Thirty male and twenty female workers, many of them teen-age girl spinners, produced 750 tons of cordage annually from hemp, oil and Archangel tar. The ropewalk was eventually absorbed by Consumer Cordage of

Montreal and later disappeared.[56] A third well-established ropery, at Gros Pin, Charlesbourg, carried on business from at least 1840 to 1868, though changing hands twice during that period. In the 1860s, the owners experimented growing hemp on their land behind the walk and claimed that they obtained fibres nine feet long and of an extraordinary whiteness, every bit as good as any imported. They urged farmers to cultivate the crop, and like Talon, volunteered to give them the seed provided they agreed to return an equal amount after harvest.[57] By 1870, however, their business had closed down.

Whether made in the time-honoured way, or with Patented machinery, ropemaking embraced three distinct processes: preparation of the hemp or other fibre for spinning, spinning the fibre to form a continuous yarn and twisting the yarn to form the rope. Traditionally, they were carried out by three different tradesmen: the hatcheller, the spinner and the ropemaker.[58] In the course of their three to seven-year apprenticeships, generally until the age of twenty or twenty-one, they learned only one of the three trades.[59] Dried and cured hemp from the supplier was first sorted into bundles of fibres of one or various qualities according to the grade of rope to be made. Then each bundle was repeatedly combed by the hatcheller on a board covered with rows of spikes, known as a "hatchel" or "heckle," until all the fibres were lying in the same direction and any waste had been removed. The spinners then took over, one man working at each of the seven or eight hooks or "whirls" on a spinning frame, with a man or boy behind him turning the handle of the drum which served to rotate the hooks. The first spinner took an armful of hemp and placed it around his waist and then, making a loop with some of the fibres, slipped it on one of the whirls and started walking away backwards down the ropewalk, feeding out the hemp as he went. When he had gone a few feet, the next man started, and so on. The thickness of the yarn was controlled by the speed at which the spinner walked and the amount of pressure he applied as the hemp passed through his hand. A man stationed beside the frame removed each thread of yarn from the whirl as it was completed and spliced it into the main coil lying beside the spinning frame, so that the work of all the spinners became part of one long continuous thread. When the coil reached the prescribed size, it was stored, unless it required tarring, in which case it was passed through a steaming hot tar bath and then through rollers to remove the excess tar.

The actual ropemaking then began. It consisted in twisting two or more lengths of spun yarn or fibre separately in one direction, a process known as the "foreturn," and then putting them together while twisting them in the opposite direction, the "afterturn." First, the threads of yarn were laid out side by side the length of the ropewalk and then they were each fixed at one end to a whirl on a stationary frame and at the other, directly opposite, to a whirl mounted on a structure on wheels known as a "breast board." In between, the yarn was kept off the ground by a series of props with pegs to keep the strands apart called "stakeheads." Because the twisting was done under pressure, the whirls at both ends were driven by geared wheels and not by a belt as in spinning. As the gears turned, the yarn twisted and became shorter and the breast board moved forward. Tension was maintained on the strand by means of a capstan, which held back the sledge on which the breast board

The Shipbuilding Trades

Figure 182: *Spinner at Work in a Ropewalk in Great Yarmouth, 1885. Photo courtesy National Museums and Galleries on Merseyside, with thanks to Mike Stammers.*

Figure 183: *Preparation of a cable laid rope made with three ropes. The afterturn. Engraving J.H. Roding, Allgemeines Worterbuch der Marine, 1798.*

Figure 184: *Ropewalk in the outskirts of Quebec.*

Figure 185: *Saint Sauveur Rope Walk. The ropery which employed both men and women was an important industry in the parish until it burnt in the fire of 1866. Courtesy National Archives, Ottawa. Neg. PA 122757.*

travelled. When the strands reached the required tension, the three ends on the breast board were placed on the same hook with a wooden cone keeping them apart for the afterturn. The hook was then rotated in the opposite direction, the cone moved backwards, and the strands came together to form the rope. Cable was made by the same method, using rope for the foreturn instead of yarn. Rope was referred to as "hawser-laid" when the fibre was spun left-handed, followed by a right-handed fore-turn and a left-handed after-turn, and "plain laid" in the case of the reverse.

By 1840, chain slings for lower yards, chain topsail sheets and ties, chain gammonings and chain bobstays were commonly in use and by 1865, galvanized wire replaced hemp standing rigging.[60]

At Quebec, not only was the percentage of shipbuilding which benefitted the ropemaker severely reduced by then, but shipbuilding itself had passed its heyday. However, the shipbuilder was not the ropemaker's only customer and the trade, fast becoming an industry, survived.

The Sailmaker

Quebec sailmakers made an excellent living supplying sails for visiting ships as well as for new construction, Even when the customer supplied the canvas, working it up still amounted to a significant account. In the case of the 904 ton ship *Thomas Fielden* making nineteen sails, two tarpaulin covers, four mast and two pump coats it came to £420 17 4d[61], see Appendix E.

Sailmakers' workshops, known as sail-lofts, generally occupied the attics of buildings where there was a large uninterrupted floor space on which the sails could be laid out. In Quebec, many were to be found under the steep roofs of office and other buildings on Saint Paul and Saint Peter streets in the lower town, where there was sometimes a two-story garret to accommodate them better. Work in the loft began at seven o'clock in the morning and ended at six at night with one hour off at noon, Monday to Saturday.[62] The long hours of sewing were hard on the eyes, especially in winter when the light failed early and the sewing was done by candle-light, each sailmaker having his own "sailmaker's candlestick." In cold damp weather fingers often became chilled and numb in the draughty lofts.

The seven-year apprenticeship survived longer in sailmaking than in most other trades and through the greater part of the nineteenth century, British fathers continued to send their young sons over to learn the trade in the Quebec lofts, in particular from Devonshire to the master sailmaker James Hunt. Many of the letters the apprentices brought with them addressed to their new master are still attached to their original indentures in the notaries' greffes. Typical is one written by John Hunt of Burston, Devon in 1824:

I have taken the opportunity of sending out to you my only son Wm as you send home that you wanted a Boy and Mrs. A. Hunt send to me to know ever I was willing to sent out Wm and I was very happy in sending him under your charge . . . Please keep him to his books.

Another from the farmer John Jarvis of Heathfield, Devon, written in 1845, expresses the often stated concern of the parents for the education of the apprentices and the practice of their religion:

Figure 186: *Master Sailmaker Richard Hudson (1826–1914) of Quebec, and his family. Photo courtesy P. Hudson.*

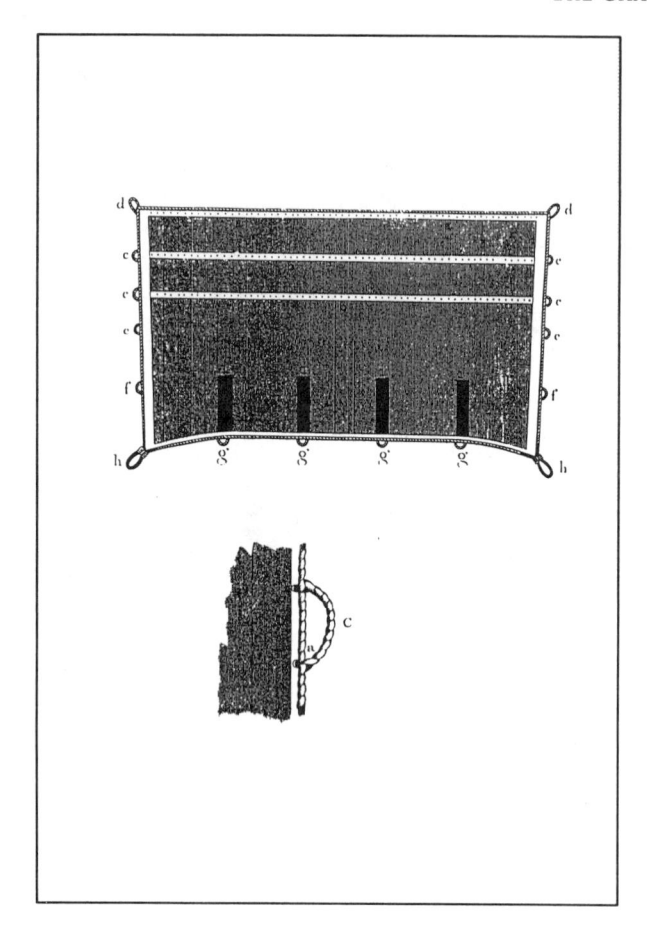

Figure 187: *Square sails, each consisting of between thirty and forty "cloths" stitched together.*

a) Tabling
b) Reef Bands
c) Cringles
d) Earing Cringles
e) Upper Bowline Cringles
f) Lower Bowline Cringles
g) Buntline Cringles
h) Clews
i) Buntline Cloths

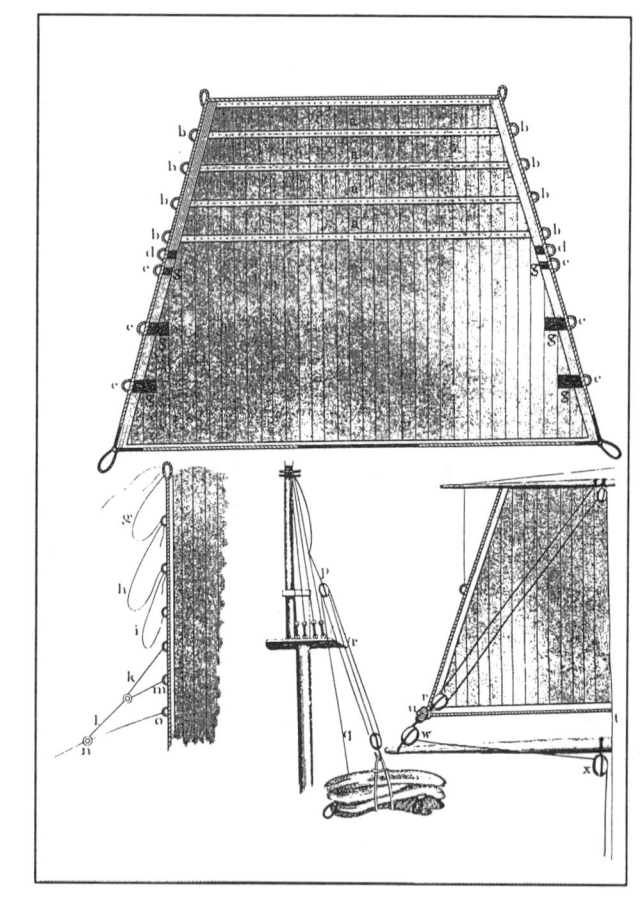

a) Reef bands
b) Cringles
c) Bowline Cringles
d) Reef-tackle Pendents
g) Patches

From Darcy Lever, The Young Sea Officer's Sheet Anchor.

... i hope sir you will do by him as you did by Cousin Robert Symons ...

... tell him to mind his Writing and please keep him Sundays to his Church.[63]

Though the young apprentice might spend some time during the first year or two generally making himself useful, running errands, delivering sails, sweeping floors and humping bolts of canvas, it was to his advantage and that of his master that he start sewing as soon as possible; as there were usually several apprentices in the loft, it is likely that he began to do so quite soon under the watchful eye of a journeyman. When he had achieved a certain efficiency in sewing, he was allowed to start "roping," or sewing rope to canvas, and later to make eyelet holes, cringles and grommets and gradually he learned all the "secrets of the trade." When he had completed his term, he became a journeyman sailmaker qualified to earn his living in a sail-loft or as a ship's sailmaker at sea.

There was no room for errors in cutting canvas, so the master sailmaker and his senior journeyman cut the pieces using a sharp knife, numbered them consecutively and handed them to a journeyman or older apprentice to sew. Each piece was joined to the next with a double seam and when all had been joined, the edges of the sail were turned over, or "tabled," thus making a wide flat hem or "tabling" all round. The parts of the sail most likely to chafe against masts, yards or ropes were then strengthened with extra strips of canvas, holes were made in the tabling into which "cringles," or rings of rope, metal or wood, were stitched and the "bolt rope" was whipped onto the edges of the sail all round, an operation which, because it was important that the rope have the right degree of twist, required considerable skill. With the rope in place, "grommets," or loops of rope, were made and sewn in the various cringles in the tabling. Lastly, reef bands were sewn across the sail, in which eyelets were made at regular intervals. Through each of these a short piece of rope, or "reef point," was passed and stitched in position with one-half lying on each side of the sail. The sailmaker's work was now complete and the sail was ready to be bent to a mast or spar.[64]

The sailmaker sat sidewise on a bench or "trestle" about fourteen inches high and six and a half feet long, that served as both seat and workbench. Two small hooks attached to the bench kept the canvas taut while he was sewing, while a grease horn filled with tallow, held his three-cornered needles free from rust. The needles varied from 2 1/4 to four inches in length, with some even longer for heavy rope-work. As he sewed, he waxed the twine with a lump of beeswax or tallow and pushed the needle through the cloth with a sailor's thimble or "seaming palm" worn round his hand. For heavier work, he used a "roping palm," which had bigger indentations to accommodate the larger needle and a leather thumb guard around which he wound the twine to pull it tight. When he wanted more leverage, he used the octagonal shaft of a stitch mallet instead and could use the indentation at its end to push the needle with extra strength.

As he worked he smoothed his seam with a small tool called a "rubber" and stretched the holes in the canvas and widened grommets and cringles with a "hand fid." For heavier work, he took the bigger "set fid," which stood on the floor. When splicing small ropes, he used a "pricker," consisting of an iron spike mounted in a wood or horn handle, and for cable or large rope, a stronger "marline spike."

Sewing machines were first used for sailmaking at Aberdeen in 1851 and at London in 1877, where they not only cut down on hand labour but also allowed some of the lofts to diversify and thus carry on through this period of decline in the industry.[65] In Quebec, gross annual production fell from $50,000 in 1870 to $11,400 in 1891, with a corresponding decrease from forty to eight workers.[66]

By far the most prominent master sailmaker in the town was James Hunt, who on his arrival from Devon in 1803 advertised his Sail Rooms at No. 18 St. Peter's Street, near the Landing Place in the Lower Town. He went on to make a fortune from his trade and other business interests. He had four daughters but no sons, and in 1840 gave one half of his sailmaking business to his former apprentice William Hunt (not a close relative) referred to above, with the right to buy the other half from his estate on his death, a right which William exercised, bringing his son into the business. Other important sailmakers at Quebec include Robert and Raymond Blakiston, James Carbry, Alexander Gibney, Charles Gortley, Richard Hudson, John Jarvis, François Rosa, Peter Simons, Thomas Stonehouse and Caleb Thorne. Unlike the other auxiliary shipbuilding trades, which disappeared long before, two of the sailmaking establishments survived until the 1980s – J. Alleyn, which specialized in awnings and canopies, and Quebec Ship Riggers and Sail Makers, which alone carried on the trades of sailmaking and rigging, adapting to new demands and conditions but able to provide a sail made in the time-honoured way to the end.

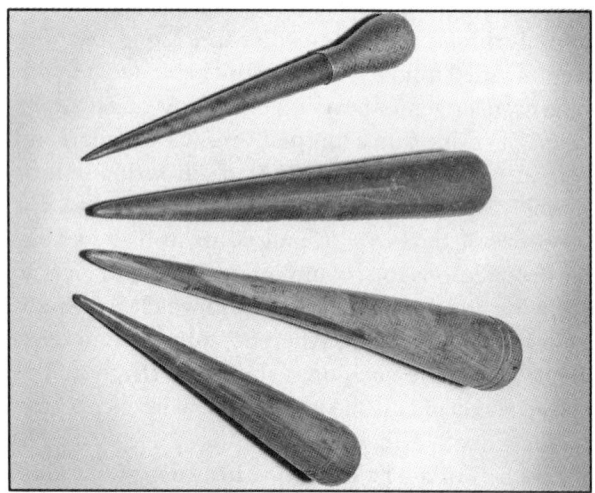

Figure 188: *Sailmakers' palms in the collection of the Canadian Museum of Civilization, Ottawa. Photo courtesy National Museums of Canada, NA–16–77–15.*

Figure 189: *Sailmakers' fids. National Museums of Canada, NA–16–77–22.*

The Shipbuilding Trades

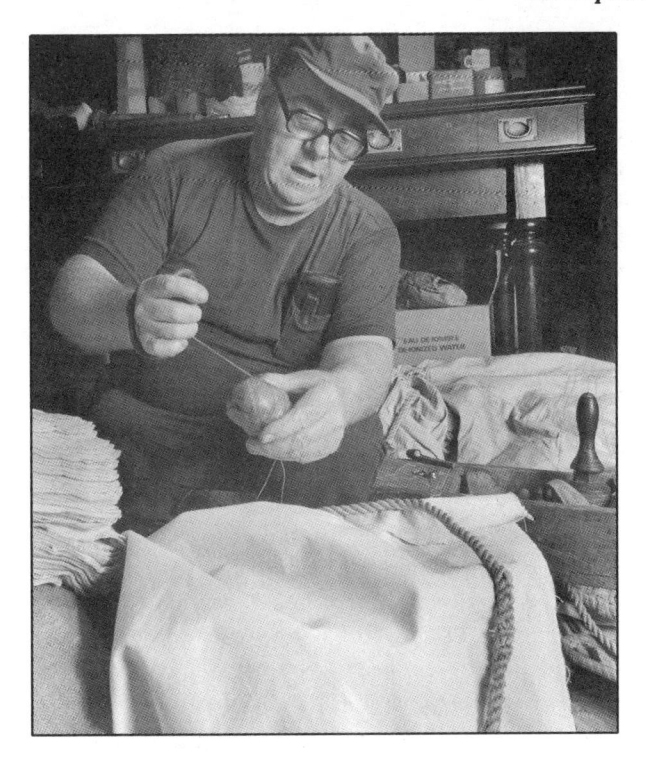

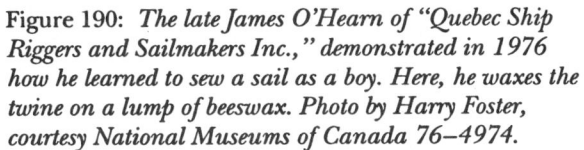

Figure 190: *The late James O'Hearn of "Quebec Ship Riggers and Sailmakers Inc.," demonstrated in 1976 how he learned to sew a sail as a boy. Here, he waxes the twine on a lump of beeswax. Photo by Harry Foster, courtesy National Museums of Canada 76–4974.*

Figure 191: *Sailmakers' hand-made wooden needle boxes, in the collection of the Canadian Museum of Civilization, Ottawa. Courtesy National Museums of Canada, NA–16–77–2.*

Figure 192: *Home of the Sailmaker Peter Simons at Lake Beauport, a few miles north of Quebec. Photo: Courtesy Colin McMichael.*

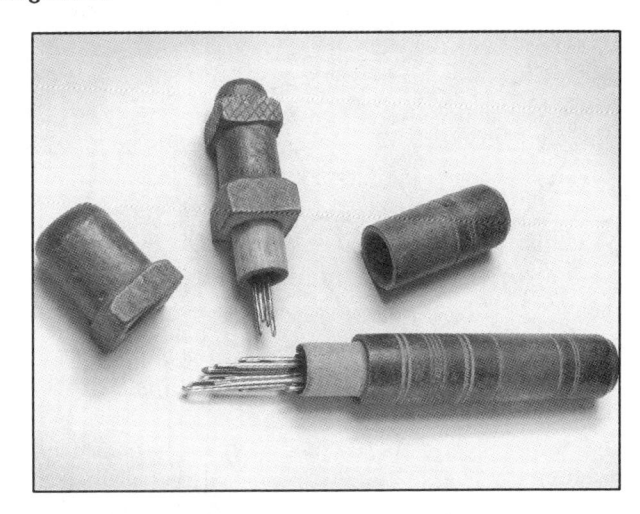

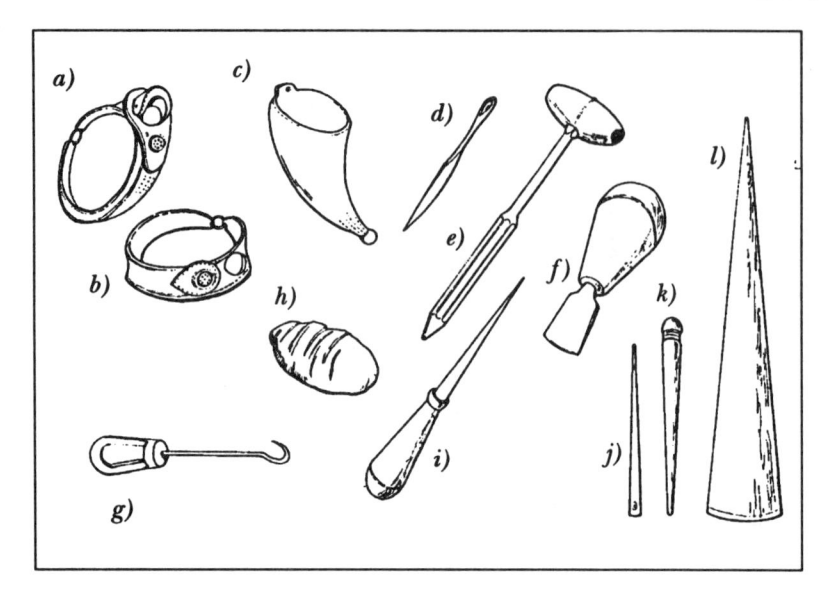

Figure 193: *Sailmakers' Tools*

a) *Roping palm*
b) *Seaming palm*
c) *Grease horn*
d) *3-cornered needle*
e) *Stitch mallet*
f) *Rubber*
g) *Sail hook*
h) *Beeswax or Tallow*
i) *Pricker*
j) *Marline spike*
k) *Hand fid*
l) *Set fid*

Adapted from R.A. Salaman, Dictionary of Tools used in the woodworking and allied trades c.1700–1970.

The Ship Rigger

A ship's rigging consists of her masts and spars, the collection of semi-permanent ropes or wires which support them, known as the "standing rigging," and the moving or movable ropes used to brace the yards, to make and take in sails, to raise and lower the masts, or do other work, known as the "running rigging." The ship rigger took the masts and spars from the mastmaker, the ironwork from the shipsmith, the ropes from the ropemaker, the pulleys from the blockmaker, the sails from the sailmaker (though some riggers did their own sailmaking) and erected the whole apparatus by which the ship used the force of the wind to sail against the resistance of the water.

Quebec being the terminal of so many voyages, rigging repairs added to the demands for rigging for new construction and kept her riggers busy. In addition, ships built above or below Quebec were sometimes sailed to the port to be rigged, and Quebec riggers at times were sent to work in an out of town yard when a ship reached the rigging stage. Riggers were required to work long hours, even through the night, to shorten the time a vessel had to remain in port or perhaps to enable her to catch a tide or take advantage of the wind and, because of the expense of keeping a ship idle, the captain would often detail some of his crew to help with the work.[67]

There were two kinds of riggers: "loft riggers" and regular riggers. Loft riggers, who were familiar with all kinds of knots, were experts at splicing, whipping and seizing both fibre and wire rope. They anticipated the requirements of the riggers and prepared the blocks, stropping them with rope and attaching a variety of thimbles, shackles, or hooks and eyes to their crowns and tails. They seized the deadeyes, made ratlines on the shrouds, and generally in the comfort of the loft, did all the work that it was not necessary to do aboard ship. Their principal tools were those used to open the lay for splicing, such as the pricker, the hand and set fid and the marline spike (see the sailmakers' tools), and the serving mallet, used to cover rope when it was necessary to protect it from chafing or becoming wet.

But the loft work was not always done locally, and one of the firms that prepared rigging for Quebec-built ships was Alexander Tough & Sons of Greenock who on at least one occasion sent instructions to the riggers in Quebec and St. John, New Brunswick, for whom they had prepared rigging:

> . . . we will feel obliged by your mentioning to them that when taking the Shrouds and other cordage of the Coils to place the coil upon the flat with the *inside end uppermost* then take the *outside or fag end* and turn it off, when it will neither put a turn in or out of the rope, by attending to this it will save much trouble and give justice to the rope. With regard to the fitted rigging shipped to "Canada" if you would mention that when setting up the shrouds to put 4 turns in every shroud and 6 turns in every Backstay, and the rest of the Rigging in proportion. In order to show the advantage of paying a little attention to what we have described permit us to quote an extract from a letter we received from Captain Ferguson of the "China" now in London, he says "You wish to know how the Rigging pleased, I must say I never saw better, it only came down 4 inches during the 14 months we were in India, it is even now as close in the lay as when it came from your Rope Work, and Stephen Groves the Rigger deserves great credit for the fitting of it."[68]

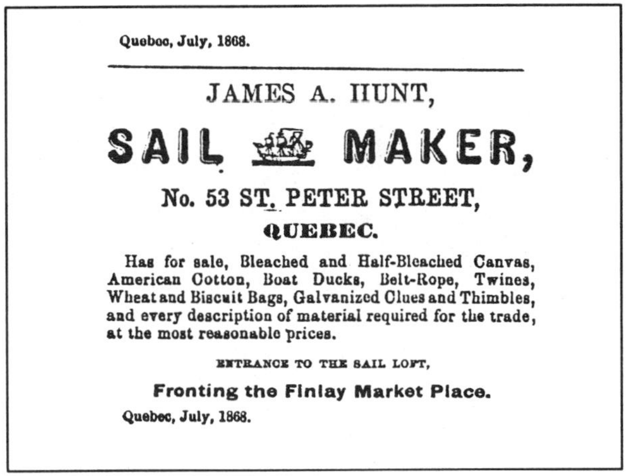
Quebec, July, 1868.

JAMES A. HUNT,

SAIL MAKER,

No. 53 ST. PETER STREET,

QUEBEC.

Has for sale, Bleached and Half-Bleached Canvas, American Cotton, Boat Ducks, Belt-Rope, Twines, Wheat and Biscuit Bags, Galvanized Clues and Thimbles, and every description of material required for the trade, at the most reasonable prices.

ENTRANCE TO THE SAIL LOFT,

Fronting the Finlay Market Place.

Quebec, July, 1868.

Figure 194: *Announcement placed by the Sailmaker James Hunt in the Quebec Directory of 1868.*

When the loft riggers had completed their work, the general riggers took over and began theirs by installing the lower masts and bowsprit, a seemingly formidable undertaking which with the use of tackles they were able to accomplish relatively easily. They first hung a wooden framework known as the "skids" over the side of the ship to protect it and by means of a parbuckle hauled two spars, which might be the top masts, aboard and set them up temporarily on deck to use as sheerlegs. That is to say, the spars were lashed together at the top and then their heels were opened out and placed on blocks known as "shoes" and the whole structure lifted perpendicular to the deck and braced fore and aft.

A system of tackles fixed both to the deck and to the sheers enabled the riggers to swing the lower mast on deck, where the tenon at its heel was wiped dry and both it and the step into which it fitted were either tarred or white leaded, or both. The mast was then lowered into place, but not before a penny was

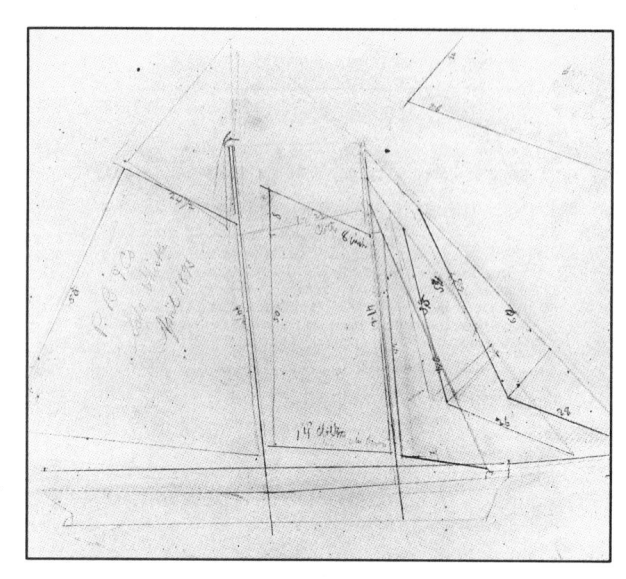

Figure 195: *Plan of the sails of the Schooner* Thistle, *ordered by P.B. & Co. (Patrick Baldwin?) Sail Plan Book of the Quebec sailmaker William Alleyn. Photo by Cedric Pearson. Courtesy C. Quinn.*

Figure 196: *Shipping a Lower Mast A lower mast being swung aboard, using sheerlegs, which have been set up on deck, and a system of tackles. The bracing of the sheerlegs – with more tackles – is not shown, in order to avoid confusion. Note the gantline block in place at the top of the mast, for use in sending up the top. From Darcy Lever,* The Young Sea Officer's Sheet Anchor.

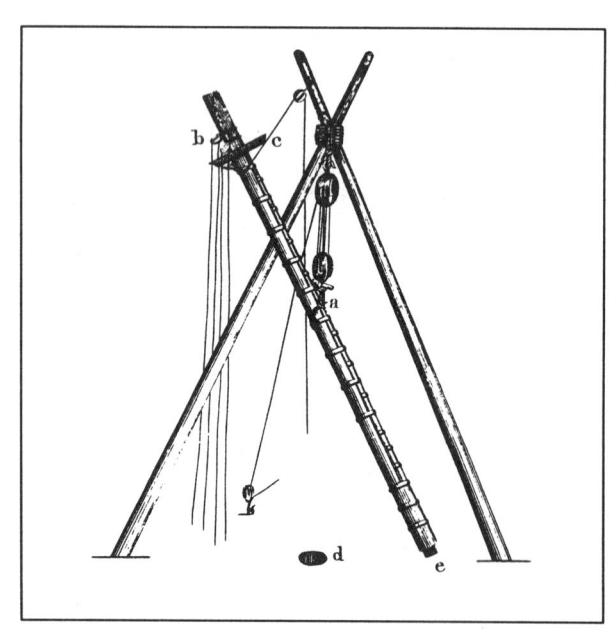

dropped into the slot that held it, for good luck. When the three lower masts were stepped, the sheerlegs were moved forward and the bowsprit was installed. Next to be put in place were the tops, the semi-circular platforms that rested on the trestletrees at the head of the mast, and the caps that held the upper and lower masts together. They were hauled up in turn using a tackle fixed to the head of the mast.

Before the topmasts were installed, the lower masts had to be rigged, beginning with the lateral supports or "shrouds," of which there were from four to six on each side. Pairs of shrouds, each made from a single hawser seized together halfway along to make an eye, were slipped over the mast alternately first for the starboard and then for the port side. If there was an odd shroud, it was either taken round the mast and seized together or seized to the corresponding shroud on the other side. Together the shrouds formed a "gang" of rigging and when they were all installed, the forestay eye was added above them.

The forestay was the first to be fixed to the deck. Its lower ends were provided with metal thimbles and were not only worked, parcelled and served but also covered with leather, were fixed to deckplates at either side of the bow, or to the knightheads or bowsprit. The ends of the shrouds, turned round and seized around upper deadeyes, were then laced with lanyards to the lower deadeye, which were fastened to chainplates on the hull, some of them crossed with ratlines forming ladders for the sailors to climb aloft. The lower main and mizzenmast rigging followed, differing only in that the stays were fixed to the deck on each side of the mast ahead, or to rollers riveted to collars on those masts.

With the lower masts secure, it was time to send

up the topmasts, which were hauled up before the lower masts through the trestletrees and tops, where gantline blocks were lashed to their heads to be used both for installing the crosstrees and for sending up the topgallant masts and later for the yards. In order to fix the rigging of the topmasts it was necessary for the bowsprit and jib boom to have been secured, after which the topmasts could be rigged as in Figure 199. It should be noted that all the top and topgallant masts were braced by back stays attached to chainplates on each side of the vessel, as well as by their stays.

When the standing rigging had been completed, the yards and the running rigging followed, the details of which can be seen in Figure 202. Unlike the standing rigging, the running rigging, as its name implies, must be easily loosened or tightened, so the free end of each rope, instead of being seized round a thimble, deadeye or other fitting, was simply wound around a belaying pin from which it could be instantly released. The yards were sent up with all their iron fittings and blocks already fixed to them, beginning with the lower yard. The manner of setting up the running rigging is complex and it is recommended that a reader who is interested should consult a rigging manual, such as *Steel's Mastmaking, Sailmaking and Rigging* (1794) or *Art of Rigging* (1818), or Darcy Lever's *The Young Sea Officer's Sheet Anchor; or a Key to the Leading of Rigging and to Practical Seamanship* (1819), of all of which there are reprints. The library of the early Quebec shipbuilder, Patrick Beatson, contained a copy of the first of these. Among more recent works are Harold Underhill's *Masting and Rigging the Clipper ship and Ocean Carrier*, originally printed in 1946, and John Harland's splendid *Seamanship in the Age of Sail* of 1984, recommended

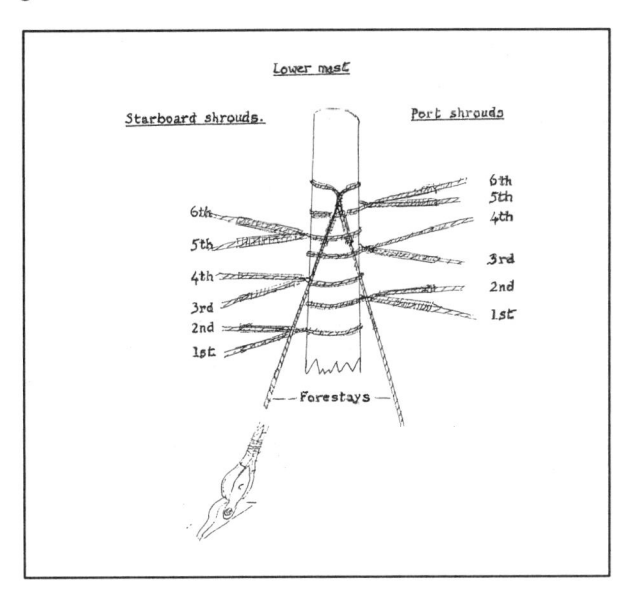

Figure 197: *Lower Mast and Shrouds*

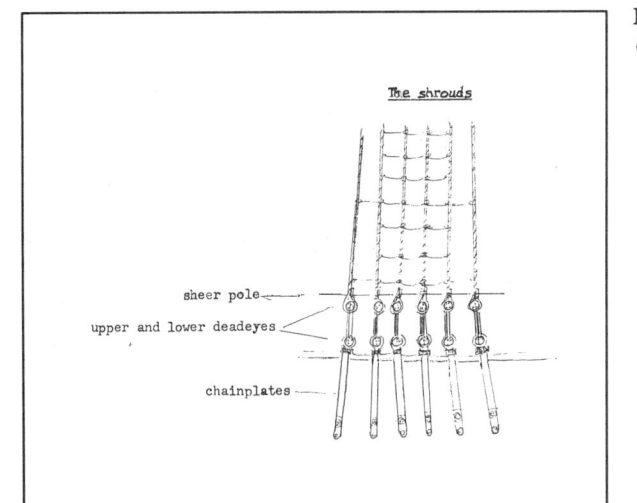

Figure 198: *Shrouds and Chainplates*

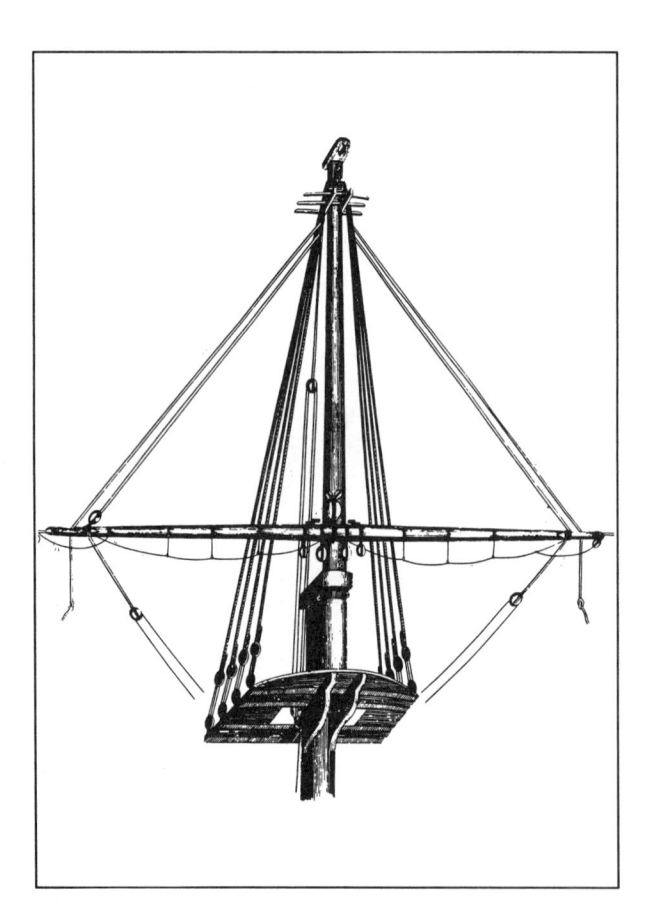

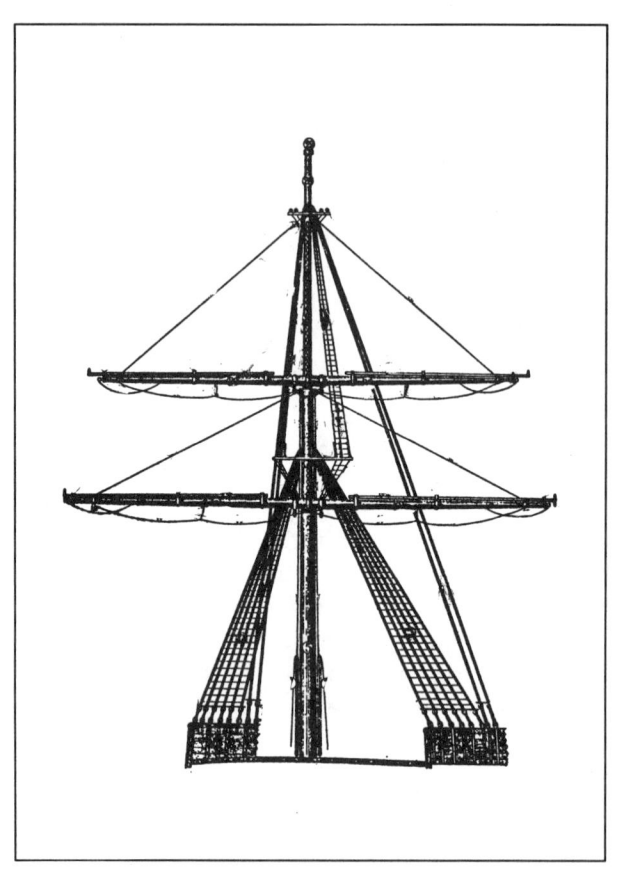

Figure 199: *Mast, complete with yards and studding sail booms and rigging.*

Figure 200: *Detail of topsail yard rigging.*

by a professional sailmaker and master of a Tall Ship, Captain Wayne Chimenti.

In every ship the rigging was set up in exactly the same way, so that a sailor could serve on any ship and if necessary handle the sails in pitch darkness, once he "knew his ropes." There was no place for alternatives or improvisations in the rigging trade and, though seamen might help them, it was essential that a qualified rigger be in charge of the job.

Other Shipyard Workers

In most shipyards, the craftsmen were supported by a number of less-skilled workers. Some, like the carters, were tradesmen in their own right; others were slightly skilled or unskilled; and still others, generally old men or boys, did such chores as tending fires and picking oakum. All were essential to keep the shipyard running efficiently and to allow the builder to make the best possible use of the more costly tradesmen's time.

"Axe-men," for instance, who commonly formed part of the work force in naval dockyards in Britain and elsewhere, were also hired in Quebec to work in the dockyard at Kingston during the War of 1812. but appear only rarely as such in contracts for work to be done in Quebec shipyards, notably in the 1810s. However, under the terms of a contract with William Carman in 1825, the undertakers were to provide "six good and capable carpenters and as many borers and axmen as necessary." Exactly how much of the work was entrusted to the axe-man is not clear, though it seems likely that it was restricted to preparing timber for the carpenter who assembled it. It seems that the job of axe-man may have been swallowed up under that of labourer by the 1850s, at least as far as ship-

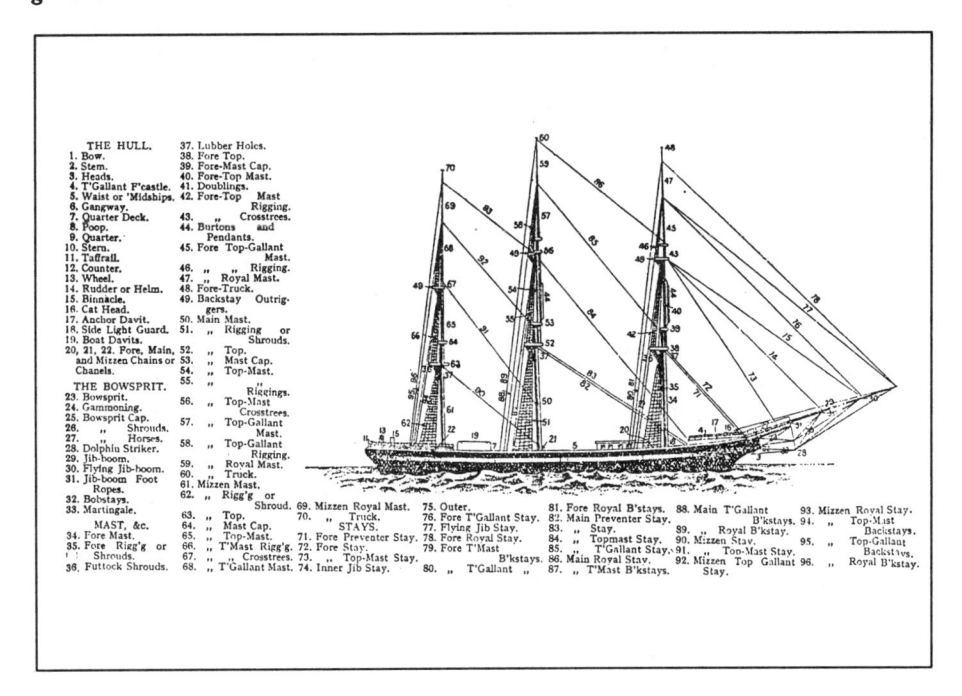

Figure 201: *Hull and Standing Rigging*. Admiralty Manual of Seamanship 1937.

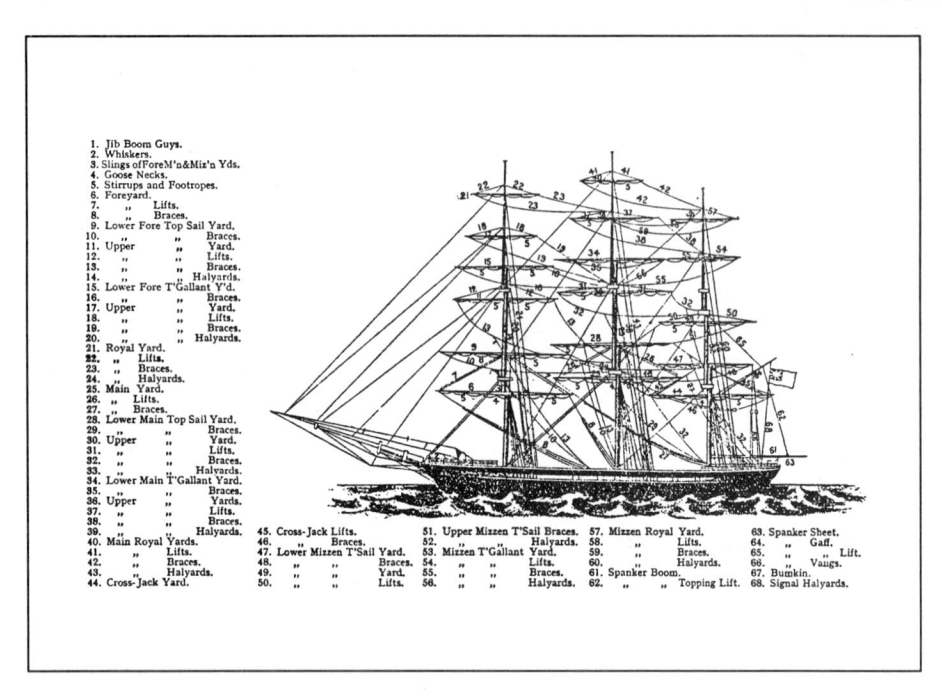

Figure 202: *Yards and Running Rigging. Admiralty Manual of Seamanship 1937.*

yards were concerned. Borers, as the name implies, bored the holes into which the trunnels or bolts were driven. Both borers and scrapers, but not axe-men, are mentioned in an itemized account for repairs carried out in 1854, along with the usual craftsmen.[69]

Making and moving the shores, scaffolds and ramps was other work that did not require the skill of a ship carpenter. It involved shoring the frames as they went up to keep them upright and "true," and then, as the plankers worked, moving them from time to time as needed. The long access ramps and scaffolds had to be erected both inside and outside the ship and removed when they were no longer required, the timber taken down and stacked, ready for the next time. This work, like that of tending the fire to make steam for the steam-box during planking operations or for heating tar kettles for caulking or simply tarring the ship's side, was often done by shipyard employees, and every planking contract clearly stipulated whether the plankers or the shipbuilder were to have the responsibility for the job. For instance, in a planking contract given out by John Bell in 1811, he agreed to supply the shores and "put up one stage round to put wales round and one gangway on each side" and in another contract made the same year Joseph Pacaud was to furnish "a steam box and a man to heat the same and to bore all the Holes in the said planking," while William Parker engaged with other plankers in 1815 to "grant them the use of the steam now in the said shipyard all the firewood that may be wanted and a man to heat the steam and keep the same agoing." However, according to George Taylor's contract with the shipwrights J.B. Cardinal and Thomas Bowman in 1818, he was to supply the steam and man, but the shipwrights were to make and set their own stages and shores.[70] It should be pointed out, however, that keeping the fire going for the steam-box did not include tending the wood that was steamed. Different types and sizes of wood required different amounts of steaming and incorrect steaming could seriously weaken the wood. An older man who understood the qualities of the different timbers was generally given the job.

Another chore that did not require a worker of tradesman's status was making treenails, of which thousands were needed for each vessel. Originally they were made by hand. The billets were split with an axe and a drawknife was used for the shaping. Although the men became proficient at their task, the treenails thus made took longer to make and could not have the precision of those that were machine-made. Once rounding equipment was available, many shipowners insisted that the treenails for the vessels they ordered be machine-made. Specifications for the *Elizabeth Yeo* built by Baldwin and Dinning for William Yeo, required them to be "1/2 in . . . caulked & wedged & to be of the same wood as driven thro' with a fair proportion of Locust in Wales and Paint Strakes. *Engine turned.*"[71] A great many different types of treenail mills were developed. One is illustrated on page 310 (fig 206).

Blocks and tackles of various types and dimensions served to lift and lower throughout the shipbuilding process, backed up at times by rudimentary cranes from at least as early as 1800. In addition, jack screws, winches and sometimes portable capstans or "crabs" lessened the burden of some of the heavier hauling jobs. For fetching and carrying materials and equipment, shipyards were generally equipped with pairs-of-wheels and drags, horse carts and sometimes dog carts. In addition, independent carters were hired for transporting over land, and boatmen or *bateliers*

Figure 203: *Shaping treenails, or "trunnels," by hand. New York Public Library Picture Collection.*

Figure 204: *A Borer piercing Holes for the treenails and bolts. New York Public Library Picture Collection.*

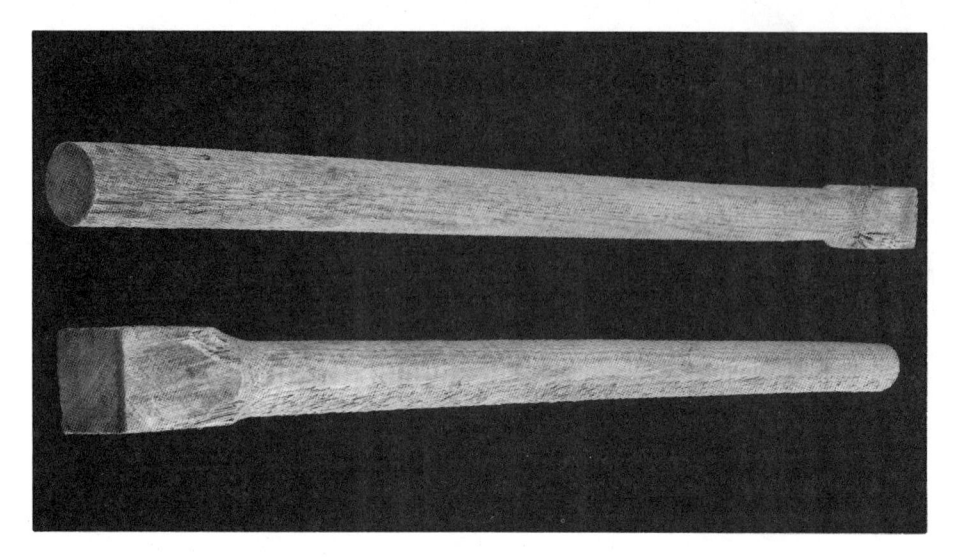

Figure 205: *Oak trunnels from the Davie Shipyard at Levis. Photo: National Museum of Canada AC 16-77-7.*

Figure 206: *Moot or Treenail Mill*

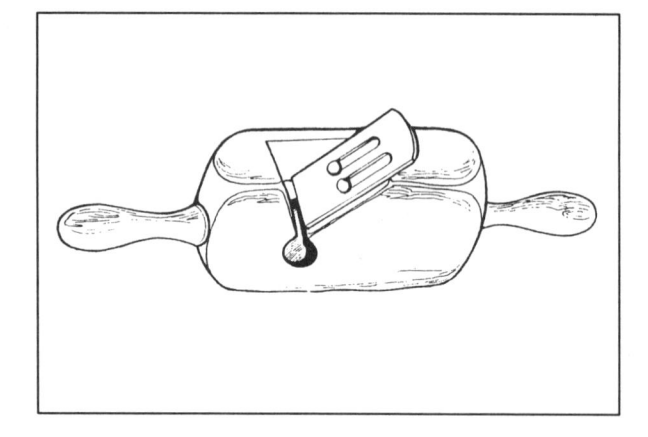

for river transport. There was, however, a constant need in the shipyard for strong men to handle timber – to receive it, stack it so that it would season correctly, or just move it from one part of the yard to another. When it came to moving the heaviest pieces, all hands joined in, dropping whatever they were doing to lend a shoulder:

The construction of wooden ships is now a thing of the past. But I still fondly remember the good old days when the worker, glistening with sweat, raised the frames of a ship as briskly and lightheartedly as if he were building his own home. His good nature had no limit when he was called upon to join in carrying the heavy timbers, the keel, the sternpost or the stempost. Then the shipyard concert would take place. If the timber was not too heavy, one of the finest vices would sing the words of a "chanson" and the others would join in the chorus. But when it was particularly heavy, we sang the "Charley-Man."

Who has not heard those deep rich voices intoning the Charley-Man, its strains drifting away to be swallowed up by the sound of the waves, without being moved to the depths of his soul? Under the rough exterieur of the worker one felt the heart of a decent, honest worker. Often of an evening mothers would take their children to the approaches of the shipyards to hear the Charley-Man.(translation).[72]

The Shipbuilding Trades

Figure 207: *Butting timber ready for export. Photo: Notman. N–1073.41. Courtesy McCord Museum.*

Notes

1. Thanks to Louis Rochette, president Davie Shipbuilding, Lauzon, and to Ladrière Samson, manager, and Wilfrid Corriveau of Davie Bros., Lévis.
2. *Quebec Gazette*, 5 March 1818.
3. S.B. Foote, *Census of Canada 1860-61* (Quebec, 1864), I, 549; I.B. Taylor, *Census of Canada 1870-71* (Ottawa, 1873), II, 319.
4. George Gale, *Quebec Twixt Old and New* (Quebec, 1915), 67.
5. A rare reference to a sawpit is in the Engagement, Toplay & Blake to Oviatt, 18 May 1812, gr J. Belanger, in which it is agreed that Oviatt will continue to provide a sawpit.
6. R.L. Salaman, *Dictionary of Tools Used in the Woodworking and Allied Trades c. 1700-1970* (London, 1975), 443.
7. Charles Holzapffel, *Turning and Mechanical Manipulation* (London, 1856), 707, cited in Chas. Hanson, "The Pit Saw," *The Museum of the Fur Trade Quarterly*, II no.4 (1975), 1-6.
8. Salaman, *Dictionary*, 426-429, 439-440.
9. Cf., Contract, 5 August 1809, gr T. Lee, in which a pair of sawyers is paid by the day at different rates, and 15 December 1809, for piece work at 5/- per 100 ft. of Pine and 7/- per 100 ft. of Oak; in 10 February 1816, gr Ed. Glackemeyer, a further distinction was made between red Pine at 7/2 and white Pine at 6/8.
10. Caulking contract, 24 June 1811, gr J. Belanger; Sawing contract, 29 January 1814, gr A. Campbell.
11. Specifications for a 430-ton ship built by John Goudie called for a "keel in three pieces," 26 October 1808, gr J. Belanger; those of a 250-ton vessel built by John Bell, a keel "in three pieces or less," 1 August 1818, gr L. McPherson. The former was to be of oak, but the latter allowed elm or oak. Many other specifications called for elm, as in the case of the 1100-ton ship built by Charland and Marquis in 1865, 7 October 1865, gr W.D. Campbell.
12. That the stern-post should be made of one piece was such an accepted fact that it was not even mentioned in contracts. On the other hand, the number of pieces of the stem-post was sometimes stipulated, see 10 July 1786, gr C. Stewart, and 26 October 1808, gr J. Belanger, for instance.
13. Exact numbers are not always given, however, over 250 were sold from the shipyard of the late A. Munn, 19 June 1812, gr A. Campbell; 288 were counted in an inventory of the Lomas and Sewell yard, 15 February 1858, *ibid.*
14. Salaman, *Dictionary*, 31-32, 41-42. The Beatson inventory of 1800 lists augers from 1/2 in. increasing by 1/8ths to 1 1/2 ins. The largest ship built by him measured 645 tons burden. Far larger bolts and consequently larger augers were obviously required for building the 2000-ton ships.
15. *Ibid.*, 133, 143.
16. It is more than likely that spirit levels, which came into use in the eighteenth century (*ibid.*, 260), were also used.
17. The ship carpenter, Joseph Alphonse Auger, cited in "Construction des Navires à Québec," *Revue du Québec Industriel*, V, No. 1, 6.
18. Two separate contracts for caulking the port and starboard sides of a ship in a five week period at £90 and £95 respectively were given by the builder Sam Finch, 24 June 1811, gr J. Belanger; contract at $6 the seam awarded by Peter Campbell, 13 May 1814, gr A. Campbell.
19. For example, in a protest registered against Wm. Lampson, reference is made to the men who were picking oakum in one of his sheds, 27 May 1841, gr A. Campbell.
20. Agreement, Lachance with Jeffery, 12 January 1841, gr J. Hunt.
21. E.g., Joinery contract, Laurencelle with Mure and Joliffe, 28 March 1809, gr J. Belanger; Shipbuilding Agreements, 15 November 1806 and 27 October 1807, gr J. Jones.
22. Frederick William Wallace, *Wooden Ships and Iron Men* (London, 1924), 271.
23. The figurehead of the *Royal Edward* and that of the *Duke of Kent* viz. "une figure ...[du] Duc de Kent en armure avec une renomée," 11 February 1800, Journal de François Baillairgé, ANQ, fall under this category, as compared with the single figure on the ship *London* of 1796, and the head of the *Earl of Moira* of 1803, Water-colour by

Baillairgé, Picture Division, NA.
24. Journal de François Baillairgé, 3 October 1793, 15 March 1796, 11 February 1800, P-398, ANQ.
25. With thanks to Annette Wolff, his great granddaughter, who owns his diaries.
26. Marius Barbeau, "Côté, sculpteur sur bois," (Ottawa, 1942), 3-11.
27. Shipbuilding contract, Marquis with Spaight, 16 February 1878, gr W.D. Campbell.
28. *Men, Ships, and the Sea*, (Washington, D.C., 1962) 198-199.
29. 6 October 1809, gr J. Belanger.
30. 26 September and 7 November 1811, gr J. Belanger.
31. Specifications for the ship *Oliver Cromwell* built by Charland and Marquis, 7 October 1865, gr W.D. Campbell.
32. M.V. Brewington, *Shipcarvers of North America* (Barre, Mass., 1962), 98-100.
33. Contract, Hadden with Clint, 29 March 1824, gr A. Campbell.
34. Described as caulkers' work in the specifications for construction, forming part of contract, Black with Halifax Steam Navigation Association, 3 September 1830, gr L. McPherson.
35. *Quebec Mercury*, 20 May 1854; Contract, Cotnam with Von Rittern, 11 January 1876, gr S. Glackemeyer.
36. "Goudronné comme ordinaire à Québec." Contract, Valin with Fabre, 23 May 1867, gr S. Glackemeyer.
37. Protest, Jeffery to Roy, 29 May 1840, gr J. Bignell.
38. Indenture, 7 November 1826, gr L. McPherson.
39. *Admiralty Manual of Seamanship* (London, 1937), I, 118, 120.
40. Lignum Vitae, a native of tropical America and Australia, was sold by weight. Four tons are listed in the blockmaker Patrick Baldwin's inventory, 29 January 1833. There is evidence of its use also during the French Regime, for example in the contract, 4 May 1730, and in the early days of the British Regime, contract, 1 March 1764, gr Louet. In both cases it is the wood of which the sheaves were to be made.
41. A detailed account of how the deadeye was made in Lunenburg, Nova Scotia, is given in John Kochiss, *The Deadeye* (Mystic, Conn., n.d.).
42. Westcott Abel, *The Shipwright's Trade*, (Cambridge, 1948), 113.
43. Inventory, 29 January 1833, gr A. Campbell.
44. Contract, 16 October 1844, gr J. Hossack.
45. Contract, 18 December 1844, gr J. Hossack.
46. A large number of early nineteenth-century contracts for spar wood from these areas are to be found in the gr of Jean Belanger, see for example, 31 April and 28 September 1807, also 14 July and 15 October 1808. These were mostly for red or Norway pine. A large number of white pine masts were also exported, as well as spruce spars in fifty to sixty foot sizes.
47. See, for example 18 April 1897 and 18 April 1808, gr J. Belanger.
48. A typical list of prices is given in the contract of 29 October 1807, gr J. Belanger.
49. See inventory, 11 December 1848, gr A. Campbell.
50. Apprenticeship, Pounder to Munn, 22 May 1827, gr A. Campbell.
51. J.G. Ross, "Unpublished Journals, 1869 and 1874."
52. Contract, Uppington with Campbell, 23 January 1819, gr A. Campbell.
53. Talon to Colbert, 13 November 1666, *RAPQ* (1930-1931), 54-62; Jacques Mathieu, *La construction navale royale à Québec 1739-1759* (Québec, 1971), 74-75.
54. *Quebec Gazette*, 16 and 23 May 1765; *Journal de Québec*, 17 April 1866, which also cites an article in the *Gazette des Campagnes*. According to James McPherson Lemoine *Maple Leaves*, *VII* (Québec, 1906), 80, John Caldwell, President of the Society of Agriculture urged the sowing of hemp to compete with foreign competition at a meeting of the Society in 1789.
55. See, for example, 18 April 1765, 15 June 1786 and 4 August 1856, *Quebec Gazette*.
56. Alexis de Barbezieux, Rév. père, *Histoire de Limoilou* (Quebec, 1921).

57. See article on the culture of hemp, *Journal de Québec*, 17 April 1866.
58. The following broad outline of rope-making is based on descriptions of the trade in *Diderot's Encyclopaedia*; John E. Horsley, *Tools of the Maritime Trades* (Newton Abbot, 1978); and D. Wilson, "Government Dockyard Workers in Portsmouth 1793-1815," Ph.D. thesis, University of Warwick, 1975, all of which describe similar methods of rope-making in the eighteenth and nineteenth centuries. The manner in which mechanization affected the Quebec rope-walks during the nineteenth century is under study.
59. Compare apprenticeship indentures, Lapointe with Dalkin, 20 March 1825, gr A. Campbell; Walsh with Brown, 17 April 1862, gr J. Clapham; Jobin with Dalkin, 11 November 1827, gr A. Campbell.
60. Specified, for instance, for the ship *Oliver Cromwell*. Contract, Charland and Marquis with Wilson, 7 October 1865, gr W.D. Campbell.
61. Pickersgill, Tibbit & Co. account with James Hunt, 8 March 1847, Pickersgill, Tibbits & Co. papers, P-202-4, ANQ.
62. See contracts, 3 July 1857, gr J. Hossack; 25 March 1809, gr T. Lee.
63. See indentures, 15 June 1809, gr T. Lee; 29 November 1824 and 27 December 1845, gr A. Campbell; 24 March 1859, gr Fisher Langlois. See also A.J.H. Richardson, "Hunt, James," *DCB*, VII, 425-27.
64. Mark Hirsch, "The Federation of Sailmakers of Great Britain and Ireland 1889-1922: A craft union in crisis. M.A. thesis. University of Warwick, 1976, 12-17.
65. Hirsch, 72.
66. *L'Evénement*, 4 January 1871; *Census of Canada 1891*, III, 280.
67. The master rigger John Richardson, for example, was sent to William Henry with two men to rig a new vessel, 11 June 1811, gr J. Voyer; Anthony Green, rigger, contracted to rig a ship building at Sorel, 12 February 1846, gr J. Hossack, and hired four seamen and a rigger to help him, 3 March 1846, *ibid.*
68. Letter Alex Tough & Son to Thomas S. Pickersgill & Co., Glasgow, 1 April 1847, Pickersgill, Tibbits & Co. papers, P-202-4, ANQ.
69. Contracts, sixteen labourers, axe-men or borers and Anderson, 15 and 16 May 1810, gr J. Voyer; various with government, 22 June 1813, gr J. Belanger; various with Carman, 21 July 1825, gr L. McPherson; Protest, Pelchat and Mercier, 17 July 1854, gr J. Clapham.
70. Agreement, Denoyers and Derome with Bell, 10 January 1811, and Connor, *et al.*, with Pacaud, 4 June 1811, gr J. Belanger; Derome, *et al.*, with Parker, 29 December 1815, *ibid.*; Taylor with Cardinal and Bowman, 30 November 1818, gr J. Belanger.
71. Contract Baldwin & Dinning with Yeo, 13 August 1855, gr O.F.Campeau.
72. Narcisse Rosa, *La construction des navires à Québec et ses environs* (Québec, 1897), 7

CHAPTER 9
Ships

The way in which ships were designated changed through the centuries – sometimes the shape of their hull gave them their name, sometimes the work they did,[1] – but from the end of the eighteenth century large sailing vessels were generally classed according to their rig and were considered to be in one of two broad categories. Those whose main driving sails were set from yards that lay square to the mast were known as "square-rigged" vessels, while those in which they were set by their luffs on masts or stays were described as "schooner-" or "fore-and-aft" rigged, see Figures 209 and 210. Square-rigged vessels were practical for ocean voyages across open seas, where full advantage could be taken of their huge sails, though they required a numerous crew to go aloft and set or trim them. Well handled, they were more manoeuvrable than a fore and after, being able to box around and sail backwards, known as boxhauling. The advantages of the fore and afters, on the other hand, were their handiness, crew size and gear economy. But whether wholly or partly fore-and-aft rigged, their size was limited because of the difficulty of handling an excessively large gaff sail until towards the end of the nineteenth century, when the donkey engine took the hard work out of setting the gaff and larger schooners, such as the Canadian *Bluenose*, came into their own.

Square-rigged vessels built at Quebec comprised ships, barques and barquentines, with three or more masts, and brigs, brigantines and snows, with two. Ships, sometimes referred to as "fully-rigged ships," were square-rigged on all their masts; barques on all but their aftermost mast; and barquentines only on their foremast. Brigs were square-rigged on both masts; brigantines on their foremast only; while snows were rigged similarly to brigs, but had an extra, small trysail mast immediately abaft the mainmast. (Figure 209) In addition, two very large vessels were launched from the Isle of Orleans in 1824 and 25 respectively, the 3690 ton *Columbus* and the 5294 ton *Baron of Renfrew*, which were rigged with three masts and a jigger or try-sail mast. They were officially registered as four-masted ships, although later they were generally referred to as four-masted barques, or more popularly, as the "large timber droghers."[2] The fore-and-aft vessels were mostly two-masted schooners, though a few had three masts, and there were also three large single-masted sloops. (Figure 210)

Quebec's specialty was undoubtedly the square-rigged vessel, which made up ninety-six percent of her production, or sixteen hundred and twenty-three vessels. Of those with three masts, nine hundred and two were fully-rigged ships,[3] four hundred and ninety-four were barques and three were barquentines. The fewer two-masted vessels comprised one hundred and

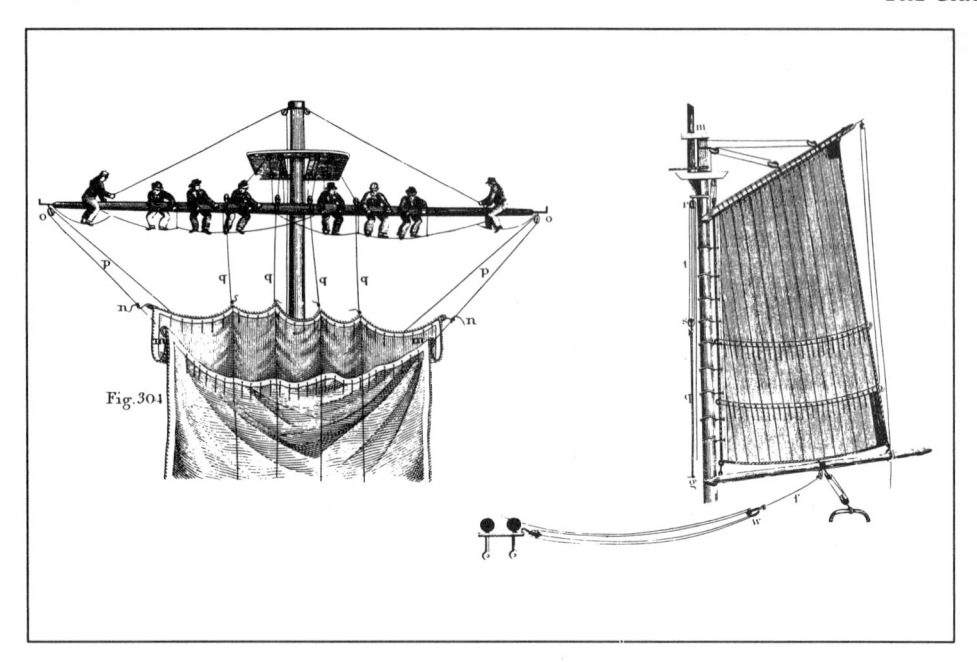

Figure 208: *Square Rig and Fore-and-Aft or Schooner Rig. The first requires a numerous crew to go aloft and set the sails; the second is handled from the deck. From Darcy Lever,* The Young Sea Officer's Sheet Anchor.

thirty-three brigs, sixty-eight brigantines and twenty-one snows. The timber droghers *Columbus* and *Baron of Renfrew* account for the other two, see Table 10.

Over the years, the changing demands of the shipping trade combined with improvements in vessel design changed the preference for one or the other rig (as shown in Table 11). From 1765 to 1804 for instance, a little over half the output of the Quebec yards consisted in quality fully-rigged ships built of oak, ordered by British merchants; the rest consisted of far smaller two-masted vessels of various rig intended in most cases for the Newfoundland or West Indies trade. During the period 1805 to 1846,[4] the barque took the place not only of the snow, but also to a certain extent of the brig, offering a larger hull with more carrying capacity for little difference in the work required to sail it. The first barque was built in 1819, and the last snow eight years later, in 1827. The ever increasing need for vessels to carry both passengers and freight over long distances, which was intensified by the Californian and Australian Gold Rushes, and then by the Crimean War, kept the demand for the large fully-rigged ship at about two thirds of Quebec production throughout the period 1847 to 65. Barques, which were still much smaller, represented roughly a quarter. From 1855 on ship design responded to the new measurement system, and quality to the presence of the Lloyd's Surveyor at Quebec, as well as to the general maturity of the industry. "The years 1850 to 1865 were," in fact, "the heyday of the wooden square-rigged merchant sailing ship.... Especially if she was built at comparatively low cost in labour and materials in Canada, she represented by far the cheapest way of carrying goods at sea."[5] But the metal-hulled ship was

Ships

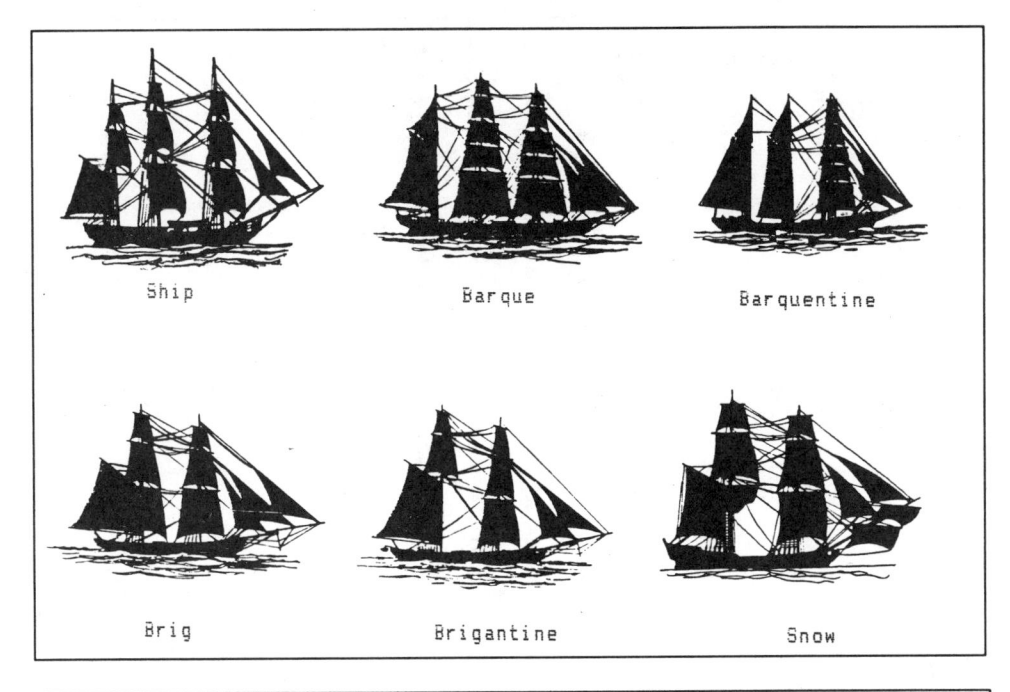

Figure 209: *Square-Rigged Vessels*

Figure 210: *Fore-and-Aft or Schooner-Rigged Vessels*
Note: *Figures 209 and 210 depict the rigs of different types of vessel. They do not illustrate their relative size, and do not necessarily have the lines of typical Quebec-built vessels.*

Table 10
Annual Production, 1787-1893

Year	Sh	Ba	Bn	Br	Be	Sn	Sc	Sl	Dr	Total	Year	Sh	Ba	Bn	Br	Be	Sn	Sc	Sl	Total
1787	1									1	1838	7	6		2	1				16
1790	1				1					2	1839	12	11		2			1		26
1791					1					1	1840	21	14		3			2		40
1792	1									1	1841	21	14					2		37
1793	1				1					2	1842	6	10		2			2		20
1794	1			1						2	1843	9	5		1			1		16
1795	1			1	1					3	1844	8	9					1		18
1796	2					1				3	1845	16	14		1			1		32
1797	4					1				5	1846	14	9							23
1798	1			1	1					3	1847	23	19		1	1				44
1799	6					1				7	1848	12	11			3				26
1800	8				1					9	1849	17	9		1					27
1801	5				1	1				7	1850	26	4			1		1		32
1802	4				2		2			8	1851	30	6		1	1		4		42
1803	3			3	3	1	2	1		13	1852	20	2		1			1		24
1804	3			1	1		2			7	1853	35	5					4		44
1805	2			1		1	1			5	1854	35	2			2		1		40
1806	3						1			4	1855	19	3					3		25
1807	3			1	1		1			6	1856	28	8		1	1		2		40
1808	6					1				7	1857	36	7		4					47
1809	3			3		1	2			9	1858	17	3		1					21
1810	8			5						13	1859	9	2		5	2				18
1811	14			3						17	1860	20	3		1	1				25
1812	3				1					4	1861	21	6		2					29
1813	3			1						4	1862	15	11							26
1814	4			1						5	1863	34	20			1				55
1815				3		1				4	1864	38	17							55
1816	2			1						3	1865	23	17		1	2				43
1817					1					1	1866	13	25			7		2		47
1818				2	1					3	1867	8	8	1	1	7				25
1819	3	2		2						7	1868	9	17		3	1				30
1820	1	1		1		2				5	1869	11	16		1	1				29
1821	1			1	2					4	1870	4	14		1			1		20
1822	3	1		1		1				6	1871	1	10					1		12
1823	2	1		3	1		1			8	1872	7	5			5		1	1	19
1824	1	7		4	1	1		1		15	1873	6	8					1		15
1825	11	18		8	1	2	1		1	42	1874	7	4							11
1826	16	10		10		4	1			41	1875	7	7		1					15
1827	3	3		9	3	1	2			21	1876	8	9							17
1828	7	2		6	2		4			21	1877	8	10	1						19
1829	8	1		6	1					16	1878	4	4							8
1830	5			4		2				11	1879	3	2							5
1831		3		1						4	1880	4	1							5
1832	2	3		4	1					10	1881		1					1		2
1833	3	5		1						9	1882	1	2							3
1834	10	3		2			1			16	1883		2					1		3
1835	7	3		2		1				13	1884					1				1
1836	10	3		2						15	1885		2							2
1837	6	8		1						15	1893				1					1

Source: Quebec Shipping Registers, Vols. 183-98, 202-203, 267-71, 375-78, NA.

Note: These figures for the Port of Quebec are a count by rig of the vessels listed in Appendix B.

Abbreviations:
- Sh Ship
- Ba Barque
- Bn Barquentine
- Dr Drogher
- Br Brig
- Be Brigantine
- Sn Snow
- Sc Schooner
- Sl Sloop

Table 11
Percentage of Total Production, Number and Average Tonnage, by Rig, 1765-1893

	sh	ba	bn	br	be	sn	sc	sl	all
	57%			12%	15%	8%	7%		
1765-	51			11	14	7	6	1	90
1804	296			121	143	164	130	115	229
	41%	19%		25%	5%	4%	6%		
1805-	139	65		84	16	14	20	1	339
1835	403	398		212	160	222	137	145	346
	50%	40%		6%		2	4%		
1836-	132	106		16	2	108	10		266
1846	736	596		228	108		163		624
	69%	22%		1%	3%		4%		
1847-	207	65		4	10		12		296
1854	1061	639		218	141		196		891
	63%	29%		3%	3%		2%		
1855-	287	132		15	16		7		457
1866	1036	493		216	198		161		808
	36%	51%	1%	1%	6%		6%		
1867-	88	128	3	3	11		14	1	245
1893	1252	694	359	341	214		192	111	835
	53%	29%		8%	4%	1%	4%		
1765-	904	496	3	133	69	21	69	3	1698
1893	879	573	359	210	169	204	164	124	675

Source: Quebec Shipping Registers, Vols. 183-98, 202-3, 67-71, 375-78, NA.

Note: Figures include all vessels in Appendix B except the two large droghers, *Columbus* and *Baron of Renfrew* of 1824 and 25 and three vessels of unknown rig, fifty-four vessels built at Pointe-aux-Trembles, eight at Saint Patrick's Hole, Isle of Orleans, and five built on the Saguenay river and completed at Quebec.

One snow of unknown tonnage included in count but not in averaging; one vessel of unknown rig included in general average.

Table 13
Tonnage of Largest Vessels Built 1787-1893 and Name of Builder

Year	Tons	Shipbuilder	Year	Tons	Shipbuilder	Year	Tons	Shipbuilder
1787	205	Duncanson, Jas	1822	325	Munn, J.	1855	2030	Parke, A. & Wm.
1790	204	King, Wm?	1823	321	Bell, J.	1856	1502	Parke, G.H.
1791	122	Black & King	1824	380	Finch, S.	1857	1558	Parke, G.H.
1792	316	Black, J.	1825	443	Jeffery, J.	1858	1230	Cotnam, Wm
1793	204	(unknown)	1826	479	Jeffery, J.	1859	1236	Dinning, H.
1794	371	Beatson, P.	1827	402	(unknown)	1860	1351	Baldwin, Wm
1795	497	Beatson, P.	1828	560	Black, Geo	1861	1305	Baldwin, W.H. & Co
1796	242	Munn, A.	1829	568	Black, Geo	1862	1752	Baldwin, W.H. & Co
1797	363	Beatson, P.	1830	443	Munn, J.	1863	1673	Valin, T.
1798	253	Beatson, P.	1831	588	Gilmour	1864	1806	Valin, P.
1799	521	Beatson, P.	1832	671	Black, Geo	1865	1444	Gingras, J.E.
1800	646	Beatson, P.	1833	659	Gilmour	1866	1303	Samson, I. & J.
1801	554	Baldwin, H.	1834	668	Gilmour	1867	1435	Gingras, J.E.
1802	561	Beatson - Baldwin	1835	707	Jeffery & Jeffery	1868	1496	Gingras, J.E.
1803	310	Baldwin, H.	1836	855	Black, Geo	1869	1747	Gingras, J.E.
1804	349	Baldwin, H.	1837	993	Munn, J.	1870	1812	Samson, I. & J.
1805	307	Munn, A.	1838	940	Baldwin, Wm	1871	1242	Baldwin, Wm
1806	419	Goudie, J.	1839	1267	Munn, J.	1872	1664	Gingras, J.E.
1807	426	Goudie, J.	1840	989	Jeffery, J.	1873	1823	Gingras, J.E.
1808	579	Munn, J. sr	1841	976	Gilmour	1874	1528	Dunn & Samson
1809	473	Goudie, J.	1842	864	Chartier, Ol	1875	1515	Oliver, J.L.
1810	575	Hooker, Phil	1843	1153	Gilmour	1876	1537	Gingras, J.E.
1811	720	Anderson - Brown	1844	1096	Munn, J.	1877	1443	Valin, P.
1812	471	Hamilton	1845	1175	Jeffery, J.	1878	1338	Gingras, J.E.
1813	421	Munn & Munn	1846	1281	Jeffery, J. & Sn	1879	1465	Samson, I. & Co.
1814	408	Labbé, Ls	1847	1230	Gilmour	1880	1384	Valin, P.
1815	207	Munn, J.	1848	1161	Oliver, T.H.	1881	792	Baldwin, P.
1816	438	Taylor, Geo?	1849	1504	Parke - Brunelle	1882	1303	Samson, Et
1817	270	Bell, J.	1850	1241	Munn, J.	1883	1301	Charland, Wm sr
1818	212	Trahan & Viger	1851	1404	Parke - Brunelle	1885	1307	Charland, Wm sr
1819	385	Taylor, Geo	1852	1757	Valin, P.	1893	396	Charland, Wm sr
1820	335	Goudie, J.	1853	2003	Parke - Brunelle			
1821	271	Black, Geo	1854	2081	Jobin, Chas			

Source: Quebec Shipping Registers, Vols. 183-98, 202-203, 267-71, 375-78, NA.

Note: Charles Wood's two timber droghers of 1824 and 1825 are not taken into consideration.

Table 12
Production of Liverpool, Bath and West Bath, Maine, St. John, N.B. and Quebec Shipyards 1815-35

	Tons						
	100-200	200-300	300-400	400-500	500-600	600-700	800-900
Liverpool	51	48	34	10	3	2	
Bath and West Bath	82	55	32	18	5		
Saint John	20	26	41	24	24	13	1
Quebec	53	65	80	31	10	8	

Sources: Francis E. Hyde, *Liverpool and the Mersey: An Economic History of a Port 1700-1970*, 39; William Avery Baker, *A Maritime History of Bath, Maine, and the Kennebec Region*, 2:820-6; Esther Clark Wright, *Saint John Ships and Their History*, 173-6.

Table 14
Production of Quebec, Saint John and Bath, Maine, Shipyards 1839-1885

	Quebec			Saint John*			Bath, Maine**		
	1000-1499t	1500-1999	over 2000	1000-1499	1500-1999	over 2000	1000-1499	1500-1999	over 2000
1839		1			1				
1840				1					
1841				2			1		
1842									
1843	3								
1844	2								
1845	5			2					
1846	5			1					
1847	7			3	1				
1848	5			1					
1849	7	1		2			1		
1850	10			2			1		
1851	20			11	2		1		
1852	9	2		12			5	1	
1853	26	4	1	24	1		11	1	
1854	20	3	1	18	2	1	19	1	
1855	13		1	7	2	1	8		
1856	11	1		17			10		
1857	9	1		14	1		4		
1858	6			6			4		
1859	5			9	2		3		
1860	8			8	3		5		
1861	8			10	2		1		
1862	12			16			3		
1863	26	2		27			8		
1864	22	3		19	3		7		
1865	18			14			7		
1866	10			10			7		
1867	8			7			4		
1868	6			6			10		
1869	8	1		6			7	2	
1870	2	1		4			1	1	
1871	1			4			3	1	
1872	5	2		6	1		2		
1873	3	3		8	1		6	3	
1874	6	1		11	3		11	5	
1875	6	1		3	4		9	3	
1876	5	1		4	4		8	5	
1877	11			4	3		8	8	
1878	6			3	1		3	4	
1879	3			6				3	
1880	4			4				2	
1881				4	1		2	6	3
1882	3			3	1		4	5	2
1883	2			3	2			6	5
1884				3					3
1885	2			1	1		3	1	*2

*Esther Clark Wright, *Saint John Ships and Their Builders.*
**William Baker, *A Maritime History of Bath, Maine, and the Kennebec River Region.*

looming larger and larger on the horizon and gradually winning over the shipowners, and in the final period, 1866 to 93, the drop in the proportion of fully-rigged ships built at Quebec is eloquent of the fact that shipowners were turning more and more to composite or metal hulls for the cream of their fleets.

Although two-masted square-rigged vessels were relatively common and accounted for thirty-five percent of the production of the shipyards from 1765 to 1804, (see Table 11), the proportion dropped to as little as six percent between 1836 and 1846 as a result of the introduction of the barque, despite the fact that the cut-off figure for tonnage between two and three-masted vessels was then considerably higher. It dropped a further two per cent between 1847 and 1866, and made only a slight comeback from 1867 on.

Schooner-rigged vessels never made up more than seven per cent of the total, with a low of two per cent in the days of greatest output of tonnage between 1855 and 1866. The Quebec yards were geared to the construction of large square-rigged vessels for exportation, and only an occasional small vessel was built there to use up the light timber, (see Table 10). Among the schooners that were built at Quebec, were several special purpose vessels, such as floating lightships, pilot

Ships

Figure 211: *The Government Revenue schooner* La Canadienne, *101 tons, built for the public Works Department by Thomas H. Oliver in 1855. Engraved by W. Scheuer.* L'Opinion Publique, *13 May 1875.*

Figure 212: *Crew of* La Canadienne. *Photo courtesy Archives Naionales du Québec, 120.6.*

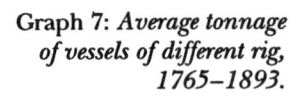

Graph 7: *Average tonnage of vessels of different rig, 1765–1893.*

Source: Quebec Shipping Registers, *183–98, 202–3, 267–71, 375–78, RG12, NA.*

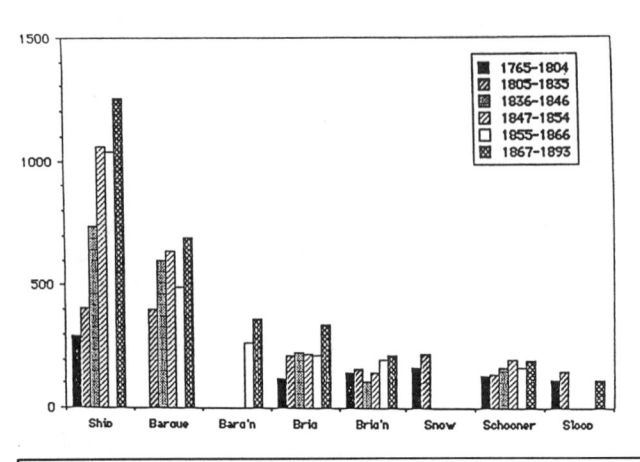

schooners, Trinity House yachts and some such as the *Saint Lawrence* of 1807, the *Gulnare* of 1852 and *La Belle Canadienne* of 1855 built for government service. Generally speaking, however, the yards in the outports and other communities supplied the domestic demand for smaller craft.

By the beginning of the nineteenth century, the average tonnage of Quebec-built ships was already relatively high. While Quebec built more three to four hundred ton vessels between 1815 and 1835 than any other size, Liverpool, for example, was mostly building

Table 15
Average Length, Breadth, and Ratio of Length to Breadth, by Rig, 1765-1893

	Ship	Barque	Barq'n	Brig	Brig'n	Snow	Schooner	Sloop
1765-	100			68	73	78	68	64
1804	27			21	22	21	21	21
	3.7			3.25	3.3	3.68	3.24	3.0
1805-	110	109		84	75	87	73	71
1835	28.5	28.1		23.7	21.8	23.9	20.7	22
	3.86	3.88		3.54	3.4	3.6	3.52	3.22
1836-	131	120		86	62		87	
1846	28.6	27		21.6	18.5		19.4	
	4.58	4.44		3.98	3.35		4.48	
1847-	164	130		87	84		102	
1854	31.1	27		22.5	20.5		21	
	5.27	4.8		3.87	4.1		4.86	
1855-	179	137	114	100	98		100	
1866	35.1	28.6	27	23.8	24.1		24	
	5.1	4.8	4.2	4.19	4.14		4.17	
1867-	196	155	140	128	101		109	96
1893	37.8	32.2	27	29	24.9		25.6	23
	5.18	4.8	5.18	4.41	4.06		4.26	4.17

Source: Quebec Shipping Registers, Vols. 183-98, 03, 267-71, 375-8, NA.

Note: Length and breadth in feet.

ships of one to two hundred tons. (See Table 12) As vessels became bigger and bigger, so the proportion of large vessels built at Quebec increased and by 1854 the average Quebec vessel measured a full one thousand tons. This spectacular increase was entirely due to the growth of the fully-rigged ship, which was far greater than that of all the other rigs and climaxed in the mid-fifties with the construction of three that each measured over two thousand tons, (see Table 13). But the fact that no others vessels of that size were subsequently laid down is a comment on the disfavour with which such large wooden hulls were received. By far the most popular sized large ship, as evidenced by their construction not only at Quebec but at other Ports such as Saint John, New Brunswick and Bath, Maine, were those that measured between 1000 and 1500 tons. Of these Quebec built no fewer than three hundred and forty-nine, (see Table 14). And, although there were also three barques of between one thousand and twelve hundred tons built in the forties, they proved impractical, and twenty-six years then elapsed before the donkey engine allowed the next one to be laid down in 1875. Similarly, in Saint John, New Brunswick, one was built in 1856, and no others until 1874.

The method of measurement for registration purposes was radically altered in the mid-nineteenth century, putting an end to the construction of overly deep hulls as a way to profit from the weakness in the measurement system, and thus paving the way to better hull design. The increase in ratio of length to breadth of the larger ships, particularly the fully-rigged ships and brigs, through the nineteenth century can be seen in Table 15. The real change in depth, however, that is to say the relative depth, was downward rather than upward. This, accompanied by the increase in length from just over four times the breadth to a little over five times, and occasionally six times, the breadth in the case of a ship, culminated in the long shallow hull of the clipper ship, no extreme clippers of greater ratio having been built at Quebec. In the 40s a ship that was one hundred and sixty foot long was frequently twenty-four foot deep, but in the 60s, it was no more than eighteen to twenty-one.

A full ninety-four per cent of the vessels built in Quebec were simple box like containers with a single deck, see the midship section of the barque *Secret*, Figure 225, p. 340, well suited for carrying their initial cargo of timber. Of these, just under forty per cent had an additional partial deck with or without some kind of deck house or deck houses that was variously described in the register as a half-deck, half-deck plus poop, poop, quarter-deck, forecastle, break deck or anchor deck, or a combination of them. However, none of these terms occur in significant numbers, except for the half-deck and the poop. A half deck was noted in the majority of single-decked vessels built between 1799 and 1836, after which the term is not found again in the register, with one exception in 1868, but this seems to be due to changes in registration procedure rather than its actual disappearance, as half decks are mentioned in many shipbuilding contracts made after that time. Use of the term ''poop'' is concentrated in the period 1832 to 1854, after which it too disappears, with one exception in 1868. And finally, almost all single-decked vessels built from 1873 onwards were fitted with a second row of beams, which acted as a strengthener, but were not covered with a deck at Quebec.

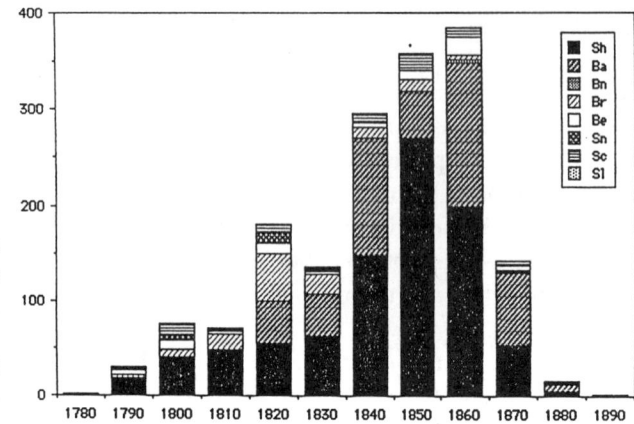

Graph 8: *Production 1780–1890 by decade and rig.*

Source: Quebec Shipping Registers, *183-98, 202-3, 267–71, 375–71, 375–78 RG12, NA.*

The ninety-six vessels with two decks, included four, which though described as single-decked on their certificates had also either a spar deck, which was a deck of lighter construction, or an awning deck, that was lighter still. One third of them were built before 1808, the Beatson shipyard alone accounting for eleven or twelve. After that there were no more until 1827, and from then on they were laid down sporadically in small numbers at certain times, except through the years 1839 to 1853 when there were none. They appear mostly to have responded to sudden specific demands. Those of the years 1836 to 1838, for instance, were destined in many cases for the emigrant trade; those of 1852 to 1854, for the expected government need for transports during the Crimean War. The fifteen that were built at that time included Quebec's three largest vessels of over 2000 tons, and four others with beams in place for a third deck. And finally in the late 60s and 70s there was a flurry of two-decked barques for French owners.

According to the registries, three-decked ships were extremely rare, and only three were registered over the entire period, Patrick Beatson's 497 ton ship *Queen* in 1795, and the 1563 ton ship *Saldanha* and 1527 ton *Norwood*, built by J.J. Nesbitt and William Cotnam respectively, in 1853,[6] though plans of W.H. Baldwin's *Eastern Empire* of 1862 and P.V. Valin's *Indian Chief* of 1864 indicate that both had three rows of beams.

Most of the plans that have come to light are midship section plans of vessels with either one deck and a row of beams for another, like the 611 ton barque *Leonard Dobbin* of 1837, or just one deck, like the 416 ton barque *Secret* of 1867.[7] They are found mostly attached to Lloyd's Surveyors' Reports, but there are a few in notarial files. Because nearly all are of vessels built in the 1860s and 70s, many are similar, but among them are the plans of Baldwin's *Lady Hincks* and Dinning's *Guinevere*, which differ considerably from the others in that they both had iron beams and stanchions, and in the case of the *Guinevere*, a diagonally planked ceiling to compensate for the lack of the customary iron strapping on the outside.

Deck plans are more rare and perhaps this is explained by the Liverpool shipowner Holderness' reply, when he was asked as a witness into the loss of the ship *Annie Jane* whether he had a plan of the deck arrangement. "We have not," he said. "Very fortunately, the sister ship, that was built at the same time, of the same dimensions within a few inches, and in all respects the same except that the class is for one year less grade, is in the Liverpool docks now . . . ; and she will give you the best idea of the *Annie Jane*."[8]

However, the arrangement of deck-houses of ships built at Quebec in later years can be seen in a number of photographs and drawings, including some

Figure 213: *The 859 ton ship* Lord Elgin *built by John J. Nesbitt in 1847, and named after the Governor General, the Earl of Elgin. The* Lord Elgin *had the typical chunky bow, square stern and huge topsails of the period. Oil painting by S.D. Skillett, photo by John Mills, courtesy National Museums and Galleries on Merseyside. Neg 27863A*

pen and ink drawings by Henry Fry,[9] and there is also information about deck houses in specifications in building contracts. Specifications in a contract between Edward Oliver and Henry Brooke of Dublin for the 869 ton barque *Lucinda* of 1840, for instance, required that the half Deck reach to "about the after part of the Mizen hatch." Another for the 900 ton ship *Elizabeth Yeo*, that was built by Baldwin and Dinning for Yeo in 1855, called for a "Poop, Forehouse about 30 foot long and half forecastle." In 1866, when Charland and Marquis built the *Oliver Cromwell* for Robert Wilson it was to have "a house and halfdeck, rail round the house instead of a poop & a monkey forecastle say four feet high & a deck house twenty feet by eighteen feet for the crew & cook house; & well fitted up."[10]

Generally speaking, the captain and the mate's quarters were in the stern of the vessel, while the crew was housed forward. The galley was somewhere between. Accommodation for passengers varied. On the *Annie Jane*, an emigrant ship, they were all over the ship –"passengers were on the main deck, half of the lower deck from the foremast forward, on the lower deck, in the poop, and in the house on the main deck."[11] Quebec shipbuilders were very often not responsible for building passenger accommodation, and certainly not the temporary accommodation set up for emigrants in the steerage.

Although the man at the wheel was often at the mercy of the elements and was very often lashed to the wheel in a storm, he was sometimes able to enjoy the relative comfort of a wheelhouse. We find, for instance in the specifications for a 980 ton barque built by William Cotnam for Gildermeister of Bremen that he was to build "from the height of the Rails a Quarter deck 14 to 15 feet long fourteen to fifteen feet long with a Wheel House on the top finished inside with lockers and a water closet; extending further forward, to Build a Round top house 27 feet long the width of the Vessel with Cabin finished according to Captns dictation; from thence forward a half deck of about 10 feet ten feet under which to have two Oak tanks one on each side to contain about 600 six hundred gallons of water each tank with Copper pump and fixings attached. The house on Deck for the Crew [was] to be about 24 feet long twenty four feet long about 16 sixteen feet in Breadth with Births [sic] &c for twelve Men and Galley with Coat Lockers &c attached."[12]

With regard to the lines of vessels, in general the shape of the bow and the stern followed the British trend. In the early days they were bluff-bowed, full-bodied and deep, carrying space being the main consideration. With the advent of the packet ship, speed became important and the lengthening of the hull was accompanied by a whittling down of the chunky bow. However, Quebec shipyards did not pursue this change to the extreme, many of their ships being described as medium-built.

As the bow changed, so did the stern. The square stern, de rigueur in merchantmen at the beginning of the century, was present long after the circular or elliptical stern had been adopted by the British Navy in 1817, even though the advantages of the circular stern were realized and many of them applied equally to merchant and fighting ships. They were listed in an article in the *Quebec Mercury*, in 1823: the method of construction of the circular stern added to the strength of the ship, it offered protection to those stationed on it both from the sea striking the stern and from the shot of the enemy, more angles could be covered for either defence or attack, and the removal of the galleries increased the sailing qualities of the vessel. The writer also noted that circular sterns had not been incorporated in any of the United States Naval vessels, with the exception of one that was under construction. But the conservatism of shipowners and shipbuilders was such, that it was not until 1849, an incredible thirty-two years after the Navy had adopted them, that the first two circular-sterned vessels were built at Quebec, both by Allan Gilmour, and even then they were only slowly accepted, square sterns predominating until 1860. In 1861 the balance finally tipped when twenty-one out of the year's production of thirty vessels were built with round or elliptical sterns. By 1870 it was rare for a square-sterned vessels to be laid down. In Figure 214 the deck plan of the 1187 ton ship *City of Montreal* of 1863 is contrasted with a plan drawn by Alexander Munn of a vessel of 1797, and shows not only the difference in the ratio of the measurements of length and breadth, but the tremendous change in the bow and the stern, the bow of the earlier vessel being even blunter than the stern of the later one, which is itself in sharp contrast to the earlier square stern.

We now the leave the hull and take a look at the remarkable and highly organized collection of sails that sailing ships carried to catch the wind and drive them forward. Their order evolved gradually, adopting an idea for an improvement here and another there. Over a considerable period the square sails on the masts and the "spritsail" under the bowsprit had furnished all the driving power. Then, at the beginning of the seventeenth century, a "sprit topsail" set on a mast at the fore end of the bowsprit was added, but it disappeared at the beginning of the eighteenth. The spritsail itself served for another hundred years and more, however, and was undoubtedly carried by many Quebec ships of the time.

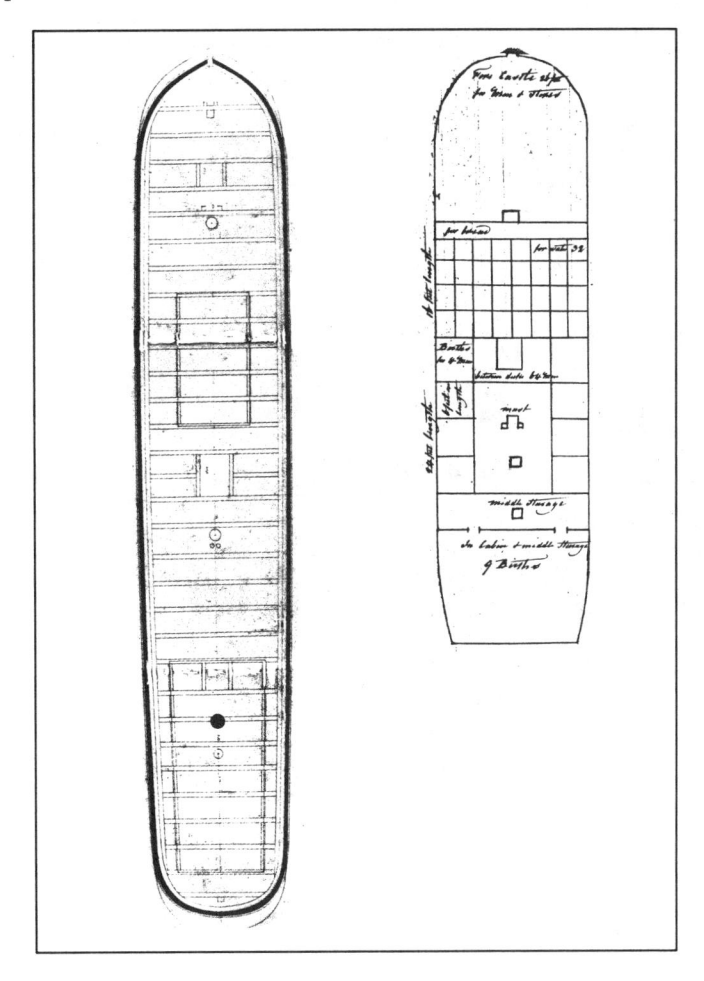

Figure 214: *Deck arrangements of vessels of 1797 and of 1862, showing the changes that took place in both the shape of the bow and stern and in their proportions.*

Figure 215: *The fully-rigged ship* Ocean Monarch, *1832 tons, of 1854. Built by Baldwin and Dinning and said to have been sold for the record figure of fifty-three dollars per ton. Drawn by Feedon. Engraving Illustrated London News, 13 October 1855.*

In the early sixteenth century only two square sails had been set on a mast, the "course," and the "topsail." By the middle of the century a third, the "topgallant," had appeared, and by 1780 a fourth, the "royal," was added. From 1815 on more extreme vessels carried "skysails," topping them sometimes with "moonsails."

In the first half of the nineteenth century the great increase in the size of sailing ship hulls led to such large unmanageable topsails that in 1841 Robert Forbes, an American captain, began experimenting to find a way to use two sails, an "upper" and a "lower" topsail, instead. He himself did not satisfactorily solve the rigging problem presented by the two sails, and it was left to another American, Captain Howes, to do so in 1854. While a large topsail can be seen in engravings of the *Ocean Monarch* of 1854, figure 215 a double topsail is apparent in most photographs of Quebec-built ships. The double topgallant, the logical next development, made its appearance in the 1870s. In light winds vessels might use extra canvas including light "studding" or "stunsails," whose yards hung below moveable extensions at each end of the yards. The barque *Montezuma* of 1845, for instance, was fitted with two top and two lower studding sails, and an unidentified vessel built for Gustavus Poppe of Bremen by T.C. Lee in 1855 had six.[13] In 1865, the ship *Moderation* and the barque *Taranaki*, T.C. Lee's last two vessels, were provided with three each.[14] Generally speaking, however, though the vessels were equipped with studding sail yards, the sails themselves were more likely to be purchased in Britain.

The rest of the ship's canvas was made up of fore-and-aft sails: triangular "headsails" or "jibs" over the bowsprit and triangular, though occasionally four-sided, "staysails" between the masts. Though small craft had set them earlier, staysails were not set on large vessels until around 1670, but once there, their usefulness was recognized, and more and more were added, their utility matching their grace. Finally "trysails," that is to say quadrilateral sails set on gaffs, might be set at the same height as the heads of the courses. They were known as "spencers" when on the foremast or main, and "spankers" on the mizen. In all, the fully-rigged ship could put on an impressive show of over forty sail, though it is unlikely that any new ship left Quebec with that many in her outfit.

Ships showed their personality at their bow and their stern in their figurehead and other carved or painted decoration. Their name was an integral part of the design and was accompanied on the stern by the name of the home port.[15] Most ships were given the names of people – sometimes a simple Christian name, such as *Anne*, *Edna*, or *Robert*, but often the name of an identifiable person, such as the builder himself, *John Bell*, or *Brunelle*, for instance, or a member of his family, such as *Young Norval*, John Goudie's son. The shipowner or broker and their families were other likely namesakes – the *Letitia Heyn*, ordered by the shipowner Gustavus Heyn of Belfast, bore his wife's name, the *Eliza Pirrie* that of the young wife of James A. Pirrie. Born in Quebec, their son William was destined to spend fifty years, 1874-1924, at the helm of the Harland and Wolff shipyard at Belfast, the largest shipyard in the world.[16] Other vessels were named after people in the public eye or fictional or mythological figures. Many bore the names of royalty or of one of the governor generals or their ladies. Indian tribes were other favourites–*Algonquin*, *Huron*, *Mic Mac* and *Mohawk* are all names that were given to more than one ship. Many vessels had place names, such as *Scotland*, *Ontario*, *Persia*, *Town of Ross*, *Callao* in the fifties and sixties, names of animals, birds and fish were popular, *Buffalo*, *Osprey* and *Salmon* among them. Human virtues were also represented, and as if two *Faith*s, half a dozen *Hope*s and a *Charity* were not enough, there was also the *Faith Hope and Charity* with all three. Some ships were given names of warships, and in later years of steamers. P.V. Valin, for instance, named the *Sarmatian*, *Sardinian* and *Polynesian* after steamers of the Allan Line. Other names in series include the Cities, *City of Kingston*, *City of Montreal*, *City of Ottawa*, the shires, *Lancashire*, *Lincolnshire*, *Staffordshire*, the Empires, *Northern Empire*, *British Empire* and *French Empire*, and precious stones, *Ruby*, *Diamond*, *Sapphire*. And the names of seventeen out of fifty-seven vessels built by the Gilmours began with the letter "A." Current events also were responsible for many of the names; some such as *War Cloud* and *Stamboul* were reminders of the Crimean War. These are just some of the subjects from which the names of the sailing ships were chosen; an examination of the names in the appendices will reveal many more.

Often the figurehead tied in with the name, and when the name had no gender an allegorical damsel was generally favoured. Of the two-thirds of the heads that represented men and women, eighty per cent were full-length figures and twenty per cent were busts. The first of the busts on a Quebec vessel was on John Munn's *Echo* of 1811, after which their popularity increased to such an extent that between 1822 and 33 they far outnumbered the full-length figures until 1857, when a full-length carving became the general rule. We do not know how often portraits were attempted, but we do know that the head on the *Earl of Elgin* was described as "an astonishingly exact likeness of His Excellency who is represented in his official costume," and that on the *Campbell* there was a "fine figurehead, the portrait of A. Campbell, Esq., Her Majesty's Notary, Quebec."[17] Men were depicted in uniform or civilian dress, as was appropriate, and there were a number in Indian dress. Women were variously attired in loose flowing garments or conventional clothes.

The sudden affinity for animal's names in the 1850s and 60s does not appear to have had a counterpart in either St. John or Bath, and possibly the ship carver William Black, whose career spanned this period, was responsible for the rash of heads, rather than a current fashion as in the case of the white figureheads that were so popular for clippers. At an earlier date, the ship carver, James McKenzie, carved a particularly fine unicorn for Abraham Joseph's sleigh, the same year, 1841, that a unicorn head graced one of the sailing ships, but on the whole, animal heads were rare.[18]

Finally, a full third of the heads were scrolls, often decorated with stylized leaf or floral designs. They are known today as "billet heads" if they turn towards the stem and "fiddleheads" if they turn outward, but were described in contemporary ship registers as "billet heads" or "scrolls," but never "fiddleheads."

Only one out of every ten Quebec ships left port without a head of some sort, though other decorative carving was optional. References can be found to carvings on trailboards, moulded or otherwise decorated panels on the counter of the stern, and of animal faces on the ends of the catheads. For example, the description of the stern carving of the ship *Eleutheria* built by Narcisse Rosa refers to a "nice piece of scrollwork, in the centre of which is the Quebec coat of arms and the motto, Natura Fortis, Industria Credit." A small vessel ordered from E.W. Sewell was to have a gilded bird head and stern molding representing a freemasons' coat of arms.[19] Some of the figureheads were very colourful, but others, particularly the damsels of the mid-nineteenth century were all white.

Unlike some of the vessels built in the Maritime Provinces, Quebec-built ships followed British design, which is what might be expected in view of the fact that the Quebec shipbuilding industry was built up by shipwrights who came from Britain and who built ships for British shipowners, whereas much of the Maritimes was peopled by Loyalists, who retained strong family and business ties with the United States. And although F.W. Wallace, in writing *Wooden Ships and Iron Men*, described the ships built in the Maritime Provinces of Nova Scotia, New Brunswick, Prince Edward Island and Quebec, collectively referring to them as British North American vessels,[20] he was sent a great deal of additional material following its publication, which considerably modified his conception of the Quebec-built ship. He wrote three years later that he had been "able to secure a few photographs and copies of paintings of Quebec ships" that showed the distinctness of the Quebec-built ship. The Quebeckers, he wrote, had full short poops without the trunk cabins common to the usual type of B.N.A. craft, and the 'half-round' style of building the poop was typically British. Another feature he noted were the painted ports, with which Quebec vessels were decorated long after the style had been discarded in Nova Scotia and New Brunswick yards."[21]

Distribution

A full two-thirds of the vessels built at Quebec accounting for almost three-quarters of the tonnage were sent to five British ports, Liverpool, London, Glasgow, Belfast and Greenock. Liverpool, however, received as much as the other four ports together. The remaining third was made up of ships sold to other British ports, a number sold to France, a few to the United States or Germany, some that remained on the Quebec Register or were Canadian owned, and those that were lost before any transfer of registry.

Until 1828, London took by far the largest share, for "London was the hub of foreign as well as domestic trade. . . . in 1750, 75 per cent of the shipping entering British ports anchored in the Thames, over two-thirds of it bringing goods from the outports . . . "

"London was therefore 'capital, metropolis, port and entrepot, all in one' (Westerfield). It offered the best shipping services to many foreign ports and secured the best naval convoys to waft them on their way. . . . Its commercial, credit, insurance, and banking facilities were far more highly developed than those of the outports. . . . London merchants exploited fully the advantages which their location, resources, and political influence gave them. They showed initiative in seeking out new fields for enterprise, such as Russia, the Levant, the Orient, and North America."[22]

And, we might add, Quebec, where the family business connection set up by the three Beatson brothers handled more than half the new vessels sent over to London at the turn of the eighteenth to nineteenth century. Built in Patrick's shipyard at Quebec, they were registered in his name and on arrival in London their ownership was shared out among various merchants, with his brothers generally retaining a part. Many were West Indiamen that were put into service in the lucrative sugar, coffee and rum trades, and like large ships at all times were liable to be chartered by the government to be used as transports, if the need arose. However, not all the ships in the Island trade were large, and many of the smaller vessels were also Quebec-built. The majority of all tonnage arriving in London from July to October was on the West Indies run, even though British timber supplies were still largely imported from the Baltic, and the main timber market for both naval and merchant shipbuilding was also at London.

During the first quarter of the nineteenth century when the Navy turned towards British North America for supplies and Admiralty contractors and other firms began shipping timber from Canada, Usborne, Mure and Joliffe, and Christopher Idle were among the London firms that had previously imported from the Baltic and now held licences to cut timber in Canadian forests. Although these and other timber merchants bought up most of the new ships at Quebec and loaded them with a first cargo of timber, they were not destined immediately to become timber ships, and after their maiden voyage generally replaced older vessels that were demoted to the timber run. For instance, only four of the twenty-three Quebec-built vessels under ten years old listed in *Lloyd's Register* of 1818 were due to return to Quebec that year. Seven sailed for India; another seven for the West Indies.

Following the cessation of hostilities with France, the British Government's decision of 1821 to retain preferential treatment of Canadian timber released a

Figure 216: *The 956 ton ship* Peter Joynson *built by H. Dinning and Company in 1863. Her long sleek lines contrast sharply with those of the* Lord Elgin, *Figure 213. Sold in Liverpool, she was sent to San Francisco in 1866 and was on the London to India run in 1872. She is shown here as seen by a Chinese artist. Courtesy Archives nationales du Québec, GH 1070–88.*

flood of timber exports, but had no immediate repercussions on Quebec shipbuilding, and it was not until 1824 that the industry came out of its post-war slump. It was that year also that Charles Wood launched the first of his two enormous droghers built of square timbers, which received so much attention in the Press, undoubtedly serving also to focus attention on the shipyards at Quebec. The forty-one new ships that were sent from Quebec to London in the next two years, 1825 and 26, seemed to augur the development of a healthy market for Quebec ships there, but it was not to be. Inevitably, the sudden heavy demand for tonnage was followed by a steep decline. Moreover, as far as the London market for Quebec ships was concerned, it had reached its peak, and though it was still the principal outlet for Quebec ships, it would cede its place to Liverpool in 1828. From then until the seventies a far smaller proportion of Quebec-built ships was disposed of in London.

Meanwhile, Quebec's commercial ties with Scotland which had accounted for a number of Scottish shipbuilders arriving in Quebec from the 1780s on, also accounted for Scottish ownership of many locally-built vessels. Like the vessels sent to London, the ships these Scots built at the turn of the century were for the most part owned by groups of merchants, and were mainly registered in Greenock or Port Glasgow. And, like those sent to London, they were used principally for trade with the West Indies, the other places including the cotton ports of the United States.

Following the establishment of the Allan Gilmour and Company shipyard at Quebec, Glasgow replaced Greenock and Port Glasgow, as the principal Scottish port to which Quebec ships were dispatched. Between 1831 and 1856, for instance, no fewer than forty-two large vessels of superior construction were built for the fleet of the parent company Pollok, Gilmour and Company at the Gilmour Wolfe's Cove yard. Another twenty were sent between 1848 and 1864 from the Russell shipyard on the south shore opposite Quebec, while between 1859 and 1876 the shipbroker James G. Ross dispatched thirty-eight, of which fourteen were from the highly productive Gingras yard. These three sources alone made up two-thirds of the sailing ships that were disposed of in Glasgow.[23]

Interestingly, their tonnage was greater on average than that of the vessels sent to the other large ports, an extraordinary turn around and one that says much for the determination of the Glaswegians, who had had spectacular improvements made to the Clyde river bed. While the vast majority of these vessels were built for Pollok, Gilmour and Company, who are said to have had a fleet of over a hundred sailing ships in the mid-nineteenth century, others were regularly bought for the Allan, Potter and Watt fleets, and many served in the Australasian and Indian trades. Other ports on the Clyde, where Quebec vessels were owned include Ardrossan, Ayr and Irvine. Of the eleven vessels registered in Irvine, five were built by the various Munns.

All told, only about thirty vessels were registered de novo on the east coast of Scotland at the ports of Leith (Edinburgh's port on the Firth of Forth), Aberdeen, Dundee, Grangemouth, Kirkcaldy, Alloa and Berwick. They were built in various yards, and the builders who were natives of the east coast do not appear to have exploited any special ties they might have had with shipping circles there. John Bell, for instance, a native of Aberdour, built only one for Leith registry in 1825 and another in 1828. George Black,

Figure 217: *Plan of the Surrey Commercial Docks, London. Notice,* right of centre, *Quebec and Canada Ponds, and lower right, Canada Dock. Published by Timber News and Sawmill Engineer. Courtesy The Museum of London Museum in Docklands Project (071 515 1162), with thanks to Robert Aspinall.*

Figure 218: *"Vessels discharging timber in the Surrey Commercial Docks, 1827," possibly a cargo from Quebec. Courtesy The Museum of London Museum in Docklands Project (071 515 1162), with thanks to Robert Aspinall.*

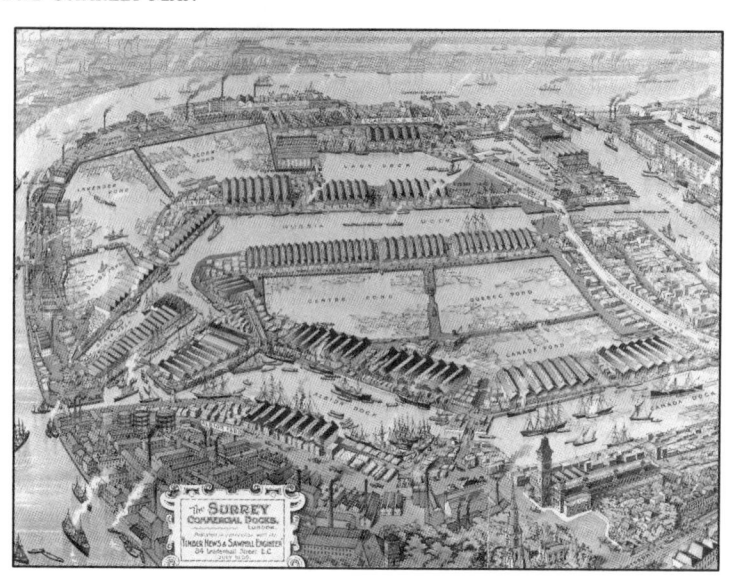

from Aberdeen, disposed of none, though one built by his son found an owner there. Twelve vessels in all were transferred to Aberdeen registry, among them the largest sailing ship built at Quebec, Charles Jobin's 2081 ton *Lord Raglan* of 1854.

During the first half of the nineteenth century the Irish merchant fleet flourished, and by the 1820s a considerable direct trade had developed between Quebec shipbuilders and Irish shipowners. Several vessels left each year to be registered at Belfast, Waterford, Dublin, Cork, or more rarely, at Londonderry or one of the smaller ports. Dublin and Waterford were then Quebec's principal Irish outlets; Londonderry, Ireland's most important port, did more business with New Brunswick shipyards. In the 30s, the situation changed and so many vessels were sent to Belfast from then on that overall more than half the Quebec ships sent to Irish ports were Belfast owned. The Irish market for Quebec ships reached its peak in the forties; thereafter, as an increasingly greater percentage of Irish goods was exported from Ireland to Liverpool or London for transshipment by steamboat, the Irish deep sea sailing ship fleets were cut back. Londonderry owners who had only occasionally bought a new Quebec ship for their fleets, made up for it in the 1860s and 70s when the Dublin, Cork, Waterford and Belfast markets had all but dried up, and two Londonderry owners, Bartholemew McCorkell and J. and J. Cooke each gave three welcome contracts to Quebec yards.

The main suppliers of the Beflast fleet were John James Nesbitt and Thomas H. Oliver, who between them built thirty-nine vessels that were Belfast owned, and George Holmes Parke, from whose yard at least another thirteen were launched. They were mostly fully-rigged ships, Nesbitt's and Oliver's averaging 645 tons, and those built by Parke, who specialized in large ships, over 1200 tons. Parke, brother-in-law of the important Belfast shipowner David Grainger, acted as agent for several other Belfast shipowners as well as Grainger, men such as Gustavus Heyn, John Dunn, James Lemon and Sinclair. Many of the vessels they bought were fitted out to carry passengers and took emigrants and general passengers to Australia, America and the West Indies. Others transported the less fortunate indentured coolies from Hong Kong or Amoy to California, the Chincha Islands or the West Indies. Often they sailed between Liverpool or Belfast and New Orleans in the cotton trade.

Of the other Irish ports, Waterford came a distant second to Belfast in her share of re-registries of Quebec ships. Waterford's main overseas trade was the timber trade with Canada, but her shipowners also bought half a dozen small vessels of under 200 tons, as most of her shipping was in the coastal or cross channel trade. Some of those that took Waterford registry in the early 1820s were bought by the merchant and shipowner Richard Pope before he set up his own shipyard around 1830, others by Hartrick and Bellord.

Cork, another port at which Quebec vessels were registered, had a prosperous farming and light industrial hinterland and traded its meat, flour, butter,[24] linen and cottons for timber and naval supplies from the Baltic and America, sugar and rum from the West Indies, wines and spirits from continental Europe and all kinds of goods from England. The Cork merchant Reuben Deaves who bought shares in the Quebec-built barque *Trio* of 1825, bought at least four other Quebec barques over the next twenty years, three of them in the 800 to 950 ton range. Later the Canadian

Figure 219: *Captain Joseph Elzéar Bernier, F.R.G.S., F.R.E.S.. A shipwright as well as a mariner. He delivered many vessels built in the Quebec shipyards and in later years served as Superintendent of Peter Baldwin's yard on the St. Charles river, before earning fame as an Arctic explorer. Photo from F.W. Wallace,* In the Wake of the Windships.

Figure 220: *Barque* Felicitas, *749 tons, of 1874, built by Peter Baldwin and sailed out by Captain Bernier in a record crossing of fifteen days and sixteen hours. He sold her to a Caernarvon owner. Courtesy Maritime Museum of the Atlantic, Wallace Collection. MP1.86.1.*

timber trade with Cork gained importance, as did the complimentary emigrant trade, though apart from seven vessels sold in the forties, only five other Quebec ships were sold there between 1803 and 1878. Like Cork, Limerick exported a great deal of farming and dairy products, and like Cork bought some Quebec ships in the forties, but only one other after that time. Finally, an average of two vessels went to Wexford, Galway, Sligo, Ross, New Ross, Tralee, Bridgewater, Donegal, Newry and Dundalk.

Tucked away under the south coast of Wales, Bristol had been an important port from early times, and had already four thousand feet of quays in 1705, which compared very favourably with London's twelve hundred for much more shipping.[25] She also had a considerable shipbuilding history of her own, and added to it in the nineteenth century, particularly in regard to sea-going steamships, which were built there as early as 1822. Nevertheless, as their Quebec agent handling the sale of their iron chain, anchors and other iron goods, William Budden was able to sell five Quebec vessels to the Acraman family, important Bristol iron founders and merchants, between 1822 and 26, before the Acramans began to build their own iron steamships. In the same way, the sugar refiners Samuel and George Lunell, who bought a 425 ton vessel built by Louis Labbé in 1825, set up their own shipyard in the thirties and built their own steam packets.[26] In the last half of the century, Quebec's main contact with Bristol was the shipping agent Henry Fry, who was born there, and sold an occasional Quebec vessel to Bristol owners.

But it was Liverpool that took the lead in 1828 and received by far the largest share of the new production of the Quebec shipyards overall. A number

Figure 221: *Ship* Calcutta, *1428 tons, built by William Charland in 1874. She went ashore in a snow storm on Grosse Isle, Magdalen Islands, in 1875 on her second outward voyage from Quebec, and was abandoned to the underwriters, but was salvaged and sailed again. She is seen here in 1890. Photo from F.W. Wallace,* In the Wake of the Windships, *616 1070–138.*

Figure 222: *Barque* Royal Visitor, *1220 tons, of 1860, built by Thomas H. Oliver and named after the Prince of Wales, who visited the shipyard during her construction. Owned by Ross & Company of Liverpool, she was later bought by Norwegians. Courtesy Maritime Museum of the Atlantic, Wallace Collection. MP2.93.1.*

of vessels joined the fleets of the great Liverpool shipping lines, others were operated from Liverpool by owners in other ports, but many of those sent to be put on the market by shipbrokers did not remain on the Liverpool register long. Some, for example, were bought by Welsh owners and registered de novo in their home ports, so that though the endorsements on the Quebec registers indicate that only twenty-four vessels were transferred to Welsh ports, the real figure for new Quebec vessels owned in Wales is closer to double that number. Slate from the Cilgerran quarries near Cardigan and from Porthmadog was used as ballast in the ships, among them some Quebeckers, that sailed from that port to Quebec to fetch timber. Though there were shipyards in and near Cardigan, it was more economical at times to buy the large vessels built on speculation in Quebec, where wood was plentiful and cheap, particularly when the market was booming and British built tonnage was not available at reasonable prices.[27]

Quebec shipbuilders would dearly have liked to sell their production to American owners, but were balked by that country's Protectionist policy. Nor was there much opportunity to sell to other countries. In 1862, however, the winds of Free Trade began clearing away the obstructions to foreign registry. The French government decided to apply the same regulations for the admission of Canadian vessels as had been negotiated between France and Great Britain and Belgium, that is to say a duty of 25 francs per ton, French measure. For this, as the French consul noted at the time, Canada did not furnish compensation. Moreover, in 1866, according to a new law passed in France, the tax on British, including Quebec-built, vessels was reduced to 2 francs a ton. Quebec shipbuilders were quick to

Figure 223: *Peter Baldwin's ship* Germanic, *1310 tons, of 1878, another vessel entrusted to Bernier. She also ended her days under the Norwegian flag. Courtesy Maritime Museum of the Atlantic, Wallace Collection. MP1.30.2.*

THE CHARLEY-MAN

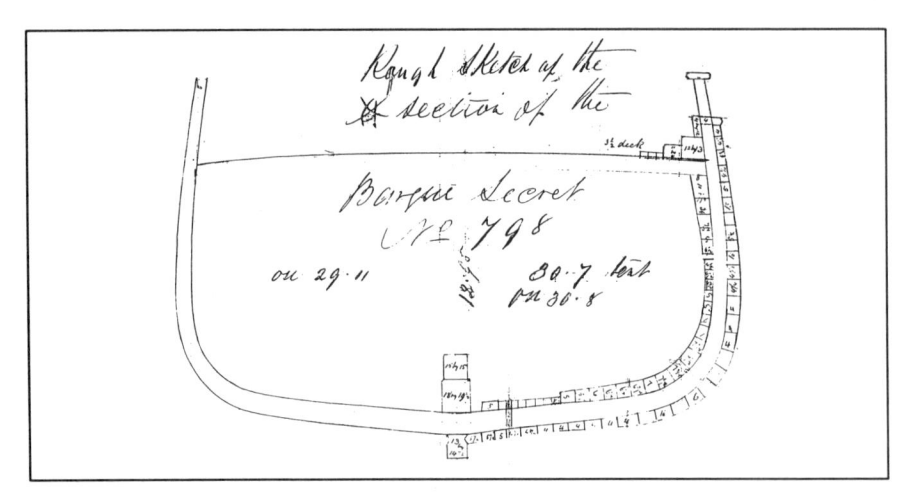

Figure 224: *Barque* Secret *of 1867, built by I. and J. Samson. "Secret of Cardiff. R. Roberts Commander. Off St. Helena in 1872." Oil on canvas. H.R. Bartlett, 1874. Courtesy Omell Gallery, London.*

Figure 225: *Midship section plan of the barque* Secret, *from the Lloyd's Survey Report No. 798.*

take advantage of this happy state of affairs, which lasted however only until 1871 when the law was revoked and the import duty on wooden sailing ships was raised to 40 francs per ton.[28] The outcry from Quebec led by Narcisse Rosa was immediate and loud. France reacted with a demand for the removal or alleviation of import duties on her wines and spirits. Powerful French shipbuilding interests fought to maintain the tax as well as for a programme of government shipbuilding subsidies, and the subsidies which came in 1881 and more particularly in 1893 effectively prevented further sales of Quebec ships to France.

However, trade with France was good while it lasted.[29] The two main links with her shipowners were Narcisse Rosa and James J. Ross. Rosa dealt directly with shipowners or brokers at the Port of Marseilles, in particular the shipowner industrialist C.-A. Verminck, who bought some vessels on the stocks at Quebec; Ross through the network of brokers with which he was connected, mainly Edmiston & Mitchell, A. Cassells and W. Ross in Britain, and A. Chrystie and Perquier at Le Havre. Perquier also handled sales of vessels for P.V. Valin. On a lesser scale, between 1863 and 1866 Hyppolite Dubord sold four vessels either to or through Paul Damas at Bordeaux, but after his death Bordes, Damas' partner, returned from South America to take charge of the business there, and no more were sold. From 1869 on E. Oulonne replaced Verminck as the main outlet for Quebec ships at Marseilles and Louis Roberge was his supplier, while Henri Bergasse et Cie., Armement Augustin Fabre, Bertrand Gorce, Oulonne, Ed. Portal, Wulfran Puget et Cie., C.-A. Verminck et Cie., all of Marseilles, also bought Quebec ships. The French did not favour large wooden sailing ships finding smaller ones more profitable. The average Quebec vessel sold to France measured 563 tons; the 830 ton *Saint-Pierre* was considered a giant ship.[30] Later, however, when high government subsidies were introduced, several French shipowners built up fleets of very large steel sailing ships.

Among the vessels disposed of elsewhere, there were at least six built for German owners between 1855 and 1883. One of these, the 430 ton barque *Friedrich Perthes* of 1876 was not registered at Quebec, and there may have been others that left port without British Registration and have not been counted. In the 60s, Quebec vessels were sold to Italy, Denmark, Holland, Australia and even Calcutta, however, after France, Norway was Quebec's main foreign customer. At least twenty new vessels were sold directly to Norwegian owners beginning in 1869, and many more were bought secondhand in later years to finish their days under the Norwegian flag.

As the 1850s advanced and the market for Quebec ships seemed to be expanding, the devastating outcome of advances in metal technology was all too evident. Though general acceptance lagged and only ninety-nine iron vessels owned in Britain were listed by Lloyd's in 1850, the more enterprising European shipowners had begun to build up their fleets with iron ships, and the "tin kettles" were showing their mettle, already some voyaged to the Pacific and the Indian Ocean. During the Crimean War, the French Emperor ordered that certain vessels be sheathed with thick iron plate and their success is said greatly to have accelerated the move towards iron ships. J.P. Corry of Belfast ordered his first iron ship in 1860, Gustave Dor of Marseilles in 1862. By the end of the 60s, at least nine large iron vessels belonged to each of the two ports. At one swoop, Bordes, the most

Figure 226: *Figurehead of the ship* Indian Chief *in the collection of The Peabody Museum, Salem, Massachusetts. The 1788 ton* Indian Chief *was built by Pierre Valin in 1864 and owned in Glasgow. She was wrecked off Mobile in 1869. Photo courtesy Peabody Museum, M2970, neg. 18236 fr.12.*

Figure 227: Canada Timber Dock, *at the north end of Liverpool. Exhibited at the Royal Academy Exhibition by Robert Dudley The Graphic, August 24th 1872. Courtesy A. Marcil.*

important shipowner in Bordeaux, matched them, ordering nine iron-hulled vessels from British shipyards. According to Henry Fry, "the days of wooden ships were fast coming to an end." In the seventies, as more former customers for Quebec's wooden ships, such as Fabre and Bergasse in Marseilles, McCorkell in Londonderry and Dixon and Corry in Belfast bought iron vessels,[31] it was evident that Quebec markets were melting away. The American Civil War shored up the shipping market generally for a few years, but when it was over the trend towards metal hulls became a landslide. Lloyd's Register of 1866 listed fourteen hundred and thirty-three iron-hulled vessels. Even owners who kept operating with wooden fleets were not interested in new Quebec ships, a wide choice of discarded wooden vessels was available to them at bargain prices.

Lastly, apart from all the vessels that changed owners and consequently their registry, there were some one hundred and forty-three vessels, or between ten and eleven per cent of the total production that were removed from the Quebec Register because they were known or presumed no longer to exist., Half of this number were "Lost" or "Missing." Thirty-four were "Stranded" or "Wrecked," and sixteen "Abandoned" or "Foundered." Another five "broke up" and the same number were "Captured" at sea. Although some fifty vessels are known to have been lost either on their maiden voyage or within a year of their launching, many served usefully for several years before meeting their fate. Others that were removed from the register after belonging to the port for a number of years include three that were "Condemned," six that "Burned," and six more whose fate was unknown and whose registry was "Closed." Undoubtedly, the trip down the Saint Lawrence could

Figure 228: *Arrangement for converting cargo space into living quarters for emigrants. Litho. J. R. Isaacs. Courtesy Liverpool Public Libraries, neg. 134 K/7.*

Figure 229: *Ship* Thornhill, *of 1855*

Figure 230: *The barque* Hope, *a 287 ton timber carrier built by P.G. Labbé and Company in 1865, and owned in New Port, Wales, loading a cargo of slate at Porthmadog, to take back to Quebec. Courtesy Gwynedd Archives, Wales, ref. XS 690/3/41.*

be hazardous, and there were years when storms were particularly bad and casualties high. But not all wrecks were due to bad weather conditions, for legislation brought in 1841 laying down punishments for those who hung out false lights with the intent of causing felony or death, who impeded efforts to save life, or destroyed wrecks or goods belonging thereto, would imply that some were man-induced.[32]

Very often, the captain was the go-between, between the builder and the shipowner, either entrusted with choosing a new vessel for his employer's fleet, or sent to supervise a vessel under construction. Other captains might be acting for the builder or broker, sometimes only being required to deliver the vessel, but at others acting as agent for its sale. Joseph-Elzéar Bernier acted in both capacities, and in the final years of shipbuilding when there were far fewer ships to deliver, spent winters superintending construction in a shipyard, while waiting for the springtime and his command. Though the registries supply no information about the crew,[33] during certain periods the captain's name was noted, either because of official requirement, or else simply due to a personal decision of the registering officer. It appears that some of the captains returned regularly to Quebec to take charge of the new ships, men such as Alexander McColl, who delivered at least twenty new vessels including fifteen built by John Munn, Joseph-Elzéar Bernier who delivered ten, the shipbuilder Andrew Neilson, who was captain of eight, A. McArthur who took over eight new additions to the Gilmour fleet, Michael O'Brien who captained seven and William Bonyman, Andrew Crawford, A. Davis, H. Gortley, Charles Grisley, Robert Maxwell and James White, who all took command of five or more. Undoubtedly the list would be much longer if the Registry entries of the

Figure 231: *The traditional celebration following a launching. This one photographed in Britain fills Captain's Bernier's description of a Quebec launching. Courtesy National Maritime Museum, B 761.*

Figure 232: Quebec *1874. R. Hinshel Wood, Engraved by J.D. Woodward, N.Y. D., Appleton.*

Figure 233: *George Taylor (1782–1861) with the commemorative silver cup presented to him by the Governor General at the launching of HMS* Kingfisher. *Oil painting by unidentified artist. Courtesy M. Anne Garneau.*

Captains' names were complete. How fortunate the shipbuilders must have considered themselves to be able to count on the services of these experienced men. Just as they heaved a sigh of relief after a safe launching, they must have heaved another on handing the vessels over to men of whose capabilities they had no doubts.

Generally speaking the native Quebecker had no love for deep sea sailing. Though very much at home on the Saint Lawrence in small craft, he was not in the least bit interested in crossing the Atlantic or distant oceans and spending long periods away from home. Men such as Captain Bernier who was not only a seasoned Atlantic shipmaster but also at a later time an Arctic explorer, were rare. In the same way, although so many ships were originally registered at Quebec, only a very small number of them remained on the Quebec register for very long. Relatively few Quebec merchants were shipowners in the real sense of the word, and those shipbuilders, who did operate their vessels, generally sold them as soon as their price was met.

Milestones

Finally, when we look over the one hundred and thirty years of wooden ship construction covered by this study, the launchings stand out like milestones, each one a triumph for the builder and the shipyard workers.

After the winter's work came the great day of launching. The workmen were required to be on hand before dawn. On his arrival each man was served a stiff drink of Canadian whisky. At dawn the work of removing blocks was begun, starting from the stern. Amidships, the men were served another drink of

Figure 234: Launching the "Royal William," Quebec, Lower Canada, April 29, 1831. *The paddle steamer* Royal William *lies alongside the moulding loft, with the steam sawmill immediately behind and the Canada Floating Dock in the foreground, at the Campbell and Black shipyard at Cape Cove. Watercolour, J.P. Cockburn, 20–I–139, neg. C 12649. Courtesy National Archives, Ottawa.*

Figure 235: *The river lapped at their back doorstep on Champlain street. Courtesy Pierre Gingras.*

Figure 236: *The homes of timber cove and shipyard workers lined the Chemin du Foulon. Courtesy National Archives, Ottawa. Neg. 85797.*

Figure 237: *A familiar sight at Quebec during the season. Shipping at Hall's booms. The "superior deep water loading berths" leased by George Robinson. Courtesy R. and E. Robinson and National Archives, Ottawa. Neg. C 90135–8.*

Figure 238: *Barque* Amity, *built on the South Shore by Thomas Dunn and Etienne Samson in 1877, and launched as the ship* Stafford. *She had been renamed* Leopold von Vangerow, *when she was sold to Norwegians who gave her the name* Amity. *Photo: Yorke, Bristol. Courtesy Maritime Museum of the Atlantic, Wallace Collection. MP2 113,1.*

whisky. By this time there were many spectators; the owners' families and friends, the workmen's families, curious strangers, and all the stragglers of the town. Just before the key was knocked out, a final drink was served to the men. Then a final blow knocked the key out, and the ship slid gracefully down the ways into the water amid thundering cheers. Her godmother stood on a platform near the bow, and as the ship started down the ways a bottle of Madeira or port, secured by ribbon, was broken against the bow.

Ships were launched without rigging, but usually with masts and deck-houses in place, and with all spars lashed on deck. As a ship reached the water she dropped anchor and came to rest in the stream. She was then towed in to a wharf to await her clothing. In the meantime, the workmen and the guests gathered around long narrow tables loaded with sandwiches, cheese and biscuits, cookies, ale and spruce-beer. The owner and his guests retired to the shipyard office where fine wines and other refreshments awaited them. On launching day, every workman was given a full day's pay.[34]

Who could watch unmoved as the infant offspring of the shipyard made her plunge into the river amid the cheers of the crowd, and then settled down serenely in her new element. When the Governor General was present, there was added pomp and ceremony enlivened by the music of military bands, and after the river steamboats came into being, they too joined in the festivities, assisting in the launching with restraining ropes and adding to the spectacle, dashing around bedecked with pennants, blowing their horns.

The first of the launchings, was that of Thompson's little snow *Cordelia* in 1765 which, according to the *Quebec Gazette* of the 25 July, was "begun and carried on by the Direction of Mr Thomson Captain of the Port, at which was present his Excellency the Governor and several other Persons of Distinction." No doubt she was a handsome vessel, for Zacharaiah Thomson was a ship's carpenter in the Royal Navy for at least thirteen years prior to receiving his discharge from *H.M.S. Vanguard* to take up new duties at the port. Thirty-five years later, Beatson will have launched an equally handsome though far larger vessel, the 497 ton three-decked ship *Queen*, for he too knew what a fine ship was, having served in what were considered the finest merchantmen afloat, the ships of the Honorable East India Company.

Then in 1813, Quebec shipwrights proved their worth to both British and United States authorities, when they topped their war time shipbuilding programme at Kingston with the launching of the 120-gun ship *H.M.S. Saint Lawrence*, to a royal gun salute. Fourteen years later at Quebec, George Taylor's 18-gun brig *H.M.S. Kingfisher*, built for George Douglas and Thomas Harby of London, but with a five year charter to the government, drew an appreciative gift for the builder of a "silver cup . . . ornamented with the arms of the Dalhousie family, and an unicorn, which is the figure of the head of the brig . . . raised from the lid."[35] A portrait of the builder in oils was also presented to Taylor on that occasion.[36] But best known of the ceremonial launchings is one not of a sailing ship, though a number of sailing ship builders were stockholders in the company that owned and operated her, but of the 364 ton paddle steamer *Royal William*, in 1831. On the 28 April 1831 the *Quebec Gazette* reported:

Figure 239: *Barque* Edinburgh, *built by William Charland junior in 1883. Courtesy Maritime Museum of the Atlantic, Wallace Collection. MP2 101.1.*

Figure 240: *The last of the Quebec-built square-riggers, the 396 ton barquentine* White Wings *built by Guillaume Charland in 1893, seen here on the day of her launching. Fonds Wurtele, G–7, courtesy Archives nationales du Québec.*

Lady Aylmer and His Excellency Lord Aylmer and his staff went yesterday afternoon to Munn's Cove, on the St. Lawrence, to attend the launch of the St. Nicholas Ferry Steamboat. His lordship performed the usual ceremonies of naming the vessel "Lady Aylmer," when she went off the stocks, from an awning decorated with flags; several thousand persons crowded the adjacent wharfs and heights. The Tow Boat Company had, in an extremely handsome manner placed the Steamer Richelieu at the service of the public, and Colonel Maitland, with his usual kindness permitted the excellent band of the 32nd regiment to attend on board. The boat was crowded and lay off the wharf in a position advantageous to witness the launch, which was effected in a manner to gratify every one. The increasing spectators then set out to Mr. Campbell's shipyard where Lady Aylmer performed the ceremony at the launching of the Quebec and Halifax company's steamship "Royal William.". . . She went off beautifully amid cheers and firing of cannon, and when she floated looked a gallant ship.

The memory of that launching was still green when in 1839, John Munn's 1267 ton ship *United Kingdom* was sent down the ways, hailed as the first Quebec-built vessel to pass the 1000 ton mark. He followed her up with the 1079 ton *Scotland* four years later, and both vessels sailed under his flag until 1849. The launching of the 1205 ton ship *Countess of Elgin* by Baldwin and Dinning on the 23 April 1852 was another particularly happy and auspicious event, as she was the first to be launched that was built under the superintendence of Lloyd's Surveyor, Thomas Menzies.[37] In 1853, George H. Parke's 2003 ton ship *Persia* was the first Quebec vessel to break 2000 tons, and a year later Charles Jobin's ship *Lord Raglan* raised the record to 2081 tons, a figure that would not be bettered.

Each launching was an occasion for the pundits to air their views: "Mr Rosa had committed an error," they predicted in 1863, "in putting her up on this spot, there being too short a run for what could be called a safe launch . . . the topmasts ought not to have been up for she was sure to roll over, not having ballast." But evidently the 1497 ton ship *Dreadnought* was in cahoots with the builder, for she "glided like a thing of life, so smooth and easy that the motion was scarcely perceptible. She sat plumb, and as graceful as a swan."[38] We are not told how the prophets of doom explained Rosa's success.

Unfortunately though, there were times when the crowd got more of a spectacle than they were bargaining for, for the builders had their share of launchings that went wrong. When Beatson's ship *Caledonia* stuck on her ways in 1799,[39] comparisons were undoubtedly drawn with the breaking up of the French Naval vessel *L'Orignal* at her launching at the Cul-de-Sac in 1750. Some were perhaps there on both occasions; others would have heard the story. Launching into the Saint Charles River took particular skill, but even when that was not lacking, some situations could not be foreseen by the shipwright in charge, for instance, when those responsible for restraining the new vessel failed in their job.

And there were also times when the crowd got less of a spectacle than they hoped for. There were many who said that Charles Wood's *Columbus* would never float but remain on the blocks where she was built, a monument to the stupendous folly of her projectors. They were wrong, but those who gathered from far and wide the following year to see the great *Baron of Renfrew* slide majestically down the ways were sadly disappointed. She moved only a little more than half her own length and then settled down refusing all efforts to set her in motion. She was finally launched a week later without ceremony, after having had holes drilled in the ways and filled with gunpowder, the little explosions that were set off gradually getting her to move.[40]

The length of the ways at the Gilmour yard added extra interest to the launchings there; whether the Gilmours ever resorted to the use of gunpowder, I do not know. One wonders also whether they indulged in the little game that some of the shipbuilders played – keeping the name of a vessel a secret until the bottle was broken on her bow. We are told that a special cheer went up when Valin's 1324 ton ship *Chattanooga* was given her name at her launching.

Most launchings took place in the morning according to newspaper reports. Americus Vidal added drama to the spectacle when his 688 ton bark *Lanarkshire* slid slowly down into the river at seven o'clock on an October evening, with lighted pitch barrels at the end of the ways illuminating the scene.[41]

But the time came when launchings were so commonplace and the reporters' clichés so worn, that it might merely be announced in the paper that "four other vessels were also launched," yet few realized that the time was not so far away when the last of the square-riggers would leave the ways and there would be no more.

Notes

1. The broad categories of hull in the eighteenth century were the frigate-built, hagboat, pink, cat and bark. David MacGregor, *Square Rigged Sailing Ships* (Watford, Herts, 1977), 10, citing F.H. Chapman.
2. David Williams, "Bulk Carriers and Timber Imports: The British North American Trade and the Shipping Boom in 1824-5," *Mariner's Mirror*, LIV (1968); Eileen Marcil, "Ship-Rigged Rafts and the Export of Quebec Timber," *The American Neptune*, XLVIII, No. 2 (Spring 1988), 77.
3. These figures and those that follow have been compiled from the Shipping Registers of the Port of Quebec and, unless otherwise indicated, cover all sailing vessels of over one hundred tons built within the limits described on p. 24 of the introduction. The *Columbus* and the *Baron of Renfrew* are not included in figures for ships in table 11.
4. In graph 6 and tables 11 and 15, the period of growth, 1805 to 1846, and the years when the industry was at its height, 1847 to 1865, have each been sub-divided into the two periods because of the change in tonnage measurement in 1836 and 1855, which prevents averaging of tonnages.
5. Basil Greenhill, *The Ship: The Life and Death of the Merchant Sailing Ship 1815-1965* (London, 1980), 28.
6. RPQ 33/1795, 94 and 98/1853.
7. L.S. 798; Contract, Oliver with Brooke, 16 December 1836, gr L. McPherson.
8. *Report of the Investigation into the Loss of the "Annie Jane," made by direction of the Board of Trade* (London, 1854), 2.
9. Henry Fry, "Reminiscences" (unpublished ms., 1891).
10. Contract, Oliver with Brooke, 30 October 1840, gr L. McPherson; Shipbuilding contract, Baldwin and Dinning with Yeo, 13 August 1855, gr C.F. Campeau; Contract, Charland and Marquis with Wilson, 7 October 1865, gr W.D. Campbell. The monkey forecastle was "a short low forecastle open on the after side and used solely for anchor gear (windlass and so on)." René de Kerchove, *International Maritime Dictionary* (New York, 1961), 518.
11. Holderness' testimony, see note 8.
12. Contract, Cotnam with Gildermeister, 11 January 1876, gr S. Glackemeyer.
13. Shipbuilding contracts, 24 December 1845 and 27 July 1855, gr A. Campbell.
14. See Contract, 18 August 1865, gr S. Glackemeyer.
15. See notes to the appendix.
16. Michael Moss and John R. Hume, *Shipbuilders to the World: 125 Years of Harland & Wolff, Belfast, 1861-1986* (Belfast, 1986), 36-243.
17. *Morning Chronicle*, 8 May 1852 and 6 October 1857.
18. Joseph's unpublished diary, December 1839 to January 1840, (courtesy Annette Wolff); George Gale, *Quebec: Twixt Old and New* (Québec, 1915), 68.
19. *Morning Chronicle*, 27 October 1862; 21 July 1866, gr W.D. Campbell.
20. Frederick William Wallace, *Wooden Ships and Iron Men* (London, 1924), 152-161.
21. Frederick William Wallace, *In the Wake of the Windships* (Toronto, 1927), 77-78.
22. Herbert Heaton, *Economic History of Europe* (New York, 1936), 121.
23. Various members of the Gillespie firm of London, Glasgow and Quebec, important brokers who financed several Quebec shipbuilders, acted for Wm. Russell from 1848 to 57. Ross' Glasgow agents were Edmiston and Mitchell.
24. The British Navy was entirely supplied with beef and butter from Cork. Ernest B. Anderson, *Sailing Ships of Ireland* (Dublin, 1984), 94.
25. John Pudney, *London's Docks* (London, 1975), 14.
26. Grahame Farr, *Shipbuilding in the Port of Bristol* (London, 1977), ix, 7, 10; advertisement for chain cable, etc., *Quebec Gazette*, 4 June 1821.
27. Emrys Hughes and Aled Eames, *Porthmadog Ships* (Gwynedd, 1975); Susan Campbell-Jones, *Welsh Sail* (Dyfed, 1976); Basil Greenhill, *The Ship: The Life and Death of the Merchant Sailing Ship* (London, 1980), 17.
28. Letter to the editor of the *Globe*, reprinted *Morning*

Chronicle, 21 March 1862; *Acte du Tarif Conventionnel*, December 1866, reported in *L'Evénement*, 15 November 1877; 28 February 1872, *L'Evénement*.
29. The French refer to the sale of foreign vessels to French shipowners as "francisation."
30. Henri Picard, *Marseille & Marine en bois 1860-1925* (Marseilles, 1983), 29.
31. Moss and Hume, *Shipbuilders to the World*, 19, 40, 507-510; Anderson, *Sailing Ships*, 284-287; Picard, *Marseille et Marine*, 168, 172, 176; Louis Lacroix, *Les Derniers Cap-Horniers Français* (Paris, 1957), 13; Fry, "Reminiscences," 38.
32. *Statutes of Canada*, 4 and 5 Vict., c. 25 and c. 26.
33. Many of the crew lists, however, are in the safekeeping of the Maritime History Archives at Memorial University, St. John's, Newfoundland.
34. J.-E. Bernier, *Master Mariner*, 171.
35. *Quebec Gazette*, 14 May 1827.
36. Family sources.
37. *Morning Chronicle*, 26 April 1852.
38. *Ibid.*, 22 May 1863.
39. Power of attorney, Beatson to Tod, Monro, Palsgrave, Frost and Hosier, 30 June 1798, gr C. Stewart.
40. *Quebec Mercury*, 25 June 1865; letter from a passenger, ANQ. Edward Oliver's ship *Wellington* also stopped on the ways on 24 April 1839, but fortunately floated off on the 30th without damage having been done. *Quebec Mercury*, 4 May 1839.
41. *Morning Chronicle*, 1 October 1863; *Quebec Mercury*, 13 October 1840.

Conclusion

"The construction of wooden vessels was an outstanding achievement of nineteenth century Quebec."[1] So wrote Albert Faucher, and there is much to support his statement. Shipbuilding was Quebec's first large-scale manufacturing industry in terms of employment, scale, and above all, output: 1633 sailing ships, over a million tons of shipping, in a period of 130 years. A full two-thirds of the vessels were built between 1840 and 1870, thirty years during which a parade of the vessels launched in many a season would have outshone the finest parade of "Tall Ships" today.

Over those years a great change took place in their appearance. The chunky bluff-bowed fully-rigged ship of the eighteenth century slimmed its lines, while reaching three times its former length and ten times its original tonnage. Changes in the brigs and brigantines were less radical, though they too increased in size, and from the 1820s the elegant three-masted barques that were relatively more economical to operate frequently took their place. The construction of snows came to an end in 1827; the first barquentine appeared in 1863.

Changes in the ships and the expansion of the shipping market led to changes in the shipyards. Not only did larger ships require longer and more commodious slips and larger lofts, but more slips were required to accommodate their increasing numbers. This in turn led to a larger workforce, greater specialization and more sub-contracting. More capital had to be found and greater risks accepted.

By the 1850s, the Quebec-built vessel had found its special comparative advantages. It succeeded in doing so not only because of its large capacity, but also because it would carry relatively more cargo and travel faster, and consequently was much appreciated as a long-distance packet ship. Moreover, it was built with strict concern about cost. It was a matter of expedience, not of ignorance, when work, fittings or equipment was left to be supplied in Britain, for the pride that the shipbuilder had in completing the vessel had always to be tempered by economic reality. In the highly-competitive nineteenth-century shipping industry Quebec vessels scored high marks for their combination of low cost, ample cargo space and speed. Soundly built with good quality materials, they did not pretend to have the high finish of those built in London or New York, nor were they sold for the same high prices. Vessels built on speculation met the classification standard, while vessels built to order were given as much or as little finish as the purchaser required. When the purchaser was willing to pay, the Quebec shipbuilder was not at a loss to provide extra luxuries. The Dublin merchant, Joseph Wilson Brooke committed an extra fifty pounds over and above the agreed contract price for additional ornament of the *Leonard Dobbin* of 1837, if the builder, Thomas Oliver, agreed to do the same,[2] — an obvious appeal to Oliver's pride. But not all shipowners placed the same importance on extras if their absence did not affect the security or improve its profitability. In fact, even Allan Gilmour was unwilling to spend on a figurehead for the Gilmour ships, considering it more important to have a "figure-head" on the poop![3]

Nor were technological improvements neglected. While not indulging in fashionable extremes, shipbuilders adopted those that proved their worth when shipowners were willing to pay for them. Quebec vessels were being fitted with iron knees in 1810, and iron cable before or soon after the end of the Napoleonic Wars, in both cases long before it had become standard practice. In the last half of the nineteenth century, however, it was no longer a matter of choice. Regulations issued from time to time by Lloyd's constantly updated construction procedures and the class a vessel might obtain depended on their being carried out. Sometimes, and in some cases, such as in the use of iron beams and spars, the builders chose to surpass the minimum requirements.

The task of the early master shipwrights was difficult, but they were men who had served their apprenticeships, were steeped in its traditions and had confidence in the shipbuilding skills they had acquired. For the builders born overseas, conditions at Quebec were vastly different from those to which they were accustomed, but they succeeded nevertheless in structuring the industry, training the next and larger generation of builders and by offering a quality product at a reasonable price, securing a place for Quebec ships on the British market. That Governor Prevost should have requested John Goudie to build the fleet at Kingston in 1813, in spite of the fact that a government dockyard already existed there, was a remarkable tribute to him personally as well as to the vigour of the industry that had been established at Quebec. That he and his team of builders and shipyard workers were able to justify that faith was a feather in all their caps which, together with their success in building HMS *Saint Lawrence*, must surely have spawned great confidence. It was in that spirit that the fledgling industry went forward, thanks to the infectious dynamism of men such as Goudie.

Goudie's steam sawmill of 1818, his diving-bell of 1817 and deep-water wharf of 1819, Wood's *Columbus* and *Baron of Renfrew*, Black's floating dock of 1827, James Goudie's steamboat *Royal William* of 1831, Davie's marine railway of 1832, Sewell's icebreaker *Northern Light* of 1876, were all products of the practical unshackled spirit that the shipbuilders shared. Unshackled, yet informed, for though Quebec was far from shipbuilding centres in Britain and the United States, the builders were well aware of developments in shipbuilding technology. Not only did hundreds of shipmasters visit the port each year bringing news but also shipwrights arriving from different countries, from merchant and naval shipyards, kept the discussion fresh. Moreover, inveterate travellers that they were, for whom the Atlantic was just a pond, the shipbuilders were not men who would wait passively for ideas to be put before them. Leaving their shipyard in the hands of a capable foreman, they set out frequently in search of new technology, new business, and, when they felt it was necessary, key personnel.

Nor were the shipbuilders fair-weather sailors, ready to leave Quebec when the going became tough. They received no government subsidies, yet felt a responsibility to provide work for the shipyard workers, even when it involved personal financial risk. They adapted well and learned to turn disadvantage to advantage, particularly in the case of the climate. Mrs. Fleur Whitworth, George T. Davie's great-granddaughter, put it simply, "If you live in Quebec, you have to learn to live with its weather." Her ancestors were among the shipbuilders who did just that. Built in what might appear to be impossible winter conditions, every spring found a number of sailing ships waiting to be released from the stocks.

The shipbuilders were able to take full advantage of Quebec's single largest industry, the timber trade: of the selection of timber that the great quantities rafted to the port afforded, of the many physical and business facilities that were set up to support it, of the financing and other ship brokerage it often provided, of an initial outward cargo of timber, of repair and salvage work required by vessels of the very large timber fleet, and occasionally of an order for a ship.

Also, they could depend on a large hard-working work force–skilled ship carpenters, blacksmiths, mastmakers, blockmakers, sailmakers and other specialized workers, and unspecialized workers, who were skilled, nevertheless, in working with wood. Unlike the ship labourers or dockers, among whom there was frequent strife, particularly between the native Quebeckers and the Irish, French and English-speaking shipyard workers seem to have enjoyed harmonious relations both among themselves and with the shipbuilders, the latter broken only rarely by a strike. The immigrant shipbuilders took their adopted city to heart, and the vast majority remained there until they died, integrating into the community and winning the confidence of the workers. Some might complain today that the attitude of the shipbuilders was paternalistic, but more than one descendant of a shipyard worker has informed the writer that his grandfather appreciated the concern. Relief from paying the rent accompanied by a basket of groceries when the bread-winner of the family was unable to work was well-received at a time when there was no welfare state.

But even as Quebec's shipbuilding industry appeared to be hitting its stride, the age of the large wooden sailing ship was drawing to a close, victim of the technological evolution that was already well under way in the early part of the century. In the mid-1850s, Quebec still held the edge in the production of large, fast, inexpensive wooden ships, and some, such as Thomas Oliver and James Goudie, found it hard to believe that there would not always be a place for them. Yet the day arrived when it was all too apparent that the large wooden ships had become obsolete and the clock could not be put back—metal ships were stronger, they rarely leaked, their annual depreciation was far less, and their insurance rates far lower.[4]

Fortunately, when conditions were ripe there were men ready to play their part in establishing a wooden shipbuilding industry of which any town in the world might be proud. Making the most of both advantage and disadvantage, they put pride of purpose and excitement into the lives of the workers as they stepped from the age of the craftsman into the industrial age.

Notes

1. Albert Faucher, "The Decline of Shipbuilding at Quebec in the 19th Century," *Canadian Journal of Economics and Political Science*, XXIII (May 1957).
2. Contract, Oliver with Brooke, 16 December 1836, gr L. McPherson.
3. John Rankin, *A History of Our Firm: Being Some Account of the Firm of Pollok, Gilmour and Co. and Its Offshoots and Connections 1804-1920* (Liverpool, 1921), 313.
4. Goudie to editor, "Wooden or Iron Vessels," *Morning Chronicle*, 20 March 1860; *Fourth Report of the Select Committee Appointed to Inquire into the General Condition of the Building of Merchant Vessels in the Dominion of Canada . . .* (Ottawa, 1868), Oliver and Fry's testimony, Appendix 11, 13.

Appendix A

Shipbuilders

Name		Born	Died	Wife	First ship	Last ship	No	Tonnage
Baldwin	Henry	1770	1832	Elizabeth	1801	1812	18	4168
Baldwin	Peter	1839	1917	Mary Skinner	1872	1881	11	9548
Baldwin	Wm H.	1827	1894	Anne Jane Lee	1851	1875	34	47972
Beatson	Patrick	1758	1800	-	1794	1800	15	4416
Bell	John	1779	1841	Hutton, Greig, Wilson	1811	1836	25	8536
Black	George	1778	1854	Jane Gilley	1820	1846	49	21921
Brunelle	Pierre jr	1829	1903	Esther Collins	1854	1865	13	12617
Brunelle	Pierre	1807	1866	Marguerite Duval	1849	1865	22	24865
Campbell	Charles	1793			1819	1826	10	3062
Campbell	John S.	1787	1855	Jane Hamilton, M. Vivian	1823	1838	41	15182
Charland	Guillaume	1824	1901	Mathilde Marquis	1864	1893	36	34805
Cotnam	Wm C.	1805	1879	Janet, Eliz Meyer	1845	1868	28	21336
Dinning	Henry	1830	1884	Etta Carpenter	1851	1877	45	45531
Dugal	Léandre			Philomène Trahan	1862	1860	12	11522
Dunn	Thomas	1811	1891	Catherine	1866	1877	19	20818
Finch	Sam	1765	1838	Elizabeth Holmes	1811	1834	23	7406
Gilmour	Allan	1805	1884	-	1831	1867	57	49225
Gingras	J.-Elie	1804	1891	Labbé, Lacroix, Godbout	1851	1880	63	56821
Goudie	John	1775	1824	Jane Black	1801	1823	33	9848
Jeffery	James	1787	1868	Nancy, N. Foy, C. Neal	1833	1848	23	16297
Jeffery	John	1794	1846	Ann Phillips	1827	1847	28	19474
Jobin	Charles			Flore Bertrand	1848	1856	11	7564
Jones	Horatio N.		1884		1850	1859	13	14999
Labbé	Louis	1779	1839	Rosalie Roy	1814	1832	13	4009
Labbé	P.-Gab		1828	Solomie Julien	1861	1866	16	8685
Lampson	William	1789	1873	Elizabeth Duncomb	1838	1844	14	7355
Lee	Thos C.	1810	1865	A. Black, L. VanFelson	1841	1866	61	50553
Marquis	F.-X.			Marcelline L. Sanschagrin	1864	1878	15	25136
McKay	Lauchlan	1811	1895	Judith Coombs	1864	1877	32	17714
Munn	Alexander	1766	1812	Agnes Galloway	1796	1812	21	5571
Munn	John	1769	1814	Frances Farrie	1799	1813	18	5668
Munn	John	1788	1859	-	1811	1857	93	56127
Nesbitt	John Jas	1803	1882	M. Cannon, C. Slevin	1835	1856	54	38582
Oliver	Edward	1817	1911		1838	1841	11	6247
Oliver	James E.	1813	1867	Eliza McDerment	1843	1853	13	13225
Oliver	Thos H.	1810	1880	Jane Eliz. Jameson	1834	1877	123	87945
Parke	George H.	1807	1900	M. Anderson, A. Smith	1849	1857	12	15481
Ray	Walter	1820	1893	Jane LeSueur	1845	1858	12	10940
Rosa	Narcisse	1823	1907	Julie Côté, F. Roy	1855	1877	50	29418
Russell	Wm G.	1807	1864	Catherine Morrison	1838	1863	37	31681
Samson	Isidore	1827	1890	Eléonore Soucy	1855	1879	23	19456
Samson	Julien			Anne Shaveran	1855	1879	23	19456
Samson	Etienne	1815	1893	M. Beland, A. Labadie	1855	1885	26	27055
Sewell	Edm W.	1828	1882	Lucie A. Cloutier	1850	1874	19	12207
Sheppard	William	1784	1867	Harriet Campbell	1823	1826	10	3062
Trahan	Edouard	1810	1865	M. Jeanne Bedard, Esther Hamel	1853	1860	10	10083
Valin	Pierre		1819	M. Anne Roy, Marie Payette	1845	1868	36	33866
Valin	Pierre V.	1827	1897	M. Talbot, M. Bardy	1864	1880	37	34780
Valin	Toussaint			M. Tremblay	1857	1863	14	12003
Warner	Henry		1893	Rebecca Elizabeth Coombs	1864	1877	31	17471

Sources: *Quebec and Montreal Shipping Registers*
Parish Registers and Notarial Deeds

Note: *Only shipbuilders who are known to have built ten or more ships in the Port of Quebec are included. Each of the partners is credited with the partnership's construction.*

Notes to Appendices B & C

A certificate of registry entitles a vessel to operate under the flag of the country where she is registered and provides her with a means of identification. Compulsory registration enables a country to know the strength and composition of its merchant marine at all times, and if it so wishes, to control the carriers of its trade.

Customs officers in designated "Ports of Registry" are responsible for the registration of vessels owned within the limits of their port, the term "port" signifying a certain distance of coast line and the ports it contains, as well as the port of registry itself. Port limits are modified to suit circumstances from time to time. Thus, Montreal, was within the "Port of Quebec" from the 1760s until 1832 when it became a Port of Registry in its own right.

Although registration existed far earlier – Port of Quebec registers date from 1763[1] – the first comprehensive British registration system was introduced by the *Act for the further Increase and Encouragement of Shipping and Navigation* of 1786.[2] From that time, all British owned decked vessels of fifteen tons and upward were required to be registered in their home port, i. e., the port from and to which the vessel usually traded and in which or near which she was owned. Conversely, no foreign-owned nor foreign-built vessel, except Prizes, could thenceforth obtain British registry.

According to the Act of 1786 each vessel was surveyed and measured by a customs officer or other authtorized person, and her tonnage was calculated according to a fixed procedure and, on bond being given by the Master and by the owner, a Certificate of Registry was given to the master. The Port of Registry retained an exact copy of the certificate in its Register Book, and sent another to the Commissioners of Customs in London within a month. The Master was obliged to produce the certificate at every British port of call under penalty of a one hundred pound fine for non-compliance, and the vessel was subject to forfeiture if she left port without a valid certificate. The Act also required that the entire text on the certificate be included in each deed of transfer of ownership or part ownership of the vessel, failing which, the deed would be void.

Registration certificates were numbered in a port series, beginning with number one each year, e.g., 1/1787, and contained the following information: the name or names of the subscribing and non-subscribing owners(s) (those not present at the registration), with their occupations and places of residence, the name of the vessel, her home port, Master, place and date of construction as given in the Builders's Certificate (a document which was essential for the registration of new vessels). In the case of a Prize, the place and date she was made free were noted instead. The surveying officer certified that she was British, Foreign or Plantation built, and gave details of her construction: the number of decks and masts, length, breadth and height between decks or depth of hold, tonnage, rig and type of contruction, whether carvel or clinker-built, whether she had galleries, and what type of head, if any. A Customs Officer signed the certificate.

The Act also required that certificates and their corresponding entries in the Port Registers be endorsed with the details of every change of Master or of owner or part-owner. When a vessel was altered in such a way that her description in the Register became inaccurate, the certificate had to be replaced. If a vessel was lost, her registry had to be endorsed with the date, manner and place of loss, and her certificate, if it survived, had to be surrendered. Any change of home port required re-registration at the new port, which would issue a new certificate and report the fact to her former home port, where the original entry in the Register Book was endorsed "reg. de novo," the name of the new home port, and the date or port number and year. In each case, the Commissioners in London had to be advised.

The Act was repealed when the new *Act for the registering of Vessels* was passed in 1823,[3] which retained the general principles of the old act, including the method of measuring and calculating tonnage, but introduced new rules for the meaurement of steam vessels, for the granting of a Governor's Pass, regarding ownership by several owners or ownership by a joint stock company and for the control of mortgages on vessels.

In 1835 the *Act to regulate the Admeasurement of the Tonnage and Burthen of the Merchant Shipping of the United Kingdom*,[4] put an end to the antiquated measurement system. Though not one hundred percent perfect, it was a big step in the right direction.

Many vessels trading in Canadian inland waters were not covered by the these registration and measurement Acts and in order to regularize the situation, an Act was passed by the Canadian Legislature in 1845 entitled *An Act to secure the right of property in British Plantation Vessels navigating the Inland Waters of this province, and not registered under the Act of the Imperial Parliament of the United Kingdom, passed in the third and fourth years of the Reign of His late Majesty King William the Fourth, intituled "An Act for the Registering of British Vessels," and to facilitate transfers of the same, and to prevent the fraudulent assignment of any property in such Vessels*.[5] Registration, including measurement and ownership regulations of all Canadian vessels was thus standardized.

By the mid-nineteenth century, new shipping laws were required to regulate the unprecedented numbers of immigrants and other travellers undertaking sea voyages, and ever increasing quantities of goods transported by sea. Moreover the time had come for all matters relating to merchantships and seamen to be administered by one strong central authority. The *Merchant Shipping Act* of 1854 provided them, and gave full power to superintend and implement all laws pertaining thereto to the Board of Trade.[6] Other parts of the act covered the safety and prevention of accidents, pilotage, lighthouses, etc.; it is Part II, however, relating to the ownership, measurement and registry of British vessels, that concerns us here. The act amended and consolidated registration procedures, introduced new measurement rules, see page 366, and provided for each vessel to be given an "official number," which she was to retain throughout her life.

In 1856, persistent lobbying by the trade led to the *Canadian Act to encourage shipbuilding within this Province*[7] which encouraged investment in shipbuilding by providing for contracts between the builder and the advancer of money or goods for building a vessel to be registered in the local Registry Office and for the registration certificate to be granted in the advancer's name.

A further *Act to amend the Merchant Shipping Act* of 1867, concerned the health of seamen, and made provision for their accommodation to be inspected and if found to be in accordance with the law, for the space to be deducted from the registered tonnage of the vessel.[8]

Finally, the British *Act relating to shipping, and for the registration, inspection and classification thereof*, of 1873, resolved the inconsistencies between the method of measurement of inland and seagoing vessels in Canada, caused by the *Merchant Shipping Act* of 1854.[9] It also made provision for better security for persons advancing money for shipbuilding, and gave the authority to make rules and regulations for the inspection and classification of ships built and registered in Canada to the Canadian Governor in Council, and the administering thereof to the Minister of Marine and Fisheries.

The registration of vessels built at Quebec between 1786 and 1873 was thus governed by a series of British and Canadian laws and their amendments, the most important of which were the *Registration Act* of 1786, instituting general registry, and the *Merchant Shipping Act* of 1854, which finally brought in satisfactory measurement rules. By the time that Britain passed the new *Act to consolidate Enactments relating to Merchant Shipping* in 1894,[10] Quebec's wooden sailing ship industry had ended.

Fortunately, an unbroken series of Register Books of the Port of Quebec from 1787 on has survived, with the added bonus of a few earlier registers. From these was drawn up Appendix B. which lists the square rigged vessels and schooners of over one hundred tons built in the port of Quebec that were granted Quebec registry or left Quebec under a Governor's Pass, and fifteen vessels built prior to 1787, identified from newpaper accounts of launchings or from *Lloyd's Registers*, as indicated. Appendix C lists the vessels of over 100 tons built in the outports and registered at Quebec.

The amount of information recorded in port registers increased greatly over the years. While the registers of 1787 devote one eighth of a page to each registration with scant information about the ownership of vessels, by the 1870s, the registration took up two full sheets and for those heavily endorsed with mortgages, sales, etc., even more.

Included in the appendixes are the date of registry of the vessel, name, rig, tonnage, measurements, builder's name and, in the case of a vessel built after 1854, official number, see notes below. Other information recorded in the registries and not included in the appendixes, though recorded by the author, is discussed in Chapter 9.

Date of registry

With the exception of vessels built prior to 1787, which have been listed under the year in which they were built, all vessels are listed under the year in which they were first registered or in which they received a Governor's Pass. The Governor's Pass was a document which permitted a vessel built for an overseas owner to proceed to her home port for registration.

Name of the vessel

Though a vessel might be given a temporary name during construction, under which she might be launched, from the time she was registered, the name on her registration certificate became the only one under which she might legally be described. The law required that name to be painted on her stern, and from 1854 on, on her bow as well, in white or yellow letters as close to four inches high as possible, on a black background, together with the name of her home port. In Canada, her registered name could only be changed by permission of the Governor in Council, and when permission was granted, her certificate of registry, the copy in the Port Register and the identification on the vessel had to be immediately changed. Names of vessels in the appendixes are the official names under which the vessel was originally registered. Time has not permitted research into name changes of Quebec ships, but some that have come to light during other research, have been included after the original name.

Rig

Classed at times according to the form of their hull and at others according to their function, by the end of the eighteenth century sailing vessels were being increasingly described according to their rig, and by 1825, this system was generally adopted. It is also how sailing vessels are classified in the Register Books and consequently in the lists that follow. Three masted vessels listed include ships (sh), barques (ba), barquentines (bn); Two masted vessels include brigs (br), brigantines (be) and schooners (sc), and until 1827, snows (sn), which carried a third small mast close abaft the mainmast. Listed also are three sloops with a single mast, and two large timber droghers.

Tonnage

Originally, a vessel's capacity to carry cargo, or her "burthen," was measured by the number of tuns she could carry. The word "tonnage" was used to denote charter costs, and later, certain fourteenth century taxes, both of which were reckoned at so much a ton of a vessel's burthen. Eventually, tonnage came to be used as an alternative for the word "burthen" and to be calculated from the vessel's measurements, and an equitable method to do so slowly evolved. The registration act of 1786 required vessels to be measured in the manner described in the earlier *Customs Act of 1773 for the better ascertaining of the Tonnage and Burthen of Ships and Vessels* .... Three-fifths of the breadth was subtracted from the length, and the result was multiplied by the breadth and then by half the breadth, and the whole was then divided by 94.

$$\frac{(L - 3/5B) \times B \times 1/2B}{94}$$

Dimensions were taken in feet and inches. Tonnage, as a result of the formula, had remainders in 94ths. Though seriously flawed because the depth of the vessel was ignored, this system of "Builder's Measurement," or as it was known later "Old Measurement" or O.M., remained in effect until 1836.

The Act of 1835, which finally brought in the "New Measurement" or N.M. system, required measurements to be taken in feet and decimal parts of a foot, and for the first time, the depth of the hold was taken into account in the formula used for calculating the tonnage. The vessel was divided into six equal parts along her length, and a series of measurements were taken at the foremost, the middle and aftermost of the points of division. The tonnage was found by multiplying the "sum of the depths" by the "sum of the breadths", by the length, dividing the product by 3500 and adding the amount of covered deck space. Consequently, instead of having remainders in 94ths, tonnages then had remainders in 3500ths.

$$\frac{(D^1 + 2D_2 + D^3) \times (B^1 + B^2 + 3B^3 + B^4 + B^5 + 2B^6) \times L}{3500} \text{ plus deckspace}$$

Although a step in the right direction, this was still far from perfect, and it was superseded in 1855 by what was known as "New Measurement" or N.N.M., a method of measurement devised by a committee appointed for that purpose, under the chairmanship of Admiral Moorsom, R.N.

Moorsom's Rules, as they have come to be known, have stood the test of time. They were adopted by the United States in 1864, and they are still the basis of the tonnage measurement systems of most countries. The procedure requires the vessel to be divided into four to twelve transverse sections of equal length and the transverse area at each of the dividing points to be calculated. A formula is then used to find the cubic content of the vessel, which, when divided by one hundred gives the tonnage. Remainders are in decimals. Below, a vessel of from 121 to 180 feet, has been divided, as required, into eight parts. "I" represents the interval between the transverse areas.

$$\frac{(A^1 + 4A^2 + 2A^3 + 4A^4 + 2A^5 + 4A^6 + A^7) \times I/3}{100} \text{ plus closed-in deck-space}$$

A modification in 1867 required that the cubic content of the crew's quarters be subtracted from the gross tonnage, and that the net tonnage so obtained be shown on the certificate of registration along with the gross tonnage. The appendixes, it should be noted, show the gross tonnage figures.

Measurements

Measurements of length and breadth are rounded to the nearest whole number, depth to one decimal.

The length is that of a line along the rabbet of the keel from the back of the main stern post to a perpendicular line from the forepart of the main stem under the bowsprit.

The breadth is that of the widest part of the vessel from outside plank to outside plank above or below the water-line.

The depth is that of the hold from tonnage deck to ceiling amidships. In the case of vessels with more than one deck, the depth given is that of the height between decks.

Builders

Though a builder's certificate was a requirement for the registration of all new vessels, it was not mandatory that the builder's name be recorded. For long periods, however, registration officers in the Port of Quebec noted it as a matter of course. The resulting gaps have been filled from newspaper reports of launchings, surveyor's reports, etc. but for many vessels built before 1829, it has not been possible to do so.

Often a builder sub-contracted the construction of a vessel to another. In such cases, the name of the actual builder, when known, follows a hyphen, as it does if the financer of the project or another party signed the builder's certificate, so that his name appears on the register instead of that of the builder.

Official Numbers

According to the *Merchant Shipping Act* of 1854 official numbers were given to every British vessel that was registered and the number was carved into the main beam of the vessel together with her tonnage. These numbers remained the same throughout her life and are therefore a valuable means of identification.

Notes
1. RG68, V. 202, microfilm C-3948, NA.
2. 26 Geo. 3, c. 60.
3. 4 Geo. 4, c. 61.
4. 5 and 6 Will. 4, c. 56.
5. Statutes of Canada, 1845, 8 Vict., c. 5.
6. 17 & 18 Vict., c. 114.
7. Statutes of Canada, 1856, 19 Vict., c. 50.
8. 30 and 31 Vict., c. 124.
9. 36 Vict., c. 128.
10. 57 and 58 Vict., c. 60.

Appendix B

Sailing Ships Built in the Port of Quebec 1765-1893

*/	1764	Malaga Packet	100	br			8/	1798	General Prescott	207	sh	84 x 24 x 6	Alexander Munn
*/	1764	Neptune (Hanover) (Firm)	200	sh			13/	1798	Saint Peter	104	br	62 x 20 x 10	Yves Picard
*/	1765	Cordelia		sn		Zach Thompson	4/	1799	Caldwell	196	sn	79 x 24 x 6	J. Normand
*/	1767	Conqueror	200	sn		Zach Thompson ?	10/	1799	Caledonia	253	sh	90 x 26 x 5	Beatson - John Munn sr
*#/	1768	Solid Carleton (Reward)	180	sh			11/	1799	Diamond	521	sh	119 x 30 x 6	Patrick Beatson
#/	1768	Betsey	140	sh		Zach Thompson	13/	1799	Quebec	221	sh	89 x 25 x 6	Alexander Munn
*/	1770	Dolphin	120				15/	1799	Phoenix	181	sh	81 x 23 x 4	Patrick Beatson
*#/	1773	Hector	240	sh			18/	1799	Duke of Kent	283	sh	95 x 26 x 6	Patrick Beatson
*/	1774	Canadian	120	br			19/	1799	Britannia	257	sh	91 x 26 x 6	John Munn sr
*/	1774	Jane	300	sh			1/	1800	Glasgow	168	be	78 x 23 x 5	Patrick Beatson ?
*#/	1774	British Queen	250	sh	68 x 25 x 11	Jos Parent	12/	1800	Duke of Kent	337	sh	105 x 27 x 5	Alexander Munn
*/	1774	James	125	br			13/	1800	Governor Milnes	300	sh	97 x 27 x 6	Wm King
*/	1774	James and Rebecca	120	br	68 x 21 x 7		15/	1800	Monarch	646	sh	127 x 34 x 6	Patrick Beatson
*/	1775	Peggy	275	sh			16/	1800	Dundas	333	sh	105 x 27 x 5	John Munn sr
/	1776	William Wilson				taken to Lake Champlain	24/	1800	Nancy	347	sh	108 x 27 x 6	John Munn sr
*/	1786	Roman Eagle	104	be	66 x 20 x 4	Jas Duncanson	25/	1800	Aimwell	303	sh	102 x 26 x 5	Alexander Munn
*/	1786	Mary S Scallan	165	sh			26/	1800	Harriet	158	sh	80 x 21 x 5	Patrick Beatson
7/	1787	Alfred	205	sh	79 x 25 x 5	Jas Duncanson	27/	1800	Queen	430	sh	117 x 29 x 6	Patrick Beatson
10/	1790	Lord Dorchester	171	be	79 x 25 x 5		9/	1801	Atlas	554	sh	119 x 33 x 6	Wm Baldwin
12/	1790	General Wolfe	204	sh	82 x 23 x 4	Wm King ?	11/	1801	Rebecca	191	sn	82 x 20 x 5	John Munn sr
8/	1791	General Clarke	122	be	67 x 20	John Black & Wm King	12/	1801	Juno	279	sh	103 x 25 x 5	Alexander Munn
/	1792	Prince Edward	316	sh	98 x 27 x 16	John Black	20/	1801	Alexander	279	sh	98 x 26 x 6	Henry Baldwin
5/	1793	Iroquois	118	be	68 x 21 x 4	Wm King ?	27/	1801	Maitland	364	sh	110 x 27 x 6	John Munn sr
/	1793	Maria	204	sh			31/	1801	George and Bridget	424	sh	113 x 29 x 6	John Goudie
9/	1794	True Briton	125	br	65 x 21 x 10	Patrick Beatson ?	/	1801	Sainte Anne	120	be		
11/	1794	Royal Edward	371	sh	110 x 28 x 6	Patrick Beatson	13/	1802	Ocean	561	sh	121 x 33 x 7	Beatson - Henry Baldwin
2/	1795	Sisters	103	be	65 x 21 x 12	Geo Bradford Lane	14/	1802	Kilby	302	sh	107 x 26 x 5	Alexander Munn
33/	1795	Queen	497	sh	120 x 31 x 6	Patrick Beatson	15/	1802	William Pitt	216	sc	84 x 24 x 5	John Goudie
/	1795	Drummond	102	br			16/	1802	Atlanta	107	sc	65 x 20 x 9	John Goudie ?
11/	1796	Active	148	sh	84 x 21 x 5	Patrick Beatson	21/	1802	Aid	149	be	76 x 21 x 5	Beatson - Henry Baldwin
12/	1796	Albion	115	sh	73 x 20 x 4	Patrick Beatson	23/	1802	Hope	158	be	80 x 21 x 4	Beatson - Henry Baldwin
14/	1796	London	242	sh	95 x 25 x 6	Alexander Munn	28/	1802	Mary	377	sh	106 x 28 x 6	John Munn sr
8/	1797	Adelphi	157	sn	87 x 21 x 5	Patrick Beatson	30/	1802	Diana	261	sh	97 x 25 x 6	John Munn sr
9/	1797	Neptune	363	sh	111 x 27 x 6	Patrick Beatson	4/	1803	Aurora	268	sh	95 x 25 x 5	Alexander Munn
11/	1797	Canada	260	sh	87 x 27 x 6	Alexander Munn ?	6/	1803	Minerva	136	br	72 x 21 x	John Goudie
/	1797	Experiment	220	sh			14/	1803	William	208	be	84 x 24 x 5	John Goudie
/	1797	Mary	203	sh			16/	1803	Marguerite	115	sl	64 x 21 x 10	Henry Baldwin
4/	1798	Christian	126	be	63 x 21 x 12								

Appendices

17/ 1803	Beaver	111	sc	64 x 20 x 10	John Goudie	22/ 1810	Mary Ann	111	br	64 x 20 x 5	Hamilton
20/ 1803	Irvine	148	be	75 x 21 x 5	David Munn	27/ 1810	Pompey	401	sh	108 x 29 x 7	John Goudie
24/ 1803	John Craigie	124	sc	64 x 22 x 8	John Goudie ?	29/ 1810	Martha	411	sh	109 x 29 x 7	John Goudie
28/ 1803	Eleanor	126	br	68 x 21 x 4	Alexander Munn	34/ 1810	Diamond	371	sh	102 x 29 x 7	Alexander Munn
29/ 1803	Jeany	130	be	69 x 22 x 12		36/ 1810	Sarah	158	br	72 x 23 x 4	Sam Brown
30/ 1803	City of Edinburgh	310	sh	97 x 27 x 6	Henry Baldwin	39/ 1810	Emperor	575	sh	124 x 32 x 7	Philip Hooker
34/ 1803	General Hunter	124	sn	67 x 21 x 10	Henry Baldwin	42/ 1810	Richard	343	sh	110 x 27 x 19	Hamilton
35/ 1803	William Pitt	258	sh	91 x 26 x 5	John Goudie	47/ 1810	Fanny	277	sh	94 x 27 x 6	Geo Charles
39/ 1803	Little George	154	br	77 x 21 x 12		10/ 1811	Eliza	150	br	73 x 22 x 4	Alexander Munn
9/ 1804	Desire	103	sc	64 x 19 x 10	H. Baldwin ?	11/ 1811	British Army	459	sh	119 x 30 x 7	Frs Robitaille
14/ 1804	Anna Maria	349	sh	106 x 28 x 19	H. Baldwin	16/ 1811	Harrison	720	sh	127 x 36 x 7	Anderson - Sam Brown
16/ 1804	Flora	119	br	66 x 20 x 10	Alexander Munn	18/ 1811	Echo	126	br	69 x 21 x 5	John Munn
18/ 1804	Bear	278	sh	93 x 26 x 5	John Goudie	25/ 1811	Caesar	438	sh	114 x 29 x 7	John Goudie
26/ 1804	Active (Langdon Cheeves)	205	br	83 x 24 x 6	John Munn sr	29/ 1811	Aberdeen	466	sh	115 x 30 x 7	J. Henry & P. Leitch
30/ 1804	Ann	176	be	80 x 23 x 14	H. Baldwin	31/ 1811	Union	258	br	94 x 26 x 5	Bell & Robitaille
/ 1804	Jane	120	sc	69 x 20 x 10		32/ 1811	Sir J. H. Craig	268	sh	95 x 26 x 5	Bell & Robitaille
7/ 1805	L'Industrie	108	sc	64 x 20 x 11	Frs & Romain Robitaille	34/ 1811	Mercator	285	sh	94 x 26 x 6	Atkinson - Walter Gilley
10/ 1805	Alexander	227	sh	87 x 24 x 6	John Goudie	40/ 1811	Sir Geo. Prevost	574	sh	125 x 32 x 7	Ph Hooker - Baldwin
18/ 1805	Lord Gardner	307	sh	99 x 27 x 6	Alexander Munn						& Ray
19/ 1805	Leeds	227	sn	88 x 24 x 5		47/ 1811	Saint Patrick	540	sh	123 x 32 x 24	Hamilton - Wm Grant
21/ 1805	President Dunn	142	br	73 x 21 x 12		48/ 1811	Crescent	403	sh	109 x 29 x 7	Jas Morrison
22/ 1806	Lauzon	115	sc	74 x 19 x 9	(at Etchemin)	49/ 1811	Contest	300	sh	99 x 26 x 6	John Munn sr
25/ 1806	Roberts	419	sh	109 x 30 x 20	John Goudie	50/ 1811	Benson	573	sh	126 x 32 x 7	Sam Finch
27/ 1806	Sisters	288	sh	94 x 27 x 6	Alexander Munn	52/ 1811	John	462	sh	120 x 30 x 7	John Goudie
28/ 1806	Mary	364	sh	105 x 28 x 6	John Munn	59/ 1811	Caldecot	470	sh	116 x 30 x 7	John Bell
9/ 1807	Mentor	224	be	90 x 24 x 6	Frs Robitaille	61/ 1811	Lord Wellington	288	sh	95 x 26 x 6	John Goudie
10/ 1807	Adelaide	149	sc	72 x 22 x 11	John Goudie	16/ 1812	Goudies	361	sh	105 x 28 x 20	John Goudie
12/ 1807	Traveller	406	sh	101 x 30 x 7	John Munn sr ?	19/ 1812	Harp	471	sh	119 x 30 x 21	Hamilton -
17/ 1807	Doubt	426	sh	112 x 30 x 20	John Goudie	27/ 1812	Industry	116	sc	66 x 21 x 12	A. Caven, A. Martin et al
21/ 1807	General Craig	374	sh	105 x 29 x 6	Alexander Munn	44/ 1812	Diana	419	sh	108 x 30 x 6	Alexander Munn
22/ 1807	Quebec	211	br	84 x 25 x 16	H. Baldwin	4/ 1813	James	230	be	86 x 25 x 5	Late Alexander Munn
10/ 1808	Canada	288	sh	90 x 27 x 19	John Goudie	15/ 1813	Hope	385	sh	105 x 29 x 7	John Bell
15/ 1808	Answell	428	sh	112 x 29 x 21	John Goudie	17/ 1813	Cossack	421	sh	109 x 30 x 7	John Munn sr &
18/ 1808	Atlantic	221	sc	83 x 27 x 15	Henry Baldwin						John Munn
19/ 1808	Neptune	555	sh	126 x 31 x 23	John Goudie	27/ 1813	Ayrshire	337	sh	105 x 27 x 6	David Munn
20/ 1808	Mint	469	sh	121 x 30 x 7	Alexander Munn	17/ 1814	Ottawa	340	sh	96 x 29 x 6	Hamilton -
22/ 1808	London	579	sh	122 x 31 x 23	John Munn sr	18/ 1814	Paris	408	sh	113 x 29 x 7	Louis Labbé
29/ 1808	Olive Branch	475	sh	123 x 30 x 24	John Munn sr	23/ 1814	Edward	365	sh	105 x 28 x 7	Peter Campbell
11/ 1809	Nancy	137	br	68 x 22 x 4	Alexander Munn	25/ 1814	Hadlow	380	sh	104 x 29 x 7	
16/ 1809	Briton	473	sh	119 x 31 x 8	John Goudie	29/ 1814	Earsdon	174	be	77 x 23 x 5	Peter Campbell
18/ 1809	Nancy	162	br	77 x 23 x 5	Alexander Munn	16/ 1815	Champion				
23/ 1809	John	121	be	64 x 21 x 11	Wm Grant	28/ 1815	Swift	140	sc	71 x 22 x 10	John Goudie
24/ 1809	Ajax	439	sh	113 x 29 x 24	John Goudie	34/ 1815	Olive Branch	207	br	83 x 24 x 5	John Munn
32/ 1809	Elisabeth	211	sn	83 x 24 x 6	Wm Grant	46/ 1815	Lady of the Lake	118	br	72 x 20 x 6	John Steples et al
33/ 1809	Sampson	381	sh	104 x 29 x 6		58/ 1815	Fame	205	br	83 x 24 x 5	John Goudie
34/ 1809	New Liverpool	181	sc	74 x 23 x 12	Henry Baldwin	7/ 1816	Greek	438	sh	109 x 30 x 7	Geo Taylor ?
20/ 1817	Saint Lawrence	122	sc	69 x 20 x 9	John Goudie (1809)	14/ 1816	Lowland Lass	145	br	71 x 22 x 12	Sam Brown
4/ 1810	Robert	108	br	64 x 20 x 6	Hamilton	15/ 1816	Highland Lad	319	sh	103 x 26 x 6	John Goudie
9/ 1810	Margaret	195	br	81 x 24 x 5	John Munn sr	6/ 1817	Favourite	270	be	93 x 26 x 5	John Bell
14/ 1810	Hussar	374	sh	117 x 27 x 7	John Goudie	14/ 1818	Betsey	212	br	85 x 24 x 6	Ol Trahan & Ben Viger
17/ 1810	Richard	145	br	69 x 22 x 5	Henry Baldwin	15/ 1818	Elizabeth	193	sn	85 x 23 x 5	Sam Finch
19/ 1810	Betsy	214	sh	85 x 24 x 5	John Munn sr	35/ 1818	Margaret	145	br	70 x 22 x 12	Robt Orkney

Figure 241: *The Customs House, in which business was carried out in the traditional British Custom House "Long Room." The Register Books that were carefully kept there serve as a solid basis for the history of shipbuilding in the Port and to a lesser extent, of other locations on the river. Fonds Michael Ayre, photo L.P. Vallée, N 80–2–20, courtesy Archives nationales du Québec.*

Appendices

No./Year	Name	Tons	Type	Dimensions	Builder/Notes
1/ 1819	Saint Lawrence	275	ba	99 x 25 x 6	John Bell
2/ 1819	Sir James Kempt	340	ba	102 x 27 x 18	Campbell & Sheppard
3/ 1819	Henry	385	sh	107 x 29 x 20	Geo Taylor
4/ 1819	Montmorency	381	sh	106 x 29 x 20	Geo Taylor
11/ 1819	Young Norval	286	sh	98 x 26 x 6	John Goudie
25/ 1819	Rob Roy	201	br	79 x 24 x 14	Robt Orkney
26/ 1819	Maria	201	br	84 x 23 x 6	Sam Finch
3/ 1820	John Howard	273	ba	93 x 26 x 17	Pat Fleming
5/ 1820	May Flower	139	sn	70 x 21 x 12	Jas Young
8/ 1820	Catherine	170	br	78 x 22 x 13	Geo Black
9/ 1820	London	335	sh	103 x 27 x 6	John Goudie
19/ 1820	Harriet	261	sn	94 x 25 x 6	Sam Finch
2/ 1821	Eleanor	271	br	94 x 26 x 6	Geo Black
3/ 1821	Dalhousie	128	be	74 x 20 x 13	
10/ 1821	Countess of Dalhousie	262	sh	95 x 25 x 5	John Goudie
32/ 1821	Saguenay	179	be	81 x 22 x 10	
6/ 1822	Saint Charles	281	br	98 x 25 x 6	John Bell
10/ 1822	Nimrod	181	sh	86 x 22 x 14	(at C. Hunter's shipyard)
11/ 1822	Quebec Packet	313	sh	98 x 27 x 6	John Munn - Geo Black
12/ 1822	Flora	325	sh	102 x 27 x 19	John Munn
21/ 1822	Constantia	239	sh	92 x 24 x 6	Campbell & Sheppard
23/ 1822	George the Fourth	259	sn	98 x 24 x 6	
10/ 1823	Thames	315	sh	101 x 26 x 6	John S. Campbell
13/ 1823	Emma	202	br	83 x 24 x 5	Sam Finch
14/ 1823	Caroline	303	sh	99 x 27 x 5	Geo Black
27/ 1823	President	124	be	66 x 21 x 10	Sam Finch
37/ 1823	London	178	br	78 x 23 x 6	John Goudie
39/ 1823	Phoebe (Marianne)	230	br	89 x 24 x 5	Sam Finch
40/ 1823	Martha and Eliza	147	sc	74 x 22 x 12	Sheppard & Campbell
41/ 1823	General Wolfe	321	ba	104 x 26 x 6	John Bell
1/ 1824	Saint David	353	ba	109 x 27 x 6	John Bell
GP/ 1824	Sir Watkin	234	ba	93 x 24 x 5	
2/ 1824	Bride	340	ba	102 x 28 x 20	Shep & Campbell - Harper
4/ 1824	Argyle	329	ba	103 x 27 x 6	Geo Black
5/ 1824	Harlequin	380	sh	111 x 28 x 7	Sam Finch
8/ 1824	Choice	122	be	71 x 20 x 12	Wm & Robt Carman
12/ 1824	Columbus	3690	dr	301 x 51 x 29	Chas Wood
14/ 1824	Columbine	279	sn	95 x 26 x 6	
26/ 1824	Union Jacket	222	br	87 x 24 x 17	Sheppard & Campbell
GP/ 1824	Ontario	297	br	96 x 26 x 6	John Bell
32/ 1824	Cato	344	ba	105 x 27 x 6	Geo Black
33/ 1824	Miriam and Jane	310	ba	103 x 26 x 19	Ed Henley
35/ 1824	Richard Pope	330	ba	102 x 27 x 7	Sam Finch
36/ 1824	Wellwood	218	br	85 x 24 x 5	John Bell
GP/ 1824	William Parke	268	br	94 x 25 x 5	John Munn
9/ 1825	Thomas Laurie	294	br	96 x 26 x 6	John Munn
10/ 1825	Duncan Gibb	361	ba	105 x 28 x 7	John Munn
GP/ 1825	Royal George	330	ba	102 x 27 x 6	John Bell
11/ 1825	Trio	307	sh	95 x 27 x 6	Geo Black
13/ 1825	Jessie Lawson	321	sh	103 x 26 x 7	Sheppard & Campbell
14/ 1825	Parmelia	443	ba	118 x 29 x 20	Shep & Cam - J. Jeffery
15/ 1825	Carrington	159	br	75 x 22 x 13	Carman - Sam Brown ?
20/ 1825	Tottenham	309	ba	95 x 27 x 6	Geo Black
22/ 1825	Lord Melville	425	sh	111 x 29 x 20	Geo Taylor
21/ 1825	William Huskisson	301	sh	96 x 27 x 7	Atkinson - ?
25/ 1825	Mansfield	372	sh	103 x 28 x 20	Louis Labbé
27/ 1825	Lord Byron	380	ba	106 x 29 x 20	Alex Martin
30/ 1825	Aid	306	ba	98 x 27 x 20	Robt Alden
32/ 1825	George Channing	424	sh	112 x 29 x 20	Sam Finch ?
33/ 1825	Thomas Wallace	301	ba	96 x 27 x 20	Atkinson - Robitaille
39/ 1825	Baron of Renfrew	5294	dr	304 x 61 x 35	Chas Wood
42/ 1825	Fortune	314	ba	99 x 27 x 18	Sam Finch
46/ 1825	Elvira	412	sh	114 x 29 x 20	Wm McAlpine
54/ 1825	Susan	204	br	86 x 24 x 15	Wm & Robt Carman
62/ 1825	City of Waterford	375	sh	109 x 28 x 6	Geo Black
65/ 1825	Charlotte and Maria	371	ba	105 x 28 x 20	Robt Wood - Pat Fleming
69/ 1825	Maxfield	343	ba	107 x 27 x 7	Campbell & Sheppard
75/ 1825	Rose Maroon	175	sn	81 x 22 x 14	Wm Bell
79/ 1825	Leonidas	383	ba	110 x 28 x 20	Carman & Finch
80/ 1825	Sir Francis N. Burton	191	br	85 x 23 x 14	Sam Finch
81/ 1825	Admiral Benbow	372	ba	106 x 28 x 6	
82/ 1825	Sir Francis Burton	411	sh	111 x 29 x 7	Sam Finch
85/ 1825	Jean Baptiste	239	br	87 x 25 x 6	Louis Labbé
86/ 1825	Anne	235	br	85 x 25 x 6	Louis Labbé
87/ 1825	Canadian	413	sh	110 x 29 x 7	Louis Labbé
88/ 1825	Thomas Ritchie	385	ba	109 x 28 x 7	John Munn
83/ 1825	Juliana	276	br	98 x 25 x 5	
92/ 1825	Belfast	246	br	87 x 26 x 6	John Munn-Robt Orkney?
93/ 1825	Julia	107	sc	71 x 18 x 12	Geo Black
GP/ 1825	Dalhousie Castle	274	sn	94 x 26 x 18	John Bell
GP/ 1825	Quebec Trader	319	ba	98 x 27 x 18	Geo Black
GP/ 1825	Flora	411	sh	111 x 29 x 19	Sam Finch
GP/ 1825	Walrus	363	ba	104 x 28 x 6	Sam Finch
GP/ 1825	Surrey	364	ba	102 x 28 x 20	McD & Hows-Louis Labbé
GP/ 1825	Brothers	296	ba	96 x 26 x 18	
GP/ 1825	Alicia	425	sh	113 x 29 x 7	Louis Labbé
2/ 1826	Manlius	479	sh	121 x 30 x 20	Sheppard & Campbell
GP/ 1826	Susan	208	sn	83 x 24 x 17	Wm Newton
33/ 1826	Georgianna	404	ba	109 x 29 x 6	Wm Newton
36/ 1826	Vibilia	361	sh	106 x 28 x 20	Geo Black
39/ 1826	Corinthian	391	ba	107 x 28 x 20	Wm Newton
GP/ 1826	Ulster	349	sh	106 x 27 x 7	Wm Bell
60/ 1826	Saint Ann	132	br	69 x 21 x 12	Jos Berte (at Baie des Chaleurs?)
GP/ 1826	Eveline	301	sh	99 x 26 x 6	Friend - McArthy, Boyd et
91/ 1826	Harlequin	352	sh	104 x 28 x 7	Sam Finch
GP/ 1826	Lycurges	329	sh	100 x 27 x 19	McD & Hows - J. Desnoyers
94/ 1826	Branches	452	sh	116 x 29 x 21	Geo Taylor
95/ 1826	Orwell	408	sh	109 x 29 x 6	John Munn
96/ 1826	Home	410	sh	111 x 29 x 7	John Munn
97/ 1826	Welcome	293	br	97 x 26 x 6	John Munn
104/ 1826	Jane Vilet	310	ba	100 x 26 x 18	Wright - Jas Adams
GP/ 1826	Superior	254	sh	93 x 25 x 6	Wm Bell

Appendices

GP/	1826	Othello	404	sh	110 x 28 x 6	Wm Bell	32/	1828	Gulnare	146	sc	75 x 21 x 10	Geo Taylor
106/	1826	Marmion	412	sh	111 x 29 x 7	Sam Finch	34/	1828	Golconda	560	sh	128 x 31 x 7	Geo Black
109/	1826	Saint Leonard	352	ba	106 x 27 x 21		35/	1828	Caroline	425	sh	111 x 29 x 7	Geo Black
110/	1826	Edward	366	ba	106 x 28 x 20	Carman-Allan, Murphy al	38/	1828	Prompt	240	br	91 x 24 x 5	John Munn
113/	1826	Unicorn	400	sh	109 x 29 x 7	J.Olivier Brunet	39/	1828	Shamrock	106	sc	63 x 20 x 10	Campbell ?
130/	1826	Newry	379	ba	107 x 28 x 20	John Munn	40/	1828	Henry	337	ba	103 x 27 x 7	Jas Young
GP/	1826	Enterprise	167	sn	80 x 22 x 13		41/	1828	Thames	283	sh	106 x 25 x 6	Geo Black
137/	1826	Anastasia	211	br	86 x 23 x 17		44/	1828	Eldon	403	sh	108 x 29 x 7	John Munn
GP/	1826	Persian	386	sh	111 x 28 x 6	Geo Black	45/	1828	British Sovereign	350	sh	103 x 28 x 6	Farrington - Viger, Ernst
145/	1826	Agnes & Ann	413	ba	113 x 29 x 6	Alex Martin	67/	1828	Amelia Matilda	192	br	81 x 23 x	Sam Finch jr
147/	1826	Dalusia	188	br	85 x 22 x 6	Sheppard & Campbell	GP/	1828	Naparina	308	ba	101 x 26 x 6	John Bell
154/	1826	Harriet	248	br	89 x 25 x 5	Atkinson - ?	82/	1828	Fulwood	329	sh	101 x 27 x 7	
166/	1826	Hope	455	sh	116 x 29 x 7	Geo Taylor	87/	1828	Lion Hill	163	sc	79 x 21 x 13	Geo Black
175/	1826	Mary Ann	241	sn	92 x 25 x 7	(at St Roch)	GP/	1828	Lois	161	br	72 x 23 x 14	J.O. Brunet
176/	1826	Pericles	247	sn	92 x 25 x 16		88/	1828	Olive Nailer	312	sh	99 x 27 x 6	John Munn
188/	1826	Jamaica	111	br	64 x 20 x 13	Geo Taylor	89/	1828	Margaret Balfour	250	br	92 x 25 x 5	
190/	1826	Champlain	300	ba	97 x 27 x 17	John S. Campbell	1/	1829	John Porter	303	sh	99 x 26 x 7	Geo Black
191/	1826	Brazila	306	br	99 x 27 x 17	John S. Campbell	6/	1829	John Kerr	113	be	62 x 21 x 11	Louis Labbé
194/	1826	Bob Logic	128	br	71 x 20 x 13	Robt Orkney	GP/	1829	William	331	sh	104 x 27 x 6	Geo Black
200/	1826	Sophia	420	ba	111 x 29 x 7	Louis Labbé	8/	1829	Margaret	312	br	102 x 26 x 6	John Bell
203/	1826	Try Again	291	br	95 x 26 x 6	John Munn	9/	1829	Strathisle	332	sh	105 x 26 x 7	Geo Black
206/	1826	Morgianna	354	sh	103 x 28 x 7	Sam Finch	14/	1829	Quebec	198	br	81 x 24 x 14	Geo Black
208/	1826	Ann and Mary	253	br	86 x 26 x 6		18/	1829	Huron	264	br	94 x 25 x 6	John Munn
GP/	1826	Town of Ross	283	ba	98 x 25 x 6	John Bell	GP/	1829	John Campbell	348	ba	105 x 27 x 18	Ls Labbé - Geo Black
213/	1826	Abeona	118	sc	65 x 21 x 9	(at Diamond Harbour)	28/	1829	Quintin Leitch	425	sh	112 x 29 x 6	John Munn
2/	1827	Kamaskda	324	ba	104 x 27 x 7	John S. Campbell	34/	1829	Edward	352	sh	106 x 27 x 6	Geo Black
8/	1827	America	391	sh	108 x 28 x 6	Pat Fleming	41/	1829	Ann	313	br	103 x 27 x 6	John Bell
9/	1827	John Binner	161	be	79 x 21 x 14	Geo Black	46/	1829	Corrib	198	br	84 x 23 x 16	Allison Davie
14/	1827	Caroline	105	be	64 x 20 x 12	J.Olivier Brunet	53/	1829	Mail	281	br	97 x 26 x 6	John Munn
15/	1827	Fanny	141	be	71 x 21 x 13	John S. Campbell	55/	1829	Silistria	154	br	73 x 23 x 13	Frs Lemieux
18/	1827	Bonaparte	134	br	70 x 21 x 13	J.Olivier Brunet	56/	1829	Onondaga	568	sh	127 x 32 x 23	Geo Black
21/	1827	Marianne	261	br	90 x 26 x 6	Sam Finch	GP/	1829	Wexford	279	sh	99 x 25 x 5	John Bell
25/	1827	Kingfisher	221	br	91 x 23 x 7	Geo Taylor	1/	1830	Brilliant	150	sc	72 x 22 x 6	John Bell
GP/	1827	Thomas	362	sh	106 x 28 x 6	Pat Fleming	2/	1830	Grenada	224	br	89 x 24 x 15	Allison Davie
29/	1827	Columbus	154	sc	87 x 20 x 7		3/	1830	Breeze	325	br	104 x 26 x 6	John Bell
32/	1827	Ariadne	333	sh	102 x 27 x 6	John Munn	4/	1830	Portia	339	sh	105 x 27 x 18	Geo Black
40/	1827	Eliza	296	br	98 x 26 x 6	John Munn	5/	1830	Thomas Tucker	141	sc	77 x 20 x 13	Geo Black
56/	1827	Esther	178	br	81 x 22 x 6	Jeffery	6/	1830	Robert Watt	221	br	89 x 24 x 15	Geo Black
GP/	1827	Hibernia	402	ba	110 x 29 x 19		19/	1830	Elizabeth Robertson	328	sh	103 x 27 x 17	Geo Black
61/	1827	Beatrix	224	sn	88 x 24 x 16	John Bell ?	23/	1830	Fanny	325	sh	101 x 27 x 6	John Munn
71/	1827	Sarah Maria	169	br	75 x 23 x 6	Baldwin, Ruddock, et al	31/	1830	Carouge	391	sh	109 x 28 x 7	Sam Finch (at Carouge)
75/	1827	Roberts	323	ba	104 x 27 x 6	John S. Campbell - Jas Young	33/	1830	Isabella	281	br	96 x 26 x 6	John Munn
77/	1827	Grace	126	br	69 x 21 x 13	J.Olivier Brunet	42/	1830	Janet	443	sh	115 x 29 x 6	John Munn
89/	1827	Brilliant	236	br	91 x 24 x 5	John Munn	8/	1831	Agnes	280	br	96 x 26 x 6	John Munn
91/	1827	Betsy	116	sc	69 x 20 x 11		18/	1831	Royal Adelaide	410	ba	112 x 28 x 19	Louis Labbé
95/	1827	Saint Andrew	112	br	63 x 21 x 11	John S. Campbell (?)	GP/	1831	Wolfe's Cove	588	ba	125 x 32 x 22	Allan Gilmour & Co.
10/	1828	Diligent	128	sc	77 x 19 x 10	Louis Labbé	GP/	1831	Quebec	586	ba	125 x 32 x 22	Allan Gilmour & Co.
11/	1828	Wiliam	121	be	71 x 20 x 12	Bennett's yard	9/	1832	Dorchester	417	sh	111 x 29 x 7	Sam Finch jr
25/	1828	Catherine	165	br	74 x 23 x 13	Sam Finch	12/	1832	Lord Aylmer (Aliquis)	671	sh	137 x 33 x 23	Geo Black
27/	1828	Betsey	291	br	98 x 26 x 6	John Bell	17/	1832	Equimaux	162	br	76 x 22 x 14	Jas Goudie
31/	1828	Montcalm	214	be	87 x 23 x 16		19/	1832	Buckingham	293	br	99 x 26 x 6	John Munn
							20/	1832	Mansfield	290	ba	99 x 26 x 6	John Munn

Appendices

24/ 1832	Lord Ramsay	346	br	106 x 27 x 6	John Bell
GP/ 1832	Glasgow	584	ba	125 x 32 x 22	Allan Gilmour & Co.
31/ 1832	Hyppolite	121	be	67 x 21 x 11	Olivier Chartier
33/ 1832	Wave	134	br	77 x 20 x 13	Louis Labbé
GP/ 1832	Mearns	587	ba	125 x 32 x 22	Allan Gilmour & Co.
7/ 1833	Aurora	361	ba	110 x 27 x 6	John Bell
8/ 1833	Pekin	288	br	99 x 25 x 6	John Munn
14/ 1833	Sir James Anderson	499	sh	123 x 30 x 21	Geo Black
18/ 1833	William Herdman	344	sh	108 x 27 x 7	Jas & John Jeffery
25/ 1833	William Rodger	497	ba	121 x 30 x 22	John Munn
35/ 1833	John McLellan	571	sh	125 x 32 x 22	Geo Black
GP/ 1833	Bengal	657	ba	136 x 32 x 22	Allan Gilmour & Co.
40/ 1833	Watt	505	ba	122 x 30 x 22	John Munn
GP/ 1833	Ganges	659	ba	136 x 32 x 22	Allan Gilmour & Co.
9/ 1834	John Bell	455	sh	118 x 29 x 6	John Bell
12/ 1834	Malay	298	br	102 x 25 x 6	John Munn
13/ 1834	British Heroine	611	sh	130 x 32 x 22	Jas & John Jeffery
GP/ 1834	Coromandel	662	sh	134 x 33 x 23	Geo Black
GP/ 1834	Aberfoil	281	sh	100 x 25 x 17	Sam Finch jr
GP/ 1834	Perfect	658	sh	133 x 33 x 23	Geo Black
GP/ 1834	Europe (Europa)	272	br	99 x 25 x 6	Thomas H. Oliver
GP/ 1834	William Ritchie	422	sh	115 x 28 x 7	Sam Finch
26/ 1834	Dibdin	571	sh	129 x 31 x 22	John Munn
27/ 1834	Blake	569	ba	129 x 31 x 22	John Munn
GP/ 1834	Canton	665	ba	138 x 32 x 8	Allan Gilmour & Co.
GP/ 1834	Catherine	449	sh	120 x 29 x 7	Sam Finch
GP/ 1834	Springfield	304	sh	105 x 25 x 7	J.S.Campbell
32/ 1834	Canada	145	sl	71 x 22 x 7	Théo Lamothe
GP/ 1834	Gilmour	668	ba	138 x 32 x 8	Allan Gilmour & Co.
GP/ 1834	Maria	275	sh	105 x 24 x 6	Thomas H. Oliver
4/ 1835	William	187	br	86 x 22 x 14	Thomas H. Oliver
6/ 1835	Cornubia	409	sh	111 x 29 x 19	John James Nesbitt
GP/ 1835	Malabar	687	sh	137 x 33 x 23	Geo Black
10/ 1835	Pink	294	br	101 x 25 x 6	John Munn
GP/ 1835	Borneo	458	sh	120 x 29 x 6	John Bell
14/ 1835	Calcutta	707	sh	132 x 34 x 23	Jas & John Jeffery
GP/ 1835	Napoleon	443	sh	122 x 28 x 7	Thomas H. Oliver
18/ 1835	Lord Canterbury	599	ba	133 x 31 x 22	John Munn
21/ 1835	Crusader	584	sh	132 x 31 x 22	Wm Sharples Son - Milling
GP/ 1835	Pekin	668	ba	138 x 32 x 22	Allan Gilmour & Co.
GP/ 1835	Indus	670	ba	138 x 32 x 22	Allan Gilmour & Co.
30/ 1835	Quebec	108	sc	77 x 17 x 6	Jas George
40/ 1835	Lord Sidmouth	595	sh	133 x 31 x 22	John Munn
1/ 1836	Jesse Maria	174	br	74 x 21 x 12	John Nicholson
2/ 1836	Robert Thomas	576	sh	120 x 28 x 20	Jas & John Jeffery
GP/ 1836	Jessie Logan	855	sh	145 x 30 x 21	Geo Black
3/ 1836	Favorite	431	sh	111 x 25 x 19	John Bell
4/ 1836	Gannet	322	br	98 x 23 x 18	John Munn
8/ 1836	Syllerie	824	sh	139 x 30 x 22	Wm Sharples Son - Milling
9/ 1836	Victory	591	sh	122 x 27 x 21	Thomas H. Oliver
12/ 1836	Harrison	651	sh	123 x 28 x 21	Geo Bell
GP/ 1836	Harriet Scott	377	sh	104 x 24 x 18	Thomas H. Oliver
13/ 1836	Jane	485	sh	116 x 25 x 19	Thomas H. Oliver
22/ 1836	Albatross	734	sh	129 x 28 x 22	John Munn
GP/ 1836	Pollock	815	ba	139 x 31 x 19	Allan Gilmour & Co.
GP/ 1836	Letitia	375	ba	107 x 24 x 17	John James Nesbitt
29/ 1836	Tamarac	768	sh	131 x 30 x 21	Wm Sharples Son - Milling
GP/ 1836	Renfrewshire	841	ba	134 x 30 x 22	Allan Gilmour & Co.
10/ 1837	Suir	431	ba	102 x 26 x 19	Geo Black
GP/ 1837	William Sharples	794	sh	145 x 33 x 21	Wm Sharples Son - Milling
GP/ 1837	Mangalore	876	sh	139 x 30 x	Geo Black
13/ 1837	Josepha	421	ba	104 x 25 x 19	Thomas H. Oliver
GP/ 1837	Agitator	425	ba	97 x 24 x 19	John Jeffery
GP/ 1837	Petrel	336	br	99 x 23 x	John Munn
GP/1837	Sophia	586	sh	118 x 26 x	Andrew Neilson
GP/ 1837	Marchioness of Abercorn	875	ba	140 x 32 x 21	Allan Gilmour & Co.
27/ 1837	Caledonia	736	sh	129 x 28 x 22	John Munn
28/ 1837	John Bolton	993	sh	142 x 32 x 24	John Munn
34/1837	Leonard Dobbin	611	ba	121 x 29 x 20	Thomas H. Oliver
36/ 1837	England	940	sh	147 x 32 x 23	John Munn
GP/ 1837	Fingalton	860	ba	136 x 31 x 22	Allan Gilmour & Co.
38/ 1837	Crescent	575	sh	114 x 27 x 20	Andrew Neilson
GP/ 1837	Fanny	515	ba	117 x 27 x 16	Wm Sharples Son - Milling
GP/ 1838	Java	572	sh	120 x 26 x 19	Geo Black
10/ 1838	Wetherall	153	br	76 x 20 x 13	Nicholson & Russell
15/ 1838	Guiana	172	br	79 x 21 x 14	Campbell & Black
16/ 1838	Providence	660	sh	129 x 29 x 21	John Jeffery
18/ 1838	Premier	299	ba	96 x 23 x 17	Ed Oliver
19/ 1838	Robert Alexander Parke	389	ba	105 x 24 x 18	Thomas H. Oliver
25/ 1838	Matthew Bell	532	sh	119 x 26 x 19	Wm Lampson
26/ 1838	Elizabeth	419	ba	99 x 25 x 20	Wm Lampson
GP/ 1838	Spencer	371	sh	101 x 25 x 18	Geo Black
GP/ 1838	Broom	888	sh	141 x 32 x 22	Allan Gilmour & Co.
33/ 1838	Earl of Durham	109	be	62 x 19 x 12	Marcel Dufour
36/ 1838	England	940	sh	147 x 32 x 23	John Munn
37/ 1838	Scotland	937	sh	141 x 32 x 24	John Munn
GP/ 1838	Mearns	757	ba	127 x 30 x 22	Allan Gilmour & Co.
46/ 1838	Prompt	398	ba	105 x 24 x 18	John Munn
GP/ 1838	Georgianna	529	sh	115 x 26 x 20	Thomas H. Oliver
6/ 1839	Urgent	622	sh	125 x 28 x 21	Andrew Neilson
9/ 1839	Briton's Queen	705	sh	129 x 29 x 22	John Jeffery
10/ 1839	Wellington	539	sh	117 x 26 x 20	Ed Oliver
14/ 1839	Queen Victoria	634	ba	122 x 28 x 21	Nicholson & Russell
GP/ 1839	Crusader	619	sh	124 x 29 x 19	Geo Black
GP/ 1839	Glenview	644	sh	125 x 29 x 20	Geo Black
19/ 1839	Belinda	346	ba	94 x 24 x 17	John James Nesbitt
20/ 1839	Token	579	ba	122 x 27 x 20	John Munn
22/ 1839	Benjamin Hart	323	ba	97 x 23 x 17	Thomas H. Oliver

Appendices

GP/	1839	Independence	692	sh	129 x 27 x 20	Thomas H. Oliver	61/	1840	Lady Flora Hastings	675 ba 131 x 28 x 21	John Munn
24/	1839	William Pirrie	553	sh	120 x 27 x 20	Thomas H. Oliver	62/	1840	Coolock	262 br 92 x 22 x 16	Thomas H. Oliver
26/	1839	Iona	393	ba	106 x 25 x 18	John Munn	63/	1840	Vitula	296 ba 96 x 23 x 17	Ed Oliver
GP/	1839	Salem	787	ba	131 x 30 x 23	Wm Lampson	66/	1840	Lanarkshire	688 ba 134 x 28 x 21	Americus Vidal
GP/	1839	Ann Moore	239	br	87 x 23 x 15	John James Nesbitt	67/	1840	Ottawa	553 sh 114 x 26 x 19	Nicholson - Russell
GP/	1839	Belfast	519	ba	93 x 23 x 17	Thomas H. Oliver	4/	1841	Rockshire	563 ba 126 x 27 x 20	Wm Lampson
GP/	1839	Euxine	895	ba	139 x 32 x 22	Allan Gilmour & Co.	6/	1841	Compton	547 sh 123 x 27 x 20	Jas Jeffery & Co.
32/	1839	Manlius	703	sh	130 x 30 x 22	John Jeffery	7/	1841	Good Hope	551 sh 122 x 26 x 20	Jas Jeffery & Co.
38/	1839	John Bull	436	sh	102 x 26 x 19	Thomas H. Oliver	8/	1841	Cremona	506 sh 116 x 26 x 20	Jas Jeffery & Co.
39/	1839	United Kingdom	1267	sh	199 x 32 x 23	John Munn	11/	1841	Liverpool	902 sh 144 x 30 x 22	Jas Jeffery & Co.
GP/	1839	Ritchie	916	ba	141 x 32 x 22	Allan Gilmour & Co.	13/	1841	Jeanie Deans	319 ba 96 x 23 x 17	John Munn
GP/	1839	Rival	191	sc	81 x 20 x 13	Thomas H. Oliver	17/	1841	Caroline	540 sh 118 x 26 x 19	John James Nesbitt
43/	1839	Wandsworth	826	sh	141 x 31 x 21	Andrew Neilson	GP/	1841	Conqueror	651 sh 124 x 28 x 20	John James Nesbitt
48/	1839	Great Britain	404	ba	103 x 25 x 18	Nicholson & Russell	18/	1841	Parmelia	817 sh 141 x 31 x 22	John Jeffery
49/	1839	Marquess of Normanby	247	br	87 x 23 x 15	John James Nesbitt	21/	1841	Anthony Anderson	499 sh 114 x 26 x 19	John James Nesbitt
51/	1839	Thistle	612	ba	125 x 28 x 20	John Munn	22/	1841	Tom Moore	278 ba 96 x 22 x 16	John James Nesbitt
52/	1839	Huron	449	sh	108 x 25 x 18	Thomas H. Oliver	25/	1841	Palestine	809 sh 140 x 30 x 22	Wm Lampson
2/	1840	Sophia	176	sc	80 x 20 x 14	John Jeffery	27/	1841	China	636 sh 130 x 28 x 20	John Jeffery
3/	1840	Devonport	767	sh	130 x 29 x 22	Jas Jeffery	28/	1841	The Duke	683 ba 132 x 28 x 21	John Munn
5/	1840	Jane	179	sc	70 x 20 x 15	John Jeffery	33/	1841	Universe	719 sh 127 x 29 x 22	Thomas H. Oliver
GP/	1840	Merton (Mertoun)	703	sh	128 x 29 x 21	Geo Black	35/	1841	Camillus	616 sh 123 x 27 x 20	Ed Oliver
GP/	1840	Windsor Castle	818	sh	133 x 31 x 21	Geo Black	36/	1841	Arabian	581 sh 124 x 27 x 20	J. McLure Muckle
15/	1840	Ocean Queen	803	sh	132 x 30 x 23	Ed Oliver	37/	1841	Jane Black	579 sh 124 x 28 x 20	T.C. Lee
16/	1840	Royal Albert	872	sh	139 x 30 x 22	Nicholson & Russell	GP/	1841	Parsee Merchant	636 sh 122 x 27 x 20	Ed Oliver
17/	1840	Robert Benn	810	sh	134 x 30 x 22	Jas Jeffery	GP/	1841	Philopontus	629 sh 121 x 28 x 21	Ed Oliver
19/	1840	Corea	734	sh	135 x 29 x 20	John James Nesbitt	39/	1841	Temperance	104 sc x 18 x 11	Marcel Dufour
23/	1840	Marquess of Bute	562	ba	126 x 27 x 20	Wm Lampson	GP/	1841	Victoria	714 sh 129 x 29 x 22	Thomas H. Oliver
24/	1840	Union	751	sh	129 x 29 x 22	Jas Jeffery & Co.	44/	1841	Afghan	691 ba 134 x 29 x 21	Americus Vidal
25/	1840	Covenanter	613	ba	126 x 27 x 21	John Munn	47/	1841	Princess Royal	605 sh 124 x 26 x 20	Nicholson & Russell
GP/	1840	Leonidas	494	sh	111 x 26 x 20	John James Nesbitt	49/	1841	Lord Sandon	678 ba 131 x 28 x 21	John Munn
28/	1840	Constitution	574	sh	118 x 27 x 20	Thomas H. Oliver	50/	1841	Bayfield	395 ba 104 x 26 x 17	Wm Lampson
29/	1840	Carthaginian	565	ba	120 x 26 x 20	Ed Oliver	GP/	1841	Lucinda	869 ba 139 x 30 x 22	Ed Oliver
GP/	1840	Cataraqui	802	sh	138 x 30 x 22	Wm Lampson	GP/	1841	Barbara	995 ba 148 x 32 x 23	Allan Gilmour & Co.
31/	1840	Osceola	568	sh	122 x 28 x 20	Geo Black	56/	1841	Henry	657 sh 127 x 27 x 20	Jas Jeffery & Co.
34/	1840	Macao	483	sh	110 x 26 x 19	John James Nesbitt	GP/	1841	GP - no details		John Jeffery
35/	1840	Royal Sovereign	505	sh	116 x 26 x 19	Thomas H. Oliver	64/	1841	Hero of Acre	663 ba 131 x 28 x 20	John Munn
36/	1840	Lord Seaton	731	sh	131 x 29 x 22	Thomas H. Oliver	GP/	1841	Union Yacht	126 sc	Geo T. Davie
37/	1840	John Munn	638	ba	127 x 28 x 20	Americus Vidal	75/	1841	Charlotte Harrison	573 ba 115 x 30 x 20	Pierre Labbé
38/	1840	Vixen	199	br	81 x 21 x 15	Wm Russell	79/	1841	Ann Best	336 ba 98 x 23 x 17	Americus Vidal
39/	1840	Ayrshire	631	ba	128 x 28 x 21	John Munn	81/	1841	Harbinger	325 ba 97 x 23 x 17	Thomas H. Oliver
40/	1840	James Dean	395	ba	106 x 24 x 18	John Munn	GP/	1841	Bolton Abbey	620 sh 121 x 27 x 20	Thomas H. Oliver
GP/	1840	Helen Sharples	861	sh	134 x 31 x 22	Sharples, Wainwright Co.	GP/	1841	Lochlibo	976 ba 146 x 32 x 23	Allan Gilmour & Co.
44/	1840	Goliath	989	ba	153 x 32 x 23	John Jeffery	12/	1842	Douce Davie	414 ba 107 x 25 x 18	John Munn
GP/	1840	Brooke	678	ba	131 x 28 x 22	Ed Oliver	16/	1842	Eagle	370 ba 103 x 24 x 18	Pierre Thorn
GP/	1840	Countess of Arran	317	ba	97 x 23 x 17	Ed Oliver	23/	1842	England	181 sc 106 x 19 x 10	Wm Lampson
GP/	1840	Ann Rankin	458	ba	113 x 26 x 18	Allan Gilmour & Co.	24/	1842	Scotland	184 sc 106 x 19 x 10	Wm Lampson
GP/	1840	Margaret Pollock	918	ba	140 x 32 x 22	Allan Gilmour & Co.	GP/	1842	Rasalama	781 sh 129 x 29 x 22	Thomas H. Oliver
51/	1840	Saint Lawrence	817	sh	138 x 30 x 22	Wm Lampson	GP/	1842	Syria	581 ba 126 x 27 x 20	Wm Lampson
53/	1840	Ann Jeffery	941	sh	143 x 31 x 23	John Jeffery	34/	1842	Eliza	633 sh 125 x 27 x 20	Nicholson & Russell
56/	1840	Wild Irish Girl	552	ba	126 x 27 x 20	Wm Lampson	36/	1842	Letitia Heyn	619 sh 124 x 27 x 20	John James Nesbitt
58/	1840	Unicorn	262	br	92 x 22 x 16	John James Nesbitt	GP/	1842	Lord Palmerston	449 ba 110 x 24 x 19	Thomas H. Oliver
GP/	1840	Agnes Gilmour	899	ba	139 x 32 x 22	Allan Gilmour & Co.	44/	1842	Highland Mary	428 ba 108 x x 25	John Munn

374 Appendices

No/Year	Name	Tons	Type	Dimensions	Builder
GP/1842	Warren Hastings	699	sh	122 x 28 x 20	Thomas H. Oliver
46/1842	Aramienta	617	sh	123 x 27 x 20	John James Nesbitt
51/1842	Sir Howard Douglas	715	ba	132 x 29 x 21	John Munn
52/1842	Agnes Jane	250	ba	102 x 22 x 13	John James Nesbitt
58/1842	Amoy	648	sh	123 x x 28	Geo Black
GP/1842	Lady Bagot	443	ba	113 x 24 x 18	Thomas H. Oliver
68/1842	Saguenay	736	ba	131 x 29 x 20	T.C. Lee
69/1842	Kitty	388	ba	103 x 24 x 18	John Munn
GP/1842	Pride	205	br	85 x 21 x 14	Thomas H. Oliver
GP/1842	Ararat	205	br	85 x 21 x 14	Thomas H. Oliver
5/1843	Mail	412	ba	108 x 25 x 18	John Munn
8/1843	Henrietta	548	sh	115 x 27 x 21	John Jeffery jr
15/1843	Annie	645	sh	127 x 27 x 20	John James Nesbitt
GP/1843	Aim	206	br	84 x 21 x 14	Thomas H. Oliver
35/1843	Chusan	460	ba	111 x 25 x 19	Thomas H. Oliver
37/1843	Miltiades	675	sh	126 x 27 x 20	John James Nesbitt
47/1843	Scotland	1079	sh	148 x 32 x 24	John Munn
GP/1843	Ganges	706	sh	128 x 28 x 21	Thomas H. Oliver
50/1843	Isabella	691	sh	126 x 28 x 22	Thomas H. Oliver
GP/1843	Bytown	615	ba	125 x 27 x 20	Allan Gilmour & Co.
GP/1843	Ottawa	1153	ba	156 x 32 x 24	Allan Gilmour & Co.
GP/1843	Oregon	177	sc	87 x 20 x 13	Antoine Ernst
58/1843	Lady Peel	567	sh	119 x 27 x 20	T.C. Lee
GP/1843	Henrietta Mary	845	sh	140 x 31 x 22	Jas E. Oliver
GP/1843	Rankin	1120	ba	156 x x 31	Allan Gilmour & Co.
60/1843	Melissa	794	sh	135 x 29 x 21	Thomas H. Oliver
7/1844	Hannibal	821	sh	130 x 31 x 23	John Jeffery jr
GP/1844	Foam	332	ba	98 x 23 x 17	Thomas H. Oliver
11/1844	Ambrosine	670	ba	127 x 27 x 20	Jas Jeffery
12/1844	Sapphiras	714	ba	129 x 28 x 21	Jas Jeffery
13/1844	Jane	658	sh	128 x 27 x 20	John James Nesbitt
15/1844	Prince Charlie	733	ba	131 x 29 x 20	John Munn
16/1844	Gem	171	sc	80 x 21 x 13	Wm Lampson
GP/1844	Asenath	321	ba	96 x 23 x 17	Thomas H. Oliver
17/1844	James T. Foord	790	sh	131 x 29 x 22	Thomas H. Oliver
19/1844	Cromwell	1096	sh	149 x 32 x 23	Thomas H. Oliver
21/1844	Stadacona	619	sh	119 x 27 x 21	T.C. Lee
GP/1844	Emigrant	946	ba	142 x 30 x 22	Thomas H. Oliver
45/1844	Coromandel	1035	sh	139 x 31 x 25	John Jeffery
55/1844	Elizabeth	691	sh	131 x 28 x 20	John James Nesbitt
57/1844	Rose	643	sh	124 x 27 x 22	T.C. Lee
59/1844	Fame	732	ba	133 x 28 x 20	John Munn
61/1844	Mayfield	825	ba	136 x 30 x 22	Thomas H. Oliver
GP/1844	Oceana	799	ba	134 x 30 x	Thomas H. Oliver
1/1845	Erin	1135	sh	147 x 32 x 24	Wm Henry
2/1845	Junior	677	ba	128 x 28 x 20	Geo Black
3/1845	Lightship	137	sc	85 x 18 x 11	Nicholson & Russell
GP/1845	Fag-an-Bealac	524	ba	123 x 27 x 19	Thomas H. Oliver
16/1845	Ann McLester	439	sh	112 x 24 x 18	John James Nesbitt
19/1845	Ayrshire	750	ba	132 x 29 x 21	John Munn
20/1845	Sir Robert Peel	903	sh	139 x 31 x 22	T.C. Lee
21/1845	James Fagan	660	sh	126 x 28 x 21	T.C. Lee
22/1845	Princess Alice	684	ba	129 x 28 x 22	Jas Jeffery
23/1845	Rosina	681	ba	129 x 28 x 22	Jas Jeffery
GP/1845	Belinda	758	sh	138 x 27 x 20	John James Nesbitt
25/1845	Arethusa	712	sh	134 x 28 x 20	John James Nesbitt
26/1845	Yorkshire Lass	389	ba	102 x 25 x 18	Wm Cotnam
27/1845	City of York	1091	sh	143 x 32 x 24	John Jeffery
GP/1845	Sea King	661	sh	130 x 27 x 20	Thomas H. Oliver
28/1845	Polly John Munn	710	ba	134 x 29 x 21	John Munn
29/1845	Manchester	824	ba	142 x 30 x 22	Walter Ray
GP/1845	John Farnworth	266	ba	93 x 21 x 15	Thomas H. Oliver
30/1845	Ben Lomond	947	ba	142 x 30 x 23	Thomas H. Oliver
33/1845	Lord Metcalfe	523	ba	120 x 26 x 18	Thomas H. Oliver
GP/1845	Dunbrody	458	ba	110 x 27 x 19	Thomas H. Oliver
43/1845	Malabar	1175	sh	155 x 33 x 24	John Jeffery
GP/1845	Agamemnon	1167	sh	157 x 32 x 24	Allan Gilmour & Co.
GP/1845	Argo	1164	sh	156 x 32 x 24	Allan Gilmour & Co.
GP/1845	Achilles	654	ba	128 x 27 x 20	Allan Gilmour & Co.
48/1845	Charlotte	694	sh	139 x 29 x 22	T.C. Lee
50/1845	Empire	709	sh	135 x 27 x 20	John James Nesbitt
51/1845	Eliza Morison	798	sh	140 x 28 x 20	John James Nesbitt
54/1845	Flint	307	br	95 x 23 x 17	Geo Black
GP/1845	Admiral	787	ba	138 x 30 x 22	Thomas H. Oliver
56/1845	Ceylon	778	sh	129 x 28 x 23	John Jeffery
GP/1845	Jane Morison	538	sh	117 x 26 x 19	Thomas H. Oliver
5/1846	Charlotte	760	ba	138 x 29 x 22	Jas Jeffery
6/1846	Elizabeth	711	ba	131 x 29 x 22	Jas Jeffery
8/1846	Erin's Queen	822	sh	141 x 29 x 21	John James Nesbitt
GP/1846	Harry Lorriquer	985	ba	146 x 31 x 23	Thomas H. Oliver
GP/1846	Kalma	568	ba	122 x 26 x 19	Thomas H. Oliver
11/1846	Rosalinda	813	sh	141 x 28 x 21	John James Nesbitt
GP/1846	Mary Seton	422	sh	108 x 26 x 18	Geo Wm Usborne
13/1846	Lord Dufferin	708	sh	134 x 28 x 21	T.C. Lee
GP/1846	Sophia Moffat	550	sh	122 x 27 x 19	Wm Russell
14/1846	Omega	1278	sh	157 x 33 x 25	Geo Black
GP/1846	Queen Pomare	715	ba	134 x 28 x 22	Thomas H. Oliver
16/1846	Moodkee	326	ba	98 x 23 x 17	Thomas H. Oliver
17/1846	Oregon	1004	sh	151 x 32 x 22	Pick Tibbits - Walter Ray
19/1846	Jessy	821	sh	138 x 29 x 22	T.C. Lee
GP/1846	Montezuma	525	ba	118 x 26 x 19	Wm Cotnam
22/1846	Marianne	797	sh	139 x 28 x 21	Rich Jeffery
27/1846	Glen Helen	1051	sh	157 x 31 x 23	Thomas H. Oliver
33/1846	Virginius	821	sh	141 x 28 x 21	John James Nesbitt
42/1846	Sobraon	1281	sh	168 x 32 x 24	John Jeffery & Son
45/1846	Jane Glassin	835	ba	137 x 29 x 22	Jas Jeffery
48/1846	Free Trader	803	sh	141 x 28 x 21	John James Nesbitt
52/1846	Margaretta	677	ba	128 x 28 x 21	Thomas H. Oliver
55/1846	Eliza	393	ba	107 x 25 x 17	Wm Cotnam
9/1847	Lumina	816	sh	140 x 30 x 22	T.C. Lee
GP/1847	Emma	623	sh	129 x 27 x 20	John James Nesbitt
12/1847	Eliza Pirrie	598	sh	127 x 27 x 20	John James Nesbitt
13/1847	Sarah	127	be	73 x 18 x 11	Thos Boyd
14/1847	Scottish Maid	482	ba	147 x 24 x 19	Geo Black jr

#	Year	Name	Tons	Type	Dimensions	Builder
19/	1847	Celina	922	ba	143 x 30 x 23	Thomas H. Oliver
24/	1847	Ringfield	1024	sh	158 x 30 x 22	Pierre Valin
25/	1847	Euterpe	857	ba	144 x 28 x 22	Rich Jeffery
27/	1847	Conrad	841	sh	142 x 30 x 23	T.C. Lee
31/	1847	Fingal	930	sh	146 x 32 x 22	Wm Henry - Edmund Sewell
32/	1847	Sarah	730	ba	136 x 28 x 21	Wm Henry - Edmund Sewell
33/	1847	Hyperion	753	ba	135 x 29 x 21	Wm Cotnam
GP/	1847	Brandon	1196	sh	163 x 32 x 24	Thomas H. Oliver
34/	1847	Lord Elgin	859	sh	142 x 30 x 22	John James Nesbitt
35/	1847	Thomas Fielden	904	sh	151 x 32 x 22	Pick Tibbits - Walter Ray
36/	1847	Jeannie Johnston	408	ba	106 x 24 x 18	John Munn
37/	1847	England	725	ba	134 x 28 x 21	John Munn
38/	1847	Riverdale	844	sh	145 x 29 x 21	Pierre Valin
40/	1847	Lady Elgin	851	ba	143 x 29 x 22	Jas Jeffery
41/	1847	Cromwell	708	ba	136 x 28 x 21	John Munn
GP/	1847	Emperor	768	sh	127 x 28 x 22	Thomas H. Oliver
45/	1847	City of Lincoln	891	sh	151 x 28 x 22	John Jeffery
51/	1847	Viceroy	1187	sh	166 x 31 x 24	Thomas H. Oliver
54/	1847	Jenny Lind	484	ba	118 x 26 x 20	T.C. Lee
GP/	1847	Acme	1230	sh	164 x 33 x 24	Allan Gilmour & Co
GP/	1847	Adept	1194	sh	160 x 32 x 24	Allan Gilmour & Co.
60/	1847	Madawaska	562	sh	127 x 26 x 19	Pick Tibbits - Walter Ray
61/	1847	Chippewa	846	sh	140 x 30 x 22	Jas Jeffery
62/	1847	Saint John	267	br	82 x 22 x 16	Geo Commerford
63/	1847	Mary Jane	547	ba	120 x 26 x 20	Jas E. Oliver
66/	1847	Retriever	351	ba	109 x 21 x 17	John Jeffery
GP/	1847	Jessie Stephens	428	ba	114 x 25 x 18	Wm Cotnam
GP/	1847	Actaon	610	ba	133 x 27 x 20	Allan Gilmour & Co.
GP/	1847	Abeona	618	ba	134 x 27 x 19	Allan Gilmour & Co.
81/	1847	Gipsy Queen	840	ba	144 x 29 x 21	John Jeffery
82/	1847	Erin Go Bragh	644	sh	134 x 28 x 20	John James Nesbitt
83/	1847	Isabella	1018	sh	159 x 32 x 23	Wm Cotnam - Edmund Sewell
GP/	1847	Wanderer	686	sh	133 x 27 x 20	John James Nesbitt
85/	1847	Blake	732	ba	136 x 29 x 21	John Munn
86/	1847	New Liverpool	722	ba	130 x 28 x 21	Wm Benson - John Jeffery ?
87/	1847	Wilson Kennedy	1130	sh	157 x 32 x 24	Thomas H. Oliver
GP/	1847	Shannon	306	ba	96 x 23 x 16	John James Nesbitt
M7/	1847	Liverpool	919	sh	151 x 28 x 22	John Jeffery
M8/	1847	Jane	700	sh	129 x 27 x 21	Wm Russell
7/	1848	Eliza	912	ba	145 x 30 x 22	Jas Jeffery
8/	1848	Kate	904	ba	145 x 30 x 22	Jas Jeffery
13/	1848	Elizabeth	986	sh	145 x 31 x 23	David Vaughan
15/	1848	Hercyna	857	ba	146 x 29 x 23	John Jeffery
16/	1848	Stella Maris	113	be	77 x 21 x 9	F.X. Mailhot
GP/	1848	Heroine	545	ba	122 x 26 x 20	John James Nesbitt
18/	1848	Thornhill	699	sh	136 x 28 x 21	John James Nesbitt
19/	1848	Baron of Renfrew	1127	sh	159 x 32 x 24	John Munn
20/	1848	Medusa	866	sh	146 x 29 x 21	Pierre Valin
21/	1848	Mary Ann	475	ba	114 x 25 x 19	Pierre Valin
22/	1848	Robina	792	sh	154 x 28 x 20	Geo Black jr
23/	1848	Jacques Cartier	115	be	68 x 20 x 10	Jos Lacombe
24/	1848	Harbinger	751	sh	131 x 29 x 21	Wm Benson (New Lpl)
GP/	1848	Lucy	1150	sh	159 x 32 x 24	Thomas H. Oliver
26/	1848	Clara Symes	887	ba	151 x 29 x 22	John Jeffery
27/	1848	Virginie	123	be	80 x 21 x 10	Chas Jobin
GP/	1848	Lydia	1146	sh	158 x 31 x 24	Thomas H. Oliver
31/	1848	Eglinton	462	ba	117 x 24 x 18	John Munn
32/	1848	Marion	739	sh	141 x 27 x 22	Wm Russell
33/	1848	Gertrude	605	ba	127 x 26 x 21	Thomas H. Oliver
35/	1848	Spalpeen	296	ba	96 x 22 x 17	Jas Kelly
GP/	1848	Anna	1050	sh	159 x 32 x 24	Jas Tibbits
38/	1848	Queen of the West	1161	sh	158 x 31 x 24	Thomas H. Oliver
49/	1848	Home	480	ba	117 x 24 x 19	John Munn
54/	1848	Challenger	816	sh	135 x 28 x 22	John James Nesbitt
GP/	1849	Sea Serpent	709	ba	135 x 29 x 22	Wm Henry - Edmund Sewell
15/	1849	Niagara	843	ba	145 x 30 x 23	T.C. Lee
GP/	1849	Dalniada	1504	sh	184 x 34 x 25	Parke & Co. - Pierre Brunelle
20/	1849	John Knox	1195	sh	164 x 33 x 24	John Munn
GP/	1849	City of Manchester	1205	sh	161 x 33 x 24	Thomas H. Oliver
GP/	1849	Lydia McHenry	884	sh	140 x 30 x 23	Thomas H. Oliver
GP/	1849	Edward	671	ba	131 x 28 x 20	Thomas H. Oliver
GP/	1849	Victoria	810	sh	141 x 29 x 22	John James Nesbitt
GP/	1849	Lydia	360	ba	107 x 24 x 17	J. Greaves Clapham
24/	1849	Theodore	1064	ba	160 x 31 x 23	Geo Black jr
26/	1849	California	487	ba	119 x 26 x 20	T.C. Lee
27/	1849	William Stevenson	806	sh	142 x 30 x 22	Wm Cotnam
37/	1849	Tinto	779	sh	146 x 29 x 22	Wm Russell
39/	1849	Lord Stanley	770	ba	141 x 29 x 21	John Munn
GP/	1849	Elspeth	283	ba	96 x 22 x 16	Thomas H. Oliver
GP/	1849	Grace McVia	882	sh	140 x 30 x 24	Thomas H. Oliver
GP/	1849	Sultan	931	sh	148 x 31 x 23	Thomas H. Oliver
GP/	1849	Tara	1137	sh	156 x 34 x 23	Parke & Co. - Pierre Brunelle
GP/	1849	Marchmont	1277	sh	168 x 33 x 24	Allan Gilmour & Co.
GP/	1849	Ronochan	1270	sh	168 x 33 x 24	Allan Gilmour & Co.
GP/	1849	Augusta	975	sh	148 x 31 x 23	Pierre Valin
59/	1849	Saint Hilda	792	sh	144 x 29 x 22	Wm Henry - Edmund Sewell
70/	1849	Lord George Bentinck	528	ba	121 x 26 x 19	John Munn
GP/	1849	Arthur	987	sh	155 x 30 x 23	Allan Gilmour & Co.
GP/	1849	Allan	994	sh	156 x 30 x 24	Allan Gilmour & Co.
82/	1849	Maria	1014	sh	150 x 32 x 23	Thomas H. Oliver
85/	1849	Panama	223	br	86 x 21 x 15	Wm Cotnam
2/	1850	Justyn	913	ba	145 x 30 x 23	Richard Jeffery
7/	1850	Aurelie	111	be	72 x 19 x 11	Théophile Jolicoeur
GP/	1850	Sunbeam	838	sh	141 x 29 x 22	John James Nesbitt
9/	1850	Kelpie	496	ba	130 x 26 x 19	Edmund Sewell
15/	1850	Australia	1029	sh	153 x 31 x 23	Pierre Valin

376 Appendices

GP/	1850	Windsor	1100	sh	158 x 32 x 23	T.C. Lee	GP/	1851	Ailsa	1458	sh	180 x 35 x 24	Allan Gilmour & Co.
GP/	1850	Coriolanus	1177	sh	163 x 33 x 23	Parke - Pierre Brunelle	GP/	1851	Arran	1065	sh	159 x 31 x 23	Allan Gilmour & Co.
GP/	1850	Garland	969	sh	153 x 31 x 23	Wm Cotnam	41/	1851	Superior	337	sc	134 x 23 x 12	Allan Gilmour & Co.
GP/	1850	Clontarf	1091	sh	157 x 31 x 23	H.N. Jones	GP/	1851	Georgiana	799	ba	137 x 29 x 21	T.C. Lee
GP/	1850	Lady Gough	975	sh	147 x 31 x 23	John James Nesbitt	43/	1851	John Bunyan	981	sh	149 x 32 x 23	John Munn
GP/	1850	Washington	1089	sh	157 x 32 x 23	T.C. Lee	45/	1851	Covenanter	1274	sh	168 x 34 x 23	John Munn
GP/	1850	Rajah Go Paul	969	sh	151 x 31 x 22	Thomas H. Oliver	48/	1851	Earl of Derby	1048	sh	163 x 32 x 23	Thomas H. Oliver
24/	1850	Martin Luther	1241	sh	165 x 33 x 23	John Munn	GP/	1851	Squaw	165	br	86 x 25 x 12	Jean Lemelin
25/	1850	John Calvin	885	sh	143 x 31 x 22	John Munn	53/	1851	Confiance	928	sh	148 x 30 x 23	John James Nesbitt
32/	1850	Glencairn	949	sh	153 x 31 x 23	Wm Russell	58/	1851	Eliza	943	sh	144 x 30 x 23	Jas E. Oliver
33/	1850	Marion	919	sh	145 x 31 x 22	Chas Jobin	61/	1851	Medina	960	sh	149 x 30 x 23	John James Nesbitt
38/	1850	Constitution	992	sh	149 x 31 x 23	Pierre Valin	GP/	1851	Columbine	970	sh	161 x 30 x 23	H.N. Jones
GP/	1850	Lady Eveline	876	sh	141 x 29 x 22	John James Nesbitt	GP/	1851	Tyendanaga	1024	sh	152 x 32 x 23	Wm Cotnam
GP/	1850	Epaminondas	1171	sh	161 x 34 x 23	Parke & Co. - P. Brunelle	62/	1851	Bannockburn	731	sh	137 x 28 x 22	Wm Russell
59/	1850	Sybil	108	sc	79 x 19 x 11	Edmund Sewell	5/	1852	Gulnare	164	sc	83 x 21 x 12	Thomas H. Oliver
GP/	1850	American Lass	766	ba	137 x 29 x 21	T.C. Lee	7/	1852	Eleanor	427	ba	115 x 26 x 18	Davidson & Goudie
GP/	1850	JKL	758	sh	137 x 29 x 22	Jas E. Oliver	8/	1852	Magyar	216	br	96 x 22 x 13	Jean Lemelin
GP/	1850	Delgany	910	sh	149 x 32 x 22	Thomas H. Oliver	9/	1852	Countess of Elgin	1205	sh	166 x 33 x 23	Baldwin & Dinning
GP/	1850	Arundel	868	sh	141 x 31 x 22	Thomas H. Oliver	13/	1852	Harriet	935	sh	144 x 30 x 23	Théo St Jean
GP/	1850	Hibernia	1065	sh	167 x 31 x 23	Jas E. Oliver	19/	1852	America	1484	sh	193 x 34 x 23	Parke - Pierre Brunelle
GP/	1850	Woodstock	967	sh	152 x 31 x 22	Thomas H. Oliver	20/	1852	Caroline	989	sh	148 x 30 x 23	Théo St Jean
76/	1850	Catherine	687	sh	134 x 26 x 21	Wm Russell	21/	1852	Gulnare	1107	sh	160 x 33 x 23	Thomas H. Oliver
78/	1850	Mangerton	1099	sh	159 x 32 x 23	H.N. Jones	23/	1852	Emigrant	935	sh	151 x 30 x 23	Thomas H. Oliver
80/	1850	Pilgrim	963	sh	147 x 32 x 23	John Munn	25/	1852	Derry Castle	942	ba	144 x 31 x 23	Edward P. Lee
81/	1850	Progress	541	ba	122 x 26 x 19	John Munn	26/	1852	Premier	905	sh	149 x 30 x 23	Thomas H. Oliver
82/	1850	Olivia	900	sh	147 x 30 x 22	Jas E. Oliver	27/	1852	Rhea Sylvia	882	sh	152 x 30 x 23	Jas E. Oliver
5/	1851	Marie Leocadie	170	ba	96 x 22 x 9	J.E. Gingras	28/	1852	Montcalm	1135	sh	165 x 32 x 23	T.C. Lee
GP/	1851	Fanny	951	sh	136 x 30 x 22	John James Nesbitt	33/	1852	Culloden	909	sh	157 x 30 x 23	Wm Russell
GP/	1851	Europa	1088	sh	158 x 33 x 23	T.C. Lee	36/	1852	Ebba Brake	1757	sh	193 x 36 x 30	Pierre Valin
8/	1851	Birmingham	1034	sh	165 x 31 x 22	Baldwin & Dinning	38/	1852	Earl of Elgin	1128	sh	165 x 32 x 23	Jean Elie Gingras
GP/	1851	Panola	966	sh	150 x 30 x 22	John James Nesbitt	47/	1852	Chesterholme	761	sh	140 x 29 x 20	Chas Jobin
10/	1851	Alice	133	be	74 x 21 x 11	Wm Davison	GP/	1852	Sarah and Emma	1195	sh	176 x 32 x 23	Jas E. Oliver
GP/	1851	Prince Arthur	1146	sh	164 x 32 x 23	T.C. Lee	60/	1852	Albinus	495	sh	133 x 25 x 18	T.C. Lee
GP/	1851	Thorwaldsden	903	ba	143 x 31 x 23	Edward P. Lee	65/	1852	Abdalla	962	sh	163 x 29 x 22	John James Nesbitt
16/	1851	Lady Bulmer	1115	sh	162 x 31 x 23	H.N. Jones	66/	1852	Sabrina	673	sh	152 x 26 x 20	Pierre Valin
GP/	1851	Plantagenet	1110	sh	162 x 31 x 23	H.N. Jones	GP/	1852	Advance	1614	sh	199 x 35 x 24	Allan Gilmour & Co.
GP/	1851	James Carson	1189	sh	176 x 32 x 23	Jas E. Oliver	GP/	1852	Advice	1373	sh	184 x 33 x 24	Allan Gilmour & Co.
18/	1851	Asia	1349	sh	178 x 33 x 23	Parke - Pierre Brunelle	68/	1852	Cameo	785	sh	144 x 27 x 21	Wm Russell
24/	1851	Sarah Mary	970	sh	156 x 30 x 23	Wm Russell	6/	1853	Hinda	300	ba	107 x 23 x 14	Vaughan - Frs Lachance
25/	1851	Forest Monarch	977	sh	149 x 31 x 23	Pierre Valin	GP/	1853	Sillery	1077	sh	170 x 30 x 22	John James Nesbitt
GP/	1851	Lady Louisa	1029	sh	143 x 31 x 22	Thomas H. Oliver	10/	1853	Lady Elma Bruce	1007	sh	170 x 31 x 22	Pelchat & Mercier
GP/	1851	Valleyfield	427	ba	116 x 24 x 18	Chas Jobin	13/	1853	Boomerang	1824	sh	204 x 36 x 29	Théo St Jean
26/	1851	Africa	1401	sh	185 x 34 x 23	Parke - Pierre Brunelle	14/	1853	The Duke of Wellington	1262	sh	181 x 32 x 23	Jean Elie Gingras
27/	1851	Marina	581	ba	125 x 25 x 20	Jas E. Oliver	GP/	1853	Volant	500	ba	129 x 26 x 18	Wm Cotnam
GP/	1851	Lord Warriston	1163	sh	165 x 33 x 23	Wm Cotnam	15/	1853	Persia	2003	sh	205 x 35 x 31	Parke - Pierre Brunelle
31/	1851	Mary	108	sc	78 x 19 x 8	Thomas H. Oliver	16/	1853	Wynnstay	528	sh	156 x 27 x 18	Théo St Jean
32/	1851	Martha	104	sc	77 x 19 x 8	Thomas H. Oliver	GP/	1853	Fulwood	1215	sh	197 x 31 x 22	H.N. Jones
GP/	1851	Bellcarrigg	938	sh	148 x 30 x 23	Thomas H. Oliver	GP/	1853	Glendalough	1077	sh	171 x 31 x 23	H.N. Jones
37/	1851	Ontario	338	sc	134 x 23 x 12	Allan Gilmour & Co.	18/	1853	Sapphire	1140	sh	179 x 30 x 23	Wm Russell
GP/	1851	Charles	1049	sh	163 x 32 x 22	T.C. Lee	21/	1853	Argonaut	1237	sh	179 x 33 x 22	Baldwin & Dinning
39/	1851	Childe Harold	1124	sh	166 x 31 x 23	Miles Kelly & D. Vaughan	22/	1853	Annie Jane	1294	sh	179 x 32 x 23	Baldwin & Dinning
							GP/	1853	James McHenry	1778	sh	197 x 36 x 28	Jas E. Oliver
GP/	1851	Julia	1057	sh	163 x 32 x 23	H.N. Jones	25/	1853	Number 1	255	sc	125 x 23 x 10	Allan Gilmour & Co.

26/ 1853	Number 2	259	sc	128 x 23 x 10	Allan Gilmour & Co.		GP/ 1854	Tudor	1649	sh	229 x 37 x 23	H.N. Jones
27/ 1853	Number 3	177	sc	104 x 21 x 9	Allan Gilmour & Co.		62/ 1854	Fanny Forsyth	1497	sh	203 x 35 x 23	Thomas H. Oliver 24099
28/ 1853	Number 4	178	sc	105 x 21 x 10	Allan Gilmour & Co.		63/ 1854	Starling	174	be	102 x 20 x 10	Lomas & Sewell
32/ 1853	Sheridan Knowles	954	ba	146 x 32 x 22	T.C. Lee		66/ 1854	Louis Napoleon	743	sh	174 x 29 x 18	T.C. Lee 23199
34/ 1853	British Lion	1370	sh	190 x 36 x 23	Pierre Valin		67/ 1854	Tiger	1102	sh	189 x 30 x 20	P. Valin & Co.
36/ 1853	Bonaventure	1125	sh	169 x 32 x 23	John Munn		71/ 1854	Empress Eugenie	1689	sh	224 x 34 x 23	Jean Elie Gingras
37/ 1853	Melbourne	1170	sh	172 x 32 x 23	Davidson & Goudie		72/ 1854	Finchley	575	ba	139 x 27 x 19	Drolet & Leblond
41/ 1853	Almora	1239	sh	198 x 32 x 22	John James Nesbitt		74/ 1854	Agnes Anderson (Florence)	1178	sh	192 x 32 x 22	Pelchat & Mercier
42/ 1853	Shooting Star	1363	sh	202 x 35 x 22	T.C. Lee		78/ 1854	Danube	1104	sh	171 x 31 x 22	A. & W. Parke
GP/ 1853	William Miles	1225	sh	196 x 32 x 22	Chas Jobin		GP/ 1854	Lord Raglan	2081	sh	226 x 37 x 29	Chas Jobin
64/ 1853	Arabia	1022	sh	180 x 32 x 21	Parke - Pierre Brunelle		83/ 1854	Moira	934	sh	158 x 29 x 23	Jas Nelson & Co. 33122
70/ 1853	Rock City	598	sh	156 x 28 x 18	T.C. Lee		85/ 1854	Alliance	604	ba	148 x 27 x 18	Isaie Julien & Co.
75/ 1853	Cap Rouge	1101	sh	172 x 32 x 23	Jas E. Oliver		89/ 1854	Jasper	629	sh	145 x 27 x 18	Ray & Dean
GP/ 1853	Hilton	1441	sh	192 x 34 x 23	Jas E. Oliver		91/ 1854	Bomarsund	673	sh	147 x 27 x 19	Michel Laprise&Co. 24329
94/ 1853	Saldanha	1563	sh	193 x 33 x 29	John James Nesbitt		93/ 1854	Swordfish	157	be	92 x 21 x 11	Fraser Wyatt & Co. 32905
97/ 1853	Daylesford	680	sh	142 x 27 x 22	Geo T. Davie		GP/ 1854	Wideawake	906	sh	156 x 30 x 22	John James Nesbitt
98/ 1853	Norwood	1527	sh	182 x 33 x 30	Wm Cotnam		6/ 1866	La Canadienne	101	sc	92 x 24 x 10	T.C. Lee (in 1855) 53842
101/ 1853	Prompt	768	ba	150 x 27 x 21	John Munn		GP/ 1855	Meteor	516	ba		T.C. Lee
106/ 1853	Admiral Boxer	1116	sh	181 x 31 x 23	Pelchat & Mercier		12/ 1855	Glenalva	1051	sh	186 x 35 x 21	E. J. & I. Samson 32800
107/ 1853	Meteor	755	sh	159 x 28 x 21	Baldwin & Dinning		18/ 1855	Alma	1071	sh	178 x 37 x 23	W.C. Richardson 32886
108/ 1853	Carpentaria	1460	sh	209 x 34 x 22	Pierre Valin		19/ 1855	Florence	961	sh	177 x 35 x 22	Pelchat & Mercier 32901
109/ 1853	Eveline	909	sh	161 x 30 x 21	J. Lemelin jr		23/ 1855	Zouave	1324	sh	212 x 38 x 23	Edouard Trahan 32927
110/ 1853	Cheviot	1066	sh	179 x 31 x 22	Walter Ray		24/ 1855	Amethyst	1164	sh	179 x 38 x 23	Ray & Dean 32929
112/ 1853	Wildfire	457	sh	133 x 25 x 17	Davidson & Goudie		26/ 1855	Mont Lilac	1172	sh	180 x 40 x 23	Baldwin & Dinning 32933
115/ 1853	Nugget	1128	sh	179 x 32 x 22	Edouard Trahan		30/ 1855	Acadia	2030	sh	225 x 41 x 21	Andrew&Wm Parke 32955
116/ 1853	Cairngorm	1161	sh	181 x 31 x 23	Wm Russell		31/ 1855	Amoor	1344	sh	203 x 39 x 23	Julien, Labbé & Co.32956
118/ 1853	War Cloud	1251	sh	188 x 32 x 22	Jean Elie Gingras		32/ 1855	Tricolour	1239	sh	189 x 39 x 23	H.N. Jones 32963
120/ 1853	Leicester	744	sh	165 x 29 x 19	T.C. Lee		35/ 1855	Liverpool	1455	sh	218 x 40 x 23	John Munn 32982
125/ 1853	Chance	477	ba	128 x 24 x 19	Baldwin & Dinning		36/ 1855	North	1210	sh	193 x 37 x 23	John Munn 32983
5/ 1854	Utility	217	sc	107 x 21 x 11	Davidson & Goudie		39/ 1855	Inkerman	810	sh	170 x 35 x 19	Jean Elie Gingras 2994
14/ 1854	Eclipse	1304	sh	195 x 34 x 23	Walter Ray							& Son
GP/ 1854	Monica	1364	sh	200 x 34 x 22	John James Nesbitt		41/ 1855	Victory	786	sh	165 x 32 x 18	Jean Elie Gingras 33002
18/ 1854	Captain Cook	1272	sh	191 x 34 x 23	Drolet & Leblond							& Son
19/ 1854	Lancashire Witch	1386	sh	201 x 32 x 23	Lomas & Sewell		55/ 1855	Alma	186	sc	107 x 23 x 10	W.C. Richardson 33060
24/ 1854	Bucephalus	1197	sh	187 x 34 x 22	Jean Lemelin jr 24126		56/ 1855	Azot	166	sc	105 x 23 x 10	W.C. Richardson ? 33061
25/ 1854	Ocean Monarch	1832	sh	226 x 37 x 23	Baldwin & Dinning		66/ 1855	Redan	829	sh	166 x 34 x 21	Rosa et frère 33080
26/ 1854	Montmorency	751	sh	166 x 29 x 19	T.C. Lee		67/ 1855	Thornhill	1068	sh	191 x 36 x 21	Chas Jobin & Son 33081
29/ 1854	Chapultepec	1084	sh	181 x 30 x 23	Isaie Julien & Co.		69/ 1855	Clutha	1060	sh	186 x 35 x 23	Wm Russell 33088
31/ 1854	Aliquis	1247	sh	182 x 32 x 23	John Munn		70/ 1855	Telegraph	375	ba	128 x 26 x 16	Andrew & 33090
GP/ 1854	Agamemnon	756	sh	155 x 29 x 18	Jean Elie Gingras							Wm Parke
35/ 1854	Typhoon	1403	sh	209 x 33 x 23	Andrew & Wm Parke		78/ 1855	Ardmillan	987	sh	180 x 35 x 22	Robt McCord 33104
36/ 1854	Exodus	1237	sh	189 x 32 x 23	Théo St Jean		81/ 1855	Tchernaya	1222	sh	199 x 38 x 22	T.C. Lee 33106
38/ 1854	The Kildare	702	sh	146 x 28 x 19	Jean Lemelin jr		86/ 1855	Brunelle	1122	sh	200 x 39 x 23	Pierre Brunelle 33118
39/ 1854	Echo	1189	sh	181 x 32 x 23	Wm Russell							& Son
GP/ 1854	Napoleon the Third	1462	sh	195 x 35 x 23	Thomas H. Oliver		90/ 1855	Gleaner	486	ba	143 x 27 x 18	John Munn 33122
40/ 1854	Nazarene	935	sh	163 x 29 x 21	John James Nesbitt		10/ 1856	Veteran	1104	sh	176 x 37 x 23	Baldwin & Dinning 33151
42/ 1854	Antartic	757	sh	168 x 29 x 19	T.C. Lee		12/ 1856	General Wyndham	865	sh	175 x 33 x 22	Blais & Co. 33155
44/ 1854	Silistria	1025	sh	177 x 31 x 20	Bidegaré Jolic'r Lachance		13/ 1856	Elizabeth Yeo	895	sh	167 x 34 x 22	Baldwin & Dinning 33156
45/ 1854	Jane	756	sh	154 x 27 x 20	P. Valin & Co. 34851		14/ 1856	Naval Brigade	1238	sh	215 x 36 x 22	Lomas & Sewell - 33157
48/ 1854	Caribou	1208	sh	192 x 33 x 23	Pierre Brunelle & Son							Ray
GP/ 1854	Ultonia	1398	sh	204 x 32 x 23	Edouard Trahan		16/ 1856	Glen Isla	1069	sh	177 x 36 x 22	John James Nesbitt 33159
50/ 1854	Czar	1252	sh	184 x 32 x 23	Robt McCord & Son		18/ 1856	Crimea	1080	sh	185 x 35 x 23	Pierre Valin 33161
GP/ 1854	Empress Eugenie	892	sh	169 x 29 x 20	Pierre Valin		19/ 1856	Young King	114	be	79 x 22 x 10	Julien & Labbé 33162

20/ 1856	Elizabeth	487	ba	139 x 28 x 18	Fortier & Co.	33163	22/ 1857	Frenchman	1156	sh	195 x 36 x 23	Henry Dinning	33312
21/ 1856	New Liverpool	176	sc	112 x 22 x 9	(at New Liverpool)	33165	25/ 1857	Floating Light	1195	sh	192 x 37 x 23	John Munn	33312
23/ 1856	Louisiana	1264	sh	202 x 37 x 22	T.C. Lee	33167	26/ 1857	Aetna	950	sh	165 x 35 x 21	Pierre Valin	33313
26/ 1856	Matilda	408	ba	137 x 28 x 17	Jas Goudie	33172	27/ 1857	Michigan	846	sh	160 x 34 x 20	T.C. Lee	33314
27/ 1856	Kate Cleather	372	ba	133 x 28 x 15	Wm Power	33173	28/ 1857	Polly	173	br	97 x 23 x 12	G.H. Parke	33315
28/ 1856	Fox	266	sh	105 x 25 x 15	Jean Lemelin	33174	31/ 1857	Nanette	386	ba	118 x 29 x 18	T. Valin	33318
29/ 1856	William Kirk	738	sh	170 x 33 x 20	Thomas H. Oliver	33176	32/ 1857	Sapphire	749	sh	160 x 32 x 20	Walter G. Ray	33320
31/ 1856	Vortigirn	910	sh	175 x 35 x 23	Edouard Trahan	33178	34/ 1857	Resolute	1072	sh	177 x 37 x 23	H.N. Jones	33322
35/ 1856	Snowdrop (Malabar)	936	sh	176 x 33 x 22	Robt McCord & Son	33182	35/ 1857	Canadian Lass	174	br	88 x 23 x 13	Wiseman & Co.	33323
							36/ 1857	Iona	847	sh	161 x 35 x 21	E. Samson & Frères	33324
36/ 1856	Dream	1106	sh	187 x 36 x 23	Wm Russell	33184	37/ 1857	Minnehaha	785	sh	162 x 23 x 20	Wm Cotnam	33325
38/ 1856	Hiawatha	491	sh	145 x 29 x 18	Pierre Valin	33186	45/ 1857	Pekin	539	sh	148 x 29 x 19	Thomas H. Oliver	33332
40/ 1856	Gladiator	1502	sh	221 x 41 x 23	G.H. Parke	33188	47/ 1857	Flora	444	ba	127 x 29 x 17	Narcisse Rosa	33334
48/ 1856	Marshall Pellissier	743	sh	165 x 32 x 20	Jean Elie Gingras & Son	33200	49/ 1857	Dr Kane	607	ba	157 x 29 x 18	Wm Power	33335
							52/ 1857	Eaglet	169	br	96 x 22 x 11	Wm Power	33338
50/ 1856	Sardinian	1208	sh	207 x 39 x 22	Pierre Brunelle	33203	53/ 1857	Hardy	374	ba	118 x 27 x 16	Jos Hardy	33164
53/ 1856	Esmeralda	1188	sh	192 x 37 x 23	Wm Cotnam	33206	54/ 1857	Oshawa	771	sh	161 x 32 x 21	Jean Elie Gingras & Son	33340
54/ 1856	Admiral Lyons	1133	sh	189 x 37 x 23	Jean Elie Gingras	33207							
55/ 1856	Marmelon	737	sh	149 x 33 x 20	Laprise & Co.	33209	56/ 1857	Gondola	337	ba	113 x 26 x 16	Narcisse Rosa	33344
58/ 1856	Piverton	239	ba	114 x 25 x 11		33213	57/ 1857	Lady Eyre	921	sh	167 x 34 x 22	Laprise & Co.	33345
62/ 1856	Broomielaw	523	ba	149 x 29 x 18	Edouard Trahan	33218	58/ 1857	Cygnet	237	br	105 x 24 x 15	Wm Power	33346
66/ 1856	Rachel	952	sh	179 x 37 x 21	Bidegaré - T.C. Lee	33223	59/ 1857	Woodfield	509	ba	132 x 28 x 19	Thomas H. Oliver	33347
68/ 1856	Sir William Eyre	1316	sh	204 x 39 x 23	Thomas H. Oliver	33230	60/ 1857	Minnesota	828	sh	159 x 34 x 21	T.C. Lee	33348
71/ 1856	Forth	788	sh	157 x 33 x 21	Samson & Co.	33233	66/ 1857	Storm Queen	1022	sh	182 x 35 x 23	Wm Baldwin	33356
73/ 1856	Zuleika	906	sh	172 x 35 x 21	Wm Baldwin	33236	67/ 1857	Electric	1106	sh	177 x 37 x 23	H.N. Jones	33357
74/ 1856	Eweretta	465	ba	132 x 28 x 17	Jean Lemelin	33238	71/ 1857	Margaret Blais	511	ba	137 x 29 x 18	Blais & Co.	33362
78/ 1856	Sauguen	482	ba	142 x 28 x 18	H. Dubord - Wm Power	33241	76/ 1857	Orso	748	sh	154 x 33 x 20	Narcisse Rosa	33370
79/ 1856	Indiana	852	ba	160 x 34 x 21	T.C. Lee	33242	77/ 1857	Virginia	839	sh	159 x 34 x 20	T.C. Lee	33371
83/ 1856	Scotia	921	sh	172 x 35 x 22	Henry Dinning	33250	78/ 1857	Nestorian	790	sh	164 x 32 x 21	Jean Elie Gingras & Son	33372
87/ 1856	Faith	619	sh	162 x 30 x 19	Pierre Valin	33255							
88/ 1856	Illustrious	1172	sh	205 x 35 x 23	Allan Gilmour & Co.	33256	79/ 1857	Campbell	680	sh	148 x 33 x 19	Toussaint Valin	33373
							83/ 1857	Gananoque	785	sh	158 x 33 x 21	Geo T. Davie	33377
90/ 1856	Myrtle	782	sh	156 x 34 x 21	Wm Russell	33260	86/ 1857	Matilda	1035	sh	178 x 36 x 22	Wm Russell	33380
93/ 1856	Mississippi	852	sh	160 x 34 x 21	T.C. Lee	33265	87/ 1857	Pladda	982	sh	189 x 33 x 21	Pierre Brunelle & Son	33381
95/ 1856	Lidias	195	br	101 x 23 x 12	Jobin & Sons	33268							
99/ 1856	Entreprise	124	sc	86 x 23 x 8		33274	6/ 1858	General Havelock	1124	sh	183 x 35 x 23	Wm Baldwin	41574
4/ 1857	Englishman	1055	sh	187 x 35 x 23	Henry Dinning	33289	9/ 1858	Lady Havelock	856	sh	159 x 34 x 20	T.C. Lee	41576
5/ 1857	Elinor	658	sh	156 x 30 x 19	Blais & Co.	33290	11/ 1858	Queen of England	1196	sh	195 x 37 x 23	Henry Dinning	41578
6/ 1857	Lady Head	664	sh	152 x 32 x 20	Jean Lemelin	33291	14/ 1858	Messenger	247	br	110 x 24 x 13	G. Garneau	41582
7/ 1857	Maid of the Mist	1121	sh	178 x 36 x 23	Wm Baldwin	33292	15/ 1858	Egeria	876	sh	158 x 34 x 21	Laprise & Co	41583
8/ 1857	Souriquois	911	sh	176 x 33 x 23	Blais & Co.	33293	18/ 1858	General Neill	970	sh	173 x 35 x 23	Edouard Trahan	41586
9/ 1857	Missouri	818	sh	157 x 34 x 20	T.C. Lee	33295	21/ 1858	Cameronian	878	sh	163 x 34 x 21	Walter G. Ray	41591
10/ 1857	Blackwater	777	sh	157 x 32 x 21	H. Dubord	33296	24/ 1858	Trenton	983	sh	219 x 33 x 20	Allan Gilmour & Co.	41594
12/ 1857	Scotsman	618	sh	152 x 30 x 18	Walter G. Ray	33298							
13/ 1857	Comet	337	ba	122 x 25 x 16	Geo T. Davie	33302	30/ 1858	Maxwell	1000	sh	168 x 36 x 23	Thomas H. Oliver	41601
14/ 1857	Milton Lockhart	750	sh	160 x 32 x 21	Jean Elie Gingras	33303	35/ 1858	Brandon	731	sh	162 x 32 x 19	Pierre Valin	41606
16/ 1857	Black Eagle	1558	sh	211 x 37 x 20	G.H. Parke	33304	38/ 1858	Gartsherrie	319	ba	110 x 27 x 16	Wm Cotnam	41609
17/ 1857	Wacousta	983	sh	169 x 35 x 21	Julien, Labbé & Co.	33305	39/ 1858	Wallace	1112	sh	189 x 35 x 22	Wm Russell	41610
							40/ 1858	Celuta	668	sh	160 x 31 x 19	Pierre Valin	41611
19/ 1857	Staffa	922	sh	169 x 33 x 21	John Munn	33307	43/ 1858	Natalie	843	sh	170 x 32 x 11	Laprise & Co.	41615
20/ 1857	Bruce	1110	sh	190 x 36 x 23	Wm Russell	33307	46/ 1858	Powerful	1230	sh	198 x 36 x 23	Wm Cotnam	41618
21/ 1857	Jura	774	sh	162 x 34 x 19	Brunelle & Son	33308	48/ 1858	Rosalie	907	sh	168 x 36 x 22	Narcisse Rosa	41931
							50/ 1858	Storm King	790	sh	164 x 33 x 20	Toussaint Valin	41933

#	Year	Name	Tons	Rig	Dimensions	Builder	No.
51/	1858	Maria	747	sh	149 x 32 x 21	Samson & Co.	41934
52/	1858	Peerless	1005	sh	191 x 33 x 22	Brunelle	41935
54/	1858	Vancouver	456	ba	124 x 30 x 19	T.C. Lee	41937
59/	1858	Forest Queen	527	ba	135 x 29 x 19	T.C. Lee	41941
3/	1859	Nyssia	223	br	93 x 24 x 15	Ed Rosa	41945
4/	1859	Prince Consort	1236	sh	198 x 37 x 22	Henry Dinning	41946
6/	1859	W.W. Scott	203	br	99 x 24 x 13	Julien & Co.	41949
8/	1859	Petite Hermine	143	br	85 x 21 x 11	Toussaint Valin	41951
20/	1859	Bravo	1012	sh	178 x 37 x 21	Oliver & Co.	41966
21/	1859	Leven	301	br	111 x 25 x 16	T.C. Lee	41967
22/	1859	Excellent	1212	sh	193 x 36 x 22	Wm Baldwin	41968
23/	1859	Mohawk	578	sh	146 x 31 x 18	Jean Elie Gingras	41969
24/	1859	Palinurus	1082	sh	177 x 36 x 22	Pierre Valin	41970
25/	1859	Trebolgan	1199	sh	179 x 37 x 22	H.N. Jones	41971
32/	1859	Iphigenia	848	sh	161 x 34 x 20	T.C. Lee	41978
34/	1859	Kelvin	280	br	106 x 24 x 15	Labbé-Gingras & Sons	41980
36/	1859	Queensland	993	sh	168 x 36 x 23	Thomas H. Oliver	41981
38/	1859	Glengarnock	593	ba	144 x 30 x 18	Wm Cotnam	41983
39/	1859	Award	846	sh	183 x 31 x 21	Allan Gilmour & Co.	41984
40/	1859	Salmon	178	be	97 x 23 x 12	M. Laprise & P. Letarte	41986
41/	1859	Solferino	107	be	76 x 21 x 10	Narcisse Rosa	41987
44/	1859	Venetia	566	ba	144 x 30 x 18	T.C. Lee	41991
GP/	1860	Glenora	396	ba	133 x 27 x 17	Pierre Valin	
13/	1860	Nagasaki	1114	sh	175 x 35 x 22	Wm Baldwin	36624
25/	1860	Quebec	1258	sh	181 x 39 x 22	Wm Baldwin	36634
28/	1860	Devonshire	858	sh	162 x 35 x 21	Henry Dinning & Co.	36637
31/	1860	City of Ottawa	884	sh	170 x 33 x 21	Gingras & Co.	36640
32/	1860	Burnside	382	ba	125 x 25 x 17	Gingras & Co.	36641
35/	1860	Sydney	1117	sh	187 x 35 x 23	Wm Russell	36643
37/	1860	Anomia	688	sh	153 x 32 x 19	Brunelle & Son	36645
38/	1860	Victoria Bridge	836	sh	156 x 33 x 22	I. & J. Samson	36646
39/	1860	Reform	407	ba	140 x 26 x 15	John Gilmour	36647
41/	1860	Pride of England	1338	sh	205 x 37 x 23	Henry Dinning & Co.	36649
42/	1860	Belle Isle	1180	sh	185 x 37 x 22	T.C. Lee	36650
44/	1860	Summerlee	806	sh	165 x 32 x 21	Toussaint Valin	37068
45/	1860	Ocean Phantom	598	sh	154 x 30 x 19	Thomas H. Oliver	37070
46/	1860	Pontiac	608	sh	152 x 30 x 19	Edouard Trahan & Son	37071
47/	1860	Canada	719	sh	157 x 31 x 20	Wm Cotnam	37072
48/	1860	Indian Empire	1351	sh	211 x 37 x 23	Wm Baldwin	37073
49/	1860	Otago	1001	sh	182 x 34 x 22	Wm Russell	37074
52/	1860	Julien and Brothers	154	be	84 x 23 x 12	Julien (at Bic & Quebec)	37077
53/	1860	Melanie	198	br	91 x 25 x 14	N. Rosa & Co.	37078
55/	1860	Ceres	861	sh	158 x 33 x 23	Gingras & Co.	37080
57/	1860	Laurel	620	sh	141 x 32 x 19	Rosa & Co.	37083
58/	1860	Rosa	635	sh	147 x 32 x 19	Rosa & Co.	37084
61/	1860	Nova Scotian	999	sh	168 x 35 x 22	T.C. Lee	37085
62/	1860	Royal Visitor	1220	sh	192 x 37 x 23	Thomas H. Oliver	37086
6/	1861	Mary Fry	986	sh	166 x 36 x 22	Henry Dinning & Co.	37092
7/	1861	Ariadne	671	sh	151 x 32 x 20	Dinning & Baldwin	37093
9/	1861	Staffa	923	sh	167 x 34 x 22	Jean Elie Gingras & Son	37094
11/	1861	Cherub	209	br	103 x 24 x 13	P.G. Labbé & Co.	37095
16/	1861	Maggie Lauder	997	sh	171 x 35 x 22	T.C. Lee	37097
GP/	1861	Colleen Bawn	531	sh	137 x 29 x 18	Toussaint Valin	
23/	1861	Colonial Empire	1305	sh	198 x 38 x 23	W.H. Baldwin & Co.	42706
GP/	1861	Beaconsfield	810	sh	162 x 32 x 20	Pierre Valin & Co.	
25/	1861	Rowena	729	sh	159 x 32 x 20	Pierre Brunelle	42708
26/	1861	Melita	914	sh	172 x 34 x 21	I. & J. Samson	42709
28/	1861	Fanny Laure	320	ba	118 x 27 x 13	Rosa	42712
29/	1861	Scotland	1170	sh	193 x 35 x 23	Wm Russell	42713
31/	1861	Ocean Empress	1068	sh	172 x 36 x 23	Thomas H. Oliver	42716
GP/	1861	Review	955	sh	178 x 34 x 21	Toussaint Valin	
GP/	1861	Ethelontes	831	sh	156 x 34 x 22	Oliver & Co.	
32/	1861	Celestial Empire	1278	sh	197 x 38 x 22	W.H. Baldwin & Co.	42717
33/	1861	Ino	462	ba	130 x 27 x 18	Wm Cotnam	42718
34/	1861	Tinto	874	sh	165 x 32 x 22	Wm Russell	42719
36/	1861	Glasgow	1180	sh	184 x 38 x 23	Gingras	42721
38/	1861	Ontario	1062	sh	178 x 34 x 23	Henry Dinning & Co.	42723
39/	1861	Duke of Newcastle	993	sh	171 x 35 x 22	T.C. Lee	42724
42/	1861	Sea Vision	259	ba	107 x 27 x 13	Thomas H. Oliver	42727
45/	1861	Countess Russell	965	sh	171 x 35 x 22	Rosa, Frs Julien	42728
49/	1861	Marie Louise	373	ba	132 x 28 x 13	Rosa	42732
52/	1861	Viola	1133	sh	187 x 35 x 21	Brunelle & Son	42735
55/	1861	Carolina	432	ba	137 x 26 x 16	Jean Elie Gingras	42736
57/	1861	Earl Russell	1042	sh	170 x 35 x 22	N. Rosa & Co.	42737
58/	1861	Lady Monck	189	br	96 x 25 x 11	Rosa	42738
7/	1862	Culdee	364	ba	128 x 27 x 16	I. & J. Samson	42748
10/	1862	Western Empire	1282	sh	191 x 38 x 23	W.H. Baldwin & Co.	42750
11/	1862	Diana	262	ba	110 x 25 x 13	Geo Lemelin	43446
13/	1862	May Queen	1067	sh	177 x 36 x 22	Henry Dinning & Co.	43447
14/	1862	Orpheus	472	ba	135 x 29 x 18	P.G. Labbé	43449
15/	1862	Stadacona	1080	sh	185 x 35 x 23	Ls Labbé & J.E. Gingras	43450
23/	1862	Lincolnshire	1250	sh	191 x 38 x 23	Toussaint Valin	43456
GP/	1862	Ellen Erie	956	sh	169 x 35 x 21	Toussaint Valin	
31/	1862	Euretta	654	ba	149 x 30 x 20	Toussaint Valin	43463
34/	1862	Alicia Bland	1185	sh	187 x 36 x 15	Henry Dinning & Co.	43466
36/	1862	Nepenthe	314	ba	118 x 27 x 13	Thomas H. Oliver	43468
37/	1862	White Rose	1193	sh	203 x 38 x 24	T.C. Lee	43469
38/	1862	Clydesdale	1355	sh	202 x 37 x 23	Ls Labbé	43470
39/	1862	India	1163	sh	194 x 35 x 23	Wm Russell	43471
40/	1862	Reserve	339	ba	120 x 27 x 14	Oliver & Co.	43472

44/1862	Passing Cloud	518 ba 138 x 31 x 18	N. Rosa & Co.	43476
GP/1862	Devonshire Belle	706 sh 159 x 31 x 20	Thomas H. Oliver	
47/1862	Barelaw	1034 sh 180 x 34 x 22	Wm Russell	43481
GP/1862	Jessie Scott	884 sh 165 x 33 x 21	Valin & Dugal	
52/1862	Ocean Nymph	310 ba 118 x 27 x 13	N. Rosa & Co.	43486
GP/1862	Southern Belle	1129 sh 185 x 37 x 24	Thomas H. Oliver	
53/1862	Petica	435 ba 138 x 26 x 16	Ls Labbé & J.E. Gingras	43487
54/1862	Eastern Empire	1752 sh 201 x 39 x 30	W.H. Baldwin & Co.	43488
66/1862	Gatineau	1165 sh 179 x 37 x 24	John Gilmour	43499
GP/1862	Canada Belle	655 ba 153 x 30 x 19	Wm Cotnam	
GP/1862	Eleutheria	795 sh 163 x 33 x 19	Narcisse Rosa	
2/1863	Eleanor Stevenson	314 ba 126 x 25 x 13	Ed Sewell	46176
4/1863	Princess of Wales	525 ba 141 x 29 x 18	Ls Labbé	46178
5/1863	Chippewa	1096 sh 187 x 36 x 23	Ls Labbé	46179
7/1863	Tyrol	547 ba 141 x 30 x 18	P.G. Labbé	46181
9/1863	French Empire	1368 sh 194 x 39 x 25	W.H. Baldwin & Co.	46183
10/1863	Southern Empire	1143 sh 174 x 36 x 23	W.H. Baldwin & Co.	46184
11/1863	Shannon	1102 sh 178 x 35 x 23	Dinning-Trahan & Son	46185
13/1863	Eleanor Wood	508 ba 145 x 29 x 18	I. & J. Sampson	46187
16/1863	Viceroy	1673 sh 211 x 38 x 29	Toussaint Valin	46190
17/1863	Princess Dagmar	1010 sh 173 x 35 x 23	Geo Lemelin	46191
18/1863	Six Freres	119 be 90 x 23 x 11	Michon-Chas Jobin Co	46192
19/1863	British Empire	1414 sh 205 x 39 x 25	W.H. Baldwin & Co.	46193
20/1863	City of Montreal	1187 sh 181 x 37 x 23	Wm Cotnam	46194
21/1863	Eastward Ho	607 sh 159 x 30 x 19	T.C. Lee	46195
23/1863	Staffordshire	1158 sh 189 x 36 x 23	Toussaint Valin	46197
GP/1863	White Water	780 sh 168 x 32 x 20	Thomas H. Oliver (Montrose)	
29/1863	Cora Linn	1172 sh 184 x 36 x 23	Lachance & Flanagan	46201
30/1863	Humberstone	322 ba 120 x 26 x 15	Chas Jobin	46202
31/1863	Ruby	551 ba 141 x 29 x 18	Louis Labbé	46203
33/1863	Prince Waldemar	464 ba 130 x 29 x 17	Geo Lemelin	46205
34/1863	Europa	1254 sh 194 x 37 x 23	Wm Russell	46206
36/1863	Dreadnought	1497 sh 218 x 38 x 25	Narcisse Rosa	46208
37/1863	Romania	1152 sh 191 x 36 x 23	P.G. Labbé	46209
GP/1863	Queen of Beauty	1327 sh 207 x 37 x 24	Oliver & Co.	
GP/1863	Red Rose	1454 sh 217 x 38 x 24	T.C. Lee	
GP/1863	Ocean Dart	407 ba 141 x 26 x 15	Oliver & Co.	
40/1863	Northern Empire	1379 sh 205 x 39 x 25	Wm Baldwin & Co.	46671
43/1863	Challenge	1264 sh 197 x 35 x 24	Pierre Brunelle & Son	46674
GP/1863	Magnificent	1283 sh 190 x 37 x 25	Valin & Dugal	
46/1863	Annie Froste	1236 sh 191 x 36 x 25	Henry Dinning & Co.	46677
49/1863	Julia Maxwell	354 ba 123 x 25 x 15	Max & Stev -Ed Sewell	46680
GP/1863	Queenstown	324 ba 120 x 26 x 15	Chas Jobin	
51/1863	Glenlyon	1446 sh 211 x 38 x 24	Ls Labbé-J.E. Gingras	46682
54/1863	Princess Alexandra	1187 sh 192 x 36 x 23	Toussaint Valin	46684
55/1863	Nydia	834 sh 163 x 34 x 22	Toussaint Valin	46685
56/1863	Peter Joynson	956 sh 170 x 34 x 23	Henry Dinning & Co.	46686
58/1863	China	1086 sh 182 x 34 x 23	Wm Russell	46687
60/1863	James Lister	982 sh 172 x 35 x 22	Narcisse Rosa	46688
65/1863	Anevoca	597 ba 151 x 30 x 19	I. & J. Samson	46692
67/1863	Emerald	607 ba 151 x 30 x 19	Lachance & Flanagan	46693
71/1863	Teviotdale	1484 sh 209 x 38 x 24	Ls Labbé-J.E. Gingras	46697
73/1863	Banner	1195 sh 183 x 37 x 24	John Gilmour	46699
78/1863	Nyanza	561 ba 145 x 29 x 19	Wm Baldwin & Co.	48154
79/1863	Etta	1154 sh 181 x 36 x 24	Henry Dinning & Co.	48155
GP/1863	Chattanooga (Sumatra)	1324 sh 194 x 38 x 25	Valin & Dugal	
80/1863	Olive Mount	583 sh 157 x 30 x 19	T.C. Lee	48156
GP/1863	Castle Avon	823 sh 178 x 32 x 21	Oliver & Co.	
83/1863	Pei-Ho	403 ba 138 x 31 x 13	T.C. Lee	48161
84/1863	Abergeldie	629 ba 154 x 29 x 20	Pierre Brunelle	48162
GP/1863	Eudora	454 ba 137 x 30 x 17	Narcisse Rosa	
89/1863	Gowanside	533 ba 142 x 29 x 18	Ls Labbé-J.E. Gingras	48166
GP/1863	Lorena	475 ba 137 x 30 x 17	Narcisse Rosa	
GP/1863	Eerie	1011 sh 178 x 34 x 23	Henry Dinning & Co	
GP/1863	Deeside (Rachel Blackw'd)	524 ba 143 x 29 x 18	Valin & Dugal	
G/1863	Hiawatha	621 ba 148 x 31 x 19	Wm Cotnam	
5/1864	Tea Taster	909 sh 174 x 34 x 22	Max & Stev-Edl Sewel	48171
7/1864	Herald of the Morning	670 sh 160 x 31 x 20	Maxwell & Stevenson	48173
9/1864	Angelique	956 sh 175 x 34 x 23	P.V. Valin	48174
GP/1864	Star of Peace	447 ba 139 x 28 x 15	Wm Baldwin & Co.	
10/1864	Highlander	694 ba 152 x 32 x 20	Narcisse Rosa	48175
GP/1864	Castiglione	1081 sh 178 x 35 x 23	Geo Lemelin	
17/1864	Rosalind	547 ba 142 x 29 x 18	Ls Labbé-J.E. Gingras	48183
18/1864	Thistle	683 ba 151 x 32 x 20	P.G. Labbé	48184
21/1864	Chillian Wallah	1249 sh 183 x 39 x 25	Lachance & Flanagan	48187
23/1864	Indian Chief	1806 sh 214 x 43 x 21	P.V. Valin	48188
24/1864	Maythorn	641 ba 155 x 31 x 19	P.V. Valin	48189
GP/1864	Rhoda	1122 sh 186 x 34 x 22	C. Russell	
GP/1864	Miningu	952 sh 166 x 34 x 22	Wm Charland	
25/1864	Lanarkshire	1439 sh 211 x 39 x 24	Ls Labbé-J.E. Gingras	48190
26/1864	Mandarin	799 sh 169 x 33 x 20	I. & J. Samson	48191
29/1864	Strathspey	525 ba 141 x 29 x 18	Ls Labbé-J.E. Gingras	48194

Appendices 381

30/ 1864	Huron	774	sh	165 x 32 x 20	Henry Dinning & Co.	48195	
31/ 1864	Far Away	422	ba	142 x 26 x 16	Thomas H. Oliver	48196	
32/ 1864	Silver Swan	535	ba	138 x 31 x 18	T.E. Sherwood	48197	
35/ 1864	Superior	1375	sh	202 x 38 x 25	Dinning-Valin & Dugal	48200	
GP/ 1864	Fidelity	586	ba	142 x 31 x 19	Geo Lemelin		
38/ 1864	Golden Eagle	766	sh	160 x 33 x 20	Thos Edward Sherwood	50703	
41/ 1864	Royal Tar	717	sh	159 x 32 x 20	Lachance & Flanagan	50706	
44/ 1864	Phaola	657	sh	161 x 30 x 19	Pelchat	50709	
GP/ 1864	Silvery Wave	834	sh	177 x 32 x 21	Thomas H. Oliver		
46/ 1864	Calcutta	1403	sh	205 x 40 x 24	P.G. Labbé	50711	
47/ 1864	Queen of the Lakes	1154	sh	181 x 37 x 23	Shaw & Patterson	50712	
48/ 1864	Desdemona	1160	sh	191 x 37 x 24	Pierre Brunelle	50713	
49/ 1864	Early Morn	1087	sh	184 x 36 x 23	McKay & Warner	50714	
54/ 1864	Jenny Lemelin	251	ba	111 x 24 x 13	Geo Lemelin	50719	
55/ 1864	Florence Lee	754	sh	161 x 33 x 21	T.C. Lee	50720	
59/ 1864	Her Majesty	1342	sh	203 x 38 x 23	Dinning - Ed Trahan	50721	
60/ 1864	L'Agouhanna	1115	sh	187 x 36 x 23	Ls Labbé - J.E. Gingras	50722	
61/ 1864	Benefactress	1276	sh	202 x 37 x 24	P.V. Valin	50723	
GP/ 1864	Eumenides	1114	sh	179 x 36 x 23	G. Charland		
GP/ 1864	Persia	1290	sh	208 x 37 x 23	C. Russell		
65/ 1864	Tri-Wave	767	sh	164 x 32 x 21	Wm Cotnam	50727	
68/ 1864	Ondine	383	ba	123 x 27 x 16	Geo T. Davie	50730	
69/ 1864	Mary Magdaleine	348	ba	134 x 29 x 13	Narcisse Rosa	50731	
71/ 1864	Wild Rose	1615	sh	233 x 39 x 24	T.C. Lee	50733	
72/ 1864	Evie	652	ba	149 x 32 x 21	Narcisse Rosa	50734	
74/ 1864	City of Liverpool	1420	sh	193 x 39 x 24	Narcisse Rosa	50735	
76/ 1864	City of Richmond	1255	sh	185 x 39 x 23	T.C. Lee	50737	
77/ 1864	Kedar	532	ba	141 x 29 x 18	Jean Elie Gingras	50738	
78/ 1864	Rock Light	778	sh	166 x 32 x 21	Dinning - Ed Trahan	50739	
81/ 1864	Mauldslie	637	ba	155 x 31 x 19	P.V. Valin	50742	
90/ 1864	Caribou	1160	sh	183 x 38 x 24	I. & J. Samson	50750	
GP/ 1864	Golden Sea	1418	sh	207 x 38 x 24	Thomas H. Oliver		
91/ 1864	Oriental	733	ba	153 x 32 x 19	Wm Baldwin & Co.	51501	
93/ 1864	Jarnia	802	sh	158 x 33 x 21	Narcisse Rosa	51503	
96/ 1864	Defiant	1325	sh	202 x 39 x 23	Wm Cotnam	51506	
99/ 1864	Wimbledon	1584	sh	212 x 41 x 24	Valin & Dugal	51508	
GP/ 1864	Arabia	1210	sh	200 x 36 x 23	Catherine Russell		
101/ 1864	Bonniton	593	ba	149 x 30 x 19	Jean Elie Gingras	51510	
108/ 1864	Annie (River Dey)	900	sh	161 x 33 x 22	H. Dubord	51515	
12/ 1865	Lady Bird	111	be	87 x 24 x 10	Jean Elie Gingras	51530	
14/ 1865	The Royal Family	1199	sh	192 x 36 x 24	Wm Baldwin	51532	
15/ 1865	Her Royal Highness	1245	sh	192 x 37 x 24	Wm Baldwin	51533	
21/ 1865	Kenilworth	860	sh	175 x 33 x 20	Ed Berry of Kingston	51538	
24/ 1865	Mongolian	1013	sh	182 x 35 x 22	P.V. Valin	51541	
25/ 1865	True Briton	1406	sh	204 x 38 x 24	Henry Dinning & Co.	51542	
26/ 1865	Fleetwing	1232	sh	191 x 37 x 23	Charland & Marquis	51543	
27/ 1865	Troopial	692	ba	151 x 31 x 20	T.E. Sherwood & Co	51544	
34/ 1865	Bonniton	1064	sh	174 x 36 x 23	Geo T. Davie	51550	
GP/ 1865	Annie Fleming	911	sh	176 x 33 x 21	Thomas H. Oliver		
36/ 1865	Pride of Wales	906	sh	195 x 33 x 20	P.G. Labbé	52451	
37/ 1865	Dunedin	1298	sh	203 x 38 x 24	Pierre Brunelle	52452	
43/ 1865	Amaranthe	1199	sh	183 x 37 x 24	A. Gilmour & Co.	52458	
44/ 1865	Annie Lisle	347	ba	133 x 26 x 13	P.G. Labbé	52459	
47/ 1865	Taradale	1133	sh	183 x 37 x 22	Charland & Marquis	52461	
52/ 1865	Rothesay	1444	sh	214 x 40 x 24	Jean Elie Gingras	52466	
53/ 1865	Strathavon	637	ba	155 x 30 x 19	Jean Elie Gingras	52467	
58/ 1865	Sophie	187	ba	112 x 22 x 10	Frs Julien	52472	
59/ 1865	Moderation	1284	sh	200 x 37 x 24	T.C. Lee	52473	
62/ 1865	Ancilla	715	sh	165 x 30 x 20	Pierre Brunelle	52476	
GP/ 1865	Adelaide	765	ba	157 x 32 x 20	Narcisse Rosa		
63/ 1865	Michigan	1027	sh	177 x 35 x 23	Henry Dinning	52477	
65/ 1865	Glen Tilt	1015	sh	171 x 35 x 23	Valin & Dugal	52479	
69/ 1865	Taranaki	566	ba	141 x 30 x 18	T.C. Lee	52482	
70/ 1865	John Elliott	1198	sh	199 x 37 x 23	McKay & Warner	52483	
GP/ 1865	Truce	760	sh	162 x 32 x 20	McKay & Warner		
GP/ 1865	Henrietta	445	ba	135 x 27 x 16	Ed. Sewell		
73/ 1865	North Wind	808	sh	168 x 33 x 21	Richard & Co.	52486	
74/ 1865	Ardenlee	732	ba	165 x 31 x 20	I. & J. Samson	52487	
77/ 1865	W.G.Russell	1264	sh	201 x 37 x 23	Catherine Russell	52490	
79/ 1865	Augustina	297	ba	130 x 29 x 13	Narcisse Rosa	52492	
GP/ 1865	Lena	1062	sh	180 x 35 x 23	Dubord - Desnoyers		
100/ 1865	Faith	293	ba	116 x 26 x 13	P.G. Labbé & Co.	53825	
101/ 1865	Hope	287	ba	116 x 26 x 13	P.G. Labbé & Co.	53826	
102/ 1865	Charity	297	br	116 x 26 x 13	P.G. Labbé & Co.	53827	
109/ 1865	Robert McM Spearing	404	be	115 x 29 x 11	McKay & Warner	53831	
114/ 1865	Coq du Village	317	ba	131 x 26 x 13	H. Dubord	53836	
115/ 1865	Ivy	319	ba	126 x 28 x 13	Richard & Co.	53837	
117/ 1865	Fidelle	316	ba	131 x 27 x 13	H. Dubord	53839	
G/ 1865	Hengist	518	ba		Wm Cotnam		
FR/ 1865	Charles Verminck	644	ba	162 x 35 x 17	Narcisse Rosa		
FR/ 1865	Progres	399	ba	142 x 32 x	Narcisse Rosa		
M/ 1865	Oneida	1155	sh	186 x 37 x 23	P.G. Labbé & Co.		
GP/ 1866	Tamarac (Eden Iron)	500	ba	139 x 29 x 18	Wm Baldwin		
GP/ 1866	Euroclydon 1280 (Siberian)		sh	191 x 39 x 24	Wm Baldwin		
8/ 1866	Friga	1135	sh	186 x 36 x 23	Henry Dinning	53844	
9/ 1866	Mora	600	ba	155 x 31 x 18	Henry Dinning	53845	
GP/ 1866	Caroline Mary (JPhillips)	520	ba	140 x 28 x 18	Ed. Sewell		
10/ 1866	L'Avenir	149	be	84 x 23 x 12	Ls Rosa	53846	
GP/ 1866	Laina (Noranside)	608	ba	154 x 31 x 17	McKay & Warner		

11/ 1866	Saint James	1188	sh	185 x 40 x 24	P.V. Valin	53847
12/ 1866	Beatrice	633	ba	155 x 31 x 19	P.V. Valin	53848
15/ 1866	Canada	384	ba	130 x 29 x 16	P.V. Valin	53851
19/ 1866	Oliver Cromwell	1112	sh	184 x 36 x 23	Charland & Marquis	53854
20/ 1866	Twilight	779	ba	166 x 32 x 21	Charland & Marquis	53855
24/ 1866	Mathilde Octavie	860	ba	143 x 31 x 13	Lachance & Cauchon	53858
25/ 1866	Psyche	665	sh	160 x 32 x 19	Henry Dinning	53859
28/ 1866	Buffalo (Robert Kerr)	1202	sh	191 x 38 x 24	Narcisse Rosa	53862
30/ 1866	Osprey	245	be	111 x 25 x 12	Shaw & Patterson	53864
31/ 1866	Homer	539	ba	150 x 30 x 17	McKay & Warner	53865
33/ 1866	Decision	1204	sh	186 x 37 x 24	John Gilmour	53877
36/ 1866	Union	595	ba	150 x 31 x 19	Bonhomme & Leclerc	53870
GP/ 1866	Sirocco	1253	sh	190 x 39 x 24	Wm Baldwin	
44/ 1866	Lumina	143	sc	110 x 24 x 8	Narcisse Rosa	53877
50/ 1866	Eclair	231	sc	88 x 29 x 11	Narcisse Rosa	53882
51/ 1866	Sketty Belle	171	be	103 x 23 x 13	P.G. Labbé & Co.	53883
53/ 1866	Tarifa (Mathilde)	685	ba	155 x 31 x 20	Jean Elie Gingras	53884
54/ 1866	Tripoli	696	ba	156 x 31 x 20	Jean Elie Gingras	53885
57/ 1866	Austerlitz	613	ba	151 x 30 x 19	Thomas H. Oliver	53888
61/ 1866	Winona	344	ba	128 x 26 x 13	P.G. Labbé & Co.	53891
64/ 1866	Coromandel	1233	sh	199 x 37 x 23	Charland & Marquis	53893
65/ 1866	Northumbria	1303	sh	197 x 38 x 24	I. & J. Samson	53894
69/ 1866	James Childs	756	ba	170 x 31 x 20	Ed Sewell	53897
70/ 1866	Rose	426	be	123 x 29 x 13	Narcisse Rosa	53898
73/ 1866	Eglantine	336	ba	121 x 29 x 14	McKay & Warner	55851
77/ 1866	Provence	622	ba	155 x 31 x 19	Valin & Dugal	55854
81/ 1866	Justine	426	ba	130 x 29 x 12	Narcisse Rosa	55857
94/ 1866	Samuel	360	ba	130 x 28 x 14	Valin & Dugal	55869
96/ 1866	Fiona	772	sh	160 x 33 x 20	Dunn & Samson	55871
GP/ 1866	Hope	633	ba	147 x 31 x 20	Narcisse Rosa	
97/ 1866	Niagara	673	ba	156 x 35 x 18	Rosa & Jacques Auger	55872
98/ 1866	Success	592	ba	147 x 33 x 13	Rosa & Jacques Auger	55873
99/ 1866	Faith, Hope and Charity	125	be	99 x 25 x 10	Ed Sewell	55874
100/ 1866	Armistice (Banare II)	490	ba	135 x 30 x 13	McKay & Warner	55875
101/ 1866	Albina	813	sh	164 x 33 x 21	Lachance & Cauchon	55876
102/ 1866	Micmac	1148	sh	185 x 37 x 23	Jean Elie Gingras	55877
103/ 1866	Adria	210	be	103 x 23 x 13	P.G. Labbé & Co.	55878
104/ 1866	Queen Emma	209	be	103 x 23 x 13	P.G. Labbé & Co.	55879
M11/ 1866	Grace Redpath	515	ba	137 x 30 x 18	Henry Dinning	
M12/ 1866	Helen Drummond	512	ba	137 x 30 x 18	Henry Dinning	
7/ 1867	Luxembourg	865	ba	159 x 33 x 21	Narcisse Rosa	55887
12/ 1867	Otonabel	225	sc	125 x 26 x 10	McKay & Warner	55890
13/ 1867	Aurora	234	sc	125 x 26 x 10	McKay & Warner	55891
14/ 1867	Cavalier	299	bn	137 x 26 x 12	McKay & Warner	55892
16/ 1867	Maria Annett	228	sc	125 x 26 x 10	McKay & Warner	55893
GP/ 1867	New Dominion	1299	sh	197 x 39 x 24	Wm Baldwin	
25/ 1867	Confederation	358	sc	139 x 26 x 13	Narcisse Rosa	55900
28/ 1867	Ariel	162	sc	111 x 25 x 9	McKay & Warner	55901
31/ 1867	Oriental	656	ba	158 x 31 x 19	P.V. Valin	55904
33/ 1867	Martinique	408	ba	128 x 29 x 17	P.V. Valin	55905
34/ 1867	Aldershot	1312	sh	199 x 38 x 25	Valin & Dugal	55906
35/ 1867	Avon	1027	sh	182 x 35 x 22	Charland & Marquis	55907
36/ 1867	Muscatel	195	be	100 x 24 x 12	Jean Elie Gingras	55908
38/ 1867	Curlew	1224	sh	188 x 37 x 24	John Gilmour	55910
43/ 1867	Undaunted	867	sh	166 x 34 x 22	Charland & Marquis	55914
44/ 1867	Secret	416	ba	146 x 31 x 13	I. & J. Samson	55915
49/ 1867	Pladda	1200	sh	199 x 36 x 23	Dunn & Samson	55920
57/ 1867	New Dominion	182	sc	115 x 26 x 9	McKay & Warner	55924
58/ 1867	Westminster	1435	sh	214 x 39 x 25	Jean Elie Gingras	55925
60/ 1867	Ravenscliffe	472	ba	131 x 29 x 19	Thomas H. Oliver	55927
68/ 1867	Aleppo	674	ba	154 x 31 x 20	Jean Elie Gingras	55932
69/ 1867	Corsica	677	ba	154 x 31 x 20	Jean Elie Gingras	55933
73/ 1867	Rivoli	406	ba	128 x 29 x 17	P.V. Valin	55936
79/ 1867	Stag	1124	sh	185 x 37 x 23	I. & J. Samson	55941
81/ 1867	Letitia	161	sc	87 x 26 x 11	N. Rosa & Co.	55942
GP/ 1868	Abyssinian	1297	sh	196 x 39 x 24	Wm Baldwin	
3/ 1868	Saint Andrew	1381	sh	202 x 40 x 24	P.V. Valin	55944
4/ 1868	Eleonore	680	ba	154 x 31 x 20	P.V. Valin	55945
8/ 1868	Barbadoes	429	ba	134 x 30 x 13	Valin & Dugal	55947
9/ 1868	Magdala	165	sc	105 x 25 x 9	McKay & Warner	55948
12/ 1868	Carluke	416	ba	129 x 28 x 17	P.V. Valin	59841
GP/ 1868	Lady Belleau	683	ba	151 x 32 x 20	Wm Baldwin	
13/ 1868	Rock City	825	sh	172 x 33 x 25	McKay & Warner	59842
16/ 1868	Little Annie	228	be	106 x 23 x 13	Wm Cotnam	59845
17/ 1868	Napier	1177	sh	184 x 37 x 24	Charland & Marquis	59846
18/ 1868	Aberdeen	375	ba	123 x 27 x 16	Charland & Marquis	59847
9/ 1868	Loraine	315	ba	117 x 27 x 13	Jos Rosa	59848
20/ 1868	Niagara	1360	sh	204 x 39 x 24	Dunn & Samson	59849
GP/ 1868	Beverly	500	ba	141 x 29 x 18	Wm Baldwin	
26/ 1868	Oriana	889	sh	168 x 34 x 22	Charland & Marquis	59855
30/ 1868	Stornoway	1496	sh	223 x 38 x 25	Jean Elie Gingras	59859
31/ 1868	Ismailia	700	ba	155 x 31 x 20	Jean Elie Gingras	59860
37/ 1868	Lord Napier	1228	sh	200 x 37 x 24	McKay & Warner	59865
41/ 1868	Dacelo	695	ba	157 x 32 x 20	McKay & Warner	59869
43/ 1868	Wapiti	666	ba	156 x 33 x 18	I. & J. Samson	59871
47/ 1868	Adria	846	sh	166 x 35 x 21	Dunn & Samson	59875
48/ 1868	Louvre	783	ba	158 x 33 x 20	Julien & Labbé	59876
57/ 1868	Victoire	211	be	99 x 26 x 11	E.T. Gauvereau	59882
59/ 1868	Wandering Sprite	770	ba	160 x 35 x 20	McKay & Warner	59883
61/ 1868	Skiddan	685	ba	154 x 32 x 20	Jean Elie Gingras	59885
62/ 1868	Snowdon	682	ba	156 x 31 x 20	Jean Elie Gingras	59886

63/ 1868	Endourne	436	ba	126 x 30 x 18	Ls Roberge	59887	34/ 1870	Contest	992	sh	175 x 36 x 22	Dunn & Samson	59973
64/ 1868	Octavie	423	ba	127 x 29 x 17	Regis Roy	59888	39/ 1870	Eleonore	679	ba	148 x 33 x 13		59976
65/ 1868	Surprise	443	ba	150 x 31 x 13	I. & J. Samson	59889	41/ 1870	New Republic	580	ba	148 x 31 x 18	McKay & Warner	59977
66/ 1868	Coral	304	be	125 x 25 x 14	Henry Dinning	59890	43/ 1870	Alphonse	293	br	122 x 29 x 13	Ls Rosa	59978
4/ 1869	Aurelie	548	ba	137 x 34 x 17	Narcisse Rosa	59894	16/ 1871	Peter Mitchell	100	sc	90 x 24 x 9		59993
6/ 1869	Eugenie	670	ba	155 x 31 x 20	P.V. Valin	59896	18/ 1871	Woodbine	446	ba	134 x 28 x 17	P.V. Valin	59995
7/ 1869	Harriet	398	ba	129 x 29 x 16	P.V. Valin	59897	19/ 1871	Lady Lisgar	1242	sh	202 x 38 x 24	Wm Baldwin	59996
8/ 1869	City of Kingston	1306	sh	190 x 37 x 24	Henry Dinning	59898	20/ 1871	Galeon	332	ba	120 x 30 x 13		59997
9/ 1869	Cherokee	1157	sh	181 x 37 x 23	Charland & Marquis	59899	21/ 1871	Saigon	786	ba	167 x 33 x 20	F.X. Marquis	59998
10/ 1869	Italia	899	sh	171 x 34 x 22	Charland &	59900	23/ 1871	Lady Hincks	700	ba	157 x 32 x 20	Wm Baldwin	60000
11/ 1869	Lady McDonald (Jane Law)	1299	sh	196 x 39 x 24	Wm Baldwin Marquis	59901	25/ 1871	Fairy Belle	641	ba	159 x 33 x 18	Thomas H. Oliver	64942
							34/ 1871	Jules	376	ba	139 x 30 x 13	Narcisse Rosa	64950
12/ 1869	Lady Cartier	693	ba	155 x 32 x 20	Wm Baldwin	59902	37/ 1871	Princess Louise	762	ba	161 x 33 x 20	P.V. Valin	64953
15/ 1869	Tecumseh	237	sh	191 x 38 x 21	Jean Elie Gingras	59905	43/ 1871	Monarch	899	ba	171 x 34 x 21	Wm Charland	64959
17/ 1869	Manoah (J.P. Smith)	777	ba	156 x 35 x 20	McKay & Warner	59907	65/ 1871	J.L. Pendergast	558	ba	157 x 31 x 18	Dunn & Samson	64979
18/ 1869	Canute	1218	sh	197 x 38 x 23	McKay & Warner	59908	80/ 1871	Marie Eliza	889	ba	162 x 37 x 20	Narcisse Rosa	64991
20/ 1869	Glengary	651	ba	150 x 33 x 20	Regis Roy	59910	5/ 1872	Scotia	111	sl	96 x 23 x 7	J. McKenzie	64997
25/ 1869	Velocipede	546	ba	142 x 30 x 18	McKay & Warner	59913	8/ 1872	Lady Bird	173	be	94 x 25 x 12	Samson Bros	65000
28/ 1869	Saint Peter	1427	sh	206 x 40 x 24	P.V. Valin	59915	9/ 1872	Lady Allan	1265	sh	199 x 36 x 24	Wm Baldwin	65001
29/ 1869	Manitou	508	ba	138 x 30 x 18	Charland & Marquis	55916	14/ 1872	JLB	148	be	101 x 22 x 12	McKay & Warner	66005
							17/ 1872	Lady Mary	167	be	94 x 25 x 12	I. & J. Samson & Co.	66008
30/ 1869	Montreal	1061	sh	183 x 36 x 22	Julien & Labbé	55917	18/ 1872	Bertha	866	ba	169 x 33 x 21	F.X. Marquis	66009
31/ 1869	Versailles	724	ba	155 x 32 x 20	Jean Elie Gingras	59918	20/ 1872	Wheatlandside	1103	sh	185 x 35 x 22	Wm Charland	66011
32/ 1869	Edna	736	ba	159 x 32 x 20	Thomas H. Oliver	59919	24/ 1872	Aurelia	124	sc	97 x 24 x 8	D. Boucher	66014
34/ 1869	Alia	448	ba	126 x 30 x 18	Ls Roberge	59920	25/ 1872	Beulah	746	ba	157 x 33 x 20	McKay & Warner	66015
36/ 1869	Manilla	1356	sh	202 x 38 x 23	Dunn & Samson	59922	37/ 1872	Marianne	213	be	95 x 25 x 12	Julien & Allard	66026
50/ 1869	Geneva	998	sh	175 x 35 x 23	Dunn & Samson	59933	42/ 1872	Saint George	1511	sh	209 x 40 x 25	P.V. Valin	66029
53/ 1869	Julie	310	be	105 x 27 x 16	Ls Roberge	59935	43/ 1872	Saint Vincent	1404	sh	200 x 38 x 24	Dunn & Samson	66030
54/ 1869	Oneata	589	ba	146 x 32 x 18	McKay & Warner	59936	45/ 1872	Success	477	ba	138 x 29 x 17	Wm Charland	66032
57/ 1869	Corsica	791	ba	152 x 33 x 21	Julien & Labbé	59938	GP/ 1872	Edinburgh	1664	sh	212 x 40 x 25	Jean Elie Gingras	
60/ 1869	Mona	409	ba	118 x 28 x 17	Thomas H. Oliver	59940	50/ 1872	Hawk	196	be	95 x 27 x 11	Narcisse Rosa	66037
61/ 1869	Wasp	443	br	133 x 30 x 18	McKay & Warner	59941	GP/ 1872	Callao	1001	sh	179 x 35 x 22	F.X. Marquis	
62/ 1869	Atlantic	1747	sh	223 x 43 x 25	Jean Elie Gingras	59942	58/ 1872	Countess of Dufferin	563	ba	143 x 33 x 17	Narcisse Rosa	66042
65/ 1869	Amelie	636	ba	149 x 34 x 20	Ls Roberge	59945	65/ 1872	Lady Dufferin	1337	sh	183 x 39 x 24	T. H. Oliver	66048
6/ 1870	Lady Young	595	ba	144 x 32 x 19	Henry Dinning	59947	72/ 1872	Newfoundland	897	ba	212 x 29 x 23	Peter Baldwin	66054
7/ 1870	Caribou	722	ba	155 x 32 x 20	P.V. Valin	59948	11/ 1873	Ella	985	ba	178 x 36 x 21	P.V. Valin	66068
9/ 1870	Manitoba	744	ba	158 x 33 x 20	Jean Elie Gingras	59949	14/ 1873	Minnie Sewell	106	sc	84 x 27 x 8	Ed. Sewell	66070
10/ 1870	Verona	649	ba	153 x 32 x 19	McKay & Warner	59950	18/ 1873	Rosario	530	ba	145 x 32 x 17	Wm Charland	66074
11/ 1870	Marie Louise	715	ba	155 x 32 x 20	P.V. Valin	59951	26/ 1873	Clydesdale	1823	sh	233 x 43 x 25	Jean Elie Gingras	66082
12/ 1870	Alice C	859	ba	174 x 36 x 21	McKay & Warner	59952	28/ 1873	Greenock	1241	sh	198 x 38 x 23	F.X. Marquis	66083
15/ 1870	Sophia	736	ba	157 x 32 x 20	Jean Elie Gingras	59955	29/ 1873	Lady Fletcher	732	ba	162 x 32 x 20	Peter Baldwin	66084
16/ 1870	Anna Craig	260	sc	129 x 26 x 11		59956	30/ 1873	Cleveland	1264	sh	208 x 38 x 23	Wm Charland	66085
18/ 1870	Jessie Cassels	721	ba	156 x 32 x 20	P.V. Valin	59957	32/ 1873	Scotia	1527	sh	212 x 40 x 24	Dunn & Samson	66086
20/ 1870	Ismalia	749	ba	161 x 33 x 20	Jean Elie Gingras	59959	35/ 1873	Earl of Dufferin	1777	sh	227 x 42 x 25	P.V. Valin	66089
21/ 1870	England	1812	sh	231 x 42 x 25	I. & J. Samson	59960	40/ 1873	Lady Muriel May	527	ba	145 x 31 x 13	Thomas H. Oliver	66094
22/ 1870	Karnak	569	ba	145 x 32 x 18	F.X. Marquis	59961	41/ 1873	Roseneath	622	ba	153 x 31 x 19	F.X. Marquis	66095
25/ 1870	Leonie	459	ba	127 x 29 x 13		59964	55/ 1873	Leilah	732	ba	156 x 33 x 20	Jean Elie Gingras	69582
30/ 1870	Guinevere	1021	sh	190 x 35 x 22	Dinning - Wm Cotnam	59969	60/ 1873	Adgillus	415	ba	142 x 29 x 13	J.M. Oliver	69587
							61/ 1873	Frostedina	402	ba	142 x 29 x 13	J.M. Oliver	69588
31/ 1870	Ireland	1005	sh	180 x 35 x 22	Oliver - Julien & Labbé	59970	GP/ 1873	Orient	1025	sh	174 x 36 x 23	Dunn & Samson	
							10/ 1874	Ossian	594	ba	153 x 31 x 18	F.X. Marquis	69600
32/ 1870	Gwenissa	517	ba	138 x 31 x 19	Henry Dinning	59971	12/ 1874	Concordian	742	ba	164 x 32 x 20	Peter Baldwin	69602

Appendices 383

#	Year	Name	Tons	Type	Dimensions	Builder	Reg #
14/	1874	Laurentine	692	ba	159 x 32 x 19	Wm Charland	69604
16/	1874	Malabar	1322	sh	206 x 38 x 24	F.X. Marquis	69605
17/	1874	Calcutta	1428	sh	209 x 40 x 24	Wm Charland	69606
30/	1874	Forest Belle	1097	sh	184 x 36 x 22	Ed. Sewell	69618
33/	1874	Rona	1369	sh	201 x 39 x 24	Jean Elie Gingras & Son	69621
36/	1874	White Rose	1528	sh	212 x 40 x 24	Dunn & Samson	69624
41/	1874	Tintern Abbey	1346	sh	196 x 40 x 24	P.V. Valin	69628
44/	1874	Felicitas	750	ba	163 x 32 x 20	Peter Baldwin	69631
58/	1874	Reciprocity	1481	sh	206 x 41 x 24	Thomas H. Oliver	69644
10/	1875	Arabella	714	ba	163 x 33 x 19	Wm Charland	69661
15/	1875	Dominion	1287	sh	199 x 38 x 24	Peter Baldwin	69667
16/	1875	Princess Beatrice	742	ba	160 x 32 x 20	Wm Baldwin	69668
18/	1875	Lakefield	1039	sh	177 x 36 x 23	Dunn & Samson	69670
23/	1875	William	287	br	128 x 27 x 10	Wm Charland jr	69675
26/	1875	Havelock	1117	sh	181 x 37 x 22	Wm Charland sr	72933
28/	1875	Seringapatam	1154	sh	189 x 38 x 23	F.X. Marquis	72935
30/	1875	Woodfield	995	sh	172 x 35 x 23	Jean Elie Gingras & Co	72937
39/	1875	Staghound	1013	ba	175 x 35 x 23	Thos. Dunn	72946
44/	1875	Buckhorn	791	ba	164 x 33 x 20	F.X. Marquis	73001
45/	1875	Enterprise	1515	sh	210 x 41 x 25	Thomas H. Oliver	73002
50/	1875	Windsor	1443	sh	207 x 40 x 25	P.V. Valin	73007
62/	1875	Queen's Cliff	611	ba	153 x 32 x 18	Wm Charland jr	73018
90/	1875	Tarifa	634	ba	157 x 31 x 19	Dunn & Samson	73051
91/	1875	Pondichery	802	ba	164 x 36 x 19	Narcisse Rosa	73052
4/	1876	Glengarry	566	ba	156 x 32 x 17	F.X.Marquis	73971
11/	1876	Supreme	762	ba	160 x 33 x 20	Peter Baldwin	73977
13/	1876	Sterling	766	ba	160 x 33 x 20	Peter Baldwin	73978
15/	1876	Queensland	1249	sh	195 x 38 x 23	Wm Charland	73980
16/	1876	Glenalla	772	ba	167 x 33 x 20	Wm Charland	73981
17/	1876	Elma	795	ba	164 x 34 x 20	Wm Charland jr	73982
22/	1876	Devonshire	1537	sh	210 x 40 x 25	Jean Elie Gingras & Co	73987
23/	1876	Circassian	1495	sh	213 x 40 x 25	P.V. Valin	73988
24/	1876	Peruvian	1060	sh	188 x 36 x 21	P.V. Valin	73989
36/	1876	Benguela	669	ba	160 x 33 x 19	Wm Charland jr	74261
37/	1876	Madura	970	ba	187 x 36 x 21	F.X.Marquis	74262
38/	1876	Souvenir	493	ba	140 x 29 x 18	P.V. Valin	74263
43/	1876	Stratford	1389	sh	207 x 39 x 24	Dunn, Samson & Co	74267
47/	1876	Rainbow	823	ba	167 x 34 x 20	Dunn & Samson	74271
49/	1876	Bokhara	1143	sh	183 x 38 x 24	I. Samson & Co.	74273
3/	1877	Natrona	293	ba	123 x 29 x 16	McKay & Dix	74286
4/	1877	ETG	950	ba	167 x 36 x 22	Narcisse Rosa	74287
5/	1877	Indian Chief	1238	sh	198 x 37 x 22	Dunn & Samson	74288
8/	1877	Dunsyre	1084	sh	184 x 36 x 24	Jean Elie Gingras	74290
11/	1877	Ivigtut	331	ba	122 x 29 x 16	McKay & Dix	74292
13/	1877	Sardinian	1443	sh	212 x 40 x 25	P.V. Valin	74294
14/	1877	Sarmatian	1105	ba	190 x 37 x 23	P.V. Valin	74295
15/	1877	Tanjore	868	ba	172 x 35 x 21	Wm Charland sr	74296
18/	1877	Belstane	1072	ba	182 x 37 x 22	Wm Charland jr	74299
24/	1877	Cosmo	1220	sh	200 x 37 x 23	Henry Dinning	75654
25/	1877	Signet	574	ba	146 x 31 x 18	Jean Elie Gingras	75655
26/	1877	Batavia	1110	sh	189 x 38 x 23	F.X. Marquis	75656
29/	1877	Modern	757	ba	161 x 32 x 20	Peter Baldwin	75659
35/	1877	Citadel	1401	sh	207 x 38 x 24	I. Samson & Co.	75665
40/	1877	Verity	1022	ba	178 x 36 x 22	Wm Charland sr	75669
41/	1877	Stafford	1116	sh	184 x 37 x 22	Dunn & Samson	75670
44/	1877	Chelmsford	381	bn	142 x 27 x 15	W. Warner	75673
GP/	1877	Lorenzo	1244	sh	193 x 38 x 24	Henry Dinning	
GP/	1877	Mary Graham	699	ba	168 x 33 x 18	Thomas H. Oliver	
2/	1878	Nydia	555	ba	152 x 29 x 18	P.V. Valin	75682
3/	1878	Polynesian	1294	sh	199 x 38 x 23	P.V. Valin	55683
4/	1878	Germanic	1296	sh	199 x 39 x 24	Peter Baldwin	75684
5/	1878	Assyrian	1157	sh	186 x 37 x 23	Wm Charland sr	75685
9/	1878	Shannon	1156	sh	191 x 38 x 23	F.X. Marquis	75689
15/	1878	Mohawk	1338	sh	193 x 39 x 24	Jean Elie Gingras	75695
22/	1878	Cyprus	939	sh	173 x 35 x 21	Wm Charland jr	77861
32/	1878	Oriental	1056	ba	180 x 37 x 22	Jean Elie Gingras	77869
5/	1879	Montagnais	1298	sh	202 x 38 x 23	Samson & Russell	77876
7/	1879	Electric Light (Wenonah)	767	ba	162 x 33 x 20	Peter Baldwin	77878
9/	1879	Vicereine	1465	sh	217 x 40 x 25	I. Samson & Co.	77880
14/	1879	Geraldine	1214	sh	196 x 38 x 23	Wm Charland	77885
16/	1879	Ivy	547	ba	158 x 29 x 18	P.V. Valin	77887
7/	1880	Lancashire	1159	sh	190 x 38 x 23	Gingras & Martineau	80732
8/	1880	Braidwood	980	ba	177 x 35 x 21	Blakis. & Charland	80733
16/	1880	Lauderdale	1259	sh	200 x 38 x 23	Wm Charland sr	80740
19/	1880	Parisian	1384	sh	208 x 38 x 24	P.V. Valin	80743
25/	1880	Emblem	1152	sh	192 x 36 x 23	Etienne Samson	80749
6/	1881	Keewatin	792	ba	168 x 33 x 20	Peter Baldwin	80757
7/	1881	A.D. Boucher	185	sc	99 x 25 x 10	A.D. Boucher	80758
3/	1882	Brandon	1250	ba	197 x 38 x 23	Wm Charland sr	83355
6/	1882	Edmonton	1298	ba	200 x 38 x 24	Wm Charland jr	83358
12/	1882	Winnipeg	1303	sh	205 x 38 x 23	Etienne Samson	83362
5/	1883	GTD	196	sc	95 x 27 x 11	Geo T. Davie	85456
9/	1883	Wolseley	1301	sh	199 x 38 x 24	Wm Charland	85460
25/	1883	Edinburgh	1299	sh	203 x 39 x 24	Wm Charland jr	85741
/	1884	President Roca	174	be	100 28 9	Etienne Samson	
7/	1885	Cambria	1252	ba	202 x 38 x 24	Etienne Samson	88311
8/	1885	Cheshire	1307	ba	198 x 39 x 24	Wm Charland sr	88312
28/	1893	White Wings	396	bn	142 x 29 x 13	Wm Charland sr	100866

Note: Only ships of over 100 tons included
   GP Denotes vessel left Quebec under a Governor's Pass
   FR Vessel built for French owner
   G Vessel built for German owner

Sources: Port of Quebec Shipping Registers, except where marked
M Port of Montreal Registers
* Early Lloyd's Registers
# Local newspaper reports

Appendix C

Outport Construction of Square-Rigged Vessels & Large Schooners and Sloops

Year	Name	Tonnage	Rig	Builder	Where built
1781	Trompeuse	100	sc		Bécancour
1790	Critique	116	sc		Bécancour
1792	Margaritte	128	sc		Bécancour
1793	Dorchester	111	sc		Bécancour
1794	If	194	sh		Paspébiac
1795	Victory	105	sc		Bécancour
1796	Sorel	132	br	Polley, John	Sorel
1796	Truth	205	sh	Day, Jas	Baie-des-Chaleurs
1797	Betsey	257	sh	Parent, Jos	Sorel
1797	General Hope	102	sl		Bécancour
1798	Coch	124	br	Cormier, Frs	Bécancour
1798	Richmond	139	be		New Richmond
1799	Beaver	130	sn		Bécancour
1799	General Prescott	127	br	Parent, Jos	Baie-Saint-Paul
1800	Margueritte	109	sc	Cormier, Frs	Bécancour
1800	New Century	210	sh	Day, Jas	Gaspé
1801	Barrones	120	be		Baie-Saint-Paul
1801	Charlotte	90	br		Gaspé
1801	Charlotte	108	br		Baie-Saint-Paul
1801	Denault	235	sh	Robitaille, Frs	Baie-Saint-Paul
1801	Fly	123	sh		Baie-des-Chaleurs
1802	Governor Milnes	160	be		Berthier-en-Bas
1802	Homely	210	sh		Baie-des-Chaleurs
1802	Sainte Anne	126	sc		Cap-Santé
1803	Pamela	123	sc		Cap-Santé
1804	Cod Hook	181	sh		Paspébiac
1805	Nancy	308	sh	Munn, D	Montreal
1806	Day	185	sh		Paspébiac
1806	Dunlop	332	sh		Montreal
1807	Lord Melville	372	sh		Montreal
1807	Montreal	259	sh		Montreal
1808	Cumberland	473	sh		Montreal
1808	Dolphin	104	sc		Bécancour
1808	Habnab	133	be		Paspébiac
1808	Margaret	346	sh	Munn, D.	Montreal
1809	Nancy	112	sc		Sorel
1809	Nimrod	384	sh	Munn, D.	Montreal
1809	Quebec	323	sh	Munn, D.	Montreal
1810	Betsey	114	br	Munn, D.	Montreal
1810	Grog	149	br		Paspébiac
1810	Jane	331	sh	Munn, D.	Montreal
1810	Janet	127	br		Montreal
1810	Janet Dunlop	182	be		Montreal
1810	Montreal Packet	159	be		Sorel
1810	Port Neuf	473	sh		Portneuf
1810	Saint Lawrence	126	sn		Montreal
1810	Trader	227	sh	Munn, D.	Montreal
1811	Amelia	140	be		Baie-Saint-Paul
1811	Canada	281	sh	Munn, D.	Montreal
1811	Christopher	450	sh		Portneuf
1811	Diana	339	sh		Sorel
1811	Glory	405	sh		Sorel
1811	Harriet	125	sn		New Carlisle
1811	Hermes	258	sh		Montreal
1811	Isaac Todd	351	sh		Trois-Rivières
1811	James Dunlop	426	sh		Montreal
1811	James and Agnes	258	sh		Montreal
1811	Little Belt	174	sn		Sorel
1811	Lord Wellington	472	sh		Montreal
1811	Magdalen	180	be		Iles-de-la-Madeleine
1811	Martha	197	br		L'Ange-Gardien
1811	Mary and Jane	152	sn	Baldwin, H.	Matane
1811	Prince Regent	264	sh		Montreal
1811	Rachel	194	br		Terrebonne
1811	Sir James Henry Craig	686	sh		Sorel

Year	Name	Tons	Type	Builder	Location	Year	Name	Tons	Type	Builder	Location
1811	Susanne	100	sc	Casault, Frs	Saint-Thomas	1822		182	br		New Richmond
1811	True Briton	398	sh		Portneuf	1823	Canadienne	104	sc		Saint-Ours
1811	William	455	sh		Montreal	1823	Caroline	101	sc		Saint-Jean-Port-Joli
1811	William Henry	100	sc	Sorel		1823	Elizabeth	266	sn		Montreal
1812	Mary	366	sh	Gilley et al	Ile d'Orléans	1823	Hercules	278	sn		Montreal
1812	Wolfe's Cove	363	sh	Baldwin et al	Ile d'Orléans	1824	Indian	276	sn		Montreal
1812	Thomas Henry	407	sh	Ray, John	Ile d'Orléans	1824	Niagara	278	sn		Montreal
1812	Adeona	140	sc		L'Islet	1824	President	102	sc		Deschambault
1812	Fame	489	sh	Hughes, Thos	Sorel	1824	Pyramus	290	sn		Montreal
1812	Gaspee	242	sh		Gaspé	1824	Sainte-Anne	101	sc		Saint-Thomas
1812	George Canning	482	sh		Montreal	1824	Sarah	274	sn		Montreal
1812	Harmony	280	sh		Montreal	1824	True Friend	115	be		St-Jean-Port-Joli
1812	Hunter	169	br		Montreal	1824	Veronica	330	sn		Montreal
1812	Little Ann	160	br		Sorel	1824	Oliver	72	be		Baie-des-Chaleurs
1812	Louisa	127	be		Baie-Saint-Paul	1825	Abeona	118	sc		Rivière Chambly
1812	Lucy	109	sc		Bécancour	1825	Alexander Henry	300	sn		Montreal
1812	Mary Ann	105	sc		Maria	1825	Canadian	305	sn		Montreal
1812	Reine Blanche	137	sc		Deschambault	1825	Charming Nancy	148	br		Gaspé
1812	Stirling	394	sh		Montreal	1825	Emelie	121	sc		Saint-Joseph
1812	Triton	429	sh		Portneuf	1825	Faith	131	br		Saint-Jean-Port-Joli
1813	Britannia	173	be	Munn, D	Montreal	1825	Favourite	293	ba		Montreal
1813	Commerce	424	sc	Munn, D.	Sorel	1825	Frederick	396	ba		Montreal
1813	General Kempt	381	sh		Portneuf	1825	George	139	br	Brunet, J.O.	Trois-Rivières
1813	James Dunlop	310	sh		Montreal	1825	Helen	322	sh		Montreal
1813	Sainte-Anne	112	sc		Deschambault	1825	Lady Rowena	323	sh		Montreal
1814	Hannah	371	sh	Robitaille, Rom.	Ile d'Orléans	1825	Mohawk	257	sn		Montreal
1814	Choyenne	105	sc		Rivière-du-Loup	1825	Montreal	315	sh		Montreal
1814	Earl of Buckinghamshire	539	sh	Munn, D.	Montreal	1825	Oldham	277	sn		Montreal
1814	Marie	103	sc		Baie-des-Chaleurs	1825	Sir Francis N. Burton	126	br	Brunet, J.O.	Deschambault
1815	Blucher	122	br		L'Ange-Gardien	1825	Sir John Newport	144	be		Montreal
1815	Greenock	182	br	Munn, D	Montreal	1825	Sophia	244	sn		Montreal
1815	John	103	sc	Munn, D.	Montreal	1825	Wilberforce	395	ba		Montreal
1815	Larch	244	sh		Paspébiac	1825	William Maitland	244	sn		Montreal
1815	Prompt	333	sh	Munn, D.	Montreal	1826	Barbados	134	be		Saint-Thomas
1816	Eliza	235	br		Montreal	1826	Caledonia	209	br		Deschambault
1816	Experiment	159	sl		Sorel	1826	Cecilia	142	br		Saint-Grégoire
1816	Brock	229	sn		Montreal	1826	Chieftain	325	sh		Montreal
1817	Palm	177	br		Bonaventure	1826	Priam	336	ba	Barallier, J Ls	Ile d'Orléans
1818	Alexander	171	be	Sherar & Melvin	New Carlisle	1826	Curler	372	sh		Ile d'Orléans
1818	Duke of Richmond	211	br	D.	Montreal	1826	Egyptian	318	sh	for Capt Friend	Montreal
1819	Harriet	246	sn		Sorel	1826	Erie	391	sh		Montreal
1819	Nancy	376	sh		Montreal	1826	Experience	105	sc		Deschambault
1819	Oliver Blaunchard	250	sh		Paspébiac	1826	Gaspé	147	be		Gaspé
1820	Clarkstone	252	br		Montreal	1826	Hero	310	ba		La Malbaie
1820	William Parker	226	br		Montreal	1826	Jane	168	br	Berte, Jos ?	Carleton
?1821	Hesione	158	sc		Montreal	1826	Mary Stewart	254	sn		Montreal
1821	Broad Axe		br		Paspébiac	1826	Ocean	368	ba		Ile d'Orléans
1821	Mary	82	be		Gaspé	1826	Rifleman	302	sh		Montreal
1821	Olive Branch	124	br	Berchevaise, Philip	Gaspé	1826	Saint Andrew	304	sh		Montreal
1821	Saint Lawrence	226	sn	Munn	Montreal	1826	Saint George	310	sh		Montreal
1822	Canadian	231	sn		Montreal	1826	Saint-Laurence	121	br		Saint-Ours

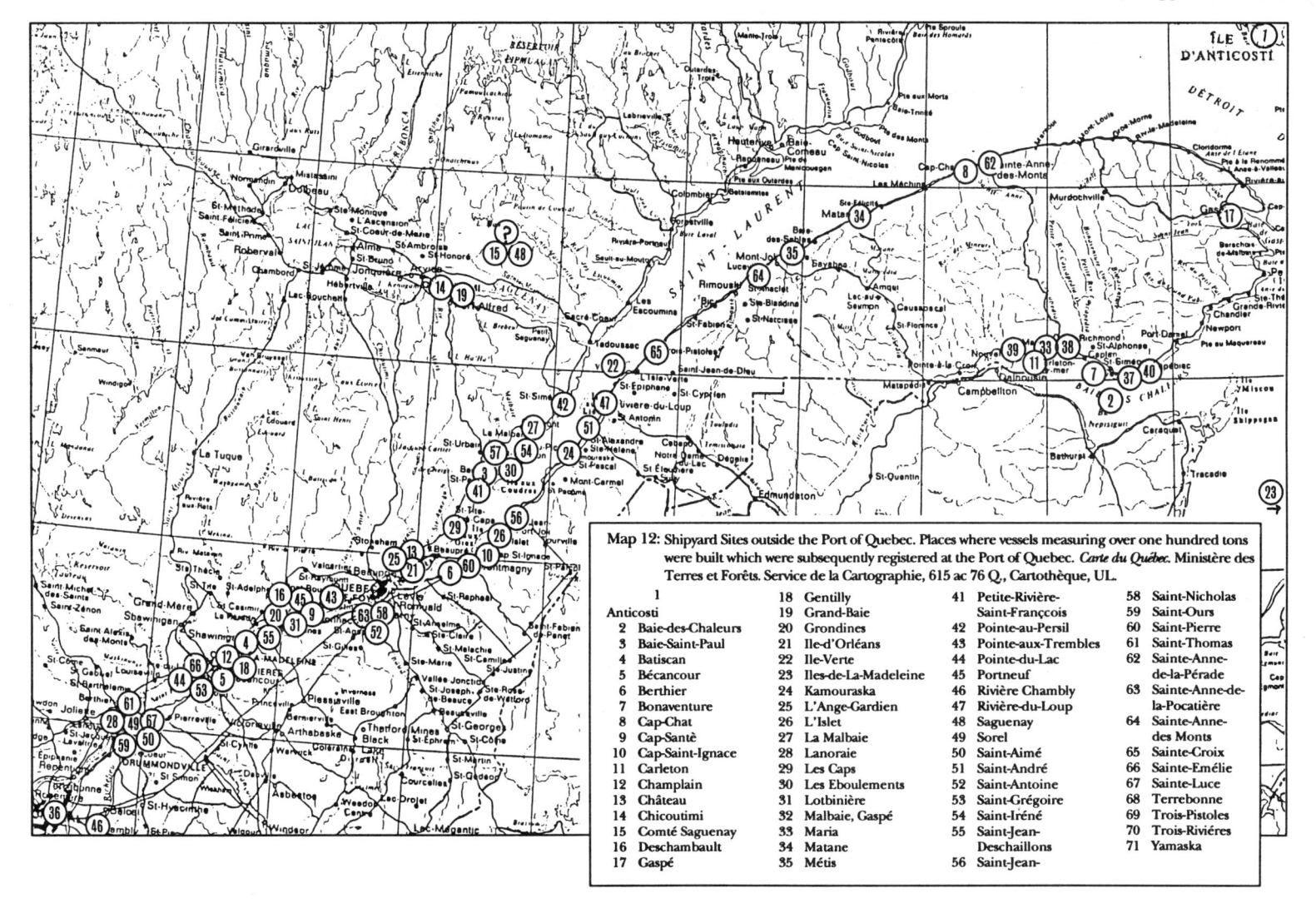

Appendices 387

Map 12: Shipyard Sites outside the Port of Quebec. Places where vessels measuring over one hundred tons were built which were subsequently registered at the Port of Quebec. *Carte du Québec*. Ministère des Terres et Forêts. Service de la Cartographie, 615 ac 76 Q., Cartothèque, UL.

1 Anticosti	18 Gentilly	41 Petite-Rivière-Saint-Françcois
2 Baie-des-Chaleurs	19 Grand-Baie	42 Pointe-au-Persil
3 Baie-Saint-Paul	20 Grondines	43 Pointe-aux-Trembles
4 Batiscan	21 Ile-d'Orléans	44 Pointe-du-Lac
5 Bécancour	22 Ile-Verte	45 Portneuf
6 Berthier	23 Iles-de-La-Madeleine	46 Rivière Chambly
7 Bonaventure	24 Kamouraska	47 Rivière-du-Loup
8 Cap-Chat	25 L'Ange-Gardien	48 Saguenay
9 Cap-Santè	26 L'Islet	49 Sorel
10 Cap-Saint-Ignace	27 La Malbaie	50 Saint-Aimé
11 Carleton	28 Lanoraie	51 Saint-André
12 Champlain	29 Les Caps	52 Saint-Antoine
13 Château	30 Les Eboulements	53 Saint-Grégoire
14 Chicoutimi	31 Lotbinière	54 Saint-Iréné
15 Comté Saguenay	32 Malbaie, Gaspé	55 Saint-Jean-Deschaillons
16 Deschambault	33 Maria	56 Saint-Jean-
17 Gaspé	34 Matane	
	35 Métis	
58 Saint-Nicholas		
59 Saint-Ours		
60 Saint-Pierre		
61 Saint-Thomas		
62 Sainte-Anne-de-la-Pérade		
63 Sainte-Anne-de-la-Pocatière		
64 Sainte-Anne-des Monts		
65 Sainte-Croix		
66 Sainte-Emélie		
67 Sainte-Luce		
68 Terrebonne		
69 Trois-Pistoles		
70 Trois-Riviéres		
71 Yamaska		

Year	Name	Tons	Type	Builder	Location
1826	Times	90	be		Baie-des-Chaleurs
1826	Young Samuel	164			Baie-des-Chaleurs
1827	Annabella	376	ba		Gaspé
1827	Bencooben	403	sh	Young	Montreal
1827	Doris	169	br		Malbaie
1827	Earl of Dalhousie	259	br	Adams	Sorel
1827	Hope	347	sh	Johnston	Montreal
*1827	Hylas	123	sc		Montreal
1827	John Francis	363	sh	Munn's yard	Montreal
1827	Northumberland	113	br	Cayouette, David	Baie-Saint-Paul
1827	Toronto	145	sn		Saint-Thomas
1828	Bon Vivant	76	be	Godin, Olivier	Anticosti
1828	Braganza	105	be		Les Eboulements
1828	Emancipation	217	br		Les Eboulements
1828	Francis	84	be		Gaspé
1828	Friends	113	be		Lanoraie
1828	Hesione?	198	sc		Montreal
1828	Industry	199	sc		Montreal
1828	Nymph	300	sn		Montreal
1828	Omphale	199	sc		Montreal
1828	Orleans	132	br		Deschambault
1828	Perseverance	196	sc		Montreal
1828	Polly	100	sc		Batiscan
1828	River David	260	br		Les Eboulements
1828	Spectator	132	br		Gaspé
1828	Walker	122	be		New Carlisle
1829	Minerva	385	sh	Shea, Luke	Montreal
1830	Arabian	278	sh	Campbell, Jas E.	Montreal
1830	Croesus	213	sc	Hunter, Robt	Montreal
1830	Favorite	198	sc	Johnston, Isaac	Montreal
1830	Rapid	256	sn	Hunter, Robt	Montreal
1830	William and Ann	76	be	Brown, Geo	Gaspé
1831	Dryope	341	sh	Johnston, Isaac	Montreal
1831	Megara	216	sc	Johnston, Isaac	Montreal
1831	Neptune	206	sc	Sheay, Luke H.	Montreal
1831	Queen	296	br	Campbell, John E.	Montreal
1831	Royal William	312	sh	Campbell, Jas E.	Montreal
1831	Sarah	82	be	Noel, Ls	Ile d'Orléans
1831	Superior	218	sc	Johnston, Isaac	Montreal
1832	James Edward	132	sc	Orford, John	Montreal
1832	Louisa Maria	135	sc	Orford, John	Montreal
*1832	Iolas	209	sc		Montreal
*1832	Alceus	158	sc		Montreal
1832	Hyppolite	121	be	Chartier, Frs	Pointe-au-Persil
1832	Patriot	86	be	Leblanc, D & Ls-J	Carleton
1832	Reine du Lac	129	sc	Cormier, Martin	Pointe-du-Lac
1833	Diligence	148	sl	Mirand, Pierre	Sainte-Anne
1833	Flore Sezarine	151	sc		Saint-Pierre-les-Becquets
1833	Virginia	153	br	Brown, Geo	New Richmond
1833	Voyageuse	131	sc	Petitclerc, Aug.	Deschambault
1834	Caroline	223	sc	Cormier, Pierre	Pointe-du-Lac
1834	Felicité	194	sc	Vanasse, Pierre	Yamaska
*1834	Iolas	161	sc		Montreal
1834	Marie Emilie	173	sl		Deschambault
1834	Marie Emilie	252	sl	Leclerc, Jean	Lotbinière
1834	Marie Lesperance	101	sc	Roy, Joseph	Saint-André
1834	Providence	179	sl	Hamelin, Louis	Grondines
1834	Saint Lawrence	191	sl	Gariépy, Ls	Portneuf
1834	Sainte-Antoine	184	sl	Lamothe, Jean	Riviere-du-Loup
1834	Sophie	226	sc		Grondines
*1834	Thalia	437	sh	Shea & Merritt	Montreal
*1834	Toronto	358	sh		
*1834	Trader	209	sc		Montreal
*1835	Douglas	376	sh	Merritt, E.D.	Montreal
1835	Elizabeth	122	be	Billingsly, Benj.	New Carlisle
1835	Henriette	125	sl	Saint-Cyr, Zeph	Batiscan
*1836	Glasgow		ba	Merritt, J.	
*1836	Hesione	158	sc		Montreal
1836	Horatio	71	be	Mabe, Edward	La Malbaie
*1836	Industry	156	sc	Vaughan, David	William Henry
1836	Jean Baptiste	225	ba	Chartier, Olivier	Trois-Rivières
*1836	Omphales	186	sc	Boyd, Thomas	William Henry
1836	Papineau	198	br	Chartier, Olivier	Trois-Rivières
*1836	Thistle	214	ba	Merritt, J.	
*1836	John Knox	347	ba		
1837	Harmise Josephine	103	sc	Cormier, Pierre	Saint-Pierre-les-Becquets
*1838	Colborne	340	sh		
1838	Countess of Durham	169	sc	Boyd & Forbes	Sorel
*1838	Gipsy	572	sh		
1838	Omphale	106	sl	Perron, Ignace	Deschambault
1838	Sainte-Philomène	138	sc	Cormier, Pierre	Pointe-du-Lac
1838	Wetherall	255	br	Merritt, J.	Montreal
*1839	Croesus	196	sc	Boyd, Thomas	Sorel
1839	Favorite	405	ba		Montreal
1839	Jim Crow	115	sc	Cayouette, David	Ile Verte
1839	Marten	107	be	Lemieux, Frs	Saguenay
1840	Cornwall	364	sh	Ernst, Antoine	Saint-André
1840	Helen	179	br	Dubord - Chartier, O	Pointe-aux-Trembles
1840	Hope	213	ba		Sorel
1840	Mersey	164	ba		Montreal
1840	Philippa	125	be	Bouchard, Damase	La Malbaie
1840	Retrieve	234	br	Boyd, Thos	Sorel
*1841	Blonde	676	ba	Merritt, Ed	Montreal
*1841	Brunette	348	ba	Marrett, Ed.	Montreal
1841	Conquest	145	be	Mabe, Peter	La Malbaie
*1841	Coquette	110	sc	Wiseman, James	Montreal
1841	Farmer	133	br	Collas, Sam	Malbaie (Gaspé)
*1841	Indian Chief	493	sh	Vaughan, David	Sorel
1841	Jubilee	112	sc	Vibert, Phil	Gaspé district
1841	Leonora	318	br	Nance, Wm	Batiscan
1841	Margaret	793	sh	Chartier - A St J	Pointe-aux-Trembles
1841	Saint Lawrence	142	br	Neron, Ls	Baie-Saint-Paul
1841	Sea Bird	122	sc	Grant, John	Nouvelle

Appendices

Year	Name	Tons	Type	Builder	Place
1841	Victoria	136	br	Dussault, J.B.	Baie-Saint-Paul
*1842	Hebe	205	sc	Boyd, Thomas	William Henry
*1841	Hope	202	sc	Vaughan, David	William Henry
*1841	Industry	169	sc	William Henry	
*1842	Sarah	537	sh	Vaughan, David	William Henry
*1842	Stadacona	138	sl	Boss, David	Montreal
1842	Hochelaga	142	sl	Boss, David	Montreal
1842	William Wilberforce	159	sl	Boss, David	Montreal
1842	Unicorn	133	be	Dussault, J.B.	Baie-Saint-Paul
1842	Victory	864	sh	Dubord - Chartier,O	Pointe-aux-Trembles
1843	Culzean Castle	232	br	Neron, Ls	Baie-Saint-Paul
1843	Fanny	427	ba	Adam, Jos	Pointe-aux-Trembles
1843	Gazelle	108	sc	Potvin, Thos	Baie-Saint-Paul
1843	John	108	be	Auger, Jacques	Ile d'Orléans
*1843	Sir Richard Jackson	418	sh	Vaughan, David	William Henry
*1843	Union	127	sc	Merritt, Ed.	Montreal
1844	Father Matthew	249	ba		Ste-Anne-des-Monts
1844	Guano	172	be	Bouchard, Damase	La Malbaie
1845	Algonquin	640	ba	Dubord - Chartier,O	Pointe-aux-Trembles
*1845	Anne	435	ba	McCarthy	William Henry
1845	Fame	310	ba	Dubord - Chartier,O	Pointe-aux-Trembles
*1846	Jessie Torrance	605	sh	McCarthy, D. & J.	William Henry
1846	Pemberton	1253	sh	Dubord - StJean,A	Pointe-aux-Trembles
1846	Torrance	175	br	Dubord, H.	Pointe-aux-Trembles
1847	Collector	793	ba	Dubord - StJean,A	Pointe-aux-Trembles
1847	Eliza	100	sc	Dufour, Marcel	Trois Pistoles
1847	James Gibb	814	ba	Dubord - StJean,A	Pointe-aux-Trembles
1847	Maple Leaf	858	sh	Dubord - StJean,A	Pointe-aux-Trembles
1848	Astoria	500	ba	Dubord - StJean,A	Pointe-aux-Trembles
1848	Elizabeth Browne	18	ba	Dubord, H.	Pointe-aux-Trembles
1849	Canada	917	ba	Dubord - StJean,A	Pointe-aux-Trembles
1849	Colonel Maule	438	ba	Dubord - StJean,A	Pointe-aux-Trembles
1849	Thomas	125	be	Marchildon, Jos	Batiscan
1850	Beaver	240	be	Dubord - Goudie,Jas	Pointe-aux-Trembles
1850	Chicago	215	sc	McCarthy, Daniel	Sorel
1850	Quebec	213	sc	McCarthy, Daniel	Sorel
1850	Sydney	881	ba	St Jean, Théo	Pointe-aux-Trembles
1850	Nepane	1007	sh	Dubord - Goudie,Jas	Pointe-aux-Trembles
1851	Crown	1285	sh	Dubord - Goudie,Jas	Pointe-aux-Trembles
1851	Harlequin	703	ba	Dubord - Goudie,Jas	Pointe-aux-Trembles
1851	Elzear	157	be	Bernier, Chas	Cap-Saint-Ignace
1851	Isabella	913	sh	St Jean, Théo	Pointe-aux-Trembles
1851	Martine	105	sc	Héros, Charles	Grondines
1851	Mary Ann	138	be	McCarthy, D. & J.	Sorel
1851	May Flower	92	be	Lavoie, Narcisse	Saint-Thomas
1851	Ontario	689	be	St Jean, Ant	Pointe-aux-Trembles
1851	Wolfe	1264	sh	Dubord - Goudie,Jas	Pointe-aux-Trembles
1852	Auguste	117	be	Lavoie, Narcisse	L'Islet
1852	Banker's Daughter	1122	sh	St Jean, Ant	Pointe-aux-Trembles
1852	Emperatrice Eugénie	130	sc		Grondines
1852	Frederick	863	sh	Dubord - Goudie,Jas	Pointe-aux-Trembles
1852	Julia	1071	sh	Dubord - Goudie,Jas	Pointe-aux-Trembles
1852	New Zealand	111	sc	Dion, Zéphirin	Saint-Pierre-les-Becquets
1852	Progress	106	be	Desjardins, Jos	Saint-André
1852	Temiscouata	187	br	April, Frs	Saint-André
1853	Balmarino	168	be	Miller, Matthew	Saguenay
*1853	Fleur de Marie	156	be		Lanoraie
1853	Highland Mary	121	be	Harrower, David A	L'Islet
1853	Isabella Peck	115	be	St Jean, Ant	Pointe-aux-Trembles
*1853	Jacques Cartier	147	be	Champagne, Gab.	Lanoraie
1853	James Goudie	110	sc	James Goudie	Pointe-aux-Trembles
1853	Lucinda	104	sc	Guilbault, Chas	Grondines
1853	Marie Flore	106	sc	Lavoie, Roger	Saguenay
1853	Marie Helene	139	sc	Beaulieu, Louis	Trois-Rivières
1853	Rimouski	210	sc	Taché, Jos-Chas	Rimouski
1853	Seabird	124	sc	Germain, Nérée	Sainte-Anne
1853	Sir Allan McNab	840	sh	Dubord - Desnoyers	Pointe-aux-Trembles
1853	Stamboul	1274	sh	Dubord - Desnoyers	Pointe-aux-Trembles
1853	Waterwitch	289	sc	Cantin, Augustin	Montreal
1854	Bridgitt	129	sc	Beaulieu, Louis	Trois-Rivières
1854	C.S.M.	208	br	Bois, les freres	Kamouraska
1854	Experiment	179	bg	Beaudry, Jos	Sainte-Anne-de-Tilly
1854	Canadienne	127	sc	Genest, Louis	Grondines
1854	Constantine	392	ba	Vachon, freres	Baie-Saint-Paul
1854	Constantinople	1298	sh	Dubord,E - Desnoyers	Pointe-aux-Trembles
1854	Eleonore	135	sc		Saint-Pierre-les-Becquets
1854	Feu Follet	117	sc	Grondines, Eust.	Grondines
1854	Flavien	111	be	Lapointe, Flavien	Saint-André
1854	Francois Hubert	130	be	Bernier, Hubert	L'Islet
1854	Handy	126	sc	Arcand, Charles	Grondines
1854	St. Jean Baptiste	141	be	Legros dit St L	Saint-Jean-Port-Joli
1854	Lucien	234	br	Chalifour, Simon	Sainte-Luce
1854	Marie Denis	120	sc	Chamberland, S	Kamouraska
1854	Mermaid	147	br	Tremblay, Ephraim	Chicoutimi
1854	Saint Paul	125	be		Baie-Saint-Paul
1854	Santa Clara	138	sc	Paquin, Hyppolite	Portneuf
1855	Adelaide	210	br		Saguenay
1855	Azoff	369	ba		Grondines
1855	De Salaberry	854	ba	Dubord - Laroche & Angers	Pointe-aux-Trembles
1855	Ebouloise	120	sc		Les Eboulements
1855	Jenny Lind	125	sc		Grondines
1855	Ketch	245	br		Saint-Pierre
1855	L'Aurore	125	sc		Deschambault
1855	Lady Head	239	br	Hudon, Damase	Grande-Baie
1855	Malakoff	1104	sh		Grande-Baie
1855	Maldon	1187	sh	Dubord,E & Desnoyers	Pointe-aux-Trembles
1855	Marie Ann	104	sc		Saint-Antoine-de-Tilly
1855	Nazaire	121	be		Saint-Thomas-de-Montmagny
1855	Olive	101	be		Saint-Thomas-de-Montmagny

Appendices

Year	Name	Tons	Type	Builder	Place
1855	Piednez (Harald)	531	sh	Dubord - Desnoyers	Pointe-aux-Trembles
1855	Sebastopol	610	ba	Chalifour, Simon	Sainte-Luce
1855	Venture	116	sc		Les Eboulements
1855	Virginie	104	sc		Lotbinière
1855	William Dargan	137	be		Chateau-Richer
1855	Wolfetown	332	ba		L'Islet
1856	Adélaide	136	sc		Portneuf
1856	Albert	195	br		Grondines
1856	Bramley Moore	882	sh	Dubord - Laroche	Pointe-aux-Trembles
1856	Dolphine	110	sc		Gentilly
1856	Hawk	137	be		Saint-André
1856	Hope	1104	sh	Valin - Roy, Chas	Saguenay
*1856	Louis Alma Inkerman	174	be		Saint Joseph de Lanoraie
1856	Province	101	sc	Thibodeau, Alphée	Lotbinière
*1856	Saint Jean Baptiste	124	be		Saint Jean Port Joli
1857	Blackwater	777	sh	Dubord, H.	Pointe-aux-Trembles
1857	Dalkeith	848	sh	Valin - Roy, Chas	Saguenay
1857	Adonis	83	be		Les Eboulements
1857	Alvina	188	sc		Deschambault
1857	Carioca	315	ba	Dubord - Laroche	Pointe-aux-Trembles
1857	Confidence	850	sh	Dubord - Laroche	Pointe-aux-Trembles
1857	Marie Flora	100	sc		Cap-Saint-Ignace
1857	Marie Georgiana	101	sc		Cap-Saint-Ignace
1858	Arbitrator	587	ba	Dubord - Laroche	Pointe-aux-Trembles
1858	British Columbia	540	sh	Valin - Roy, Chas	Saguenay-Bagotville
1858	Leandre	110	be		Cap-Saint-Ignace
1859	Castor	799	sh	Dubord - Angers,Jos	Pointe-aux-Trembles
1859	Sainte-Anne	104	sc		Sainte-Anne-de-la-Pocatière
1861	Bridget	934	sh	Dubord - Angers,Jos	Pointe-aux-Trembles
1861	Bonaventure	282	ba	Dubord - Angers,Jos	Pointe-aux-Trembles
1861	Josephine	106	sc	Sauvageau, Marc.	Grondines
*1861	Ontario	433	ba	Cantin, Augustin	Montreal
1862	E. Lacourciere	109	sc	Lacourcière, Eus.	Batiscan
1862	Marie Eleonore	116	sc	Maud, Hilaire	Deschambault
1862	Saint-Michel	103	sl		Saint-Jean-Deschaillons
1862	Zélée	100	sc	Onézime	Grondines
1863	Adeline	128	sc	Marchildon, Jos	Saint-Pierre-les-Becquets
1863	Blue Wave	266	bn	Max. & Stevenson	Portneuf
1863	Calumet	1628	sh	Dubord - Angers,Jos	
1863	Canadienne	104	sc	Beaudet, Ovide	Lotbinière
*1863	Cromwell	442	ba	Janes, W.D.B.	Montreal
1863	Marie Catherine	493	ba	Dubord, H.	Pointe-aux-Trembles
1863	Norfolk	235	ba	Hutchinson, G. jr	Portneuf
1863	Ocean Spray	262	bn	Max Stev - Laroche	Portneuf
1863	Suffolk	231	ba	St Jean & Laroche	Portneuf
1864	Aigle de Mer	130	sc	Maguy, Charles	Batiscan
1864	Alice	107	sc	Tremblay, Ephrem	Chicoutimi
*1864	Annie Mackenzie	437	ba	Goudie, James	Montreal
1864	B.L. George	120	be	Deroy, Basile	L'Islet
1864	Babineau et Gaudry	156	sc	Grondines, Eust.	Grondines
1864	Canadienne	109	sc	Guilbault, C.	Grondines
1864	Christina	550	ba	Dubord - Angers,Jos	Pointe-aux-Trembles
1864	Delin	147	sc	Portelance, Louis	Grondines
1864	Francis K. Dumas	1209	sh	Dubord - Angers,Jos	Pointe-aux-Trembles
1864	Jean Baptiste	114	sc	Gouin, F.X.	Batiscan
*1864	Kathleen	250	ba	Cas ?b?y, Xavier	Sorel
1864	Myrah	150	be	Slevin, Edward	Les Caps Chrlvx
1864	Passe Partout	304	ba	Dubord - Angers,Jos	Pointe-aux-Trembles
1864	Stewart Lane	1180	sh	Dubord - Angers,Jos	Pointe-aux-Trembles
1864	Sundown	144	sc	Germain, Nérée	Sainte-Anne-de-la-Pocatière
*1864	Victor Hudon	160	be	St. Cyr, Hubert	Batiscan
1864	Violet	230	be	Dubord - Angers,Jos	Pointe-aux-Trembles
1865	Alexina	109	be	Savard, Roger	Les Eboulements
1865	Arrogante	333	ba	Dubord - Angers,Jos	Pointe-aux-Trembles
1865	Diligence (Waterloo)	1245	sh	Dubord - Angers,Jos	Pointe-aux-Trembles
1865	Elegante	335	ba	Dubord - Angers,Jos	Pointe-aux-Trembles
1865	Josephine	116	sc	Chenard, Jos	Saint-Jean-Deschaillons
1865	Lusteria	104	sc	Bergeron, Phil.	Les Eboulements
1865	Marie Beatrice	118	sc	Mercier, Xavier	Saint-Nicolas
1865	Mary	115	sc	Bouchard, Léandre	Les Eboulements
1865	Pierre Nolasque	166	br	Beaudry, Jos	Saint-Pierre-les-Becquets
1865	Sainte-Anne	107	sc	Houde, Samuel	Grondines
*1865	Tina Forbes	493	ba	Tate, Power & Co.	Montreal
1865	Volage	729	ba	Dubord - Angers,Jos	Pointe-aux-Trembles
1866	Canadienne	888	sh	Dubord - Angers,Jos	Pointe-aux-Trembles
1866	L. Edouard	108	be	Richard, Octave	Cap-Saint-Ignace
1866	Marie Olvine	105	sc	Tremblay, Louis	Saint-Irénée
1866	Mary Lydia	107	sc	Simard, Arsène	Baie-Saint-Paul
*1866	Porto Rico	232	be	Cantin, Augustin	Montreal
1866	Saint Joseph	216	be	Bernier, Thos	L'Islet
1866	Sainte-Luce	129	sc	Lavoie, Ignace	Sainte-Luce
1866	Sea Gull	224	be	Price - Roy, Chas	Saguenay
1867	Algonquin	1499	sh	Dubord - Angers	Pointe-aux-Trembles
1867	Amelia	118	sc	Desjardins, David	Saint-André
1867	Beaver	181	be	Roy, Chas	Saguenay
1867	Foederis Arca	123	sc	Carbonneau, Ed.	Berthier
1867	Marie Erselie	111	sc	Lemieux, Antonin	L'Islet
1867	Modesty	979	sh	Dubord - Angers,Jos	Pointe-aux-Trembles
1867	Queen Victoria	105	sc	Sauvageau, Marc.	Grondines
1867	Reine de la Prévoyance	112	sc	Raymond, Eleuth.	Saint-Irénée
1868	Alfred	280	ba	Marchildon, Jos	Sainte-Emélie
1868	Halewood	557	ba	Angers, Jos	Pointe-aux-Trembles
1869	Fidelite	293	ba	Dubord - Angers,Jos	Pointe-aux-Trembles
1869	Black Duck	127	be	Duval - Hillier	Métis
1869	Lady Young	107	sc	Raymond, I.	Les Eboulements
1869	Prince	251	br	Roy, Chas	Saguenay
1870	John Day	136	sl		Saint-Aimé
1870	Saint Michel	460	be	Bernier, Thos	L'Islet
1871	Catherine	612	ba	Methot, Léandre	Cap-Saint-Ignace
1871	Emmanuel	104	sc		Saint-Antoine-de-Tilly
1871	Hélène	111	sc		L'Islet

Year	Name	Tons	Type	Builder	Place
1871	New Dominion	124	be	Joncas, Isaie	St-Thomas-de-Montmagny
1871	North Star	728	ba	Angers & Bertrand	Pointe-aux-Trembles
1871	Reine Elisabeth	109	sc		Portneuf
1871	Reine Victoria	116	sc		Champlain
1872	Alexina	114	sc		Grondines
1872	Baupré	163	sl		Yamaska
1872	Elie	121	be	Roy, Elie	Baie-Saint-Paul
1872	Fabiola	147	sc		Deschambault
1872	Marie Alberta	105	sc		Saint-Irénèe
1872	Marie Anna	116	sc		Saint-Irénèe
1872	Mary Queen of Scots	109	sc		La Malbaie
1872	Regina	129	sc		Grondines
1872	Star	109	be		Les Eboulements
1872	Toronto	800	ba	Angers & Bertrand	Pointe-aux-Trembles
1873	Audet et Robitaille	101	sc	Auger, Nazaire-E.	Sainte-Anne-de-la-Pocatière
1873	Biona (Marie Jeanne)	128	sc	Houde, S.	Grondines
*1873	Corinne	22	be	Lavoie, Roger	Les Eboulements
1873	Julia	482	ba	Angers & Bertrand	Pointe-aux-Trembles
1873	Marie Georgiana	158	sc	Sauvageau, Edmond	Champlain
1873	Marie Stella	138	sc	Côté, Pierre	Grondines
1873	Zoila	934	sh	Methot, Léandre	Cap-Saint-Ignace
1874	Albany	132	sc	Durand, Jos	Champlain
1874	Alphonsine	106	sc		L'Islet
1874	Camilla	127	sc	Talbot, Onésime'	Cap-Saint-Ignace
1874	Canadienne	128	sc	Rivard, Aimé	Grondines
1874	Emma	237	sc	Bélanger, A.	Cap-Saint-Ignace
1874	Emélie	101	sc	Gagnon, Antoine	Comté Saguenay
1874	Hedwidge	898	ba	Methot, Léandre	Cap-Saint-Ignace
1874	Louisiana	106	c	Audet, Théodore	Grondines
1874	Marie Adèle	149	sc	Rivard, Olivier	Grondines
1874	Marie Anne	134	sc	Duval, Pierre	Batiscan
1874	Zelia	143	sc	Lavoie, Roger	Les Eboulements
1875	Alexina	209	be		Les Eboulements
1875	Emma V.	413	ba	Ross, John	Cap-Chat
1875	J. Savard	139	sc	Savard, J.	Les Eboulements
1875	Laliberté	135	sl	Laliberté, Jos	Saint-Jean-Deschaillons
1875	Orleans	207	be	Warren, Nap	La Malbaie
1875	Saint Francois	282	be	Normand, Raymond	L'Islet
1875	Saint Joseph	233	be	Auger, Elzéar	Cap-Saint-Ignace
1875	Saint Louis	195	be		Sainte-Irénèe
1875	Seabird	104	sc	Barabé, Gédéon	Saint-Jean-Deschaillons
1875	Stadacona	132	sc	Bergeron, Max	Les Eboulements
1876	Alice	754	ba	Methot, Léandre	Cap-Saint-Ignace
1877	Eugénie	196	sc	Méthot, Léandre	Cap-Saint-Ignace
1877	S. Fortin	240	be	Begin & Fortin	Cap-Saint-Ignace
1879	Aurore	106	sc	Tremblay, Epiph.	Rimouski
1879	Marie Vigilante	114	sc	Roy, Elie	Baie-Saint-Paul
1879	Zelia	126	sc	Anctil, Barth	Sainte-Anne-de-la-Pocatière
1880	Sainte-Anne	125	sc	Tremblay, Alexis	Les Eboulements
1883	Albani	110	sc	Tremblay, Jean	Les Eboulements
1883	Jeannette	198	sc	Bouchard, Théod.	Petite-Riv-St-Fran\ois
1886	Marie Elmire	155	sc	Bergeron, Jos	Les Eboulements
1886	Mignonette	150	sc	Price, Evan John	Saguenay
1887	Thistle	114	sc	Price, Evan John	Chicoutimi
1889	Albatros	130	sc	Arcand, Liboire	Sainte-Anne-de-la-Pocatière
1890	Sarah Alice	209	be	Gauthier, E, H, X	Sainte-Irénèe
1891	Marie Anne	108	sc	Desruisseaux, Cas	Sainte-Croix

Note: *Only vessels registered at the Ports of Quebec or Montreal are listed. Builders of some Pointe-aux-Trembles vessels as identified by M. Rouleau, La construction navale à Québec et à Neuville au XIXe siècle, 39-42.*

* Montreal registry

Appendix D

Shipyards and Shipbuilders by District

QUEBEC 1.1 - 1.7

1.1	Saint Nicholas Dockyard	1765-1774	Zacharaiah Thompson
1.2	Bell's Shipyard	1794-1802	John Munn
		1805-1807	François Robitaille
		1811	John Bell and Robitaille Romain
		1813-1825	John Bell
		1825-1826	William Bell
		1826-1836	John Bell
		1836	Thomas H. Oliver completes ship begun by Bell
		1838-1842	John Nicholson and William G. Russell
1.3	The Canoterie - George Taylor	1810	John Bell
		1807-1816	Sam Brown for Anderson & Bruce
		1816	Etienne Derome
		1819-1825	George Taylor
		1825-1830	George Taylor and Allison Davie
1.4	Lepper's Wharf	1854-1857	Isaie Julien and Co. = Joseph, Isaie & Louis Julien and P. Labbé
1.5	Tremain and Hunters' Wharf	1835	John Nicholson and William Newton
1.6	Cul de Sac Dockyard	1796-1806	Alexander Munn
1.7	Molson's Wharf	1824-1825	William and Robert Carman
1.*	Lowndes & Patton Wharf	1845	Richard Jeffery
1.*	J. Marmette's Yard (St Paul St)	1849	Clapham

SAINT LAWRENCE NORTH 2.1 - 2.7

2.1	Diamond Harbour - (after 1824, divided sometimes into two separate yards)		
		1786-1787	James Duncanson
		1790-1792	William King and John Black
		1794-1800	Patrick Beatson
		1801-1804	Henry Baldwin for John Beatson
		1807-1812	Alexander Munn
		1813	David Munn
		1815	John Munn
		1824-1826	Louis Labbée
		1824	Jean Desnoyé for McDonald and Hows
		1827	James Young
		1824	[Vessel built for Captain Edward Henley]
		1825	[Vessel built for Captain James Clint]
		1827	Paul Viger & Antoine Ernst
		1833-1836	James and John Jeffery
		1840	William Lampson

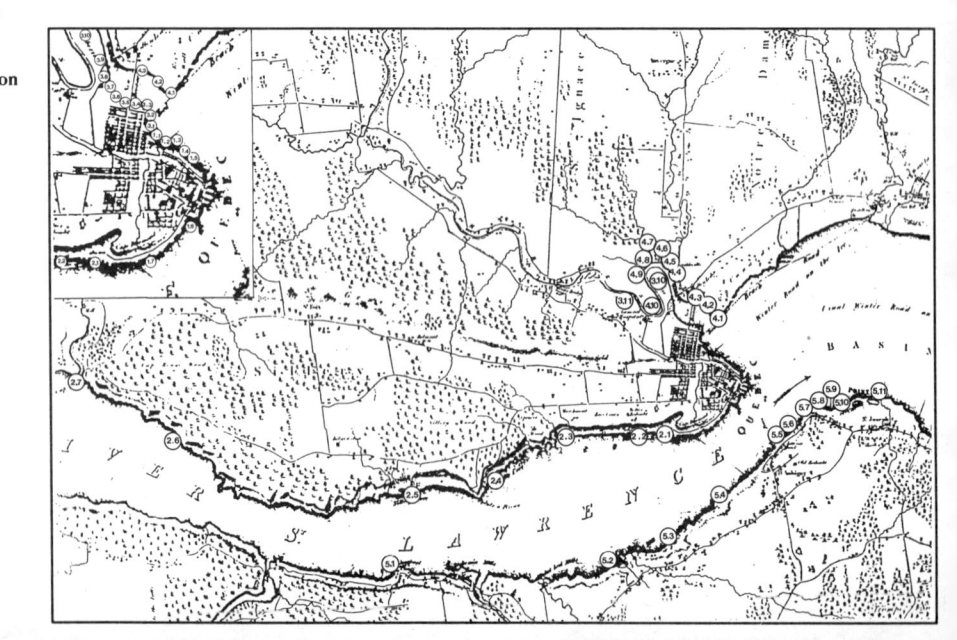

2.2	Cape Cove Shipyard	1818	Benjamin Viger and Olivier Trahan					John Jeffery jr.
		1825-1837	John S. Campbell and George Black				1850-1852	Pierre Valin
		1837-1846	George Black					Lemelin
		1846-1849	George Black jr				1855-1858	Walter G. Ray
		1851-1856	William H. Baldwin and				1860-1863	William Cotnam
			Henry Dinning				1863-1874	Pierre V. Valin
		1858	Edmund Black and J.G. Shaw	3.6	Nesbitt's Shipyard	1837-1856	John J. Nesbitt
		1859-1865	Henry Dinning and Company		Dalhousie St	1856-1866	William H. Baldwin
		1865-1877	Henry Dinning			1859	Edward Dodd (for W.H.B.)
2.3	Wolfe's Cove	1795	George Bradford Lane	3.7	Vacherie	1857	William Power
		1815	William Simons (of Greenock)			1865	Narcisse Rosa
		1819-1826	Charles Campbell & William Sheppard	3.8	Marine Hospital Cove	1810	François Robitaille
		1831-1865	Allan Gilmour & Co.					(for Mure and Joliffe)
		1866-1867	John Gilmour			1838-1840	Andrew Neilson
2.4	Saint Michael's Cove	1825	Patrick Fleming			1841-1850	Thomas C. Lee
2.5	Sillery Cove	1811	Walter Gilley			1851-1852	Edward P. Lee
		1825	William McAlpine and			1853	Joseph Leblond and Antonio Drolet
			John Richardson			1854	P. Bidegaré, François Jolicoeur &
		1826	James Adams				P. Lachance
		1835-1840	Mr. Milling for Wm Sharples & Son			1855	Thomas C. Lee
2.6	Crescent Cove, Cap Rouge	1810	James Morrson			1856	Pierre Valin
2.7	Atkinson's, Cap Rouge	1825	François Robitaille			1861-1862	Pierre Gabriel Labbé & Ovide Richard
		1830	Sam Finch jr			1863	Flanagan & Roche
						1866	Joseph Lachance & Edouard Cauchon
ST ROCH and ST SAUVEUR 3.1 - 3.11				3.9	Thomas Lee's		
					Shipyard	1839-1849	James Jeffery & Co.
3.1	Land of the Recollet Chapel	1774	Joseph Parent			1850-1865	Thomas C. Lee
		1792	John Black			1870	William H. Baldwin
	Goudie's First Shipyard	1801-18??	John Goudie			1872	Peter Baldwin
		1826	Alex Martin	3.10	Hare Point Lot 1	1854	Pierre Valin
		1845	John Munn (?)			1862	Henry Dinning & Co.
3.2	John Munn's Shipyard	1803-18??	John Munn			1865-1869	Pierre Valin & Leandre Dugal
		18??-1813	John Munn & Son			1869	Narcisse Rosa
		1813	Peter Campbell			1869	Louis Roberge
		1818-1821	Sam Finch			1872-1874	Narcisse Rosa
		1821-1857	John Munn		Hare Point Lot 2	1864	Regis Roy, Louis & Edouard Rosa
		1864-1866	Patterson & Shaw			1870	Narcisse Rosa
3.3	John Campbell's Property		John Goudie		Hare Point Lot 5	1867-1869	Regis Roy & Louis Rosa
			Sam Finch		Hare Point Lot 6	1862-18	Narcisse, Louis and Edouard Rosa
		1835	John Munn			1864-185	Regis Roy, Louis and Edouard Rosa
		1840-1841	Aymerick Vidal			1866	Louis Rosa
			J. Oliver?			1866	Narcisse Rosa
3.4	Goudie's Sawmill	1803-1824	John Goudie			1867	Narcisse Rosa & François Julien
		1834	John S. Campbell			1868	François Julien
		1834-1859	Thomas H. Oliver		Hare Point Lot 7	1851-1857	J. Lemelin, Valin
		1859	James Goudie			1862-1864	Georges Lemelin
	Goudie's Shipyard	1803-1824				1865-1866	Edmund W. Sewell
		1838-1839	William Lampson			1868	William Cotnam
		1839-	Edward Oliver		Hare Point Lot 8	1854	Pierre Valin
		18??	Edward and James E. Oliver			1855-1856	Fortier, Laurencelle & Vezina
		18??	Oliver & Co.			1862-1863	Edouard Trahan
		1860	Thomas H. Oliver			1866	L. Leclerc & C. Bonhomme
3.5	John Jeffery's Shipyard	1825	Robert Alden				(Union Society of Quebec)
		1828-1832	Louis Labbé		Hare Point (southwest)	1869	Louis Roberge (?)
		1836	John Jeffery	3.11	Little River (1)	1850-1856	Jean Elie Gingras
			John Jeffery & Son			1856-1858	Jean Elie and Pierre Elie Gingras

394 Appendices

		1859-1870	Jean Elie Gingras
		1871-1876	Jean Elie and Pierre Elie Gingras
		1877	Jean Elie and Alfred Gingras
		1879-1880	Jean Elie Gingras and Ferdinand Martineau
	Little River (2)		J.-B. Dion & Hilaire Blouin
			Charles Jobin & fils
		1856-1856	Walter G. Ray
			Jobin & Dion
	Little River (3)	1853-1855	Pelchat & Mercier
		1856	Walter G. Ray
		186	Jobin & Dion
			Charles Jobin & fils

ST ROCH NORTH 4.1 - 4.10

4.1	New Waterford Cove	1849-18	William Simons for Horation N. Jones
4.2	Beauport Cove	1849	William Cotnam
		1850-1852	Charles Jobin
		1853-1857	Edouard Trahan
4.3	Hedley Beach	1812	Philip Hooker
		1849	John James Nesbitt
		1853-1855	René Pelchat & Louis Mercier
4.4	Smithville	1854	James Nelson & Co.
		1863-1873	Lauchlan M'Kay and Henry Warner
		1873	Lauchlan M'Kay
		1874	Peter Baldwin
4.5	St. Charles Shipyard	1847	George H. Parke
		1848	Pierre Valin
		1849-1853	Pierre Brunelle
	James Nelson		
		1854-1855	Alexander and William Parke
		1856-1857	George H. Parke
		1863	Robert Maxwell & James Black Stevenson
		1864	Stevenson, Douglas & Co.
		1864	Edmund Sewell
4.6	Lairet	1852	Letarte, Drouin,
		1856	Michel Laprise
		1862	E.O. Richard
		1862-1865	William Cotnam
		1880	Peter Baldwin
4.7	Gros Pin	1850-1854	William Cotnam
		1855	E., J, and I. Samson
		1856-1862	William Cotnam

4.7-8 New Yard from 1862 made up of Parts of 4.7 and 4.8 and divided in two by Bickell's Bridge road

		1862-1872	P.G. Labbé
4.8	The Bridge	1850-1853	Théophile St. Jean
		1853-1856	Etienne Samson
		1856-1861	J. & I. Samson
		1862	Julien & Labbé
4.9	Saint Michael's Stream	1854-1857	Pierre Valin & Gonzague Vallerand
		1857	Narcisse Rosa
		1857-1863	Toussaint Valin

		1863	Pierre Valin & Gonzague Vallerand
		1863-1864	Pierre Valin
		1865	Valin & Vallerand (?)
4.10	Pointe aux Vaches	1852	Pierre Valin
		1857-1864	Narcisse Rosa

ST LAWRENCE SOUTH 5.1 - 5.11

5.1	New Liverpool	1810-1814	George & William Hamilton
		1846-1848	William Chapman Benson
		1855	Robert McCord
5.2	Hadlow Cove	1826-1828	William Price ?
		1854-1856	Lomas & Sewell
5.3	(Charles') Tibbit's Cove	1810	George Charles
		1845-1847	Walter G. Ray
5.4	Russell's Shipyard	1843-1845	William G. Russell and John Nicholson
		1845-1864	William G. Russell
		1864-1865	Catherine Russell
		1866-1877	Thomas Dunn & Etienne Samson
		1879	Alexander Russell and Etienne Samson
5.5	Dubord's Shipyard	1864-1865	Edouard Desnoyers
5.6	Davie's Patent Slip	1841	George Taylor
		1853-1883	George T. Davie
5.7.	Saint Lawrence Cove (a)	1849	Edmund W. Sewell
		1853	Charles Jobin
	Saint Lawrence Cove (b)	1846	Edmund W. Sewell
5.8	Glenburnie Cove Guillaume Charland jr Yard	1875-1883	Guillaume Charland jr
5.9	Glenburnie Cove Davie's Lower Yard	1874	Edmund Sewell
5.10	Glenburnie Cove Brunelle's Yard	1854-1862	Pierre Brunelle & Son

5.10.a Charland & Marquis Shipyard (northern end of former Brunelle property. Southern end was leased to the St. Lawrence Tow Boat Company).

		1864-1869	Guillaume (William) Charland & F.X. Marquis
5.10.a.1	South End of 5.9.a		
		1869-1893	Guillaume (William) Charland
5.10.a.2	North End of 5.9.a		
		1869-1878	F. X. Marquis
5.11	Lauzon	1863-1865	Pierre Brunelle & Son for Duncan Patton

ISLE OF ORLEANS 6.1 - 6.2

6.1	Saint Patrick's Hole	1811	Sam Finch) under
		1812	Walter Gilley et al) supervision of
		1812	John Ray) George Taylor
		1814	Romain Robitaille)
		1826	Joseph Louis Barallier
6.2	Saint Pierre	1824-1825	Charles Wood

Note: *These dates cover the years when new ships built by the shipbuilders concerned were registered, not those of their occupation of the yard.*

Appendix E

Deeds and Other Documents

1. George Black's account of the stages and labour in building the brig *Eleanor* of 1821

2. Henry Baldwin's account for blockmaking and turning for the ship *Manchester*, 1845

3. Account of Alexander Tough of Greenock for cordage for the ship *Quebec*, 1847.

4. Inventory of J.J. Nesbitt's shipyard, 1848

5. Agreements respecting the building of a ship between Pierre Valin and Anderson & Swinburn

6. J. Anger's account of expenses for the ship *Bridget* of 1860

7. Fire Insurance

8. Builder's Certificate signed by Richard Jeffery for the barque *Agenoria* of 1849

9. Handing over of a Treenail

10. Copy of Charter-party for a voyage of the vessel *Bee* from Liverpool to Quebec, 1847

11. Articles of Agreement of the crew of the ship *Sisters* bound from Dublin to Quebec, 1831

12. Narcisse Rosa's protest concerning a crew member who deserted

13. Ship's Carpenter's certificate of discharge at the end of a one-way journey.

14. Lloyd's Form of the Report of Original Survey

15. Lloyd's Table 1 - The different descriptions of timber, of good quality, to be used in the Timbering of Ships ...

16. Lloyd's Table A - Exhibiting the number of years to be assigned to the different descriptions of timber used in ships

17. Lloyd's Table B - Minimum dimensions of timber ...

18. Lloyd's Table C - Siding and moulding of beams.

19. Lloyd's Table D - Sizes of bolts, pintles of rudder and treenails.

20. Lloyd's Table E - Number of hanging knees

21. Lloyd's Table F - Minimum dimensions of iron knees and knee riders for British North American built ships and fir ships

22. Lloyd's circular letter of 26 June 1869.

Appendices

1. George Black's account for the construction of the brig Eleanor *of 1821, George Black's journal, P-1000, ANQ, from Richard Rice, "Shipbuilding in British America, 1878-1890: An Introductory Study," 181.*

\multicolumn{4}{c	}{Stages and Labour in Building the Brig *ELEANOR*, 1820-1}
Framing	Knees & hull 'beams'	Decks, stringers & 'stenchions'	Channels, rudder & 'linching etc.'
867 1/2 days (10 weeks, 1 day)	1,024 days (10 weeks, 5 days)	295 days	250 days
	Planking	Spinning oakum &	Cabin (joiners)
	576 days	230 days	195 days
			Making masts, spars & crosstrees 46 days
Stage totals: 867 1/2 days	1600 days	525 days	491 days
			TOTAL **3,483 1/2 days**

Source: 'George Black's Book', Archives Nationales, Québec.

2. Henry Baldwin's account for the blockmaker's outfit for the ship Manchester *built at Pickersgill Tibbits' yard in 1845. Pickersgill & Tibbit papers, P 0202/1, ANQ.*

3. Account of Alexander Tough of Greenock for cordage for the ship Quebec *of 1847. Pickersgill & Tibbits Co. papers, P-0202/1, ANQ.*

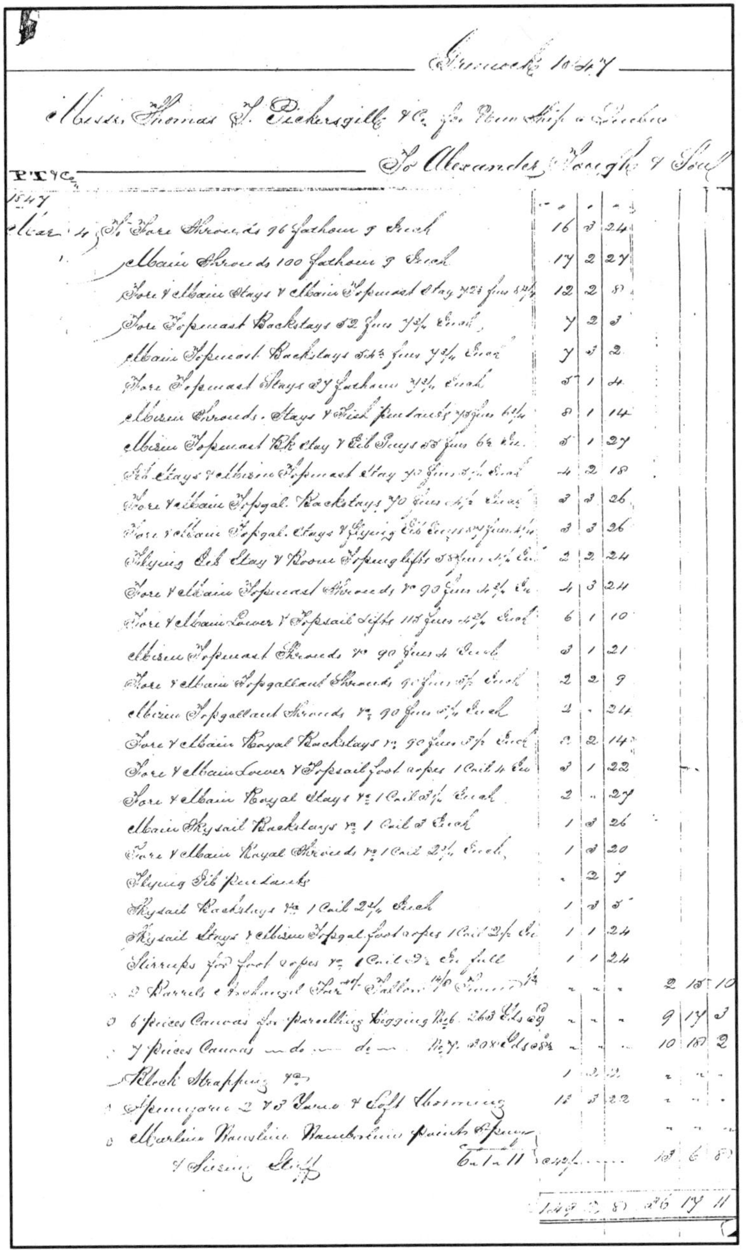

Greenock 1847

Messrs Thomas T. Pickersgill & Co. for New Ship Quebec

To Alexander Tough & Son

PT&Co.

1847						
Mar 4 To Fore Shrouds 96 fathom 9 Inch	16	3	24			
Main Shrouds 100 fathom 9 Inch	17	2	27			
Fore & Main Stays & Main Topmast Stay 72½ fms 8¾	12	2	8			
Fore Topmast Backstays 52 fms 7¾ Inch	7	2	3			
Main Topmast Backstays 54½ fms 7¾ Inch	7	3	2			
Fore Topmast Stays 27 fathom 7¾ Inch	5	1	4			
Mizen Shrouds, Stays & Fish pendants 70 fms 6¾	8	1	14			
Mizen Topmast Bk stay & Jib Guys 55 fms 6½ In.	5	1	27			
Jib Stays & Mizen Topmast Stay 70 fms 5¼ Inch	4	2	18			
Fore & Main Topgal. Backstays 70 fms 4½ Inch	3	3	26			
Fore & Main Topgal. Stays & Flying Jib Guys 115 fms 4¼	3	3	26			
Flying Jib Stay & Boom Topping lifts 58 fms 4½ In.	2	2	24			
Fore & Main Topmast Shrouds &c 90 fms 4¾ In	4	3	24			
Fore & Main Lower & Topsail Lifts 115 fms 4¾ Inch	6	1	10			
Mizen Topmast Shrouds &c 90 fms 4 Inch	3	1	21			
Fore & Main Topgallant Shrouds 90 fms 3½ Inch	2	2	9			
Mizen Topgallant Shrouds &c 90 fms 3¼ Inch	2	-	24			
Fore & Main Royal Backstays &c 90 fms 3½ Inch	2	2	14			
Fore & Main Lower & Topsail foot ropes 1 Coil 4 In	3	1	22			
Fore & Main Royal Stays &c 1 Coil 3¼ Inch	2	-	27			
Main Skysail Backstays &c 1 Coil 3 Inch	1	3	26			
Fore & Main Royal Shrouds &c 1 Coil 2¾ Inch	1	3	20			
Flying Jib Pendants	-	2	7			
Skysail Backstays &c 1 Coil 2¾ Inch	1	3	5			
Skysail Stays & Mizen Topgal. foot ropes 1 Coil 2½ In	1	1	24			
Stirrups for foot ropes &c 1 Coil 3½ In full	1	1	24			
2 Barrels Archangel Tar 40/- Tallow 14/6 Twine 1/4	-	-	-	2	15	10
6 pieces Canvas for parcelling Rigging No. 6 263 Yds @ 9d	-	-	-	9	17	3
7 pieces Canvas — do — do — No. 7 308 Yds @ 8½	-	-	-	10	18	2
Block Strapping &c	1	2	2	-	-	-
Spunyarn 2 & 3 Yarns & Soft Worming	12	3	22	-	-	-
Marline Houseline Hambroline points Spun & Seizing Stuff — Total @ 42/-				13	6	8
	149	2	8	36	17	11

3. (cont.) Alexander Tough's account, page 2.

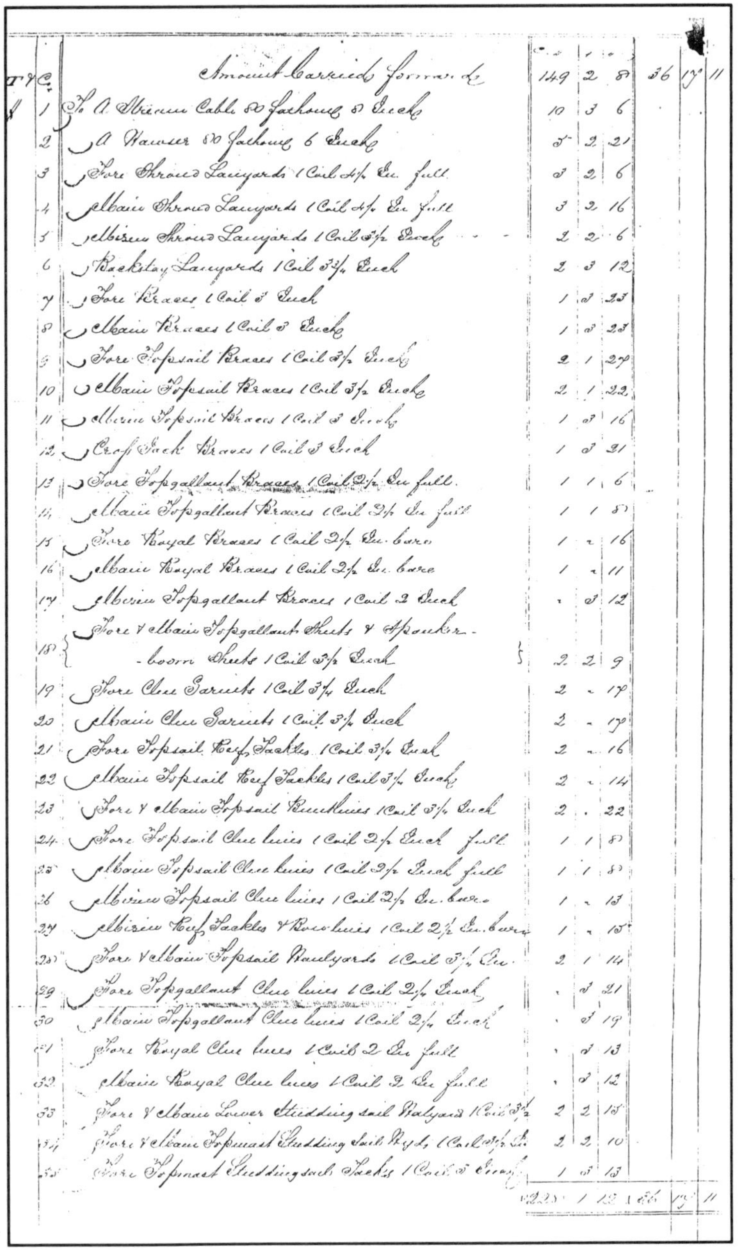

T&Co. Amount Carried forward	149	2	8	36	17	11
1 To A Mizen Cable 80 fathoms 8 Inch	10	3	6			
2 A Hawser 80 fathoms 6 Inch	5	2	21			
3 Fore Shroud Lanyards 1 Coil 4½ In. full	3	2	6			
4 Main Shroud Lanyards 1 Coil 4½ In full	3	2	16			
5 Mizen Shroud Lanyards 1 Coil 3½ Inch	2	2	6			
6 Backstay Lanyards 1 Coil 3¾ Inch	2	3	12			
7 Fore Braces 1 Coil 3 Inch	1	3	23			
8 Main Braces 1 Coil 3 Inch	1	3	23			
9 Fore Topsail Braces 1 Coil 3½ Inch	2	1	27			
10 Main Topsail Braces 1 Coil 3½ Inch	2	1	22			
11 Mizen Topsail Braces 1 Coil 3 Inch	1	3	16			
12 Cross Jack Braces 1 Coil 3 Inch	1	3	21			
13 Fore Topgallant Braces 1 Coil 2½ In full	1	1	6			
14 Main Topgallant Braces 1 Coil 2½ In full	1	1	8			
15 Fore Royal Braces 1 Coil 2½ In. bare	1	-	16			
16 Main Royal Braces 1 Coil 2½ In. bare	1	-	11			
17 Mizen Topgallant Braces 1 Coil 2 Inch	-	3	12			
18 Fore & Main Topgallant Sheets & Spanker-boom Sheets 1 Coil 3½ Inch	2	2	9			
19 Fore Clue Garnets 1 Coil 3¼ Inch	2	-	17			
20 Main Clue Garnets 1 Coil 3¼ Inch	2	-	17			
21 Fore Topsail Reef Tackles 1 Coil 3¼ Inch	2	-	16			
22 Main Topsail Reef Tackles 1 Coil 3¼ Inch	2	-	14			
23 Fore & Main Topsail Buntlines 1 Coil 3¼ Inch	2	-	22			
24 Fore Topsail Clue lines 1 Coil 2½ Inch full	1	1	8			
25 Main Topsail Clue lines 1 Coil 2½ Inch full	1	1	8			
26 Mizen Topsail Clue lines 1 Coil 2½ In. bare	1	-	13			
27 Mizen Reef Tackles & Bow lines 1 Coil 2½ In. bare	1	-	15			
28 Fore & Main Topsail Haulyards 1 Coil 3¼ In.	2	1	14			
29 Fore Topgallant Clue lines 1 Coil 2¼ Inch	-	3	21			
30 Main Topgallant Clue lines 1 Coil 2¼ Inch	-	3	19			
31 Fore Royal Clue lines 1 Coil 2 In full	-	3	13			
32 Main Royal Clue lines 1 Coil 2 In full	-	3	12			
33 Fore & Main Lower Studding sail Halyards 1 Coil 3½	2	2	15			
34 Fore & Main Topmast Studding Sail Hyds 1 Coil 3½ In	2	2	10			
35 Fore Topmast Studding sail Tacks 1 Coil 3 Inch	1	3	13			
	225	1	12	36	17	11

3. (cont.) Alexander Tough's account, page 3.

4. Inventory of J.J. Nesbitt's shipyard effects offered for sale on 11 December 1848, filed the same date in the greffe of notary Archibald Campbell.

INVENTORY
OF THE
EFFECTS BELONGING TO THE ESTATE OF
J. J. NESBITT.
TO BE SOLD ON
MONDAY MORNING,
The 11th instant,
AT ELEVEN O'CLOCK,
AT HIS SHIP-YARD, ST. ROCHS,
BY ORDER OF THE ASSIGNEES:

Nos.
1.—Lot of Treenails,
2.—Lot of Treenail Wedges,
3.—Lot of Large Wedges,
4.—1 Ladder,
5.—1 Lot Treenails, Wedges, and Boat-hook Handles,
6.—1 Lot of Blocks,
7.—1 do. Rope Cuttings,
8.—Part of Barrel of American Tar,
9.—Large Stove,
10.—5 Iron Levers,
11.—1 Lot Stove Pipes, and a Tub,
12.—2 Ship's Figure-heads,
13.—1 Lot Rudderband Moulds,
14.—1 do. Paint Tubs and Kegs,
15.—1 do. Paint, various colours,
16.—3 Boats' Davits,
17.—Book Case, Office Desk and Stool,
18.—Stove and Pipes.
19.—3 Barrels American Tar,
20.—2 do. Varnish,
21.—1 do. Cod Oil,
22.—24 do. Pitch,
23.—20½ Barrels Rosin,
24.—4 Shovels and lot of Spikes,
25.—6 Cant-hooks, and a Boat's Grapple, lot of Chain, and 4 Tar Brushes,
26.—9 Pitch Kettles,
27.—Lot of American and other Augurs,
28.—1 Cask Board Nails and Augurs,
29.—4 Bars Copper, & Composition Pump Chamber,
30.—11 Metal belaying Pins, & Lead Pump,
31.—1 Lot of New Dead Eyes,
32.—1 do. Rope, Sheerpole, and 1 Block,
33.—1 Barrel, 7 Scrapers, and 4 Lignum Vitæ Beetles,
34.—3 Bellows, and 2 Anvils,
35.—1 Punching and a Cutting Machine,
36.—2 Barrels Clinching Plates,

Nos.
37.—Lot of Chain and Ship's Iron Tiller,
38.— Do. Forge Tools,
39.— Do. Ribband Nails and Dogs,
40.— Do. Scrap Iron,
41.— Do. do.
42.— Do. Old Iron Work,
43.— Do. do. do.
44.—2 Pieces Square Iron, and a Lot Riming Irons,
45.—1 Lot of Ring Bolts,
46.—1 do. Sett Bolts,
47.—1 do. Smith's Coals,
48.—Joiner's Bench and lot of Loose Boards,
49.—Lot of Moulds,
50.— Do. Augurs, Punches, Grindstone, and 4 Joiners' Boxes,
51.—Lot of Mouldings,
52.— Do. Boards,
53.—Ships' Moulds, and Sheer Battens,
54.—Lot of Bulwark Boards,
55.—1 Joiners' Bench and Lot of Cuttings,
56.—Lot of Pine Plank and Boards,
57.— Do. Beam Moulds,
58.—4 Spar Maker's Stools, 1 Pair Ash Oars, and 2 Ladders,
59.—Lot of Harpings, Pitch Pine, and other Plank,
60.— Do. White Pine Boards,
61.—3 Ladders,
62.—60 Pieces Square Tamarac,
63.—Windlass body and part of patent,
64.—3 Lower Masts,
65.—2 Piles of Oak, Elm, and Pine Blocks,
66.—2 Pine Shear Legs,
67.—Lot of Elm, Oak, Pine & Tamarac Plank,
68.— Do. Stage Plank,
69.—1 Sett Launching Ways,
70.—8 Pieces of Red Pine,
71.—1 Crab,
72.—Lot Stage Poles and Shores,

4. con.) J. Nesbitt's shipyard efects offered for sale, continued.

```
                              2
73.—2 Birch 1st Futtocks,        93.— Do.  Ring Bolts,
74.— 80 Pieces Elm Timber,       94.— Do.  Rock Salt,
75.—200 do.  Flat Tamarac,       95.—2 Tackle Falls,
76.—  6 do.  Oak,                96.—1 Nunn Buoy,
77.—  8 do.  Ash,                97.—Lot Lignum Vitæ Beetles and Shovels,
78.—1 Red Pine Top-sail Yard,    98.— Do.  Blocks, Dead & Bull's Eyes, &c.,
79.—Lot of Empty Casks, and part of Barrel  99.— Do.  Old Rope,
     of Coal Tar,               100.—1 do.    do.
80.—Lot of Bar Iron, round, square and flat, 101.—1 do.    do.
81.—Old Pump and lot of Metal,  102.—6 Screw Clamps, 2 Swivel Shackles,
82.—Lot of Square Tamarac Knees,      and Lot of Iron Work,
83.— Do.  Round-house Knees,    103.—1 Demi-John and lot of Jars, &c.,
84.—2 Gratings and Steering Wheel Barrel, 104.—Part of Stove and Jackscrew,
85.—2 Winches,                  105.—Ship's Figure-head, lot of Reinstaffs,
86.—1 Grindstone,                     Belaying Pins, and Deck Plugs,
87.—1 Pair Scales,              106.—1 Lot of Oakum,
88.—1 lot of Chain,             107.—2 Sails,
89.—Tyzack & Dobson's Windlass, patent 108.—1 Lot of Handspikes,
     purchase,                  109.—5 Boats' Rudders, and 2 Ships' Caps,
90.—2 Anchors,                  110.—1 Pitch Kettle,
91.—Lot of Iron Knees,          111.—1 Pair Purchase Blocks, & lot of Spiles,
92.—Lot of Flat Tamarac, about 200 pieces, 112.—1 Lot of Deck Lights.
```

Thomas Hamilton, A. & B.

Quebec, 6th December, 1848.

5. Agreements between Pierre Valin and Anderson & Swinburn respecting the financing of the construction of the 491 ton ship Hiawatha, made before the notary Archibald Campbell on 27 November 1855 and 20 June 1856.

No. 14355

Agreement respecting the building of a ship–between–Pierre Valin–and–Anderson & Swinburn 27 November 1855.

On this day, the twenty-seventh of November, in the year of Our Lord one thousand eight hundred and fifty-five, Before the undersigned Notaries duly admitted and sworn in and for that part of the Province of Canada heretofore called Lower Canada, dwelling in the City of Quebec, in the said Province, personally came and appeared Pierre Valin, of the City of Quebec, Ship-builder, Of the One part, and James Swinburn, Esquire, of London, Merchant, acting as well for himself as for and in the name of his partner in trade William Danson Anderson, also of London, Merchant, they, the said James Swinburn and William Danson Anderson carrying on trade in London in that part of the United Kingdom of Great Britain and Ireland called England, under the name, style and firm of "Anderson & Swinburn," of the other part; which said Pierre Valin did and by these presents doth bind and oblige himself, his heirs and assigns, to build and construct in a good, strong and substantial manner at the ship-yard of the said Pierre Valin, in the Suburbs of Saint Roch, Hare Point, a ship or vessel for the said Anderson and Swinburn, upon the conditions and for the considerations hereinafter mentioned, - Which ship is to be of the following dimensions: Length of Keel, one hundred and thirty-two feet with eight feet rake, Figure-head, bust of an Indian Warrior, Extreme breadth, twenty-eight feet; depth of hold, eighteen feet, elliptic stern, and is to be of the burthen of about five hundred Tons, old measurement, to be built in the best possible style for a regular trader, but without cabin or state rooms - The deck to be flush fore and aft, with wheel house, with berths and top-gallant bulwarks - temporary berths for Captain and Crew in cabin and fore-castle and the cabin deck laid as far forward as mid-way between the main-mast and mizzen-mast. And the said Pierre Valin did, and by these presents he doth bind and oblige himself to and with the said Anderson & Swinburn to do, perform and execute in a good, strong and workmanlike manner the whole of the work necessary to finish and complete the said ship in a faithful manner, under the inspection of Lloyd's Surveyor, and to class seven years A I at Lloyd's, and shall be launched on or before the thirtieth day of May next, the said Pierre Valin furnishing and providing good materials, iron, copper, rigging, sails, anchors, chains, boats and everything that may be found necessary to complete the said ship in a style fit for the purpose of a regular trader as aforesaid, the outfit to be equal to that of Other vessels usually built at Quebec. - The said vessel to be delivered to the said Anderson & Swinburn safe afloat in the month of May next, accidents of launching and fire expected - The said Anderson & Swinburn to insure against the risk of accidents of launching, charging the said Pierre Valin with the premium of Insurance.

In consideration of which the said James Swinburn did and by these presents doth bind and oblige himself and his said partner to pay for the said ship at and after the rate of Ten Pounds Currency, per Ton, old measurement, which sum it is agreed shall and will be paid to Henry Atkinson, Esquire, of Quebec, Merchant, who has agreed to advance to the said Pierre Valin the necessary funds and monies to enable the said Pierre Valin to build and complete the said ship or vessel, and he, the said Pierre Valin, did and doth therefore assign, transfer and make over to the said Henry Atkinson, accepting hereof, all the sum or sums of money that may become due, payable and owing to him under the present Contract. - And the said James Swinburn, acting as aforesaid, did & doth hereby bind and oblige himself to furnish, without loss of time, and to forward from london direct to Boston or Portland all the standing rigging and metal rods required and whatever may be ordered by the said Pierre Valin, and for which the said Pierre Valin obliges himself to pay at the Invoice cost and expenses, with the usual commission of five per cent; And the said James Swinburn doth further agree to ship by the first vessels from London for Quebec the anchors, cables, sails and running rigging for the said ship, all which to be deducted from the sum or sums that the said Anderson & Swinburn agreed to be paid for the said ship as aforesaid at the market price, with charges and five percent Commission, that is to say:- the same shall be received by the said Pierre Valin on account of the present Contract or consideration of the said ship, the balance of the said Ten Pounds per Ton, Currency, the said James Swinburn binds and obliges himself, acting as aforesaid, to pay to the said Henry Atkinson as aforesaid, by the Drafts of the said Pierre Valin in favour of the said Henry Atkinson on the said Anderson & Swinburn, one half at sixty days and the other half at ninety days, on the sailing of the said ship, the payment of which drafts to be secured by a mortgage of the said ship to and in favour of the said Henry Atkinson with power to sell, in the event of the non-payment of the said drafts at maturity. - The ship to be insured at London by the said Anderson & Swinburn and the Policy to be approved and lodged with William Atkinson, Esquire, of London, for account of the said Henry Atkinson on behalf of the said Pierre Valin, the premium of Insurance to be paid by the said Anderson & Swinburn. It is agreed that the mortgage of the said ship for the security of the advances intended to be made by the said Henry Atkinson to the said Pierre Valin, to enable him to build and complete the said ship and to fulfil the present Contract, shall be sent to the said William Atkinson, to be cancelled and discharged, on payment of the sum due thereon; and for his trouble and Agency in the premises, he, the said William Atkinson, shall and will be allowed at Net Commission of two and one half per cent by the said Anderson & Swinburn. - And, in order to secure to the said Henry Atkinson the payment of all sum and sums that he may advance to the said Pierre Valin, to enable him to build and complete the said ship as aforesaid, it is agreed that the said ship shall and will, while on the stocks, be assigned and transferred to the said Henry Atkinson and be held by him as his own property, until he obtain the mortgage aforesaid, it being understood that such transfer and Assignment or any security the said Henry Atkinson may deem it expedient to take upon the said ship shall not in any manner vitiate the present Contract or Agreement and shall be as binding on the said Pierre Valin and the said Anderson & Swinburn as if no such security, transfer or Assignment had been made, and shall not prejudice the right of the said Anderson & Swinburn on the said ship or present Contract, provided they the said Anderson & Swinburn, do pay to the said Henry Atkinson the consideration or price agreed to be paid for the said ship; And, should they not pay the same, then and in that case the said Henry Atkinson shall and will sell and dispose of the said ship, in order to be paid and satisfied for the sum or sums advanced by him as aforesaid, and any surplus shall be paid by him the said Henry Atkinson to the said Pierre Valin, should any balance be due by the said Anderson & Swinburn, or to the said Anderson & Swinburn, in the event of a balance being due to them upon the said sale. - It is agreed that after the said ship is safely moored at a wharf in the Lower Town of Quebec, she shall then be in the charge and care of the said Anderson & Swinburn, they paying wharfage of the same. -

It is agreed by and between the said parties that the said ship shall and will be fitted out and equipped in every respect and particular as the generality of ships built at Quebec, guaranteed to class seven years.

Thus done and passed at Quebec, in the Office of Archibald Campbell, one of the undersigned notaries the day, month and year first above written, under the number fourteen thousand and three hundred and fifty five.

In Witness whereof the said parties have hereunto set their hands these presents being first duly read, according to law.

                (s) P. Valin

                     James Swinburn

                     Henry Atkinson

O.F. Campeau   Arch Campbell
Not.   *Not Pub.*

No. 14432

And on this day the Twentieth of June in the year of our Lord one thousand eight hundred and fifty six Before the undersigned Notaries residing at Quebec personally came and appeared William Danson Anderson of London in England Merchant at present at Quebec acting as well for himself as for his partner James Swinburn of the same place Merchant his partner in trade, they the said William Danson Anderson and James Swinburn carrying on business at London aforesaid under the firm of Anderson & Swinburn and Pierre Valin of the City of Quebec Merchant and Henry Atkinson Esquire also of the said City of Quebec Merchant the parties names in the foregoing agreement, who did declare and agree to and with each other in manner and form following that is to say:- That he the said Pierre Valin hath this day at the time of the execution hereof granted a Bill of Sale of the ship "Hiawatha" in favor of the said William Danson Anderson, and it is declared and agreed that the said sale is so made for the sake of facilitating the registration of the said ship and in order to comply the more readily with the provisions of the "Merchant Shipping Act of 1854," and the said William Danson Anderson did declare and agree that the said Bill of Sale though made in his own name is so accepted by him for and on behalf of the said firm of Anderson & Swinburn, and the said William Danson Anderson, acting as aforesaid, and the said Pierre Valin did and do hereby declare and agree that the said Bill of Sale now executed by the said Pierre Valin shall not in any way novate or alter any of the clauses, conditions and obligations in the foregoing agreement and further, that in pursuance and compliance with the said foregoing agreement he the said William Danson Anderson shall and will execute to and in favor of the therein named Henry Atkinson a good and valid mortgage of the said ship or vessel for the amount of advances on the said vessel now remaining due to him to with the sum of Three thousand seven hundred and sixty four pounds five shillings and two pence - current money of this Province, for which balance he hath handed to the said Henry Atkinson his the said William Danson Anderson's drafts or bills of Exchange on the said firm of Anderson & Swinburn to wit one for sixteen hundred pounds sterling payable sixty days after sight and the other for fifteen hundred and fifteen pounds one shilling and one penny payable ninety days after sight both dated his day.

Thus done and passed at Quebec aforesaid in the office of Archibald Campbell one of us the undersigned notaries on the day and year first above written under the number Fourteen thousand four hundred and thirty two. In faith and testimony whereof the said parties have signed these presents with us the said notaries, being first duly read according to law. -

    (s) Henry Atkinson
        P. Valin
        O.F. Campeau   W. D. Anderson
        Not.

402 Appendices

6. Contracts signed for construction of the ship Bridget, 900 tons, at Pointe aux Trembles, by Mr. J. Angers (data provided by Mr. Marc Rouleau)

Date	Contractors	Work	Paid	£	s	Days' work	Total
5/11/1860	Gabriel Rancourt Narcisse Bougie	Sawing all the wood for the ship *Bridget*, including the scaffolding - £150.	27/10/60 - 10/05/61				£178 0
3/11/1860	Jos. Ledoux	The elm treenails, large and small wedges, turning spruce and elm, driving in after planking done	10/60 - 05/61			207 @ 3/-	22 0 9 0
13/11/1860	Nicolas Tardif Jos. Leight Alex. Vaillancourt	The masting completely finished to J. Angers's taste, boring out the scuppers, boring the windlass, mortising the blocks and davits, making the tops and crosstrees, fishing the masts, and also the bowsprit if necessary. Must be better done than the work for the last ship - £40	1/12/60 1/01/61 1/02/61 1/03/61 1/04/61 1/05/61 25/05/61	10 16 9 17 2	10 10 13 10 6 0	200 @ 4/-	40 0
19/11/1860	R. Duchéneau	The ironwork as well as all the clinch rings - £85 (£2 10s deducted for work done in Quebec)	27/10/60 18/06/61			220 @ 7/6	82 10
	Narcisse Parent Frs. Vezina Narcisse Doré	Assembling the vessel at 9/- per pair of frames - 62 pairs	1/12/60 1/01/61	13 14	10 8	160 @ 3/6	27 18
4/12/1860	Ferdinand Labbé Jean Bédard	All the work in the hold, fitting the wooden beams, the knees, all the rest of the hold except the small keelson, fitting the /battens?/ to the stanchions, the curved pieces to the hog, i.e. the completed hold except for the clinched bolting - £140	1/01/61 1/02/61 1/03/61 1/04/61 1/05/61	12 28 37 41 22	0 0 0 0 0	560 @ 5/-	140 0
	Jos. Alain Dolbec	Making the hog, fitting it, finishing the large keelson, fitting the small keelsons and the stem and stern knees to the hog - £3	1/01/61 1/02/61	2	10 10		3 0
	Jos. Noel	The upper beams and the lower beams for 2/6 apiece	1/01/61 1/02/61 1/03/61	1 1	10 17	767 @ 2/-	3 15

Date	Contractors	Work	Paid	£	s	Days' work	Total
12/12/1860	Elie Lefebvre	Bolting the main keelson, the hog, the knees	1/1/61	2	0		
					10		2 10
	Pierre Côté	Making the counter, the rudder, the cutwater, the windlass,	1/1/61	3	0		
		the two upper ports, fitting the copper "platines" fore and	1/2/61	5	0		
		aft, all the rudder fittings	1/3/61	5	0		
			1/4/61	5	0		
			1/5/61	5	0		
			1/6/61	3	0		
			1/7/61	3	0		
			8/7/61	3	0	82½ @ 7/9	32 0
20/12/1860	Hyppolite Belanger Pierre Tremblay	The carpentry work complete, i.e. like the *Quebec*, with three houses - £166. 8 a.m. to 5 p.m. 4/-; 6 a.m. to 6 p.m. 5/-	1/1/61	2	10		
			1/2/61	10	18		
			1/3/61	17	0		
			1/4/61	36	14		
			1/5/61	46	8		
			1/6/61	38	13		
			1/7/61	14	15	@ 4/-	
			14/7/61	8	19	@ 5/-	
		Plus £9 10s for overtime					175 10
9/01/1861	François Julien Jos. Morissette	All the upper works of the ship, i.e. the deck the passageway, everything having to do with the top except for the windlass. The carpentry work and clinched bolting, installing all the fittings in the upper works, except the mast fittings (must take on Quebec people if there is a need)	1/2/61	9	0		
			1/3/61	12	10		
			1/4/61	24	17		
			1/5/61	33	15		
			1/6/61	5	0		
			14/7/61	9	18		
						380 @ 5/-*	95 0

(* because they did very good work)

Date	Contractors	Work	Paid	£	s	Days' work	Total
9/01/1861	Narcisse Parent Narcisse Doré Pierre Berthiaume Octave Bourgette	Planking the ship 45 strakes, about $14 each	1/2/61 1/3/61 /4/61	39 74 41	0 0 0	(@ 5/- (@ 6/3	155 0
5/03/1861	Louis Laperrière Elisé Vezina Bruno Girard I. Falardeau Louis Savard Desaulniers	Upper knees	1/4/61	9	10	40 @ 4/9	9 10
20/03/1861	X. Léveillé F. Vermette N. Rochette M. Côté	Boring out the bottom knees, the passageway over the ends of the lower beams, also the three rows of stringers in the tween decks. Bore the holes, drive them in and punch them. The breasthook fore and aft and the riders aft £4 and £5 5s. Three rows of stringers in the hold up from the foot waling, driving them in and punching them £1 5s.	1/4/61 1/5/61	4 6	0 10	68 @ 3/1	10 10
9/04/1861	Ed Dolbec Narcisse Drolet Lazare Soulard John Noel	48 molds for the two sides @ 1/6 £3 12 24 knees on one side @ 4/- 4 16 26 stanchions @ 3/6 4 11 Extra work 9	1/5/61 1/6/61			71½ @ 3/9	13 8
4/04/1861	L. Laperrière Elisée Vezina Bruno Girard Jos Laperrière	Making and fitting the tween-deck stanchions and fitting the knees that go over the "battens" in the tween decks. Also, making the molds for the iron knees for 1/6 each. Fitting one side of the knees for the top ports 4/-. Wedging the masts.	1/5/61	8	0	35½ @ 4/6	13 8
1/04/1861	Gabriel Rancourt Narcisse Bougie	Completely calking the ship. Horsing up three times if necessary to ensure good work, doing the "adonnage" of the joints and fitting the pieces that will go into the planking at £125 (they paid their men 5/- the first period, 5/6 the second; they themselves may have earned 7/6 per day throughout)	1/4/61 1/5/61 6/6/61	35 45 44	0 0 0	@ 7/6	125 0

Date	Contractors	Work	Paid	£	s	Days' work	Total
1/04/1861	Xavier Léveillé M. Côté	Boring 4 points, i.e. 8 pieces with knees. Boring them, driving them in and clinching them. Boring the mast carlings £2 13s 6d	1/5/61	2	13		2 13
9/04/1861	El. Dubuc	Boring three rows of stringers in the hold, i.e. from the foot waling up, and the strake above, in addition, boring the /battens?/ in the tween decks, as well as the kneeing that goes under the deck. Bore holes in them, drive them in and clinch them @ 4 sous per bolt. 238 bolts @ 2d £1 19 8 70 doz. clinch bolts @ 3_ 1 0 5 50 doz. clinch bolts @ 3_ 14 7	1/5/61 1/6/61	1 2	18 11		4 9
9/04/1861	L. Laperrière P. Angers E. Vésina Jos Laperrière	Fitting the blocks in the air spaces in the tween decks, fitting the gussets, making the four ballast ports, fitting the two riders and the breasthook of the tween-decks port. Fitting the pieces into the stringers, fitting the small pointed pieces forward, fitting one piece at each side of the upper ports and "wedging" the masts, the whole for £8	1/5/61				8 0
16/04/1861	L. Laperrière P. Angers E. Vésina Jos Laperrière	Making and fitting the diamond points, clinching the rings @ 2/6 per knee in the hold, starting work on 16/4/61; also the moulds of the tween-decks knees; fitting the knees @ 3/- per knee. Fitting 48 iron knees @ 3/- £7 4 Fitting and clinching points 6 0 Fitting and clinching diamond points of tween-decks knees 3 10	1/5/61 1/6/61	13 3	4 10		16 4
18/04/1861	A. Vaillancourt	Painting the ship same as the *Quebec*, two coats throughout, and a third if necessary, all the varnishing tween decks, the hold; starting at the foot waling and up to upper beams fir the sum of £26.	1/5/61 1/6/61 1/7/61	7 11 7	10 10 0		26 0
10/04/1861	Jos. Noel	Fitting the iron knees in the hold all on one side at 2/6 per knee. 24 knees £3.	1/5/61	3	0	@ 4/3 - 4/6d	3 0

Date	Contractors	Work				Paid	£	s	Days' work	Total	
18/04/1861	Honoré Auger	Boring the bottom planks on the inside, driving in and clinching at 3_d per bolt. Also all the butt bolts at the same price, in addition boring the "battens" and the lower knees of the hog at 2d per bolt.									
		330 bottom planks and butt bolts	£4	16	3						
		90 bottom planks and butt bolts	1	6	3	1/5/61	3	0	5 a.m.-7 p.m.		
		234 "battens" and hogs @ 2d	1	19	0	1/6/61	5	1	@ 4/6	8	1
29/04/1861	Italien John	Rigging the ship, i.e. taking coil wire and doing all the rigging, tying up the ship at the wharf, lining the sails, mounting the anchors and chains for £120.				1/5/61	25	0			
						1/6/61	47	0			
						10/6/61	12	0			
						15/6/61	35	0		120	0

Ship *Bridget* 979 tons at 40/- per ton			£1,949		
Received payment for only 933 tons @ 40/-			1,866		
less accounts totalling			1,801	5	11d
balance			£64	14	1d
to my brother	$30				
P. Tremblay	18				
finishing at Quebec	60	$108	£27	0	0
			£37	14	1

I collected a salary of 5/- per day for the
period, October 1860 to 8 June 1861,
and made a profit at the end of £37 14 1d.

Translation from French courtesy Parks Canada

Appendices

7. Fire Insurance policy issued by the Aetna Insurance Company in the amount of £100 on the wooden building in John James Nesbitt's shipyard on Prince Edward Street used as a moulding loft. The moulds and shipbuilding materials in the building were insured for a further £50. Dated 6th August 1853.

8. Builder's Certificate signed by Richard Jefferyy for the barque Agenoria of 1849.

9. Pierre Valin hands Henry Atkinson a treenail of the vessel he is building for him as a symbol of his delivery of the vessel to him. Recorded by the notary Archibald Campbell, 12th February 1856.

> N° 14.387
> Delivery
> — by —
> P. Valin
> — to —
> H. Atkinson
>
> 12th Feby 1856
>
> And on the Twelfth day of February in the year of our Lord one thousand eight hundred and fifty six the hull or frame and body of the ship mentioned and described in the foregoing Agreement was delivered and assigned over in the presence of us the said Notaries by the said Pierre Valin to the said Henry Atkinson in the shipyard in which the said ship is being built at the River St. Charles, the said Pierre Valin handing to the said Henry Atkinson a treenail of the said vessel in seizin and delivery thereof. —
> In witness whereof the said parties have signed with us the said Notaries these presents being first duly read & recorded in the office of Archibald Campbell one of us the

10. *Copy of Charter-party for a voyage of the vessel* Bee *bound from Liverpool to Quebec, 1847.* Pickersgill and Tibbits papers, P-0202/1, ANQ.

11. *Articles of Agreement of the crew of the 198 ton vessel* Sisters *bound from Dublin to Quebec in April 1831.*

410 *Appendices*

12. a) *Narcisse Rosa follows the usual practice in his attempt to see that a crew member does not skip ship by authorizing the Captain to pay him £20 three days after sailing; and*
    b) *is thwarted by his jumping overboard thirty-six hours after the ship leaves port.*

13. *Certificate of Discharge of David Goudie, son of James Goudie, who signed on as ship's carpenter for the journey of the ship Ruby to Liverpool. 24th September 1863.*

Appendices 411

14. Lloyd's Form of the Report of Original Survey

15. Lloyd's Table 1 of minimum timber requirements. Lloyd's Register 1866.

16. Lloyd's Table A of classification standards
Lloyd's Register 1866.

TABLE A.

EXHIBITING THE NUMBER OF YEARS TO BE ASSIGNED TO THE DIFFERENT DESCRIPTIONS OF TIMBER USED IN SHIPS, THE SAME TO BE OF GOOD QUALITY, PROPERLY SEASONED, AND FREE FROM DEFECTS.

		TIMBERING							**Rudder and Windlass.**	**OUTSIDE PLANK**					**INSIDE PLANK, &c.**		
		Floors.	First Foothooks.	Second Foothooks.	Third Foothooks and Top Timbers.	Main and Rider Keelsons.	Transoms, Knightheads, Hawse-Timbers, Apron, and Deadwood* Stem and Stern Post.	Beams and Hooks.	Knees.	Main Pieces.	Keel to First Futtock Heads.	First Futtock Heads to Light Mark.	Light Mark to Wales.	Wales, Black-Strakes, Topsides, and Sheer-strakes.	Upper deck Waterway, Spirk'tting, and Planksh'rs.	Shelves, Clamps, Limber and Bilge Strakes, Ceiling in Hold and betwixt Decks, also Spirketting and Waterway below the Upper Deck.		
1	English, African, and Live Oak, Adriatic, Italian, Spanish, Portuguese, and French Oak; East-India Teak, Morung Saul, Greenheart, Morra, and Iron Bark	12	12	12	12	12	12	12	12	12	12	12	12	12	12	12	English, African, and Live Oak, Adriatic, Italian, Spanish, Portuguese, and French Oak; East-India Teak, Morung Saul, Greenheart, Morra, and Iron Bark	1
2	Mahogany of Hard Texture, Cuba Sabicu, Pencil Cedar, Angelly, and Venatica	10	10	10	10	10	10	12	12	10	12	12	10	10	10	12	Mahogany of Hard Texture, Cuba Sabicu, Pencil Cedar, Angelly, and Venatica	2
3	Other Continental White Oak, Spanish Chesnut, and Blue Gum	9	9‡	7	7	9	7	8	8	7	12	12	9	8	9	10	Other Continental White Oak, Spanish Chesnut, and Blue Gum	3
4	N. American White Oak, American Sweet Chesnut, Stringy Bark, and Red Cedar	8	8‡	7	7	8	7	7	7	7	12	10	8	7	7	9	N. American White Oak, American Sweet Chesnut, Stringy Bark, and Red Cedar	4
5	Pitch Pine, Larch, Hackmatack, Tamarac, and Juniper	7	7	7	7	8	7	8	8	7‖	12	10	8	8	10	8	Pitch Pine, Larch, Hackmatack, Tamarac, and Juniper	5
6	Second-hand English Oak, African Oak, and East-India Teak §§	7	7	6	6	6	6	6	6	5	—	—	—	—	5	5	Second-hand English Oak, African Oak, and East-India Teak §§	6
7	Cowdie, Huon Pine	6¶	6	6	7	7	6	7	7	—	10	9	8	7	10	8	Cowdie, Huon Pine	7
8	Baltic and American Red Pine	5	5	5	7	7	5	7	7	5‖	9	9	8	7	10	8	Baltic and American Red Pine	8
9	English Ash	7	6	5	5	5	4	5	5	5‖	10	7	4	—	—	5	English Ash	9
10	Foreign Ash	5	5	4	4	5	4	5	5	—	10	7	4	—	—	5	Foreign Ash	10
11	American Rock Elm and Hickory	6¶	6	5	5	6	5	5	5	4	12§	8	6	5	5	6†	American Rock Elm and Hickory	11
12	European and American Grey Elm	5	5	4	4	4	4	5	5	—	12§	8	5	4	4	4	European and American Grey Elm	12
13	Black Birch and Black Walnut	5¶	5**	4	4	4	4	4	4	4‖	10	7	4	4	—	5	Black Birch and Black Walnut	13
14	Spruce Fir	5	5**	4	4	4	4	5	7	5‖	6	6	5	5	5	5	Spruce Fir	14
15	White Cedar	5	5	4	7	4	4	4	7	4‖	6	6	5	4	4	5	White Cedar	15
16	Beech	5¶	4	—	—	4	—	—	—	4‖	12§	8	4	—	—	5	Beech	16
17	Yellow Pine	—	—	4	4	4	4	4	—	6	5	5	5	5††	5	Yellow Pine		17
18	Hemlock	4	4	4	4	4	4	4	4	—	4	4	4	4	4	4	Hemlock	18

* This Table applies as to the Deadwood so far as regards the Material to be used from the height of two feet above the rabbet of the Keel. † American Rock Elm allowed for Limber Strakes, Bilge Strakes, and Ceiling between them in Ships of the 7 years' grade.
‡ If the First Foothooks run up above the Light Watermark, the use of Foreign White Oak is allowed for the 7 years' grade only.
§ The use of Elm and Beech, in Ships above the 8 years' grade, to be restricted to a height from the lower part of the Main Keel, of one-third of the internal depth of the Ship measured, in midships, from the top of the Limber Strake to the top of the Upper Deck Beams.
¶ Black Birch, Beech, American Rock Elm, and Cowdie, allowed for Floors in Midships, to an extent not exceeding one-half the entire length of the Keel, in Ships of the 7 years' grade.
** Black Birch and Spruce allowed for First Futtocks amidships, to the same extent in Ships of the 6 years' grade.
†† Yellow Pine allowed for Waterways of Upper Deck in Ships of the 7 years' grade, if properly fastened, as prescribed in Table B, and provided the Beams are well secured independently of the Waterways.
Mem.—The word "English" includes Timber the growth of the United Kingdom.
‖ The Materials marked thus ‖ under the head of "Rudder and Windlass," allowed in Ships of 300 Tons and under *only*.
§§ In cases where second-hand Teak of approved quality is proposed to be used, application may be made to the Committee with a view to its being allowed a higher grade (not exceeding two years) than as set forth above.

Lloyd's Register of Shipping, London,
21st September, 1865.

17. Lloyd's Tables B and C - minimum dimensions for timber and beams. Lloyd's Register 1866.

18. Lloyd's Tables D and E of bolt sizes and requirements for hanging knees
Lloyd's Register 1866.

TABLE D.

SIZES OF BOLTS, PINTLES OF RUDDER, AND TREENAILS. *Section 46.*

	50	100	150	200	250	300	350	400	450	500	700	900	1350
Tonnage													
Heel-Knee, Stemson, and Deadwood Bolts ...... Inches	14/16	15/16	1	1	1 1/16	1 2/16	1 2/16	1 3/16	1 4/16	1 4/16	1 5/16	1 6/16	1 8/16
Bolts in Sister Keelsons, Scarphs of Keel,* Arms of Breast Hooks, Pointers, Crutches, Riders, Hanging and Lodging Knees to Hold or Lower Deck Beams (except in and out Throat Bolts of Hanging Knees, which must be larger), also in and out Bolts of Shelf, Clamp, and Waterway of Hold or Lower Deck Beams, and the in and out Throat Bolts of Upper Deck Hanging Knees.	11/16	12/16	12/16	12/16	13/16	14/16	14/16	15/16	15/16	1	1 2/16	1 3/16	1 4/16
Keelson Bolts (one through Keel at each Floor), Throats of Transoms, Throats of Breasthooks, and Throats of Hanging Knees to Hold or Lower Deck Beams	12/16	13/16	14/16	14/16	15/16	1	1	1 1/16	1 2/16	1 2/16	1 3/16	1 4/16	1 6/16
Bilge, Limber Strake, and Through Butt Bolts	9/16	10/16	10/16	11/16	11/16	12/16	12/16	12/16	13/16	14/16	14/16	15/16	1
Other Butt Bolts	9/16	10/16	10/16	10/16	11/16	11/16	11/16	12/16	12/16	12/16	13/16	13/16	14/16
Bolts through heels of cant timbers at fore and after Deadwood. In and out Bolts of Upper Deck Waterway, Shelf and Clamp, also Arms of Hanging and Lodging Knees, except in and out Throat Bolts of Hanging Knees, which must be larger	10/16	11/16	11/16	11/16	12/16	13/16	13/16	14/16	14/16	14/16	15/16	1	1 2/16
Pintles of Rudder { The Braces of which must extend so as to receive not less than Two Bolts on the Planking on each side.	1 7/8	2	2	2 1/4	2 3/8	2 1/2	2 5/8	2 3/4	3	3	3 1/4	3 1/2	3 1/2
Hardwood Treenails	1	1	1	1 1/8	1 1/8	1 1/8	1 1/4	1 1/4	1 1/4	1 3/8	1 3/8	1 3/8	1 1/2

* NUMBER OF BOLTS IN SCARPHS OF KEEL:—
In Ships of 150 Tons and under .... 6 Bolts
„ above 150 Tons and under 500 Tons .... 7 do.
„ 500 Tons and above .... 8 do.

N.B.—Bolts to be through and clenched, as prescribed in *Section 46*, and to be of good quality, well made with suitable heads and be tightly driven.

Lloyd's Register of Shipping, 16th May, 1861.

TABLE E.

NUMBER OF HANGING KNEES *Section 41.*

Tons.	To Hold Beams. Pairs.	To Upper Deck Beams. Pairs.
150	—	4
200	4	6
250	5	7
300	6	8
350	7	9
400	8	10
450	8	11
500	9	12
550	9	13
600	10	14
650	10	15
700	11	16
750	11	17
800	12	18
900	13	20
1000	14	22
1100	15	24
1350	17	26

19. Lloyd's Table F of dimensions of iron knees and knee riders.
Lloyd's Register 1866.

TABLE F.

MINIMUM DIMENSIONS OF IRON KNEES AND KNEE RIDERS FOR BRITISH NORTH AMERICAN BUILT SHIPS AND FIR SHIPS.—*Section 62.*

TONNAGE ....TONS	150	200	250	300	350	400	450	500	550	600	650	700	750	800	900	1000	1100	1200	1300	1400	1500	1600	1700	1800	1900	2000
Number of Hanging Knees to Hold or Lower Deck Beams ....Pairs	3*	4	6	8	9	Upwards, one Knee Rider to every Beam, or Knees and Riders as per Section 62																				
Number of Hanging Knees to Upper and Middle Deck Beams ....Pairs	4	6	7	8	9	10	11	12	13	14	15	16	17	18	Upwards, one to every Beam											
Breadth of Knees and Riders to Hold or Lower Deck Beams ....Inches	3	3	3	3	3	3	3¼	3¼	3½	3½	3¾	3¾	4	4	4¼	4¼	4½	4½	4¾	4¾	5	5	5¼	5¼	5½	5½
Breadth of Upper Deck Knees, where there are two Decks, and of Middle Deck Knees, where there are three Decks ....Inches	3	3	3	3	3	3	3¼	3¼	3½	3½	3½	3½	3¾	3¾	4	4	4¼	4¼	4½	4½	4½	4½	4¾	4¾	4¾	4¾
Thickness of Riders at the joints or butts of the Timbers ....Inches	1¼	1¼	1½	1½	1½	1½	1¾	1¾	2	2	2¼	2¼	2½	2½	2¾	2¾	3	3	3¼	3¼	3½	3½	3½	3½	3¾	3¾
Thickness of Knees to Lower Deck or Hold Beams and Knee Riders at the Angle of the Throat ....Inches	2½	2½	2¾	2¾	3	3	3¼	3¼	3½	3½	3¾	3¾	4	4	4¼	4¼	4½	4½	4¾	4¾	5	5	5¼	5¼	5½	5½
Thickness of Knees to Lower Deck or Hold Beams and Knee Riders at the Throat Bolts.................................... Inches	1¾	1¾	2	2	2¼	2¼	2½	2½	2¾	2¾	2¾	2¾	3	3	3	3	3¼	3¼	3¼	3¼	3½	3½	3½	3½	3¾	3¾
Thickness of Knees to Upper or Middle Deck at the Throat Bolts † .... Inches	1½	1½	1¾	1¾	2	2	2¼	2¼	2½	2½	2½	2½	2¾	2¾	2¾	2¾	3	3	3	3	3¼	3¼	3¼	3¼	3½	3½
Thickness of Hanging Knees (not Riders) at the ends ....Inches	⅝	⅝	¾	¾	¾	¾	⅞	⅞	⅞	⅞	1	1	1	1	1	1	1	1	1	1	1	1	1	1	1	1
Length of Beam Arms of Knees and Knee Riders for Lower Deck or Hold Beams ‡ ...	2 ft. 6 in.	2 ft. 6 in.	2 ft. 9 in.	2 ft. 9 in.	3 ft. 0 in.	3 ft. 0 in.	3 ft. 3 in.	3 ft. 3 in.	3 ft. 3 in.	3 ft. 6 in.	3 ft. 6 in.	3 ft. 6 in.	3 ft. 9 in.	3 ft. 9 in.	3 ft. 9 in.	3 ft. 9 in.	4 ft. 0 in.	4 ft. 0 in.	4 ft. 0 in.	4 ft. 0 in.	4 ft. 0 in.	4 ft. 0 in.	4 ft. 0 in.	4 ft. 0 in.	4 ft. 0 in.	4 ft. 0 in.

NOTE.—The Bolts in all Iron Riders in Hold, to be not more than twenty-one inches apart on the average. Standards upon the Beams of such Ships are not admitted as substitutes for Hanging Knees below them. For sizes of Bolts, see Table D.

* Provided the depth of hold be 13ft. or upwards.

† Breadth and thickness of Knees for Upper Deck, where there are Three Decks, may be one sixth less. ‡ Beam Arms of Upper an[illegible]le Deck Knees, may be three inches shorter than those of the Lower Deck.

Side Arms of Hanging Knees not to be less in length, than one and a half the length of their Beam Arms. Beam Arms of Knees and Knee Riders, which are 3[illegible] in length, to have not less than Four Bolts; and shorter than that length, to have not less than Three Bolts.

Side Arms of all Hanging Knees to have at least One Bolt more than in the Beam Arms.

Lloyd's Register of Shipping,
27th May, 1858.

LLOYD'S REGISTER OF SHIPPING,
2, WHITE LION COURT, CORNHILL.
26th June, 1869.

SIR,

Considering the acknowledged improvement which has taken place in the construction and efficiency of Vessels built in the North American Colonies since this Society appointed Surveyors to superintend them while building, and after carefully considering the memorials of the Quebec Shipbuilders of the 18th February, 1869, and of the Glasgow Shipowners of the 17th March, 1869, with the various letters from the Colonial Surveyors and others, and also the able report by the Liverpool Surveyors, who have given the subject so much attention, and who have so much experience of the exigencies of these vessels; we have come to the following opinion respecting modes of constructing them which we think might warrant the Committee in increasing the number of years of classification for vessels built of *Spruce* or *Hackmatack*, that is to say:—if in vessels built of Spruce (which are at present limited by Table A to 5 years) the stem, apron, and inner and outer sternposts were made of Pitch Pine or Hackmatack, and if the treenails used from the lower part of the chocks of the short floor heads to the upper part of the bilges for half the vessel's length amidships were of approved hardwood, and the rest of the treenails of good seasoned Hackmatack, and the spaces between the timbers of the frame and transoms were filled with *salt* while the vessel is being built, and thick garboard strakes crossbolted were fitted, and all the in and out bolts of the iron riders and hanging knees below the hold beams, and the bolts of keel scarphs and stem scarphs were of copper or yellow metal (although the bolts of the thick strakes on the short floor heads were of *Iron* driven from the inside and clenched on the frame, and the middle line bolts were also of *Iron*) such vessel might in our opinion be allowed *one* year additional classification.

Or, if a vessel built of such materials were copper or yellow metal fastened down from one-fifth the depth of hold below the upper deck, including the bilge and middle line bolting; and the keelsons, shelves, waterways, sheerstrake, and transoms, with the stem, apron, and sternposts were of Pitch Pine, Hackmatack, or Red Pine and *salted*, then *two* years additional might be allowed, say 7 A with the usual additions for extra copper bolting or for being built under a roof. And vessels built of *Hackmatack*, which are at present limited by Table A to 7 years, if constructed and *salted* as above described for the Spruce vessels of the 6 A class, might be raised to the 8 years, and if copper or yellow metal fastened from one-fifth the depth of hold below the upper deck might be classed 9 years, with the usual extension of class for extra copper bolting or for being built under a roof. The state of the salting to be ascertained and reported upon at the Half-time or other Special Surveys, and if deemed necessary, the vessel to be re-salted.

We submit herewith Table A amended (in red figures) as would be necessary if the above alterations in classification were sanctioned by the Committee. We beg to add that, as the thicknesses of the planking in Colonial built ships usually exceed the requirements of the rules, it is desirable that the St. John and Quebec Surveyors be allowed to submit amended tables of thicknesses of planking for these vessels, as proposed in Messrs. Tucker and Besant's letter, No. 438, of the 9th February, 1869.

We also agree in the following remarks made by the Liverpool Surveyors on the subject of opening Colonial built ships for re-classification, as stated on the third page of their report of the 10 March, 1869, viz.:—"With regard to the re-classification of these vessels, we would suggest "that the removal of the strake of outside planking between wales and the light line be dispensed "with, defects but very rarely existing in that part; and if the opening at the turn of the bilge be "considered by the Committee to be necessary, we would submit that it be made imperative, and "not as at present optional, to open the ship *outside* instead of inside *amidships*, and at the ends "*inside*, thus preventing weakening the vessel where strength is required."

We are, Sir,
Your obedient Servants.
J. H. RITCHIE.
J. MARTIN.
B. WAYMOUTH.

To G. B. SEYFANG, Esq.
  Secretary.

20. Lloyd's Circular Letter of 26th June, 1869.

Bibliography

Principal Manuscript Sources

1. CANADA

Archives civiles de Québec
    Notaries' records 1838-1887
    Parish records 1875-1910

Archives nationales du Québec
    Biens des Jésuites
        Correspondence 1821-1829   E 196
    Court Records
        Superior Court 1809-1880   T 0011
    Notaries' records 1760-1894   CN 301
    Parish Registers 1760-1875   CEO 301
    Port of Quebec
        Bureau Veritas Letter Book 1883-1905   F0002 16
        Lloyd's Agency Registers of
        Casualties 1856-1889   F0002 18
        Port Wardens' Report Books 1872-1907   F0002 1-5, 7, 13
        Quebec Exchange Daily Reports 1832-1833   F0002 14, 21
        Trinity House Meetings Book 1818-21   F0002 21
    Surveyors' records 1760-1917   CA 301

Archives of the Port of Quebec
    Trinity House
    Letter Books, 1 and 2 1804-1816
    Minute Books 1804-1812
    Maps

Archives de la Ville de Québec
    Chemins
    Surveyor's reports and plans
    Conseil de Ville
    Letters and petitions received 1840-1888
    Letters sent 1833-36, 1840-1880
    Role of evaluation 1844-56
    Juges de Paix
    Sessions of the Peace 1814-33, 1836-40

National Archives of Canada
    Admiralty papers   MG 12
    Census returns for Quebec   MG 8
    Lower Canada Land Papers   RG 1, L 3L
    Lower Canada Marriage Bonds   RG 4, B 28
    Military C-series   RG 8
    Registers of the Port of Quebec 1787-1893   RG 12
    William Bell Papers   MG 24, F 3

Registry Office Levis
    Registered land deeds 1880-1890

Registry Office Quebec
    Registered land deeds 1820-1890

2. UNITED KINGDOM

Custom House, Greenock
    Registers of Shipping 1786-1819

Custom House, London
    Bills of Entry for British Ports, 1855.

India House - India Office
    Memorials   L/MAR/C/655
    Birth Certificates   L/MAR/C/669
    Records   B/108

National Maritime Museum, Greenwich
    C.W. Kellock papers 1855
    Lloyd's Survey Reports for Quebec 1852-1880
    Transcripts of Liverpool Shipping Registers 1786-1812
    Transcripts of London Shipping Registers, 1786-1822

Public Record Office, Kew, England

ADMIRALTY
Records of Naval Yards 1813-1816:
Lake Champlain   ADM 37/5000-5001, 42/2167, 2170, 2174, 38/2294
Lake Erie   ADM 42/2167, 2170, 2173-4, 2177-78, 2180-81
Lake Ontario   ADM 32/254, 37/5000-5002, 42/2167, 2169-70, 2172, 2174-2175, 2177-2181
Letters to and from Admiralty 1814-1816
ADM 106/1997, 106/3179
BOARD OF TRADE
London Shipping Register   BT 107/112
North Britain Shipping Register 1814   BT 107/113

Registrar-General for Scotland, Edinburgh
Old parish registers of baptisms, burials and marriages:
Irvine   OPR 595/1
Kilmarnock   OPR 597/3,4
North Leith   OPR 692/3
Port Glasgow   OPR 574/7

Scottish Record Office
Register of Deeds
Register of Saisines, Ayr and Fife
Register of Wills, Testaments and Inventories

Maps and Plans

The majority of plans of shipyard sites were filed with records of notaries or surveyors and are now at the Cartothèque of the Archives nationales du Québec. Others were found in the Map Department of the National Archives, Ottawa and at the Archives de la Ville de Québec. Maps were obtained from all these sources and from the Cartothèque of the Université Laval, an important series being the Fortification Surveys of the Royal Engineers.

Reference Works and Tools

Much useful information concerning shipbuilders and tradesmen was found in the decennial censuses of Canada from 1830 to 1880 in both their manuscript (on microfilm) and published forms, as well as in city directories for the years of the period under study. The card indexes for the *Quebec Gazette*, the Lower Canada Land Papers, the Lower Canada Marriage Bonds and the Military "C" series at the National Archives of Canada were of great help in cutting down research time, as were the card indexes of marriages in Catholic parish registers, and of births, marriages and deaths in local Protestant registers at the Archives nationales du Quebec. Those of the past century are at the Archives civiles at the Palais de Justice. As far as the ships were concerned, the Lloyd's Survey Reports supplied a great deal of data, while the most useful published reference books were undoubtedly the *Lloyd's Registers* from 1767 on.

Government Documents

Canada. Parliamentary Papers (1824). A Report from the Select Committee of the Legislative Council of the Province of Lower-Canada To whom the Petition from several Merchants and Ship-Owners of the Port of Quebec, was referred, with instruction to the said Committee, to enquire into the means of extending and securing the Coasting Trade of this Province; also, the Trade carried on between this province and the other possessions of His Majesty in North-America.

Canada. Petition of ship-builders of Quebec, for the protection of their interests, by a reduction of duties or otherwise, (1846).

Canada. Petition of merchants and others interested in the trade of Ship-building at Quebec, for a law to secure a lien on ships to parties contributing to the building or repairing thereof, (1849).

Canada. Parliamentary Papers. Appendix No.11 (1868). Third and Fourth Reports of the Select Committee Appointed to inquire into the general condition of the building of merchant vessels in the Dominion of Canada and as to the means of promoting its development.

Canada. "Certified copy of a Report of a Committee of the Honorable the Privy Council, approved by His Excellency the Governor General in Council on the 28th February 1894" [re the *S.S. Royal William*]. Appendix G. *Report of the Secretary of State of Canada for the Year Ended 31st December 1894*.

Great Britain. Parliamentary Papers. Vol.III (1820). First Report of the Select Committee of the House of Lords appointed to inquire into the means of extending and securing the Foreign Trade of the Country.

Great Britain. Parliamentary Papers. Vol.III (1821). First Report of the Select Committee appointed to consider the best means of maintaining and improving the Foreign Trade of the Country.

Great Britain. Parliamentary Papers. Vol. XIX (1835). Report from the Select Committee appointed to take into consideration the Duties on Timber.

Great Britain. Parliamentary Papers. Vol.IX (1839). Report from the Select Committee appointed to inquire into Shipwrecks of Timber Ships, and Loss of Life attendant thereon, and whether any means can be adopted to reduce the amount thereof in the future.

Great Britain. Parliamentary papers. Vol. V (1840). Report from the Select Committee on Import Duties Together with Minutes of Evidence.

Great Britain. Parliamentary Papers. Vol. XX, part 2 (1847/48). First Report from the Select Committee of the House of Lords appointed to inquire into the policy and operation of the Navigation Acts.

Great Britain. Parliamentary Papers. Report of the Investigation into the Loss of the "Annie Jane," made by direction of the Board of Trade by Captain W.W. Beechey, R.N. (1854) Presented to both Houses of Parliament by Command of Her Majesty.

Newpapers and Journals

Le Journal de Québec 1858-1859, 1864-1866
Liverpool Telegraph 1854-1855
Morning Chronicle 1852, 1858-1859, 1867-1870
Quebec Gazette 1764-1890
Quebec Mercury 1839-1851, 1853-1863

Studies (Books and Pamphets)

ABEL, WESTCOTT. *The Shipwright's Trade*. Cambridge: Cambridge University Press, 1948.

ALBION, ROBERT GREENHALGH. *Forests and Sea Power. The Timber Problem of the Royal Navy, 1652-1862*. Cambridge, Mass.: Harvard University Press, 1926.

_____. *The Rise of New York Port, 1815-1860*. Boston: Northeastern University Press, 1939.

_____. *Square-Riggers on Schedule, The New York Sailing Packets to England, France and the Cotton Ports*. Princeton: Princeton University Press, 1938.

ALEXANDER, DAVID AND ROSEMARY OMMER (eds.). *Volumes not Values: Canadian Sailing Ships and World Trades*. Saint John's: Maritime History Group, 1979.

ANDERSON, ERNEST B. *Sailing Ships of Ireland*. Dublin: Morris, 1984.

APPLETON, THOMAS E. *Ravenscraig: The Allan Royal Mail Line*. Toronto: McClelland and Stewart, 1974.

ARMOUR, CHARLES A. and THOMAS LACKEY. *Sailing Ships of the Maritimes*. Toronto: McGraw Hill Ryerson, 1975.

BAKER, WILLIAM AVERY. *A Maritime History of Bath, Maine, and the Kennebec Region*. 2 vols. Portland: Marine Research Society of Bath, 1973.

BARBEAU, MARIUS. *Louis Jobin, statuaire*. Montreal: Beauchemin, 1968.

DE BARBEZIEUX, ALEXIS. *Histoire de Limoilou*. Quebec: Imprimerie de l'Action Sociale, 1921.

BEATSON, ROBERT. *Naval and Military Memoirs of Great Britain from 1727 to 1783*. London: N.P., 1804.

BEERS, J.H. & CO. *History of the Great Lakes*, I. Toronto, 1899. Reprinted as *Trading and Shipping on the Great Lakes*. Toronto: Coles, 1980.

BERNIER, GABRIEL. *Le quartier Saint-Sauveur de Québec*. Quebec: The Author, 1978.

BERNIER, J.E. *Master Mariner and Arctic Explorer*. Ottawa: Le Droit, 1939.

BLACKBURN, ISAAC. *A Treatise on the Science of Ship-Building with Observations on the British Navy and the Extraordinary Decay of the Men-of-War*. London: N.P., 1817.

BOORSTIN, DANIEL J. (ed.) *Subject-Matter Index of Patents for Inventions Issued by the United States patent Office from 1790 to 1873, Inclusive*. Arno Press, New York, 1976.

BOUCHETTE, JOS. *A Topographical Description of Lower Canada with Remarks upon Upper Canada and the Relative Connection of Both Provinces with the United States of America* London: Faden, 1815.

BOWEN, N.H. *An Historical Sketch of the Isle of Orleans*. Quebec: Mercury, 1860.

BRISSON, REAL. *La charpenterie navale à Québec sous le Régime français*. Québec: Institut quebécois de recherche sur la culture, 1983.

BROOKES, IVAN. *The Lower Saint Lawrence*. Cleveland: Freshwater Press, 1974.

Bibliography

BUNKER, JOHN G. *Harbor and Haven.* California: Windsor Publications, 1979.

CALVIN, D.D. *A Saga of the Saint Lawrence.* Toronto: Ryerson Press, 1945.

CAMPBELL-JONES, SUSAN. *Welsh Sail.* Dyfed, Wales: Gomer, 1976.

CARSE, ROBERT. *The Twilight of Sailing Ships.* New York: Galahad, 1965.

CHAPELLE, HOWARD I. *The Baltimore Clipper.* New York: Bonanza, 1930.

_____. *The History of American Sailing Ships.* New York: Norton, 1935.

_____. *The History of the American Sailing Navy.* New York: Bonanza, 1949.

CHARBONNEAU, ANDRE; DESLOGES, YVON, and MARC LAFRANCE. *Québec, The Fortified City: From the 17th to the 19th Century.* Ottawa: Queen's Printer, 1972.

CIMON, HECTOR. *Un siècle de yachting sur le St-Laurent 1861-1964.* Québec: Librairie Garneau, 1966.

CLARKE, J.F. *Power on Land and Sea: A History of R. & W. Hawthorne Leslie & Co.* Newcastle: N.P., 1977.

COCKERELL, H.A.L. and EDWIN GREEN. *The British Insurance Business.* London: Heineman Educational Books, 1976.

COMISSIONERS OF PATENTS, *Abridgements of the Specifications Relating to Ship Building, Repairing, Sheathing Launching, &*, London; Great Seal Patent Office, 1862.

COOKE, SHOLTO. *The Maiden City.* Dublin: Morris and Co., n.d.

CRAIG, ROBERT and RUPERT JARVIS. *Liverpool Registry of Merchant Ships.* Manchester: Manchester University Press, 1967.

CRAIG, ROBIN. *The Ship: Steam Tramps and Cargo Liners 1850-1950.* London: HMSO, 1980.

CREIGHTON, DONALD G. *The Commercial Empire of the Saint Lawrence 1760-1850.* Toronto: Ryerson, 1937.

_____. *The Empire of the Saint Lawrence.* Toronto: MacMillan, 1956.

DAHL, E.H.; ESPESSET, H.; LAFRANCE, M. and T. RUDDELL. *La Ville de Québec: un inventaire de cartes et plans, 1800-1850.* Ottawa: National Museum of Man, 1975.

DAVIS, CHARLES G. *Ships of the Past.* New York: Bonanza, 1979.

DAVIS, RALPH. *The Rise of the Atlantic Economies.* Ithaca, New York: Cornell University Press, 1973.

_____. *The Rise of the English Shipping Industry in the Seventeenth and Eighteenth Centuries.* London: MacMillan, 1962.

DE HARTOG, JAN. *Les voiliers.* New York: Odyssey Press, 1964.

DE KERCHOVE, RENE. *International Maritime Dictionary.* 2nd edition. Princeton: D. Van Nostrand Company, 1961.

DE LA ROCHE, MAZO. *Quebec Historic Seaport.* New York: Doubleday, 1944.

DENISON, MERILL, *The Barley and the Stream: The Molson Story, A Footnote to Canadian History.* Toronto: McClelland and Stewart, 1955.

DESGAGNES, MICHEL. *Les goélettes de Charlevoix.* Ottawa: Leméac, 1977.

DESMOND, CHARLES. *Wooden Shipbuilding.* New York: Rudder, 1919.

DORION-ROBITAILLE, YOLANDE. *Le capitaine J.E. Bernier et la souveraineté du Canada dans l'Arctique.* Ottawa: Department of Indian and Northern Affairs, 1978.

DOUGAN, DAVID. *The History of North East Shipbuilding.* London: George Allen and Unwin, 1968.

DOUGLAS, W.A.B. *Gunfire on the Lakes.* Ottawa: National Museum of Man, 1977.

DUNCAN, JOHN M. *Travels Through Part of the United States and Canada in 1818 and 1819.* New York: W.B. Gilley, 1823.

DUPONT, JEAN-CLAUDE. *L'Artisan Forgeron.* Quebec: PUL/Editeur officiel du Québec, 1979.

ESTEP, H. Cole. *How Wooden Ships are Built.* Cleveland: Penton Publishing, 1918; reprint; New York: W.W. Norton, 1983.

FARR, GRAHAME E. "Custom House Ship Registers of the West Country." In H.E.S. Fisher (ed.). *The South West and the Sea.* Exeter: University of Exeter, 1968.

_____. *Shipbuilding in North Devon.* Greenwich: National Maritime Museum, 1976.

____. *Shipbuilding in the Port of Bristol.* Greenwich: National Maritime Museum, 1977.

FINGARD, JUDITH. *Jack in Port.* Toronto: University of Toronto Press, 1982.

____. "'Those Crimps of Hell and Goblins Damned': The Image and Reality of Quebec's Sailortown Bosses." In Rosemary Ommer and Gerald Panting (eds.). *Working Men Who Got Wet.* St. John's: Maritime History Group, 1980.

FISCHER, LEWIS R. and ERIC W. SAGER (eds.) *The Enterprising Canadians: Entrepreneurs and Economic Development in Eastern Canada, 1820-1914.* St. John's: Maritime History Group, 1979.

____. *Merchant Shipping and Economic Development in Atlantic Canada.* St. John's: Maritime History Group, 1982.

FRANCK, ALAIN. *Les goélettes à voiles du Saint-Laurent.* L'Islet-sur-mer, Québec: Musée Maritime Bernier, 1984.

FRY, HENRY. *The History of North Atlantic Steam Navigation.* London: Sampson Low, Marston and Company, 1896.

GALE, GEORGE. *Historic Tales of Old Quebec.* Quebec: Telegraph Printing Company, 1920.

____. *Twixt Old and New.* Quebec: Telegraph Printing Company, 1915.

GAMACHE, J-CHARLES. *Histoire de Saint Roch et de ses institutions 1829-1929.* Québec: Charrier et Dugal, 1929.

GIFFARD, ANN. *Towards Quebec.* London: HMSO, 1981.

GOLDENBERG, J.A. *Shipbuilding in Colonial America.* Charlottesville: University Press of Virginia, 1976.

GOODMAN, W.L. *The History of Woodworking Tools.* London: Bell, 1962.

GOSSELIN, DAVID. *Figures d'hier et d'aujourd'hui, à travers Saint Laurent, I.O.* Québec: Imprimerie Franciscaines Missionaires, 1919.

GRAHAM, GERALD S. *British Policy and Canada 1774-1791: A Study in 18th Century Trade Policy.* London: Longmans, Green and Co., 1930. Reprint; Westport, Conn: Greenwood Press, 1974.

____. *The Politics of Naval Supremacy: Studies in British Maritime Ascendancy.* Cambridge: Cambridge University Press, 1965.

GRANT, ALLISON. *Sailing Ships and Emigrants in Victorian Times.* London: Longman, 1972.

GREENHILL, BASIL. *The Merchant Schooners.* 2 vols. New York: Augustus M. Kelley, 1968.

____. *A Quayside Camera 1845-1917.* Middletown, Conn.: Wesleyan University Press, 1975.

____. *The Ship. The Life and Death of the Merchant Sailing Ship 1815-1965.* London: HMSO, 1980.

____. *Westcountrymen in Prince Edward's Isle.* Toronto: University of Toronto Press, 1967.

____. and ANN GIFFARD. *Victorian and Edwardian Sailing Ships From Old Photographs.* London: B.T. Batsford, 1976.

HAMELIN, JEAN. *Economie et société en Nouvelle France.* Québec: Les Presses de l'Université Laval, 1970.

____. (ed.). *Histoire du Québec.* Saint-Hyacinthe: EDISEM, 1977.

____. et Y. ROBY. *Histoire économique du Québec 1851-1896.* Saint-Hyacinthe: Fides, 1971.

HAMILTON, GEORGE. *A History of the House of Hamilton.*

HARDY, JEAN-PIERRE et D.T. RUDDEL. *Les apprentis artisans à Québec: 1660-1815.* Montréal: Les Presses de l'Université du Québec, 1977.

HARLAND, JOHN. *Seamanship in the Age of Sail: An Account of the Shiphandling of the Sailing Man-of-War 1600-1860, Based on Contemporary Sources.* London: Conway Maritime, 1984.

HASSLOF, OLOF. *Ships and Shipyards, Sailors and Fishermen.* Copenhagen: University Press, 1972.

HAWS, GEORGE W. *The Haws Family and Their Seafaring Kin.* Dunfermline: N.P., 1932.

Bibliography

HAWTHORNE, DANIEL. *The Clipper Ship.* New York: Dodd, Mead and Company, 1928.

HEATON, HERBERT. *Economic History of Europe.* New York: Harper and Row, 1936.

HILL, JOHN C.G. *Shipshape and Bristol Fashion.* Bristol: Redcliffe, 1951.

HOLLAND, A.J. *Ships of British Oak.* Newton Abbot: David and Charles, 1971.

HOLLETT, D. *Fast Passage to Australia.* London: Fairplay, 1986.

HOLZAPFFEL, CHARLES. *Turning and Mechanical Manipulation.* London: 1856.

HORSLEY, JOHN E. *Tools of the Maritime Trades.* Newton Abbot: David and Charles, 1978.

HUGHES, EMRYS and ALED EAMES. *Porthmadog Ships.* Gwynned: Gwynned Archives Service, 1975.

HUOT. *Annuaire du commerce et de l'industrie de Québec pour 1873.*

HUTCHINS, JOHN G.B. *The American Maritime Industries and Public Policy 1789-1914.* Cambridge, Mass.: Harvard University Press, 1941.

JENKINS, J. GERAINT. *Maritime Heritage. The Ships and Seamen of Southern Ceredigion.* Dyfed, Wales: Gomer Press, 1982.

JOBIN, ALBERT. *La petite histoire de Québec.* Québec: Institut St-Jean Bosco, 1948.

KAUFFMAN, HENRY. *American Axes.* Vermont: Stephen Greene, 1972.

KEMP, PETER. *Encyclopaedia of Ships and Seafaring.* London: Stanford Maritime, 1980.

_____. *The History of Ships.* London: Orbis, 1978.

_____. (comp.). *The Oxford Companion to Ships and the Sea.* Oxford: Oxford University Press, 1976.

DE KERCHOVE, RENE (comp.). *International Maritime Dictionary.* New York: Van Nostrand Reinhold, 1961.

KOCHISS, JOHN. *The Deadeye.* Mystic, Conn.: Marine Historical Association, n.d.

KONVITZ, JOSEF. *Cities and the Sea.* Baltimore: John Hopkins University Press, 1978.

LABERGE, LIONEL. *Charles Aubert de la Chesnay et la construction des vaisseaux dans la rivière Saint-Charles.* Quebec, 1969.

LACROIX, LOUIS. *Les derniers Cap-Horniers français.* Paris: Pierre Amiot, 1957.

LAING, ALEXANDER. *American Sail.* New York: Dutton, 1961.

_____. *Seafaring America.* New York: McGraw Hill, 1974.

LAMONTAGNE, P-A. *L'histoire de Sillery 1630-1950.* Robert Rumilly, 1952.

LARN, RICHARD and CLIVE CARTER. *Cornish Shipwrecks.* New York: Taplinger, 1969.

LEMOINE, JAMES MCPHERSON. *Maple Leaves. VII Series.* Quebec: Carrel, 1906.

_____. *Picturesque Quebec.* Montreal: Dawson, 1882.

LEVER, DARCY. *The Young Sea Officer's Sheet Anchor; or, a Key to the Leading of Rigging, and to Practical Seamanship.* Reprint; Boston: Lauriat, 1938 of First Philadelphia Edition, from second London edition: Carey, 1819.

LLOYD'S. *Annals of Lloyd's Register.* London: Lloyd's, 1934.

LOWER, A.R.M. *The North American Assault on the Canadian Forest.* Toronto: Ryerson, 1938.

MABER, JOHN M. *The Ship Channel Packets and Ocean Liners 1850-1970.* London: HMSO, 1980.

MACGREGOR, DAVID R. *Square Rigged Sailing Ships.* Watford, Herts: Argus Books, 1977.

MANNING, SAMUEL F. *New England Masts and the King's Broad Arrow.* Kennebunk, Me.: Thomas Murphy, 1979.

MANNY, LOUISE. *Ships of Miramichi.* Saint John: New Brunswick Museum, 1960.

_____. *Ships of Kent County New Brunswick.* Sackville: Tribune Press, 1949.

MARCIL, EILEEN REID. "Beatson, Patrick," vol. IV, 1979; "Goudie, John," vol. VI, 1987; "Munn, John," vol. VIII, 1985; "Wood, Charles," vol. VII, 1988; "Baldwin, William Henry," "Fry, Henry" and Valin, Pierre Vincent," vol. XII, 1990; "Davie, George Taylor," vol. XII, forthcoming, *Dictionary of Canadian Biography.* Toronto and Quebec: University of Toronto and Laval University Press.

MARSHALL, JAMES SCOTT. *The Life and Times of Leith.* Edinburgh: John Donald, 1986.

MATHIEU, JACQUES. *La construction navale royale à Québec 1739-1759.* Québec: La Société historique de Québec, 1971.

_____. "Levasseur, René Nicolas." *Dictionary of Canadian Biography.* Vol. IV. Toronto and Quebec: University of Toronto and Laval University Press, 1979.

MATTHEWS, KEITH and GERALD PANTING (eds.). *Ships and Shipbuilding in the North Atlantic Region.* St. John's: Maritime History Group, 1978.

MATTHIAS, PETER. *The First Industrial Nation: An Economic History of Britain.* London: 1969.

MCGOWAN, ALAN. *The Ship. The Century before Steam: The Development of the Sailing Ship 1700-1820.* London: HMSO, 1980.

_____. *The Ship. Tiller and Whipstaff: The Development of the Sailing Ship 1400-1700.* London: HMSO, 1981.

McIVOR, CRAIG. *Canadian Monetary Policy, Banking and Fiscal Development.* Toronto: MacMillan, c. 1958.

MACKENZIE, KENNETH, et al. "Dinning, Henry." *Dictionary of Canadian Biography.* Vol. XI. Toronto and Quebec: University of Toronto and Laval University Press, 1982.

McPHERSON, Mrs. DANIEL. *Old Memories: Amusing and Historical.* Montreal: N.P., n.d.

M'KAY, LAUCHLAN. *The Practical Shipbuilder.* New York: N.P., 1839.

MEAD, HILARY P. *Trinity House.* London: Sampson Low, Marston and Company, 1946.

MILLS, JOHN M. *Canadian Coastal and Inland Steam Vessels 1809-1930.* Providence, R.I.: Steamship Historical Society of America, 1979.

MITCHELL, B.R. (comp.). *Abstract of British Historical Studies.* Cambridge: Cambridge University Press, 1962.

MORISON, SAMUEL ELIOT. *The Ropemakers of Plymouth: A History of the Plymouth Cordage Company, 1824-1949.* Cambridge, Mass.: Riverside Press, 1950.

MORRISON, JOHN H. *History of the New York Shipyards.* New York: William F. Sametz, 1909.

MOSS, MICHAEL and JOHN R. HUME. *Shipbuilders to the World: 125 Years of Harland and Wolff, Belfast 1861-1986.* Belfast: Blackstaff, 1986.

_____. *Workshop of the British Empire.* London: 1977.

NAISH, GEORGE. "Shipbuilding." In Charles Singer, et al. *A History of Technology.* Vol. IV. Oxford: Clarendon Press, 1954.

NARES, GEORGE S. *Seamanship 1862.* Reprint Old Woking, Surrey: Unwin, 1979.

NORTON, PETER. *Figureheads.* Greenwich: National Maritime Museum, 1972.

_____. *Ships' Figureheads.* New York: Barre, 1976.

OMMER, ROSEMARY and GERALD PANTING (eds.). *Working Men who Got Wet.* St. John's: Maritime History Group, 1980.

OUELLET, FERNAND. *Histoire économique et sociale du Québec 1760-1850: structures et conjoncture.* Montréal: 1966; reprinted Montreal: 1971.

PAASCH, Capitaine. *From Keel to Truck. Dictionary of Naval Terms.* 4th edition. London: David Nutt, 1908.

PARKER. JOHN P. *Cape Breton Ships and Men.* Toronto: George J. McLeod, 1967.

_____. *Sails of the Maritimes.* North Sydney: The Author, 1960.

PICARD, HENRI. *Marseille & Marine en bois 1860-1925.* Marseille: Schefer, 1983.

PICKETT, GERTRUDE M. *Portsmouth's Heyday in Shipbuilding.* Jo Sawtelle, 1979.

PILKINGTON, WOODFORD. *On Methods Adopted in Carrying out Dock and Harbour Works at Quebec with Descriptions of Plant Employed.* London: Institution of Civil Engineers, 1899.

PUDNEY, JOHN. *London Docks*. London: Thames and Hudson, 1975.

PULLEN, H.F. *Atlantic Schooners*. Fredericton: Brunswick Press, 1967.

RANKIN, JOHN. *A History of our Firm*. Liverpool: Henry Young, 1921.

RAYMOND, W.O. *The River St. John*. Sackville: Tribune, 1910.

RICHARDSON, A.J.H. "Hunt, James." *Dictionary of Canadian Biography*. Vol. VII. Toronto and Quebec: University of Toronto and Laval University Press, 1988.

RITCHIE, L.A. *Modern British Shipbuilding. A Guide to Historical Records*. London: HMSO, 1980.

ROSA, NARCISSE. *La construction des navires à Québec et ses environs*, Quebec: Leger Brousseau, 1897.

ROSE, WALTER. *The Village Carpenter*. Cambridge: Cambridge University Press, 1937.

ROWE, WILLIAM HUTCHINSON. *The Maritime History of Maine*, Maine: Bond Wheelwright, 1948.

ROY, J. EDMOND. *Histoire de la Seigneurie de Lauzon*. 5 vols. Lévis: The Author, 1904.

ROY, PIERRE-GEORGES. *La Chambre de Commerce de Lévis 1872-1947*. Lévis: Le Quotidien, 1947.

———. *Profils lévisiens*. 2 volumes. Levis: 1948.

RUSSELL, WILLIS. *Quebec: As It Was, and As It Is*. Quebec: N.P., 1857.

SALAMAN, R.A. *Dictionary of Tools*. London: George Allen and Unwin, 1975.

SANSOM, JOSEPH. *Travels in Lower Canada*. London: Sir Richard Phillips, 1820.

SILLIMAN, BENJAMIN. *Remarks made on a Short Tour between Hartford and Quebec in the Autumn of 1819*. London: P. Phillips and Co., 1822.

SLAVEN, A. "The Shipbuilding Industry." In Roy Church (ed.). *The Dynamics of Victorian Business: Problems and Perspectives to the 1870s*. London: George Allen and Unwin, 1980.

SLOANE, ERIC. *A Museum of Early American Tools*. New York: Ballantyne, 1964.

SMITH, HERVEY GARRETT. *Boat Carpentry*. Princeton: Van Nostrand, 1955.

SPICER, STANLEY T. *Masters of Sail*. Toronto: Ryerson, 1968.

SPRATT, H. PHILIP. *Transatlantic Paddle Steamers*. Glasgow: Brown, Son and Ferguson, 1951.

STEEL's Elements of Mastmaking, Sailmaking and Rigging (From the 1794 Edition), Arranged by Claude E. Gill. Largo, Florida: Edward W. Sweetman, 1982.

STEEL's Art of Rigging. Brighton: Fisher Nautical Press, 1974, reprint of 1818 edition.

STORY, DANA. *The Building of a Wooden Ship "Sawn frames and Trunnel Fastened"*. Barre, Mass.: Barre Publishers, 1971.

SVENSSON, SAM. "Spars and Rigging." In Try Tryckare (ed.). *The Lore of the Ship*. Gothenburg: AB Nordbok, 1975.

SYRETT, DAVID. *Shipping and the American War 1775-83*. London: Athlone Press, 1970.

TALBOT, ALLEN (ed.). *Five Years Residence in the Canadas*, London: Longman, Hurst, Rees, Orme, Brown and Green, 1824. Reprint; New York: Johnson, 1968.

TAYLOR, GEORGE, et al. (eds.). *The International Book of Wood*. London: Beazley, 1976.

TERRIEN, PAUL. *Québec à l'âge de la voile*. Hull: Asticou, 1984.

TETU, HORACE. *Résumé historique de l'industrie et du commerce de Québec de 1775 à 1800*. Québec: N.P., 1899.

Trading and Shipping on the Great Lakes. Reprinted from History of the Great Lakes, vol. 1, 1899. Toronto: Coles, 1980.

TRYCKARE, TRY. *The Lore of Ships*. Gothenburg: AB Nordbok, 1975.

TURCOTTE, L.P. *L'Ile d'Orléans*. Quebec: Atelier Typographique du Canadien, 1867.

UDEN, GRANT and RICHARD COOPER. *A Dictionary of British Ships and Seamen.* New York: St. Martin's, 1980.

UNDERHILL, HAROLD A. *Masting and Rigging the Clipper Ship and Ocean Carrier.* Glasgow: Brown, Son and Ferguson, 1946.

WALKER, FRED M. *Song of the Clyde.* Cambridge: Patrick Stephens, 1984.

WALLACE, FREDERICK WILLIAM. *In the Wake of the Windships.* Toronto: Musson, 1927.

_____. *Record of Canadian Shipping.* Toronto: Musson, 1929.

_____. *Wooden Ships and Iron Men.* London: Hodder and Stoughton, 1924.

WEEKS, EZRA. *A Statement in Relation to the Concerns of the New-York Dry Dock Company.* New York: N.P., 1825.

WHITTON, CHARLOTTE. *A Hundred Years A-Fellin, the Story of the Gillies on the Ottawa.* Ottawa: Runge, 1943.

WOOD, C. *Ballast.* Glasgow: John Clark, 1836.

WRIGHT, ESTHER CLARK. *Saint John Ships and their Builders.* Wolfville, N.S.: The Author, 1976.

Articles and Periodicals

AYLMER, LADY. "Recollections of Canada." *RAPQ* (1934-1935), 282-318.

BARBEAU, MARIUS. "Côté, sculpteur sur bois." *Mémoires de la Société Royale du Canada,* Section 1 (1942), 3-11.

_____. "Constructeurs de navires: Les voiliers de Québec." *Le Canada français,* XXVIII, No. 8 (April 1941), 805-14, continued XXVI, No.9 (May 1941), 899-907.

CALVIN, D.D. "Rafting on the Saint Lawrence." *Canadian Geographical Journal,* III, No. 4 (October 1931), 276-286.

CRUICKSHANK, E.A. "Notes on the History of Shipbuilding and Navigation on Lake Ontario up to 1816." *Ontario Historical Society, Papers and Records,* XXIII (1926), 33-44.

DESJARDINS, GEORGES. "Un chantier naval à la Pointe-Sèche de Kamouraska." *Mémoires de la Société généalogique Canadienne-Française,* XXI (1970), 212.

DUFOUR, PIERRE. "La construction navale à Québec, 1760-1825: sources inexplorées et nouvelles perspectives de recherches." *Revue d'histoire de l'Amérique française,* XXXV, No. 2 (September 1981), 231-251.

FAUCHER, ALBERT. "The Decline of Shipbuilding at Quebec in the Nineteenth Century." *Canadian Journal of Economics and Political Science,* II (1957), 195-215.

FRY, HENRY. "Shipbuilding in Quebec." *The Canadian Magazine,* I (1895), 3-8.

HANSON, CHARLES. "The Pit Saw." *The Museum of the Fur Trade Quarterly,* II No.4 (1975), 1-6.

IGNOTUS. "La construction des vaisseaux sous le règime français." *BRH,* X, No. 6 (1904), 179-187.

LEVASSEUR. "La construction des navires à Québec." *Bulletin de la Société de Géographie,* II, No. 4 (1917), 187-201.

MARCIL, EILEEN REID. "Ship-Rigged Rafts and the Export of Quebec Timber." *The American Neptune,* No. 2 (Spring 1988), 67-76.

OMMER, ROSEMARY. "Anticipating the Trend: The Pictou Ship Register, 1840-1889," *Acadiensis,* X, No. 2 (Spring 1981), 67-89.

POLLARD, S. "The Decline of Shipbuilding on the Thames." *Economic History Review,* 2nd series, No. 3 (1950-1951), 72-89.

RICHARDSON, A.J.H. "Indications for Research in the History of Wood-Processing Technology." *APT,* III (1974), 35-146.

ROY, PIERRE-GEORGES. "La construction Royale à Quebec." *Les Cahiers des Dix,* XI (1946), 141-190.

RUBIN, NORMAN N. "Quebec Figureheads and Ship-carving." *Nautical Research Journal,* XVIII, No. 2 (Summer 1971), 75-89.

RUSSELL, J. SCOTT. "On the Late Mr. John Wood and Mr. Charles Wood, Naval Architects, of Port Glasgow." Institute of Naval Architects *Proceedings,* I (March 1881), 141-148.

SELECT COMMITTEE OF THE FRANKLIN INSTITUTE. "Report ... on a Dry Dock, projected by Commodore James Barron, and also, one by Thomas Caldwell," *The Franklin Journal and American Mechanics Magazine*, III, No. 1 (January 1827).

Unpublished Material

DUFOUR, BENOIT. "Le développement d'un mécanisme de crédit et la croissance économique d'une communauté d'affaires. Les marchands et les industriels de la Ville de Québec au dix-neuvième siècle." Ph.D. thesis, Université Laval, 1987.

FRY, HENRY. "Reminiscences." Autobiography written for his son, 1891.

GUINARD, LUC, "La localisation des chantiers navals sur la rivière Saint Charles 1840-1870." Mémoire de licence, Université Laval, 1972.

HIRSCH, MARK. "The Federation of Sailmakers of Great Britain and Ireland 1889-1922: a craft union in crisis." M.A. thesis, University of Warwick, 1976.

LEMELIN, ANDRE. "Le déclin du port de Québec et la reconversion économique à la fin du 19e siècle." Typescript, 1981.

McCLELLAND, PETER. "The New Brunswick Economy in the Nineteenth Century." Ph.D. thesis, Harvard University, 1966.

McMICHAEL, GERTRUDE. "My Ain Folk." A typescript history of the Simons family. Montreal, 1987.

RICE, RICHARD. "Shipbuilding in British America 1789-1890: An Introductory Study," Ph.D. thesis, University of Liverpool, 1977.

RUDDELL, THIERRY. "The Evolution of a Colonial Town." Ph.D. thesis, Université Laval, 1981.

Index of Ships Names

A.D. Boucher 384
Aaron Manby 67
Abdalla 274, 376
Abeona 371, 375, 386
Aberdeen 368, 382
Aberfoil 372
Abergeldie 380
Abyssinian 382
Acadia 377
Accommodation 53, 55, 56
Achilles 374
Acme 375
Actaon 375
Active 367, 368
Adélaide 368, 381, 389
Adeline 390
Adelphi 367
Adeona 386
Adept 375
Adgillus 383
Admiral 374
Admiral Benbow 370
Admiral Boxer 377
Admiral Lyons 378
Adonis 390
Adria 382
Advance 376
Advice 376
Aetna 378
Afghan 373
Africa 80, 376
Agamemnon 245, 374, 377
Agenoria 407
Agitator 372
Agnes 189, 371
Agnes & Ann 371

Agnes Anderson 189, 377
Agnes Gilmour 373
Agnes Jane 374
Aid 367, 370
Aigle de Mer 390
Ailsa 376
Aim 374
Aimwell 367
Ajax 368
Albani 391
Albania 271
Albany 391
Albatros 391
Albatross 372
Albert 390
Albina 382
Albinus 376
Albion 220, 367
Alceus 388
Aldershot 382
Aleppo 382
Alexander 367, 368, 386
Alexander Henry 386
Alexina 390, 391
Alfred 75, 93, 156, 213, 223, 272, 367, 390
Algonquin 329, 389, 390
Alia 383
Alice 376, 390, 391
Alice C 383
Alicia 370, 379
Alicia Bland 379
Aliquis 371, 377
Allan 375
Alliance 377
Almora 377

Alphonse 383
Alphonsine 391
Alvina 390
Amaranthe 381
Ambrosine 374
Amelia 386, 390
Amelia Matilda 371
Amelie 383
America 80, 246, 371, 376
American Lass 376
Amethyst 377
Amity 350
Amoor 108, 377
Amoy 335, 374
Anastasia 371
Ancilla 381
Anevoca 380
Angelique 192, 380
Ann 371
Ann and Mary 371
Ann Best 373
Ann Jeffery 373
Ann McLester 374
Ann Moore 373
Ann Rankin 373
Anna 116, 375
Anna Craig 383
Anna Maria 368
Annabella 388
Anne 329, 370, 389
Annie 374, 381
Annie Fleming 381
Annie Froste 380
Annie Jane 232, 249, 324, 326, 356, 376
Annie Lisle 381
Annie Mackenzie 390
Anomia 247, 379
Answell 368

Antartic 377
Anthony Anderson 191, 373
Arabella 384
Arabia 80, 377, 381
Arabian 373, 388
Aramienta 374
Ararat 374
Arbitrator 390
Ardenlee 381
Ardmillan 377
Arethusa 374
Argo 374
Argonaut 376
Argyle 370
Ariadne 371, 379
Ariel 382
Armistice 382
Arran 376
Arrogante 390
Arthur 375
Arundel 376
Asenath 374
Asia 80, 376
Assyrian 384
Astoria 389
Athol 223
Atlanta 367
Atlantic 236, 368, 383
Atlas 367
Augusta 375
Auguste 389
Augustina 381
Aurelia 383
Aurelie 375, 383
Aurora 367, 372, 382
Aurore 389, 391
Austerlitz 382
Australia 375
Avon 382

Award 379
Ayrshire 368, 373, 374
Azoff 389
Azot 377
B.L. George 390
Babineau et Gaudry 390
Balmarino 389
Banare II 382
Banker's Daughter 389
Banner 380
Bannockburn 376
Barbadoes 382
Barbados 386
Barbara 373
Barelaw 380
Baron of Renfrew 17, 35, 65, 77, 154, 204, 315, 316, 319, 354, 356, 360, 370, 375
Barrones 385
Batavia 384
Bayfield 373
Beaconsfield 250, 379
Bear 368
Beatrice 382
Beatrix 371
Beaupré 276, 391
Beaver 368, 385, 389, 390
Bee 409
Belfast 370, 373
Belinda 372, 374
Bellcarrigg 376
Belle Isle 379
Belmont 71
Belstane 237, 384
Ben Lomond 374
Bencooben 388

Benefactress 381
Bengal 372
Benguela 33, 384
Benjamin Hart 372
Benson 368
Bertha 343, 383
Betsey 73, 367, 368, 371, 385
Betsy 368, 371
Beulah 190, 383
Beverly 382
Biona 391
Birmingham 189, 376
Black Duck 390
Black Eagle 378
Blackwater 378, 390
Blake 372, 375
Blonde 388
Blucher 386
Bluenose 315
Blue Wave 390
Bob Logic 371
Bokhara 384
Bolton Abbey 373
Bomarsund 377
Bon Vivant 388
Bonaparte 371
Bonaventure 377, 390
Bonniton 192, 381
Boomerang 189, 376
Borneo 372
Braganza 388
Braidwood 200, 38
Bramley Moore 390
Branches 370
Brandon 375, 378, 384
Bravo 379
Brazila 371
Breeze 371

Index of Ships' names

Bride 370
Bridget 211, 367, 390, 402-406
Bridgitt 38
Brilliant 371
Britannia 367, 386
British Army 36
British Columbia 390
British Empire 329, 380
British Heroine 372
British Lion 189, 377
British Queen 73, 367
British Sovereign 371
Briton 223, 368
Briton's Queen 372
Broad Axe 386
Brooke 202, 373
Broom 372
Broomielaw 378
Brothers 370
Bruce 206, 363, 378
Brunelle 329, 377
Brunette 388
Bucephalus 8, 134, 189, 274, 377
Buckhorn 384
Buckingham 371
Buffalo 63, 329, 382
Burnside 379
Bytown 374
C.S.M. 389
Caesar 368
Cairngorm 377
Calcutta 337, 372, 381, 384
Caldecot 368
Caldwell 367
Caledonia 54, 58, 106, 354, 367, 372, 386
California 375

Callao 329, 383
Calumet 390
Cambria 69, 144, 384
Cameo 376
Cameronian 270, 378
Camilla 391
Camillus 373
Campbell 330, 378
Canada 100, 194, 270, 367, 368, 372, 379, 382, 385, 389
Canada Belle 380
Canadian 367, 370, 386
Canadian Lass 378
Canadienne 386, 389-391
Canton 372
Canute 383
Cap Rouge 377
Captain Cook 377
Car of Commerce 54, 58
Carcajou 222
Caribou 30, 192, 377, 381, 383
Carioca 245, 390
Carluke 382
Caroline 370, 371, 373, 376, 386, 388
Caroline Mary 381
Carouge 371
Carpentaria 377
Carrington 370
Carthaginian 373
Castiglione 380
Castle Avon 380
Castor 390
Cataraqui 373
Catherine 370-372, 376, 391
Cato 370

Cavalier 382
Cecilia 386
Celestial Empire 379
Celina 375
Celuta 378
Ceres 379
Ceylon 374
Challenge 380
Challenger 375
Champion 368
Champlain 371
Chance 377
Chapultepec 377
Charity 329, 381
Charles 376
Charles Verminck 381
Charlotte 374, 385
Charlotte and Maria 370
Charlotte Dundas 53
Charlotte Harrison 373
Charming Nancy 386
Chattanooga 380
Chelmsford 384
Cherokee 383
Cherub 379
Cheshire 69, 144, 384
Chesterholme 376
Cheviot 377
Chicago 389
Chieftain 386
Childe Harold 376
Chillian Wallah 380
China 202, 373, 380
Chippewa 375, 380
Choice 370
Choyenne 386
Christian 367
Christina 390
Christopher 224, 386
Chusan 374

Circassian 384
Citadel 384
City of Edinburgh 368
City of Kingston 329, 383
City of Lincoln 375
City of Liverpool 381
City of Manchester 375
City of Montreal 327, 329, 380
City of Ottawa 329, 379
City of Richmond 381
City of Waterford 370
City of York 374
Clara Symes 375
Clarkstone 386
Clermont 53
Cleveland 234, 383
Clontarf 376
Clutha 377
Clydesdale 379, 383
Coch 385
Cod Hook 385
Colborne 388
Collector 389
Colleen Bawn 379
Colonel Maule 389
Colonial Empire 379
Columbine 370, 376
Columbus 8, 17, 35, 65, 77, 151, 152, 154, 315, 316, 319, 354, 356, 360, 370, 371
Comet 378
Commerce 386
Compton 373
Concordian 383
Confederation 382
Confiance 7, 62, 376
Confidence 390

Conqueror 367, 373
Conquest 388
Conrad 375
Constantia 370
Constantine 250, 389
Constantinople 389
Constitution 373, 376
Contest 368, 383
Coolock 373
Coq du Village 381
Cora Linn 380
Coral 383
Cordelia 7, 73, 101, 102, 351, 367
Corea 373
Corinne 391
Corinthian 370
Coriolanus 80, 376
Cornubia 372
Cornwall 388
Coromandel 372, 374, 382
Corrib 371
Corsica 382, 383
Cosmo 8, 119, 193, 195, 199, 270, 384
Cossack 368
Countess of Dalhousie 370
Countess of Dufferin 383
Countess of Durham 388
Countess of Elgin 354, 376
Countess Russell 379
Covenanter 373, 376
Cremona 373
Crescent 120, 368, 372
Crimea 377
Critique 385

Croesus 388
Cromwell 374, 375, 390
Crown 389
Crusader 202, 372
Culdee 8, 233, 379
Culloden 376
Culzean Castle 389
Cumberland 385
Curler 386
Curlew 382
Cygnet 378
Cyprus 384
Czar 377
Dacelo 382
Dalhousie 388
Dalhousie Castle 370
Dalkeith 390
Dalniada 375
Dalusia 371
Danube 377
Day 385, 390
Daylesford 377
De Salaberry 250, 389
Decision 382
Deeside 380
Defiant 192, 381
Delgany 376
Delina 390
Denault 385
Derry Castle 376
Desdemona 381
Desire 368
Detroit 59, 61
Devonport 373
Devonshire 193, 379, 384
Devonshire Belle 380
Diamond 329, 367
Diana 367, 368, 379, 385
Dibdin 372
Diligence 388, 390

Index of Ships' names

Diligent 371
Dolphin 367, 385
Dolphine 390
Dominion 384
Dorchester 371, 385
Doris 388
Doubt 368
Douce Davie 373
Douglas 388
Dr Kane 378
Dreadnought 354, 380
Dream 378
Drummond 367
Dryope 388
Duke of Gloucester 61
Duke of Kent 274, 312, 367
Duke of Newcastle 379
Duke of Richmond 386
Dunbrody 374
Duncan Gibb 370
Dundas 367
Dunedin 381
Dunlop 385
Dunsyre 384
E. Lacourciere 390
Eagle 373
Eaglet 378
Earl of Buckinghamshire 386
Earl of Dalhousie 388
Earl of Derby 376
Earl of Dufferin 383
Earl of Durham 372
Earl of Elgin 330, 376
Earl of Moira 61, 312
Early Morn 381
Earsdon 368
Eastern Empire 324, 380
Eastward Ho 380
Ebba Brake 189, 376

Ebouloise 389
Echo 368, 377
Eclair 382
Eclipse 377
Eden Iron 381
Edinburgh 236, 275, 352, 383, 384
Edmonton 274, 276, 384
Edna 329, 383
Edward 368, 371, 375
Eerie 380
Egeria 378
Eglantine 382
Eglinton 375
Egyptian 386
Eldon 371
Eleanor 246, 368, 370, 376, 396
Eleanor Stevenson 380
Eleanor Wood 380
Electric 378
Electric Light 384
Elegante 232, 390
Eleonore 382, 383, 389
Eleutheria 330, 380
Elie 391
Elinor 378
Elisabeth 368, 391
Eliza 368, 371, 373, 374, 375, 376, 386, 389
Eliza Morison 374
Eliza Pirrie 329, 374
Elizabeth 93, 368, 372, 374, 375, 378, 386, 388
Elizabeth Robertson 371
Elizabeth Yeo 7, 116, 309, 326, 377

Ella 383
Ellen Erie 379
Elma 384
Elspeth 375
Elvira 370
Elzear 389
Emancipation 388
Emblem 144, 384
Emelie 386, 391
Emerald 380
Emigrant 374, 376
Emma 370, 374, 391
Emmanuel 390
Emperor 368, 375
Empire 374
Empress Eugenie 377
Endourne 383
England 372, 373, 375, 383
Englishman 378
Enterprise 22, 74, 167, 331, 371, 384
Epaminondas 80, 376
Equimaux 371
Erie 59, 61, 76, 386
Erin 374
Erin Go Bragh 375
Erin's Queen 374
Esmeralda 378
Esther 371
ETG 384
Ethelontes 379
Etna 270
Etta 380
Eudora 380
Eugénie 383, 391
Eumenides 381
Euretta 379
Euroclydon 381
Europa 372, 376, 380
Europe 372
Euterpe 375
Euxine 373

Eveline 370, 377
Evie 381
Eweretta 75, 378
Excellent 379
Exodus 377
Experience 386
Experiment 367, 386, 389
Fabiola 391
Fag-an-Bealac 374
Fairy Belle 383
Faith 329, 378, 381, 386
Faith, Hope and Charity 382
Fame 368, 374, 386, 389
Fanny 368, 371, 372, 376, 389
Fanny Forsyth 250, 377
Fanny Laure 379
Far Away 239, 381
Farmer 388
Father Matthew 389
Favorite 372, 388
Favourite 368, 386
Felicitas 336, 384
Félicité 388
Feu Follet 389
Fidelite 390
Fidelity 381
Fidelle 381
Finchley 377
Fingal 375
Fingalton 372
Fiona 382
Firm 367
Flavien 389
Fleetwing 381
Fleur de Marie 389
Flint 374

Floating Light 378
Flora 368, 370, 378
Flore Sezarine 388
Florence 377
Florence Lee 381
Fly 385
Foam 374
Foederis Arca 390
Forest Belle 146, 229, 384
Forest Monarch 274, 376
Forest Queen 379
Forth 378
Fortune 370
Fox 378
Francis 388
Francis K. Dumas 390
Francois Hubert 389
Frederick 386, 389
Free Trader 374
French Empire 329, 380
Frenchman 378
Friends 388
Friga 381
Frostedina 383
Fulwood 371, 376
Galeon 383
Gananoque 378
Ganges 372, 374
Gannet 372
Garland 376
Gartsherrie 378
Gaspé 386
Gaspee 386
Gatineau 380
Gazelle 389
Gem 374
General Brock 386
General Clarke 367
General Craig 368

General Havelock 378
General Hope 385
General Hunter 61, 368
General Kempt 386
General Neill 378
General Prescott 73, 367, 385
General Wolfe 367, 370
General Wyndham 377
Geneva 383
George 386
George and Bridget 367
George Canning 386
George Channing 370
George the Fourth 370
Georgiana 376
Georgianna 370, 372
Geraldine 384
Germanic 10, 339, 384
Gertrude 375
Gilmour 372
Gipsy 388
Gipsy Queen 375
Gladiator 378
Glasgow 367, 372, 379, 388
Gleaner 377
Glen Helen 374
Glen Isla 377
Glen Tilt 381
Glenalla 231, 384
Glenalva 377
Glencairn 376
Glendalough 376
Glengarnock 379
Glengarry 237, 384
Glengary 382

Index of Ships' names

Glenlyon 380
Glenora 379
Glenview 372
Glory 386
Golconda 371
Golden Eagle 381
Golden Sea 381
Goliath 373
Gondola 378
Good Hope 373
Goudies 213, 368
Governor Milnes 367, 385
Gowanside 380
Grace 371
Grace McVia 375
Grace Redpath 382
Great Britain 373
Great Eastern 20
Greek 368
Greenock 234, 383, 386
Grenada 371
Grog 385
GTD 384
Guano 194, 389
Guiana 372
Guinevere 236, 324, 383
Gulnare 189, 322, 371, 376
Gwenissa 383
Habnab 385
Hadlow 368
Halewood 390
Handy 389
Hannibal 374
Hanover 367
Harbinger 373, 375
Hardy 378
Harlequin 370, 389
Harmise Josephine 388
Harmony 386

Harp 368
Harriet 367, 370, 371, 376, 383, 385, 386
Harriet Scott 372
Harrison 368, 372
Harry Lorriquer 374
Havelock 384
Hawk 383, 390
Hebe 389
Hector 367
Hedwidge 391
Helen 150, 386, 388
Helen Drummond 382
Helen Sharples 373
Hélène 390
Hengist 381
Henrietta Mary 374
Henriette 388
Henry 370, 371, 373
Her Majesty 192, 330, 381
Her Royal Highness 381
Herald of the Morning 380
Hercules 56, 164, 386
Hercyna 375
Hermes 385
Hero 386
Hero of Acre 373
Heroine 375
Hesione 386, 388
Hiawatha 239, 378, 380, 399-401
Hibernia 371, 376
Highland Lad 213, 368
Highland Mary 373, 389
Highlander 9, 275, 380
Hilton 377
Hinda 376

HMS Albermarle 180
HMS Inflexible 61
HMS Kingfisher 346, 351
HMS St. Lawrence 61-64, 351
HMS Vanguard 351
Hochelaga 389
Home 370, 375
Homely 385
Homer 382
Hope 329, 344, 367, 368, 371, 381, 382, 388-390
Horatio 388
Humberstone 380
Hunter 386
Huron 192, 249, 329, 371, 373, 381
Hussar 368
Hylas 388
Hyperion 375
Hyppolite 372, 388
If 385
Illustrious 247, 378
Independence 373
India 379
Indian 386
Indian Chief 10, 192, 324, 341, 380, 384, 389
Indian Empire 379
Indiana 378
Indus 189, 372
Industry 224, 368, 388, 389
Inkerman 377, 390
Ino 379
Iolas 388
Iona 50, 215, 232, 233, 245, 373, 378
Iphigenia 379
Ireland 383

Iroquois 224, 367
Irvine 368
Isaac Todd 385
Isabella 371, 374, 375, 389
Isabella Peck 389
Ismailia 382
Ismalia 383
Italia 383
Ivigtut 384
Ivy 381, 384
J. Savard 391
J.L. Pendergast 383
J.P. Smith 383
Jacques Cartier 375, 389
Jamaica 371
James 367, 368
James and Agnes 386
James and Rebecca 367
James Carson 376
James Childs 382
James Dean 373
James Dunlop 385, 386
James Edward 388
James Fagan 374
James Gibb 389
James Goudie 389
James Lister 380
James McHenry 243, 376
James T. Foord 374
James Watt 56
Jane 367, 368, 372-5, 377, 385, 386
Jane Black 373
Jane Glassin 374
Jane Law 383
Jane Morison 374
Jane Vilet 370
Janet 371, 385

Janet Dunlop 385
Jarnia 381
Jasper 377
Java 372
Jean Baptiste 370, 388, 389
Jeanie Deans 373
Jeannette 391
Jeannie Johnston 375
Jeany 368
Jenny 93
Jenny Lemelin 381
Jenny Lind 56, 375, 389
Jesse Maria 372
Jessie Cassels 383
Jessie Lawson 370
Jessie Logan 372
Jessie Scott 380
Jessie Stephens 375
Jessie Torrance 389
Jessy 374
Jim Crow 388
JKL 376
JLB 383
John 368, 389
John Bell 372
John Binner 371
John Bolton 372
John Bull 373
John Bunyan 376
John Calvin 376
John Campbell 371
John Craigie 368
John Day 390
John Elliott 381
John Farnworth 374
John Francis 388
John Howard 370
John Kerr 371
John Knox 375, 388
John McLellan 372
John Munn 80, 373

John Porter 371
Josepha 372
Josephine 388, 390
Jubilee 388
Jules 383
Julia 370, 376, 389, 391
Julia Maxwell 380
Juliana 370
Julie 383
Julien and Brothers 379
Junior 374
Juno 367
Jura 92, 378
Justine 382
Justyn 375
Kalma 374
Kamaskda 371
Karnak 383
Kate 375
Kate Cleather 378
Kathleen 390
Kedar 381
Keewatin 76, 136, 384
Kelpie 375
Kelvin 379
Kenilworth 381
Ketch 389
Kilby 367
Kingfisher 346, 351, 371
Kitty 374
L. Edouard 390
L'Agouhanna 192, 381
L'Aurore 389
L'Avenir 381
L'Industrie 368
L'Orignal 101, 354
La Belle Canadienne 322

Index of Ships' names

La Canadienne 321, 377
La Grande Hermine 34
La Québec 51
Lady Allan 383
Lady Bagot 374
Lady Belleau 382
Lady Bird 381, 383
Lady Bulmer 376
Lady Cartier 383
Lady Dufferin 383
Lady Elgin 375
Lady Elma Bruce 376
Lady Eveline 376
Lady Eyre 378
Lady Fletcher 383
Lady Flora Hastings 373
Lady Gough 376
Lady Havelock 378
Lady Head 378, 390
Lady Hincks 236, 324, 383
Lady Lisgar 8, 178, 383
Lady Louisa 376
Lady Mary 383
Lady McDonald 383
Lady Monck 379
Lady Muriel May 383
Lady of the Lake 368
Lady Peel 374
Lady Sherbrooke 54, 58
Lady Young 383, 390
Laina 381
Lakefield 384
Laliberté 391
Lanarkshire 355, 373, 380
Lancashire 384
Lancashire Witch 377
Larch 223, 227, 386
Lauderdale 200, 227, 384
Laurel 379
Laurentine 384
Lauzon 55, 368
Leandre 390
Leeds 368
Leicester 377
Leilah 383
Lena 381
Leonard Dobbin 324, 360, 372
Leonidas 232, 370, 373
Leonie 383
Leonora 388
Letitia 372, 382
Letitia Heyn 329, 373
Levant 274
Leven 379
Lidias 378
Lightship 374
Lincolnshire 329, 379
Linnet 62
Lion Hill 371
Little Ann 386
Little Annie 382 Little Belt 385
Little George 368
Liverpool 373, 375, 377
Lochlibo 373
Lois 371
London 105, 119, 274, 312, 367, 368, 370
Loraine 382
Lord Aylmer 354, 371
Lord Byron 370
Lord Canterbury 372
Lord Dorchester 367
Lord Dufferin 374
Lord Elgin 202, 325, 332, 375
Lord Gardner 368
Lord George Bentinck 375
Lord Melville 61, 370, 385
Lord Metcalfe 374
Lord Napier 382
Lord Palmerston 373
Lord Raglan 335, 354, 377
Lord Ramsay 372
Lord Sandon 373
Lord Seaton 373
Lord Sidmouth 372
Lord Stanley 375
Lord Warriston 376
Lord Wellington 224, 368, 385
Lorena 380
Lorenzo 119, 123, 384
Louis Napoleon 377
Louisa 386
Louisa Maria 388
Louisiana 378, 391
Louvre 382
Lowland Lass 368
Lucien 389
Lucinda 232, 326, 373, 389
Lucy 375, 386
Lumina 374, 382
Lusteria 390
Luxembourg 382
Lycurges 370
Lydia 375
Lydia McHenry 375
Madawaska 50, 202, 375
Madura 194, 384
Magdala 382
Magdalen 337, 385
Maggie Lauder 379
Magnificent 380
Magyar 376
Maid of the Mist 378
Mail 371, 374
Maitland 367
Malabar 372, 374, 378, 384
Malaga Packet 367
Malakoff 390
Malay 372
Maldon 7, 29, 243, 390
Malsham 54
Manchester 374, 396
Mandarin 192, 380
Mangalore 372
Mangerton 376
Manilla 383
Manitoba 383
Manitou 383
Manlius 370, 373
Manoah 383
Mansfield 370, 371
Maple Leaf 389
Marchioness of Abercorn 372
Marchmont 375
Margaret 368, 371, 385, 388
Margaret Balfour 371
Margaret Blais 378
Margaret Pollock 373
Margaretta 374
Margaritte 385
Marguerite 367
Margueritte 385
Maria 201, 367, 370, 372, 375, 379
Maria Annett 382
Marianne 370, 371, 374, 383
Marie 386
Marie Adèle 391
Marie Alberta 391
Marie Anna 391
Marie Anne 390, 391
Marie Beatrice 390
Marie Catherine 390
Marie Denis 389
Marie Elénore 390
Marie Eliza 383
Marie Elmire 391
Marie Emilie 388
Marie Erselie 390
Marie Flora 390
Marie Flore 389
Marie Georgiana 390, 391
Marie Helene 389
Marie Leocadie 376
Marie Lesperance 388
Marie Louise 379, 383
Marie Olvine 390
Marie Stella 391
Marie Vigilante 391
Marina 376
Marion 375, 376
Marmelon 378
Marmion 371
Marquess of Normanby 373
Marshall Pellissier 378
Marten 388
Martha 235, 368, 376, 385
Martha and Eliza 370
Martin Luther 376
Martine 389
Martinique 382
Mary 235, 367, 368, 376, 386, 390
Mary and Jane 385
Mary Ann 189, 368, 371, 375, 386, 389
Mary Fry 8, 195, 379
Mary Graham 73, 384
Mary Jane 375
Mary Lydia 390
Mary S Scallan 367
Mary Seton 374
Mary Stewart 386
Mathilde Octavie 382
Matilda 371, 378
Matthew Bell 372
Mauldslie 192, 381
Maxfield 370
Maxwell 378
May Flower 370, 389
May Queen 379
Mayfield 374
Maythorn 192, 380
Mearns 372
Medina 376
Medusa 375
Megara 388
Melanie 379
Melbourne 377
Melissa 374
Melita 379
Menier Consol 185
Mentor 368
Mercator 120, 368
Mermaid 389
Mersey 388
Merton 373
Mertoun 373
Messenger 378
Meteor 377
Mic Mac 329, 386
Michigan 378, 381
Micmac 382
Mignonette 391
Miltiades 374
Milton Lockhart 378
Minerva 367, 388
Miningu 380
Minnehaha 378

Index of Ships' names

Minnesota 378
Minnie Sewell 383
Mint 368
Miriam and Jane 370
Mississippi 378
Missouri 378
Moderation 328, 381
Modern 384
Modesty 390
Mohawk 329, 379, 384, 386
Moira 377
Mona 383
Monarch 367, 383
Mongolian 381
Monica 377
Mont Lilac 377
Montagnais 148, 384
Montcalm 246, 371, 376
Montezuma 328, 374
Montmorency 370, 377
Montreal 58, 383, 385, 386
Montreal Packet 385
Montrose 380
Moodkee 374
Mora 381
Morgianna 371
Muscatel 382
Myrah 390
Myrtle 378
Nagasaki 379
Nancy 367, 368, 385, 386
Nanette 378
Naparina 371
Napier 382
Napoleon 372
Napoleon the Third 377

Natalie 378
Natrona 384
Naval Brigade 377
Nazaire 390
Nazarene 377
Nepane 389
Nepenthe 379
Neptune 367, 368, 388
Nestorian 378
New Century 385
New Dominion 382, 391
New Liverpool 375, 378
New Republic 383
New Swiftsure 54
New Zealand 389
Newfoundland 383
Newry 371
Niagara 62, 375, 382, 386
Nimrod 370, 385
Noranside 381
Norfolk 246, 390
North 377
North River Steamboat 53
North Star 194, 391
North Wind 381
Northern Empire 329, 380
Northern Light 78, 146, 360
Northumberland 388
Northumbria 382
Norwood 189, 324, 377
Nova Scotian 379
Nugget 239, 377
Number 1 376
Number 2 377

Number 3 377
Number 4 377
Nyanza 380
Nydia 380, 384
Nymph 388
Nyssia 379
Ocean 367, 386
Ocean Dart 380
Ocean Empress 379
Ocean Monarch 10, 119, 190, 214, 215, 246, 328, 377
Ocean Nymph 380
Ocean Phantom 379
Ocean Queen 373
Ocean Spray 390
Oceana 374
Octavie 383
Oldham 386
Olive 389
Olive Branch 368, 386
Olive Mount 380
Olive Nailer 371
Oliver Blaunchard 386
Oliver Cromwell 9, 242, 278, 313, 314, 326, 382
Olivia 376
Omega 374
Omphale 388
Omphales 388
Ondine 381
Oneata 383
Oneida 381
Onondaga 371
Ontario 329, 370, 376, 379, 389, 390
Oregon 374
Oriana 382
Orient 331, 383

Oriental 381, 382, 384
Orleans 388, 391
Orpheus 379
Orso 378
Orwell 370
Osceola 373
Oshawa 378
Osprey 329, 382
Ossian 383
Otago 379
Othello 371
Otonabel 382
Ottawa 368, 373, 374
Palestine 373
Palinurus 233, 379
Palm 386
Pamela 385
Panama 375
Panola 189, 376
Papineau 388
Paris 368
Parisian 384
Parmelia 370, 373
Parsee Merchant 373
Passe Partout 390
Passing Cloud 380
Patriot 388
Peerless 379
Peggy 367
Pei-Ho 380
Pekin 372, 378
Pemberton 389
Perfect 288, 372
Pericles 371
Perseverance 388
Persia 20, 80, 329, 354, 376, 381
Persian 371
Peruvian 384
Peter Joynson 10, 332, 380
Peter Mitchell 383

Petica 380
Petite Hermine 379
Petrel 372
Phaola 381
Philippa 388
Philopontus 373
Phoebe 370
Phoenix 367
Piednez 390
Pierre Nolasque 390
Pilgrim 376
Pink 372
Piverton 378
Pladda 205, 378, 382
Plantagenet 376
Pollock 372, 373
Polly 378, 388
Polynesian 329, 384
Pompey 368
Pondichery 384
Pontiac 379
Port Neuf 385
Portia 371
Porto Rico 390
Powerful 378
Premier 247, 372, 376
President 370, 386
President Dunn 368
President Roca 384
Priam 386
Pride 374
Pride of England 379
Prince 390
Prince Arthur 376
Prince Charlie 374
Prince Consort 379
Prince Edward 104, 367
Prince Regent 61, 385
Prince Waldemar 380
Princess Alexandra 380
Princess Alice 374

Princess Beatrice 384
Princess Charlotte 7, 60, 61
Princess Dagmar 380
Princess Louise 383
Princess of Wales 380
Princess Royal 116, 373
Progres 381
Progress 376, 389
Prompt 371, 372, 377, 386
Provence 382
Providence 372, 388
Province 390
Psyche 382
Pyramus 386
Quebec 23, 54, 56, 224, 367, 368, 371, 372, 379, 385, 389, 391, 394, 395, 397
Quebec Packet 370
Quebec Trader 370
Queen 112, 324, 351, 367, 388
Queen Charlotte 61
Queen Emma 382
Queen of Beauty 380
Queen of England 239, 378
Queen of the Lakes 192, 381
Queen of the West 375
Queen Pomare 374
Queen Victoria 372, 390
Queen's Cliff 384
Queensland 379, 384
Queenstown 380
Quintin Leitch 371
Rachel 378, 385
Rachel Blackwood 380
Rainbow 384

Index of Ships' names

Rajah Go Paul 376
Rankin 373, 374
Rapid 192, 283, 388
Rasalama 373
Ravenscliffe 382
Rebecca 367
Reciprocity 384
Red Rose 380
Redan 377
Reform 222, 379
Regina 391
Reine Blanche 386
Reine du Lac 388
Reine Elisabeth 391
Reine Victoria 391
Renfrewshire 372
Reserve 379
Resolute 378
Retrieve 388
Retriever 375
Review 379
Reward 367
Rhea Sylvia 376
Rhoda 380
Richard 368
Richard Pope 335, 370
Richelieu 56, 71, 354
Richmond 385
Rifleman 386
Rimouski 389
Ringfield 179, 277, 375
Ritchie 373
Rival 373
River David 388
River Dey 381
Riverdale 277, 375
Rivoli 382
Rob Roy 370
Robert 329, 368

Robert Alexander Parke 372
Robert Benn 373
Robert Kerr 382
Robert McM Spearing 381
Robert Thomas 372
Roberts 270, 368, 371
Robina 375
Rock City 8, 195, 377, 382
Rock Light 192, 381
Rockshire 373
Roman Eagle 93, 367
Romania 380
Rona 384
Ronochan 375
Rosa 379
Rosalie 378
Rosalind 167, 192, 380
Rosalinda 374
Rosario 383
Rose 374, 382
Rose Maroon 370
Roseneath 383
Rosina 374
Rothesay 381
Rowena 379
Rowland Hill 80
Royal Adelaide 371
Royal Edward 9, 272, 273, 312, 367
Royal George 61, 370
Royal Sovereign 373
Royal Visitor 10, 338, 379
Royal William 7, 8, 10, 17, 55, 56, 64, 65, 78, 82, 117, 119, 164, 170-173, 215, 226, 227, 281, 347, 351, 354, 360, 388

Ruby 329, 380, 410
S. Fortin 391
Sabrina 376
Saguenay 370, 374
Saigon 383
Saint Andrew 202, 371, 382, 386
Saint Ann 370
Saint Charles 370
Saint David 281, 370
Saint Francois 391
Saint George 236, 383, 386
Saint Hilda 375
Saint James 236, 382
Saint John 375
Saint Joseph 390, 391
Saint Lawrence 61, 62, 63, 213, 230, 288, 322, 368, 370, 373, 385, 386, 388
Saint Leonard 371
Saint Louis 391
Saint Michel 390
Saint Patrick 224, 368
Saint Paul 389
Saint Peter 367, 383
Saint Vincent 383
Saint-Laurence 386
Saint-Michel 390
Saint-Pierre 341
Sainte Anne 367, 385, 388, 390
Sainte-Anne 386, 391
Sainte-Antoine 388
Sainte-Luce 390
Sainte-Philomène 388
Saldanha 324, 377
Salem 373
Salmon 275, 329, 379
Sampson 368, 380
Samuel 382, 388, 390

Santa Clara 389
Santa Maria 277
Sapphiras 374
Sapphire 329, 376, 378
Sarah 368, 371, 374-376, 386, 388, 389, 391
Sarah Alice 391
Sarah and Emma 376
Sarah Maria 371
Sarah Mary 376
Sardinian 247, 329, 378, 384
Sarmatian 329, 384
Saugueen 378
Savannah 35
Scotia 39, 48, 74, 86, 152, 269, 291, 313, 330, 378, 383
Scotland 329, 354, 372-374, 379
Scotsman 378
Scottish Maid 374
Sea Bird 388
Sea Gull 390
Sea Serpent 117, 375
Sea Vision 379
Seabird 389, 391
Sebastopol 390
Secret 323, 324, 340, 382
Seringapatam 384
Shamrock 371
Shannon 162, 238, 250, 274, 275, 375, 380, 384
Sheridan Knowles 377
Shooting Star 78, 94, 377
Siberian 381
Signet 384

Silistria 371, 377
Sillery 376
Silver Swan 381
Silvery Wave 381
Sir Francis Burton 370
Sir Francis N. Burton 370, 386
Sir Georges Prevost 224, 368
Sir Howard Douglas 374
Sir Isaac Brock 61
Sir J. H. Craig 368
Sir James Anderson 372
Sir James Henry Craig 385
Sir James Kempt 370
Sir John Newport 386
Sir Richard Jackson 389
Sir Robert Peel 374
Sir Watkin 370
Sir William Eyre 378
Sirius 20
Sirocco 382
Sisters 120, 367, 368, 409
Six Freres 199, 380
Sketty Belle 382
Skiddan 382
Snowdon 382
Snowdrop 378
Sobraon 374
Solferino 379
Solid Carleton 367
Sophia 371-374, 383, 386
Sophia Moffat 374
Sophie 381, 388
Sorel 385, 386, 388-390

Souriquois 378
Southern Belle 380
Southern Empire 380
Souvenir 384
Spalpeen 375
Spectator 388
Spencer 372
Springfield 372
Squaw 376
Stadacona 374, 379, 389, 391
Staffa 247, 378, 379
Stafford 350, 384
Staffordshire 329, 380
Stag 205, 382
Staghound 216, 384
Stamboul 189, 329, 389
Star 391
Star of Peace 380
Starling 377
Stella Maris 375
Sterling 384
Stewart Lane 390
Stirling 386
Storm King 378
Storm Queen 378
Stornoway 382
Stratford 384
Strathavon 381
Strathisle 371
Strathspey 192, 380
Success 382, 383
Suffolk 390
Suir 372
Sultan 375
Sumatra 380
Summerlee 379
Sunbeam 375
Sundown 39
Superior 192, 370, 376, 381, 388

Index of Ships' names

Supreme 384
Surprise 383
Surrey 370
Susan 370
Susanne 386
Swift 368
Swiftsure 54, 55, 58
Swordfish 377
Sybil 376
Sydney 245, 379, 389
Syllerie 372
Syria 373
Tamarac 290, 372, 381
Tanjore 384
Tara 80, 375
Taradale 381
Taranaki 328, 381
Tarifa 231, 382, 384
Tchernaya 377
Tea Taster 380
Tecumseh 383
Telegraph 54, 58, 377
Temiscouata 389
Temperance 373
Teviotdale 380
Thalia 388
Thames 370, 371
The Duke 189, 373
The Duke of Wellington 37
The Kildare 377
The Royal Family 381
Theodore 375, 391
Thistle 9, 192, 304, 373, 380, 388, 391
Thomas 371, 389
Thomas Henry 386
Thomas Laurie 370
Thomas Ritchie 370
Thomas Tucker 37
Thomas Wallace 370
Thornhill 10, 375, 377
Thorwaldsden 376
Tiger 377
Times 388
Tina Forbes 390
Tintern Abbey 384
Tinto 375, 379
Token 372
Tom Moore 373
Toronto 388, 391
Torrance 389
Tottenham 370
Town of Ross 329, 371
Trader 385
Traveller 368
Trebolgan 379
Trenton 378
Tri-Wave 381
Tricolour 171, 377
Trio 335, 370
Tripoli 382
Triton 235, 386
Trompeuse 385
Troopial 381
Truce 381
True Briton 367, 381, 385
True Friend 386
Truth 385
Try Again 371
Tubal Cain 236
Tudor 247, 377
Twilight 382
Tyendanaga 376
Typhoon 189, 377
Tyrol 380
Ulster 370
Ultonia 232, 377
Undaunted 382
Unicorn 371, 373, 389
Union 368, 373, 382, 389
Union Jacket 370
Union Yacht 373
United Kingdom 354, 373
Universe 373
Urgent 372
Utility 377
Valleyfield 376
Vancouver 379
Velocipede 383
Venetia 379
Venture 390
Verity 384
Verona 190, 383
Veronica 386
Versailles 383
Veteran 377
Vibilia 370
Vicereine 384
Viceroy 375, 380
Victoire 382
Victor Hudon 390
Victoria 373, 375, 389
Victoria Bridge 379
Victory 62, 372, 377, 385, 389
Viola 379
Violet 390
Virginia 378, 388
Virginie 375, 390
Virginius 374
Vitula 373
Vixen 373
Volage 390
Volant 376
Vortigirn 378
Voyageuse 388
W.G. Russell 381
W.W. Scott 379
Wacousta 378
Walker 388
Wallace 378
Walrus 370
Wanderer 375
Wandering Sprite 382
Wandsworth 373
Wapiti 382
War Cloud 329, 377
Warren Hastings 374
Washington 376
Wasp 383
Waterwitch 389
Watt 372
Wave 372
Welcome 370
Wellington 357, 372
Wellwood 370
Wenonah 384
Western Empire 379
Westminster 205, 382
Wetherall 372, 388
Wexford 371
Wheatlandside 383
White Rose 245, 250, 379, 384
White Water 380
Wideawake 377
Wilberforce 386
Wild Irish Girl 373
Wild Rose 381
Wildfire 377
Wiliam 371
William 367, 371, 372, 384, 385
William and Ann 388
William Dargan 390
William Henry 386
William Herdman 372
William Huskisson 370
William Kirk 378
William Maitland 386
William Miles 377
William Parke 365, 370
William Parker 386
William Pirrie 373
William Pitt 367, 368
William Ritchie 372
William Rodger 372
William Sharples 372
William Stevenson 375
William Wilberforce 389
William Wilson 367
Wilson Kennedy 375
Wimbledon 381
Windsor 376, 384
Windsor Castle 373
Winnipeg 384
Winona 382
Wolfe 61, 367, 389
Wolfe's Cove 371, 386
Wolfetown 390
Wolseley 384
Woodbine 383
Woodfield 378, 384
Woodstock 274, 376
Wynnstay 376
Yorkshire Lass 374
Young Norval 329, 370
Young Oliver 386
Young Samuel 388
Zélée 390
Zoila 391
Zouave 377
Zuleika 378

General Index

Aberdeen 20, 76, 300, 335
Aberdour 76, 333
Acraman 337
Alden, Robert 393
Allan Line 109, 329
Alleyn, J. 300
Alleyn, William 304
American Shipmasters' Assn 200
Amherstburg 59, 61, 76
Anderson, David 207
Anderson & Swinburn 399-401
Angers, Joseph 79, 186, 211, 390, 391, 402-406
apprentices 27, 81-83, 86, 94, 132, 217, 277, 282, 299
Archer, Joseph 237, 278
Ardrossan 333
army bills 48
Atkinson 120, 156-158, 193, 216, 368, 370, 371, 393, 408
Australia 67, 214, 313, 335
Aylmer, Lady 354
Aylmer, Lord 354
Baie Saint Paul 73
Baldwin 63, 76, 289, 392-394, 363, 367, 368, 371, 376-386
Baldwin & Dinning 116, 119, 180, 190, 215, 309, 314, 326, 328, 354, 376, 377
Baldwin, Henry 76, 86, 94, 207, 319, 367, 368, 396
Baldwin, Patrick 284, 285, 287, 304, 313
Baldwin, Peter 80, 86, 89, 136, 154, 211, 319, 336, 339, 383, 384, 393, 394
Baldwin, William H. 22, 77, 80, 81, 86, 94, 119, 129, 130, 157, 171, 178, 182, 190, 236, 319, 324, 363, 379, 380, 393
Baltic 37-40, 42, 43, 75, 120, 223-225, 227, 230, 231, 331, 335
banks
    Bank of Canada 49
    Bank of Montreal 49
    Bank of Quebec 49
    banking 48, 191
    Banque nationale 192
    City Bank 159
    Union Bank 192
Barallier, Joseph 149, 386, 394
Bath (Maine) 11, 167, 185, 242, 250, 294, 319, 323, 330
Battle of Plattsburg 62
Beatson 22, 75-77, 113, 155-157, 173, 180, 207, 218, 331, 363, 367, 392
Beatson, John 95, 112
Beatson, Patrick 22, 83, 84, 109-112, 156, 169, 177, 180, 186, 223, 238, 248, 249, 273, 305, 312, 319, 324, 354, 363, 367, 392
Beatson, Robert 71
Beatson, William 112, 163, 212
Behan, John 120
Belfast 77, 134, 244, 250, 277, 329, 335, 341, 343, 356
Bell, George 55, 87
Bell, John 12, 55, 76, 83, 88, 91, 93-95, 105, 107, 108, 132, 155, 209, 213, 216-218, 248, 281, 288, 308, 312, 314, 319, 333, 363, 368, 370-372, 392
Bell, William 59, 61, 76, 93, 135, 185, 250, 370, 371, 392
Bennett, John 56
Bennett's yard 371
Bergasse, Henri 341, 343
Berry, Father 104
Berwick 333
Bidegaré, Pierre 377, 378, 393
Black, Edmund 174, 393
Black, George 22, 55, 56, 73, 76, 78, 83, 91, 94, 117, 119, 156, 157, 164, 167, 173, 180, 183, 187, 206, 210, 216, 218, 234, 313, 319, 333, 347, 360, 363, 370-374, 396
Black, George jr 117, 119, 374, 375
Black, John 71, 74, 75, 78, 91, 93, 94, 98, 100, 104, 107, 112, 155-157, 164, 182, 274, 319, 363, 367, 392, 393
Black, William 274, 330
Blais, Jacques 113, 156, 249, 377, 378
Blakiston, Raymond 300
blockade 40, 42
boats (see ships and boats)
Bonyman, William 345
Bordeaux 341, 343
Bordes, Antoine Dom. 341
Boucher, A.D. 36
Boulton and Watt 56
bow 230, 256, 275, 277, 325-327, 329, 351, 355
Bowman, Thomas 308
bowsprits 225, 231, 234, 236
Boyd, Thomas 374, 388, 389
Bremen 200, 243, 326, 328
Bristol 31, 193, 337, 356
Britain 11, 21, 32, 37-40, 42, 45, 49, 53, 58, 65, 67, 68, 73, 75, 77, 78, 81, 83, 106, 169, 170, 173, 188-192, 197, 200-202, 208, 209, 212, 213, 214, 223-227, 236, 238, 239, 246, 251, 252, 267, 277, 278, 284, 286, 287, 307, 314,14, 328, 330, 339, 341, 345, 359, 360
Brodie, Augustus McGhee 225
Brooke, Jas Wilson 202, 359
Brown, George 388
Brown, John (ropemaker) 243, 293, 311, 314
Brown, Sam 207, 217, 319, 368, 370, 392
Brown, Sir Samuel 235
Bruce and Anderson 206
Brunelle, Pierre 79, 80, 88, 136, 139, 141, 146, 159, 163, 173, 187, 215-16, 247, 329, 363, 375-381, 394
Brunet, J.O. 371, 386
Budden, William 337
Bureau Veritas 76, 88, 93, 95, 128, 200, 216
cabin 212, 213, 218, 232, 249, 270, 271, 281, 282, 326
Caldwell, Henry 53, 120, 127, 158, 170
Caldwell, Thomas 164, 185
Campbell, Archibald 31, 78, 114, 209, 330
Campbell, Charles 40, 78, 87, 119, 120, 157, 250, 363, 370, 393
Campbell, James E. 388
Campbell, John 107, 126, 127, 157, 159, 249, 393
Campbell, John Saxton 55, 56, 64, 76, 78, 94, 114, 117, 120, 126, 154, 156, 164, 170, 187, 216, 291, 313, 347, 354, 363, 370, 371, 372, 393
Campbell, Peter 312, 368, 393
Cap Blanc 113
Cap Rouge 23, 45, 117, 120, 157
Cape Cove 17, 56, 76, 78, 116, 117, 119, 130, 156, 164, 167, 170, 173, 174, 180, 187, 222, 347, 393
capstan 167, 232, 274, 292, 294
captains 44, 49, 56, 75, 78, 84, 134, 201, 345
Cardinal, J.B. 308
Carman, Robert 109
Carman, William 87, 109, 307
Cauchon, Edouard 393
Chamber of Commerce 48, 91, 137, 209
Chambre des Arts et Manufacturiers 91
Charland, Guillaume (William) 33, 69, 79, 87, 88, 91, 139, 141, 146, 159, 163, 226, 227, 231, 278, 312, 313, 319, 326, 337, 352, 353, 363, 380-382, 383, 384, 394
Charles, George 202, 394
Chartier de Lotbinière, Michel 120
Chartier, Olivier 372
Chaussegros de Léry 100, 149, 155
Chimenti, Wayne 307
Chrystie 194
Citadel 65, 384
Civil War 68, 213, 343
classification 11, 88, 190, 196-200, 202, 222, 226, 227, 229, 236, 238, 245, 359
Clint, Capt. James 112
Clyde 20, 53, 68, 72, 75, 236, 333
Coker, Charles 199, 200
Commerford, George 375
contract to build 25, 26, 201-203
Cooke, J. 335
copper 53, 149, 177, 201, 212-214, 220, 221, 227, 238, 244, 266, 267, 281, 326
cordage 17, 236, 242-244, 293, 303
    cable 177, 235, 242, 243, 293, 295, 296, 300
    Consumer Cordage 293
    hemp 58, 174, 236, 239, 242, 243, 293, 294, 296, 313, 314
    John Brown's Patent Cordage Works 243, 293
    ropewalk 51, 53, 133, 136, 243, 244
    small stuff 242, 243, 293
Cork 335, 337, 356
Corriveau, Wilfrid 312
Corry, J.P. 343
Côté, Jean Baptiste 274
Côté, Pierre 391
Cotnam, William 88, 128, 136, 194, 200, 207, 216, 221, 236, 243, 282, 319, 324, 326, 363, 374-383, 393, 394
Crimean War 67, 213, 316, 324, 329, 341
crimps 65, 66, 72
Crosbie, Robert 74, 93, 156
Cul-de-Sac 51, 100, 101, 105, 106, 354
Cunard 55
Dalkin 133, 156, 293, 314
Damas 341
Davidson 376, 377
Davie 154, 160, 165, 160, 166, 183
Davie, Allison 55, 77, 83, 107, 108, 138, 141, 159, 167, 180, 182, 183, 185, 186, 360, 371, 392, 394
Davie Allison II, 146
Davie Brothers Ltd. 34, 251, 265, 267, 312,
Davie, Elizabeth 85, 141, 143
Davie, George Duncan 176
Davie, George Taylor 83, 85, 89, 91, 138, 141, 146, 166, 167, 185, 211, 361, 373, 377, 378, 378, 381, 384, 394
Davie (Lauzon) 70, 146, 185, 251
Davis, A. 50
Dean, James 149
Deaves, Reuben 335
deck house 211, 270, 323, 326
decks 23, 48, 56, 62, 112, 244
Desnoyers, Edouard 394
Desnoyers, Jean 29, 93, 112, 392
Dick, John 187
Dinning, Henry 22, 77, 86, 91, 94, 119, 166, 180, 187, 190, 193, 197, 199, 236, 246, 270, 378-384, 394
Dion, Zéphirin 389
Dix, Charles 84, 134

Dixon, Thomas 343
Dobell's timber cove 149
dockyards, naval
   British 37, 39, 53, 58, 169, 220, 223-225, 228, 235, 248, 277, 284, 307
   Halifax 38, 104,
   Lakes 58, 61, 64, 73, 76-78, 80, 81, 107, 202, 207, 226, 307, 360
   Quebec 15, 16, 34, 51, 74, 99-101, 104, 222, 360, 392
Dor, Gustave 341
Drapeau 107, 155
Drolet 377, 393
Dublin 50, 120, 201, 202, 244, 326, 335, 356, 359, 409
Dubord, Edmond 29, 79, 389, 390
Dubord, Hyppolite 22, 79, 85, 194, 341, 381, 389, 390, 394
Dufour, Marcel 372, 373, 389
Dugal, Léandre 132, 158, 363, 393
Duncanson, James 74, 75, 93, 112, 202, 213, 223, 272, 319, 367, 392
Dunière, Louis 110, 112, 156, 186, 274
Dunlop, James 62, 120
Dunn, John 335
Dunn, Thomas 78, 138, 144, 159, 192, 231, 319, 350, 363, 382-384, 394
East India Company 75, 235, 351
Eckford, Henry 78, 104
Edgeley, Edward 207
Edmiston, Robert 194, 341, 356
Ernst, Antoine 78, 94, 112, 156, 374, 388, 392
Etchemin 53, 137, 170, 368
Fabre, Augustin 281, 313, 341, 343
Fairrie, James 74, 75, 156, 202, 218, 248
Farrington, Joseph 164, 371
Fernie, John 117, 156, 170
ferry 55, 78, 138, 354
Finch, Sam 77, 88, 107, 123, 183, 250, 312, 319, 363, 368, 370-372, 393, 394
fire 37, 126, 127, 129, 130, 133, 156, 170, 173, 175, 177, 178, 180, 202, 236, 293, 296, 308
Flanagan 220, 393
Fleming, Patrick 61, 72, 88, 370, 371, 381, 393
Forbes, Robert 328
Forsyth & Bell 47, 112, 191, 19
Fortier, F.X. 378, 393
France 15-17, 34, 39, 51, 67, 71, 92, 132, 209, 226, 231, 237, 251, 252, 287, 293, 331, 339, 341
Free Trade 43, 339
French ownership 136, 281, 313, 324, 339, 341, 357
French Regime 16, 17, 34, 49, 51, 52, 64, 74, 76, 81, 98, 99-101, 164, 169, 208, 209, 230, 237, 239, 248, 251, 253, 273, 274, 354, 357, 380, 384

Friend, Captain 226, 370, 386
Fry, Henry 18, 22, 35, 77, 95, 132, 159, 192-195, 216, 224, 226, 227, 249, 326, 337, 343, 356, 362, 379
Fulton, Robert 53, 54
galley 270, 326
gangs (work gangs) 162, 206, 211, 244
Gaspé 21, 23, 46, 385, 386, 388
Gauvereau, E.T. 382
Germany 331
Gibney, Alexander 300
Gildermeister 200, 216, 326, 356
Gillespie, James 149
Gilley, Walter 76, 120, 393, 394
Gilmour, Allan 22, 76, 120, 122, 123, 157, 217, 222, 248, 319, 327, 333, 345, 355, 360, 363, 371-380, 382, 393
Gilmour, Allan & Co. 45, 66, 72, 76, 120, 121, 123, 154, 157, 166, 171, 173, 175, 177-179, 186, 187, 205, 206, 217, 222, 247, 279, 319, 327, 329, 333, 355, 371-379, 393
Gilmour, John 76, 121, 379, 380, 382, 393
Gingras, Jean Elie 79, 87, 91, 131, 132, 158, 184, 194, 197, 211, 215, 216, 236, 245, 249, 319, 333, 348, 363, 376-379, 381-384, 393, 394
Glasgow 30, 35, 62, 77, 120, 170, 194, 314, 331, 333, 341, 356
Gobeil, Edouard 87, 95
Gold rush 214
Gorce, Bertrand 341
Goudie, James 56, 78, 186, 215, 319, 360-362, 371, 376-378, 389, 390, 393, 410
Goudie, Jane 158
Goudie, John 22, 53-56, 58, 60, 61-63, 67, 71, 72, 75, 77, 83, 88, 91, 93-95, 104, 107, 126, 127, 133, 157, 170, 171, 180, 183, 186, 207-210, 213, 217, 218, 223, 248, 249, 270, 277, 293, 312, 319, 329, 360, 363, 367, 368, 370-71, 393-94
Gould, Nathaniel 227
Grainger, David 77, 134, 159, 335
Grant, James 72
Grant, William 206, 207, 368
Gray, Dugald 82
Gray, Ralph 155
Greenock 62, 74-76, 83, 120, 236, 244, 303, 331, 333, 393, 397
Grisley, Charles 345
Grosse Isle 337
Hamilton, George and William 85, 94, 138, 156, 158, 206, 210, 319, 363, 368, 394
Hamilton, James 128
Harby, Thomas 351
Hardy, Joseph 378
Hare Point 130, 132-134, 136, 159, 174, 183, 393

Harland and Wolff 329
Hartrick and Bellord 335
Havre 194, 341
Henderson, Patrick 30
Henley, Capt. Ed. 112, 370
Henley, John 84
Hermitage 98, 100, 101, 104, 106
Heyn, Gustavus 329, 335
Hooker, Philip 319, 368, 394
Hudson, Richard 238, 297
hull
   beams 197, 211, 219, 226, 227, 235, 236, 245, 247, 256-258, 261, 262, 264, 270, 278, 323, 324, 360
   breasthook 219
   cathead 270, 275
   deadwood 226, 254, 255, 257
   deck 197, 201, 210, 219, 220, 223, 226, 227, 229, 239, 256
   floor timbers 164, 226, 232, 255, 256
   futtocks 213, 219, 223, 226, 227, 229, 234, 245, 256, 278 300
   hatches 239, 242, 256, 257, 326
   keel 62, 161, 164-166, 190, 201, 219, 223, 226, 230, 238, 254, 256, 257, 283, 310, 312
   keelson 211, 219, 223, 226, 236, 255, 256
   rudder 211, 226, 235, 238, 245, 256, 277
   stem 211, 223, 226, 230, 245, 254-256, 275, 310, 312, 330
   stern 19, 23, 24, 161, 256, 257, 270, 273-275, 282, 325-327, 329, 330, 346
   sternpost 219, 223, 226, 230, 254, 255, 257, 277, 310, 312
   strake 254, 262, 270, 281, 309
   top timbers 164, 232, 245, 256
   wales 238, 247, 262, 270, 281, 308, 309
Hunt 297
Hunt, James 22, 77, 128, 158, 250, 297, 300, 303, 314
Hunt, Thomas 273
Hunt, William 77, 300
Hunter, Capt. Thomas 150
Hunter, Robert 75
Hunter, Francis & William 120
Idle, Christopher 302, 331
insurance 177, 188, 196, 202, 361
Intendant Bigot 16
Ireland 73, 188, 189, 201, 239, 314, 335
iron 19, 37, 45, 53, 64, 67-68, 179, 212-214, 221-223, 235, 236, 237, 244, 246, 247, 259, 264-266, 278, 283, 287, 291-292, 324, 337
   beams 236, 324, 360
   bolts 173, 197, 201, 212, 214, 221, 223, 226, 230, 232, 235-239, 254, 259, 264, 266, 277, 299, 308, 309, 312

cable 97, 167, 180, 200, 235, 237, 243, 296, 337, 356, 360
hulls 12, 20, 67, 68, 70, 71, 192, 341, 343
knees 173, 212, 214, 230, 235-237, 245, 247, 258, 277, 278, 360
masts 231, 232, 236, 290, 360
pumps 235, 290
riders 173, 214, 235, 236, 246, 258, 278,
Isle of Orleans 4, 12, 17, 23, 45, 65, 77, 96, 97, 146, 149, 151, 169, 204, 245, 315, 356
Jameson, Elizabeth 363
Jameson, John 202
Jarvis, John 297
Jarvis, Rupert 93
Jeffery 77, 87, 130, 132, 158, 175, 180, 183, 207, 215, 217, 267, 282, 312, 313, 319, 371-375
Jeffery, James 91, 112, 130, 131, 206, 363, 372-375, 392, 393
Jeffery, John 88, 112, 128, 131, 158, 180, 206, 319, 363, 370, 372-375, 392, 393
Jeffery, John jr 88, 158, 374
Jeffery, Richard 130, 158, 375, 392, 407
Jeffery, William H. 88, 95, 130, 217
Jenkins, Francis 201, 244
Jobin, Charles 88, 95, 156, 181, 199, 206, 217, 274, 276, 314, 319, 335, 354, 363, 375-378, 380, 394
Jobin, Louis 274, 276
Johnston & Purss 104
Jolicoeur, Théophile 375
Jones 134, 216, 356, 363
Jones, H.N. 77, 83, 85, 134, 159, 171, 174, 187, 206, 217, 247, 363, 376-379, 394
Jones, J. 217, 218, 312
Joseph, Abraham 274, 330
Julien, Frs 88
Julien, Isaie & Company 87, 89, 108, 133, 136, 183, 211, 215, 363, 377-379, 381-383, 392-394
Julien, Paul 95
keel-blocks 254, 255
Kenny, Francis 120, 157
King, William 74, 104, 109, 112, 164, 182, 212, 213
King's wharf 12, 104-106, 108, 177
Kingston 60-62, 64, 72, 76, 95, 132, 146, 167, 207, 307, 329, 351, 360, 381
Kronstadt 164
Labbé, Jacques 206
Labbé, Louis 79, 112, 183, 206, 217, 337, 363, 368, 370-372, 380, 392, 393
Labbé, Pierre 87, 108, 373
Lachance, Ed 382
Lachance, François 380, 381
Lacombe, Jos 375
Lake Champlain 42, 52, 61, 70, 73, 101, 107, 155, 234, 367

Lake Erie 59, 61, 76
Lake Ontario 52, 61, 72, 233
Lamothe, Théo 372
Lampson, William 78, 112, 113, 156, 158, 165, 171, 206, 392, 393, 363, 372-374
Lane, George Bradford 120, 393
Laprise, Michel 87, 136, 275, 377, 378, 394
Laroche, Louis 79, 389, 390
launching 48, 91, 93, 100-102, 105, 106, 132, 137, 156, 157, 161, 162, 164, 170, 183, 198, 201, 202, 206, 222, 254, 267, 345, 346, 347, 351, 353-355
Laurencelle, Fortier 393
Laurencelle, François 87
Lauzon 12, 15, 55, 70, 79, 88, 137, 139, 141, 146, 162-164, 173, 175, 176, 185, 251, 394
Le Havre 194, 341
Lee, Edward P. 376, 393
Lee, Thomas C. 12, 71, 78, 94, 95, 130, 131, 132, 133, 158, 194, 201, 217, 245, 246, 250, 328, 363, 373-381, 393, 394
Legislative Assembly 48, 91
Leitch 72, 371
Leith 75, 77, 88, 93, 112, 180, 198, 333
Lemelin, George 132, 158, 379, 380, 381, 393
Lemelin, Jean 79, 174, 186, 274, 376, 378, 393
Lemelin, Jean jr 134, 189, 377, 393 Lemieux, François 371
Lepper, Paul 108, 155, 183, 392
Letarte, Pierre 87, 159, 275, 394
Levasseur, René Noël 17, 22, 34, 51, 52
Levis 34, 50, 69, 76, 88, 137, 139-141, 143, 145, 146, 148, 154, 159, 163, 166, 167, 175, 176, 182, 209, 226, 235, 251, 263, 265, 267, 312
Limerick 245
Liverpool 11, 29, 35, 67, 69, 73-74, 88, 126, 128, 144, 150, 188, 189, 194, 201, 202, 208, 214, 216, 231, 232, 234, 236, 239, 243, 244, 246, 290, 319, 322, 324, 331, 332, 333, 335, 337-339, 342, 409
Lloyd's 31, 71, 77, 80, 88, 95, 141, 149, 171, 197-202, 206, 214-216, 222, 224-226, 227, 230, 231, 233-238, 243- 249, 264, 266, 316, 324, 331, 340, 341, 354, 360, 384, 411-413
Lomas, Robert 312, 377, 394
London 35, 37, 38, 42, 48, 50, 67, 69, 71, 72, 77, 94, 95, 105, 119, 164, 185, 196, 216, 218, 224, 225, 227, 239, 248-250, 274, 277, 300, 303, 312, 313, 328, 331-335, 337, 351, 356, 359
Londonderry 335, 343
Lorne Dry Dock 70, 159
Lunell, Samuel and George 337
Maine 164
Marine Hospital 129, 130, 158, 393
Marquis, F.X. 79, 87, 139, 146, 159, 162, 163, 167, 194, 216, 238, 244, 274, 278, 312, 313, 314, 326, 356, 363, 381-384, 394
Marseilles 341, 343, 357
Martin, A. 368, 370, 371, 393
Martin dit Beaulieu, Jean 114, 156
Martineau, F.X. 132, 158
Maxwell, Robert 136, 345, 378, 380, 390, 394
McColl, Alexander 345
McCord, Robert 394
McCorkell, Bartholemew 335
McDonald and Hows 183
McDouall, James 62, 218
McKay, Lauchlan 67, 78, 83, 84, 86, 87, 94, 134, 171, 180, 182, 190, 194, 211, 216, 246, 363, 381-384, 394
McKenzie, James 72, 88, 95, 274, 330
Mechanics Union 91
Menzies, Thomas 77, 88, 149, 198, 199, 216, 239, 245, 246, 354
Mercier 314, 390, 394
Merritt, J. 388
Milling, Mr. 123, 127, 157, 170
Mitchell, Alex 194
Molson, John 53, 54, 56, 57, 71, 109, 156, 392
Montmorency 23, 53, 169, 170
Montreal 46, 48, 49, 53-57, 62, 64, 65, 68, 69, 70, 72, 75, 93, 97, 109, 113, 120, 164, 194, 195, 198, 234, 236, 243, 244, 294 383, 384-386, 388-391
Montreal Ocean Steamship Company 109
Morrison, Catherine 363
Morrison, James 393
Muckle, J. McLure 373
Mulholland, Henry 207
Munn, Agnes 155, 156, 180
Munn, Alexander 75, 88, 93, 104, 105, 107, 109, 111, 112, 155, 177, 186, 224, 319, 327, 363, 367, 368, 392
Munn, David 75, 88, 155, 156, 208, 217, 392, 368
Munn, John 12, 22, 27, 55, 66, 75, 76, 80, 83, 86, 87, 88, 91, 93, 94, 104-107, 109, 111, 112, 125, 126, 127, 141, 155-158, 175, 177, 179, 180, 182, 183, 184, 186, 206, 208, 213, 216-218, 230, 236, 247-250, 290, 313, 319, 329, 345, 354, 392, 393, 363, 367, 368, 370, 371, 372-378, 385, 386, 388
Muntz, J.F. 238
Mure and Joliffe 218, 312
Napoleonic Wars 40, 42, 64, 213, 238, 360
Navigation Laws 39, 74, 213
Navy 16, 27, 34, 38, 39, 50, 51, 61, 72, 73, 100, 151, 155, 169, 223, 225, 231, 235, 236, 248, 249, 296, 326, 327, 331, 351, 356
Neilson, Andrew 130, 158, 345, 372, 373, 393
Neilson, John 87, 88, 95
Nelson, James 136, 377, 394
Nelson, Lord 62, 180
Nesbitt, John James 22, 77, 78, 88, 94, 130, 158, 166, 174, 184, 185, 206, 215, 274, 335, 363, 372-377, 393, 394, 397, 398, 399, 407
New Brunswick 18, 38-40, 67, 72, 76, 120, 214, 218, 225, 231, 330, 335
New England 38, 40
New France 15-17, 51, 226, 231, 251, 287, 293
New Liverpool 45, 137, 210, 378, 394
New Waterford 134, 171, 174, 394
Newton, William 392, 370
Nichols, John 235
Nicholson, John 76, 77, 107, 166, 392, 372
Noad, H.J. 95, 166, 185
North West Company 75, 76
notary 13, 24, 26, 28, 31, 44, 50, 51, 78, 83, 114, 126, 190, 202, 209, 210, 330
Nova Scotia 39, 74, 86, 152, 330
O'Brien, Michael 345
O'Hearn, James 301
Oliver, Thomas H. 22, 73, 74, 81, 83, 93, 94, 109, 127, 154, 156, 158, 166, 171, 183-186, 189, 191, 201, 202, 206, 215-217, 247, 274, 319, 321, 335, 338, 356, 360-363, 373-384, 392, 393
Oliver, Edward 67, 73, 88, 93, 127, 158, 188, 201, 206, 208, 244, 326, 363, 372, 393
Oliver, James E. 73, 127, 208, 243, 363, 374-9, 393
Oliver, J.M. 383
Orkney, Robert 368, 370, 371
outfit 32, 73, 91, 109, 146, 175, 187, 191, 193, 196, 200, 212, 213, 237, 239, 240, 242-246, 287, 329
Parent, Joseph 101, 367, 385
Parent, Louis 73
Parke, Andrew 87, 319, 377, 394
Parke, George H. 77, 80, 85, 128, 131, 134, 136, 159, 179, 202, 250, 277, 319, 335, 354, 363, 375-378, 394
Parke, William 87, 136, 319, 377, 394
Parker, Capt. John 18
Parker, William 308, 314
Paterson, Grant & Greenshields 120
Patterson & Mure 163
Patterson & Shaw 126, 354, 381, 382
Patterson, Dyke & Company 77, 94, 169, 202, 217, 218
Patterson, Peter 53, 157, 170, 235
Patton, Duncan 139, 146, 187, 394
Pearson, Adam 218
Pearson, Silas 82
Pelchat, René & fils 381
Pelchat & Mercier 376, 377, 394
Pemberton Bros 47
penalty clause 47, 202, 205
Perquier et fils 341
Picard, Yves 367
Pickersgill and Tibbits 138, 165, 166, 185
Pirrie, James A. 329
Pirrie, William 373
Plucknett, George 61
Pointe-aux-Trembles 43, 186, 204, 208, 388-390, 402
Pollok, Gilmour and Company 120, 333, 345, 360, 362
Pope, Richard 335, 370
Poppe, Gustavus 328
Portneuf 388-390
Power, William 78, 132, 378, 393
Prevost, Sir George 61, 62, 224, 360
Price, David 390
Price, Evan John 391
Price, William 170, 394
Prince Edward Island 20, 72, 198, 214, 218
Prince Edward Street 3, 127, 133, 166, 179, 407
Princess Louise Wet Dock 70
Pryde & Jones 201
Puget, Wulfran 341
pumps 164, 165, 201, 235, 239, 244, 252, 290-292
Quebec Ship Riggers & Sail Makers 300
Quebec Steamship Company 76, 89
Ray & Dean 377
Ray, John 94, 172, 213, 218, 368, 386, 394
Ray, Walter Gilley 76, 83, 86, 88, 94, 95, 115, 128, 172, 187, 200, 215, 216, 270, 363, 374, 375, 377, 378, 393
Record, George 61
Reed, Matthew 161
registration 22-25, 31, 39, 48, 85, 190, 193, 194, 201, 209, 212, 323, 341
Richard & Co. 381
Richard, E.O. 136, 394
Richard, J. 95
Richardson, John 314
Richardson, William Cathro 202, 377
Richelieu 56, 58, 61, 62, 71, 354
Roberge, Louis 341, 383, 393
Roberge, Magloire 64
Robitaille, François 79, 213, 368, 385, 392, 393
Robitaille, Romain 107, 394
Roche, John 120, 121, 157, 166, 186
Rochette, Louis 312
Rosa et frère 377
Rosa, Edouard 379, 380, 393
Rosa, François 300
Rosa, Joseph 382
Rosa, Louis 381, 383, 393
Rosa, Narcisse 17, 21, 35, 50, 79, 89, 90, 92, 95, 131, 132, 136, 158, 159, 214, 216, 227, 236, 274, 275, 330, 341, 354, 363, 377-384, 393, 394, 410

438 *The Charley-Man*

Ross, James G. 22, 47, 69, 79, 85, 191-194, 196, 200, 205, 216-218, 231, 249, 274, 313, 333, 341, 356
Ross, W.H. 194
Ross & Co. 141, 191, 194, 198, 338
Rotherhithe (Rotherhyde) 75, 163
Roy, Régis 383, 393
Rush-Bagot Agreement 64
Russell, Alexander 12, 83, 138, 140, 141, 145, 148, 163, 165, 171, 210, 234, 394
Russell, Catherine 85, 380, 381, 384, 394
Russell, William G. 76, 78, 87, 89, 91, 94, 95, 107, 138, 145, 155, 159, 166, 183, 185, 186, 206, 235, 333, 356, 363, 372-380, 392, 394
Russia 37, 38, 42, 293, 331
Saguenay 234, 370, 374, 388-391
sails 18, 26, 44, 45, 84, 116, 201, 214, 218, 238-242, 245, 246, 250, 278, 287, 293, 296, 298, 299, 302, 304, 307, 315, 316, 327-329
   cotton 239, 250
   flax 38, 239, 242
   linen 82, 335
   Rutherford 242
Saint John 18, 21, 31, 37, 38, 50, 88, 198, 319, 323, 375
Saint Johns 58, 61
Saint Lawrence Channel 69
Saint Maurice 75, 233, 237
Saint Patrick's Hole 169, 270, 319, 356, 394
Saint Peter Street 4, 175, 285
Saint Roch 12, 44, 53, 96, 98, 124, 125, 157, 170, 171, 180, 207, 243, 252, 293
Saint-Jean 81, 83, 136, 389-391
Saint-Jean, Antoine 81
sales prices 24, 26, 31, 64, 189, 191, 194, 196, 197, 200, 202, 210, 212-215, 218, 339, 343, 346, 359, 360
Samson frères 30, 50, 79, 87, 131, 136, 138, 211, 215, 233, 250, 312, 319, 340, 363, 377, 378, 379, 380, 381-384, 394
Samson, Étienne 50, 69, 78, 138, 144, 148, 159, 186, 192, 194, 218, 231, 249, 319, 350, 363, 377, 378, 382-384, 394
Samson, Ladrière 312
Scotland 72, 75-77, 83, 112, 126, 155, 170, 223, 333
Scott, Idles and Company 42
Sewell, Edmund W. 78, 94, 132, 136, 146, 158, 159, 160, 215, 229, 274, 312, 330, 360, 363, 375-377, 380-384, 393, 394
Sharples 120, 150, 206, 372, 373, 393
sheathing 221, 238
Sheppard 40, 87, 119, 120, 157, 363, 370, 371, 394
Sheppard, William 40, 119, 120

Sherwood, Thomas 206, 381
Shickluna, Louis 82
shipbroker 47, 49, 67, 73, 79, 188-190, 225, 333
shipbuilding trades
   blockmaker 76, 86, 119, 155, 207, 213, 231, 232, 252, 282-284, 286, 287, 302, 313, 396
   deadeyes 284, 286, 302, 304
   boatbuilder 112, 146, 149, 245
   borer 309
   carver 251, 273, 274, 277, 330
   carved work 23, 24, 108, 201, 232, 270, 272-277, 312, 329, 330, 360
   caulker 43, 166, 201, 210, 213, 252, 253, 261, 262, 266, 267, 308, 312
   glazier 251, 281, 282
   joiner 61, 72, 88, 253, 264, 270, 273, 274, 287
   labourer 15, 28, 51, 52, 66, 67, 72, 90, 104, 137, 182, 206, 209, 210, 314, 361
   mastmaker 286-289, 302
   masts 43, 207, 211, 212, 225, 231, 234, 239, 242, 277, 287-291, 296, 299, 303-305, 315, 327, 328
   painter 137, 180, 281, 282
   planker 37, 80, 194, 197, 201, 207, 210, 213, 219, 220, 223, 226, 227, 229, 232, 238, 246, 252, 254, 256, 257, 262-264, 266, 267, 270, 274, 277, 308
   pumpmaker 175, 207, 213, 226, 251, 252, 285, 286, 287, 290-292
   rigger 22, 36, 207, 217, 251, 300-308, 314
   rigging 44, 80, 84, 101, 179, 187, 213, 214, 220, 231, 235, 236, 242-244, 246, 249-251, 262, 277, 283, 284, 290, 292, 293, 296, 303-305, 328, 351
   ropemaker 51, 243, 251, 293-296, 314
   sail-maker (see sails) 22, 76, 83, 116, 128, 175, 238, 250, 296, 297, 299-304, 307
   sawyer 171, 208, 251-253
   ship carpenter 73, 82, 86, 90, 113, 114, 206, 254, 261, 277, 292, 308, 312
   shipsmith 26, 48, 61, 66, 72, 75, 107, 110, 111, 112, 113, 114, 130, 136, 137, 173, 179, 182, 183, 186, 201, 207, 211-213, 217, 237, 251, 277, 278, 281, 302, 305, 361
   shipwright 76, 82, 83, 85, 86, 101, 109, 120, 161, 164, 185, 197, 206, 247, 261, 287, 313, 336, 354
ship measurement 24, 200, 212, 213, 218, 316, 323, 356
ships and boats (see also separate Index of Ships' Names for individual ships)
   barge 71, 119, 123
   barque 8-11, 69, 73, 117, 135, 136, 146, 151, 205, 221, 230-233, 235-237, 239, 243, 250, 274,

276, 287-289, 291, 315-320, 322-324, 326, 328, 335, 340, 341, 344, 350
   barquentine 15, 69, 246, 315-319, 322, 324, 353, 359
   bateau 58, 101
   boat 31, 64, 66, 67, 98, 138, 146, 149, 166, 185, 201, 213, 222, 239, 242, 244, 245, 250, 281, 287, 292, 354
   brig 61, 62, 73, 118, 167, 315-319, 322, 324, 351
   brigantine 120, 224, 275, 315-319, 322, 324
   clipper 20, 67, 78, 86, 87, 132, 134, 247, 277, 323
   gunboat 52, 61, 62, 63
   icebreaker 71, 360
   packet 326, 359
   schooner 43, 52, 56, 61, 63, 98, 113, 138, 174, 261, 304, 315-322, 324
   ship (fully-rigged) 116, 239, 241, 315-320, 322-324, 328-29, 359
   sloop 62, 98, 315, 317-319, 322, 324
   snow 73, 101, 102, 315-319, 322, 351, 324
   steamboat 44, 48, 53-58, 64, 66, 70, 72, 77, 78, 80, 83, 98, 109, 113, 119, 123, 139, 141, 146, 154, 164, 166, 175, 232, 281, 335, 351, 354, 360
   warship 51, 52, 61
ships, composite 192, 236, 320, 321
shipyard facilities:
   booms 44, 45, 88, 111, 119, 179, 181, 182, 349
   building slip 4, 100, 101, 161, 173, 251, 254
   dry dock 70, 88, 104, 149, 159, 163, 164, 185
   floating dry dock 164
   forge 101, 113, 173, 174, 237, 278
   grid iron 160, 162
   marine railway 138, 143, 154, 159, 165, 167, 183, 267, 360, 394
   Mould Loft (Moulding Loft) 45, 110, 113, 114, 118, 125, 127, 140, 149, 171, 173, 308, 309
Sillery 111, 120, 128, 150, 376, 393
Simons, Peter 76, 83, 300, 301
Simons, William 62, 76, 78, 83, 85, 88, 120, 134, 159, 187, 200, 206, 217, 236, 247, 393, 394
Sinclair, J. 335
Sorel 44, 46, 48, 56, 73, 75, 97, 98, 212, 314, 385, 386, 388-390
Spencer Cove 120, 156, 157
St. Lawrence Steamboat Company 109
Stadacona 136, 154, 171, 374, 379, 389, 391
steering-wheel 175, 232, 239, 274, 285, 292, 326
Steples 368
surveyor 73, 76, 128, 200, 231, 235
Symes, G. Burns 47, 193

Symington, William 53
Symons, Robert 299
Talon, Intendant Jean 15, 34, 51, 71, 100, 209, 293, 294
Taylor, George 55, 61, 77, 83, 94, 107, 108, 149, 155, 183, 186, 209, 249, 250, 308, 314, 319, 346, 351, 368, 370, 371, 392, 394
Thames measurement 218
Thompson, James 71, 209
Thompson, Zacharaiah 392
Thorne, Caleb 300
Three Rivers (Trois Rivières) 234
Tibbits, James 50, 138, 159, 165, 166, 185, 202, 217, 250, 314, 374, 375, 394
Timber 19, 31, 37-43, 47, 49
   Baltic timber 38, 40, 43, 224, 225, 227
   Birch 226, 232, 234, 248, 290
   British market 19, 21, 32, 37, 38, 81, 138, 191, 200, 227, 306
   carriers 17, 29, 77, 106, 118
   deck-loads 43, 170, 193
   ceiling 164, 219, 226, 230, 232, 247, 262, 264, 267, 270, 324
   chocks 245, 255, 256
   "compass" timber 38, 119,
   coves 44, 46, 85, 98, 106, 107, 110, 111, 117, 119, 120, 136, 137, 149, 165, 177, 233, 310
   culls 233
   cullers 44, 78, 94, 114, 128
   deforestation 38, 231
   dry rot 220, 221, 224, 225
   Elm 223, 226, 230, 232, 248, 254, 274, 283, 312
   finishing wood
   Fir 169, 225, 228
   Hackmatack 227
   handling 90
   knees 45, 173, 210, 212, 219, 223, 229, 230, 234-237, 245, 247, 248, 249, 257, 258, 264, 277, 278, 360
   Larch 223, 227, 386
   Lignum Vitae 231, 232, 266, 283, 285
   Locust 222, 234, 277, 309
   moulinet(te) 233
   Oak 38, 39, 42, 50, 120, 157, 164, 165, 182, 208, 213, 222-224, 225-228, 230, 232, 233, 244-246, 248, 266, 277, 282, 312, 316, 326
   Oregon 231, 290, 374
   Pine 42, 149, 164, 170, 182, 208, 213, 223, 225-228, 231, 232, 234, 248, 270, 277, 290, 292, 312, 313
   pitch Pine 232
   price 26, 38, 40, 43, 67, 233, 287, 313
   properties 34, 68, 101, 109, 126, 132, 182, 220, 228, 233

General Index

rafts 42, 44, 48, 65, 93, 105, 117, 120, 126, 164, 225, 356
rock Maple 232
salt 175, 199, 221, 222, 293
sawmills 53, 114, 117, 126, 127, 132, 134-136, 140, 141, 169-171, 182, 252, 334, 347, 360, 393
spar wood 219, 220, 230, 313
Spruce 223, 227-231, 234, 313, 351
supply 15-17, 50, 51, 53, 112, 233
Tamarac 164, 213, 223, 226, 227, 229, 230, 232-234, 236, 245, 246, 249, 290, 372, 381
Teredo worm 220, 222, 267, 270
trade 21, 22, 32, 37-43, 47, 49, 70, 77, 89, 106, 104
treenails (trunnels) 222, 230, 234, 247, 259, 262, 264, 267, 277, 308-310
Toronto 34, 50, 61, 63, 71, 72, 164, 185, 216, 356, 388, 391
Tough, Alexander 303, 314, 397, 398
79, 81, 83, 87, 94, 95, 193, 363, 377-381, 393, 394

Trahan, Joseph 132, 158
Trahan, Olivier 113, 114, 156, 319, 368, 393
Trinity House 43, 48, 50, 91
United States 20, 37, 39, 40, 67, 70, 71, 74, 78, 132, 134, 164, 167, 186, 188, 189, 214, 277, 286, 327, 330, 331, 333, 351, 360
Uppington, Richard 289, 291
Usborne, George William 374
Usborne, Henry 42, 156, 157, 193, 217, 218, 225, 331
Usborne, John 42
Vacherie 126, 129, 130, 132, 393
Valin, Gabriel 171
Valin, Pierre 22, 79, 91, 113, 128, 131, 132, 136, 156, 159, 174, 183, 186, 189, 233, 241, 249, 250, 270, 277, 319, 363, 375-379, 390, 393, 394, 399-401, 408
Valin, Pierre Vincent 79, 84, 85, 88, 91, 92, 95, 128-130, 136, 154, 178, 182, 194, 211, 217, 236, 274, 281, 313, 319, 329, 341, 355, 363, 382-384, 393, 394

Valin, Toussaint 79, 85, 136, 319, 363, 378-380, 394
Valin & Dugal 132, 158, 380-382, 393
Vallerand, Gonzague 95, 136, 182, 394
Vaughan, David 84, 166, 183, 375
Verminck 341, 381
Vezina, Arsène 87
Vidal, Aymerick (Americus) 27, 83, 86, 355, 373, 393
Viger, Paul 156, 392
Viger, Paul Benjamin 78, 112-114, 368, 393
Wales 197, 224, 337-339, 344
War of 1812 48, 54, 58, 61, 63, 76-78, 104, 126, 138, 147, 149, 210, 213, 215, 226, 307
Ward, John D. 56
Warner, Henry 87, 134, 180, 190
Waterford 77, 133, 134, 171, 174, 335, 370, 394
Watt 56, 333, 371, 372
West Indies 39, 316, 331, 333, 335
White, James 345
White, John and Company 277

William Henry (see Sorel)
Wilson, Charles 85, 241, 250
Wilson, James & Son 155
Wilson, John 66, 194
Wilson, Matthew I. 193
Wilson, Robert 216, 326, 356
windlass 201, 211, 226, 232, 292, 356
Wiseman 378, 388
Wolfe's Cove 41-43, 45, 111, 119-122, 154, 156, 157, 166, 168, 178, 279, 333, 371, 386, 393
Wood, Charles 22, 56, 93, 151, 152, 154, 333, 354, 394
Wood, Robert 370
workforce 74, 90, 203-211, 359
Wyatt 377
Yellow metal 189, 226, 238, 267
Yeo, James 62, 72
Yeo, William 116, 309, 314, 326, 356
Young (Montreal) 388
Young, James 112, 156, 392, 370, 371
Young, John 93, 106, 155